P9-EDE-203

EVERYMAN, I will go with thee,

and be thy guide,

In thy most need to go by thy side

TOBIAS GEORGE SMOLLETT

Born in 1721 in Dumbartonshire and educated at
Glasgow. Went to London in 1739 and in 1741
sailed as surgeon's mate on one of the vessels of
the Cartagena Expedition. On his return he settled
in London and devoted himself to literature.
Died in 1771.

TOBIAS SMOLLETT

Peregrine Pickle

IN TWO VOLUMES: VOLUME ONE

INTRODUCTION BY
WALTER ALLEN

DENT: LONDON
EVERYMAN'S LIBRARY
DUTTON: NEW YORK

NO. *838*

INTRODUCTION

Tobias George Smollett belongs to the great company of English hack-writers, a race still with us though now dignified by the name of professional author. As a hack, he wrote for money, and he was prepared to write anything, or almost anything, for which there seemed to be a public demand. His works included verse, plays, novels, a travel book, several histories, one of England and another, in eight volumes, 'of all the countries in known world,' an *Essay on the External Use of Water*, translations of *Gil Blas*, *Don Quixote* and the writings of Voltaire, and a mass of literary and political journalism. All that is read to-day are three of the novels, *Roderick Random*, *Peregrine Pickle*, and *Humphry Clinker*, and the travel book *Travels in France and Italy*.

Smollett was born in 1721 at Dalquhurn, in Dumbartonshire, the younger son of a younger son of a distinguished Scottish family, and his was the proverbial lot of the younger son of a younger son. He was apprenticed to a medical practitioner, which in those days meant an apothecary as well as a doctor, and probably also attended courses at Glasgow University. In 1739 he left Scotland for London, with little money in his purse, some medical knowledge, and a five-act tragedy, *The Regicide*, in his pocket. Unsuccessful in getting his play produced, he joined the Royal Navy as a surgeon's mate; he was present at the siege of Cartagena in 1741 and in all served in His Majesty's ships for five years. By 1744 he was back in London, with a wife, and had settled down in Downing Street to practise medicine. Medicine not proving lucrative, he turned to writing. Richardson's *Pamela* had appeared in 1740, Fielding's *Joseph Andrews* in 1742; a new form of the story, the novel, had come into existence. Smollett added to it, in 1748, with *Roderick Random*. From then on, though he seems to have had occasional hankerings after the profession of medicine, his life was entirely bound up with literature; a stormy life, distinguished by acrimonious feuds with fellow authors and a term in prison for libel. He died in 1771, near Leghorn, in Italy, four years too soon to inherit the family estate which would have brought him prosperity for the first time in his life. We may catch glimpses of him as a boy and as a ship's doctor in *Roderick Random*; towards the end of his life he drew a picture of himself in the character of Matthew Bramble in *Humphry Clinker*, the picture of a man choleric, irascible, warm-hearted, possessed of one skin too few for the age in which he found himself, and able to meet its brutality only with a brutality of his own.

The brutality of the mid-eighteenth century, its filth and squalor, its callous disregard for human life and what we now think of as human rights, can scarcely be overestimated. Of this brutality the best minds of the time were highly conscious; it obsessed the great novelists in their different ways, just as it is largely the theme of the great draughtsmen, of Hogarth and Rowlandson. Indeed, for the modern reader the ideal introduction to Smollett's novels would be a close look at the work of Hogarth and Rowlandson, and Rowlandson perhaps in particular. He did in fact illustrate *Peregrine Pickle*, and in the gross, almost animal figures of his cartoons, the horseplay and the roaring spirits, we have the pictorial equivalent of Smollett. We have something else too: the realization that though for us Smollett's rowdiness may seem unnaturally phrenetic and his characters often caricatures, they did not appear so to his contemporaries.

This is to say that Smollett was writing in a convention not ours, an eighteenth-century convention. Perhaps the last great novelist who belonged to it, at any rate in his characterization, was Dickens, whose love for Smollett may be found recorded in the early pages of *David Copperfield*. Both saw human beings from the outside; they looked for eccentricity; and there is a passage in *Peregrine Pickle* which throws much light on this:

. . . Nothing more easily gains credit than an imputation of madness fixed upon any person whatsoever; for when the suspicion of the world is roused, and its observation once set at work, the coolest man upon earth, will, by some particulars in his behaviour, convict himself of the charge. Every singularity in his dress and manner (and such are observable in every person), that before passed unheeded, now rise up in judgment against him, with all the exaggerations of the observer's fancy; and the sagacious examiner perceives distraction in every glance of the eye, turn of the finger, and motion of the head. When he speaks, there is a strange peculiarity in his argument and expression; when he holds his tongue, his imagination teems with some extravagant reverie; his sobriety of demeanour is no other than a lucid interval, and his passion mere delirium.

Here Smollett might have been describing his own attitude
to the men and women in the world about him. His suspicion
was always roused, his observation always at work, so that he
sees human beings as though they were mad, as though violently departing from an agreed norm of appearance and
behaviour. But the agreed norm too, we must remember, is
a convention; and what George Santayana says in his famous
essay on Dickens is almost as true of Smollett:

When people say Dickens exaggerates, it seems to me they can
have no eyes and no ears. They probably have only *notions* of what
things and people are; they accept them conventionally at their
diplomatic value. Their minds run on in the region of discourse,
where there are masks only, and no faces; ideas and no facts; they
have little sense for those living grimaces that play from moment to
moment on the countenance of the world.

Of course Smollett does exaggerate. The outstanding
instance in *Peregrine Pickle* is its greatest character, the
retired naval officer Hawser Trunnion. There never was a
naval officer quite like him; and yet he is, in one sense, merely
an extension of the traditional seafaring man, or for that
matter of any human being fixed in a well-marked profession,
as commonly observed. His professionalism has made him a
monster, a freak; he is not so much a man as a walking embodi-
ment of a vocation and, as such, he has lost the ability to adapt
himself to life outside his vocation. It is from this that the
comedy of Trunnion arises: when he sets out on horseback for
his wedding he behaves as though his horse were a ship governed
by the prevailing winds: he is mad, or we would think him mad
if we met his like in life. Yet this madness of his detracts not
a jot from his reality in the novel, as is shown from the fact that
it is from him that the finest comedy in the book springs and
from the fact that in his rendering of his death Smollett soars
to heights of comic pathos he reached nowhere else. The death
of Trunnion is one of the greatest scenes in all literature; and if
it reminds us of the death of Falstaff it does so not because it is
similar to it but because here, for once, Smollett is touched with
a truly Shakespearian spirit.

To mention Dickens along with Smollett, the pupil with the
master, is, of course, merely to be reminded of the gulf that lies
between us and the eighteenth century. Dickens appears so
much more human and humane; sympathy and pity, as well as
savage denunciation, are his hall-marks; and when his affections are engaged, comedy slides into humour. We find few

signs of sympathy and pity in Smollett. Indeed, almost certainly the first thing that strikes the modern reader of *Peregrine Pickle* is its cruelty. At times, I think we must admit, it is cruelty for its own sake. No one has ever claimed much for the hero of the novel himself. Yet Pickle is a very efficient device for Smollett's purposes. His function is, as it were, that of a joke-machine, a mechanism by which a headlong series of practical jokes are projected one after another. Some of these jokes, as I say, will seem to us merely cruel; Hawser Trunnion, Pickles's butt in the first half of the novel, is shown as anybody's game; and when we read of the jests played upon him by his ward we must be reminded of the eighteenth-century attitude to the wretched inmates of Bedlam: madness, even eccentricity, had no rights.

Later, however, as Trunnion ceases to dominate the novel, the purpose, though not the nature, of the jokes changes. They may be crude, but they are salutary. They become instruments by which folly is exposed and affectations ridiculed, and much of the satire that results still cuts deeply even to-day. One type of 'progressive,' for example, has been unerringly caught for all time in the character of the doctor (a character modelled on the poet Akenside) with whom Pickles travels in France, with his outburst, on hearing that his friend Pallet the painter has been imprisoned in the Bastille: 'In my opinion, we shall be accessory to the ruin of this poor enslaved people, if we bestir ourselves in demanding or imploring the release of our unhappy countryman; as we may thereby prevent the commission of a flagrant crime, which would fill up the vengeance of Heaven against the perpetrators, and perhaps be the means of restoring a whole nation to the unspeakable fruition of freedom.'

The faults of *Peregrine Pickle* are obvious enough. Smollett lacked any sense of form and he had no very dignified conception of the novel such as, in their different ways, his greater contemporaries Richardson and Fielding possessed. In *Humphry Clinker* he succeeded in producing a satisfactory form of his own, but *Peregrine Pickle* reads like one long improvisation; as indeed it probably was. It allowed him to incorporate his own observations and comments on the state of France and the Low Countries as he had seen them when he toured those lands in 1750, a year before the novel was published. These remain of interest. But the practice of improvisation also enabled him without scruple to insert into the novel the long and quite irrelevant 'Memoirs of a Lady of Quality.' This, the 'true confession' story of a notorious woman of the day, Lady Vane, Smollett himself probably did not write and was paid to include.

This means that in *Peregrine Pickle* the parts are much better than the whole. But how good some of the parts are! And how wonderfully Smollett keeps up his succession of practical jokes! One feels they ought to bore us; they do not. And one reason they do not is the sheer speed of Smollett's prose: there never was a more energetic master of narrative. Another reason, of course, is the excellence of the jokes them-selves, Trunnion's wedding, for example, or that scene in which Peregrine buys a gipsy's daughter and passes her off in society as a fine lady, an imposture wholly successful until an accusation of cheating at cards 'burst open the floodgates of her own natural repartee, twanged off with the appellation of b—— and w——, which she repeated with great vehemence, in an attitude of manual defiance; nay, to such an unguarded pitch was she provoked, that, starting up, she snapt her fingers, in testimony of disdain, and, as she quitted the room, applied her hand to that part which was the last of her that dis-appeared, inviting the company to kiss it, by one of its coarsest denominations.' The scene, which does not last more than five pages, contains the whole of Bernard Shaw's *Pygmalion*.

As a writer of vigorous comedy Smollett is unsurpassed, and good comedy excuses a thousand defects. And there is, of course, something else. To read Smollett is to find oneself thrown head first into the bustle, the noise, the stink, the boisterousness, of his century.

WALTER ALLEN.

1956

SELECT BIBLIOGRAPHY

COLLECTED WORKS. *Miscellaneous Works of Tobias Smollett* (novels, poems, plays, and travels), 6 vols., 1790; with memoir of life and writings by R. Anderson, 6 vols., 1796; with life of author, 12 vols., 1824; with memoir by T. Roscoe, 1841. *Works of Tobias Smollett*, selected and edited, with historical notes and life of author, by D. Herbert, 1870. *Works*, ed. J. P. Browne, 8 vols., 1872; ed. Professor George Saintsbury in 12 vols., 1895, 1925. *Works of Tobias Smollett*, with introduction by W. E. Henley, in 12 vols., 1899–1901.

Novels, with memoir by Sir Walter Scott, in 2 vols., 1821. Shakespeare Head Edition of Novels, 1925.

Poetical Works, with life of author, 1794; with life by S. W. Singer, 1822; ed. E. Sanford, 1822.

NOVELS. *The Adventures of Roderick Random*, 1748; 3rd edition, 1750; 8th edition, 1770; with six plates, 1780; with life (Cooke's edition), 1793; illustrated by George Cruikshank, 1831; with memoir by G. H. Townsend, 1857; many other editions until present day. Abridged by R. Lewis (Dublin), 1791. Translated into French as *Histoire et aventures de Roderik Random*, 1782; other editions, 1784 and 1804.

The Adventures of Peregrine Pickle, in which are included Memoirs of a Lady of Quality, 1751; 3rd edition, 1765; 7th edition, 1784; Cooke's edition, 1794, with plates by T. Rowlandson, 1805; illustrated by Phiz, 1857; illustrated by George Cruikshank, 1904; translated into French by the author of *Les Mœurs* as *Histoire et aventures de Sir Williams Pickle*, 1753. For special reference to this novel see Howard S. Buck's Study in *Smollett*, 1925.

The Adventures of Ferdinand, Count Fathom, 1753; 2nd edition, 1771; other editions, 1780, 1782; Cooke's edition, 1795, 1890; illustrated by T. Stothard, 1905; translated into French by T. P. Bertin as *Fathom et Melvil*, 1798 (?).

The Adventures of Sir Launcelot Greaves, 1762; Cooke's edition, 1793; with engravings, 1839; many other editions, until present day. Translated into French by M. de F . . . as *Les Aventures de Sir Launcelot Greaves*, 1824.

The Expedition of Humphry Clinker, 1771; 2nd edition, 1772; Cooke's edition, 1794; with memoir by T. Roscoe and illustrated by George Cruikshank, 1831; illustrated by Phiz, 1857; illustrated by Cruikshank and bibliography by J. H. Isaacs, 1895; with portrait and illustrated by Cruikshank, 1904; with introduction and notes by L. Rice-Oxley, 1925. Adapted as a farce by J. Cumberland, 1828.

PLAYS, POEMS, AND SATIRES. *The Regicide : or James the First of Scotland, a tragedy*, 1749; *The Reprisal, or the Tars of Old England, a comedy*, 1757; and other editions. *The Tears of Scotland*, 1746; *Advice, a Satire* (in verse), 1746; *Reproof, a Satire* (in verse), 1747; reprinted as *Advice and Reproof*, 1748, 1826. *Burlesque Ode on the Loss of a Grandmother*, 1747; *Ode to Independence*, published posthumously, 1773. *The History and Adventures of an Atom* (prose, a satire), 1749, 1769, 1786, and 1795.

MISCELLANEOUS WORKS. Medical treatise, entitled *An Essay on the External Use of Water*, 1752. Began in 1756 *A Complete History of England from the descent of Julius Caesar to the Treaty of Aix-la-Chapelle*, 1748;

continued in 1763 as the *Continuation of the History of England*; afterwards known as *The History of England from the Revolution to the Death of George the Second*, and published in 1790. *Travels through France and Italy* appeared in 1766; 2nd edition, 1772; with introduction by Osbert Sitwell, 1949; translated by C. Albini Petrucci, with Lady Wortley Montagu's Letters as *Impressioni italiane di viaggiatori inglesi del sec. xviii*, 1916.

Smollett also translated *Gil Blas*, 1749, and numerous later editions; *Don Quixote*, 1755, and numerous later editions; several works of Voltaire, 1761; Fénelon's *Adventures of Telemachus*, 1776.

In 1756 Smollett edited the *Critical Review*; the *British Magazine* in 1760; the *Briton* from 1762 to 1763; A Compendium of Authentic and Entertaining Voyages, 1766.

A work sometimes attributed to Smollett is the *Faithful Narrative of the base and inhuman arts that were lately practised upon the brain of Habbakkuk Hilding, by Drawcansir Alexander, Fencing-Master and Philomath*, 1752.

BIOGRAPHY AND CRITICISM. G. M. Kahrl: *Tobias Smollett: Traveller-Novelist*, 1945; L. M. Knapp: *Tobias Smollett: Doctor of Men and Manners*, 1949; L. Brander: *Tobias Smollett*, 1951.

CONTENTS

CHAPTER I

An Account of Mr. Gamaliel Pickle—The Disposition of his Sister described—He yields to her Solicitations, and retires to the Country.

IN a certain county of England, bounded on one side by the sea, and at the distance of one hundred miles from the metropolis, lived Gamaliel Pickle, Esq., the father of that hero whose adventures we purpose to record. He was the son of a merchant in London, who, like Rome, from small beginnings, had raised himself to the highest honours of the city, and acquired a plentiful fortune, though, to his infinite regret, he died before it amounted to a plum, conjuring his son, as he respected the last injunction of a parent, to imitate his industry, and adhere to his maxims, until he should have made up the deficiency, which was a sum considerably less than fifteen thousand pounds.

This pathetic remonstrance had the desired effect upon his representative, who spared no pains to fulfil the request of the deceased, but exerted all the capacity with which nature had endowed him, in a series of efforts, which, however, did not succeed; for, by the time he had been fifteen years in trade, he found himself five thousand pounds worse than he was when he first took possession of his father's effects; a circumstance that affected him so nearly, as to detach his inclinations from business, and induce him to retire from the world, to some place where he might at leisure deplore his misfortunes, and, by frugality, secure himself from want, and the apprehensions of a jail, with which his imagination was incessantly haunted. He was often heard to express his fears of coming upon the parish, and to bless God, that, on account of his having been so long a housekeeper, he was entitled to that provision. In short, his talents were not naturally active, and there was a sort of inconsistency in his character; for, with all the desire of amassing which any citizen could possibly entertain, he was encumbered by a certain indolence and sluggishness that prevailed over every interested consideration, and even hindered him from profiting by the singleness of apprehension, and moderation of appetites, which have so frequently conduced to the acquisition of immense fortunes, qualities which he possessed in a very remarkable degree. Nature, in all probability, had mixed little or nothing inflammable in his composition; or whatever seeds of excess she might have sown within him, were effectually stifled and destroyed by the austerity of his education.

The sallies of his youth, far from being inordinate or criminal, never exceeded the bounds of that decent jollity, which an extraordinary pot, on extraordinary occasions, may be supposed to have produced in a club of sedate book-keepers, whose imaginations were neither very warm nor luxuriant. Little subject to refined sensations, he was scarce ever disturbed with violent emotions of any kind. The passion of love never interrupted his tranquillity; and if, as Mr. Creech says after Horace,

> Not to admire is all the art I know,
> To make men happy, and to keep them so,

Mr. Pickle was undoubtedly possessed of that invaluable secret; at least he was never known to betray the faintest symptom of transport, except one evening at the club, where he observed, with some demonstrations of vivacity, that he had dined upon a delicate loin of veal.

Notwithstanding this appearance of phlegm, he could not help feeling his disappointments in trade; and, upon the failure of a certain underwriter, by which he lost five hundred pounds, declared his design of relinquishing business, and retiring to the country. In this resolution he was comforted and encouraged by his only sister Mrs. Grizzle, who had managed his family since the death of his father, and was now in the thirtieth year of her maidenhood, with a fortune of five thousand pounds, and a large stock of economy and devotion.

These qualifications, one would think, might have been the means of abridging the term of her celibacy, as she never expressed any aversion to wedlock; but it seems she was too delicate in her choice to find a mate to her inclination in the city; for I cannot suppose that she remained so long unsolicited, though the charms of her person were not altogether enchanting, nor her manner over and above agreeable. Exclusive of a very wan (not to call it sallow) complexion, which perhaps was the effects of her virginity and mortification, she had a cast in her eyes that was not at all engaging, and such an extent of mouth, as no art or affectation could contract into any proportionable dimension. Then her piety was rather peevish than resigned, and did not in the least diminish a certain stateliness in her

demeanour and conversation, that delighted in communicating
the importance and honour of her family, which, by the bye,
was not to be traced two generations back, by all the power of
heraldry or tradition.

She seemed to have renounced all the ideas she had acquired
before her father served the office of sheriff; and the era which
regulated the dates of all her observations, was the mayoralty
of her papa. Nay, so solicitous was this good lady for the
support and propagation of the family name, that, suppressing
every selfish motive, she actually prevailed upon her brother to
combat with his own disposition, and even surmount it so far,
as to declare a passion for the person whom he afterwards
wedded, as we shall see in the sequel. Indeed she was the spur
that instigated him in all his extraordinary undertakings; and
I question whether or not he would have been able to disengage
himself from that course of life in which he had so long mechanically moved, unless he had been roused and actuated by her
incessant exhortations. London, she observed, was a receptacle
of iniquity, where an honest unsuspecting man was every day
in danger of falling a sacrifice to craft; where innocence was
exposed to continual temptations, and virtue eternally persecuted by malice and slander; where everything was ruled by
caprice and corruption, and merit utterly discouraged and
despised. This last imputation she pronounced with such
emphasis and chagrin, as plainly denoted how far she considered
herself as an example of what she advanced; and really the
charge was justified by the constructions that were put upon
her retreat by her female friends, who, far from imputing it to
the laudable motives that induced her, insinuated, in sarcastic
commendations, that she had good reason to be dissatisfied with
a place where she had been so long overlooked; and that it was
certainly her wisest course to make her last effort in the country,
where, in all probability, her talents would be less eclipsed, and
her fortune more attractive.

Be this as it will, her admonitions, though they were powerful
enough to convince, would have been insufficient to overcome
the languor and *vis inertiæ* of her brother, had she not reinforced
her arguments by calling in question the credit of two or three
merchants, with whom he was embarked in trade.

Alarmed at these hints of intelligence, he exerted himself
effectually; he withdrew his money from trade, and laying it
out in bank stock and India bonds, removed to a house in the
country, which his father had built near the seaside, for the

convenience of carrying on a certain branch of traffic in which he had been deeply concerned.

Here, then, Mr. Pickle fixed his habitation for life, in the six-and-thirtieth year of his age; and, though the pangs he felt at parting with his intimate companions, and quitting all his former connexions, were not quite so keen as to produce any dangerous disorder in his constitution, he did not fail to be extremely disconcerted at his first entrance into a scene of life to which he was totally a stranger. Not but that he met with abundance of people in the country, who, in consideration of his fortune, courted his acquaintance, and breathed nothing but friendship and hospitality. Yet even the trouble of receiving and returning these civilities, was an intolerable fatigue to a man of his habits and disposition. He therefore left the care of the ceremonial to his sister, who indulged herself in all the pride of formality, while he himself, having made a discovery of a public-house in the neighbourhood, went thither every evening, and enjoyed his pipe and can; being very well satisfied with the behaviour of the landlord, whose communicative temper was a great comfort to his own taciturnity; for he shunned all superfluity of speech, as much as he avoided any other unnecessary expense.

CHAPTER II

He is made acquainted with the Characters of Commodore Trunnion and his Adherents; meets with them by accident, and contracts an Intimacy with that Commander.

THIS loquacious publican soon gave him sketches of all the characters in the county, and, among others, described that of his next neighbour, Commodore Trunnion, which was altogether singular and odd. "The commodore and your worship," said he, "will in a short time be hand and glove; he has a power of money, and spends it like a prince—that is, in his own way —for, to be sure, he is a little humoursome, as the saying is, and swears woundily, though I'll be sworn he means no more harm than a sucking babe. Lord help us! it will do your honour's heart good to hear him tell a story, as how he lay alongside of the French, yard-arm and yard-arm, board and board, and of heaving grapplings, and stinkpots, and grapes, and round and double-headed partridges, crows and carters—

Laud have mercy upon us! he has been a great warrior in his time, and lost an eye and a heel in the service. Then, he does not live like any other Christian land-man; but keeps garrison in his house, as if he were in the midst of his enemies, and makes his servants turn out in the night, watch and watch, as he calls it, all the year round. His habitation is defended by a ditch, over which he has laid a draw-bridge, and planted his court-yard with patereroes continually loaded with shot, under the direction of one Mr. Hatchway, who had one of his legs shot away, while he acted as lieutenant on board the commodore's ship; and now, being on half-pay, lives with him as his companion. The lieutenant is a very brave man, a great joker, and, as the saying is, hath got the length of his commander's foot; though he has another favourite in the house, called Tom Pipes, that was his boatswain's mate, and now keeps the servants in order. Tom is a man of few words, but an excellent hand at a song concerning the boatswain's whistle, hussle-cap, and chuck-farthing—there is not such another pipe in the county.

"So that the commodore lives very happy in his own manner; thof he be sometimes thrown into perilous passions and quandaries, by the application of his poor kinsmen, whom he can't abide, because as how some of them were the first occasion of his going to sea. Then he sweats with agony at the sight of an attorney; just, for all the world, as some people have an antipathy to a cat; for it seems he was once at law for striking one of his officers, and cast in a swingeing sum. He is, moreover, exceedingly afflicted with goblins that disturb his rest, and keep such a racket in his house, that you would think, God bless us! all the devils in hell had broke loose upon him. It was no longer ago than last year about this time, that he was tormented the livelong night by two mischievous spirits that got into his chamber, and played a thousand pranks about his hammock (for there is not one bed within his walls). Well, sir, he rung his bell, called up all his servants, got lights, and made a thorough search; but the devil a goblin was to be found. He had no sooner turned in again, and the rest of the family gone to sleep, than the foul fiends began their game anew. The commodore got up in the dark, drew his cutlass, and attacked them both so manfully, that, at five minutes, everything in the apartment went to pieces. The lieutenant, hearing the noise, came to his assistance. Tom Pipes, being told what was the matter, lighted his match, and, going down to the yard, fired all the patereroes as signals of distress. Well, to be sure, the whole parish was in a pucker; some thought the French had landed; others imagined the commodore's house was beset by thieves; for my own part, I called up two dragoons that are quartered upon me; and they swore with deadly oaths, it was a gang of smugglers engaged with a party of their regiment, that lies in the next village; and, mounting their horses like lusty fellows, rode up into the country as fast as their beasts could carry them.

"Ah, master! these are hard times, when an industrious body cannot earn his bread without fear of the gallows. Your worship's father, God rest his soul! was a good gentleman, and as well respected in this parish as e'er a he that walks upon neat's leather. And if your honour should want a small parcel of fine tea, or a few ankers of right Nants, I'll be bound you shall be furnished to your heart's content. But, as I was saying, the hubbub continued till morning, when the parson being sent for, conjured the spirits into the Red Sea; and the house has been pretty quiet ever since. True it is, Mr. Hatchway makes a mock of the whole affair; and told his commander in this very blessed spot, that the two goblins were no other than a couple of jackdaws which had fallen down the chimney, and made a flapping with their wings up and down the apartment. But the commodore, who is very choleric, and does not like to be jeered, fell into a main high passion, and stormed like a perfect hurricane, swearing that he knew a devil from a jackdaw as well as e'er a man in the three kingdoms. He owned, indeed, that the birds were found, but denied that they were the occasion of the uproar. For my own part, master, I believe much may be said on both sides of the question, thof, to be sure, the devil is always going about, as the saying is."

This circumstantial account, extraordinary as it was, never altered one feature in the countenance of Mr. Pickle, who, having heard it to an end, took the pipe from his mouth, saying, with a look of infinite sagacity and deliberation, "I do suppose he is of the Cornish Trunnions. What sort of a woman is his spouse?" "Spouse!" cried the other, "odds heart! I don't think he would marry the Queen of Sheba. Lack-a-day! sir, he won't suffer his own maids to lie in the garrison, but turns them into an outhouse every night before the watch is set. Bless your honour's soul, he is, as it were, a very oddish kind of a gentleman. Your worship would have seen him before now; for when he is well, he and my good master Hatchway come hither every evening, and drink a couple of cans of rumbo a-piece; but he has been confined to his house this fortnight by a plaguy fit of the gout, which, I'll assure your worship, is a good penny out of my pocket."

At that instant, Mr. Pickle's ears were saluted with such a strange noise, as even discomposed the muscles of his face, which gave immediate indications of alarm. This composition of notes at first resembled the crying of quails and croaking of bull-frogs; but, as it approached nearer, he could distinguish articulate sounds pronounced with great violence, in such a cadence as one would expect to hear from a human creature scolding through the organs of an ass. It was neither speaking nor braying, but a surprising mixture of both, employed in the utterance of terms absolutely unintelligible to our wondering merchant, who had just opened his mouth to express his curiosity, when the landlord, starting up at the well-known sound, cried, "Odds niggers! there is the commodore with his company, as sure as I live"; and with his apron began to wipe the dust off an elbow-chair placed at one side of the fire, and kept sacred for the ease and convenience of this infirm commander. While he was thus occupied, a voice still more uncouth than the former bawled aloud, "Ho! the house, ahoy!" Upon which the publican, clapping a hand to each side of his head, with his thumbs fixed to his ears, rebellowed in the same tone, which he had learned to imitate, "Hilloah." The voice again exclaimed, "Have you got any attorneys aboard?" and when the landlord replied, "No, no"; this man of strange expectation came in, supported by his two dependents, and displayed a figure every way answerable to the oddity of his character.

He was in stature at least six feet high, though he had contracted an habit of stooping, by living so long on board; his complexion was tawny, and his aspect rendered hideous by a large scar across his nose, and a patch that covered the place of one eye. Being seated in his chair with great formality, the landlord complimented him upon his being able to come abroad again; and, having in a whisper communicated the name of his fellow-guest, whom the commodore already knew by report, went to prepare, with all imaginable despatch, the first allowance of his favourite liquor, in three separate cans, for each was accommodated with his own portion apart, while the lieutenant sat down on the blind side of his commander; and Tom Pipes, knowing his distance, with great modesty, took his station in the rear. After a pause of some minutes, the conversation was begun by this ferocious chief, who, fixing his eye upon the lieutenant with a sternness of countenance not to be described, addressed him in these words: "D—n my eyes! Hatchway, I always took you to be a better seaman than to overset our chaise in such fair weather. Blood! didn't I tell you we were running bump ashore, and bid you set in the lee-brace, and haul upon a wind?" "Yes," replied the other, with an arch sneer, "I do confess as how you did give such orders, after you had run us foul of a post, so as that the carriage lay along, and could not right herself." "I run you foul of a post!" cried the commander; "d—n my heart! you're a pretty dog, an't you, to tell me so aboveboard to my face? Did I take charge of the chaise? Did I stand at the helm?" "No," answered Hatchway; "I must confess you did not steer; but howsomever, you cunned all the way, and so, as you could not see how the land lay, being blind of your larboard eye, we were fast ashore, before you knew anything of the matter. Pipes, who stood abaft, can testify the truth of what I say." "D—n my limbs!" resumed the commodore, "I don't value what you or Pipes say a rope yarn. You're a couple of mutinous—I'll say no more; but you shan't run your rig upon me, d—n ye. I am the man that learnt you, Jack Hatchway, to splice a rope, and raise a perpendicular."

The lieutenant, who was perfectly well acquainted with the trim of his captain, did not choose to carry on the altercation any farther; but, taking up his can, drank to the health of the stranger, who very courteously returned the compliment, without, however, presuming to join in the conversation, which suffered a considerable pause. During this interruption, Mr. Hatchway's wit displayed itself in several practical jokes upon the commodore, with whom, he knew, it was dangerous to tamper in any other way. Being without the sphere of his vision, he securely pilfered his tobacco, drank his rumbo, made wry faces, and, to use the vulgar phrase, cocked his eye at him, to the no small entertainment of the spectators, Mr. Pickle himself not excepted, who gave evident tokens of uncommon satisfaction at the dexterity of this marine pantomime.

Meanwhile, the captain's choler gradually subsided, and he was pleased to desire Hatchway, by the familiar and friendly diminutive of Jack, to read a newspaper that lay on the table before him. This task was accordingly undertaken by the lame lieutenant, who, among other paragraphs, read that which follows, with an elevation of voice that seemed to prognosticate something extraordinary: "We are informed, that Admiral Bower will very soon be created a British peer, for his eminent services during the war, particularly in his late engagement with the French fleet." Trunnion was thunderstruck at this piece of intelligence. The mug dropped from his hand, and shivered into a thousand pieces; his eye glistened like that of a rattlesnake, and some minutes elapsed before he could pronounce, "Avast! overhaul that article again." It was no sooner read the second time, than, smiting the table with his fist, he started up, and, with the most violent emphasis of rage and indignation, exclaimed, "D—n my heart and liver! 'tis a land lie, d'ye see; and I will maintain it to be a lie, from the spritsail-yard to the mizen-topsail-haulyards! Blood and thunder! Will Bower a peer of this realm! a fellow of yesterday, that scarce knows a mast from a manger; a snotty-nose boy, whom I myself have ordered to the gun, for stealing eggs out of the hencoops! and I, Hawser Trunnion, who commanded a ship before he could keep a reckoning, am laid aside, d'ye see, and forgotten! If so be as this be the case, there is a rotten plank in our constitution, which ought to be hove down and repaired, d—n my eyes! For my own part, d'ye see, I was none of your guinea pigs; I did not rise in the service by parliamenteering interest, or a handsome b—h of a wife. I was not hoisted over the bellies of better men, nor strutted athwart the quarter-deck in a laced doublet, and thingumbobs at the wrists. D—n my limbs! I have been a hard-working man, and served all offices on board from cook's shifter to the command of a vessel. Here, you Tunley, there's the hand of a seaman, you dog."

So saying, he laid hold on the landlord's fist, and honoured him with such a squeeze, as compelled him to roar with great vociferation, to the infinite satisfaction of the commodore, whose features were a little unbended, by this acknowledgment of his vigour; and he thus proceeded in a less outrageous strain: "They make a d—ned noise about this engagement with the French; but, egad! it was no more than a bumboat battle, in comparison with some that I have seen. There was old Rook and Jennings, and another whom I'll be d—ned before I name, that knew what fighting was. As for my own share, d'ye see, I am none of those that halloo in their own commendation; but if so be that I were minded to stand my own trumpeter, some of those little fellows that hold their heads so high would be taken all aback, as the saying is; they would be ashamed to show their colours, d—n my eyes! I once lay eight glasses alongside of the *Flour de Louse,* a French man-of-war, though her metal was heavier, and her complement larger by an hundred hands than mine. You, Jack Hatchway, d—n ye, what d'ye grin at? D'ye think I tell a story, because you never heard it before?"

"Why, look ye, sir," answered the lieutenant, "I am glad to find you can stand your own trumpeter on occasion; thof I wish you would change the tune; for that is the same you have been piping every watch for these ten months past. Tunley himself will tell you, he has heard it five hundred times."

"God forgive you, Mr. Hatchway," said the landlord, interrupting him; "as I'm an honest man and a housekeeper, I never heard a syllab of the matter."

This declaration, though not strictly true, was extremely agreeable to Mr. Trunnion, who, with an air of triumph, observed, "Aha! Jack, I thought I should bring you up, with your jibes and your jokes; but suppose you had heard it before, is that any reason why it shouldn't be told to another person? There's the stranger, belike he has heard it five hundred times too; han't you, brother?" addressing himself to Mr. Pickle; who replied, with a look expressing curiosity, "No, never"; he thus went on: "Well, you seem to be an honest quiet sort of a man; and therefore you must know, as I said before, I fell in with a French man-of-war, Cape Finisterre bearing about six leagues on the weather bow, and the chase three leagues to leeward, going before the wind; whereupon I set my studding-sails, and, coming up with her, hoisted my jack and ensign, and poured in a whole broadside, before you could count three rattlins, in the mizen shrouds; for I always keep a good look-out, and love to have the first fire." "That I'll be sworn," said Hatchway; "for the day we made the *Triumph*, you ordered the men to fire when she was hull-to, by the same token we below pointed the guns at a flight of gulls; and I won a can of punch from the gunner, by killing the first bird." Exasperated at this sarcasm, he replied with great vehemence, "You lie, lubber! d—n your bones! what business have you to come always athwart my hawse in this manner? You, Pipes, was upon deck, and can bear witness, whether or not I fired too soon. Speak, you blood of a —, and that upon the word of a seaman; how did the chase bear of us, when I gave orders to fire?"

Pipes, who had hitherto sat silent, being thus called upon to give his evidence, after divers strange gesticulations, opened his mouth like a gasping cod, and, with a cadence like that of the east wind singing through a cranny, pronounced, "Half a quarter of a league right upon our lee-beam." "Nearer, you porpuss-fac'd swab!" cried the commodore, "nearer by twelve fathom; but, howsomever, that's enough to prove the falsehood of Hatchway's jaw—and so, brother, d'ye see," turning to Mr. Pickle, "I lay alongside of the *Flour de Louse*, yard-arm and yard-arm, plying our great guns and small arms, and heaving in stinkpots, powder-bottles, and hand-grenades, till our shot was all expended, double-headed, partridge, and grape; then we loaded with iron crows, marlinspikes, and old nails; but, finding the Frenchman took a great deal of drubbing, and that he had shot away all our rigging, and killed and wounded a great number of our men, d'ye see, I resolved to run him on board upon his quarter, and so ordered our grapplings to be got ready; but Monsieur, perceiving what we were about, filled his topsails and sheered off, leaving us like a log upon the water, and our scuppers running with blood."

Mr. Pickle and the landlord paid such extraordinary attention to the rehearsal of this exploit, that Trunnion was encouraged to entertain them with more stories of the same nature; after which he observed, by way of encomium on the government, that all he had gained in the service was a lame foot and the loss of an eye. The lieutenant, who could not find in his heart to lose any opportunity of being witty at the expense of his commander, gave a loose to his satirical talent once more, saying, "I have heard as how you came by your lame foot, by having your upper decks overstowed with liquor, whereby you became crank, and rolled, d'ye see, in such a manner, that, by a pitch of the ship, your starboard heel was jammed in one of the scuppers; and as for the matter of your eye, that was knocked out by your own crew when the *Lightning* was paid off. There's poor Pipes, who was beaten into all the colours of the rainbow for taking your part, and giving you time to sheer off; and I don't find as how you have rewarded him according as he deserves." As the commodore could not deny the truth of these anecdotes, however unseasonably they were introduced, he affected to receive them with good-humour, as jokes of the lieutenant's own inventing; and replied, "Ay, ay, Jack, everybody knows your tongue is no slander; but, howsomever, I'll work you to an oil for this, you dog." So saying, he lifted up one of his crutches, intending to lay it gently across Mr. Hatchway's pate; but Jack, with great agility, tilted up his wooden leg, with which he warded off the blow, to the no small admiration of Mr. Pickle, and utter astonishment of the landlord, who, by the bye, had expressed the same amazement, at the same feat, at the same hour, every night for three months before.

Trunnion then directing his eye to the boatswain's mate, "You, Pipes," said he, "do you go about and tell people that I did not reward you for standing by me, when I was hussled by these rebellious rapscallions? d—n you, han't you been rated on the books ever since?" Tom, who indeed had no words to spare, sat smoking his pipe with great indifference, and never dreamed of paying any regard to these interrogations; which being repeated and reinforced with many oaths, that, however, produced no effect, the commodore pulled out his purse, saying, "Here, you bitch's baby, here's something better than a smart ticket!" and threw it at his silent deliverer, who received and pocketed his bounty, without the least demonstration of surprise or satisfaction; while the donor turning to Mr. Pickle, "You see, brother," said he, "I make good the old saying, 'We sailors get money like horses, and spend it like asses'; come, Pipes, let's have the boatswain's whistle, and be jovial." This musician accordingly applied to his mouth the silver instrument that hung at a button-hole of his jacket, by a chain of the same metal, and, though not quite so ravishing as the pipe of Hermes, produced a sound so loud and shrill, that the stranger (as it were instinctively) stopped his ears, to preserve his organs of hearing from such a dangerous invasion. The prelude being thus executed, Pipes fixed his eyes upon the egg of an ostrich that depended from the ceiling, and, without once moving them from that object, performed the whole cantata in a tone of voice that seemed to be the joint issue of an Irish bagpipe and a sow-gelder's horn; the commodore, the lieutenant, and landlord joined in the chorus, repeating this elegant stanza:

> Bustle, bustle, brave boys,
> Let us sing, let us toil,
> And drink all the while,
> Since labour's the price of our joys.

The third line was no sooner pronounced, than the can was lifted to every man's mouth with admirable uniformity; and the next word taken up at the end of their draught with a twang equally expressive and harmonious. In short, the company began to understand one another; Mr. Pickle seemed to relish the entertainment, and a correspondence immediately commenced between him and Trunnion, who shook him by the hand, drank to further acquaintance, and even invited him to a mess of pork and peas in the garrison. The compliment was returned, good fellowship prevailed, and the night was pretty far advanced when the merchant's man arrived with a lanthorn to light his master home; upon which the new friends parted, after a mutual promise of meeting next evening in the same place.

CHAPTER III

Mrs. Grizzle exerts herself in finding a proper Match for her Brother; who is accordingly introduced to the young Lady, whom he marries in due season.

I HAVE been the more circumstantial in opening the character of Trunnion, because he bears a considerable share in the course of these memoirs; but now it is high time to resume the consideration of Mrs. Grizzle, who, since her arrival in the country, had been engrossed by a double care, namely, that of finding a suitable match for her brother, and a comfortable yoke-fellow for herself.

Neither was this aim the result of any sinister or frail suggestion, but the pure dictates of that laudable ambition, which prompted her to the preservation of the family name. Nay, so disinterested was she in this pursuit, that, postponing her nearest concern, or at least leaving her own fate to the silent operation of her charms, she laboured with such indefatigable zeal in behalf of her brother, that, before they had been three months settled in the country, the general topic of conversation in the neighbourhood, was an intended match between the rich Mr. Pickle and the fair Miss Appleby, daughter of a gentleman who lived in the next parish, and who, though he had but little fortune to bestow upon his children, had (to use his own phrase) replenished their veins with some of the best blood in the country.

This young lady, whose character and disposition Mrs. Grizzle had investigated to her own satisfaction, was destined for the spouse of Mr. Pickle, and an overture accordingly made to her father, who being overjoyed at the proposal, gave his consent without hesitation, and even recommended the immediate execution of the project with such eagerness, as seemed to indicate either a suspicion of Mr. Pickle's constancy, or a diffidence of his own daughter's complexion, which perhaps he thought too sanguine to keep much longer cool. The previous point being thus settled, our merchant, at the instigation of Mrs. Grizzle, went to visit his future father-in-law, and was introduced to the daughter, with whom he had, that same afternoon, an opportunity of being alone. What passed in that interview, I never could learn, though, from the character of the suitor, the reader may justly conclude, that she was not much teased with the impertinence of his addresses. He was not, I believe, the less welcome for that reason; certain it is, she made no objection to his taciturnity, and when her father communicated his resolution, acquiesced with the most pious resignation. But Mrs. Grizzle, in order to give the lady a more favourable idea of his intellects than what his conversation could possibly inspire, was resolved to dictate a letter, which her brother should transcribe and transmit to his mistress, as the produce of his own understanding, and had actually composed a very tender billet for this purpose; yet her intention was entirely frustrated by the misapprehension of the lover himself, who, in consequence of his sister's repeated admonitions, anticipated her scheme, by writing for himself, and despatching the letter one afternoon, while Mrs. Grizzle was visiting at the parson's.

Neither was this step the effect of his vanity or precipitation; but, having been often assured by his sister, that it was absolutely necessary for him to make a declaration of his love in writing, he took this opportunity of acting in conformity with her advice, when his imagination was unengaged or undisturbed by any other suggestion, without suspecting the least that she intended to save him the trouble of exercising his own genius. Left, therefore, as he imagined, to his own inventions, he sat down and produced the following morceau, which was transmitted to Miss Appleby, before his sister and counsellor had the least intimation of the affair:

MISS SALLY APPLEBY

MADAM,—Understanding you have a parcel of heart, warranted sound, to be disposed of, shall be willing to treat for said commodity, on reasonable terms; doubt not shall agree for same; shall wait on you for further information, when and where you shall appoint. This the needful from

Yours, etc.,

GAM. PICKLE.

This laconic epistle, simple and unadorned as it was, met with as cordial a reception from the person to whom it was addressed, as if it had been couched in the most elegant terms that delicacy of passion and cultivated genius could supply;

nay, I believe, was the more welcome, on account of its mer-
cantile plainness: because, when an advantageous match is in
view, a sensible woman often considers the flowery professions
and rapturous exclamations of love as ensnaring ambiguities,
or at best impertinent preliminaries, that retard the treaty
they are designed to promote; whereas Mr. Pickle removed all
disagreeable uncertainty, by descending at once to the most
interesting particular.

She had no sooner, as a dutiful child, communicated this
billet-doux to her father, than he, as a careful parent, visited
Mr. Pickle, and, in presence of Mrs. Grizzle, demanded a formal
explanation of his sentiments with regard to his daughter Sally.
Mr. Gamaliel, without any ceremony, assured him he had a
respect for the young woman, and, with his good leave, would
take her for better for worse. Mr. Appleby, after having
expressed his satisfaction that he had fixed his affections in
his family, comforted the lover with the assurance of his being
agreeable to the young lady, and they forthwith proceeded to
the articles of the marriage-settlement, which being discussed
and determined, a lawyer was ordered to engross them; the
wedding-clothes were bought, and, in short, a day was appointed
for the celebration of their nuptials, to which everybody of
any fashion in the neighbourhood was invited. Among these
Commodore Trunnion and Mr. Hatchway were not forgotten,
being the sole companions of the bridegroom, with whom, by
this time, they had contracted a sort of intimacy at their
nocturnal rendezvous.

They had received a previous intimation of what was on the
anvil from the landlord, before Mr. Pickle thought proper to
declare himself; in consequence of which, the topic of the one-
eyed commander's discourse at their meeting, for several
evenings before, had been the folly and plague of matrimony,
on which he held forth with great vehemence of abuse, levelled
at the fair sex, whom he represented as devils incarnate, sent
from hell to torment mankind; and, in particular, inveighed
against old maids, for whom he seemed to entertain a singular
aversion; while his friend Jack confirmed the truth of all his
allegations, and gratified his own malignant vein at the same
time, by clenching every sentence with a sly joke upon the
married state, built upon some allusion to a ship or seafaring
life. He compared a woman to a great gun loaded with fire,
brimstone, and noise, which, being violently heated, will bounce
and fly, and play the devil, if you don't take special care of her

breechings. He said she was like a hurricane, that never blows from one quarter, but veers about to all points of the compass. He likened her to a painted galley curiously rigged, with a leak in her hold, which her husband would never be able to stop. He observed that her inclinations were like the Bay of Biscay; for why? because you may heave your deep sea lead long enough without ever reaching the bottom. That he who comes to anchor on a wife, may find himself moored in d—d foul ground, and, after all, can't for his blood slip his cable; and that, for his own part, thof he might make short trips for pastime, he would never embark in woman on the voyage of life, because he was afraid of foundering in the first foul weather.

In all probability, these insinuations made some impression on the mind of Mr. Pickle, who was not very much inclined to run great risks of any kind; but the injunctions and importunities of his sister, who was bent upon the match, overbalanced the opinion of his sea friends, who, finding him determined to marry, notwithstanding all the hints of caution they had thrown out, resolved to accept his invitation, and honoured his nuptials with their presence accordingly.

CHAPTER IV

The Behaviour of Mrs. Grizzle at the Wedding, with an Account of the Guests.

I HOPE it will not be thought uncharitable, if I advance, by way of conjecture, that Mrs. Grizzle, on this grand occasion, summoned her whole exertion, to play off the artillery of her charms upon the single gentlemen who were invited to the entertainment. Sure I am, she displayed to the best advantage all the engaging qualities she possessed. Her affability at dinner was altogether uncommon; her attention to the guests was superfluously hospitable; her tongue was sheathed with the most agreeable and infantine lisp; her address was perfectly obliging; and though, conscious of the extraordinary capacity of her mouth, she would not venture to hazard a laugh, she modelled her lips into an enchanting simper, which played upon her countenance all day long; nay, she even profited by that defect in her vision we have already observed, and securely contemplated those features which were most to her liking, while the rest of the company believed her regards were disposed in a quite contrary

direction. With what humility of complaisance did she receive
the compliments of those who could not help praising the
elegance of the banquet! and how piously did she seize that
opportunity of commemorating the honours of her sire, by
observing that it was no merit in her to understand something
of entertainments, as she had occasion to preside at so many,
during the mayoralty of her papa! Far from discovering the
least symptom of pride and exultation, when the opulence of
her family became the subject of conversation, she assumed a
severity of countenance; and, after having moralised on the
vanity of riches, declared, that those who looked upon her as
a fortune were very much mistaken; for her father had left her
no more than poor five thousand pounds, which, with what little
she had saved of the interest since his death, was all she had to
depend upon. Indeed, if she had placed her chief felicity in
wealth, she should not have been so forward in destroying her
own expectations, by advising and promoting the event at
which they were now so happily assembled; but she hoped she
should always have virtue enough to postpone any interested
consideration, when it should happen to clash with the happiness
of her friends. Finally, such was her modesty and self-denial,
that she industriously informed those whom it might concern,
that she was no less than three years older than the bride;
though had she added ten to the reckoning, she would have
committed no mistake in point of computation.

To contribute as much as lay in her power to the satisfaction
of all present, she, in the afternoon, regaled them with a tune
on the harpsichord, accompanied with her voice, which, though
not the most melodious in the world, I dare say, would have
been equally at their service, could she have vied with Philomel
in song; and as the last effort of her complaisance, when dancing
was proposed, she was prevailed upon, at the request of her
new sister, to open the ball in person.

In a word, Mrs. Grizzle was the principal figure in this festival,
and almost eclipsed the bride, who, far from seeming to dispute
the pre-eminence, very wisely allowed her to make the best of
her talents, contenting herself with the lot to which fortune
had already called her, and which she imagined would not be
the less desirable, if her sister-in-law were detached from
the family.

I believe I need scarce advertise the reader, that, during this
whole entertainment, the commodore and his lieutenant were
quite out of their element; and this, indeed, was the case with

the bridegroom himself, who, being utterly unacquainted with any sort of polite commerce, found himself under a very disagreeable restraint during the whole scene.

Trunnion, who had scarce ever been on shore till he was paid off, and never once in his whole life in the company of any females above the rank of those who herd upon the Point at Portsmouth, was more embarrassed about his behaviour, than if he had been surrounded at sea by the whole French navy. He had never pronounced the word madam since he was born; so that, far from entering into conversation with the ladies, he would not even return the compliment, or give the least nod of civility when they drank to his health; and, I verily believe, would rather have suffered suffocation, than allowed the simple phrase, *your servant*, to proceed from his mouth. He was altogether as inflexible with respect to the attitudes of his body; for, either through obstinacy or bashfulness, he sat upright without motion, insomuch that he provoked the mirth of a certain wag, who, addressing himself to the lieutenant, asked whether that was the commodore himself, or the wooden lion that used to stand at his gate? An image to which, it must be owned, Mr. Trunnion's person bore no faint resemblance.

Mr. Hatchway, who was not quite so unpolished as the commodore, and had certain notions that seemed to approach the ideas of common life, made a less uncouth appearance; but then he was a wit, and though of a very peculiar genius, partook largely of that disposition which is common to all wits, who never enjoy themselves, except when their talents meet with those marks of distinction and veneration which, in their own opinion, they deserve.

These circumstances being premised, it is not to be wondered at if this triumvirate made no objections to the proposal, when some of the grave personages of the company made a motion for adjourning into another apartment, where they might enjoy their pipes and bottles, while the young folks indulged themselves in the continuance of their own favourite diversion. Thus rescued, as it were, from a state of annihilation, the first use the two lads of the castle made of their existence, was to ply the bridgroom so hard with bumpers, that, in less than an hour, he made divers efforts to sing, and soon after was carried to bed, deprived of all manner of sensation, to the utter disappointment of the bridemen and maids, who, by this accident, were prevented from throwing the stocking, and performing certain other ceremonies practised on such occasions. As for the bride, she bore this misfortune with great good-humour; and indeed, on all occasions, behaved like a discreet woman, perfectly well acquainted with the nature of her own situation.

CHAPTER V

Mrs. Pickle assumes the Reins of Government in her own Family; her Sister-in-Law undertakes an Enterprise of great moment; but is for some time diverted from her Purpose by a very interesting Consideration.

WHATEVER deference, not to say submission, she had paid to Mrs. Grizzle before she was so nearly allied to her family, she no sooner became Mrs. Pickle, than she thought it incumbent upon her to act up to the dignity of the character; and, the very day after the marriage, ventured to dispute with her sister-in-law on the subject of her own pedigree, which she affirmed to be more honourable in all respects than that of her husband; observing that several younger brothers of her house had arrived at the station of Lord Mayor of London, which was the highest pitch of greatness that any of Mr. Pickle's predecessors had ever attained.

This presumption was like a thunderbolt to Mrs. Grizzle, who began to perceive that she had not succeeded quite so well as she imagined, in selecting for her brother a gentle and obedient yoke-fellow, who would always treat her with that profound respect which she thought due to her superior genius, and be entirely regulated by her advice and direction. However, she still continued to manage the reins of government in the house, reprehending the servants as usual; an office she performed with great capacity, and in which she seemed to take singular delight, until Mrs. Pickle, on pretence of consulting her ease, told her one day she would take that trouble upon herself, and for the future assume the management of her own family. Nothing could be more mortifying to Mrs. Grizzle than such a declaration, to which, after a considerable pause, and strange distortion of look, she replied, "I shall never refuse or repine at any trouble that may conduce to my brother's advantage." "Dear madam," answered the sister, "I am infinitely obliged to your kind concern for Mr. Pickle's interest, which I consider as my own, but I cannot bear to see you a sufferer by your friendship; and, therefore, insist upon exempting you from the fatigue you have borne so long."

In vain did the other protest that she took pleasure in the task; Mrs. Pickle ascribed the assurance to her excess of complaisance, and expressed such tenderness of zeal for her dear sister's health and tranquillity, that the reluctant maiden found herself obliged to resign her authority, without enjoying the least pretext for complaining of her being deposed.

This disgrace was attended by a fit of peevish devotion that lasted three or four weeks; during which period, she had the additional chagrin of seeing the young lady gain an ascendency over the mind of her brother, who was persuaded to set up a gay equipage, and improve his housekeeping, by an augmentation in his expense, to the amount of a thousand a year at least; though his alteration in the economy of his household effected no change in his own disposition, or manner of life; for, as soon as the painful ceremony of receiving and returning visits was performed, he had recourse again to the company of his sea friends, with whom he spent the best part of his time.   But if he was satisfied with his condition, the case was otherwise with Mrs. Grizzle, who, finding her importance in the family greatly diminished, her attractions neglected by all the male sex in the neighbourhood, and the withering hand of time hang threatening over her head, began to feel the horror of eternal virginity, and, in a sort of desperation, resolved at any rate to rescue herself from that uncomfortable situation.

Thus determined, she formed a plan, the execution of which, to a spirit less enterprising and sufficient than hers, would have appeared altogether impracticable; this was no other than to make a conquest of the commodore's heart, which the reader will easily believe was not very susceptible of tender impressions; but, on the contrary, fortified with insensibility and prejudice against the charms of the whole sex, and particularly prepossessed to the prejudice of that class distinguished by the appellation of old maids, in which Mrs. Grizzle was by this time unhappily ranked. She, nevertheless, took the field, and, having invested this seemingly impregnable fortress, began to break ground one day, when Trunnion dined at her brother's, by springing certain ensnaring commendations on the honesty and sincerity of seafaring people, paying a particular attention to his plate, and affecting a simper of approbation at everything he said, which by any means she could construe into a joke, or with modesty be supposed to hear; nay, even when he left decency on the left hand, which was often the case, she ventured to reprimand his freedom of speech with a gracious grin, saying,

"Sure you gentlemen belonging to the sea have such an odd way with you." But all this complacency was so ineffectual, that, far from suspecting the true cause of it, the commodore, that very evening, at the club, in presence of her brother, with whom by this time he could take any manner of freedom, did not scruple to d—n her for a squinting, block-faced, chattering p—s-kitchen; and immediately after drank despair to all old maids.

The toast Mr. Pickle pledged without the least hesitation, and next day intimated to his sister, who bore the indignity with surprising resignation, and did not therefore desist from her scheme, unpromising as it seemed to be, until her attention was called off, and engaged in another care, which, for some time, interrupted the progress of this design. Her sister had not been married many months, when she exhibited evident symptoms of pregnancy, to the general satisfaction of all concerned, and the inexpressible joy of Mrs. Grizzle, who, as we have already hinted, was more interested in the preservation of the family name, than in any other consideration whatever. She, therefore, no sooner discovered appearances to justify and confirm her hopes, than, postponing her own purpose, and laying aside that pique and resentment she had conceived from the behaviour of Mrs. Pickle, when she superseded her authority, or perhaps considering her in no other light than that of the vehicle which contained and was destined to convey her brother's heir to light, she determined to exert her uttermost in nursing, tending, and cherishing her, during the term of her important charge. With this view she purchased Culpeper's *Midwifery*, which, with that sagacious performance dignified with Aristotle's name, she studied with indefatigable care, and diligently perused *The Complete Housewife*, together with Quincy's *Dispensatory*, culling every jelly, marmalade, and conserve which these authors recommend as either salutary or toothsome, for the benefit and comfort of her sister-in-law, during her gestation. She restricted her from eating roots, pot-herbs, fruit, and all sorts of vegetables; and one day, when Mrs. Pickle had plucked a peach with her own hand, and was in the very act of putting it between her teeth, Mrs. Grizzle perceived the rash attempt, and running up to her, fell upon her knees in the garden, entreating her, with tears in her eyes, to resist such a pernicious appetite. Her request was no sooner complied with, than, recollecting that, if her sister's longing was balked, the child might be affected with some disagreeable mark, or deplorable disease, she begged as earnestly that she would swallow the fruit, and, in the meantime, ran for some cordial water of her own composing, which she forced upon her sister, as an antidote to the poison she had received.

This excessive zeal and tenderness did not fail to be very troublesome to Mrs. Pickle, who, having revolved divers plans for the recovery of her own ease, at length determined to engage Mrs. Grizzle in such employment as would interrupt that close attendance which she found so teasing and disagreeable. Neither did she wait long for an opportunity of putting her resolution in practice. The very next day, a gentleman happening to dine with Mr. Pickle, unfortunately mentioned a pineapple, part of which he had eaten a week before at the house of a nobleman who lived in another part of the country, at the distance of an hundred miles at least.

The name of this fatal fruit was no sooner pronounced than Mrs. Grizzle, who incessantly watched her sister's looks, took the alarm, because she thought they gave certain indications of curiosity and desire; and, after having observed that she herself could never eat pineapples, which were altogether unnatural productions, extorted by the force of artificial fire out of filthy manure, asked with a faltering voice, if Mrs. Pickle was not of her way of thinking? This young lady, who wanted neither slyness nor penetration, at once divined her meaning, and replied with seeming unconcern, that, for her own part, she should never repine, if there was not a pineapple in the universe, provided she could indulge herself with the fruits of her own country.

This answer was calculated for the benefit of the stranger, who would certainly have suffered for his imprudence by the resentment of Mrs. Grizzle, had her sister expressed the least relish for the fruit in question. It had the desired effect, and re-established the peace of the company, which was not a little endangered by the gentleman's want of consideration. Next morning, however, after breakfast, the pregnant lady, in pursuance of her plan, yawned, as it were by accident, full in the face of her maiden sister, who, being infinitely disturbed by this convulsion, affirmed it was a symptom of longing, and insisted upon knowing the object in desire, when Mrs. Pickle, assuming an affected smile, told her she had eaten a most delicious pineapple in her sleep. This declaration was attended with an immediate scream, uttered by Mrs. Grizzle, who instantly, perceiving her sister surprised at the exclamation, clasped her in her arms, and assured her, with a sort of hysterical laugh, that she could not help screaming with joy, because she had it in her power to gratify her dear sister's wish; a lady in the neighbourhood having promised to send her, in a present, a couple of delicate pineapples, which she would that very day go in quest of.

Mrs. Pickle would by no means consent to this proposal, on pretence of sparing the other unnecessary fatigue; and assured her, that if she had any desire to eat a pineapple, it was so faint, that the disappointment could produce no bad consequence. But this assurance was conveyed in a manner (which she knew very well how to adopt) that, instead of dissuading, rather stimulated Mrs. Grizzle to set out immediately, not on a visit to that lady, whose promise she herself had feigned, with a view of consulting her sister's tranquillity, but on a random search through the whole country for this unlucky fruit, which was like to produce so much vexation and prejudice to her and her father's house.

During three whole days and nights did she, attended by a valet, ride from place to place without success, unmindful of her health, and careless of her reputation, that began to suffer from the nature of her inquiry, which was pursued with such peculiar eagerness and distraction, that everybody with whom she conversed looked upon her as an unhappy person, whose intellects were not a little disordered.

Baffled in all her researches within the county, she at length resolved to visit that very nobleman, at whose house the officious stranger had been, for her so unfortunately, regaled, and actually arrived in a postchaise at the place of his habitation, where she introduced her business as an affair on which the happiness of a whole family depended. By virtue of a present to his lordship's gardener, she procured the Hesperian fruit, with which she returned in triumph.

CHAPTER VI

Mrs. Grizzle is indefatigable in gratifying her Sister's Longings—Peregrine is born, and managed contrary to the Directions and Remonstrances of his Aunt, who is disgusted upon that account, and resumes the Plan which she had before rejected.

THE success of this device would have encouraged Mrs. Pickle to practise more of the same sort upon her sister-in-law, had she not been deterred by a violent fever which seized her zealous ally, in consequence of the fatigue and uneasiness she had undergone; which, while it lasted, as effectually conduced to her repose, as any other stratagem she could invent. But Mrs. Grizzle's health was no sooner restored, than the other, being as much incommoded as ever, was obliged, in her own defence, to have recourse to some other contrivance; and managed her artifices in such a manner, as leaves it at this day a doubt whether she was really so whimsical and capricious in her appetites as she herself pretended to be; for her longings were not restricted to the demands of the palate and stomach, but also affected all the other organs of sense, and even invaded her imagination, which at this period seemed to be strangely diseased.

One time she longed to pinch her husband's ear; and it was with infinite difficulty that his sister could prevail upon him to undergo the operation. Yet this task was easy, in comparison with another she undertook for the gratification of Mrs. Pickle's unaccountable desire; which was no other than to persuade the commodore to submit his chin to the mercy of the big-bellied lady, who ardently wished for an opportunity of plucking three black hairs from his beard. When this proposal was first communicated to Mr. Trunnion by the husband, his answer was nothing but a dreadful effusion of oaths, accompanied with such a stare, and delivered in such a tone of voice, as terrified the poor beseecher into immediate silence; so that Mrs. Grizzle was fain to take the whole enterprise upon herself, and next day went to the garrison accordingly, where, having obtained entrance by means of the lieutenant, who, while his commander was asleep, ordered her to be admitted for the joke's sake, she waited patiently till he turned out, and then accosted him in the yard, where he used to perform his morning walk. He was thunderstruck at the appearance of a woman in a place which he had hitherto kept sacred from the whole sex, and immediately began to utter an apostrophe to Tom Pipes, whose turn it was then to watch; when Mrs. Grizzle, falling on her knees before him, conjured him with many pathetic supplications, to hear and grant her request, which was no sooner signified, than he bellowed in such an outrageous manner, that the whole court re-echoed the opprobrious term *bitch*, and the word *d—tion*, which he repeated with surprising volubility, without any sort of propriety or connexion; and retreated into his penetralia, leaving the baffled devotee in the humble posture she had so unsuccessfully chosen to melt his obdurate heart.

Mortifying as this repulse must have been to a lady of her stately disposition, she did not relinquish her aim, but endeavoured to interest the commodore's counsellors and adherents in her cause. With this view, she solicited the interest of Mr. Hatchway, who, being highly pleased with a circumstance so productive of mirth and diversion, readily entered into her measures, and promised to employ his whole influence for her satisfaction; and, as for the boatswain's mate, he was rendered propitious by the present of a guinea, which she slipped into his hand. In short, Mrs. Grizzle was continually engaged in this negotiation for the space of ten days, during which the commodore was so incessantly pestered with her remonstrances, and the admonitions of his associates, that he swore his people had a design upon his life, which becoming a burden to him, he at last complied, and was conducted to the scene like a victim to the altar, or rather like a reluctant bear, when he is led to the stake amidst the shouts and cries of butchers and their dogs. After all, this victory was not quite so decisive as the conquerors imagined; for the patient being set, and the performer prepared with a pair of pincers, a small difficulty occurred. She could not for some time discern one black hair on the whole superficies of Mr. Trunnion's face; when Mrs. Grizzle, very much alarmed and disconcerted, had recourse to a magnifying glass that stood upon her toilet; and, after a most accurate examination, discovered a fibre of a dusky hue, to which the instrument being applied, Mrs. Pickle pulled it up by the roots, to the no small discomposure of the owner, who, feeling the smart much more severe than he had expected, started up, and swore he would not part with another hair to save them all from d—tion.

Mr. Hatchway exhorted him to patience and resignation; Mrs. Grizzle repeated her entreaties with great humility; but finding him deaf to all her prayers, and absolutely bent upon leaving the house, she clasped his knees, and begged for the love of God, that he would have compassion upon a distressed family, and endure a little more for the sake of the poor infant, who would otherwise be born with a grey beard upon its chin. Far from being melted, he was rather exasperated by this reflection; to which he replied with great indignation, "D—n you for a yaw-sighted b—h! he'll be hanged long enough before he has any beard at all." So saying, he disengaged himself from her embraces, flung out at the door, and halted homewards with such surprising speed, that the lieutenant could not overtake him until he had arrived at his own gate; and Mrs. Grizzle was so much affected with his escape, that her sister, in pure compassion, desired she would not afflict herself, protesting that her own wish was already gratified, for she had plucked three hairs at once, having from the beginning been dubious of the commodore's patience. But the labours of this assiduous kinswoman did not end with the achievement of this adventure; her eloquence or industry was employed without ceasing, in the performance of other tasks imposed by the ingenious craft of her sister-in-law, who, at another time, conceived an insuppressible affection for a fricassee of frogs, which should be the genuine natives of France; so that there was a necessity for despatching a messenger on purpose to that kingdom. But, as she could not depend upon the integrity of any common servant, Mrs. Grizzle undertook that province, and actually set sail in a cutter for Boulogne, from whence she returned in eight-and-forty hours with a tub full of these live animals, which, being dressed according to art, her sister would not taste them, on pretence that her fit of longing was past; but then her inclinations took a different turn, and fixed themselves upon a curious implement belonging to a lady of quality in the neighbourhood, which was reported to be a very great curiosity; this was no other than a porcelain chamber-pot of admirable workmanship, contrived by the honourable owner, who kept it for her own private use, and cherished it as a utensil of inestimable value.

Mrs. Grizzle shuddered at the first hint she received of her sister's desire to possess this piece of furniture, because she knew it was not to be purchased; and the lady's character, which was none of the most amiable in point of humanity and condescension, forbade all hopes of borrowing it for a season; she therefore attempted to reason down this capricious appetite, as an extravagance of imagination which ought to be combated and repressed; and Mrs. Pickle, to all appearance, was convinced and satisfied by her arguments and advice; but, nevertheless, could make use of no other convenience, and was threatened with a very dangerous suppression. Roused at the peril in which she supposed her to be, Mrs. Grizzle flew to the lady's house, and, having obtained a private audience, disclosed the melancholy situation of her sister, and implored the benevolence of her ladyship; who, contrary to expectation, received her very graciously, and consented to indulge Mrs. Pickle's longing. Mr. Pickle began to be out of humour at the expense to which he was exposed by the caprice of his wife, who was herself alarmed at this last accident, and, for the future, kept her fancy within bounds; insomuch, that, without being subject to any more extraordinary trouble, Mrs. Grizzle reaped the long-wished-for fruits of her dearest expectation in the birth of a fine boy, whom her sister in a few months brought into the world.

I shall omit the description of the rejoicings, which were infinite, on this important occasion, and only observe, that Mrs. Pickle's mother and aunt stood godmothers, and the commodore assisted at the ceremony as godfather to the child, who was christened by the name of Peregrine, in compliment to the memory of a deceased uncle. While the mother was confined to her bed, and incapable of maintaining her own authority, Mrs. Grizzle took charge of the infant by a double claim; and superintended with surprising vigilance the nurse and midwife in all the particulars of their respective offices, which were performed by her express direction. But no sooner was Mrs. Pickle in a condition to reassume the management of her own affairs, than she thought proper to alter certain regulations concerning the child, which had obtained in consequence of her sister's orders, directing, among other innovations, that the bandages with which the infant had been so neatly rolled up, like an Egyptian mummy, should be loosened and laid aside, in order to rid nature of all restraint, and give the blood free scope to circulate; and, with her own hands, she plunged him headlong every morning in a tub full of cold water. This operation seemed so barbarous to the tender-hearted Mrs. Grizzle, that she not only opposed it with all her eloquence, shedding abundance of tears over the sacrifice when it was made, but took horse immediately, and departed for the habitation of an eminent country physician, whom she consulted in these words: "Pray, doctor, is it not both dangerous and cruel to be the means of letting a poor tender infant perish, by sousing it in water as cold as ice?" "Yes," replied the doctor, "downright murder, I affirm." "I see you are a person of great learning and sagacity," said the other; "and I must beg you will be so good as to signify your opinion in your own handwriting." The doctor immediately complied with her request, and expressed himself upon a slip of paper to this purpose:

These are to certify whom it may concern, that I firmly believe, and it is my unalterable opinion, that whosoever letteth an infant perish, by sousing it in cold water, even though the said water should not be so cold as ice, is in effect guilty of the murder of the said infant—as witness my hand.

COMFIT COLOCYNTH.

Having obtained this certificate, for which the physician was immediately acknowledged, she returned exulting, and hoping, with such authority, to overthrow all opposition. Accordingly, next morning, when her nephew was about to undergo his diurnal baptism, she produced the commission, whereby she conceived herself empowered to overrule such inhuman proceedings. But she was disappointed in her expectation, confident as it was; not that Mrs. Pickle pretended to differ in opinion from Dr. Colocynth, "for whose character and sentiments," said she, "I have such veneration, that I shall carefully observe the caution implied in this very certificate, by which, far from condemning my method of practice, he only asserts that killing is murder; an asseveration, the truth of which, it is to be hoped, I never shall dispute."

Mrs. Grizzle, who, sooth to say, had rather too superficially considered the clause by which she thought herself authorised, perused the paper with more accuracy, and was confounded at her own want of penetration. Yet, though she was confuted, she was by no means convinced that her objections to the cold bath were unreasonable; on the contrary, after having bestowed sundry opprobrious epithets on the physician, for his want of knowledge and candour, she protested in the most earnest and solemn manner against the pernicious practice of dipping the child; a piece of cruelty which, with God's assistance, she should never suffer to be inflicted on her own issue; and, washing her hands of the melancholy consequence that would certainly ensue, shut herself up in her closet, to indulge her sorrow and vexation. She was deceived, however, in her prognostic. The boy, instead of declining in point of health, seemed to acquire fresh vigour from every plunge, as if he had been resolved to discredit the wisdom and foresight of his aunt, who, in all probability, could never forgive him for this want of reverence and respect. This conjecture is founded upon her behaviour to him in the sequel of his infancy, during which she was known to torture him more than once, when she had opportunities of thrusting pins into his flesh, without any danger of being detected. In a word, her affections were in a little time altogether alienated from this hope of her family, whom she abandoned to the conduct of his mother, whose province it undoubtedly was to manage the nurture of her own child; while she herself resumed her operations upon the commodore, whom she was resolved at any rate to captivate and enslave. And it must be owned that Mrs. Grizzle's knowledge of the human heart never shone so conspicuous, as in the methods she pursued for the accomplishment of this important aim.

Through the rough unpolished husk that cased the soul of Trunnion, she could easily distinguish a large share of that vanity and self-conceit that generally predominate even in the most savage breast; and to this she constantly appealed. In his presence she always exclaimed against the craft and dishonest dissimulation of the world, and never failed of uttering particular invectives against those arts of chicanery in which the lawyers are so conversant, to the prejudice and ruin of their fellow-creatures; observing, that in a seafaring life, so far as she had opportunities of judging or being informed, there was nothing but friendship, sincerity, and a hearty contempt for everything that was mean or selfish.

This kind of conversation, with the assistance of certain particular civilities, insensibly made an impression on the mind of the commodore, and that the more effectually, as his former prepossessions were built upon very slender foundations. His antipathy to old maids, which he had conceived upon hearsay, began gradually to diminish, when he found they were not quite such infernal animals as they had been represented; and it was not long before he was heard to observe at the club, that Pickle's sister had not so much of the core of bitch in her as he had imagined. This negative compliment, by the medium of her brother, soon reached the ears of Mrs. Grizzle, who, thus encouraged, redoubled all her arts and attention; so that, in less than three months after, he in the same place distinguished her with the epithet of a d—ed sensible jade.

Hatchway taking the alarm at this declaration, which he feared foreboded something fatal to his interest, told his commander, with a sneer, that she had sense enough to bring him to under her stern; and he did not doubt but that such an old crazy vessel would be the better for being taken in tow. "But, howsomever," added this arch adviser, "I'd have you take care of your upper works; for if once you are made fast to her poop, egad, she'll spank it away, and make every beam in your body crack with straining." Our she-projector's whole plan had like to have been ruined by the effect which this malicious hint had upon Trunnion, whose rage and suspicion being wakened at once, his colour changed from tawney to a cadaverous pale, and then shifting to a deep and dusky red, such as we sometimes observe in the sky when it is replete with thunder, he, after his usual preamble of unmeaning oaths, answered in these words: "D—n ye, ye jury-legged dog, you would give all the stowage in your hold to be as sound as I am; and as for being taken in tow, d'ye see, I'm not so disabled but that I can lie my course, and perform my voyage without any assistance; and, egad! no man shall ever see Hawser Trunnion lagging astern in the wake of e'er a b—h in Christendom."

Mrs. Grizzle, who every morning interrogated her brother with regard to the subject of his overnight's conversation with his friends, soon received the unwelcome news of the commodore's aversion to matrimony; and, justly imputing the greatest part of his disgust to the satirical insinuations of Mr. Hatchway, resolved to level this obstruction to her success, and actually found means to interest him in her scheme. She had indeed, on some occasions, a particular knack at making converts, being probably not unacquainted with that grand system of persuasion, which is adopted by the greatest personages of the age, as fraught with maxims much more effectual than all the eloquence of Tully or Demosthenes, even when supported by the demonstrations of truth. Besides, Mr. Hatchway's fidelity to his new ally was confirmed by his foreseeing in his captain's marriage an infinite fund of gratification for his own cynical disposition. Thus, therefore, converted and properly cautioned, he for the future suppressed all the virulence of his wit against the matrimonial state; and, as he knew not how to open his mouth in the positive praise of any person whatever, took all opportunities of excepting Mrs. Grizzle by name from the censures he liberally bestowed upon the rest of her sex. "She is not a drunkard, like Nan Castick of Deptford," he would say; "not a nincompoop, like Peg Simper of Woolwich; not a brimstone, like Kate Coddie of Chatham; nor a shrew, like Nell Griffin on the Point at Portsmouth (ladies to whom, at different times, they had both paid their addresses); but a tight, good-humoured, sensible wench, who knows very well how to box her compass; well trimmed aloft, and well sheathed alow, with a good cargo under her hatches." The commodore at first imagined this commendation was ironical, but hearing it repeated again and again, was filled with astonishment at this surprising change in the lieutenant's behaviour; and, after a long fit of musing, concluded that Hatchway himself harboured a matrimonial design on the person of Mrs. Grizzle.

Pleased with this conjecture, he rallied Jack in his turn, and one night toasted her health as a compliment to his passion; a circumstance which the lady learned next day by the usual canal of her intelligence, and, interpreting as the result of his own tenderness for her, she congratulated herself upon the victory she had obtained; and, thinking it unnecessary to continue the reserve she had hitherto industriously affected, resolved from that day to sweeten her behaviour towards him with such a dish of affection, as could not fail to persuade him that he had inspired her with a reciprocal flame. In consequence of this determination, he was invited to dinner, and, while he staid, treated with such cloying proofs of her regard, that not only the rest of the company, but even Trunnion himself, perceived her drift; and, taking the alarm accordingly, could not help exclaiming, "Oho! I see how the land lies, and if I don't weather the point, I'll be d—ed." Having thus expressed himself to his afflicted inamorata, he made the best of his way to the garrison, in which he shut himself up for the space of ten days, and had no communication with his friends and domestics but by looks, which were most significantly picturesque.

CHAPTER VII

Divers Stratagems are invented and put in practice, in order to overcome the Obstinacy of Trunnion, who at length is teased and tortured into the Noose of Wedlock.

THIS abrupt departure and unkind declaration affected Mrs. Grizzle so much, that she fell sick of sorrow and mortification; and, after having confined herself to her bed for three days, sent for her brother, told him she perceived her end drawing near, and desired that a lawyer might be brought, in order to write her last will. Mr. Pickle, surprised at her demand, began to act the part of a comforter, assuring her that her distemper was

not at all dangerous; and that he would instantly send for a
physician, who would convince her that she was in no manner
of jeopardy; so that there was no occasion at present to employ
an officious attorney in such a melancholy task. Indeed, this
affectionate brother was of opinion, that a will was altogether
superfluous at any rate, as he himself was heir at law to his
sister's whole real and personal estate. But she insisted upon
his compliance with such determined obstinacy, that he could
no longer resist her importunities; and, a scrivener arriving,
she dictated and executed her will, in which she bequeathed to
Commodore Trunnion one thousand pounds, to purchase a
mourning ring, which she hoped he would wear as a pledge of
her friendship and affection. Her brother, though he did not
much relish this testimony of her love, nevertheless that same
evening gave an account of this particular to Mr. Hatchway,
who was also, as Mr. Pickle assured him, generously remembered
by the testatrix.

The lieutenant, fraught with this piece of intelligence, watched
for an opportunity, and as soon as he perceived the commodore's
features a little unbended from that ferocious contraction they
had retained so long, ventured to inform him that Pickle's
sister lay at the point of death, and that she had left him a
thousand pounds in her will. This piece of news overwhelmed
him with confusion, and Mr. Hatchway imputing his silence to
remorse, resolved to take advantage of that favourable moment,
and counselled him to go and visit the poor young woman, who
was dying for love of him. But his admonition happened to be
somewhat unseasonable; for Trunnion no sooner heard him
mention the cause of her disorder, than, his morosity recurring,
he burst out into a violent fit of cursing, and forthwith betook
himself again to his hammock, where he lay uttering, in a low
growling tone of voice, a repetition of oaths and imprecations,
for the space of four-and-twenty hours, without ceasing. This
was a delicious meal to the lieutenant, who, eager to enhance
the pleasure of the entertainment, and at the same time conduce
to the success of the cause he had espoused, invented a stratagem, the execution of which had all the effect he could desire.
He prevailed upon Pipes, who was devoted to his service, to get
upon the top of the chimney belonging to the commodore's
chamber, at midnight, and to lower down by a rope a bunch
of stinking whitings; which being performed, he put a speaking-
trumpet to his mouth, and hollowed down the vent, in a voice
like thunder, "Trunnion! Trunnion! turn out and be spliced,

or lie still and be d—ed." This dreadful note, the terror of which was increased by the silence and darkness of the night, as well as the echo of the passage through which it was conveyed, no sooner reached the ears of the astonished commodore, than turning his eye towards the place from whence this solemn address seemed to proceed, he beheld a glittering object that vanished in an instant. Just as his superstitious fear had improved the apparition into some supernatural messenger clothed in shining array, his opinion was confirmed by a sudden explosion, which he took for thunder, though it was no other than the noise of a pistol fired down the chimney by the boatswain's mate, according to the instructions he had received; and he had time enough to descend before he was in any danger of being detected by his commander, who could not for a whole hour recollect himself from the amazement and consternation which had overpowered his faculties.

At length, however, he got up, and rang his bell with great agitation. He repeated the summons more than once; but no regard being paid to this alarm, his dread returned with double terror; a cold sweat bedewed his limbs, his knees knocked together, his hair bristled up, and the remains of his teeth were shattered to pieces in the convulsive vibrations of his jaws.

In the midst of this agony, he made one desperate effort, and, bursting open the door of his apartment, bolted into Hatchway's chamber, which happened to be on the same floor. There he found the lieutenant in a counterfeit swoon, who pretended to wake from his trance in an ejaculation of "Lord have mercy upon us!" and, being questioned by the terrified commodore, with regard to what had happened, assured him he had heard the same voice and clap of thunder by which Trunnion himself had been discomposed.

Pipes, whose turn it was to watch, concurred in giving evidence to the same purpose; and the commodore not only owned that he had heard the voice, but likewise communicated his vision, with all the aggravation which his disturbed fancy suggested.

A consultation immediately ensued, in which Mr. Hatchway very gravely observed, that the finger of God was plainly perceivable in those signals; and that it would be both sinful and foolish to disregard his commands, especially as the match proposed was, in all respects, more advantageous than any that one of his years and infirmities could reasonably expect; declaring, that, for his own part, he would not endanger his soul and body, by living one day longer under the same roof with a man who despised the holy will of heaven; and Tom Pipes adhered to the same pious resolution.

Trunnion's perseverance could not resist the number and diversity of considerations that assaulted it; he revolved in silence all the opposite motives that occurred to his reflection; and after having been, to all appearance, bewildered in the labyrinth of his own thoughts, he wiped the sweat from his forehead, and, heaving a piteous groan, yielded to their remonstrances, in these words: "Well, since it must be so, I think we must e'en grapple. But, d—n my eyes! 'tis a d—ed hard case that a fellow of my years should be compelled, d'ye see, to beat up to windward all the rest of his life, against the current of his own inclination."

This important article being discussed, Mr. Hatchway set out in the morning to visit the despairing shepherdess, and was handsomely rewarded for the enlivening tidings with which he blessed her ears. Sick as she was, she could not help laughing heartily at the contrivance, in consequence of which her swain's assent had been obtained, and gave the lieutenant ten guineas for Tom Pipes, in consideration of the part he acted in the farce.

In the afternoon, the commodore suffered himself to be conveyed to her apartment, like a felon to execution, and was received by her in a languishing manner, and genteel dishabille, accompanied by her sister-in-law, who was, for very obvious reasons, extremely solicitous about her success. Though the lieutenant had tutored him, touching his behaviour at this interview, he made a thousand wry faces before he could pronounce the simple salutation of "How d'ye?" to his mistress; and, after his counsellor had urged him with twenty or thirty whispers, to each of which he had replied aloud, "D—n your eyes, I won't," he got up, and halting towards the couch on which Mrs. Grizzle reclined in a state of strange expectation, he seized her hand, and pressed it to his lips; but this piece of gallantry he performed in such a reluctant, uncouth, indignant manner, that the nymph had need of all her resolution to endure the compliment without shrinking; and he himself was so disconcerted at what he had done, that he instantly retired to the other end of the room, where he sat silent, broiling with shame and vexation. Mrs. Pickle, like a sensible matron, quitted the place, on pretence of going to the nursery; and Mr. Hatchway, taking the hint, recollected that he had left his tobacco pouch in the parlour, whither he immediately descended, leaving the two lovers to their mutual endearments.

Never had the commodore found himself in such a disagreeable dilemma before. He sat in an agony of suspense, as if he every moment dreaded the dissolution of nature; and the imploring sighs of his future bride added, if possible, to the pangs of his distress. Impatient of his situation, he rolled his eye around in quest of some relief, and unable to contain himself, exclaimed, "D—tion seize the fellow and his pouch too! I believe he has sheered off, and left me here in the stays." Mrs. Grizzle, who could not help taking some notice of this manifestation of chagrin, lamented her unhappy fate in being so disagreeable to him, that he could not put up with her company for a few moments without repining; and began in very tender terms to reproach him with his inhumanity and indifference. To this expostulation he replied, "Zounds! what would the woman have? Let the parson do his office when he wool; here I am ready to be reeved in the matrimonial block, d'ye see, and d—n all nonsensical palaver." So saying, he retreated, leaving his mistress not at all disobliged at his plain dealing. That same evening the treaty of marriage was brought upon the carpet, and, by means of Mr. Pickle and the lieutenant, settled to the satisfaction of all parties, without the intervention of lawyers, whom Mr. Trunnion expressly excluded from all share in the business; making that condition the indispensable pre-liminary of the whole agreement. Things being brought to this bearing, Mrs. Grizzle's heart dilated with joy; her health, which, by the bye, was never dangerously impaired, she recovered as if by enchantment; and a day being fixed for the nuptials, employed the short period of her celibacy in choosing ornaments for the celebration of her entrance into the married state.

CHAPTER VIII

Preparations are made for the Commodore's Wedding, which is delayed by an Accident that hurried him the Lord knows whither.

THE fame of this extraordinary conjunction spread all over the county; and, on the day appointed for their spousals, the church was surrounded by an inconceivable multitude. The commodore, to give a specimen of his gallantry, by the advice of his friend Hatchway, resolved to appear on horseback on the grand occasion, at the head of all his male attendants, whom he had rigged with the white shirts and black caps formerly belonging to his barge's crew; and he bought a couple of hunters for the accommodation of himself and his lieutenant. With this equipage then he set out from the garrison for the church, after having despatched a messenger to apprise the bride that he and his company were mounted. She got immediately into the coach, accompanied by her brother and his wife, and drove directly to the place of assignation, where several pews were demolished, and divers persons almost pressed to death, by the eagerness of the crowd that broke in to see the ceremony performed. Thus arrived at the altar, and the priest in attendance, they waited a whole half-hour for the commodore, at whose slowness they began to be under some apprehension, and accordingly dismissed a servant to quicken his pace. The valet, having rode something more than a mile, espied the whole troop disposed in a long field, crossing the road obliquely, and headed by the bridegroom and his friend Hatchway, who, finding himself hindered by a hedge from proceeding farther in the same direction, fired a pistol, and stood over to the other side, making an obtuse angle with the line of his former course; and the rest of the squadron followed his example, keeping always in the rear of each other like a flight of wild geese.

Surprised at this strange method of journeying, the messenger came up, and told the commodore that his lady and her company expected him in the church, where they had tarried a considerable time, and were beginning to be very uneasy at his delay; and therefore desired he would proceed with more expedition. To this message Mr. Trunnion replied, "Hark ye, brother, don't you see we make all possible speed? go back, and tell those who sent you, that the wind has shifted since we weighed anchor, and that we are obliged to make very short trips in tacking, by reason of the narrowness of the channel; and that, as we lie within six points of the wind, they must make some allowance for variation and leeway." "Lord, sir!" said the valet, "what occasion have you to go zig-zag in that manner? Do but clap spurs to your horses, and ride straight forward, and I'll engage you shall be at the church porch in less than a quarter of an hour." "What! right in the wind's eye?" answered the commander; "ahey! brother, where did you learn your navigation? Hawser Trunnion is not to be taught at this time of day how to lie his course, or keep his own reckoning. And as for you, brother, you best know the trim of your own frigate." The courier finding he had to do with people who would not be easily persuaded out of their own opinions, returned to the temple, and made a report of what he had seen and heard, to the no small consolation of the bride, who had begun to discover some signs of disquiet. Composed, however, by this piece of intelligence, she exerted her patience for the space of another half-hour, during which period, seeing no bridegroom arrive, she was exceedingly alarmed, so that all the spectators could easily perceive her perturbation, which manifested itself in frequent palpitations, heart-heavings, and alterations of countenance, in spite of the assistance of a smelling-bottle, which she incessantly applied to her nostrils.

Various were the conjectures of the company on this occasion. Some imagined he had mistaken the place of rendezvous, as he had never been at church since he first settled in that parish; others believed he had met with some accident, in consequence of which his attendants had carried him back to his own house; and a third set, in which the bride herself was thought to be comprehended, could not help suspecting that the commodore had changed his mind. But all these suppositions, ingenious as they were, happened to be wide of the true cause that detained him, which was no other than this:—The commodore and his crew had, by dint of turning, almost weathered the parson's house that stood to windward of the church, when the notes of a pack of hounds unluckily reached the ears of the two hunters which Trunnion and the lieutenant bestrode. These fleet animals no sooner heard the enlivening sound, than, eager for the chase, they sprung away all of a sudden, and strained every nerve to partake of the sport, flew across the fields with incredible speed, overleaped hedges and ditches, and everything in their way, without the least regard to their unfortunate riders. The lieutenant, whose steed had got the heels of the other, finding it would be great folly and presumption in him to pretend to keep the saddle with his wooden leg, very wisely took the opportunity of throwing himself off in his passage through a field of rich clover, among which he lay at his ease; and seeing his captain advancing at full gallop, hailed him with the salutation of "What cheer? ho!" The commodore, who was in infinite distress, eyeing him askance, as he passed, replied with a faltering voice, "O d—n you! you are safe at an anchor; I wish to God I were as fast moored." Nevertheless, conscious of his disabled heel, he would not venture to try the experiment which had succeeded so well with Hatchway, but resolved to stick as close as possible to his horse's back, until Providence should interpose in his behalf.

With this view he dropped his whip, and with his right hand laid fast hold on the pummel, contracting every muscle in his body to secure himself in the seat, and grinning most formidably, in consequence of this exertion. In this attitude he was hurried on a considerable way, when all of a sudden his view was comforted by a five-bar gate that appeared before him, as he never doubted that there the career of his hunter must necessarily end. But, alas! he reckoned without his host. Far from halting at this obstruction, the horse sprung over it with amazing agility, to the utter confusion and disorder of his owner, who lost his hat and periwig in the leap, and now began to think in good earnest that he was actually mounted on the back of the devil. He recommended himself to God, his reflection forsook him, his eyesight and all his other senses failed, he quitted the reins, and, fastening by instinct on the mane, was in this condition conveyed into the midst of the sportsmen, who were astonished at the sight of such an apparition. Neither was their surprise to be wondered at, if we reflect on the figure that presented itself to their view. The commodore's person was at all times an object of admiration; much more so on this occasion, when every singularity was aggravated by the circumstances of his dress and disaster.

He had put on, in honour of his nuptials, his best coat of blue broad-cloth, cut by a tailor of Ramsgate, and trimmed with five dozen of brass buttons, large and small; his breeches were of the same piece, fastened at the knees with large bunches of tape; his waistcoat was of red plush, lapelled with green velvet, and garnished with vellum holes; his boots bore an infinite resemblance, both in colour and shape, to a pair of leather buckets; his shoulder was graced with a broad buff belt, from whence depended a huge hanger with a hilt like that of a backsword; and on each side of his pummel appeared a rusty pistol, rammed in a case covered with a bearskin. The loss of his tie periwig and laced hat, which were curiosities of the kind, did not at all contribute to the improvement of the picture, but, on the contrary, by exhibiting his bald pate, and the natural extension of his lanthorn jaws, added to the peculiarity and extravagance of the whole. Such a spectacle could not have failed of diverting the whole company from the chase, had his horse thought proper to pursue a different route, but the beast was too keen a sporter to choose any other way than that which the stag followed; and, therefore, without stopping to gratify the curiosity of the spectators, he, in a few minutes, outstripped every hunter in the field. There being a deep hollow way betwixt him and the hounds, rather than ride round about the length of a furlong to a path that crossed the lane, he transported himself, at one jump, to the unspeakable astonishment and terror of a waggoner who chanced to be underneath, and saw this pheno- menon fly over his carriage. This was not the only adventure he achieved. The stag having taken a deep river that lay in his way, every man directed his course to a bridge in the neigh- bourhood; but our bridegroom's courser, despising all such conveniences, plunged into the stream without hesitation, and swam in a twinkling to the opposite shore. This sudden immer- sion into an element, of which Trunnion was properly a native, in all probability helped to recruit the exhausted spirits of his rider, who, at his landing on the other side, gave some tokens of sensation, by hallooing aloud for assistance, which he could not possibly receive, because his horse still maintained the advantage he had gained, and would not allow himself to be overtaken.

In short, after a long chase that lasted several hours, and extended to a dozen miles at least, he was the first in at the death of the deer, being seconded by the lieutenant's gelding, which, actuated by the same spirit, had, without a rider, followed his companion's example.

Our bridegroom finding himself at last brought up, or, in other words, at the end of his career, took the opportunity of the first pause, to desire the huntsmen would lend him a hand in dis- mounting; and was by their condescension safely placed on the grass, where he sat staring at the company as they came in, with such wildness of astonishment in his looks, as if he had been a creature of another species, dropped among them from the clouds.

Before they had fleshed the hounds, however, he recollected himself, and seeing one of the sportsmen take a small flask out of his pocket and apply it to his mouth, judged the cordial to be no other than neat Cognac, which it really was; and, expressing a desire of participation, was immediately accommodated with a moderate dose, which perfectly completed his recovery.

By this time he and his two horses had engrossed the attention of the whole crowd; while some admired the elegant proportion and uncommon spirit of the two animals, the rest contemplated the surprising appearance of their master, whom before they had only seen *en passant*; and at length one of the gentlemen, accost- ing him very courteously, signified his wonder at seeing him in such an equipage, and asked him if he had not dropped his companion by the way. "Why, look ye, brother," replied the commodore, "mayhap you think me an odd sort of a fellow, seeing me in this trim, especially as I have lost part of my rigging; but this here is the case, d'ye see: I weighed anchor from my own house this morning at ten A.M., with fair weather and a favourable breeze at south-south-east, being bound to the next church on the voyage of matrimony; but, howsomever, we had not run down a quarter of a league, when the wind shifting, blowed directly in our teeth; so that we were forced to tack all the way, d'ye see, and had almost beat up within sight of the port, when these sons of bitches of horses, which I had bought but two days before (for my own part, I believe they are devils incarnate), luffed round in a trice, and then, refusing the helm, drove away like lightning with me and my lieutenant, who soon came to anchor in an exceeding good berth. As for my own part, I have been carried over rocks, and flats, and quicksands; among which I have pitched away a special good tie periwig and an iron-bound hat; and at last, thank God! am got into smooth water and safe riding; but if ever I venture my carcass upon such a hare'em-scare'em blood of a bitch again, my name is not Hawser Trunnion, d—n my eyes!"

One of the company, struck with his name, which he had often heard, immediately laid hold on his declaration at the close of this singular account; and observing that his horses were very vicious, asked how he intended to return? "As for that matter," replied Mr. Trunnion, "I am resolved to hire a sledge or waggon, or such a thing as a jackass; for I'll be d—d if ever I cross the back of a horse again." "And what do you propose to do with these creatures?" said the other, pointing to the hunters; "they seem to have some mettle; but then they are mere colts, and will take the devil and all of breaking. Methinks this hinder one is shoulder-slipped." "D—n them," cried the commodore, "I wish both their necks were broke, thof the two cost me forty good yellow-boys." "Forty guineas!" exclaimed the stranger, who was a squire and a jockey, as well as owner of the pack, "Lord! Lord! how a man may be imposed upon! Why, these cattle are clumsy enough to go to plough; mind what a flat counter; do but observe how sharp this here one is in the withers; then, he's fired in the further fetlock." In short, this connoisseur in horse-flesh, having discovered in them all the defects which can possibly be found in that species of animals, offered to give him ten guineas for the two, saying he would convert them into beasts of burden.—The owner, who, after what had happened, was very well disposed to listen to anything that was said to their prejudice, implicitly believed the truth of the stranger's asseverations, discharged a furious volley of oaths against the rascal who had taken him in, and forthwith struck a bargain with the squire, who paid him instantly for his purchase; in consequence of which he won the plate at the next Canterbury races.

This affair being transacted to the mutual satisfaction of both parties, as well as to the general entertainment of the company, who laughed in their sleeves at the dexterity of their friend, Trunnion was set upon the squire's own horse, and led by his servant in the midst of this cavalcade, which proceeded to a neighbouring village, where they had bespoke dinner, and where our bridegroom found means to provide himself with another hat and wig. With regard to his marriage, he bore his disappointment with the temper of a philosopher; and, the exercise he had undergone having quickened his appetite, sat down at table in the midst of his new acquaintance, making a very hearty meal, and moistening every morsel with a draught of the ale, which he found very much to his satisfaction.

CHAPTER IX

He is found by the Lieutenant; reconducted to his own House; Married to Mrs. Grizzle, who meets with a small Misfortune in the Night, and asserts her Prerogative next Morning; in consequence of which, her Husband's Eye is endangered.

MEANWHILE Lieutenant Hatchway made shift to hobble to the church, where he informed the company of what had happened to the commodore; and the bride behaved with great decency on the occasion; for, as soon as she understood the danger to which her future husband was exposed, she fainted in the arms of her sister-in-law, to the surprise of all the spectators, who could not comprehend the cause of her disorder; and when she was recovered by the application of smelling-bottles, earnestly begged that Mr. Hatchway and Tom Pipes would take her brother's coach, and go in quest of their commander.

This task they readily undertook, being escorted by all the rest of his adherents on horseback; while the bride and her friends were invited to the parson's house, and the ceremony deferred till another occasion.

The lieutenant, steering his course as near the line of direction in which Trunnion went off, as the coach-road would permit, got intelligence of his track from one farm-house to another; for such an apparition could not fail of attracting particular notice; and one of the horsemen having picked up his hat and wig in a bye-path, the whole troop entered the village where he was lodged, about four o'clock in the afternoon. When they understood he was safely housed at the George, they rode up to the door in a body, and expressed their satisfaction in three cheers; which were returned by the company within, as soon as they were instructed in the nature of the salute by Trunnion, who by this time had entered into all the jollity of his new friends, and was indeed more than half seas over. The lieutenant was introduced to all present as his sworn brother, and had something tossed up for his dinner. Tom Pipes and the crew were regaled in another room; and, a fresh pair of horses being put to the coach, about six in the evening the commodore, with all his attendants, departed for the garrison, after having shook hands with every individual in the house.

Without any farther accident, he was conveyed in safety to his own gate, before nine, and committed to the care of Pipes, who carried him instantly to his hammock, while the lieutenant was driven away to the place where the bride and her friends remained in great anxiety, which vanished when he assured them that his commodore was safe, being succeeded by abundance of mirth and pleasantry at the account he gave of Trunnion's adventure.

Another day was fixed for the nuptials; and, in order to balk the curiosity of idle people, which had given great offence, the parson was prevailed upon to perform the ceremony in the garrison, which all that day was adorned with flags and pendants displayed, and at night illuminated by the direction of Hatchway, who also ordered the patereroes to be fired as soon as the marriage knot was tied. Neither were the other parts of the entertainment neglected by this ingenious contriver, who produced undeniable proofs of his elegance and art in the wedding supper, which had been committed to his management and direction. This genial banquet was entirely composed of sea-dishes; a huge pillaw, consisting of a large piece of beef sliced, a couple of fowls, and half a peck of rice, smoked in the middle of the board; a dish of hard fish swimming in oil, appeared at each end, the sides being furnished with a mess of that savoury composition known by the name of lob's cou[r]se, and a plate of salmagundy. The second course displayed a goose of a monstrous magnitude, flanked with two guinea hens, a pig barbecued, an hock of salt pork in the midst of a pease pudding, a leg of mutton roasted, with potatoes, and another boiled with yams. The third service was made up with a loin of fresh pork with apple sauce, a kid smothered with onions, and a terrapin baked in the shell; and, last of all, a prodigious sea pie was presented, with an infinite volume of pancakes and fritters. That everything might be answerable to the magnificence of this delicate feast, he had provided vast quantities of strong beer, flip, rumbo, and burnt brandy, with plenty of Barbadoes water, for the ladies; and hired all the fiddles within six miles, who, with the addition of a drum, bagpipes, and Welch harp, regaled the guests with a most melodious concert.

The company, who were not at all exceptious, seemed extremely well pleased with every particular of the entertainment; and, the evening being spent in the most social manner, the bride was by her sister conducted to her apartment, where, however, a trifling circumstance had like to have destroyed the harmony which had been hitherto maintained.

I have already observed, that there was not one standing-bed within the walls; therefore the reader will not wonder that Mrs. Trunnion was out of humour, when she found herself under the necessity of being confined with her spouse in a hammock, which, though enlarged with a double portion of canvas, and dilated with a yoke for the occasion, was at best but a disagreeable, not to say dangerous, situation. She accordingly complained with some warmth of this inconvenience, which she imputed to disrespect, and at first absolutely refused to put up with the expedient; but Mrs. Pickle soon brought her to reason and compliance, by observing that one night would soon be elapsed, and next day she might regulate her own economy.

Thus persuaded, she ventured into the vehicle, and was visited by her husband in less than an hour, the company being departed to their own homes, and the garrison left to the command of his lieutenant and mate. But it seems the hooks that supported this swinging couch were not calculated for the addition of weight which they were now destined to bear; and therefore gave way in the middle of the night, to the no small terror of Mrs. Trunnion, who perceiving herself falling, screamed aloud, and by that exclamation brought Hatchway, with a light, into the chamber. Though she had received no injury by the fall, she was extremely discomposed and incensed at the accident, which she even openly ascribed to the obstinacy and whimsical oddity of the commodore, in such petulant terms as evidently declared that she thought her great aim accomplished, and her authority secured against all the shocks of fortune. Indeed, her bedfellow seemed to be of the same opinion, by his tacit resignation; for he made no reply to her insinuations, but with a most vinegar aspect, crawled out of his nest, and betook himself to rest in another apartment, while his irritated spouse dismissed the lieutenant, and from the wreck of the hammock made an occasional bed for herself on the floor, fully determined to provide better accommodation for the next night's lodging.

Having no inclination to sleep, her thoughts, during the remaining part of the night, were engrossed by a scheme of reformation she was resolved to execute in the family; and no sooner did the first lark bid salutation to the morn, than, starting from her humble couch, and huddling on her clothes, she sallied from her chamber, explored her way through paths before unknown, and, in the course of her researches, perceived a large bell, to which she made such effectual application, as alarmed every soul in the family. In a moment she was surrounded by Hatchway, Pipes, and all the rest of the servants, half-dressed; but, seeing none of the feminine gender appear, she began to storm at the sloth and laziness of the maids, who, she observed, ought to have been at work an hour at least before she called; and then, for the first time, understood that no woman was permitted to sleep within the walls.

She did not fail to exclaim against this regulation; and, being informed that the cook and chambermaid lodged in a small office-house, that stood without the gate, ordered the drawbridge to be let down, and in person beat up their quarters, commanding them forthwith to set about scouring the rooms, which had not been hitherto kept in a very decent condition, while two men were immediately employed to transport the bed on which she used to lie, from her brother's house to her new habitation; so that, in less than two hours, the whole economy of the garrison was turned topsy-turvy, and everything involved in tumult and noise.—Trunnion being disturbed and distracted with the uproar, turned out in his shirt like a maniac, and, arming himself with a cudgel of crab-tree, made an irruption into his wife's apartment, where perceiving a couple of carpenters at work, in joining a bedstead, he, with many dreadful oaths and opprobrious invectives, ordered them to desist, swearing, he would suffer no bulk-heads nor hurricane houses to stand where he was master; but finding his remonstrances disregarded by these mechanics, who believed him to be some madman belonging to the family, who had broke from his confinement, he assaulted them both with great fury and indignation, and was handled so roughly in the encounter, that, in a very short time, he measured his length on the floor, in consequence of a blow that he received from a hammer, by which the sight of his remaining eye was grievously endangered.

Having thus reduced him to a state of subjection, they resolved to secure him with cords, and were actually busy in adjusting his fetters, when he was exempted from the disgrace, by the accidental entrance of his spouse, who rescued him from the hands of his adversaries, and, in the midst of her condolence, imputed his misfortune to the inconsiderate roughness of his own disposition.

He breathed nothing but revenge, and made some efforts to chastise the insolence of the workmen, who, as soon as they understood his quality, asked forgiveness for what they had done, with great humility, protesting that they did not know he was master of the house. But, far from being satisfied with this apology, he groped about for the bell (the inflammation of his eye having utterly deprived him of sight), and the rope being, by the precaution of the delinquents, conveyed out of his reach, began to storm with incredible vociferation, like a lion roaring in the toil, pouring forth innumerable oaths and execrations, and calling by name Hatchway and Pipes, who, being within hearing, obeyed the extraordinary summons, and were ordered to put the carpenters in irons, for having audaciously assaulted him in his own house.

His myrmidons, seeing he had been evil-entreated, were exasperated at the insult he had suffered, which they considered as an affront upon the dignity of the garrison: the more so, as the mutineers seemed to put themselves in a posture of defence, and set their authority at defiance. They therefore unsheathed their cutlasses, which they commonly wore as badges of their commission; and a desperate engagement, in all probability, would have ensued, had not the lady of the castle interposed, and prevented the effects of their animosity by assuring the lieutenant that the commodore had been the aggressor, and that the workmen, finding themselves attacked in such an extraordinary manner, by a person whom they did not know, were obliged to act in their own defence, by which he had received that unlucky contusion.

Mr. Hatchway no sooner learnt the sentiments of Mrs. Trunnion, than, sheathing his indignation, he told the commodore that he should always be ready to execute his lawful commands, but that he could not in conscience be concerned in oppressing poor people who had been guilty of no offence.

This unexpected declaration, together with the behaviour of his wife, who in his hearing desired the carpenters to resume their work, filled the breast of Trunnion with rage and mortification. He pulled off his woollen night-cap, pummell'd his bare pate, beat the floor alternately with his feet, swore his people had betrayed him, and cursed himself to the lowest pit of hell, for having admitted such a cockatrice into his family. But all these exclamations did not avail; they were among the last essays of his resistance to the will of his wife, whose influence among his adherents had already swallowed up his own, and who now peremptorily told him, that he must leave the management of everything within doors to her, who understood best what was for his honour and advantage. She then ordered a poultice to be prepared for his eye, which being applied, he was committed to the care of Pipes, by whom he was led about the house like a blind bear growling for prey, while his industrious yoke-fellow executed every circumstance of the plan she had projected; so that, when he recovered his vision, he was an utter stranger in his own house.

CHAPTER X

The Commodore being in some cases restive, his Lady has recourse to Artifice in the Establishment of her Throne—She exhibits Symptoms of Pregnancy, to the unspeakable Joy of Trunnion, who nevertheless is balked in his Expectation.

THESE innovations were not effected without many loud objections on his part; and divers curious dialogues passed between him and his yoke-fellow, who always came off victorious from the dispute; insomuch that his countenance gradually fell; he began to suppress, and at length entirely devoured his chagrin; the terrors of superior authority were plainly perceivable in his features, and in less than three months he became a thorough-paced husband. Not that his obstinacy was extinguished, though overcome; in some things he was as inflexible and mulish as ever; but then he durst not kick so openly, and was reduced to the necessity of being passive in his resentments. Mrs. Trunnion, for example, proposed that a coach and six should be purchased, as she could not ride on horseback, and the chaise was a scandalous carriage for a person of her condition; the commodore, conscious of his own inferior capacity in point of reasoning, did not think proper to dispute the proposal, but lent a deaf ear to her remonstrances, though they were enforced with every argument which she thought could soothe, terrify, shame, or decoy him into compliance.   In vain did she urge the excess of affection she had for him, as meriting some return of tenderness and condescension; he was even proof against certain menacing hints she gave, touching the resentment of a slighted woman; and he stood out against all the considerations of dignity or disgrace, like a bulwark of brass. Neither was he moved to any indecent or unkind expressions of contradiction, even when she upbraided him with his sordid disposition, and put him in mind of the fortune and honour he had acquired by his marriage, but seemed to retire within himself, like a tortoise when attacked, that shrinks within its shell, and silently endured the scourge of her reproaches, without seeming sensible of the smart.

This, however, was the only point in which she had been baffled since her nuptials; and as she could by no means digest the miscarriage, she tortured her invention for some new plan, by which she might augment her influence and authority. What her genius refused was supplied by accident; for she had not lived four months in the garrison, when she was seized with frequent qualms and retchings, her breasts began to harden, and her stomach to be remarkably prominent; in a word, she congratulated herself on the symptoms of her own fertility, and the commodore was transported with joy at the prospect of an heir of his own begetting.

She knew this was the proper season for vindicating her own sovereignty, and accordingly employed the means which nature had put in her power.   There was not a rare piece of furniture and apparel for which she did not long; and one day as she went to church, seeing Lady Stately's equipage arrive, she suddenly fainted away.   Her husband, whose vanity had never been so perfectly gratified as with this promised harvest of his own sowing, took the alarm immediately, and in order to prevent relapses of that kind, which might be attended with fatal consequences to his hope, gave her leave to bespeak a coach, horses, and liveries, to her own liking.   Thus authorised, she in a very little time exhibited such a specimen of her own taste and magnificence, as afforded speculation to the whole country, and made Trunnion's heart quake within him, because he foresaw no limits to her extravagance, which also manifested itself in the most expensive preparations for her lying-in.

Her pride, which had hitherto regarded the representative of her father's house, seemed now to lose all that hereditary respect, and prompt her to outshine and undervalue the elder branch of her family. She behaved to Mrs. Pickle with a sort of civil reserve that implied a conscious superiority, and an emulation in point of grandeur immediately commenced between the two sisters. She every day communicated her importance to the whole parish, under pretence of taking the air in her coach, and endeavoured to extend her acquaintance among people of fashion. Nor was this an undertaking attended with great difficulty; for all persons whatever, capable of maintaining a certain appearance, will always find admission into what is called the best company, and be rated in point of character according to their own valuation, without subjecting their pretensions to the smallest doubt or examination. In all her visits and parties, she seized every opportunity of declaring her present condition, observing that she was forbid by her physicians to taste such a pickle, and that such a dish was poison to a woman in her way; nay, where she was on a footing of familiarity, she affected to make wry faces, and complained that the young rogue began to be very unruly, writhing herself into divers contortions, as if she had been grievously incommoded by the metal of this future Trunnion. The husband himself did not behave with all the moderation that might have been expected. At the club he frequently mentioned this circumstance of his own vigour as a pretty successful feat to be performed by an old fellow of fifty-five, and confirmed the opinion of his strength by redoubled squeezes of the landlord's hand, which never failed of extorting a satisfactory certificate of his might. When his companions drank to the *Hans en kelder*, or, Jack in the low cellar, he could not help displaying an extraordinary complacence of countenance, and signified his intention of sending the young dog to sea, as soon as he should be able to carry a cartridge, in hopes of seeing him an officer before his own death.

This hope helped to console him under the extraordinary expense to which he was exposed by the profusion of his wife, especially when he considered that his compliance with her prodigality would be limited to the expiration of the nine months, of which the best part was by this time elapsed. Yet, in spite of all this philosophical resignation, her fancy sometimes soared to such a ridiculous and intolerable pitch of insolence and absurdity, that his temper forsook him, and he could not help wishing in secret, that her pride might be confounded in the dissipation of her most flattering hopes, even though he himself should be a principal sufferer by the disappointment. These, however, were no other than the suggestions of temporary disgusts, that commonly subsided as suddenly as they arose, and never gave the least disturbance to the person who inspired them, because he took care to conceal them carefully from her knowledge.

Meanwhile she happily advanced in her reckoning, with the promise of a favourable issue; the term of her computation expired, and in the middle of the night she was visited by certain warnings that seemed to bespeak the approach of the critical moment. The commodore got up with great alacrity, and called the midwife, who had been several days in the house; the gossips were immediately summoned, and the most interesting expectations prevailed; but the symptoms of labour gradually vanished, and, as the matrons sagely observed, this was no more than a false alarm.

Two nights after they received a second intimation; and as she was sensibly diminished in the waist, everything was supposed to be in a fair way. Yet this visitation was not more conclusive than the former; her pains wore off in spite of all her endeavours to encourage them, and the good women betook themselves to their respective homes, in expectation of finding the third attack decisive, alluding to the well-known maxim, that *number three is always fortunate.* For once, however, this apothegm failed; the next call was altogether as ineffectual as the former; and moreover attended with a phenomenon which to them was equally strange and inexplicable. This was no other than such a reduction in the size of Mrs. Trunnion as might have been expected after the birth of a full-grown child. Startled at such an unaccountable event, they sat in close divan; and, concluding that the case was in all respects unnatural and prodigious, desired that a messenger might be immediately despatched for some male practitioner in the art of midwifery.

The commodore, without guessing the cause of their perplexity, ordered Pipes immediately on this piece of duty; and in less than two hours they were assisted by the advice of a surgeon of the neighbourhood, who boldly affirmed that the patient had never been with child. This asseveration was like a clap of thunder to Mr. Trunnion, who had been, during eight whole days and nights, in continual expectation of being hailed with the appellation of father.

After some recollection, he swore the surgeon was an ignorant fellow, and that he would not take his word for what he advanced, being comforted and confirmed in his want of faith by the insinuations of the midwife, who still persisted to feed Mrs. Trunnion with hopes of a speedy and safe delivery; observing, that she had been concerned in many a case of the same nature, where a fine child was found, even after all signs of the mother's pregnancy had disappeared. Every twig of hope, how slender soever it may be, is eagerly caught hold on by people who find themselves in danger of being disappointed. To every question proposed by her to the lady with the preambles of "Ha'n't you?" or "Don't you?" an answer was made in the affirmative, whether agreeable to truth or not; because the respondent could not find in her heart to disown any symptom that might favour the notion she had so long indulged.

This experienced proficient in the obstetric art was therefore kept in close attendance for the space of three weeks, during which the patient had several returns of what she pleased herself with believing to be labour pains, till at length she and her husband became the standing joke of the parish; and this infatuated couple could scarce be prevailed upon to part with their hopes, even when she appeared as lank as a greyhound, and they were furnished with other unquestionable proofs of their having been deceived. But they could not for ever remain under the influence of this sweet delusion, which at last faded away, and was succeeded by a paroxysm of shame and confusion, that kept the husband within doors for the space of a whole fortnight, and confined his lady to her bed for a series of weeks, during which she suffered all the anguish of the most intense mortification; yet even this was subdued by the lenient hand of time.

The first respite from her chagrin was employed in the strict discharge of what are called the duties of religion, which she performed with the most rancorous severity, setting on foot a persecution in her own family, that made the house too hot for all the menial servants, even ruffled the almost invincible indifference of Tom Pipes, harassed the commodore himself out of all patience, and spared no individual but Lieutenant Hatchway, whom she never ventured to disoblige.

CHAPTER XI

Mrs. Trunnion erects a Tyranny in the Garrison, while her Husband conceives an Affection for his Nephew Perry, who manifests a Peculiarity of Disposition even in his tender Years.

HAVING exercised herself three months in such pious amusements, she appeared again in the world; but her misfortune had made such an impression on her mind, that she could not bear the sight of a child, and trembled whenever the conversation happened to turn upon a christening. Her temper, which was naturally none of the sweetest, seemed to have imbibed a double proportion of souring from her disappointment; of consequence her company was not much coveted, and she found very few people disposed to treat her with those marks of consideration which she looked upon as her due. This neglect detached her from the society of an unmannerly world; she concentred the energy of her talents in the government of her own house, which groaned accordingly under her arbitrary sway; and in the brandy-bottle found ample consolation for all the affliction she had undergone.

As for the commodore, he in a little time weathered his disgrace after having sustained many severe jokes from the lieutenant; and now his chief aim being to be absent from his own house as much as possible, he frequented the public-house more than ever; more assiduously cultivated the friendship of his brother-in-law Mr. Pickle; and, in the course of their intimacy, conceived an affection for his nephew Perry, which did not end but with his life. Indeed, it must be owned that Trunnion was not naturally deficient in the social passions of the soul, which, though they were strangely warped, disguised, and overborne, by the circumstance of his boisterous life and education, did not fail to manifest themselves occasionally through the whole course of his behaviour.

As all the hopes of propagating his own name had perished, and his relations lay under the interdiction of his hate, it is no wonder that, through the familiarity and friendly intercourse subsisting between him and Mr. Gamaliel, he contracted a liking for the boy, who by this time entered the third year of his age, and was indeed a very handsome, healthy, and promising child; and what seemed to ingratiate him still more with his uncle, was a certain oddity of disposition, for which he had been remarkable, even from his cradle. It is reported of him, that,

C 838

before the first year of his infancy was elapsed, he used very often, immediately after being dressed, in the midst of the caresses which were bestowed upon him by his mother, while she indulged herself in the contemplation of her own happiness, all of a sudden, to alarm her with a fit of shrieks and cries, which continued with great violence till he was stripped to the skin with the utmost expedition, by order of his affrighted parent, who thought his tender body was tortured by the misapplication of some unlucky pin; and when he had given them all this disturbance and unnecessary trouble, he would lie sprawling and laughing in their faces, as if he ridiculed the impertinence of their concern. Nay, it is affirmed, that one day, when an old woman, who attended in the nursery, had by stealth conveyed a bottle of cordial waters to her mouth, he pulled his nurse by the sleeve, and, by a slight glance detecting the theft, tipt her the wink with a particular slyness of countenance, as if he had said with a sneer, "Ay, ay, that is what you must all come to." But these instances of reflection in a babe nine months old are so incredible, that I look upon them as *ex post facto* observations, founded upon imaginary recollection, when he was in a more advanced age, and his peculiarities of temper became much more remarkable—of a piece with the ingenious discoveries of those sagacious observers who can discern something evidently characteristic in the features of any noted personage, whose character they have previously heard explained; yet, without pretending to specify at what period of his childhood this singularity first appeared, I can with great truth declare, that, when he first attracted the notice and affection of his uncle, it was plainly perceivable.

One would imagine he had marked out the commodore as a proper object of ridicule, for almost all his little childish satire was levelled against him. I will not deny that he might have been influenced in this particular by the example and instruction of Mr. Hatchway, who delighted in superintending the first essays of his genius. As the gout had taken up its residence in Mr. Trunnion's great toe, from whence it never removed, no, not for a day, little Perry took great pleasure in treading by accident on this infirm member; and when his uncle, incensed by the pain, used to d—n him for a hell-begotten brat, he would appease him in a twinkling, by returning the curse with equal emphasis, and asking what was the matter with old Hannibal Tough? an appellation by which the lieutenant had taught him to distinguish this grim commander.

Neither was this the only experiment he tried upon the patience of the commodore, with whose nose he used to take indecent freedoms, even while he was fondled on his knee; in one month he put him to the expense of two guineas in seal-skin, by picking his pocket of divers tobacco pouches, all of which he in secret committed to the flames. Nor did the caprice of his disposition abstain from the favourite beverage of Trunnion, who more than once swallowed a whole draught, in which his brother's snuff-box had been emptied, before he perceived the disagreeable infusion: and one day, when the commodore had chastised him by a gentle tap with his cane, he fell flat on the floor, as if he had been deprived of all sense and motion, to the terror and amazement of the striker; and, after having filled the whole house with confusion and dismay, opened his eyes, and laughed heartily at the success of his own imposition.

It would be an endless, and perhaps no very agreeable task, to enumerate all the unlucky pranks he played upon his uncle and others, before he attained the fourth year of his age; about which time he was sent, with an attendant, to a day school in the neighbourhood, that, to use his good mother's own expression, he might be out of harm's way. Here, however, he made little progress, except in mischief, which he practised with impunity, because the schoolmistress would run no risk of disobliging a lady of fortune, by exercising unnecessary severities upon her only child. Nevertheless, Mrs. Pickle was not so blindly partial as to be pleased with such unseasonable indulgence. Perry was taken out of the hands of this courteous teacher, and committed to the instruction of a pedagogue, who was ordered to administer such correction as the boy should, in his opinion, deserve. This authority he did not neglect to use; his pupil was regularly flogged twice a day; and, after having been subjected to this course of discipline for the space of eighteen months, declared the most obstinate, dull, and untoward genius that ever had fallen under his cultivation; instead of being reformed, he seemed rather hardened and confirmed in his vicious inclinations, and was dead to all sense of fear as well as shame. His mother was extremely mortified at these symptoms of stupidity, which she considered as an inheritance derived from the spirit of his father, and consequently unsurmountable by all the efforts of human care. But the commodore rejoiced over the ruggedness of his nature, and was particularly pleased when, upon inquiry, he found that Perry had beaten all the boys in the school; a circumstance from which he prognosticated everything that was fair and fortunate in his future fate; observing that, at his age, he himself was just such another. The boy, who was now turned of six, having profited so little under the birch of his unsparing governor, Mrs. Pickle was counselled to send him to a boarding-school not far from London, which was kept by a certain person very eminent for his successful method of education. This advice she the more readily embraced, because at that time she found herself pretty far gone with another child, that she hoped would console her for the disappointment she had met with in the unpromising talents of Perry, or at any rate divide her concern, so as to enable her to endure the absence of either.

CHAPTER XII

Peregrine is sent to a Boarding-School—Becomes remarkable for his Genius and Ambition.

THE commodore understanding her determination, to which her husband did not venture to make the least objection, interested himself so much in behalf of his favourite, as to fit him out at his own charge, and accompany him in person to the place of his destination; where he defrayed the expense of his entrance, and left him to the particular care and inspection of the usher, who, having been recommended to him as a person of parts and integrity, received per advance a handsome consideration for the task he undertook.

Nothing could be better judged than this piece of liberality; the assistant was actually a man of learning, probity, and good sense; and, though obliged by the scandalous administration of fortune to act in the character of an inferior teacher, had, by his sole capacity and application, brought the school to that degree of reputation, which it never could have obtained from the talents of his superior. He had established an economy, which, though regular, was not at all severe, by enacting a body of laws suited to the age and comprehension of every individual; and each transgressor was fairly tried by his peers, and punished according to the verdict of the jury. No boy was scourged for want of apprehension, but a spirit of emulation was raised by well-timed praise and artful comparison, and maintained by a distribution of small prizes, which were adjudged to those who signalised themselves either by their industry, sobriety, or genius. This tutor, whose name was Jennings, began with Perry, according to his constant maxim, by examining the soil; that is, studying his temper, in order to consult the bias of his disposition, which was strangely perverted by the absurd discipline he had undergone. He found him in a state of sullen insensibility, which the child had gradually contracted in a long course of stupefying correction; and at first he was not in the least actuated by that commendation which animated the rest of his school-fellows; nor was it in the power of reproach to excite his ambition, which had been buried, as it were, in the grave of disgrace; the usher therefore had recourse to contemptuous neglect, with which he affected to treat this stubborn spirit; foreseeing that, if he retained any seeds of sentiment, this weather would infallibly raise them into vegetation: his judgment was justified by the event; the boy in a little time began to make observations; he perceived the marks of distinction with which virtue was rewarded, grew ashamed of the despicable figure he himself made among his companions, who, far from courting, rather shunned his conversation, and actually pined at his own want of importance.

Mr. Jennings saw and rejoiced at his mortification, which he suffered to proceed as far as possible, without endangering his health. The child lost all relish for diversion, loathed his food, grew pensive, solitary, and was frequently found weeping by himself. These symptoms plainly evinced the recovery of his feelings, to which his governor thought it now high time to make application; and therefore by little and little altered his behaviour from the indifference he had put on, to the appearance of more regard and attention. This produced a favourable change in the boy, whose eyes sparkled with satisfaction one day, when his master expressed himself with a show of surprise in these words: "So, Perry! I find you don't want genius, when you think proper to use it." Such encomiums kindled the spirit of emulation in his little breast; he exerted himself with surprising alacrity, by which he soon acquitted himself of the imputation of dulness, and obtained sundry honorary silver pennies, as acknowledgments of his application: his schoolfellows now solicited his friendship as eagerly as they had avoided it before; and, in less than a twelvemonth after his arrival, this supposed dunce was remarkable for the brightness of his parts; having in that short period learnt to read English perfectly well, made great progress in writing, enabled himself to speak the French language without hesitation, and acquired some knowledge in the rudiments of the Latin tongue. The usher did not fail to transmit an account of his proficiency to the commodore, who received it with transport, and forthwith communicated the happy tidings to the parents.

Mr. Gamaliel Pickle, who was never subject to violent emotions, heard them with a sort of phlegmatic satisfaction, that scarce manifested itself either in his countenance or expressions; nor did the child's mother break forth into that rapture and admiration which might have been expected, when she understood how much the talents of her first-born had exceeded the hope of her warmest imagination. Not but that she professed herself well pleased with Perry's reputation; though she observed that, in these commendations, the truth was always exaggerated by schoolmasters, for their own interest; and pretended to wonder that the usher had not mingled more probability with his praise. Trunnion was offended at her indifference and want of faith; and, believing that she refined too much in her discernment, swore that Jennings had declared the truth, and nothing but the truth; for he, himself, had prophesied from the beginning that the boy would turn out a credit to his family. But by this time Mrs. Pickle was blessed with a daughter, whom she had brought into the world about six months before the intelligence arrived; so that her care and affection being otherwise engrossed, the praise of Perry was the less greedily devoured. The abatement of her fondness was an advantage to his education, which would have been retarded, and perhaps ruined, by pernicious indulgence and preposterous interposition, had her love considered him as an only child; whereas, her concern being now diverted to another object, that shared, at least, one half of her affection, he was left to the management of his preceptor, who tutored him according to his own plan, without any let or interruption. Indeed, all his sagacity and circumspection were but barely sufficient to keep the young gentleman in order; for, now that he had won the palm of victory from his rivals in point of scholarship, his ambition dilated, and he was seized with the desire of subjecting the whole school by the valour of his arm. Before he could bring his project to bear, innumerable battles were fought with various success; every day a bloody nose and complaint were presented against him, and his own visage commonly bore some livid marks of obstinate contention. At length, however, he accomplished his aim; his adversaries were subdued, his prowess acknowledged, and he obtained the laurel in war as well as in wit. Thus triumphant, he was intoxicated with success. His pride rose in proportion to his power, and, in spite of all the endeavours of Jennings, who practised every method he could invent for curbing his licentious conduct, without depressing his spirit, he contracted a large proportion of insolence, which a series of misfortunes that happened to him in the sequel could scarce effectually tame. Nevertheless, there was a fund of good-nature and generosity in his composition, and, though he established a tyranny among his comrades, the tranquillity of his reign was maintained by the love rather than by the fear of his subjects.

In the midst of all this enjoyment of empire, he never once violated that respectful awe with which the usher had found means to inspire him; but he by no means preserved the same regard for the principal master, an old illiterate German quack, who had formerly practised corn-cutting among the quality, and sold cosmetic washes to the ladies, together with teeth powders, hair-dyeing liquors, prolific elixirs, and tinctures to sweeten the breath. These nostrums, recommended by the art of cringing, in which he was consummate, ingratiated him so much with people of fashion, that he was enabled to set up school with five-and-twenty boys of the best families, whom he boarded on his own terms, and undertook to instruct in the French and Latin languages, so as to qualify them for the colleges of Westminster and Eton. While this plan was in its infancy, he was so fortunate as to meet with Jennings, who, for the paltry consideration of thirty pounds a year, which his necessities compelled him to accept, took the whole trouble of educating the children upon himself, contrived an excellent system for that purpose, and, by his assiduity and knowledge, executed all the particulars to the entire satisfaction of those concerned, who, by the bye, never inquired into his qualifications, but suffered the other to enjoy the fruits of his labour and ingenuity.

Over and above a large stock of avarice, ignorance, and vanity, this superior had certain ridiculous peculiarities in his person, such as a hunch upon his back, and distorted limbs, that seemed to attract the satirical notice of Peregrine, who, young as he was, took offence at his want of reverence for his usher, over whom he sometimes chose opportunities of displaying his authority, that the boys might not displace their veneration. Mr. Keypstick, therefore, such as I have described him, incurred the contempt and displeasure of this enterprising pupil, who now, being in the tenth year of his age, had capacity enough to give him abundance of vexation. He underwent many mortifying jokes from the invention of Pickle and his confederates; so that he began to entertain suspicion of Mr. Jennings, who, he could not help thinking, had been at the bottom of them all, and spirited up principles of rebellion in the school, with a view of making himself independent. Possessed with this chimera, which was void of all foundation, the German descended so low as to tamper in private with the boys, from whom he hoped to draw some very important discovery; but he was disappointed in his expectation; and this mean practice reaching the ears of his usher, he voluntarily resigned his employment. Finding interest to obtain holy orders in a little time after, he left the kingdom, hoping to find a settlement in some of our American plantations.

The departure of Mr. Jennings produced a great revolution in the affairs of Keypstick, which declined from that moment, because he had neither authority to enforce obedience, nor prudence to maintain order among his scholars; so that the school degenerated into anarchy and confusion, and he himself dwindled in the opinion of his employers, who looked upon him as superannuated, and withdrew their children from his tuition.

Peregrine, seeing this dissolution of their society, and finding himself every day deprived of some companion, began to repine at his situation, and resolved, if possible, to procure his release from the jurisdiction of the person whom he both detested and despised. With this view he went to work, and composed the following billet, addressed to the commodore, which was the first specimen of his composition in the epistolary way:

HONOURED AND LOVING UNCLE,—Hoping you are in good health, this service to inform you, that Mr. Jennings is gone, and Mr. Keypstick will never meet with his fellow. The school is already almost broke up, and the rest daily going away; and I beg of you of all love to have me fetched away also, for I cannot bear to be any longer under one who is a perfect ignoramus, who scarce knows the declination of *musa*, and is more fit to be a scarecrow than a schoolmaster; hoping you will send for me soon, with my love to my aunt, and my duty to my honoured parents, craving their blessing and yours. And this is all at present, from, honoured uncle, your well-beloved and dutiful nephew and godson, and humble servant to command till death,

PEREGRINE PICKLE.

Trunnion was overjoyed at the receipt of this letter, which

he looked upon as one of the greatest efforts of human genius, and as such communicated the contents to his lady, whom he had disturbed for the purpose in the middle of her devotion, by sending a message to her closet, whither it was her custom very frequently to retire. She was out of humour at being interrupted, and therefore did not peruse this specimen of her nephew's understanding with all the relish that the commodore himself had enjoyed; on the contrary, after sundry paralytical endeavours to speak (for her tongue sometimes refused its office), she observed that the boy was a pert jackanapes, and deserved to be severely chastised for treating his betters with such disrespect. Her husband undertook his godson's defence, representing, with great warmth, that he knew Keypstick to be a good-for-nothing pimping old rascal, and that Perry showed a great deal of spirit and good sense in desiring to be taken from under his command; he therefore declared that the boy should not live a week longer with such a shambling son of a bitch, and sanctioned his declaration with abundance of oaths.

Mrs. Trunnion, composing her countenance into a look of religious demureness, rebuked him for his profane way of talking; and asked, in a magisterial tone, if he intended never to lay aside that brutal behaviour? Irritated at this reproach, he answered in terms of indignation, that he knew how to behave himself as well as e'er a woman that wore a head, bade her mind her own affairs, and, with another repetition of oaths, gave her to understand that he would be master in his own house.

This insinuation operated upon her spirits like friction upon a glass globe; her face gleamed with resentment, and every pore seemed to emit particles of flame. She replied with incredible fluency of the bitterest expressions. He retorted with equal rage in broken hints and incoherent imprecations. She rejoined with redoubled fury, and in conclusion he was fain to betake himself to flight, ejaculating curses against her, and muttering something concerning the brandy-bottle, which, however, he took care should never reach her ears.

From his own house he went directly to visit Mrs. Pickle, to whom he imparted Peregrine's epistle, with many encomiums upon the boy's promising parts; and finding his commendations but coldly received, desired she would permit him to take his godson under his own care.

This lady, whose family was now increased by another son, who seemed to engross her care for the present, had not seen

Perry during a course of four years, and, with regard to him, was perfectly weaned of that infirmity known by the name of maternal fondness; she therefore consented to the commodore's request with great condescension, and a polite compliment to him on the concern he had all along manifested for the welfare of the child.

CHAPTER XIII

The Commodore takes Peregrine under his own Care—The Boy arrives at the Garrison—Is strangely received by his own Mother—Enters into a Confederacy with Hatchway and Pipes, and executes a Couple of waggish Enterprises upon his Aunt.

TRUNNION having obtained this permission, that very afternoon despatched the lieutenant in a post-chaise to Keypstick's house, from whence in two days he returned with our young hero; who being now in the eleventh year of his age, had outgrown the expectation of all his family, and was remarkable for the beauty and elegance of his person. His godfather was transported at his arrival, as if he had been actually the issue of his own loins. He shook him heartily by the hand, turned him round and round, surveyed him from top to bottom, bade Hatchway take notice how handsomely he was built; squeezed his hand again, saying, "D—n ye, you dog, I suppose you don't value such an old crazy son of a bitch as me a rope's end. You have forgot how I was wont to dandle you on my knee, when you was a little urchin no bigger than the davit, and played a thousand tricks upon me, burning my bacco-pouches, and poisoning my rumbo: O, d—n ye, you can grin fast enough, I see; I warrant you have learnt more things than writing and the Latin lingo." Even Tom Pipes expressed uncommon satisfaction on this joyful occasion; and coming up to Perry, thrust forth his fore paw, and accosted him with the salutation of "What cheer, my young master? I am glad to see thee with all my heart."

These compliments being passed, his uncle halted to the door of his wife's chamber, at which he stood hallooing, "Here's your kinsman Perry; belike you won't come and bid him welcome."—"Lord! Mr. Trunnion," said she, "why will you continually harass me in this manner with your impertinent intrusion?"—"I harrow you!" replied the commodore; "'sblood, I believe your upper works are damaged; I only came to inform you that here was your cousin, whom you have not seen these four long years; and I'll be d—d if there is such another of his age within the king's dominions, d'ye see, either for make or mettle; he's a credit to the name, d'ye see; but d—n my eyes, I'll say no more of the matter; if you come, you may; if you won't, you may let it alone."—"Well, I won't come, then," answered his yoke-fellow, "for I am at present more agreeably employed."—"Oho! you are? I believe so too!" cried the commodore, making wry faces, and mimicking the action of dram-drinking. Then addressing himself to Hatchway, "Prithee, Jack," said he, "go and try thy skill on that stubborn hulk; if anybody can bring her about, I know you wool." The lieutenant accordingly taking his station at the door, conveyed his persuasion in these words: "What, won't you turn out and hail little Perry? It will do your heart good to see such a handsome young dog; I'm sure he is the very moral of you, and as like as if he had been spit out of your own mouth, as the saying is; do show a little respect for your kinsman, can't you?" —To this remonstrance she replied in a mild tone of voice, "Dear Mr. Hatchway, you are always teasing one in such a manner; sure I am, nobody can tax me with unkindness, or want of natural affection"; so saying, she opened the door, and advancing to the hall where her nephew stood, received him very graciously, and observed that he was the very image of her papa.

In the afternoon, he was conducted by the commodore to the house of his parents; and, strange to tell, no sooner was he presented to his mother, than her countenance changed, she eyed him with tokens of affliction and surprise, and, bursting into tears, exclaimed her child was dead, and this was no other than an impostor whom they had brought to defraud her sorrow. Trunnion was confounded at this unaccountable passion, which had no other foundation than caprice and whim; and Gamaliel himself was so disconcerted and unsettled in his own belief, which began to waver, that he knew not how to behave towards the boy, whom his godfather immediately carried back to the garrison, swearing all the way that Perry should never cross their threshold again with his goodwill. Nay, so much was he incensed at this unnatural and absurd renunciation, that he refused to carry on any further correspondence with Pickle, until he was appeased by his solicitations and submission, and Peregrine owned as his son and heir. But this acknowledgment was made without the privity of his wife, whose vicious aversion he was obliged, in appearance, to adopt. Thus exiled from his father's house, the young gentleman was left entirely to the disposal of the commodore, whose affection for him daily increased, insomuch that he could scarce prevail upon himself to part with him, when his education absolutely required that he should be otherwise disposed of.

In all probability, this extraordinary attachment was, if not produced, at least riveted, by that peculiar turn in Peregrine's imagination, which we have already observed; and which, during his residence in the castle, appeared in sundry stratagems he practised upon his uncle and aunt, under the auspices of Mr. Hatchway, who assisted him in the contrivance and execution of all his schemes. Nor was Pipes exempted from a share in their undertakings; for, being a trusty fellow, not without dexterity in some cases, and altogether resigned to their will, they found him a serviceable instrument for their purpose, and used him accordingly.

The first sample of their art was exhibited upon Mrs. Trunnion. They terrified that good lady with strange noises when she retired to her devotion. Pipes was a natural genius in the composition of discords; he could imitate the sound produced by the winding of a jack, the filing of a saw, and the swinging of a malefactor hanging in chains; he could counterfeit the braying of an ass, the screeching of a night owl, the cater-wauling of cats, the howling of a dog, the squeaking of a pig, the crowing of a cock; and he had learned the war whoop uttered by the Indians in North America. These talents were exerted successively at different times and places, to the terror of Mrs. Trunnion, the discomposure of the commodore himself, and the consternation of all the servants in the castle. Peregrine, with a sheet over his clothes, sometimes tumbled before his aunt in the twilight, when her organs of vision were a little impaired by the cordial she had swallowed; and the boatswain's mate taught him to shoe cats with walnut shells, so that they made a most dreadful clattering in their nocturnal excursions. The mind of Mrs. Trunnion was not a little disturbed by these alarms, which, in her opinion, portended the death of some principal person in the family; she redoubled her religious exercises, and fortified her spirits with fresh potations; nay, she began to take notice that Mr. Trunnion's constitution was very much broke, and seemed dissatisfied when people observed that they never saw him look better.

Her frequent visits to the closet, where all her consolation was deposited, inspired the confederates with a device which had like to have been attended with tragical consequences. They found an opportunity to infuse jalap in one of her case-bottles, and she took so largely of this medicine, that her constitution had wellnigh sunk under the violence of its effect. She suffered a succession of fainting fits that reduced her to the brink of the grave, in spite of all the remedies that were administered by a physician, who was called in the beginning of her disorder. After having examined the symptoms, he declared that the patient had been poisoned with arsenic, and prescribed oily draughts and lubricating injections, to defend the coats of the stomach and intestines from the vellicating particles of that pernicious mineral; at the same time hinting, with a look of infinite sagacity, that it was not difficult to divine the whole mystery. He affected to deplore the poor lady, as if she was exposed to more attempts of the same nature; thereby glancing obliquely at the innocent commodore, whom the officious son of Æsculapius suspected as the author of this expedient, to rid his hands of a yoke-fellow for whom he was well known to have no great devotion. This impertinent and malicious insinuation made some impression upon the bystanders, and furnished ample field for slander to asperse the morals of Trunnion, who was represented through the whole district as a monster of barbarity. Nay, the sufferer herself, though she behaved with great decency and prudence, could not help entertaining some small diffidence of her husband; not that she imagined he had any design upon her life, but that he had been at pains to adulterate the brandy, with a view of detaching her from that favourite liquor.

On this supposition she resolved to act with more caution for the future, without setting on foot any inquiry about the affair; while the commodore, imputing her indisposition to some natural cause, after the danger was past never bestowed a thought upon the subject; so that the perpetrators were quit of their fear, which, however, had punished them so effectually, that they never would hazard any more jokes of the same nature.

The shafts of their wit were now directed against the commander himself, whom they teased and terrified almost out of his senses. One day while he was at dinner, Pipes came and told him that there was a person below that wanted to speak with him immediately about an affair of the greatest importance, that would admit of no delay; upon which he ordered the stranger to be told that he was engaged, and that he must send up his name and business. To this demand he received for answer a message, importing that the person's name was unknown to him, and his business of such a nature, that it could not be disclosed to any one but the commodore himself, whom he earnestly desired to see without loss of time.

Trunnion, surprised at this importunity, got up with great reluctance in the middle of his meal, and, descending to a parlour where the stranger was, asked him in a surly tone what he wanted with him in such a d—ned hurry, that he could not wait till he had made an end of his mess? The other, not at all disconcerted at this rough address, advanced close up to him on his tiptoes, and, with a look of confidence and conceit, laying his mouth to one side of the commodore's head, whispered softly in his ear, "Sir, I am the attorney whom you wanted to converse with in private."—"The attorney!" cried Trunnion, staring and half choked with choler.—"Yes, sir, at your service," replied this retainer to the law, "and, if you please, the sooner we despatch the affair, the better; for it is an old observation, that delay breeds danger."—"Truly, brother," said the commodore, who could no longer contain himself, "I do confess that I am very much of your way of thinking, d'ye see; and therefore you shall be despatched in a trice"; so saying, he lifted up his walking-staff, which was something between a crutch and a cudgel, and discharged it with such energy on the seat of the attorney's understanding, that, if there had been anything but solid bone, the contents of his skull must have been evacuated.

Fortified as he was by nature against all such assaults, he could not withstand the momentum of the blow, which in an instant laid him flat on the floor, deprived of all sense and motion; and Trunnion hopped upstairs to dinner, applauding himself in ejaculations all the way for the vengeance he had taken on such an impudent pettifogging miscreant.

The attorney no sooner awaked from his trance, into which he had been so unexpectedly lulled, than he cast his eyes around in quest of evidence, by which he might be enabled the more easily to prove the injury he had sustained; but not a soul appearing, he made shift to get upon his legs again, and, with the blood trickling over his nose, followed one of the servants into the dining-room, resolved to come to an explanation with the assailant, and either extort money from him by way of satisfaction, or provoke him to a second application before witnesses. With this view he entered the room in a peal of clamour, to the amazement of all present, and the terror of

Mrs. Trunnion, who shrieked at the appearance of such a spectacle; and addressing himself to the commodore, "I'll tell you what, sir," said he, "if there be law in England, I'll make you smart for this here assault. You think you have screened yourself from a prosecution, by sending all your servants out of the way, but that circumstance will appear upon trial to be a plain proof of the malice prepense with which the fact was committed, especially when corroborated by the evidence of this here letter, under your own hand, whereby I am desired to come to your own house to transact an affair of consequence." So saying, he produced the writing, and read the contents in these words:

MR. ROGER RAVINE.

SIR,—Being in a manner prisoner in my own house, I desire you will give me a call precisely at three o'clock in the afternoon, and insist upon seeing me yourself, as I have an affair of great consequence, in which your particular advice is wanted by your humble servant,

HAWSER TRUNNION.

The one-eyed commander, who had been satisfied with the chastisement he had already bestowed upon the plaintiff, hearing him read this audacious piece of forgery, which he considered as the effect of his own villany, started up from table, and seizing a huge turkey that lay in a dish before him, would have applied it, sauce and all, by way of poultice to his wound, had he not been restrained by Hatchway, who laid fast hold on both his arms, and fixed him to his chair again, advising the attorney to sheer off with what he had got. Far from following this salutary counsel, he redoubled his threats, and set Trunnion at defiance, telling him he was not a man of true courage, although he had commanded a ship of war, or else he would not have attacked any person in such a cowardly and clandestine manner. This provocation would have answered his purpose effectually, had not his adversary's indignation been repressed by the suggestions of the lieutenant, who desired his friend in a whisper to be easy, for he would take care to have the attorney tossed in a blanket for his presumption. This proposal, which he received with great approbation, pacified him in a moment; he wiped the sweat from his forehead, and his features relaxed into a grim smile.

Hatchway disappeared, and Ravine proceeded with great fluency of abuse, until he was interrupted by the arrival of Pipes, who, without any expostulation, led him out by the hand,

and conducted him to the yard, where he was put into a carpet, and in a twinkling sent into the air by the strength and dexterity of five stout operators, whom the lieutenant had selected from the number of domestics for that singular spell of duty.

In vain did the astonished vaulter beg for the love of God and passion of Christ, that they would take pity upon him, and put an end to his involuntary gambols; they were deaf to his prayers and protestations, even when he swore, in the most solemn manner, that, if they would cease tormenting him, he would forget and forgive what was past, and depart in peace to his own habitation; and continued the game till they were fatigued with the exercise.

Ravine, being dismissed in a most melancholy plight, brought an action of assault and battery against the commodore, and subpœnaed all the servants as evidences in the cause; but as none of them had seen what happened, he did not find his account in the prosecution, though he himself examined all the witnesses, and, among other questions, asked whether they had not seen him come in like another man; and whether they had ever seen any other man in such a condition as that in which he had crawled off. But this last interrogation they were not obliged to answer, because it had reference to the second discipline he had undergone, in which they, and they only, were concerned; and no person is bound to give testimony against himself.

In short, the attorney was nonsuited, to the satisfaction of all who knew him, and found himself under the necessity of proving that he had received, in course of post, the letter, which was declared in court a scandalous forgery, in order to prevent an indictment with which he was threatened by the commodore, who little dreamed that the whole affair had been planned and executed by Peregrine and his associates.

The next enterprise in which this triumvirate engaged, was a scheme to frighten Trunnion with an apparition, which they prepared and executed in this manner: to the hide of a large ox, Pipes fitted a leathern vizor of a most terrible appearance, stretched on the jaws of a shark, which he had brought from sea, and accommodated with a couple of broad glasses instead of eyes. On the inside of these, he placed two rushlights, and, with a composition of sulphur and saltpetre, made a pretty large fuse, which he fixed between two rows of the teeth. This equipage being finished, he, one dark night chosen for the purpose, put it on, and following the commodore into a long passage, in which he was preceded by Perry with a light in his hand, kindled his fire-work with a match, and began to bellow like a bull. The boy, as it was concerted, looking behind him, screamed aloud, and dropped the light, which was extinguished in the fall; when Trunnion, alarmed at his nephew's consternation, exclaimed, "Zounds! what's the matter?" And, turning about to see the cause of his dismay, beheld a hideous phantom vomiting blue flame, which aggravated the horrors of its aspect. He was instantly seized with an agony of fear, which divested him of his reason; nevertheless, he, as it were mechanically, raised his trusty supporter in his own defence, and the apparition advancing towards him, aimed it at this dreadful annoyance with such a convulsive exertion of strength, that, had not the blow chanced to light upon one of the horns, Mr. Pipes would have had no cause to value himself upon his invention. Misapplied as it was, he did not fail to stagger at the shock, and, dreading another such salutation, closed with the commodore, and, having tripped up his heels. retreated with great expedition.

It was then that Peregrine, pretending to recollect himself a little, ran with all the marks of disturbance and affright, and called up the servants to the assistance of their master; whom they found in a cold sweat upon the floor, his features betokening horror and confusion. Hatchway raised him up, and, having comforted him with a cup of Nantz, began to inquire into the cause of his disorder; but he could not extract one word of answer from his friend, who, after a considerable pause, during which he seemed to be wrapped up in profound contemplation, pronounced aloud, "By the Lord! Jack, you may say what ye wool, but I'll be d—n'd if it was not Davy Jones himself. I know him by his saucer-eyes, his three rows of teeth, his horns and tail, and the blue smoke that came out of his nostrils. What does the blackguard hell's baby want with me? I am sure I never committed murder, except in the way of my profession, nor wronged any man whatsomever since I first went to sea." This same Davy Jones, according to the mythology of sailors, is the fiend that presides over all the evil spirits of the deep, and is often seen in various shapes, perching among the rigging on the eve of hurricanes, shipwrecks, and other disasters, to which a seafaring life is exposed; warning the devoted wretch of death and woe. No wonder then that Trunnion was disturbed by a supposed visit of this demon, which in his opinion foreboded some dreadful calamity.

CHAPTER XIV

He is also by their Advice engaged in an Adventure with the Exciseman,
who does not find his Account in his own Drollery.

HOWSOEVER preposterous and unaccountable that passion may
be, which prompts persons, otherwise generous and sympathising,
to afflict and perplex their fellow-creatures, certain it is, our
confederates entertained such a large proportion of it, that, not
satisfied with the pranks they had already played, they still
persecuted the commodore without ceasing. In the course of his
own history, the particulars of which he delighted to recount,
he had often rehearsed an adventure of deer-stealing, in which,
during the unthinking impetuosity of his youth, he had been
unfortunately concerned. Far from succeeding in that achievement, he and his associates had, it seems, been made prisoners,
after an obstinate engagement with the keepers, and carried
before a neighbouring justice of the peace, who used Trunnion
with great indignity, and, with his companions, committed
him to jail.

His own relations, and in particular an uncle, on whom he
chiefly depended, treated him during his confinement with great
rigour and inhumanity, and absolutely refused to interpose his
influence in his behalf, unless he would sign a writing obliging
himself to go to sea within thirty days after his release, under
the penalty of being proceeded against as a felon. The alternative was, either to undergo this voluntary exile, or remain
in prison disowned and deserted by everybody, and, after all,
suffer an ignominious trial, that might end in a sentence of
transportation for life. He, therefore, without much hesitation,
embraced the proposal of his kinsman, and, as he observed, was,
in less than a month after his discharge, turned adrift to the
mercy of the wind and waves.

Since that period he had never maintained any correspondence
with his relations, all of whom had concurred in sending him off;
nor would he ever pay the least regard to the humiliations and
supplications of some among them, who had prostrated themselves before him, on the advancement of his fortune; but he
retained a most inveterate resentment against his uncle, who
was still in being, though extremely old and infirm, and frequently mentioned his name with all the bitterness of revenge.

Perry, being perfectly well acquainted with the particulars of
this story, which he had heard so often repeated, proposed to

Hatchway, that a person should be hired to introduce himself to the commodore, with a supposititious letter of recommendation from this detested kinsman; an imposition that, in all likelihood, would afford abundance of diversion.

The lieutenant relished the scheme, and, young Pickle having composed an epistle for the occasion, the exciseman of the parish, a fellow of great impudence and some humour, in whom Hatchway could confide, undertook to transcribe and deliver it with his own hand, and also personate the man in whose favour it was feigned to be writ. He accordingly one morning arrived on horseback at the garrison, two hours at least before Trunnion used to get up, and gave Pipes, who admitted him, to understand, that he had a letter for his master, which he was ordered to deliver to none but the commodore himself. This message was no sooner communicated, than the indignant chief, who had been waked for the purpose, began to curse the messenger for breaking his rest, and swore he would not budge till his usual time of turning out. This resolution being conveyed to the stranger, he desired the carrier to go back and tell him, he had such joyful tidings to impart, that he was sure the commodore would think himself amply rewarded for his trouble, even if he had been raised from the grave to receive them.

This assurance, flattering as it was, would not have been powerful enough to persuade him, had it not been assisted with the exhortations of his spouse, which never failed to influence his conduct. He therefore crept out of bed, though not without great repugnance, and, wrapping himself in his morning gown, was supported downstairs, rubbing his eye, yawning fearfully, and grumbling all the way. As soon as he popped his head into the parlour, the supposed stranger made divers awkward bows, and, with a grinning aspect, accosted him in these words: "Your most humble servant, most noble commodore! I hope you are in good health; you look pure and hearty; and, if it was not for that misfortune of your eye, one would not desire to see a more pleasant countenance in a summer's day. Sure as I am a living soul, one would take you to be on this side of threescore. Laud help us! I should have known you to be a Trunnion, if I had met with you in the midst of Salisbury plain, as the saying is." The commodore, who was not at all in the humour of relishing such an impertinent preamble, interrupted him in this place, saying, with a peevish accent, "Pshaw! pshaw! brother, there's no occasion to bowse out so much unnecessary gum; if you can't bring your discourse to bear on the right subject, you had much better clap a stopper on your tongue, and bring yourself up, d'ye see. I was told you had something to deliver." "Deliver!" cried the waggish impostor, "odds heart! I have got something for you that will make your very entrails rejoice within your body. Here's a letter from a dear and worthy friend of yours. Take, read it, and be happy. Blessings on his old heart! one would think he had renewed his age, like the eagles."

Trunnion's expectation being thus raised, he called for his spectacles, adjusted them to his eye, took the letter, and, being curious to know the subscription, no sooner perceived his uncle's name, than he started back, his lip quivered, and he began to shake in every limb with resentment and surprise; nevertheless, eager to know the subject of an epistle from a person who had never before troubled him with any sort of address, he endeavoured to recollect himself, and perused the contents, which were these:

LOVING NEPHEW,—I doubt not but you will be rejoiced to hear of my welfare; and well you may, considering what a kind uncle I have been to you in the days of your youth, and how little you deserved any such thing; for you was always a graceless young man, given to wicked courses and bad company, whereby you would have come to a shameful end, had it not been for my care in sending you out of mischief's way. But this is not the cause of my present writing. The bearer, Mr. Timothy Trickle, is a distant relation of yours, being the son of the cousin of your Aunt Margery, and is not over and above well as to worldly matters. He thinks of going to London, to see for some post in the excise or customs, if so be that you will recommend him to some great man of your acquaintance, and give him a small matter to keep him till he is provided. I doubt not, nephew, but you will be glad to serve him, if it was no more but for the respect you bear to me, who am,

Loving nephew, your affectionate uncle, and servant to command,
                                        TOBIAH TRUNNION.

It would be a difficult task for the inimitable Hogarth himself to exhibit the ludicrous expression of the commodore's countenance, while he read this letter. It was not a stare of astonishment, a convulsion of rage, or a ghastly grin of revenge, but an association of all three, that took possession of his features. At length he hawked up, with incredible straining, the interjection Ah! that seemed to have stuck some time in his windpipe, and thus gave vent to his indignation. "Have I come alongside of you at last, you old stinking curmudgeon! you lie, you lousy hulk, you lie—you did all in your power to founder me when I was a stripling; and, as for being graceless, and wicked, and keeping bad company, you tell a d—ned lie again, you thief; there was not a more peaceable lad in the county, and I kept no bad company but your own, d'ye see. Therefore, you Trickle, or what's your name, tell the old rascal that sent you hither, that I spit in his face, and call him horse; that I tear his letter into rags, so; and that I trample upon it as I would upon his own villanous carcass, d'ye see." So saying, he danced in a sort of frenzy upon the fragments of the paper, which he had scattered about the room, to the inexpressible satisfaction of the triumvirate, who beheld the scene.

The exciseman having got between him and the door, which was left open for his escape, in case of necessity, affected great confusion and surprise at his behaviour, saying, with an air of mortification, "Lord be merciful unto me! is this the way you treat your own relations, and the recommendation of your best friend! Surely all gratitude and virtue has left this sinful world! What will cousin Tim, and Dick, and Tom, and good mother Pipkin, and her daughters, cousins Sue and Prue, and Peg, with all the rest of our kinsfolk, say, when they hear of this unconscionable reception that I have met with? Consider, sir, that ingratitude is worse than the sin of witchcraft, as the apostle wisely observes; and do not send me away with such unchristian usage, which will lay a heavy load of guilt upon your poor miserable soul." "What, you are on a cruise for a post, brother Trickle, an't ye?" said Trunnion, interrupting him; "we shall find a post for you in a trice, my boy. Here, Pipes, take this saucy son of a bitch, belay him to the whipping-post in the yard. I'll teach you to rowce me in the morning with such impertinent messages." Pipes, who wanted to carry the joke farther than the exciseman dreamed of, laid hold of him in a twinkling, and executed the orders of his commander, notwithstanding all his nods, winking, and significant gestures, which the boatswain's mate would by no means understand; so that he began to repent of the part he acted in this performance, which was like to end so tragically, and stood fastened to the stake, in a very disagreeable state of suspense, casting many a rueful look over his left shoulder, while Pipes was absent in quest of a cat-and-nine-tails, in expectation of being relieved by the interposition of the lieutenant, who did not, however, appear. Tom, returning with the instrument of correction, undressed the delinquent in a trice, and whispering in his ear, that he was very sorry for being employed in such an office, but durst not for his soul disobey the orders of his commander, flourished the scourge about his head, and, with admirable dexterity, made such a smarting application to the offender's back and shoulders, that the distracted gauger performed sundry new cuts with his feet, and bellowed hideously with pain, to the infinite satisfaction of the spectators. At length, when he was almost flea'd from his rump to the nape of his neck, Hatchway, who had purposely absented himself hitherto, appeared in the yard, and, interposing in his behalf, prevailed upon Trunnion to call off the executioner, and ordered the malefactor to be released.

The exciseman, mad with the catastrophe he had undergone, threatened to be revenged upon his employers, by making a candid confession of the whole plot; but the lieutenant giving him to understand, that, in so doing, he would bring upon himself a prosecution for fraud, forgery, and imposture, he was fain to put up with his loss, and sneaked out of the garrison, attended with a volley of curses discharged upon him by the commodore, who was exceedingly irritated by the disturbance and disappointment he had undergone.

CHAPTER XV

The Commodore detects the Machinations of the Conspirators, and hires a Tutor for Peregrine, whom he settles at Winchester School.

THIS was not the least affliction he suffered from the unwearied endeavours and inexhausted invention of his tormentors, who harassed him with such a variety of mischievous pranks, that he began to think all the devils in hell had conspired against his peace; and accordingly became very serious and contemplative on the subject.

In the course of his meditations, when he recollected and compared the circumstances of every mortification to which he had been lately exposed, he could not help suspecting that some of them must have been contrived to vex him; and, as he was not ignorant of his lieutenant's disposition, nor unacquainted with the talents of Peregrine, he resolved to observe them both for the future with the utmost care and circumspection. This resolution, aided by the incautious conduct of the conspirators, whom, by this time, success had rendered heedless and indiscreet, was attended by the desired effect. He in a little time detected Perry in a new plot, and, by dint of a little chastisement, and a great many threats, extorted from him a confession of all the contrivances in which he had been concerned. The commodore was thunderstruck at the discovery, and so much incensed against Hatchway for the part he had acted in the whole, that he deliberated with himself, whether he should demand satisfaction with sword and pistol, or dismiss him from the garrison, and renounce all friendship with him at once. But he had been so long accustomed to Jack's company, that he could not live without him; and, upon more cool reflection, perceiving that what he had done was rather the effect of wantonness than malice, which he himself would have laughed to see take place upon any other person, he determined to devour his chagrin, and extend his forgiveness even to Pipes, whom, in the first sally of his passion, he had looked upon in a more criminal light than that of a simple mutineer. This determination was seconded by another, which he thought absolutely necessary for his own repose, and in which his own interest and that of his nephew concurred.

Peregrine, who was now turned of twelve, had made such advances under the instruction of Jennings, that he often disputed upon grammar, and was sometimes thought to have the better in his contests with the parish priest, who, notwithstanding this acknowledged superiority of his antagonist, did great justice to his genius, which he assured Mr. Trunnion would be lost for want of cultivation, if the boy was not immediately sent to prosecute his studies at some proper seminary of learning.

This maxim had been more than once inculcated upon the commodore by Mrs. Trunnion, who, over and above the deference she paid to the parson's opinion, had a reason of her own for wishing to see the house clear of Peregrine, at whose prying disposition she began to be very uneasy. Induced by these motives, which were joined by the solicitation of the youth himself, who ardently longed to see a little more of the world, his uncle determined to send him forthwith to Winchester, under the immediate care and inspection of a governor, to whom he allowed a very handsome appointment for that purpose. This gentleman, whose name was Mr. Jacob Jolter, had been school-fellow with the parson of the parish, who recommended him to Mrs. Trunnion as a person of great worth and learning, in every respect qualified for the office of a tutor. He likewise added, by way of eulogium, that he was a man of exemplary piety, and particularly zealous for the honour of the church of which he was a member, having been many years in holy orders, though he did not then exercise any function of the priesthood. Indeed, Mr. Jolter's zeal was so exceedingly fervent, as on some occasions to get the better of his discretion; for, being a high churchman, and of consequence a malcontent, his resentment was habituated into an unsurmountable prejudice against the present disposition of affairs, which, by confounding the nation with the ministry, sometimes led him into erroneous, not to say absurd calculations; otherwise a man of good morals, well versed in mathematics and school divinity, studies which had not at all contributed to sweeten and unbend the natural sourness and severity of his complexion.

This gentleman being destined to the charge of superintending Perry's education, everything was prepared for their departure; and Tom Pipes, in consequence of his own petition, put into livery, and appointed footman to the young squire. But, before they set out, the commodore paid the compliment of communicating his design to Mr. Pickle, who approved of the plan, though he durst not venture to see the boy; so much was he intimidated by the remonstrances of his wife, whose aversion to her firstborn became every day more inveterate and unaccountable. This unnatural caprice seemed to be supported by a consideration which, one would imagine, might have rather vanquished her disgust. Her second son Gam, who was now in the fourth year of his age, had been rickety from the cradle, and as remarkably unpromising in appearance as Perry was agreeable in his person. As the deformity increased, the mother's fondness was augmented, and the virulence of her hate against the other son seemed to prevail in the same proportion.

Far from allowing Perry to enjoy the common privileges of a child, she would not suffer him to approach his father's house, expressed uneasiness whenever his name happened to be mentioned, sickened at his praise, and in all respects behaved like a most rancorous stepmother. Though she no longer retained that ridiculous notion of his being an impostor, she still continued to abhor him, as if she really believed him to be such; and when any person desired to know the cause of her surprising dislike, she always lost her temper, and peevishly replied, that she had reasons of her own, which she was not obliged to declare; nay, so much was she affected by this vicious partiality, that she broke off all commerce with her sister-in-law and the commodore, because they favoured the poor child with their countenance and protection.

Her malice, however, was frustrated by the love and generosity of Trunnion, who, having adopted him as his own son, equipped him accordingly, and carried him and his governor in his own coach to the place of destination, where they were settled on a very genteel footing, and everything regulated according to their desires.

Mrs. Trunnion behaved with great decency at the departure of her nephew, to whom, with a great many pious advices and injunctions to behave with submission and reverence towards his tutor, she presented a diamond ring of small value, and a gold medal, as tokens of her affection and esteem. As for the lieutenant, he accompanied them in the coach; and such was the friendship he had contracted for Perry, that, when the commodore proposed to return, after having accomplished the intent of his journey, Jack absolutely refused to attend him, and signified his resolution to stay where he was.

Trunnion was the more startled at this declaration, as Hatchway was become so necessary to him in almost all the purposes of his life, that he foresaw he should not be able to exist without his company. Not a little affected with this consideration, he turned his eye ruefully upon the lieutenant, saying, in a piteous tone, "What! leave me at last, Jack, after we have weathered so many hard gales together? D—n my limbs! I thought you had been more of an honest heart. I looked upon you as my foremast, and Tom Pipes as my mizen; now he is carried away; if so be as you go too, my standing rigging being decayed, d'ye see, the first squall will bring me by the board. D—n ye, if in case I have given offence, can't you speak above board, and I shall make you amends."

Jack being ashamed to own the true situation of his thoughts, after some hesitation, answered with perplexity and incoherence, "No, d—me! that an't the case neither; to be sure you always used me in an officer-like manner, that I must own, to give the devil his due, as the saying is; but for all that, this here is the case, I have some thoughts of going to school myself, to learn your Latin lingo; for, as the saying is, *Better mend late than never*. And I am informed as how one can get more for the money here than anywhere else."

In vain did Trunnion endeavour to convince him of the folly of going to school at his years, by representing that the boys would make game of him, and that he would become a laughing-stock to all the world; he persisted in his resolution to stay, and the commodore was fain to have recourse to the mediation of

Pipes and Perry, who employed their influence with Jack, and at last prevailed upon him to return to the garrison, after Trunnion had promised he should be at liberty to visit them once a month. This stipulation being settled, he and his friend took leave of the pupil, governor, and attendant, and next morning set out for their habitation, which they reached in safety that same night.

Such was Hatchway's reluctance to leave Peregrine, that he is said, for the first time in his life, to have looked misty at parting: certain I am, that, on the road homewards, after a long pause of silence, which the commodore never dreamed of interrupting, he exclaimed all of a sudden, "I'll be d—n'd if the dog ha'n't given me some stuff to make me love him." Indeed, there was something congenial in the disposition of these two friends, which never failed to manifest itself in the sequel, howsoever different their education, circumstances, and connexions happened to be.

CHAPTER XVI

Peregrine distinguishes himself among his Schoolfellows, exposes his Tutor, and attracts the particular Notice of the Master.

THUS left to the prosecution of his studies, Peregrine was in a little time a distinguished character, not only for his acuteness of apprehension, but also for that mischievous fertility of fancy, of which we have already given such pregnant examples. But, as there was a great number of such luminaries in this new sphere to which he belonged, his talents were not so conspicuous, while they shone in his single capacity, as they afterwards appeared, when they concentred and reflected the rays of the whole constellation.

At first he confined himself to piddling game, exercising his genius upon his own tutor, who attracted his attention, by endeavouring to season his mind with certain political maxims, the fallacy of which he had discernment enough to perceive. Scarcely a day passed in which he did not find means to render Mr. Jolter the object of ridicule; his violent prejudices, ludicrous vanity, awkward solemnity, and ignorance of mankind, afforded continual food for the raillery, petulance, and satire of his pupil, who never neglected an opportunity of laughing, and making others laugh at his expense.

Sometimes, in their parties, by mixing brandy in his wine, he decoyed this pedagogue into a debauch, during which his caution forsook him, and he exposed himself to the censure of the company. Sometimes, when the conversation turned upon intricate subjects, he practised upon him the Socratic method of confutation, and, under pretence of being informed, by an artful train of puzzling questions, insensibly betrayed him into self-contradiction.

All the remains of authority which he had hitherto preserved over Peregrine soon vanished; so that, for the future, no sort of ceremony subsisted betwixt them; and all Mr. Jolter's precepts were conveyed in hints of friendly advice, which the other might either follow or neglect at his own pleasure. No wonder, then, that Peregrine gave a loose to his inclinations, and, by dint of genius and an enterprising temper, made a figure among the younger class of heroes in the school.

Before he had been a full year at Winchester, he had signalised himself in so many achievements in defiance to the laws and regulations of the place, that he was looked upon with admiration, and actually chosen *Dux*, or leader, by a large body of his co-temporaries. It was not long before his fame reached the ears of his master, who sent for Mr. Jolter, communicated to him the informations he had received, and desired him to check the vivacity of his charge, and redouble his vigilance in time to come, else he should be obliged to make a public example of his pupil for the benefit of the school.

The governor, conscious of his own unimportance, was not a little disconcerted at this injunction, which it was not in his power to fulfil by any compulsive means. He therefore went home in a very pensive mood, and, after mature deliberation, resolved to expostulate with Peregrine in the most familiar terms, and endeavour to dissuade him from practices which might affect his character as well as interest. He accordingly frankly told him the subject of the master's discourse, represented the disgrace he might incur by neglecting this warning, and, putting him in mind of his own situation, hinted the consequences of the commodore's displeasure, in case he should be brought to disapprove of his conduct. These insinuations made the greater impression, as they were delivered with many expressions of friendship and concern. The young gentleman was not so raw but that he could perceive the solidity of Mr. Jolter's advice, to which he promised to conform, because his pride was interested in the affair; and he considered his own reformation as the only means of avoiding that infamy which, even in idea, he could not bear.

His governor, finding him so reasonable, profited by these moments of reflection; and, in order to prevent a relapse, proposed that he should engage in some delightful study that would agreeably amuse his imagination, and gradually detach him from those connexions which had involved him in so many troublesome adventures. For this purpose, he, with many rapturous encomiums, recommended the mathematics, as yielding more rational and sensible pleasures to a youthful fancy than any other subject of contemplation, and actually began to read Euclid with him that same afternoon.

Peregrine entered upon this branch of learning with all that warmth of application which boys commonly yield on the first change of study; but he had scarce advanced beyond the *Pons Asinorum*, when his ardour abated; the test of truth by demonstration did not elevate him to those transports of joy with which his preceptor had regaled his expectation; and before he arrived at the fortieth-and-seventh proposition, he began to yawn drearily, make abundance of wry faces, and thought himself but indifferently paid for his attention, when he shared the vast discovery of Pythagoras, and understood that the square of the hypothenuse was equal to the squares of the other two sides of a right-angled triangle. He was ashamed, however, to fail in his undertaking, and persevered with great industry, until he had finished the first four books, acquired plain trigonometry, with the method of algebraical calculation, and made himself well acquainted with the principles of surveying; but no consideration could prevail upon him to extend his inquiries farther in this science, and he returned with double relish to his former avocations, like a stream, which, being dammed, accumulates more force, and, bursting over its mounds, rushes down with double impetuosity.

Mr. Jolter saw with astonishment and chagrin, but could not resist the torrent. His behaviour was now no other than a series of licence and effrontery; prank succeeded prank, and outrage followed outrage, with surprising velocity. Complaints were every day preferred against him; in vain were admonitions bestowed by the governor in private, and menaces discharged by the masters in public; he disregarded the first, despised the latter, divested himself of all manner of restraint, and proceeded in his career to such a pitch of audacity, that a consultation was held upon the subject, in which it was determined that this untoward spirit should be humbled by a severe and ignominious flogging for the very next offence he should commit. In the meantime, Mr. Jolter was desired to write, in the master's name, to the commodore, requesting him to remove Tom Pipes from the person of his nephew, the said Pipes being a principal actor and abettor in all his malversations; and to put a stop to the monthly visitations of the mutilated lieutenant, who had never once failed to use his permission, but came punctual to a day, always fraught with some new invention. Indeed, by this time, Mr. Hatchway was as well known, and much better beloved by every boy in the school, than the master who instructed him, and always received by a number of scholars, who used to attend Peregrine when he went forth to meet his friend, and conduct him to his lodging with public testimonies of joy and applause.

As for Tom Pipes, he was not so properly the attendant of Peregrine, as master of the revels to the whole school. He mingled in all their parties, and superintended their diversions, deciding between boy and boy, as if he acted by commission under the great seal. He regulated their motions by his whistle, instructed the young boys in the games of hustle-cap, leap-frog, and chuck-farthing; imparted to those of a more advanced age the sciences of cribbage and all-fours, together with the method of storming the castle, acting the comedy of Prince Arthur, and other pantomimes, as they are commonly exhibited at sea; and instructed the seniors, who were distinguished by the appellation of bloods, in cudgel-playing, dancing the St. Giles's hornpipe, drinking flip, and smoking tobacco. These qualifications had rendered him so necessary and acceptable to the scholars, that, exclusive of Perry's concern in the affair, his dismission, in all probability, would have produced some dangerous convulsion in the community. Jolter, therefore, knowing his importance, informed his pupil of the directions he had received, and very candidly asked how he should demean himself in the execution; for he durst not write to the commodore without this previous notice, fearing that the young gentleman, as soon as he should get an inkling of the affair, would follow the example, and make his uncle acquainted with certain anec-dotes, which it was the governor's interest to keep concealed. Peregrine was of opinion that he should spare himself the trouble of conveying any complaints to the commodore, and, if questioned by the master, assure him he had complied with his desire; at the same time he promised faithfully to conduct himself with such circumspection for the future, that the masters should have no temptation to revive the inquiry. But the resolution attending this extorted promise was too frail to last, and, in less than a fortnight, our young hero found himself entangled in an adventure, from which he was not extricated with his usual good fortune.

CHAPTER XVII

He is concerned in a dangerous Adventure with a certain Gardener—Sublimes his Ideas, commences Gallant, and becomes acquainted with Miss Emily Gauntlet.

HE, and some of his companions, one day entered a garden in the suburbs, and having indulged their appetites, desired to know what satisfaction they must make for the fruit they had pulled. The gardener demanded what, in their opinion, was an exorbitant price; and they, with many opprobrious terms, refused to pay it. The peasant being surly and untractable, insisted upon his right; neither was he deficient nor sparing in the eloquence of vulgar abuse. His guests attempted to retreat; a scuffle ensued, in which Peregrine lost his cap; and the gardener, being in danger, from the number of his foes, called to his wife to let loose the dog, who instantly flew to his master's assistance, and, after having tore the leg of one, and the shoulder of another, put the whole body of the scholars to flight. Enraged at the indignity which had been offered them, they solicited a reinforcement of their friends, and, with Tom Pipes at their head, marched back to the field of battle. Their adversary, seeing them approach, called his apprentice, who worked at the other end of the ground, to his assistance, armed him with a mattock, while he himself wielded an hoe, bolted his door on the inside, and, flanked with his man and mastiff, waited the attack without flinching. He had not remained three minutes in this posture of defence, when Pipes, who acted as the enemy's forlorn hope, advanced to the gate with great intrepidity, and clapping his foot to the door, which was none of the stoutest, with the execution and despatch of a petard, split it into a thousand pieces. This sudden execution had an immediate effect upon the 'prentice, who retreated with great precipitation, and escaped at a postern. But the master placed himself like another Hercules in the breach; and when Pipes, brandishing his cudgel, stepped forward to engage him, levelled his weapon

with such force and dexterity at his head, that, had the skull
been made of penetrable stuff, the iron edge must have cleft
his pate in twain. Casemated as he was, the instrument cut
sheer even to the bone, on which it struck with such amazing
violence, that sparks of real fire were produced by the collision.
And let not the incredulous reader pretend to doubt the truth
of this phenomenon, until he shall have first perused the ingenious Peter Kolben's *Natural History of the Cape of Good Hope*,
where the inhabitants commonly used to strike fire with the
shin-bones of lions, which have been killed in that part of Africa.

Pipes, though a little disconcerted, far from being disabled
by the blow, in a trice retorted the compliment with his trun-
cheon; which, had not his antagonist expeditiously slipped his
head aside, would have laid him breathless across his own
threshold; but, happily for him, he received the salutation upon
his right shoulder, which crashed beneath the stroke, and the
hoe dropped instantly from his tingling hand. Tom perceiving,
and being unwilling to forego the advantage he had gained,
darted his head into the bosom of this son of earth, and overturned him on the plain, being himself that instant assaulted
by the mastiff, who fastened upon the outside of his thigh.
Feeling himself incommoded by this assailant in his rear, he
quitted the prostrate gardener to the resentment of his associates,
who poured upon him in shoals, and, turning about, laid hold
with both his hands of this ferocious animal's throat, which he
squeezed with such incredible force and perseverance, that the
creature quitted his hold, his tongue lolled out of his jaws,
the blood started from his eyes, and he swung a lifeless trunk
between the hands of his vanquisher.

It was well for his master that he did not longer exist; for
by this time he was overwhelmed by such a multitude of foes,
that his whole body scarce afforded points of contact to all the
fists that drummed upon it, consequently, to use a vulgar phrase,
his wind was almost knocked out, before Pipes had leisure to
interpose in his behalf, and persuade his offenders to desist,
by representing that the wife had gone to alarm the neighbourhood, and that in all probability they would be intercepted in
their return. They accordingly listened to his remonstrances,
and marched homewards in triumph, leaving the gardener in
the embraces of his mother earth, from which he had not power
to move when he was found by his disconsolate helpmate and
some friends, whom she had assembled for his assistance.
Among these was a blacksmith and farrier, who took cognisance

of his carcass, every limb of which having examined, he declared there was no bone broke, and, taking out his fleam, blooded him plentifully as he lay. He was then conveyed to his bed, from which he was not able to stir during a whole month. His family coming upon the parish, a formal complaint was made to the master of the school, and Peregrine represented as the ringleader of those who committed this barbarous assault. An inquiry was immediately set on foot, and the articles of impeachment being fully proved, our hero was sentenced to be severely chastised in the face of the whole school. This was a disgrace, the thoughts of which his proud heart could not brook. He resolved to make his elopement rather than undergo the punishment to which he was doomed; and having signified his sentiments to his confederates, they promised, one and all, to stand by him, and either screen him from the chastisement, or share his fate.

Confiding in this friendly protestation, he appeared unconcerned on the day that was appointed for his punishment; and, when he was called to his destiny, advanced towards the scene, attended by the greatest part of the scholars, who intimated their determination to the master, and proposed that Peregrine should be forgiven. The superior behaved with that dignity of demeanour which became his place, represented the folly and presumption of their demand, reprehended them for their audacious proceeding, and ordered every boy to his respective station. They obeyed his command, and our unfortunate hero was publicly horsed, *in terrorem* of all whom it might concern.

This disgrace had a very sensible effect upon the mind of Peregrine, who, having by this time passed the fourteenth year of his age, began to adopt the pride and sentiments of a man. Thus dishonourably stigmatised, he was ashamed to appear in public as usual; he was incensed against his companions for their infidelity and irresolution, and plunged into a profound reverie that lasted several weeks, during which he shook off his boyish connexions, and fixed his view upon objects which he thought more worthy of his attention.

In the course of his gymnastic exercises, at which he was very expert, he contracted intimacies with several youths who were greatly his superiors in point of age, and who, pleased with his aspiring genius and address, introduced him into parties of gallantry which strongly captivated his inclination. He was by nature particularly adapted for succeeding in adventures of this kind; over and above a most engaging person, that improved with his years, he possessed a dignified assurance, an agreeable ferocity which enhanced the conquest of the fair who had the good fortune to enslave him, unlimited generosity, and a fund of humour which never failed to please. Nor was he deficient in the more solid accomplishments of youth; he had profited in his studies beyond expectation, and besides that sensibility of discernment which is the foundation of taste, and in consequence of which he distinguished and enjoyed the beauties of the classics, he had already given several specimens of a very promising poetic talent.

With this complexion and these qualifications, no wonder that our hero attracted the notice and affections of the young Delias in town, whose hearts had just begun to flutter for they knew not what. Inquiries were made concerning his condition; and no sooner were his expectations known, than he was invited and caressed by all the parents, while their daughters vied with each other in treating him with particular complacency. He inspired love and emulation wherever he appeared; envy and jealous rage followed of course; so that he became a very desirable, though a very dangerous acquaintance. His moderation was not equal to his success; his vanity took the lead of his passions, dissipating his attention, which might otherwise have fixed him to one object; and he was possessed with the rage of increasing the number of his conquests. With this view he frequented public walks, concerts, and assemblies, became remarkably rich and fashionable in his clothes, gave entertainments to the ladies, and was in the utmost hazard of turning out a most egregious coxcomb.

While his character thus wavered between the ridicule of some and the regard of others, an accident happened, which, by contracting his view to one object, detached him from those vain pursuits that would in time have plunged him into an abyss of folly and contempt. Being one evening at the ball which is always given to the ladies at the time of the races, the person who acted as master of the ceremonies, knowing how fond Mr. Pickle was of every opportunity to display himself, came up and told him that there was a fine young creature at the other end of the room, who seemed to have a great inclination to dance a minuet, but wanted a partner, the gentleman who attended her being in boots.

Peregrine's vanity being aroused at this intimation, he went up to reconnoitre the young lady, and was struck with admiration at her beauty. She seemed to be of his own age, was tall, and, though slender, exquisitely shaped; her hair was auburn, and in such plenty, that the barbarity of dress had not been able to prevent it from shading both sides of her forehead, which was high and polished; the contour of her face was oval, her nose very little raised in the aquiline form, that contributed to the spirit and dignity of her aspect; her mouth was small, her lips plump, juicy, and delicious, her teeth regular and white as driven snow, her complexion incredibly delicate and glowing with health, and her full blue eyes beamed forth vivacity and love. Her mien was at the same time commanding and engaging, her address perfectly genteel, and her whole appearance so captivating, that our young Adonis looked, and was overcome.

He no sooner recollected himself from his astonishment, than he advanced to her with a graceful air of respect, and begged she would do him the honour to walk a minuet with him. She seemed particularly pleased with his application, and very frankly complied with his request. The pair was too remarkable to escape the particular notice of the company; Mr. Pickle was well known by almost everybody in the room; but his partner was altogether a new face, and of consequence underwent the criticism of all the ladies in the assembly. One whispered, "She has a good complexion, but don't you think she is a little awry?" a second pitied her for her masculine nose; a third observed, that she was awkward for want of seeing company; a fourth distinguished something very bold in her countenance; and, in short, there was not a beauty in her whole composition which the glass of envy did not pervert into a blemish.

The men, however, looked upon her with different eyes: among them her appearance produced an universal murmur of applause; they encircled the space on which she danced, and were enchanted by her graceful motion. While they launched out in the praise of her, they expressed their displeasure at the good fortune of her partner, whom they d—ed for a little finical coxcomb, that was too much engrossed by the contemplation of his own person, to discern or deserve the favour of his fate. He did not hear, therefore could not repine at these invectives; but while they imagined he indulged his vanity, a much more generous passion had taken possession of his heart.

Instead of that petulance of gaiety for which he had been distinguished in his public appearance, he now gave manifest signs of confusion and concern; he danced with an anxiety which impeded his performance, and blushed to the eyes at every false step he made. Though this extraordinary agitation was overlooked by the men, it could not escape the observation of the ladies, who perceived it with equal surprise and resentment; and when Peregrine led this fair unknown to her seat, expressed their pique in an affected titter, which broke from every mouth at the same instant, as if all of them had been informed by the same spirit.

Peregrine was nettled at this unmannerly mark of disapprobation, and, in order to increase their chagrin, endeavoured to enter into particular conversation with their fair rival. The young lady herself, who neither wanted penetration, nor the consciousness of her own accomplishments, resented their behaviour, though she triumphed at the cause of it, and gave her partner all the encouragement he could desire. Her mother, who was present, thanked him for his civility, in taking such notice of a stranger, and he received a compliment of the same nature from the young gentleman in boots, who was her own brother.

If he was charmed with her appearance, he was quite ravished with her discourse, which was sensible, spirited, and gay. Her frank and sprightly demeanour excited his own confidence and good-humour; and he described to her the characters of those females who had honoured them with such a spiteful mark of distinction, in terms so replete with humorous satire, that she seemed to listen with particular complacency of attention, and distinguished every nymph thus ridiculed with such a significant glance, as overwhelmed her with chagrin and mortification. In short, they seemed to relish each other's conversation, during which our young Damon acquitted himself with great skill in all the duties of gallantry; he laid hold of proper opportunities to express his admiration of her charms, had recourse to the silent rhetoric of tender looks, breathed divers insidious sighs, and attached himself wholly to her during the remaining part of the entertainment.

When the company broke up, he attended her to her lodgings, and took leave of her with a squeeze of the hand, after having obtained permission to visit her next morning, and been informed by the mother that her name was Miss Emilia Gauntlet.

All night long he closed not an eye, but amused himself with plans of pleasure, which his imagination suggested, in consequence of this new acquaintance. He rose with the lark, adjusted his hair into an agreeable negligence of curl, and, dressing himself in a genteel grey frock, trimmed with silver binding, waited with the utmost impatience for the hour of ten, which no sooner struck than he hied him to the place of appointment, and, inquiring for Miss Gauntlet, was shown into a parlour. Here he had not waited above ten minutes, when Emilia entered in a most enchanting undress, with all the graces of nature playing about her person, and in a moment riveted the chains of his slavery beyond the power of accident to unbind.

Her mother being still a-bed, and her brother gone to give orders about the chaise, in which they proposed to return that same day to their own habitation, he enjoyed her company *tête-à-tête* a whole hour, during which he declared his love in the most passionate terms, and begged that he might be admitted into the number of those admirers whom she permitted to visit and adore her.

She affected to look upon his vows and protestations as the ordinary effects of gallantry, and very obligingly assured him, that, were she to live in that place, she should be glad to see him often; but, as the spot on which she resided was at a considerable distance, she could not expect he would go so far upon such a trifling occasion, as to take the trouble of providing himself with her mamma's permission.

To this favourable hint he answered with all the eagerness of the most fervid passion, that he had uttered nothing but the genuine dictates of his heart; that he desired nothing so much as an opportunity of evincing the sincerity of his professions; and that, though she lived at the extremity of the kingdom, he would find means to lay himself at her feet, provided he could visit her with her mother's consent, which he assured her he would not fail to solicit.

She then gave him to understand, that her habitation was about sixteen miles from Winchester, in a village which she named, and where, as he could easily collect from her discourse, he would be no unwelcome guest.

In the midst of this communication they were joined by Mrs. Gauntlet, who received him with great courtesy, thanking him again for his politeness to Emy at the ball, and anticipated his intentions, by saying that she should be very glad to see him at her house, if ever his occasions should call him that way.

CHAPTER XVIII

He inquires into the Situation of this Young Lady, with whom he is enamoured—Elopes from School—Is found by the Lieutenant, conveyed to Winchester, and sends a Letter with a Copy of Verses to his Mistress.

HE was transported with pleasure at this invitation, which he assured her he should not neglect; and, after a little more conversation on general topics, took his leave of the charming Emilia and her prudent mamma, who had perceived the first emotions of Mr. Pickle's passion for her daughter, and been at some pains to inquire about his family and fortune.

Neither was Peregrine less inquisitive about the situation and pedigree of his new mistress, who, he learned, was the only daughter of a field officer, who died before he had it in his power to make suitable provision for his children; that the widow lived in a frugal, though decent manner, on her pension, assisted by the bounty of her relations; that the son carried arms as a volunteer in the company which his father had commanded; and that Emilia had been educated in London, at the expense of a rich uncle, who was seized with the whim of marrying at the age of fifty-five; in consequence of which, his niece had returned to her mother, without any visible dependence, except on her own conduct and qualifications.

This account, though it could not diminish his affection, nevertheless alarmed his pride; for his warm imagination had exaggerated all his own prospects; and he began to fear that his passion for Emilia might be thought to derogate from the dignity of his situation. The struggle between his interest and love produced a perplexity which had an evident effect upon his behaviour; he became pensive, solitary, and peevish, avoided all public diversions, and grew so remarkably negligent in his dress, that he was scarce distinguishable by his own acquaintance. This contention of thoughts continued several weeks, at the end of which the charms of Emilia triumphed over every other consideration. Having received a supply of money from the commodore, who acted towards him with great generosity, he ordered Pipes to put up some linen, and other necessaries, in a sort of knapsack which he could conveniently carry, and, thus attended, set out early one morning on foot for the village where his charmer lived, at which he arrived before two o'clock in the afternoon; having chosen this method of travelling, that his route might not be so easily discovered as it must have been, had he hired horses, or taken a place in the stage-coach.

The first thing he did was to secure a convenient lodging at the inn where he dined; then he shifted himself, and, according to the direction he had received, went to the house of Mrs. Gauntlet in a transport of joyous expectation. As he approached the gate, his agitation increased, he knocked with impatience and concern, the door opened, and he had actually asked if Mrs. Gauntlet was at home, before he perceived that the portress was no other than his dear Emilia. She was not without emotion at the unexpected sight of her lover, who instantly recognising his charmer, obeyed the irresistible impulse of his love, and caught the fair creature in his arms. Nor did she seem offended at this forwardness of behaviour, which might have displeased another of a less open disposition, or less used to the freedom of a sensible education; but her natural frankness had been encouraged and improved by the easy and familiar intercourse in which she had been bred; and therefore, instead of reprimanding him with a severity of look, she with great good-humour rallied him upon his assurance, which, she observed, was undoubtedly the effect of his own conscious merit, and conducted him into a parlour, where he found her mother, who in very polite terms expressed her satisfaction at seeing him within her house.

After tea, Miss Emy proposed an evening walk, which they enjoyed through a variety of little copses and lawns, watered by a most romantic stream, that quite enchanted the imagination of Peregrine.

It was late before they returned from this agreeable excursion; and when our lover wished the ladies good-night, Mrs. Gauntlet insisted upon his staying to supper, and treated him with particular demonstrations of regard and affection. As her economy was not encumbered with an unnecessary number of domestics, her own presence was often required in different parts of the house; so that the young gentleman was supplied with frequent opportunities of promoting his suit, by all the tender oaths and insinuations that his passion could suggest. He protested her idea had taken such entire possession of his heart, that, finding himself unable to support her absence one day longer, he had quitted his studies, and left his governor by stealth, that he might visit the object of his adoration, and be blessed in her company for a few days without interruption.

She listened to his addresses with such affability as denoted approbation and delight, and gently chid him as a thoughtless truant, but carefully avoided the confession of a mutual flame; because she discerned, in the midst of all his tenderness, a levity of pride which she durst not venture to trust with such a declaration. Perhaps she was confirmed in this caution by her mother, who very wisely, in her civilities to him, maintained a sort of ceremonious distance, which she thought not only requisite for the honour and interest of her family, but likewise for her own exculpation, should she ever be taxed with having encouraged or abetted him in the imprudent sallies of his youth. Yet, notwithstanding this affected reserve, he was treated with such distinction by both, that he was ravished with his situation, and became more and more enamoured every day.

While he remained under the influence of this sweet intoxication, his absence produced great disturbance at Winchester. Mr. Jolter was grievously afflicted at his abrupt departure, which alarmed him the more, as it happened after a long fit of melancholy which he had perceived in his pupil. He communicated his apprehensions to the master of the school, who advised him to apprise the commodore of his nephew's disappearance, and in the meantime inquire at all the inns in town, whether he had hired horses, or any sort of carriage, for his conveyance, or was met with on the road by any person who could give an account of the direction in which he travelled.

This scrutiny, though performed with great diligence and minuteness, was altogether ineffectual; they could obtain no intelligence of the runaway. Mr. Trunnion was well-nigh distracted at the news of his flight; he raved with great fury at the imprudence of Peregrine, whom, in his first transports, he d—ed as an ungrateful deserter; then he cursed Hatchway and Pipes, who he swore had foundered the lad by their pernicious counsels; and, lastly, transferred his execrations upon Jolter, because he had not kept a better look-out; finally, he made an apostrophe to that son of a bitch the gout, which for the present disabled him from searching for his nephew in person. That he might not, however, neglect any means in his power, he immediately despatched expresses to all the seaport towns on that coast, that he might be prevented from leaving the kingdom; and the lieutenant, at his own desire, was sent across the country, in quest of this young fugitive.

Four days had he unsuccessfully carried on his inquiries with great accuracy, when, resolving to return by Winchester, where he hoped to meet with some hints of intelligence, by which he might profit in his future search, he struck off the common road, to take the benefit of a nearer cut, and, finding himself benighted near a village, took up his lodgings at the first inn to which his horse directed him. Having bespoke something for supper, and retired to his chamber, where he amused himself with a pipe, he heard a confused noise of rustic jollity, which being all of a sudden interrupted, after a short pause his ear was saluted with the voice of Pipes, who, at the solicitation of the company, began to entertain them with a song.

Hatchway instantly recognised the well-known sound, in which indeed he could not possibly be mistaken, as nothing in nature bore the least resemblance to it; he threw his pipe into the chimney, and, snatching up one of his pistols, ran immediately to the apartment from whence the voice issued; he no sooner entered, than, distinguishing his old shipmate in a crowd of country peasants, he in a moment sprung upon him, and, clapping his pistol to his breast, exclaimed, "D—n you, Pipes, you are a dead man, if you don't immediately produce young master."

This menacing application had a much greater effect upon the company than upon Tom, who, looking at the lieutenant with great tranquillity, replied, "Why, so I can, Mr. Hatchway." "What! safe and sound?" cried the other. "As a roach," answered Pipes, so much to the satisfaction of his friend Jack, that he shook him by the hand, and desired him to proceed with his song. This being performed, and the reckoning discharged, the two friends adjourned to the other room, where the lieutenant was informed of the manner in which the young gentleman had made his elopement from college, as well as of the other particulars of his present situation, as far as they had fallen within the sphere of the relater's comprehension.

While they sat thus conferring together, Peregrine, having taken leave of his mistress for the night, came home, and was not a little surprised when Hatchway, entering his chamber in a sea attitude, thrust out his hand by way of salutation. His old pupil received him, as usual, with great cordiality, and expressed his astonishment at meeting him in that place; but when he understood the cause and intention of his arrival, he started with concern, and, his visage glowing with indignation, told him he was old enough to be judge of his own conduct, and, when he should see it convenient, would return of himself; but those who thought he was to be compelled to his duty would find themselves egregiously mistaken.

The lieutenant assured him, that, for his own part, he had no intention to offer him the least violence; but at the same time he represented to him the danger of incensing the commodore, who was already almost distracted on account of his absence; and, in short, conveyed his arguments, which were equally obvious and valid, in such expressions of friendship and respect, that Peregrine yielded to his remonstrances, and promised to accompany him next day to Winchester.

Hatchway, overjoyed at the success of his negotiation, went immediately to the hostler, and bespoke a post-chaise for Mr. Pickle and his man, with whom he afterwards indulged himself in a double can of rumbo, and, when the night was pretty far advanced, left the lover to his repose, or rather to the thorns of his own meditation; for he slept not one moment, being incessantly tortured with the prospect of parting from his divine Emilia, who had now acquired the most absolute empire over his soul. One minute he proposed to depart early in the morning, without seeing his enchantress, in whose bewitching presence he durst not trust his own resolution. Then the thoughts of leaving her in such an abrupt and disrespectful manner interposed in favour of his love and honour. This war of sentiments kept him all night upon the rack, and it was time to rise before he had determined to visit his charmer, and candidly impart the motives that induced him to leave her.

He accordingly repaired to her mother's house with a heavy heart, being attended to the gate by Hatchway, who did not choose to leave him alone; and, being admitted, found Emilia just risen, and, in his opinion, more beautiful than ever.

Alarmed at his early visit, and the gloom that overspread his countenance, she stood in silent expectation of hearing some melancholy tidings; and it was not till after a considerable pause that he collected resolution enough to tell her he was come to take his leave. Though she strove to conceal her sorrow, nature was not to be suppressed; every feature of her countenance saddened in a moment, and it was not without the utmost difficulty that she kept her lovely eyes from overflowing. He saw the situation of her thoughts, and, in order to alleviate her concern, assured her that he should find means to see her again in a very few weeks; meanwhile he communicated his reasons for departing, in which she readily acquiesced; and, having mutually consoled each other, their transports of grief subsided, and, before Mrs. Gauntlet came downstairs, they were in a condition to behave with great decency and resignation.

This good lady expressed her concern when she learned his resolution, saying, she hoped his occasions and inclination would permit him to favour them with his agreeable company another time.

The lieutenant, who began to be uneasy at Peregrine's stay, knocked at the door, and, being introduced by his friend, had the honour of breakfasting with the ladies; on which occasion his heart received such a rude shock from the charms of Emilia, that he afterwards made a merit with his friend of having constrained himself so far as to forbear commencing his professed rival.

At length they bade adieu to their kind entertainers, and, in less than an hour setting out from the inn, arrived about two o'clock in Winchester, where Mr. Jolter was overwhelmed with joy at their appearance.

The nature of this adventure being unknown to all except those who could be depended upon, everybody who inquired about the cause of Peregrine's absence was told that he had been with a relation in the country, and the master condescended to overlook his indiscretion; so that Hatchway, seeing everything settled to the satisfaction of his friend, returned to the garrison, and gave the commodore an account of his expedition.

The old gentleman was very much startled when he heard there was a lady in the case, and very emphatically observed, that a man had better be sucked into the Gulf of Florida, than once get into the indraught of a woman; because, in one case, he may with good pilotage bring out his vessel safe between the Bahamas and the Indian shore; but in the other there is no outlet at all, and it is in vain to strive against the current; so that of course he must be embayed, and run chuck upon a lee shore. He resolved, therefore, to lay the state of the case before Mr. Gamaliel Pickle, and concert such measures with him as should be thought likeliest to detach his son from the pursuit of an idle amour, which could not fail of interfering in a dangerous manner with the plan of his education.

In the meantime, Perry's ideas were totally engrossed by his amiable mistress, who, whether he slept or waked, was still present in his imagination, which produced the following stanzas in her praise:

> Adieu, ye streams that smoothly flow,
> Ye vernal airs that softly blow,
> Ye plains by blooming spring array'd,
> Ye birds that warble through the shade!

Unhurt from you my soul could fly,
Nor drop one tear, nor heave one sigh;
But forc'd from Celia's charms to part,
All joy deserts my drooping heart.

O! fairer than the rosy morn,
When flowers the dewy fields adorn;
Unsullied as the genial ray
That warms the balmy breeze of May,

Thy charms divinely bright appear,
And add new splendour to the year;
Improve the day with fresh delight,
And gild with joy the dreary night!

This juvenile production was enclosed in a very tender billet to Emilia, and committed to the charge of Pipes, who was ordered to set out for Mrs. Gauntlet's habitation with a present of venison, and a compliment to the ladies; and directed to take some opportunity of delivering the letter to Miss, without the knowledge of her mamma.

CHAPTER XIX

His Messenger meets with a Misfortune, to which he applies a very extraordinary Expedient, that is attended with strange Consequences.

As a stage-coach passed within two miles of the village where she lived, Tom bargained with the driver for a seat on the box, and accordingly departed on this message, though he was indifferently qualified for commissions of such a nature. Having received particular injunctions about the letter, he resolved to make that the chief object of his care, and very sagaciously conveyed it between his stocking and the sole of his foot, where he thought it would be perfectly secure from all injury and accident. Here it remained until he arrived at the inn where he had formerly lodged, when, after having refreshed himself with a draught of beer, he pulled off his stocking, and found the poor billet sullied with dust, and torn in a thousand tatters by the motion of his foot in walking the last two miles of his journey. Thunderstruck at this phenomenon, he uttered a long and loud *whew!* which was succeeded by an exclamation of "D—n my old shoes! a bite, by God!" then he rested his elbows on the table, and his forehead upon his two fists, and in that attitude deliberated with himself upon the means of remedying this misfortune.

As he was not distracted by a vast number of ideas, he soon concluded, that his best expedient would be to employ the clerk of the parish, who he knew was a great scholar, to write another epistle according to the directions he should give him; and never dreaming that the mangled original would in the least facilitate this scheme, he very wisely committed it to the flames, that it might never rise up in judgment against him.

Having taken this wise step, he went in quest of the scribe, to whom he communicated his business, and promised a full pot by way of gratification. The clerk, who was also schoolmaster, proud of an opportunity to distinguish his talents, readily undertook the task; and repairing with his employer to the inn, in less than a quarter of an hour produced a morsel of eloquence so much to the satisfaction of Pipes, that he squeezed his hand by way of acknowledgment, and doubled his allowance of beer. This being discussed, our courier betook himself to the house of Mrs. Gauntlet, with the haunch of venison and this succedaneous letter, and delivered his message to the mother who received it with great respect, and many kind inquiries about the health and welfare of his master, attempting to tip the messenger a crown, which he absolutely refused to accept, in consequence of Mr. Pickle's repeated caution. While the old gentlewoman turned to a servant, in order to give directions about the disposal of the present, Pipes looked upon this as a favourable occasion to transact his business with Emilia, and therefore shutting one eye, with a jerk of his thumb towards his left shoulder, and a most significant twist of his countenance, he beckoned the young lady into another room, as if he had been fraught with something of consequence, which he wanted to impart. She understood the hint, howsoever strangely communicated, and, by stepping to one side of the room, gave him an opportunity of slipping the epistle into her hand, which he gently squeezed at the same time in token of regard; then, throwing a side glance at the mother, whose back was turned, clapped his finger on the side of his nose, thereby recommending secrecy and discretion.

Emilia, conveying the letter into her bosom, could not help smiling at Tom's politeness and dexterity; but lest her mamma should detect him in the execution of his pantomime, she broke off this intercourse of signs, by asking aloud when he proposed to set out on his return to Winchester. When he answered, "To-morrow morning," Mrs. Gauntlet recommended him to the hospitality of her own footman, desiring him to make much of

Mr. Pipes below, where he was kept to supper, and very cordially
entertained. Our young heroine, impatient to read her lover's
billet, which made her heart throb with rapturous expectation, retired to her chamber as soon as possible, with a view
of perusing the contents, which were these:

DIVINE EMPRESS OF MY SOUL!—If the refulgent flames of your
beauty had not evaporated the particles of my transported brain,
and scorched my intellects into a cinder of stolidity, perhaps the
resplendency of my passion might shine illustrious through the
sable curtain of my ink, and in sublimity transcend the galaxy
itself, though wafted on the pinions of a grey goose quill! But ah!
celestial enchantress! the necromancy of thy tyrannical charms
hath fettered my faculties with adamantine chains, which unless
thy compassion shall melt, I must eternally remain in the Tartarean
gulf of dismal despair. Vouchsafe, therefore, O thou brightest
luminary of this terrestrial sphere! to warm as well as shine; and
let the genial rays of thy benevolence melt the icy emanations of
thy disdain, which hath frozen up the spirits of—angelic pre-
eminence!—thy most egregious admirer and superlative slave,

PEREGRINE PICKLE.

Never was astonishment more perplexing than that of Emilia,
when she read this curious composition, which she repeated
verbatim three times, before she could credit the evidence of
her own senses. She began to fear in good earnest that love
had produced a disorder in her lover's understanding; but, after
a thousand conjectures, by which she attempted to account
for this extraordinary fustian of style, she concluded that it was
the effect of mere levity, calculated to ridicule the passion he
had formerly professed. Irritated by this supposition, she
resolved to balk his triumph with affected indifference, and in
the meantime endeavour to expel him from that place which
he possessed within her heart. And, indeed, such a victory
over her inclinations might have been obtained without great
difficulty; for she enjoyed an easiness of temper that could
accommodate itself to the emergencies of her fate; and her
vivacity, by amusing her imagination, preserved her from the
keener sensations of sorrow. Thus determined and disposed,
she did not send any sort of answer, or the least token of remembrance by Pipes, who was suffered to depart with a general
compliment from the mother, and arrived at Winchester the
next day.

Peregrine's eyes sparkled when he saw his messenger come in,
and he stretched out his hand in full confidence of receiving
some particular mark of his Emilia's affection; but how was he

confounded, when he found his hope so cruelly disappointed!
In an instant his countenance fell. He stood for some time
silent and abashed, then thrice repeated the interrogation of
"What! not one word from Emilia?" and dubious of his courier's
discretion, inquired minutely into all the particulars of his
reception. He asked, if he had seen the young lady; if she was
in good health; if he had found an opportunity of delivering his
letter, and how she looked, when he put it into her hand? Pipes
answered, that he had never seen her in better health or higher
spirits; that he had managed matters so as not only to present
the billet unperceived, but also to ask her commands in private
before he took his leave, when she told him that the letter
required no reply. This last circumstance he considered as a
manifest mark of disrespect, and gnawed his lips with resentment. Upon further reflection, however, he supposed that
she could not conveniently write by the messenger, and would
undoubtedly favour him by the post. This consideration consoled him for the present, and he waited impatiently for the
fruits of his hope; but after he had seen eight days elapsed
without reaping the satisfaction with which he had flattered
himself, his temper forsook him, he raved against the whole
sex, and was seized with a fit of sullen chagrin; but his pride
in a little time came to his assistance, and rescued him from the
horrors of the melancholy fiend. He resolved to retort her own
neglect upon his ungrateful mistress; his countenance gradually
resumed its former serenity; and though by this time he was
pretty well cured of his foppery, he appeared again at public
diversions with an air of gaiety and unconcern, that Emilia
might have a chance of hearing how much, in all likelihood, he
disregarded her disdain.

There are never wanting certain officious persons, who take
pleasure in promoting intelligence of this sort. His behaviour
soon reached the ears of Miss Gauntlet, and confirmed her in the
opinion she had conceived from his letter; so that she fortified
herself in her former sentiments, and bore his indifference with
great philosophy. Thus a correspondence which had commenced
with all the tenderness and sincerity of love, and every promise
of duration, was interrupted in its infancy by a misunderstanding
occasioned by the simplicity of Pipes, who never once reflected
upon the consequences of his deceit.

Though their mutual passion was by these means suppressed
for the present, it was not altogether extinguished, but glowed
in secret, though even to themselves unknown, until an occasion,

which afterwards offered, blew up the latent flame, and love resumed his empire in their breasts.

While they moved, as it were, without the sphere of each other's attraction, the commodore, fearing that Perry was in danger of involving himself in some pernicious engagement, resolved, by advice of Mr. Jolter and his friend the parish priest, to recal him from the place where he had contracted such imprudent connexions, and send him to the university, where his education might be completed, and his fancy weaned from all puerile amusements.

This plan had been proposed to his own father, who, as hath been already observed, stood always neuter in everything that concerned his eldest son; and as for Mrs. Pickle, she had never heard his name mentioned since his departure, with any degree of temper or tranquillity, except when her husband informed her that he was in a fair way of being ruined by this indiscreet amour. It was then she began to applaud her own foresight, which had discerned the mark of reprobation in that vicious boy, and launched out in comparison between him and Gammy, who, she observed, was a child of uncommon parts and solidity, and, with the blessing of God, would be a comfort to his parents, and an ornament to the family.

Should I affirm that this favourite, whom she commended so much, was in every respect the reverse of what she described; that he was a boy of mean capacity, and, though remarkably distorted in his body, much more crooked in his disposition; and that she had persuaded her husband to espouse her opinion, though it was contrary to common sense, as well as to his own perception; I am afraid the reader will think I represent a monster that never existed in nature, and be apt to condemn the economy of my invention; nevertheless, there is nothing more true than every circumstance of what I have advanced; and I wish the picture, singular as it is, may not be thought to resemble more than one original.

CHAPTER XX

Peregrine is summoned to attend his Uncle—Is more and more hated by his own Mother—Appeals to his Father, whose Condescension is defeated by the Dominion of his Wife.

BUT, waiving these reflections, let us return to Peregrine, who received a summons to attend his uncle, and in a few days arrived with Mr. Jolter and Pipes at the garrison, which he filled with joy and satisfaction. The alteration which, during his absence, had happened in his person, was very favourable in his appearance, which, from that of a comely boy, was converted into that of a most engaging youth. He was already taller than a middle-sized man, his shape ascertained, his sinews well knit, his mien greatly improved, and his whole figure as elegant and graceful as if it had been cast in the same mould with the Apollo of Belvidere.

Such an outside could not fail of prepossessing people in his favour. The commodore, notwithstanding the advantageous reports he had heard, found his expectation exceeded in the person of Peregrine, and signified his approbation in the most sanguine terms. Mrs. Trunnion was struck with his genteel address, and received him with uncommon marks of complacency and affection; he was caressed by all the people in the neighbourhood, who, while they admired his accomplishments, could not help pitying his infatuated mother, for being deprived of that unutterable delight which any other parent would have enjoyed in the contemplation of such an amiable son.

Divers efforts were made by some well-disposed people to conquer, if possible, this monstrous prejudice; but their endeavours, instead of curing, served only to inflame the distemper, and she never could be prevailed upon to indulge him with the least mark of maternal regard. On the contrary, her original disgust degenerated into such inveteracy of hatred, that she left no stone unturned to alienate the commodore's affection from this her innocent child, and even practised the most malicious defamation to accomplish her purpose. Every day did she abuse her husband's ear with some forged instance of Peregrine's ingratitude to his uncle, well knowing that it would reach the commodore's knowledge at night.

Accordingly, Mr. Pickle used to tell him at the club, that his hopeful favourite had ridiculed him in such a company, and aspersed his spouse upon another occasion; and thus retail the

little scandalous issue of his own wife's invention.   Luckily for
Peregrine, the commodore paid no great regard to the authority
of his informer, because he knew from what channel his intelligence flowed; besides, the youth had a staunch friend in Mr.
Hatchway, who never failed to vindicate him when he was thus
unjustly accused, and always found argument enough to confute
the assertions of his enemies.   But, though Trunnion had been
dubious of the young gentleman's principles, and deaf to the
remonstrances of the lieutenant, Perry was provided with a
bulwark strong enough to defend him from all such assaults.
This was no other than his aunt, whose regard for him was
perceived to increase in the same proportion as his own mother's
diminished; and indeed the augmentation of the one was, in all
probability, owing to the decrease of the other; for the two
ladies, with great civility, performed all the duties of good
neighbourhood, and hated each other most piously in their
hearts.

Mrs. Pickle having been disobliged at the splendour of her
sister's new equipage, had, ever since that time, in the course
of her visiting, endeavoured to make people merry with satirical
jokes on the poor lady's infirmities; and Mrs. Trunnion seized
the very first opportunity of making reprisals, by inveighing
against her unnatural behaviour to her own child; so that
Peregrine, as on the one hand he was abhorred, so on the other
was he caressed, in consequence of this contention; and I firmly
believe that the most effectual method of destroying his interest
at the garrison, would have been the show of countenancing
him at his father's house; but, whether this conjecture be
reasonable or chimerical, certain it is the experiment was never
tried, and therefore Mr. Peregrine ran no risk of being disgraced.
The commodore, who assumed, and justly too, the whole merit
of his education, was now as proud of the youth's improvements,
as if he had actually been his own offspring; and sometimes his
affection rose to such a pitch of enthusiasm, that he verily
believed him to be the issue of his own loins.   Notwithstanding
this favourable predicament in which our hero stood with his
aunt and her husband, he could not help feeling the injury he
suffered from the caprice of his mother; and, though the gaiety
of his disposition hindered him from afflicting himself with
reflections of any gloomy cast, he did not fail to foresee that,
if any sudden accident should deprive him of the commodore,
he would in all likelihood find himself in a very disagreeable
situation.   Prompted by this consideration, he one evening

accompanied his uncle to the club, and was introduced to his father, before that worthy gentleman had the least inkling of his arrival.

Mr. Gamaliel was never so disconcerted as at this rencounter. His own disposition would not suffer him to do anything that might create the least disturbance, or interrupt his evening's enjoyment; so strongly was he impressed with the terror of his wife, that he durst not yield to the tranquillity of his temper; and, as I have already observed, his inclination was perfectly neutral. Thus distracted between different motives, when Perry was presented to him, he sat silent and absorbed, as if he did not, or would not, perceive the application; and when he was urged to declare himself by the youth, who pathetically begged to know how he had incurred his displeasure, he answered in a peevish strain, "Why, good now, child, what would you have me to do? your mother can't abide you."—"If my mother is so unkind, I will not call it unnatural," said Peregrine, the tears of indignation starting from his eyes, "as to banish me from her presence and affection, without the least cause assigned, I hope you will not be so unjust as to espouse her barbarous prejudice."

Before Mr. Pickle had time to reply to this expostulation, for which he was not at all prepared, the commodore interposed, and enforced his favourite's remonstrance, by telling Mr. Gamaliel, that he was ashamed to see any man drive in such a miserable manner under his wife's petticoat. "As for my own part," said he, raising his voice, and assuming a look of importance and command, "before I would suffer myself to be steered all weathers by any woman in Christendom, d'ye see, I'd raise such a hurricane about her ears, that"—here he was interrupted by Mr. Hatchway, who, thrusting his head towards the door, in the attitude of one that listens, cried, "Ahey! there's your spouse come to pay us a visit." Trunnion's features that instant adopted a new disposition. Fear and confusion took possession of his countenance; his voice, from a tone of vociferation, sunk into a whisper of "Sure you must be mistaken, Jack"; and in great perplexity he wiped off the sweat which had started on his forehead at this false alarm. The lieutenant having thus punished him for the rodomontade he had uttered, told him with an arch sneer, that he was deceived with the sound of the outward door creaking upon its hinges, which he mistook for Mrs. Trunnion's voice, and desired him to proceed with his admonitions to Mr. Pickle. It is not to be denied that this arrogance was a little unseasonable in the commodore, who was in all respects as effectually subdued to the dominion of his wife, as the person whose submission he then ventured to condemn, with this difference of disposition—Trunnion's subjection was like that of a bear, chequered with fits of surliness and rage; whereas Pickle bore the yoke like an ox, without repining. No wonder then that this indolence, this sluggishness, this stagnation of temper, rendered Gamaliel incapable of withstanding the arguments and importunity of his friends, to which he at length surrendered. He acquiesced in the justice of their observations, and, taking his son by the hand, promised to favour him for the future with his love and fatherly protection.

But this laudable resolution did not last. Mrs. Pickle, still dubious of his constancy, and jealous of his communication with the commodore, never failed to interrogate him every night about the conversation that happened at the club, and regulate her exhortations according to the intelligence she received. He was no sooner, therefore, safely conveyed to bed (that academy in which all notable wives communicate their lectures) than her catechism began; and she in a moment perceived something reluctant and equivocal in her husband's answers. Aroused at this discovery, she employed her influence and skill with such success, that he disclosed every circumstance of what had happened; and, after having sustained a most severe rebuke for his simplicity and indiscretion, humbled himself so far as to promise that he would next day annul the condescensions he had made, and for ever renounce the ungracious object of her disgust. This undertaking was punctually performed in a letter to the commodore, which she herself dictated in these words:

SIR,—Whereas my good-nature being last night imposed upon, I was persuaded to countenance and promise, I know not what, to that vicious youth, whose parent I have the misfortune to be; I desire you will take notice that I revoke all such countenance and promises, and shall never look upon that man as my friend, who will henceforth in such a cause solicit,

Sir, yours, etc.
GAM. PICKLE.

CHAPTER XXI

Trunnion is enraged at the Conduct of Pickle—Peregrine resents the Injustice of his Mother, to whom he explains his Sentiments in a Letter—Is entered at the University of Oxford, where he signalises himself as a Youth of an enterprising Genius.

UNSPEAKABLE were the transports of rage to which Trunnion was incensed by this absurd renunciation. He tore the letter with his gums—teeth he had none—spit with furious grimaces, in token of the contempt he entertained for the author, whom he not only d—ed as a lousy, scabby, nasty, scurvy, skulking, lubberly noodle, but resolved to challenge to single combat with fire and sword; but he was dissuaded from this violent measure, and appeased by the intervention and advice of the lieutenant and Mr. Jolter, who represented the message as the effect of the poor man's infirmity, for which he was rather an object of pity than of resentment; and turned the stream of his indignation against the wife, whom he reviled accordingly. Nor did Peregrine himself bear with patience this injurious declaration, the nature of which he no sooner understood from Hatchway, than equally shocked and exasperated, he retired to his apartment, and, in the first emotions of his ire, produced the following epistle, which was immediately conveyed to his mother:

MADAM,—Had nature formed me a bugbear to the sight, and inspired me with a soul as vicious as my body was detestable, perhaps I might have enjoyed particular marks of your affection and applause; seeing you have persecuted me with such unnatural aversion, for no other visible reason than that of my differing so widely in shape, as well as disposition, from that deformed urchin who is the object of your tenderness and care. If those be the terms on which alone I can obtain your favour, I pray God you may never cease to hate, Madam,

Your much injured son,
PEREGRINE PICKLE.

This letter, which nothing but his passion and inexperience could excuse, had such an effect upon his mother, as may be easily conceived. She was enraged to a degree of frenzy against the writer; though at the same time she considered the whole as the production of Mrs. Trunnion's particular pique, and represented it to her husband as an insult that he was bound in honour to resent, by breaking off all correspondence with the commodore and his family. This was a bitter pill to Gamaliel, who, through a long course of years, was so habituated to

Trunnion's company, that he could as easily have parted with a limb, as have relinquished the club all at once. He therefore ventured to represent his own incapacity to follow her advice, and begged that he might at least be allowed to drop the connexion gradually; protesting that he would do his endeavour to give her all manner of satisfaction.

Meanwhile preparations were made for Peregrine's departure to the university, and in a few weeks he set out, in the seventeenth year of his age, accompanied by the same attendants who lived with him at Winchester. His uncle laid strong injunctions upon him to avoid the company of immodest women, to mind his learning, to let him hear of his welfare as often as he could spare time to write, and settled his appointments at the rate of five hundred a-year, including his governor's salary, which was one-fifth part of the sum. The heart of our young gentleman dilated at the prospect of the figure he should make with such an handsome annuity, the management of which was left to his own discretion; and he amused his imagination with the most agreeable reveries during his journey to Oxford, which he performed in two days. Here being introduced to the head of the college, to whom he had been recommended, accommodated with genteel apartments, entered as gentleman commoner in the books, and provided with a judicious tutor, instead of returning to the study of Greek and Latin, in which he thought himself already sufficiently instructed, he renewed his acquaintance with some of his old schoolfellows, whom he found in the same situation, and was by them initiated in all the fashionable diversions of the place.

It was not long before he made himself remarkable for his spirit and humour, which were so acceptable to the bucks of the university, that he was admitted as a member of their corporation, and, in a very little time, became the most conspicuous personage of the whole fraternity; not that he valued himself upon his ability in smoking the greatest number of pipes, and drinking the largest quantity of ale; these were qualifications of too gross a nature to captivate his refined ambition. He piqued himself on his talent for raillery, his genius and taste, his personal accomplishments, and his success at intrigue. Nor were his excursions confined to the small villages in the neighbourhood, which are commonly visited once a week by the students for the sake of carnal recreation. He kept his own horses, traversed the whole county in parties of pleasure, attended all the races within fifty miles of Oxford, and made frequent jaunts to London, where he used to lie incognito during the best part of many a term.

The rules of the university were too severe to be observed by a youth of his vivacity; and therefore he became acquainted with the proctor by times. But all the checks he received were insufficient to moderate his career; he frequented taverns and coffee-houses, committed midnight frolics in the streets, insulted all the sober and pacific class of his fellow-students; the tutors themselves were not sacred from his ridicule; he laughed at the magistrate, and neglected every particular of college discipline.

In vain did they attempt to restrain his irregularities by the imposition of fines; he was liberal to profusion, and therefore paid without reluctance. Thrice did he scale the windows of a tradesman, with whose daughter he had an affair of gallantry; as often was he obliged to seek his safety by a precipitate leap; and one night would, in all probability, have fallen a sacrifice to an ambuscade that was laid by the father, had not his trusty squire Pipes interposed in his behalf, and manfully rescued him from the clubs of his enemies.

In the midst of these excesses, Mr. Jolter, finding his admonitions neglected, and his influence utterly destroyed, attempted to wean his pupil from his extravagant courses, by engaging his attention in some more laudable pursuit. With this view he introduced him into a club of politicians, who received him with great demonstrations of regard, accommodated themselves more than he could have expected to his jovial disposition, and, while they revolved schemes for the reformation of the state, drank with such devotion to the accomplishment of their plans, that, before parting, the cares of their patriotism were quite overwhelmed.

Peregrine, though he could not approve of their doctrine, resolved to attach himself for some time to their company; because he perceived ample subject for his ridicule, in the characters of these wrong-headed enthusiasts. It was a constant practice with them, in their midnight consistories, to swallow such plentiful draughts of inspiration, that their mysteries commonly ended like those of the Bacchanalian Orgia; and they were seldom capable of maintaining that solemnity of decorum which, by the nature of their functions, most of them were obliged to profess. Now, as Peregrine's satirical disposition was never more gratified than when he had an opportunity of exposing grave characters in ridiculous attitudes, he laid a mischievous snare for his new confederates, which took effect in this manner. In one of their nocturnal deliberations, he promoted such a spirit of good-fellowship, by the agreeable sallies of his wit, which were purposely levelled against their political adversaries, that by ten o'clock they were all ready to join in the most extravagant proposal that could be made. They broke their glasses in consequence of his suggestion, drank healths out of their shoes, caps, and the bottoms of the candlesticks that stood before them, sometimes standing with one foot on a chair, and the knee bent on the edge of the table; and, when they could no longer stand in that posture, setting their bare posteriors on the cold floor. They huzzaed, hallooed, danced, and sung, and, in short, were elevated to such a pitch of intoxication, that when Peregrine proposed that they should burn their periwigs, the hint was immediately approved, and they executed the frolic as one man. Their shoes and caps underwent the same fate by the same instigation; and in this trim he led them forth into the street, where they resolved to compel everybody they should find to subscribe to their political creed, and pronounce the Shibboleth of their party. In the achievement of this enterprise, they met with more opposition than they expected; they were encountered with arguments which they could not well withstand; the noses of some, and eyes of others, in a very little time, bore the marks of obstinate disputation. Their conductor having at length engaged the whole body in a fray with another squadron, which was pretty much in the same condition, he very fairly gave them the slip, and slily retreated to his apartment, foreseeing that his companions would soon be favoured with the notice of their superiors; nor was he deceived in his prognostic; the proctor, going his round, chanced to fall in with this tumultuous uproar, and, interposing his authority, found means to quiet the disturbance. He took cognisance of their names, and dismissed the rioters to their respective chambers, not a little scandalised at the behaviour of some among them, whose business and duty it was to set far other examples to the youth under their care and direction.

About midnight, Pipes, who had orders to attend at a distance, and keep an eye upon Jolter, brought home that unfortunate governor upon his back, Peregrine having beforehand secured his admittance in the college; and among other bruises he was found to have received a couple of contusions on his face, which next morning appeared in a black circle that surrounded each eye.

This was a mortifying circumstance to a man of his character and deportment, especially as he had received a message from the proctor, who desired to see him forthwith. With great humility and contrition he begged the advice of his pupil, who, being used to amuse himself with painting, assured Mr. Jolter, that he would cover those signs of disgrace, with a slight coat of flesh-colour so dexterously, that it would be almost impossible to distinguish the artificial from the natural skin. The rueful governor, rather than expose such opprobrious tokens to the observation and censure of the magistrates, submitted to the expedient. Although his counsellor had overrated his own skill, he was persuaded to confide in the disguise, and actually attended the proctor, with such a staring addition to the natural ghastliness of his features, that his visage bore a very apt resemblance to some of those ferocious countenances that hang over the doors of certain taverns and alehouses, under the denomination of the Saracen's Head.

Such a remarkable alteration of physiognomy could not escape the notice of the most undiscerning beholder, much less the penetrating eye of his severe judge, already whetted with what he had seen overnight. He was therefore upbraided with this ridiculous and shallow artifice, and, together with the companions of his debauch, underwent such a cutting reprimand for the scandalous irregularity of his conduct, that all of them remained crestfallen, and were ashamed, for many weeks, to appear in the public execution of their duty.

Peregrine was too vain of his finesse to conceal the part he acted in this comedy, with the particulars of which he regaled his companions, and thereby entailed upon himself the hate and resentment of the community, whose maxims and practices he had disclosed; for he was considered as a spy, who had intruded himself into their society with a view of betraying it; or, at best, as an apostate and renegado from the faith and principles which he had professed

CHAPTER XXII

He is insulted by his Tutor, whom he lampoons—Makes a considerable Progress in polite Literature; and, in an Excursion to Windsor, meets with Emilia by Accident, and is very coldly received.

AMONG those who suffered by his craft and infidelity was Mr. Jumble, his own tutor, who could not at all digest the mortifying affront he had received, and was resolved to be revenged on the insulting author. With this view he watched the conduct of Mr. Pickle with the utmost rancour of vigilance, and let slip no opportunity of treating him with disrespect, which he knew the disposition of his pupil could less brook than any other severity it was in his power to exercise.

Peregrine had been several mornings absent from chapel; and as Mr. Jumble never failed to question him in a very peremptory style about his non-attendance, he invented some very plausible excuses; but at length his ingenuity was exhausted; he received a very galling rebuke for his profligacy of morals, and, that he might feel it the more sensibly, was ordered, by way of exercise, to compose a paraphrase, in English verse, upon these two lines in Virgil:—

> Vane Ligur, frustraque animis elate superbis,
> Nequicquam patrias tentâsti lubricus artes.

The imposition of this invidious theme had all the desired effect upon Peregrine, who not only considered it as a piece of unmannerly abuse levelled against his own conduct, but also as a retrospective insult on the memory of his grandfather, who, as he had been informed, was in his lifetime more noted for his cunning than candour in trade.

Exasperated at this instance of the pedant's audacity, he had well-nigh, in his first transports, taken corporal satisfaction on the spot; but foreseeing the troublesome consequence that would attend such a flagrant outrage against the laws of the university, he checked his indignation, and resolved to revenge the injury in a more cool and contemptuous manner. Thus determined, he set on foot an inquiry into the particulars of Jumble's parentage and education. He learned that the father of this insolent tutor was a bricklayer, that his mother sold pies, and that the son, at different periods of his youth, had amused himself in both occupations before he converted his views to the study of learning. Fraught with this intelligence, he composed the following ballad in doggerel rhymes, and next

day presented it as a gloss upon the text which the tutor
had chosen:

> Come listen, ye students of ev'ry degree,
> I sing of a wit and a tutor *perdie*;
> A statesman profound, a critic immense,
> In short, a mere jumble of learning and sense;
> And yet of his talents, though laudably vain,
> His own family arts he could never attain.
>
> His father intending his fortune to build,
> In his youth would have taught him the trowel to wield,
> But the mortar of discipline never would stick,
> For his skull was secur'd by a facing of brick;
> And with all his endeavours of patience and pain,
> The skill of his sire he could never attain.
>
> His mother, an housewife, neat, artful, and wise,
> Renown'd for her delicate biscuit and pies,
> Soon alter'd his studies, by flatt'ring his taste,
> From the raising of walls to the rearing of paste!
> But all her instructions were fruitless and vain;
> The pie-making myst'ry he ne'er could attain.
>
> Yet true to his race, in his labours were seen
> A jumble of both their professions, I ween;
> For, when his own genius he ventur'd to trust,
> His pies seem'd of brick, and his houses of crust.
> Then, good Mr. Tutor, pray be not so vain,
> Since your family arts you could never attain.

This impudent production was the most effectual vengeance
he could have taken on his tutor, who had all the supercilious
arrogance and ridiculous pride of a low-born pedant. Instead
of overlooking this petulant piece of satire with that temper
and decency of disdain that became a person of his gravity and
station, he no sooner cast his eye over the performance, than the
blood rushed into his countenance, which immediately after
exhibited a ghastly pale colour. With a quivering lip he told
his pupil that he was an impertinent jackanapes, and he would
take care that he should be expelled from the university, for
having presumed to write and deliver such a licentious and
scurrilous libel. Peregrine answered with great resolution, that,
when the provocation he had received should be known, he was
persuaded that he should be acquitted in the opinion of all
impartial people; and that he was ready to submit the whole to
the decision of the master.

This arbitration he proposed, because he knew the master
and Jumble were at variance; and for that reason the tutor
durst not venture to put the cause on such an issue. Nay,
when this reference was mentioned, Jumble, who was naturally

jealous, suspected that Peregrine had a promise of protection before he undertook to commit such an outrageous insult; and this notion had such an effect upon him, that he resolved to devour his vexation, and wait for a more proper opportunity of gratifying his hate. Meanwhile copies of the ballad were distributed among the students, who sung it under the very nose of Mr. Jumble, to the tune of *A cobbler there was, etc.*, and the triumph of our hero was complete. Neither was his whole time devoted to the riotous extravagances of youth. He enjoyed many lucid intervals; during which he contracted a more intimate acquaintance with the classics, applied himself to the reading of history, improved his taste for painting and music, in which he made some progress; and above all things, cultivated the study of natural philosophy. It was generally after a course of close attention to some of these arts and sciences, that his disposition broke out into those irregularities and wild sallies of a luxuriant imagination, for which he became so remarkable; and he was perhaps the only young man in Oxford, who, at the same time, maintained an intimate and friendly intercourse with the most unthinking, as well as with the most sedate students at the university.

It is not to be supposed that a young man of Peregrine's vanity, inexperience, and profusion, could suit his expense to his allowance, liberal as it was; for he was not one of those fortunate people who are born economists, and knew not the art of withholding his purse when he saw his companion in difficulty. Thus, naturally generous and expensive, he squandered away his money, and made a most splendid appearance upon the receipt of his quarterly appointment; but long before the third month was elapsed, his finances were consumed; and, as he could not stoop to ask an extraordinary supply, was too proud to borrow, and too haughty to run in debt with tradesmen, he devoted those periods of poverty to the prosecution of his studies, and shone forth again at the revolution of quarter-day.

In one of these irruptions, he and some of his companions went to Windsor, in order to see the royal apartments in the castle, whither they repaired in the afternoon; and, as Peregrine stood contemplating the picture of Hercules and Omphale, one of his fellow-students whispered in his ear, "Zounds! Pickle, there are two fine girls." He turned instantly about, and, in one of them, recognised his almost forgotten Emilia. Her appearance acted upon his imagination like a spark of fire that falls among gunpowder; that passion which had lain dormant for the space of two years flashed up in a moment, and he was seized with an universal trepidation. She perceived and partook of his emotion; for their souls, like unisons, vibrated with the same impulse. However, she called her pride and resentment to her aid, and found resolution enough to retire from such a dangerous scene. Alarmed at her retreat, he recollected all his assurance, and, impelled by love, which he could no longer resist, followed her into the next room, where, in the most disconcerted manner, he accosted her with "Your humble servant, Miss Gauntlet"; to which salutation she replied, with an affectation of indifference, that did not, however, conceal her agitation, "Your servant, sir"; and immediately extending her finger towards the picture of Duns Scotus, which is fixed over one of the doors, asked her companion in a giggling tone, if she did not think he looked like a conjuror. Peregrine, nettled into spirits by this reception, answered for the other lady, "that it was an easy matter to be a conjuror in those times, when the simplicity of the age assisted his divination; but were he, or Merlin himself, to rise from the dead now, when such deceit and dissimulation prevail, they would not be able to earn their bread by the profession." "O! sir," said she, turning full upon him, "without doubt they would adopt new maxims; 'tis no disparagement in this enlightened age for one to alter one's opinion." "No, sure, madam," replied the youth, with some precipitation, "provided the change be for the better." "And, should it happen otherwise," retorted the nymph with a flirt of her fan, "inconstancy will never want countenance from the practice of mankind." "True, madam," resumed our hero, fixing his eyes upon her, "examples of levity are everywhere to be met with." "O Lord, sir," cried Emilia, tossing her head, "you'll scarce ever find a fop without it." By this time his companion, seeing him engaged with one of the ladies, entered into conversation with the other; and, in order to favour his friend's gallantry, conducted her into the next apartment, on pretence of entertaining her with the sight of a remarkable piece of painting.

Peregrine, laying hold on this opportunity of being alone with the object of his love, assumed a most seducing tenderness of look, and, heaving a profound sigh, asked if she had utterly discarded him from her remembrance. Reddening at this pathetic question, which recalled the memory of the imagined slight he had put upon her, she answered in great confusion,

"Sir, I believe I once had the pleasure of seeing you in a ball in Winchester." "Miss Emilia," said he, very gravely, "will you be so candid as to tell me what misbehaviour of mine you are pleased to punish, by restricting your remembrance to that single occasion?" "Mr. Pickle," she replied in the same tone, "it is neither my province nor inclination to judge your conduct; and therefore you misapply your question, when you ask such an explanation of me." "At least," resumed our lover, "give me the melancholy satisfaction to know for what offence of mine you refused to take the least notice of that letter which I had the honour to write from Winchester, by your own express permission." "Your letter," said Miss, with great vivacity, "neither required, nor, in my opinion, deserved an answer; and, to be free with you, Mr. Pickle, it was but a shallow artifice to rid yourself of a correspondence you had deigned to solicit."

Peregrine, confounded at this repartee, replied, that howsoever he might have failed in point of elegance or discretion, he was sure he had not been deficient in expressions of respect and devotion for those charms which it was his pride to adore. "As for the verses," said he, "I own they were unworthy of the theme, but I flattered myself that they would have merited your acceptance, though not your approbation, and been considered not so much the proof of my genius, as the genuine effusion of my love." "Verses!" cried Emilia, with an air of astonishment, "what verses? I really don't understand you." The young gentleman was thunderstruck at this exclamation, to which, after a long pause, he answered, "I begin to suspect, and heartily wish it may appear, that we have misunderstood each other from the beginning. Pray, Miss Gauntlet, did you not find a copy of verses enclosed in that unfortunate letter?" "Truly, sir," said the lady, "I am not so much of a connoisseur as to distinguish whether that facetious production, which you merrily style an unfortunate letter, was composed in verse or prose; but, methinks, the jest is a little too stale to be brought upon the carpet again." So saying, she tripped away to her companion, and left her lover in a most tumultuous suspense. He now perceived that her neglect of his addresses, when he was at Winchester, must have been owing to some mystery which he could not comprehend. And she began to suspect, and to hope, that the letter which she received was spurious, though she could not conceive how that could possibly happen, as it had been delivered to her by the hands of his own servant.

However, she resolved to leave the task of unravelling the

affair to him, who, she knew, would infallibly exert himself for his own as well as her satisfaction. She was not deceived in her opinion. He went up to her again at the staircase, and, as they were unprovided with a male attendant, insisted upon squiring the ladies to their lodgings. Emilia saw his drift, which was no other than to know where she lived; and, though she approved of his contrivance, thought it was incumbent upon her, for the support of her own dignity, to decline the civility. She therefore thanked him for his polite offer, but would by no means consent to his giving himself such unnecessary trouble, especially as they had a very little way to walk. He was not repulsed by this refusal, the nature of which he perfectly understood; nor was she sorry to see him persevere in his determination. He therefore accompanied them in their return, and made divers efforts to speak with Emilia in particular. But she had a spice of the coquette in her disposition, and, being determined to whet his impatience, artfully baffled all his endeavours, by keeping her companion continually engaged in the conversation, which turned upon the venerable appearance and imperial situation of the place. Thus tantalised, he lounged with them to the door of the house in which they lodged, when his mistress, perceiving, by the countenance of her comrade, that she was on the point of desiring him to walk in, checked her intention with a frown; then turning to Mr. Pickle, dropped him a very formal curtsey, seized the other young lady by the arm, and saying, "Come, cousin Sophy," vanished in a moment.

CHAPTER XXIII

After sundry unsuccessful Efforts, he finds means to come to an Explanation with his Mistress; and a Reconciliation ensues.

PEREGRINE, disconcerted at their sudden disappearance, stood for some minutes gaping in the street, before he could get the better of his surprise; and then deliberated with himself whether he should demand immediate admittance to his mistress, or choose some other method of application. Piqued at her abrupt behaviour, though pleased with her spirit, he set his invention to work, in order to contrive some means of seeing her; and, in a fit of musing, arrived at the inn, where he found his companions, whom he had left at the Castle gate. They had already made inquiry about the ladies, in consequence of which he learnt, that Miss Sophy was daughter of a gentleman in town, to whom his mistress was related; that an intimate friendship subsisted between the two young ladies; that Emilia had lived about a month with her cousin, and appeared at the last assembly, where she was universally admired; and that several young gentlemen of fortune had since that time teased her with addresses.

Our hero's ambition was flattered, and his passion inflamed with this intelligence; and he swore within himself, that he would not quit the spot until he should have obtained an indisputed victory over all his rivals.

That same evening he composed a most eloquent epistle, in which he earnestly entreated that she would favour him with an opportunity of vindicating his conduct; but she would neither receive his billet, nor see his messenger. Balked in this effort, he enclosed it in a new cover, directed by another hand, and ordered Pipes to ride next morning to London, on purpose to deliver it at the post-office, that, coming by such conveyance, she might have no suspicion of the author, and open it before she should be aware of the deceit.

Three days he waited patiently for the effect of this stratagem, and, in the afternoon of the fourth, ventured to hazard a formal visit, in quality of an old acquaintance. But here, too, he failed in his attempt; she was indisposed, and could not see company. These obstacles served only to increase his eagerness. He still adhered to his former resolution; and his companions, understanding his determination, left him next day to his own inventions. Thus relinquished to his own ideas, he doubled his assiduity, and practised every method his imagination could suggest, in order to promote his plan.

Pipes was stationed all day long within sight of her door, that he might be able to give his master an account of her motions; but she never went abroad, except to visit in the neighbourhood, and was always housed before Peregrine could be apprised of her appearance. He went to church with a view of attracting her notice, and humbled his deportment before her; but she was so mischievously devout as to look at nothing but her book, so that he was not favoured with one glance of regard. He frequented the coffee-house, and attempted to contract an acquaintance with Miss Sophy's father, who, he hoped, would invite him to his house; but this expectation was also defeated. That prudent gentleman looked upon him as one of those forward fortune-hunters who go about the country seeking whom they may devour, and warily discouraged all his advances. Chagrined by so many unsuccessful endeavours, he began to despair of accomplishing his aim; and, as the last suggestion of his art, paid off his lodging, took horse at noon, and departed, in all appearance, for the place from whence he had come. He rode, however, but a few miles, and, in the dusk of the evening, returned unseen, alighted at another inn, ordered Pipes to stay within doors, and, keeping himself incognito, employed another person as a sentinel upon Emilia.

It was not long before he reaped the fruits of his ingenuity. Next day, in the afternoon, he was informed by his spy, that the two young ladies were gone to walk in the park, whither he followed them on the instant, fully determined to come to an explanation with his mistress, even in presence of her friend, who might possibly be prevailed upon to interest herself in his behalf.

When he saw them at such a distance that they could not return to town before he should have an opportunity of putting his resolution in practice, he mended his pace, and found means to appear before them so suddenly, that Emilia could not help expressing her surprise in a scream. Our lover putting on a mien of humility and mortification, begged to know if her resentment was implacable; and asked, why she had so cruelly refused to grant him the common privilege that every criminal enjoyed? "Dear Miss Sophy," said he, addressing himself to her companion, "give me leave to implore your intercession with your cousin; I am sure you have humanity enough to espouse my cause, did you but know the justice of it; and I flatter myself, that, by your kind interposition, I may be able to rectify that fatal misunderstanding which hath made me wretched." "Sir," said Sophy, "you appear like a gentleman, and I doubt not but your behaviour has been always suitable to your appearance; but you must excuse me from undertaking any such office in behalf of a person whom I have not the honour to know." "Madam," answered Peregrine, "I hope Miss Emy will justify my pretensions to that character, notwithstanding the mystery of her displeasure, which, upon my honour, I cannot for my soul explain." "Lord! Mr. Pickle," said Emilia, who had by this time recollected herself, "I never questioned your gallantry and taste, but I am resolved that you never shall have cause to exercise your talents at my expense; so that you tease yourself and me to no purpose. Come, Sophy, let us walk home again." "Good God! madam," cried the lover with great emotion, "why will you distract me with such indifference? Stay, dear Emilia! I conjure you on my knees to stay and hear me. By all that is sacred! I was not to blame; you must have been imposed upon by some villain who envied my good fortune, and took some treacherous method to ruin my love."

Miss Sophy, who possessed a large stock of good-nature, and to whom her cousin had communicated the cause of her reserve, seeing the young gentleman so much affected with that disdain, which she knew to be feigned, laid hold on Emilia's sleeve, saying with a smile, "Not quite so fast, Emily, I begin to perceive that this is a love-quarrel, and therefore there may be hopes of a reconciliation; for I suppose both parties are open to conviction." "For my own part," cried Peregrine, with great eagerness, "I appeal to Miss Sophy's decision. But why do I say appeal? Though I am conscious of having committed no offence, I am ready to submit to any penance, let it be ever so rigorous, that my fair enslaver herself shall impose, providing it will entitle me to her favour and forgiveness at last." Emily, well-nigh overcome by this declaration, told him, that, as she taxed him with no guilt, she expected no atonement; and pressed her companion to return into town. But Sophy, who was too indulgent to her friend's real inclination to comply with her request, observed, that the gentleman seemed so reasonable in his concessions, she began to think her cousin was in the wrong, and felt herself disposed to act as umpire in the dispute.

Overjoyed at this condescension, Mr. Pickle thanked her in the most rapturous terms, and, in the transport of his expectation, kissed the hand of his kind mediatrix; a circumstance which had a remarkable effect on the countenance of Emilia, who did not seem to relish the warmth of his acknowledgment.

After many supplications on one hand, and pressing remonstrances on the other, she yielded at length, and, turning to her lover, while her face was overspread with blushes, "Well, sir," said she, "supposing I were to put the difference on that issue, how could you excuse the ridiculous letter which you sent to me from Winchester?" This expostulation introduced a discussion of the whole affair, in which all the circumstances were canvassed; and Emilia still affirmed, with great heat, that the letter must have been calculated to affront her; for she could not suppose the author was so weak as to design it for any other purpose.

Peregrine, who still retained in his memory the substance of his unlucky epistle, as well as the verses which were enclosed, could recollect no particular expression which could have justly given the least umbrage; and therefore, in the agonies of perplexity, begged that the whole might be submitted to the judgment of Miss Sophy, and faithfully promised to stand to her award.

In short, this proposal was, with seeming reluctance, embraced by Emilia, and an appointment made to meet next day, in the same place, whither both parties were desired to come, provided with their credentials, according to which definitive sentence would be pronounced.

Our lover having succeeded thus far, overwhelmed Sophy with acknowledgments on account of her generous mediation, and, in the course of their walk, which Emilia was now in no hurry to conclude, whispered a great many tender protestations in the ear of his mistress, who nevertheless continued to act upon the reserve until her doubts should be more fully resolved.

Mr. Pickle having found means to amuse them in the fields till the twilight, was obliged to wish them good-evening, after having obtained a solemn repetition of their promise to meet him at the appointed time and place; and then retreated to his apartment, where he spent the whole night in various conjectures on the subject of this letter, the Gordian knot of which he could by no means untie. One while he imagined that some wag had played a trick upon his messenger, in consequence of which Emilia had received a supposititious letter; but, upon further reflection, he could not conceive the practicability of any such deceit. Then he began to doubt the sincerity of his mistress, who perhaps had only made that an handle for discarding him, at the request of some favourite rival; but his own integrity forbade him to harbour this mean suspicion; and therefore he was again involved in the labyrinth of perplexity.

Next day he waited on the rack of impatience for the hour of five in the afternoon, which no sooner struck, than he ordered Pipes to attend him, in case there should be occasion for his evidence, and repaired to the place of rendezvous, where he had not tarried five minutes before the ladies appeared. Mutual compliments being passed, and the attendant stationed at a convenient distance, Peregrine persuaded them to sit down upon the grass, under the shade of a spreading oak, that they might be more at their ease; while he stretched himself at their feet, and desired that the paper on which his doom depended might be examined. It was accordingly put into the hands of his fair arbitress, who read it immediately with an audible voice. The first two words of it were no sooner pronounced, than he started with great emotion, and raised himself on his hand and knee, in which posture he listened to the rest of the sentence; then sprung upon his feet in the utmost astonishment, and, glowing with resentment at the same time, exclaimed, "Hell and the devil! what's all that? Sure you make a jest of me, madam." "Pray, sir," said Sophy, "give me the hearing for a few moments, and then urge what you shall think proper in your own defence." Having thus cautioned him, she proceeded: but, before she had finished one-half of the performance, her gravity forsook her, and she was seized with a violent fit of laughter, in which neither of the lovers could help joining, notwithstanding the resentment which at that instant prevailed in the breasts of both. The judge, however, in a little time resumed her solemnity, and having read the remaining part of this curious epistle, all three continued staring at each other alternately for the space of half a minute, and then broke forth at the same instant into another paroxysm of mirth.

From this unanimous convulsion, one would have thought that both parties were extremely well pleased with the joke; yet this was by no means the case. Emilia imagined, that, notwithstanding his affected surprise, her lover, in spite of himself, had renewed the laugh at her expense, and, in so doing, applauded his own unmannerly ridicule. This supposition could not fail of raising and reviving her indignation, while Peregrine highly resented the indignity with which he supposed himself treated, in her attempting to make him the dupe of such a gross and ludicrous artifice. This being the situation of their thoughts, their mirth was succeeded by a mutual gloominess of aspect; and the judge, addressing herself to Mr. Pickle, asked if he had anything to offer why sentence should not be pronounced? "Madam," answered the culprit, "I am sorry to find myself so low in the opinion of your cousin, as to be thought capable of being deceived by such a shallow contrivance." "Nay, sir," said Emilia, "the contrivance is your own; and I cannot help admiring your confidence in imputing it to me." "Upon my honour, Miss Emily," resumed our hero, "you wrong my understanding as well as my love, in accusing me of having written such a silly, impertinent performance; the very appearance and address of it is so unlike the letter which I did myself the honour to write, that I dare say my man, even at this distance of time, will remember the difference."

So saying, he extended his voice, and beckoned to Pipes, who immediately drew near. His mistress seemed to object to the evidence, by observing that, to be sure, Mr. Pipes had his cue; when Peregrine, begging she would spare him the mortification of considering him in such a dishonourable light, desired his valet to examine the outside of the letter, and recollect if it was the same which he had delivered to Miss Gauntlet about two years ago. Pipes having taken a superficial view of it, pulled up his breeches, saying, "Mayhap it is, but we have made so many trips, and been in so many creeks and corners since that time, that I can't pretend to be certain; for I neither keep journal nor log-book of our proceedings." Emilia commended him for his candour, at the same time darting a sarcastic look at his master, as if she thought he had tampered with his servant's integrity in vain; and Peregrine began to rave and to curse his fate for having subjected him to such mean suspicion, attesting heaven and earth in the most earnest manner, that, far from having composed and conveyed that stupid production, he had never seen it before, nor been privy to the least circumstance of the plan.

Pipes, now for the first time, perceived the mischief which he had occasioned, and, moved with the transports of his master, for whom he had a most inviolable attachment, frankly declared he was ready to make oath that Mr. Pickle had no hand in the letter which he delivered. All three were amazed at this confession, the meaning of which they could not comprehend. Peregrine, after some pause, leaped upon Pipes, and seizing him by the throat, exclaimed in an ecstasy of rage, "Rascal! tell me this instant what became of the letter I entrusted to your care." The patient valet, half-strangled as he was, squirted a collection of tobacco-juice out of one corner of his mouth, and with great deliberation replied, "Why,—burnt it; you wouldn't have me give the young woman a thing that shook all in the wind in tatters, would you?" The ladies interposed in behalf of the distressed squire, from whom, by dint of questions, which he had neither art nor inclination to evade, they extorted an explanation of the whole affair.

Such ridiculous simplicity and innocence of intention appeared in the composition of his expedient, that even the remembrance of all the chagrin which it had produced could not rouse their indignation, or enable them to resist a third eruption of laughter, which they forthwith underwent.

Pipes was dismissed with many menacing injunctions to

beware of such conduct for the future; Emilia stood with a confusion of joy and tenderness in her countenance; Peregrine's eyes kindled into rapture, and when Miss Sophy pronounced the sentence of reconciliation, advanced to his mistress, saying, "Truth is mighty, and will prevail"; then clasping her in his arms, very impudently ravished a kiss, which she had not power to refuse. Nay, such was the impulse of his joy, that he took the same freedom with the lips of Sophy, calling her his kind mediatrix and guardian angel, and behaved with such extravagance of transport as plainly evinced the fervour and sincerity of his love.

I shall not pretend to repeat the tender protestations that were uttered on one side, or describe the bewitching glances of approbation with which they were received on the other; suffice it to say, that the endearing intimacy of their former connexion was instantly renewed, and Sophy, who congratulated them upon the happy termination of their quarrel, favoured with their mutual confidence. In consequence of this happy pacification, they deliberated upon the means of seeing each other often; and, as he could not, without some previous introduction, visit her openly at the house of her relation, they agreed to meet every afternoon in the park till the next assembly, at which he would solicit her as a partner, and she be unengaged, in expectation of his request. By this connexion he would be entitled to visit her next day, and thus an avowed correspondence would of course commence. This plan was actually put in execution, and attended with a circumstance which had well-nigh produced some mischievous consequence, had not Peregrine's good fortune been superior to his discretion.

CHAPTER XXIV

He achieves an Adventure at the Assembly, and quarrels with his Governor.

AT the assembly were no fewer than three gentlemen of fortune, who rivalled our lover in his passion for Emilia, and who had severally begged the honour of dancing with her upon that occasion. She had excused herself to each, on pretence of a slight indisposition that she foresaw would detain her from the ball, and desired they would provide themselves with other partners. Obliged to admit her excuse, they accordingly followed her advice; and, after they had engaged themselves beyond the power of retracting, had the mortification to see her there unclaimed.

They in their turn made up to her, and expressed their surprise and concern at finding her in the assembly unprovided, after she had declined their invitation; but she told them that her cold had forsaken her since she had the pleasure of seeing them, and that she would rely upon accident for a partner. Just as she pronounced these words to the last of the three, Peregrine advanced as an utter stranger, bowed with great respect, told her he understood she was unengaged, and would think himself highly honoured in being accepted as her partner for the night; and he had the good fortune to succeed in his application.

As they were by far the handsomest and best accomplished couple in the room, they could not fail of attracting the notice and admiration of the spectators, which inflamed the jealousy of his three competitors, who immediately entered into a conspiracy against this gaudy stranger, whom, as their rival, they resolved to affront in public. Pursuant to the plan which they projected for this purpose, the first country dance was no sooner concluded, than one of them, with his partner, took place of Peregrine and his mistress, contrary to the regulation of the ball. Our lover, imputing his behaviour to inadvertency, informed the gentleman of his mistake, and civilly desired he would rectify his error. The other told him, in an imperious tone, that he wanted none of his advice, and bade him mind his own affairs. Peregrine answered with some warmth, and insisted upon his right; a dispute commenced, high words ensued, in the course of which our impetuous youth, hearing himself reviled with the appellation of scoundrel, pulled off his antagonist's periwig, and flung it in his face. The ladies immediately shrieked, the gentlemen interposed, Emilia was seized with a fit of trembling, and conducted to her seat by her youthful admirer, who begged pardon for having discomposed her, and vindicated what he had done, by representing the necessity he was under to resent the provocation he had received.

Though she could not help owning the justice of his plea, she was not the less concerned at the dangerous situation in which he had involved himself, and, in the utmost consternation and anxiety, insisted upon going directly home. He could not resist her importunities; and her cousin being determined to accompany her, he escorted them to their lodgings, where he wished them good-night, after having, in order to quiet their apprehensions, protested, that, if his opponent was satisfied, he should never take any step towards the prosecution of the quarrel. Meanwhile the assembly-room became a scene of tumult and uproar. The person who conceived himself injured, seeing Peregrine retire, struggled with his companions, in order to pursue and take satisfaction of our hero, whom he loaded with terms of abuse, and challenged to single combat.

The director of the ball held a consultation with all the subscribers who were present; and it was determined, by a majority of votes, that the two gentlemen who had occasioned the disturbance should be desired to withdraw. This resolution being signified to one of the parties then present, he made some difficulty of complying, but was persuaded to submit by his two confederates, who accompanied him to the street-door, where he was met by Peregrine on his return to the assembly.

This choleric gentleman, who was a country squire, no sooner saw his rival, than he began to brandish his cudgel in a menacing posture, when our adventurous youth, stepping back with one foot, laid his hand upon the hilt of his sword, which he drew halfway out of the scabbard. This attitude, and the sight of the blade, which glistened by moonlight in his face, checked, in some sort, the ardour of his assailant, who desired he would lay aside his toaster, and take a bout with him at equal arms. Peregrine, who was an expert cudgel-player, accepted the invitation; then exchanging weapons with Pipes, who stood behind him, put himself in a posture of defence, and received the attack of his adversary, who struck at random, without either skill or economy. Pickle could have beaten the cudgel out of his hand at the first blow; but as, in that case, he would have been obliged in honour to give immediate quarter, he resolved to discipline his antagonist without endeavouring to disable him, until he should be heartily satisfied with the vengeance he had taken. With this view he returned the salute, and raised such a clatter about the squire's pate, that one who had heard, without seeing the application, would have mistaken the sound for that of a salt-box, in the hand of a dexterous merry-andrew, belonging to one of the booths at Bartholomew Fair. Neither was this salutation confined to his head; his shoulders, arms, thighs, ankles, and ribs were visited with amazing rapidity, while Tom Pipes sounded the charge through his fist. Peregrine, tired with this exercise, which had almost bereft his enemy of sensation, at last struck the decisive blow, in consequence of which the squire's weapon flew out of his grasp, and he allowed our hero to be the better man. Satisfied with this acknowledgment, the victor walked upstairs, with such elevation of spirits, and insolence of mien, that nobody chose to intimate the resolution which had been taken in his absence. There having amused himself for some time in beholding the country dances, he retreated to his lodging, where he indulged himself all night in the contemplation of his own success.

Next day, in the forenoon, he went to visit his partner; and the gentleman at whose house she lived, having been informed of his family and condition, received him with great courtesy, as the acquaintance of his cousin Gauntlet, and invited him to dinner that same day.

Emilia was remarkably well pleased, when she understood the issue of his adventure, which began to make some noise in town, even though it deprived her of a wealthy admirer. The squire, having consulted an attorney about the nature of the dispute, in hopes of being able to prosecute Peregrine for an assault, found little encouragement to go to law. He therefore resolved to pocket the insult and injury he had undergone, and to discontinue his addresses to her who was the cause of both.

Our lover being told by his mistress, that she proposed to stay a fortnight longer at Windsor, he determined to enjoy her company all that time, and then to give her a convoy to the house of her mother, whom he longed to see. In consequence of this plan, he every day contrived some fresh party of pleasure for the ladies, to whom he had by this time free access; and entangled himself so much in the snares of love, that he seemed quite enchanted by Emilia's charms, which were now indeed almost irresistible. While he thus heedlessly roved in the flowery paths of pleasure, his governor at Oxford, alarmed at the unusual duration of his absence, went to the young gentlemen who had accompanied him in his excursion, and very earnestly intreated them to tell him what they knew concerning his pupil. They accordingly gave him an account of the rencounter that happened between Peregrine and Miss Emily Gauntlet in the castle, and mentioned circumstances sufficient to convince him that his charge was very dangerously engaged.

Far from having an authority over Peregrine, Mr. Jolter durst not even disoblige him; therefore, instead of writing to the commodore, he took horse immediately, and that same night reached Windsor, where he found his stray sheep very much surprised at his unexpected arrival

The governor desiring to have some serious conversation with him, they shut themselves up in an apartment, when Jolter, with great solemnity, communicated the cause of his journey, which was no other than his concern for his pupil's welfare; and very gravely undertook to prove, by mathematical demonstration, that this intrigue, if farther pursued, would tend to the young gentleman's ruin and disgrace. This singular proposition raised the curiosity of Peregrine, who promised to yield all manner of attention, and desired him to begin without further preamble.

The governor, encouraged by this appearance of candour, expressed his satisfaction in finding him so open to conviction, and told him he would proceed upon geometrical principles. Then, hemming thrice, he observed, that no mathematical inquiries could be carried on, except upon certain *data*, or concession to truths, that were self-evident; and therefore he must crave his assent to a few axioms, which he was sure Mr. Pickle would see no reason to dispute. "In the first place, then," said he, "you will grant, I hope, that youth and discretion are, with respect to each other, as two parallel lines, which, though infinitely produced, remain still equidistant, and will never coincide; and then you must allow, that passion acts upon the human mind in a ratio compounded of the acuteness of sense and constitutional heat; and, thirdly, you will not deny that the angle of remorse is equal to that of precipitation. The *postulata* being admitted," added he, taking pen, ink, and paper, and drawing a parallelogram, "let youth be represented by the right line A B, and discretion by another right line C D, parallel to the former. Complete the parallelogram A B C D, and let the point of intersection, B, represent perdition. Let passion, represented under the letter C, have a motion in the direction C A. At the same time, let another motion be communicated to it, in the direction C D, it will proceed in the diagonal C B, and describe it in the same time that it would have described the side C A by the first motion, or the side C D by the second. To understand the demonstration of this corollary, we must premise this obvious principle, that when a body is acted upon by a motion of power parallel to a right line given in position, this power, or motion, has no effect to cause the body to approach towards that line, or recede from it, but to move in a line parallel to a right line only, as appears from the second law of motion; therefore C A being parallel to D B"—

His pupil having listened to him thus far, could contain

himself no longer, but interrupted the investigation with a loud laugh, and told him, that his *postulata* put him in mind of a certain learned and ingenious gentleman, who undertook to disprove the existence of natural evil, and asked no other *datum* on which to found his demonstration, but an acknowledgment that *everything that is, is right.* "You may, therefore," said he, in a peremptory tone, "spare yourself the trouble of torturing your invention; for after all, I am pretty certain that I shall want capacity to comprehend the discussion of your lemma, and, consequently, be obliged to refuse my assent to your deduction."

Mr. Jolter was disconcerted at this declaration, and so much offended at Peregrine's disrespect, that he could not help expressing his displeasure, by telling him flatly, that he was too violent and headstrong to be reclaimed by reason and gentle means; that he (the tutor) must be obliged, in the discharge of his duty and conscience, to inform the commodore of his pupil's imprudence; that, if the laws of this realm were effectual, they would take cognisance of the gipsy who had led him astray; and observed, by way of contrast, that, if such a preposterous intrigue had happened in France, she would have been clapped up in a convent two years ago.

Our lover's eyes kindled with indignation, when he heard his mistress treated with such irreverence. He could scarce refrain from inflicting manual chastisement on the blasphemer, whom he reproached in his wrath as an arrogant pedant, without either delicacy or sense; and cautioned him against using any such impertinent freedoms with his affairs for the future, on pain of incurring more severe effects of his resentment.

Mr. Jolter, who entertained very high notions of that veneration to which he thought himself entitled by his character and qualifications, had not bor[n]e, without repining, his want of influence and authority over his pupil, against whom he cherished a particular grudge ever since the adventure of the painted eye; and therefore, on this occasion, his politic forbearance had been overcome by the accumulated motives of his disgust. Indeed, he would have resigned his charge with disdain, had he not been encouraged to persevere, by the hopes of a good living which Trunnion had in his gift, or known how to dispose of himself for the present to better advantage.

CHAPTER XXV

He receives a Letter from his Aunt, breaks with the Commodore, and disobliges the Lieutenant, who, nevertheless, undertakes his Cause.

MEANWHILE he quitted the youth in high dudgeon, and that same evening despatched a letter for Mrs. Trunnion, which was dictated by the first transports of his passion, and of course replete with severe animadversions on the misconduct of his pupil.

In consequence of this complaint, it was not long before Peregrine received an epistle from his aunt, wherein she commemorated all the circumstances of the commodore's benevolence towards him, when he was helpless and forlorn, deserted and abandoned by his own parents, upbraided him for his misbehaviour, and neglect of his tutor's advice, and insisted upon his breaking off all intercourse with that girl who had seduced his youth, as he valued the continuance of her affection and her husband's regard.

As our lover's own ideas of generosity were extremely refined, he was shocked at the indelicate insinuations of Mrs. Trunnion, and felt all the pangs of an ingenuous mind that labours under obligations to a person whom it contemns. Far from obeying her injunction, or humbling himself by a submissive answer to her reprehension, his resentment buoyed him up above every selfish consideration; he resolved to attach himself to Emilia, if possible, more than ever; and although he was tempted to punish the officiousness of Jolter, by recriminating upon his life and conversation, he generously withstood the impulse of his passion, because he knew that his governor had no other dependence than the good opinion of the commodore. He could not, however, digest in silence the severe expostulations of his aunt; to which he replied by the following letter, addressed to her husband:

SIR,—Though my temper could never stoop to offer, nor, I believe, your disposition deign to receive, that gross incense which the illiberal only expect, and none but the base-minded condescend to pay, my sentiments have always done justice to your generosity, and my intention scrupulously adhered to the dictates of my duty. Conscious of this integrity of heart, I cannot but severely feel your lady's unkind (I will not call it ungenerous) recapitulation of the favours I have received; and, as I take it for granted, that you knew and approved of her letter, I must beg leave to assure you, that, far from being swayed by menaces and reproach, I am determined to embrace the most abject extremity of fortune, rather than submit to such a dishonourable compulsion. When I am treated in a more delicate and respectful manner, I hope I shall behave as becomes,

Sir, your obliged

P. PICKLE.

The commodore, who did not understand those nice distinctions of behaviour, and dreaded the consequence of Peregrine's amour, against which he was strangely prepossessed, seemed exasperated at the insolence and obstinacy of his adopted son; to whose epistle he wrote the following answer, which was transmitted by the hands of Hatchway, who had orders to bring the delinquent along with him to the garrison:

HEARK YE, CHILD,—You need not bring your fine speeches to bear upon me. You only expend your ammunition to no purpose. Your aunt told you nothing but truth; for it is always fair and honest to be above board, d'ye see. I am informed as how you are in chase of a painted galley, which will decoy you upon the flats of destruction, unless you keep a better look-out and a surer reckoning than you have hitherto done; and I have sent Jack Hatchway to see how the land lies, and warn you of your danger. If so be as you will put about ship, and let him steer you into this harbour, you shall meet with a safe berth and friendly reception; but if you refuse to alter your course, you cannot expect any further assistance from yours, as you behave,

HAWSER TRUNNION.

Peregrine was equally piqued and disconcerted at the receipt of this letter, which was quite different from what he had expected, and declared in a resolute tone to the lieutenant, who brought it, that he might return as soon as he pleased, for he was determined to consult his own inclination, and remain for some time longer where he was.

Hatchway endeavoured to persuade him by all the arguments which his sagacity and friendship could supply, to show a little more deference for the old man, who was by this time rendered fretful and peevish by the gout, which now hindered him from enjoying himself as usual, and who might, in his passion, take some step very much to the detriment of the young gentleman, whom he had hitherto considered as his own son. Among other remonstrances, Jack observed that mayhap Peregrine had got under Emilia's hatches, and did not choose to set her adrift; and, if that was the case, he himself would take charge of the vessel, and see her cargo safely delivered; for he had a respect for the young woman and his needle pointed towards matrimony; and as, in all probability, she could not be much the worse for the wear, he would make shift to scud through life with her under an easy sail.

Our lover was deaf to all his admonitions, and, having thanked him for this last instance of his complaisance, repeated his resolution of adhering to his first purpose. Hatchway, having profited so little by mild exhortations, assumed a more peremptory aspect, and plainly told him he neither could nor would go home without him; so he had best make immediate preparation for the voyage.

Peregrine made no other reply to this declaration than by a contemptuous smile, and rose from his seat in order to retire; upon which the lieutenant started up, and posting himself by the door, protested, with some menacing gestures, that he would not suffer him to run ahead neither. The other, incensed at his presumption in attempting to detain him by force, tripped up his wooden leg, and laid him on his back in a moment; then walked deliberately towards the park, in order to indulge his reflection, which at that time teemed with disagreeable thoughts. He had not proceeded two hundred steps, when he heard something blowing and stamping behind him; and, looking back, perceived the lieutenant at his heels, with rage and indignation in his countenance. This exasperated seaman, impatient of the affront he had received, and forgetting all the circumstances of their former intimacy, advanced with great eagerness to his old friend, saying, "Look ye, brother, you're a saucy boy, and if you was at sea, I would have your backside brought to the davit for your disobedience; but as we are on shore, you and I must crack a pistol at one another; here is a brace, you shall take which you please."

Peregrine, upon recollection, was sorry for having been laid under the necessity of disobliging honest Jack, and very frankly asked his pardon for what he had done. But this condescension was misinterpreted by the other, who refused any other satisfaction but that which an officer ought to claim; and, with some irreverent expressions, asked if Perry was afraid of his bacon. The youth, inflamed at this unjust insinuation, darted a ferocious look at the challenger, told him he had paid but too much regard to his infirmities, and bade him walk forward to the park, where he would soon convince him of his error, if he thought his concession proceeded from fear.

About this time, they were overtaken by Pipes, who, having heard the lieutenant's fall, and seen him pocket his pistols, suspected that there was a quarrel in the case, and followed him with a view of protecting his master. Peregrine, seeing him arrive, and guessing his intention, assumed an air of serenity, and pretending that he had left his handkerchief at the inn, ordered his man to go thither and fetch it to him in the park, where he would find them at his return. This command was twice repeated before Tom would take any other notice of the message, except by shaking his head; but being urged with many threats and curses to obedience, he gave them to understand that he knew their drift too well to trust them by themselves. "As for you, Lieutenant Hatchway," said he, "I have been your shipmate, and know you to be a sailor, that's enough; and as for master, I know him to be as good a man as ever stepped betwixt stem and stern, whereby, if you have anything to say to him, I am your man, as the saying is. Here's my sapling, and I don't value your crackers of a rope's end." This oration, the longest that ever Pipes was known to make, he concluded with a flourish of his cudgel, and enforced with such determined refusals to leave them, that they found it impossible to bring the cause to mortal arbitrement at that time, and strolled about the park in profound silence; during which, Hatchway's indignation subsiding, he all of a sudden thrust out his hand as an advance to reconciliation, which being cordially shaken by Peregrine, a general pacification ensued; and was followed by a consultation about the means of extricating the youth from his present perplexity. Had his disposition been like that of most other young men, it would have been no difficult task to overcome his difficulties; but such was the obstinacy of his pride, that he deemed himself bound in honour to resent the letters he had received; and, instead of submitting to the pleasure of the commodore, expected an acknowledgment from him, without which he would listen to no terms of accommodation. "Had I been his own son," said he, "I should have bor[n]e his reproof, and sued for forgiveness; but, knowing myself to be on the footing of an orphan, who depends entirely upon his benevolence, I am jealous of everything that can be construed into disrespect, and insist upon being treated with the most punctual regard. I shall now make application to my father, who is obliged to provide for me by the ties of nature, as well as the laws of the land; and if he shall refuse to do me justice, I can never want employment while men are required for his Majesty's service."

The lieutenant, alarmed at this intimation, begged he would

take no new step until he should hear from him; and that very evening set out for the garrison, where he gave Trunnion an account of the miscarriage of his negotiation, told him how highly Peregrine was offended at the letter, communicated the young gentleman's sentiments and resolution, and, finally, assured him, that unless he should think proper to ask pardon for the offence he had committed, he would, in all appearance, never more behold the face of his godson.

The old commodore was utterly confounded at this piece of intelligence; he had expected all the humility of obedience and contrition from the young man; and, instead of that, received nothing but the most indignant opposition, and even found himself in the circumstances of an offender, obliged to make atonement, or forfeit all correspondence with his favourite. These insolent conditions at first threw him into an agony of wrath, and he vented execrations with such rapidity, that he left himself no time to breathe, and had almost been suffocated with his choler. He inveighed bitterly against the ingratitude of Peregrine, whom he mentioned with many opprobrious epithets, and swore that he ought to be keel-hauled for his presumption; but when he began to reflect more coolly upon the spirit of the young gentleman, which had already manifested itself on many occasions, and listened to the suggestions of Hatchway, whom he had always considered as an oracle in his way, his resentment abated, and he determined to take Perry into favour again; this placability being not a little facilitated by Jack's narrative of our hero's intrepid behaviour at the assembly, as well as in the contest with him in the park. But still this plaguey amour occurred like a bugbear to his imagination; for he held it as an infallible maxim, that woman was an eternal source of misery to man. Indeed, this apothegm he seldom repeated since his marriage, except in the company of a very few intimates, to whose secrecy and discretion he could trust. Finding Jack himself at a nonplus in the affair of Emilia, he consulted Mrs. Trunnion, who was equally surprised and offended, when she understood that her letter did not produce the desired effect; and, after having imputed the youth's obstinacy to his uncle's unseasonable indulgence, had recourse to the advice of the parson, who, still with an eye to his friend's advantage, counselled them to send the young gentleman on his travels, in the course of which he would, in all probability, forget the amusements of his greener years. The proposal was judicious, and immediately approved, when Trunnion going into his closet, after divers efforts, produced the following billet, with which Jack departed for Windsor that same afternoon:

MY GOOD LAD,—If I gave offence in my last letter, I'm sorry for't, d'ye see; I thought it was the likeliest way to bring you up; but, in time to come, you shall have a larger swing of cable. When you can spare time, I shall be glad if you will make a short trip and see your aunt, and him who is

Your loving godfather and humble servant,

HAWSER TRUNNION.

P.S.—If you want money, you may draw upon me, payable at sight.

CHAPTER XXVI

He becomes melancholy and despondent—Is favoured with a condescending Letter from his Uncle—Reconciles himself to his Governor, and sets out with Emilia and her Friend for Mrs. Gauntlet's House.

PEREGRINE, fortified as he was with pride and indignation, did not fail to feel the smarting suggestions of his present situation; after having lived so long in an affluent and imperious manner, he could ill brook the thoughts of submitting to the mortifying exigencies of life. All the gaudy schemes of pomp and pleasure, which his luxuriant imagination had formed, began to dissolve, a train of melancholy ideas took possession of his thoughts, and the prospect of losing Emilia was not the least part of his affliction. Though he endeavoured to suppress the chagrin that preyed upon his heart, he could not conceal the disturbance of his mind from the penetration of that amiable young lady, who sympathised with him in her heart, though she could not give her tongue the liberty of asking the cause of his disorder; for, notwithstanding all the ardour of his addresses, he never could obtain from her the declaration of a mutual flame; because, though he had hitherto treated her with the utmost reverence and respect, he had never once mentioned the final aim of his passion. However honourable she supposed it to be, she had discernment enough to foresee, that vanity or interest, co-operating with the levity of youth, might one day deprive her of her lover, and she was too proud to give him any handle of exulting at her expense. Although he was received by her with the most distinguished civility, and even an intimacy of friendship, all his solicitations could never extort from her an acknowledgment of love; on the contrary, being of a gay disposition, she sometimes coquetted with other admirers, that his attention thus whetted might never abate, and that he might see she had other resources, in case he should flag in his affection.

This being the prudential plan on which she acted, it cannot be supposed that she would condescend to inquire into the state of his thoughts, when she saw him thus affected; but she, nevertheless, imposed that task on her cousin and confidant, who, as they walked together in the park, observed that he seemed to be out of humour. When this is the case, such a question generally increases the disease; at least, it had that effect upon Peregrine, who replied, somewhat peevishly, "I assure you, madam, you never was more mistaken in your observations." "I think so too," said Emilia, "for I never saw Mr. Pickle in higher spirits."—This ironical encomium completed his confusion; he affected to smile, but it was a smile of anguish, and in his heart he cursed the vivacity of both. He could not for his soul recollect himself so as to utter one connected sentence; and the suspicion that they observed every circumstance of his behaviour, threw such a damp on his spirits, that he was quite overwhelmed with shame and resentment, when Sophy, casting her eyes towards the gate, said, "Yonder is your servant, Mr. Pickle, with another man who seems to have a wooden leg." Peregrine started at this intelligence, and immediately underwent sundry changes of complexion, knowing that his fate in a great measure depended upon the information he would receive from his friend.

Hatchway advancing to the company, after a brace of sea bows to the ladies, took the youth aside, and put the commodore's letter into his hand, which threw him into such an agitation, that he could scarce pronounce, "Ladies, will you give me leave?" When, in consequence of their permission, he attempted to open the billet, he fumbled with such manifest disorder, that his mistress, who watched his motions, began to think there was something very interesting in the message; and so much was she affected with his concern, that she was fain to turn her head another way, and wipe the tears from her lovely eyes.

Meanwhile, Peregrine no sooner read the first sentence, than his countenance, which before was overcast with a deep gloom, began to be lighted up, and every feature unbending by degrees, he recovered his serenity. Having perused the letter, his eyes sparkling with joy and gratitude, he hugged the lieutenant in his arms, and presented him to the ladies as one of his best friends. Jack met with a most gracious reception, and shook Emilia by the hand, telling her, with the familiar appellation of *old acquaintance*, that he did not care how soon he was master of such another clean-going frigate as herself.

The whole company partook of this favourable change that evidently appeared in our lover's recollection, and enlivened his conversation with such an uncommon flow of sprightliness and good-humour, as even made an impression on the iron countenance of Pipes himself, who actually smiled with satisfaction as he walked behind them.

The evening being pretty far advanced, they directed their course homeward; and, while the valet attended Hatchway to the inn, Peregrine escorted the ladies to their lodgings, where he owned the justness of Sophy's remark, in saying he was out of humour, and told them he had been extremely chagrined at a difference which had happened between him and his uncle, to whom, by the letter which they had seen him receive, he now found himself happily reconciled.

Having received their congratulations, and declined staying to sup with them, on account of the longing desire he had to converse with his friend Jack, he took his leave, and repaired to the inn, where Hatchway informed him of everything that had happened in the garrison upon his representations. Far from being disgusted, he was perfectly well pleased with the prospect of going abroad, which flattered his vanity and ambition, gratified his thirst after knowledge, and indulged that turn for observation, for which he had been remarkable from his most tender years. Neither did he believe a short absence would tend to the prejudice of his love, but, on the contrary, enhance the value of his heart, because he should return better accomplished, and consequently a more welcome offering to his mistress. Elevated with these sentiments, his heart dilated with joy, and the sluices of his natural benevolence being opened by this happy turn of his affairs, he sent his compliments to Mr. Jolter, to whom he had not spoken during a whole week, and desired he would favour Mr. Hatchway and him with his company at supper.

The governor was not weak enough to decline this invitation; in consequence of which he forthwith appeared, and was cordially welcomed by the relenting pupil, who expressed his sorrow for the misunderstanding which had prevailed between them, and assured him, that, for the future, he would avoid giving him any just cause of complaint. Jolter, who did not want affection, was melted by this acknowledgment, which he could not have expected, and earnestly protested, that his chief study had always been, and ever should be, to promote Mr. Pickle's interest and happiness.

The best part of the night being spent in the circulation of a cheerful glass, the company broke up; and next morning Peregrine went out with a view of making his mistress acquainted with his uncle's intention of sending him out of the kingdom for his improvement, and of saying everything which he thought necessary for the interest of his love.   He found her at breakfast with her cousin; and, as he was very full of the subject of his visit, had scarce fixed himself in his seat, when he brought it upon the carpet, by asking with a smile, if the ladies had any commands for Paris?   Emilia, at this question, began to stare, and her confidant desired to know who was going thither? He no sooner gave them to understand that he himself intended in a short time to visit that capital, than his mistress, with great precipitation, wished him a good journey, and affected to talk with indifference about the pleasures he would enjoy in France. But when he seriously assured Sophy, who asked if he was in earnest, that his uncle actually insisted upon his making a short tour, the tears gushed in poor Emilia's eyes, and she was at great pains to conceal her concern, by observing that the tea was so scalding hot, as to make her eyes water.   This pretext was too thin to impose upon her lover, or even deceive the observation of her friend Sophy, who, after breakfast, took an opportunity of quitting the room.

Thus left by themselves, Peregrine imparted to her what he had learned of the commodore's intention, without, however, mentioning a syllable of his being offended at their correspondence, and accompanied his information with such fervent vows of eternal constancy and solemn promises of a speedy return, that Emilia's heart, which had been invaded by a suspicion that this scheme of travelling was the effect of her lover's inconstancy, began to be more at ease; and she could not help signifying her approbation of his design.

This affair being amicably compromised, he asked how soon she proposed to set out for her mother's house; and, under-standing that her departure was fixed for next day but one, and that her cousin Sophy intended to accompany her in her father's chariot, he repeated his intention of attending her.   In the meantime he dismissed his governor and the lieutenant to the garrison, with his compliments to his aunt and the commodore, and a faithful promise of his being with them in six days at farthest.

These previous measures being taken, he, attended by Pipes, set out with the ladies; and they had also a convoy for twelve miles from Sophy's father, who at parting recommended them piously to the care of Peregrine, with whom, by this time, he was perfectly well acquainted.

CHAPTER XXVII

They meet with a dreadful Alarm on the Road—Arrive at their Journey's End—Peregrine is introduced to Emily's Brother—These two young Gentlemen misunderstand each other—Pickle departs for the Garrison.

As they travelled at an easy rate, they had performed something more than one-half of their journey, when they were benighted near an inn, at which they resolved to lodge. The accommodation was very good; they supped together with great mirth and enjoyment, and it was not till after he had been warned by the yawns of the ladies, that he conducted them to their apartment; where wishing them good-night, he retired to his own, and went to rest.

The house was crowded with country people who had been at a neighbouring fair, and now regaled themselves with ale and tobacco in the yard; so that their consideration, which at any time was but slender, being now overwhelmed by this debauch, they staggered into their respective kennels, and left a lighted candle sticking to one of the wooden pillars that supported the gallery.—The flame in a little time laid hold on the wood, which was as dry as tinder, and the whole gallery was on fire, when Peregrine suddenly awaked, and found himself almost suffocated. He sprung up in an instant, slipped on his breeches, and throwing open the door of his chamber, saw the whole entry in a blaze.

Heavens! what were the emotions of his soul, when he beheld the volumes of flame and smoke rolling towards the room where his dear Emilia lay! Regardless of his own danger, he darted himself through the thickest of the gloom, when knocking hard, and calling at the same time to the ladies, with the most anxious intreaty to be admitted, the door was opened by Emilia in her shift, who asked, with the utmost trepidation, what was the matter? He made no reply, but snatching her up in his arms,

like another Æneas, bore her through the flames to a place of
safety; where, leaving her before she could recollect herself,
or pronounce one word, but "Alas! my cousin Sophy!" he flew
back to the rescue of that young lady, and found her already
delivered by Pipes, who, having been alarmed by the smell of
fire, had got up, rushed immediately to the chamber where he
knew these companions lodged, and (Emily being saved by her
lover) brought off Miss Sophy with the loss of his own shock
head of hair, which was singed off in his retreat.

By this time the whole inn was alarmed; every lodger, as well
as servant, exerted himself in order to stop the progress of this
calamity; and there being a well-replenished horse-pond in the
yard, in less than an hour the fire was totally extinguished,
without having done any other damage than that of consuming
about two yards of the wooden gallery.

All this time our young gentleman closely attended his fair
charges, each of whom had swooned with apprehension; but
as their constitutions were good, and their spirits not easily
dissipated, when upon reflection they found themselves and
their company safe, and that the flames were happily quenched,
the tumult of their fears subsided, they put on their clothes,
recovered their good-humour, and began to rally each other on
the trim in which they had been secured. Sophy observed,
that now Mr. Pickle had an indisputable claim to her cousin's
affection; and therefore she ought to lay aside all affected reserve
for the future, and frankly avow the sentiments of her heart.
Emily retorted the argument, putting her in mind, that, by
the same claim, Mr. Pipes was entitled to the like return from
her. Her friend admitted the force of the conclusion, provided
she could not find means of satisfying her deliverer in another
shape; and turning to the valet, who happened to be present,
asked, if his heart was not otherwise engaged? Tom, who did
not conceive the meaning of the question, stood silent according
to custom; and the interrogation being repeated, answered, with
a grin, "Heart-whole as a biscuit, I'll assure you, mistress."
"What?" said Emilia, "have you never been in love, Thomas?"
"Yes, forsooth," replied the valet without hesitation, "sometimes of a morning." Peregrine could not help laughing, and
his mistress looked a little disconcerted at this blunt repartee;
while Sophy slipping a purse into his hand, told him there was
something to purchase a periwig. Tom, having consulted his
master's eyes, refused the present, saying, "No, thank ye as much
as if I did." And though she insisted upon his putting it in his

pocket, as a small testimony of her gratitude, he could not be
prevailed upon to avail himself of her generosity; but, following
her to the other end of the room, thrust it into her sleeve without
ceremony, exclaiming, "I'll be d—d to hell if I do." Peregrine
having checked him for his boorish behaviour, sent him out of
the room, and begged that Miss Sophy would not endeavour to
debauch the morals of his servant, who, rough and uncultivated
as he was, had sense enough to perceive that he had no pretension to any such acknowledgment. But she argued with great
vehemence, that she should never be able to make an acknowledgment adequate to the service he had done her, and that she
should never be perfectly easy in her own mind, until she found
some opportunity of manifesting the sense she had of the obliga
tion. "I do not pretend," said she, "to reward Mr. Pipes; but
I shall be absolutely unhappy, unless I am allowed to give him
some token of my regard."

Peregrine, thus earnestly solicited, desired that, since she was
bent upon displaying her generosity, she would not bestow upon
him any pecuniary gratification, but honour him with some trin-
ket, as a mark of consideration; because he himself had such a
particular value for the fellow, on account of his attachment and
fidelity, that he should be sorry to see him treated on the footing
of a common mercenary domestic.

There was not one jewel in the possession of this grateful
young lady, that she would not have gladly given as a recompense
or badge of distinction to her rescuer; but his master pitched
upon a seal ring of no great value, that hung at her watch, and
Pipes being called in, had permission to accept that testimony of
Miss Sophy's favour. Tom received it accordingly with sundry
scrapes, and, having kissed it with great devotion, put it on his
little finger, and strutted off, extremely proud of his acquisition.

Emilia, with a most enchanting sweetness of aspect, told her
lover, that he had instructed her how to behave towards him;
and, taking a diamond ring from her finger, desired he would
wear it for her sake. He received the pledge as became him, and
presented another in exchange, which she at first refused, alleging
that it would destroy the intent of her acknowledgment; but
Peregrine assured her, he had accepted her jewel, not as a proof
of her gratitude, but as the mark of her love; and that, if she
refused a mutual token, he should look upon himself as the object
of her disdain. Her eyes kindled, and her cheeks glowed with
resentment, at this impudent intimation, which she considered
as an unseasonable insult; and the young gentleman perceiving

her emotion, stood corrected for his temerity, and asked pardon for the liberty of his remonstrance, which he hoped she would ascribe to the prevalence of that principle alone which he had always taken pride in avowing.

Sophy, seeing him disconcerted, interposed in his behalf, and chid her cousin for having practised such unnecessary affectation; upon which Emilia, softened into compliance, held out her finger as a signal of her condescension. Peregrine put on the ring with great eagerness, mumbled her soft white hand in an ecstasy which would not allow him to confine his embraces to that limb, but urged him to seize her by the waist, and snatch a delicious kiss from her love-pouting lips; nor would he leave her a butt to the ridicule of Sophy, on whose mouth he instantly committed a rape of the same nature; so that the two friends, countenanced by each other, reprehended him with such gentleness of rebuke, that he was almost tempted to repeat the offence.

The morning being now lighted up, and the servants of the inn on foot, he ordered some chocolate for breakfast, and, at the desire of the ladies, sent Pipes to see the horses fed, and the chariot prepared, while he went to the bar, and discharged the bill.

These measures being taken, they set out about five o'clock, and, having refreshed themselves and their cattle at another inn on the road, proceeded in the afternoon. Without meeting with any other accident, they safely arrived at the place of their destination, where Mrs. Gauntlet expressed her joy at seeing her old friend Mr. Pickle, whom, however, she kindly reproached for the long discontinuance of his regard. Without explaining the cause of that interruption, he protested, that his love and esteem had never been discontinued, and that, for the future, he should omit no occasion of testifying how much he had her friendship at heart. She then made him acquainted with her son, who at that time was in the house, being excused from his duty by furlough.

This young man, whose name was Godfrey, was about the age of twenty, of a middling size, vigorous make, remarkably well shaped, and the scars of the smallpox, of which he bore a good number, added a peculiar manliness to the air of his countenance. His capacity was good, and his disposition naturally frank and easy; but he had been a soldier from his infancy, and his education was altogether in the military style. He looked upon taste and letters as mere pedantry, beneath the consideration of a gentleman; and every civil station of life as mean, when compared with the profession of arms. He had made great progress in the gymnastic sciences of dancing, fencing, and riding, played perfectly well on the German flute, and, above all things, valued himself upon a scrupulous observance of all the points of honour.

Had Peregrine and he considered themselves upon equal footing, in all probability they would have immediately entered into a league of intimacy and friendship. But this sufficient soldier looked upon his sister's admirer as a young student, raw from the university, and utterly ignorant of mankind; while Squire Pickle beheld Godfrey in the light of a needy volunteer, greatly inferior to himself in fortune, as well as every other accomplishment. This mutual misunderstanding could not fail of producing animosities. The very next day after Peregrine's arrival, some sharp repartees passed between them in presence of the ladies, before whom each endeavoured to assert his own superiority. In these contests our hero never failed of obtaining the victory, because his genius was more acute, and his talents better cultivated than those of his antagonist, who therefore took umbrage at his success, became jealous of his reputation, and began to treat him with marks of scorn and disrespect. His sister saw, and dreading the consequences of his ferocity, not only took him to task in private for his impolite behaviour, but also intreated her lover to make allowances for the roughness of her brother's education. He kindly assured her, that, whatever pains it might cost him to vanquish his own impetuous temper, he would for her sake endure all the mortifications to which her brother's arrogance might expose him; and, after having stayed with her two days, and enjoyed several private interviews, during which he acted the part of a most passionate lover, he took his leave of Mrs. Gauntlet overnight, and told the young ladies he would call early next morning to bid them farewell.

He did not neglect this piece of duty, and found the two friends and breakfast already prepared in the parlour. All three being extremely affected with the thoughts of parting, a most pathetic silence for some time prevailed, till Peregrine put an end to it, by lamenting his fate, in being obliged to exile himself so long from the dear object of his most interesting wish. He begged, with the most earnest supplications, that she would now, in consideration of the cruel absence he must suffer, give him the consolation which she had hitherto refused, namely, that of knowing he possessed a place within her heart. The confidant seconded his request, representing that it was now no time to disguise her sentiments, when her lover was about to leave the kingdom, and might be in danger of contracting other connexions, unless he was confirmed in his constancy, by knowing how far he could depend upon her love; and, in short, she was plied with such irresistible importunities, that she answered, in the utmost confusion: "Though I have avoided literal acknowledgments, methinks the circumstances of my behaviour might have convinced Mr. Pickle, that I do not regard him as a common acquaintance." "My charming Emily!" cried the impatient lover, throwing himself at her feet, "why will you deal out my happiness in such scanty portions? Why will you thus mince the declaration which would overwhelm me with pleasure, and cheer my lonely reflection, while I sigh amid the solitude of separation?" His fair mistress, melted by this image, replied, with the tears gushing from her eyes, "I'm afraid I shall feel that separation more severely than you imagine." Transported at this flattering confession, he pressed her to his breast, and, while her head reclined upon his neck, mingled his tears with hers in great abundance, breathing the most tender vows of eternal fidelity. The gentle heart of Sophy could not bear this scene unmoved; she wept with sympathy, and encouraged the lovers to resign themselves to the will of fate, and support their spirits with the hope of meeting again on happier terms. Finally, after mutual promises, exhortations, and endearments, Peregrine took his leave, his heart being so full, that he could scarce pronounce the word *Adieu!* and, mounting his horse at the door, set out with Pipes for the garrison.

CHAPTER XXVIII

Peregrine is overtaken by Mr. Gauntlet, with whom he fights a Duel, and contracts an intimate Friendship—He arrives at the Garrison, and finds his Mother as implacable as ever—He is insulted by his Brother Gam, whose Preceptor he disciplines with a Horse-whip.

IN order to expel the melancholy images that took possession of his fancy, at parting from his mistress, he called in the flattering ideas of those pleasures he expected to enjoy in France; and, before he had rode ten miles, his imagination was effectually amused.

While he thus prosecuted his travels by anticipation, and indulged himself in all the insolence of hope, at the turning of a lane he was all of a sudden overtaken by Emilia's brother on horseback, who told him he was riding the same way, and should be glad of his company. This young gentleman, whether prompted by personal pique, or actuated with zeal for the honour of his family, had followed our hero, with a view of obliging him to explain the nature of his attachment to his sister. Peregrine returned his compliment with such disdainful civility, as gave him room to believe that he suspected his errand; and therefore, without further preamble, he declared his business in these words: "Mr. Pickle, you have carried on a correspondence with my sister for some time, and I should be glad to know the nature of it." To this question our lover replied, "Sir, I should be glad to know what title you have to demand that satisfaction." "Sir," answered the other, "I demand it in the capacity of a brother, jealous of his own honour, as well as of his sister's reputation; and, if your intentions are honourable, you will not refuse it." "Sir," said Peregrine, "I am not at present disposed to appeal to your opinion for the rectitude of my intentions; and I think you assume a little too much importance, in pretending to judge my conduct." "Sir," replied the soldier, "I pretend to judge the conduct of every man who interferes with my concerns, and even to chastise him, if I think he acts amiss." "Chastise!" cried the youth, with indignation in his looks, "sure you dare not apply that term to me!" "You are mistaken," said Godfrey; "I dare do anything that becomes the character of a gentleman." "Gentleman, God wot!" replied the other, looking contemptuously at his equipage, which was none of the most superb; "a very pretty gentleman, truly!" The soldier's wrath was inflamed by this ironical repetition, the contempt of which his conscious poverty made him feel; and he called his antagonist Presumptuous Boy! Insolent Upstart! with other epithets, which Perry retorted with great bitterness. A formal challenge having passed between them, they alighted at the first inn, and walked into the next field, in order to decide their quarrel by the sword.

Having pitched upon the spot, helped to pull off each other's boots, and laid aside their coats and waistcoats, Mr. Gauntlet told his opponent, that he himself was looked upon in the army as an expert swordsman; and that, if Mr. Pickle had not made that science his particular study, they should be upon a more equal footing in using pistols. Peregrine was too much incensed to thank him for his plain dealing, and too confident of his own skill, to relish the other's proposal, which he accordingly rejected. Then, drawing his sword, he observed, that, were he to treat Mr. Gauntlet according to his deserts, he would order his man to punish his audacity with a horse-whip. Exasperated at this expression, which he considered as an indelible affront, he made no reply, but attacked his adversary with equal ferocity and address. The youth parried his first and second thrust, but received the third in the outside of his sword arm. Though the wound was superficial, he was transported with rage at the sight of his own blood, and returned the assault with such fury and precipitation, that Gauntlet, loth to take advantage of his unguarded heat, stood upon the defensive. In the second longe, Peregrine's weapon entering a kind of network in the shell of Godfrey's sword, the blade snapped in two, and left him at the mercy of the soldier, who, far from making an insolent use of the victory he had gained, put up his Toledo with great deliberation, like a man who had been used to that kind of rencounters, and observed, that such a blade as Peregrine's was not to be trusted with a man's life. Then, advising the owner to treat a gentleman in distress with more respect for the future, he slipped on his boots, and, with sullen dignity of demeanour, stalked back to the inn.

Though Pickle was extremely mortified at his miscarriage in this adventure, he was also struck with the behaviour of his antagonist, which affected him the more, as he understood that Godfrey's *fierté* had proceeded from the jealous sensibility of a gentleman declined into the vale of misfortune. Gauntlet's valour and moderation induced him to put a favourable construction on all those circumstances of that young soldier's conduct, which had before given him disgust. Though, in any other case, he would have industriously avoided the least appearance of submission, he followed his conqueror to the inn, with a view of thanking him for his generous forbearance, and of soliciting his friendship and correspondence. Godfrey had his foot in the stirrup, to mount, when Peregrine, coming up to him, desired he would defer his departure for a quarter of an hour, and favour him with a little private conversation. The soldier, who mistook the meaning of the request, immediately quitted his horse, and followed Pickle into a chamber, where he expected to find a brace of pistols loaded on the table; but he was very agreeably deceived when our hero, in the most respectful terms, acknowledged his noble deportment in the field, owned, that till then he had misunderstood his character, and begged that he would honour him with his intimacy and correspondence.

Gauntlet, who had seen undoubted proofs of Peregrine's courage, which had considerably raised him in his esteem, and had sense enough to perceive that this concession was not owing to any sordid or sinister motive, embraced his offer with demonstrations of infinite satisfaction. When he understood the terms on which Mr. Pickle was with his sister, he proffered his service in his turn, either as agent, mediator, or confidant.   Nay, to give his new friend a convincing proof of his sincerity, he disclosed to him a passion which he had for some time entertained for his cousin Miss Sophy, though he durst not reveal his sentiments to her father, lest he should be offended at his presumption, and withdraw his protection from the family.   Peregrine's generous heart was wrung with anguish, when he understood that this young gentleman, who was the only son of a distinguished officer, had carried arms for the space of five years, without being able to obtain a subaltern's commission, though he had always behaved with remarkable regularity and spirit, and acquired the friendship and esteem of all the officers under whom he had served.

He would, at that time, with the utmost pleasure, have shared his finances with him; but, as he would not run the risk of offending the young soldier's delicacy of honour, by a premature exertion of his liberality, he resolved to insinuate himself into an intimacy with him, before he would venture to take such freedoms; and, with that view, pressed Mr. Gauntlet to accompany him to the garrison, where he did not doubt of having influence enough to make him a welcome guest.   Godfrey thanked him very courteously for his invitation, which he said he could not immediately accept; but promised, if he would favour him with a letter, and fix the time at which he proposed to set out for France, he would endeavour to visit him at the commodore's habitation, and from thence give him a convoy to Dover.   This new treaty being settled, and a dossil of lint, with a snip of plaster, applied to our adventurer's wound, he parted from the brother of his dear Emilia, to whom, and his friend Sophy, he sent his kindest wishes; and, having lodged one night upon the road, arrived next day in the afternoon at the garrison, where he found all his friends in good health, and overjoyed at his return.

The commodore, who was by this time turned of seventy, and altogether crippled by the gout, seldom went abroad; and, as his conversation was not very entertaining, had but little company within doors; so that his spirits must have quite stagnated, had they not been kept in motion by the conversation of Hatchway, and received, at different times, a wholesome fillip from the discipline of his spouse, who, by the force of pride, religion, and cognac, had erected a most terrible tyranny in the house.   There was such a quick circulation of domestics in the family, that every suit of livery had been worn by figures of all dimensions Trunnion himself had, long before this time, yielded to the torrent of her arbitrary sway, though not without divers obstinate efforts to maintain his liberty; and now that he was disabled by his infirmities, when he used to hear his empress singing the loud Orthyan song among the servants below, he would often, in whispers, communicate to the lieutenant hints of what he would do, if so be as how he was not deprived of the use of his precious limbs. Hatchway was the only person whom the temper of Mrs. Trunnion respected, either because she dreaded his ridicule, or looked upon his person with eyes of affection. This being the situation of things in the garrison, it is not to be doubted that the old gentleman highly enjoyed the presence of Peregrine, who found means to ingratiate himself so effectually with his aunt, that, while he remained at home, she seemed to have exchanged the disposition of a tigress, for that of a gentle kid. But he found his own mother as implacable, and his father as much henpecked as ever.

Gamaliel, who now very seldom enjoyed the conversation of his old friend the commodore, had some time ago entered into an amicable society consisting of the barber, apothecary, attorney, and exciseman of the parish, among whom he used to spend the evening at Tunley's, and listen to their disputes upon philosophy and politics with great comfort and edification, while his sovereign lady domineered at home as usual, visited with great pomp in the neighbourhood, and employed her chief care in the education of her darling son Gam, who was now in the fifteenth year of his age, and so remarkable for his perverse disposition, that, in spite of his mother's influence and authority, he was not only hated, but also despised, both at home and abroad. She had put him under the tuition of the curate, who lived in the family, and was obliged to attend him in all his exercises and excursions. This governor was a low-bred fellow, who had neither experience nor ingenuity, but possessed a large fund of adulation and servile complaisance, by which he had gained the good graces of Mrs. Pickle, and presided over all her deliberations, in the same manner as his superior managed those of Mrs. Trunnion.

He had one day rode out to take the air with his pupil, who, as I have already observed, was odious to the poor people, for having killed their dogs, and broken their enclosures, and, on account of his hump, was distinguished by the title of My Lord, when in a narrow lane they chanced to meet Peregrine on horseback. The young squire no sooner perceived his elder brother, against whom he had been instructed to bear the most inveterate grudge, than he resolved to insult him *en passant*, and actually rode against him full gallop. Our hero, guessing his aim, fixed himself in his stirrups, and, by a dexterous management of the reins, avoided the shock in such a manner, as that their legs only should encounter, by which means My Lord was tilted out of his saddle, and, in a twinkling, laid sprawling in the dirt. The governor, enraged at the disgrace of his charge, advanced with great insolence and fury, and struck at Peregrine with his whip. Nothing could be more agreeable to our young gentleman than this assault, which furnished him with an opportunity of chastising an officious wretch, whose petulance and malice he had longed to punish. He therefore, spurring up his horse towards his antagonist, overthrew him in the middle of a hedge. Before he had time to recollect himself from the confusion of the fall, Pickle alighted in a trice, and exercised his horse-whip with such agility about the curate's face and ears, that he was fain to prostrate himself before his enraged conqueror, and implore his forbearance in the most abject terms. While Peregrine was thus employed, his brother Gam had made shift to rise and attack him in the rear; for which reason, when the tutor was quelled, the victor faced about, snatched the weapon out of his hand, and having broken it to pieces, remounted his horse and rode off, without deigning to honour him with any other notice.

The condition in which they returned produced infinite clamour against the conqueror, who was represented as a ruffian who had lain in ambush to make away with his brother, in whose defence the curate was said to have received those cruel stripes, that hindered him from appearing for three whole weeks in the performance of his duty at church. Complaints were made to the commodore, who, having inquired into the circumstances of the affair, approved of what his nephew had done; adding, with many oaths, that, provided Peregrine had been out of the scrape, he wished Crookback had broke his neck in the fall.

CHAPTER XXIX

He projects a Plan of Revenge, which is executed against the Curate.

OUR hero, exasperated at the villainy of the curate in the treacherous misrepresentation he had made of this rencounter, determined to practise upon him a method of revenge, which should be not only effectual, but also unattended with any bad consequence to himself. For this purpose he and Hatchway, to whom he imparted his plan, went to the alehouse one evening, and called for an empty room, knowing there was no other but that which they had chosen for the scene of action. This apartment was a sort of parlour that fronted the kitchen, with a window towards the yard; where, after they had sat some time, the lieutenant found means to amuse the landlord in discourse, while Peregrine, stepping out into the yard, by the talent of mimicry, which he possessed in a surprising degree, counterfeited a dialogue between the curate and Tunley's wife. This reaching the ears of the publican, for whose hearing it was calculated, inflamed his naturally jealous disposition to such a degree, that he could not conceal his emotion, but made an hundred efforts to quit the room; while the lieutenant, smoking his pipe with great gravity, as if he neither heard what passed, nor took notice of the landlord's disorder, detained him on the spot by a succession of questions which he could not refuse to answer, though he stood sweating with agony all the time, stretching his neck every instant towards the window through which the voices were conveyed, scratching his head and exhibiting sundry other symptoms of impatience and agitation. At length, the supposed conversation came to such a pitch of amorous complaisance, that the husband, quite frantic with his imaginary disgrace, rushed out at the door, crying, "Coming, sir." But, as he was obliged to make a circuit round one-half of the house, Peregrine had got in by the window before Tunley arrived in the yard.

According to the feigned intelligence he had received, he ran directly to the barn, in expectation of making some very extraordinary discovery; and having employed some minutes in rummaging the straw to no purpose, returned in a state of distraction to the kitchen, just as his wife chanced to enter at the other door. The circumstance of her appearance confirmed him in the opinion that the deed was done. As the disease of being henpecked was epidemic in the parish, he durst not express the least hint of his uneasiness to her, but resolved to take vengeance on the libidinous priest, who, he imagined, had corrupted the chastity of his spouse.

The two confederates, in order to be certified that their scheme had taken effect, as well as to blow up the flame which they had kindled, called for Tunley, in whose countenance they could easily discern his confusion. Peregrine, desiring him to sit down and drink a glass with them, began to interrogate him about his family, and, among other things, asked him "how long he had been married to that handsome wife?" This question, which was put with an arch significance of look, alarmed the publican, who began to fear that Pickle had overheard his dishonour; and this suspicion was not at all removed, when the lieutenant, with a sly regard, pronounced, "Tunley, wan't you noosed by the curate?" "Yes, I was," replied the landlord with an eagerness and perplexity of tone, as if he thought the lieutenant knew that *thereby hung a tale*; and Hatchway supported this suspicion, by answering, "Nay, as for that matter, the curate may be a very sufficient man in his way." This transition from his wife to the curate, convinced him that his shame was known to his guests; and, in the transport of his indignation, he pronounced with great emphasis, "A sufficient man! odds heart! I believe they are wolves in sheep's clothing. I wish to God I could see the day, master, when there shall not be a priest, an exciseman, or a custom-house officer in this kingdom. As for that fellow of a curate, if I do catch him—It don't signify talking—But, by the Lord!—Gentlemen, my service to you."

The associates being satisfied, by these abrupt insinuations, that they had so far succeeded in their aim, waited with impatience two or three days, in expectation of hearing that Tunley had fallen upon some method of being revenged for this imaginary wrong: but finding that either his invention was too shallow or his inclination too languid, to gratify their desire of his own accord, they determined to bring the affair to such a crisis, that he should not be able to withstand the opportunity of executing his vengeance. With this view they one evening hired a boy to run to Mr. Pickle's house, and tell the curate, that Mrs. Tunley being taken suddenly ill, her husband desired he would come immediately, and pray with her. Meanwhile, they had taken possession of a room in the house; and Hatchway engaging the landlord in conversation, Peregrine, in his return from the yard, observed, as if by accident, that the parson was gone into the kitchen, in order, as he supposed, to catechise Tunley's wife.

The publican started at this intelligence, and, under pretence of serving another company in the next room, went out to the barn, where arming himself with a flail, he repaired to a lane through which the curate was under a necessity of passing in his way home. There he lay in ambush, with fell intent; and, when the supposed author of his shame arrived, greeted him in the dark with such a salutation, as forced him to stagger backward three paces at least. If the second application had taken effect, in all probability, that spot would have been the boundary of the parson's mortal peregrination; but, luckily for him, his antagonist was not an expert in the management of his weapon, which by a twist of the thong that connected the legs, instead of pitching upon the head of the astonished curate, descended in an oblique direction on his own pate, with such a swing, that the skull actually rung like an apothecary's mortar, and ten thousand lights seemed to dance before his eyes. The curate recollecting himself during the respite he obtained from this accident, and believing his aggressor to be some thief who lurked in that place for prey, resolved to make a running fight, until he should arrive within cry of his habitation. With this design he raised up his cudgel for the defence of his head, and, betaking himself to his heels, began to roar for help with the lungs of a Stentor. Tunley, throwing away the flail, which he durst no longer trust with the execution of his revenge, pursued the fugitive with all the speed he could exert; and the other, either unnerved by fear, or stumbling over a stone, was overtaken before he had run a hundred paces. He no sooner felt the wind of the publican's fist that whistled round his ears, than he fell flat upon the earth at full length, and the cudgel flew from his unclasping hand; when Tunley, springing like a tiger upon his back, rained such a shower of blows upon his carcass, that he imagined himself under the discipline of ten pairs of fists at least; yet the imaginary cuckold, not satisfied with annoying the priest in this manner, laid hold on one of his ears with his teeth, and bit so unmercifully, that the curate was found almost entranced with pain by two labourers, at whose approach the assailant retreated unperceived.

The lieutenant had posted himself at the window, in order to see the landlord at his first return; and no sooner perceived him enter the yard, than he called him into the apartment, impatient to learn the effects of their stratagem. Tunley obeyed the summons, and appeared before his guests in all the violence of rage, disorder and fatigue; his nostrils were dilated more than one-half beyond their natural capacity, his eyes rolled, his teeth chattered, he snored in breathing as if he had been oppressed by the nightmare, and streams of sweat flowed down each side of his forehead.

Peregrine, affecting to start at sight of such an uncouth figure, asked if he had been wrestling with a spirit; upon which he answered, with great vehemence, "Spirit! No, no, master, I have had a roll and tumble with the flesh. A dog! I'll teach him to come a-caterwauling about my doors." Guessing from this reply that his aim was accomplished, and curious to know the particulars of the rencounter, "Well then," said the youth, "I hope you have prevailed against the flesh, Tunley." "Yes, yes," answered the publican, "I have cooled his capissens, as the saying is: I have played such a tune about his ears, that I'll be bound he shan't long for music this month. A goatish ram-faced rascal! Why, he's a perfect parish bull, as I hope to live."

Hatchway, observing that he seemed to have made a stout battle, desired he would sit down and recover wind; and after he had swallowed a brace of bumpers, his vanity prompted him to expatiate upon his own exploit in such a manner, that the confederates, without seeming to know the curate was his antagonist, became acquainted with every circumstance of the ambuscade.

Tunley had scarce got the better of his agitation, when his wife, entering the room, told them by way of news, that some waggish body had sent Mr. Sackbut the curate to pray with her. This name inflamed the husband's choler anew; and, forgetting all his complaisance for his spouse, he replied, with a rancorous grin, "Add rabbit him! I doubt not but you found his admonitions deadly comfortable!" The landlady, looking at her vassal with a sovereign aspect, "What crotchets," said she, "have you got in your fool's head, I trow? I know no business you have to sit here like a gentleman with your arms a-kimbo, when there's another company in the house to be served." The submissive husband took the hint, and, without further expostulation, sneaked out of the room.

Next day it was reported, that Mr. Sackbut had been waylaid, and almost murdered by robbers, and an advertisement was pasted upon the church door, offering a reward to any person that should discover the assassin; but he reaped no satisfaction from this expedient, and was confined to his chamber a whole fortnight by the bruises he had received.

CHAPTER XXX

Mr. Sackbut and his Pupil conspire against Peregrine, who, being apprised of their Design by his Sister, takes Measures for counterworking their Scheme, which is executed by mistake upon Mr. Gauntlet—This young Soldier meets with a cordial Reception from the Commodore, who generously decoys him into his own Interest.

WHEN he considered the circumstances of the ambuscade, he could not persuade himself that he had been assaulted by a common thief, because it was not to be supposed that a robber would have amused himself in pommelling rather than in rifling his prey. He therefore ascribed his misfortune to the secret enmity of some person who had a design upon his life; and, upon mature deliberation, fixed his suspicion upon Peregrine, who was the only man on earth from whom he thought he deserved such treatment. He communicated his conjecture to his pupil, who readily adopted his opinion, and advised him strenuously to revenge the wrong by a like contrivance, without seeking to make a narrower inquiry, lest his enemy should be thereby put upon his guard.

This proposal being relished, they in concert revolved the means of retorting the ambush with interest, and actually laid such a villainous plan for attacking our hero in the dark, that, had it been executed according to their intention, the young gentleman's scheme of travelling would have been effectually marred. But their machinations were overheard by Miss Pickle, who was now in the seventeenth year of her age, and, in spite of the prejudice of education, entertained in secret a most sisterly affection for her brother Perry, though she had never spoken to him, and was deterred by the precepts, vigilance, and menaces of her mother, from attempting any means of meeting him in private. She was not, however, insensible to his praise, which was loudly sounded forth in the neighbourhood, and never failed of going to church, and every other place, where she thought she might have an opportunity of seeing this amiable brother. With these sentiments it cannot be supposed that she would hear the conspiracy without emotion. She was shocked at the treacherous barbarity of Gam, and shuddered at the prospect of the danger to which Peregrine would be exposed from their malice. She durst not communicate this plot to her mother, because she was afraid that lady's unaccountable aversion for her first-born would hinder her from interposing in his behalf, and consequently render her a sort of accomplice in the guilt of his assassins. She therefore resolved to warn Peregrine of the conspiracy, an account of which she transmitted to him in an affectionate letter, by means of a young gentleman in that neighbourhood, who made his addresses to her at that time, and who, at her request, offered his service to our hero, in defeating the projects of his adversaries.

Peregrine was startled when he read the particulars of their scheme, which was no other than an intention to sally upon him when he should be altogether unprovided against such an attack, cut off his ears, and otherwise mutilate him in such a manner, that he should have no cause to be vain of his person for the future.

Incensed as he was against the brutal disposition of his own father's son, he could not help being moved at the integrity and tenderness of his sister, of whose inclinations towards him he had been hitherto kept in ignorance. He thanked the gentleman for his honourable dealing, and expressed a desire of being better acquainted with his virtues; told him that, now he was cautioned, he hoped there would be no necessity for giving him any further trouble; and wrote by him a letter of acknowledgment to his sister, for whom he expressed the utmost love and regard, beseeching her to favour him with an interview before his departure, that he might indulge his fraternal fondness, and be blessed with the company and countenance of one at least belonging to his own family.

Having imparted this discovery to his friend Hatchway, they came to a resolution of countermining the plan of their enemies. As they did not choose to expose themselves to the insinuations of slander, which would have exerted itself at their expense, had they, even in defending themselves, employed any harsh means of retaliation, they invented a method of disappointing and disgracing their foes, and immediately set Pipes at work to forward the preparations.

Miss Pickle having described the spot which the assassins had pitched upon for the scene of their vengeance, our triumvirate intended to have placed a sentinel among the corn, who should come and give them intelligence when the ambuscade was laid; and, in consequence of that information, they would steal softly towards the place, attended by three or four of the domestics, and draw a large net over the conspirators, who, being entangled in the toil, should be disarmed, fettered, heartily scourged, and suspended between two trees in the snare, as a spectacle to all passengers that should chance to travel that way.

The plan being thus digested, and the commodore made acquainted with the whole affair, the spy was set upon duty, and everybody within doors prepared to go forth upon the first notice. One whole evening did they spend in the most impatient expectation; but, on the second, the scout crept into the garrison, and assured them that he had perceived three men skulking behind the hedge, on the road that led to the public-house, from which Peregrine and the lieutenant used every night to return about that hour. Upon this intelligence, the confederates set out immediately with all their implements. Approaching the scene with as little noise as possible, they heard the sound of blows; and, though the night was dark, perceived a sort of tumultuous conflict on the very spot which the conspirators had possessed. Surprised at this occurrence, the meaning of which he could not comprehend, Peregrine ordered his myrmidons to halt, and reconnoitre; and immediately his ears were saluted with an exclamation of " You shan't 'scape me, rascal."   The voice being quite familiar to him, he all at once divined the cause of that confusion which they had observed; and running up to the assistance of the exclaimer, found a fellow on his knees begging his life of Mr. Gauntlet, who stood over him with a naked hanger in his hand.

Pickle instantly made himself known to his friend, who told him that, having left his horse at Tunley's, he was, in his way to the garrison, set upon by three ruffians, one of whom, being the very individual person now in his power, had come behind him, and struck with a bludgeon at his head, which, however, he missed, and the instrument descended on his left shoulder; that, upon drawing his hanger, and laying about him in the dark, the other two fled, leaving their companion, whom he had disabled, in the lurch.

Peregrine congratulated him upon his safety, and having ordered Pipes to secure the prisoner, conducted Mr. Gauntlet to the garrison, where he met with a very hearty reception from the commodore, to whom he was introduced as his nephew's intimate friend; not but that, in all likelihood, he would have abated somewhat of his hospitality, had he known that he was the brother of Perry's mistress; but her name the old gentleman had never thought of asking, when he inquired into the particulars of his godson's amour.

The captive being examined, in presence of Trunnion and all his adherents, touching the ambuscade, owned, that, being in the service of Gam Pickle, he had been prevailed upon, by the solicitations of his master and the curate, to accompany them in their expedition, and undertake the part which he had acted against the stranger, whom he and his employers mistook for Peregrine.   In consideration of this frank acknowledgment, and a severe wound he had received in his right arm, they resolved to inflict no other punishment on this malefactor, than to detain him all night in the garrison, and next morning carry him before a justice of the peace, to whom he repeated all that he had said overnight, and, with his own hand, subscribed his confession, copies of which were handed about the neighbourhood, to the unspeakable confusion and disgrace of the curate and his promising pupil.

Meanwhile Trunnion treated the young soldier with uncommon marks of respect, being prepossessed in his favour by this adventure, which he had so gallantly achieved, as well as by the encomiums that Peregrine bestowed upon his valour and generosity. He liked his countenance, which was bold and hardy, admired his Herculean limbs, and delighted in asking questions concerning the service he had seen.

The day after his arrival, while the conversation turned on this last subject, the commodore, taking the pipe out of his mouth, "I'll tell you what, brother," said he, "five-and-forty years ago, when I was third lieutenant of the *Warwick* man-of-war, there was a very stout young fellow on board, a subaltern officer of marines; his name was not unlike your own, d'ye see, being Guntlet, with a G. I remember he and I could not abide one another at first, because, d'ye see, I was a sailor and he a landsman, till we fell in with a Frenchman, whom we engaged for eight glasses, and at length boarded and took. I was the first man that stood on the enemy's deck, and should have come scurvily off, d'ye see, if Guntlet had not jumped to my assistance; but we soon cleared ship, and drove them to close quarters, so that they were obliged to strike; and from that day Guntlet and I were sworn brothers as long as he remained on board. He was exchanged into a marching regiment, and what became of him afterwards, Lord in Heaven knows; but this I'll say of him, whether he be dead or alive, he feared no man that ever wore a head, and was, moreover, a very hearty messmate."

The stranger's breast glowed at this eulogium, which was no sooner pronounced, than he eagerly asked if the French ship was not the *Diligence*? The commodore replied with a stare, "The very same, my lad." "Then," said Gauntlet, "the person of whom you are pleased to make such honourable mention was my own father." "The devil he was!" cried Trunnion, shaking him by the hand; "I am rejoiced to see a son of Ned Guntlet in my house."

This discovery introduced a thousand questions, in the course of which the old gentleman learned the situation of his friend's family, and discharged innumerable execrations upon the ingratitude and injustice of the ministry, which had failed to provide for the son of such a brave soldier. Nor was his friendship confined to such ineffectual expressions; he that same evening signified to Peregrine a desire of doing something for his friend. This inclination was so much praised, encouraged, and promoted by his godson, and even supported by his counsellor Hatchway, that our hero was empowered to present him with a sum of money sufficient to purchase a commission.

Though nothing could be more agreeable to Pickle than this permission, he was afraid that Godfrey's scrupulous disposition would hinder him from subjecting himself to any such obligation; and therefore proposed that he should be decoyed into his own interest by a feigned story, in consequence of which he would be prevailed upon to accept of the money, as a debt which the commodore had contracted of his father at sea. Trunnion made wry faces at this expedient, the necessity of which he could not conceive, without calling in question the commonsense of Gauntlet, as he took it for granted, that such offers as those were not to be rejected on any consideration whatever. Besides, he could not digest an artifice, by which he himself must own that he had lived so many years without manifesting the least intention of doing justice to his creditor. All these objections, however, were removed by the zeal and rhetoric of Peregrine, who represented that it would be impossible to befriend him on any other terms; that his silence hitherto would be imputed to his want of information, touching the circumstances and condition of his friend; and that his remembering and insisting upon discharging the obligation, after such an interval of time, when the whole affair was in oblivion, would be the greatest compliment he could pay to his own honour and integrity.

Thus persuaded, he took an opportunity of Gauntlet's being alone with him to broach the affair, telling the young man, that his father had advanced a sum of money for him, when they sailed together, on account of the mess, as well as to stop the mouth of a clamorous creditor at Portsmouth; and that the said sum, with interest, amounted to about four hundred pounds, which he would now, with great thankfulness, repay.

Godfrey was amazed at this declaration, and, after a considerable pause, replied, that he had never heard his parents mention any such debt; that no memorandum or voucher of it was found among his father's papers; and that, in all probability, it must have been discharged long ago, although the commodore, in such a long course of time, and hurry of occupation, might have forgot the repayment. He therefore desired to be excused from accepting what, in his own conscience, he believed was not his due; and complimented the old gentleman upon his being so scrupulously just and honourable.

The soldier's refusal, which was a matter of astonishment to Trunnion, increased his inclination to assist him; and, on pretence of acquitting his own character, he urged his beneficence with such obstinacy, that Gauntlet, afraid of disobliging him, was in a manner compelled to receive a draft for the money, for which he subscribed an ample discharge, and immediately transmitted the order to his mother, whom, at the same time, he informed of the circumstances by which they had so unexpectedly gained this accession of fortune.

Such a piece of news could not fail of being agreeable to Mrs. Gauntlet, who, by the first post, wrote a polite letter of acknowledgment to the commodore, another to her own son, importing that she had already sent the draft to a friend in London, with directions to deposit it in the hands of a certain banker, for the purchase of the first ensigncy to be sold; and she took the liberty of sending a third to Peregrine, couched in very affectionate terms, with a kind postscript, signed by Miss Sophy and his charming Emilia.

This affair being transacted to the satisfaction of all concerned, preparations were set on foot for the departure of our hero, on whom his uncle settled an annuity of eight hundred pounds, being little less than one-half of his whole income. By this time, indeed, the old gentleman could easily afford to alienate such a part of his fortune, because he entertained little or no company, kept few servants, and was remarkably plain and frugal in his housekeeping; Mrs. Trunnion being now some years on the wrong side of fifty, her infirmities began to increase; and though her pride had suffered no diminution, her vanity was altogether subdued by her avarice.

A Swiss valet-de-chambre, who had already made the tour of Europe, was hired for the care of Peregrine's own person; Pipes being ignorant of the French language, as well as otherwise unfit for the office of a fashionable attendant, it was resolved that he should remain in garrison; and his place was immediately supplied by a Parisian lacquey engaged at London for that purpose. Pipes did not seem to relish this disposition of things; and though he made no verbal objections to it, looked remarkably sour at his successor upon his first arrival; but this sullen fit seemed gradually to wear off; and, long before his master's departure, he had recovered his natural tranquillity and unconcern.

CHAPTER XXXI

The two young Gentlemen display their Talents for Gallantry, in the course of which they are involved in a ludicrous Circumstance of Distress, and afterwards take Vengeance on the Author of their Mishap.

MEANWHILE our hero and his new friend, together with honest Jack Hatchway, made daily excursions into the country, visited the gentlemen in the neighbourhood, and frequently accompanied them to the chase; all three being exceedingly caressed on account of their talents, which could accommodate themselves with great facility to the tempers and turns of their entertainers.   The lieutenant was a droll in his way, Peregrine possessed a great fund of sprightliness and good humour, and Godfrey, among his other qualifications, already recited, sung a most excellent song; so that the company of this triumvirate was courted in all parties, whether male or female; and if the hearts of our young gentlemen had not been pre-engaged, they would have met with opportunities in abundance of displaying their address in the art of love; not but that they gave loose to their gallantry without much interesting their affections, and amused themselves with little intrigues, which, in the opinion of a man of pleasure, do not affect his fidelity to the acknowledged sovereign of his soul.

In the midst of these amusements, our hero received an intimation from his sister, that she should be overjoyed to meet him next day, at five o'clock in the afternoon, at the house of her nurse, who lived in a cottage hard by her father's habitation, she being debarred from all opportunity of seeing him in any other place by the severity of her mother, who suspected her inclination.

He accordingly obeyed the summons, and went at the time appointed to the place of rendezvous, where he met this affectionate young lady, who, when he entered the room, ran towards him with all the eagerness of transport, flung her arms about his neck, and shed a flood of tears in his bosom before she could utter one word, except a repetition of "My dear, dear brother!"   He embraced her with all the piety of fraternal tenderness, wept over her in his turn, assured her that this was one of the happiest moments of his life, and kindly thanked her for having resisted the example and disobeyed the injunctions of his mother's unnatural aversion.

He was ravished to find by her conversation, that she possessed a great share of sensibility and prudent reflection; for she lamented the infatuation of her parents with the most filial regret, and expressed such abhorrence and concern at the villainous disposition of her younger brother, as a humane sister may be supposed to have entertained. He made her acquainted with all the circumstances of his own fortune; and, as he supposed she spent her time very disagreeably at home, among characters which must be shockingly distressing, professed a desire of removing her into some other sphere, where she could live with more tranquillity and satisfaction.

She objected to this proposal, as an expedient that would infallibly subject her to the implacable resentment of her mother, whose favour and affection she at present enjoyed but in a very inconsiderable degree; and they had canvassed divers schemes of corresponding for the future, when the voice of Mrs. Pickle was heard at the door.

Miss Julia (that was the young lady's name) finding herself betrayed, was seized with a violent agitation of fear, and Peregrine scarce had time to encourage her with a promise of protection, before the door of the apartment being flung open, this irreconcilable parent rushed in, and, with a furious aspect, flew directly at her trembling daughter, when the son interposing, received the first discharge of her fury.

Her eyes gleamed with all the rage of indignation, which choked up her utterance, and seemed to convulse her whole frame; she twisted her left hand in his hair, and with the other buffeted him about the face till the blood gushed from his nostrils and mouth; while he defended his sister from the cruelty of Gam who assaulted her from another quarter, seeing his brother engaged. This attack lasted several minutes with great violence, till at length Peregrine, finding himself in danger of being overpowered, if he should remain any longer on the defensive, laid his brother on his back; then he disentangled his mother's hand from his own hair, and, having pushed her gently out of the room, bolted the door on the inside; finally, turning to Gam, he threw him out of the window, among a parcel of hogs that fed under it. By this time Julia was almost distracted with terror; she knew she had offended beyond all hope of forgiveness, and from that moment considered herself as an exile from her father's house. In vain did her brother strive to console her with fresh protestations of love and protection; she counted herself extremely miserable in being obliged to endure the eternal resentment of a parent with whom she had hitherto lived, and dreaded the censure of the world, which, from her mother's misrepresentation, she was sensible would condemn her unheard. That she might not, however, neglect any means in her power of averting the storm, she resolved to appease, if possible, her mother's wrath with humiliation, and even appeal to the influence of her father, weak as it was, before she would despair of being forgiven. But the good lady spared her this unnecessary application, by telling her, through the key-hole, that she must never expect to come within her father's door again; for from that hour she renounced her as unworthy of her affection and regard. Julia, weeping bitterly, endeavoured to soften the rigour of this sentence, by the most submissive and reasonable remonstrances; but, as in her vindication she of necessity espoused her elder brother's cause, her endeavours, instead of soothing, served only to exasperate her mother to a higher pitch of indignation, which discharged itself in invectives against Peregrine, whom she reviled with the epithets of a worthless abandoned reprobate.

The youth, hearing these unjust aspersions, trembled with resentment through every limb, assuring the upbraider that he considered her as an object of compassion; "for, without all doubt," said he, "your diabolical rancour must be severely punished by the thorns of your own conscience, which this very instant taxes you with the malice and falsehood of your reproaches. As for my sister, I bless God that you have not been able to infect her with your unnatural prejudice, which because she is too just, too virtuous, too humane to imbibe, you reject her as an alien to your blood, and turn her out unprovided into a barbarous world. But even there your vicious purpose shall be defeated; that same Providence that screened me from the cruelty of your hate shall extend its protection to her, until I shall find it convenient to assert by law that right of maintenance which nature, it seems, hath bestowed upon us in vain. In the meantime, you will enjoy the satisfaction of paying an undivided attention to that darling son, whose amiable qualities have so long engaged and engrossed your love and esteem."

This freedom of expostulation exalted his mother's ire to mere frenzy; she cursed him with the bitterest imprecations, and raved like a bedlamite at the door, which she attempted to burst open. Her efforts were seconded by her favourite son, who denounced vengeance against Peregrine, made furious assaults against the lock, which resisted all their applications, until our hero, espying his friends Gauntlet and Pipes stepping over a stile that stood about a furlong from the window, called them to his assistance; giving them to understand how he was besieged, he desired they would keep off his mother, that he might the more easily secure his sister Julia's retreat. The young soldier entered accordingly, and, posting himself between Mrs. Pickle and the door, gave the signal to his friend, who, lifting up his sister in his arms, carried her safe without the clutches of this she-dragon, while Pipes with his cudgel kept young master at bay.

The mother being thus deprived of her prey, sprung upon Gauntlet like a lioness robbed of her whelps, and he must have suffered sorely in the flesh, had he not prevented her mischievous intent by seizing both her wrists, and so keeping her at due distance. In attempting to disengage herself from his grasp, she struggled with such exertion, and suffered such agony of passion at the same time, that she actually fell into a severe fit, during which she was put to bed, and the confederates retired without further molestation.

In the meantime, Peregrine was not a little perplexed about the disposal of his sister whom he had rescued. He could not endure the thoughts of saddling the commodore with a new expense; and he was afraid of undertaking the charge of Julia, without his benefactor's advice and direction; for the present, however, he carried her to the house of a gentleman in the neighbourhood, whose lady was her godmother, where she was received with great tenderness and condolence; and he purposed to inquire for some creditable house, where she might be genteelly boarded in his absence, resolving to maintain her from the savings of his own allowance, which he thought might very well bear such deduction. But this intention was frustrated by the publication of the whole affair, which was divulged next day, and soon reached the ears of Trunnion, who chid his godson for having concealed the adventure; and, with the approbation of his wife, ordered him to bring Julia forthwith to the garrison. The young gentleman, with tears of gratitude in his eyes, explained his design of maintaining her at his own expense, and earnestly begged that he might not be deprived of that satisfaction. But his uncle was deaf to all his entreaties, and insisted upon her living in the garrison, though for no other reason than that of being company to her aunt, who, he observed, was lost for want of conversation.

Julia was accordingly brought home, and settled under the tuition of Mrs. Trunnion, who, whatever face she might put on the matter, could have dispensed with the society of her niece; though she was not without hope of gratifying her pique to Mrs. Pickle, by the intelligence she would receive from the daughter of that lady's economy and domestic behaviour. The mother herself seemed conscious of this advantage which her sister-in-law had now gained over her, being as much chagrined at the news of Julia's reception in the garrison, as if she had heard of her own husband's death. She even tortured her invention to propagate calumnies against the reputation of her own daughter, whom she slandered in all companies; she exclaimed against the commodore, as an old ruffian, who spirited up a rebellion among her children, and imputed the hospitality of his wife, in countenancing them, to nothing else but her inveterate enmity to their mother, whom they had disobliged. She now insisted, in the most peremptory terms, upon her husband's renouncing all commerce with the old lad of the castle and his adherents; and Mr. Gamaliel, having by this time contracted other friendships, readily submitted to her will, nay, even refused to communicate with the commodore one night, when they happened to meet by accident at the public-house.

CHAPTER XXXII

The Commodore sends a Challenge to Gamaliel, and is imposed upon by a waggish Invention of the Lieutenant, Peregrine, and Gauntlet.

THIS affront Trunnion could by no means digest. He advised with the lieutenant upon the subject; and the result of their consultation was a defiance which the old commander sent to Pickle, demanding that he would meet him at such a place on horseback with a brace of pistols, and give satisfaction for the slight he had put upon him.

Nothing could have afforded more pleasure to Jack than the acceptance of this challenge, which he delivered verbally to Mr. Gamaliel who was called out from the club at Tunley's for that purpose. The nature of this message had an instantaneous effect upon the constitution of the pacific Pickle, whose bowels yearned with apprehension, and underwent such violent agitation on the spot, that one would have thought the operation proceeded from some severe joke of the apothecary which he had swallowed in his beer.

The messenger, despairing of a satisfactory answer, left him in this woeful condition; and being loth to lose any opportunity of raising the laugh against the commodore, went immediately and communicated the whole affair to the young gentlemen, entreating them, for the love of God, to concert some means of bringing old Hannibal into the field. The two friends relished the proposal, and, after some deliberation, it was resolved that Hatchway should tell Trunnion his invitation was accepted by Gamaliel, who would meet him at the place appointed with his second, to-morrow in the twilight, because, if either should fall the other would have the better chance of escaping in the dark; that Godfrey should personate old Pickle's friend, and Peregrine represent his own father, while the lieutenant should take care, in loading the pistols, to keep out the shot, so that no damage might be done in the rencontre.

These circumstances being adjusted, the lieutenant returned to his principal with a most thundering reply from his antagonist, whose courageous behaviour, though it could not intimidate, did not fail to astonish the commodore, who ascribed it to the spirit of his wife, which had inspired him. Trunnion that instant desired his counsellor to prepare his cartridge-box, and order the quietest horse in the stable to be kept ready saddled for the occasion; his eye seemed to lighten with alacrity and pleasure at the prospect of smelling gunpowder once more before his death; and when Jack advised him to make his will, in case of accident, he rejected his counsel with disdain, saying, "What! dost think that Hawser Trunnion, who has stood the fire of so many floating batteries, runs any risk from the lousy pops of a landman? Thou shalt see, thou shalt see how I shall make him lower his topsails."

Next day Peregrine and the soldier provided themselves with horses at the public-house, from whence, at the destined hour, they rode to the field of battle, each of them being muffled in a greatcoat, which, with the dimness of the light, effectually shielded them from the knowledge of the one-eyed commander, who having taken horse on pretence of enjoying the fresh air, soon appeared with Hatchway in his rear. When they came within sight of each other, the seconds advanced, in order to divide the ground, and regulate the measures of the combat; when it was determined by mutual consent, that two pistols should be discharged on each side, and that, if neither should prove decisive, recourse must be had to the broadswords, in order to ascertain the victory. These articles being settled, the opponents rode forward to their respective stations, when Peregrine, cocking his pistol, and presenting, counterfeited his father's voice, bidding Trunnion take care of his remaining eye. The commodore took his advice, being unwilling to hazard his daylight, and very deliberately opposed the patched side of his face to the muzzle of his antagonist's piece, desiring him to do his duty without further jaw. The young man accordingly fired, and the distance being small, the wad of his pistol took place with a smart stroke on the forehead of Trunnion, who, mistaking it for a ball, which he thought was lodged in his brain, spurred up his steed in a state of desperation towards his antagonist, and holding his piece within two yards of his body, let it off without any regard to the laws of battle. Surprised and enraged to see it had made no impression, he hallooed in a terrible tone, "O d—n ye, you have got your netting stuffed, I see"; and advancing, discharged his second pistol so near his godson's head, that, had he not been defended by his greatcoat, the powder must have scorched his face.

Having thus thrown away his fire, he remained at the mercy of Peregrine, who, clapping the piece he had in reserve to his head, commanded him to beg his life, and ask pardon for his presumption. The commodore made no reply to this imperious injunction, but dropping his pistol, and unsheathing his broadsword in an instant, attacked our hero with such incredible agility, that, if he had not made shift to ward off the stroke with his piece, the adventure, in all likelihood, would have turned out a very tragical joke. Peregrine finding it would be in vain for him to think of drawing his weapon, or of standing on the defensive against this furious aggressor, very fairly clapped spurs to his nag, and sought his safety in flight. Trunnion pursued him with infinite eagerness, and his steed being the better of the two, would have overtaken the fugitive to his peril, had he not been unfortunately encountered by the boughs of a tree, that happened to stand on his blind side, and incommoded him so much, that he was fain to quit his sword, and lay hold on the mane, in order to maintain his seat. Perry perceiving his disaster, wheeled about, and now finding leisure to produce his weapon, turned upon his disarmed foe, brandishing his Ferrara, threatening to make him shorter by the head, if he would not immediately crave quarter and yield. There was nothing farther from the intention of the old gentleman than such submission, which he flatly refused to pay, alleging that he had already compelled his enemy to clap on all his sails, and that his own present misfortune was owing to accident, all one as if a ship should be attacked, after she had been obliged to heave her guns overboard in a storm.

Before Peregrine had time to answer this remonstrance, the

lieutenant interposed, and, taking cognisance of the case, established a truce, until he and the other second should discuss and decide upon the merits of the cause. They accordingly retired to a small distance, and, after having conferred a few minutes, Hatchway returned, and pronounced the commodore vanquished by the chance of war.

Never was rage more transported than that which took possession of old Hannibal when he heard the sentence. It was some time before he could utter aught, except the reproachful expression, *You lie!* — which he repeated more than twenty times, in a sort of delirious insensibility. When he recovered the further use of speech, he abused the arbitrators with such bitter invectives, renouncing their sentence, and appealing to another trial, that the confederates began to repent of having carried the joke so far; and Peregrine, in order to appease his choler, owned himself overcome.

This acknowledgment calmed the tumult of his wrath, though he could not for some days forgive the lieutenant; and the two young gentlemen rode back to Tunley's, while Hatchway, taking the commodore's horse by the bridle, reconducted him to his mansion, growling all the way to Jack for his unjust and unfriendly decree; though he could not help observing, as how he had made his words good, in making his adversary strike his topsails. "And yet," said he, "before God! I think the fellow's head is made of a woolpack; for my shot rebounded from his face like a wad of spun yarn from the side of a ship. But if so be that son of a bitch of a tree hadn't come athwart my weather-bow, d'ye see, I'll be d—ed if I hadn't snapt his main-yard in the slings, and mayhap let out his bulge-water into the bargain." He seemed particularly vain of this exploit, which dwelt upon his imagination, and was cherished as the child of his old age; for though he could not with decency rehearse it to the young men, and his wife, at supper, he gave shrewd hints of his own manhood, even at these years, and attested Hatchway as a voucher for his mettle; while the triumvirate, diverted by his vanity, enjoyed in secret the success of their imposition.

CHAPTER XXXIII

Peregrine takes his Leave of his Aunt and Sister—Sets out from the Garrison—Parts with his Uncle and Hatchway on the Road, and, with his Governor, arrives in safety at Dover.

THIS, however, was the last effort of invention which they practised upon him; and everything being now prepared for the departure of his godson, that hopeful youth, in two days, took leave of all his friends in the neighbourhood. He was closeted two whole hours with his aunt, who enriched him with many pious advices, recapitulated all the benefits which, through her means, had been conferred upon him since his infancy, cautioned him against the temptations of lewd women, who bring many a man to a morsel of bread; laid strict injunctions upon him to live in the fear of the Lord, and the true Protestant faith, to eschew quarrels and contentions, to treat Mr. Jolter with reverence and regard, and, above all things, to abstain from the beastly sin of drunkenness, which exposed a man to the scorn and contempt of his fellow-creatures, and, by divesting him of reason and reflection, rendered him fit for all manner of vice and debauchery. She recommended to him economy, and the care of his health—bade him remember the honour of his family; and, in all the circumstances of his behaviour, assured him, that he might always depend upon the friendship and generosity of the commodore. Finally, presenting him with her own picture, set in gold, and a hundred guineas from her privy purse, she embraced him affectionately, and wished him all manner of happiness and prosperity.

Being thus kindly dismissed by Mrs. Trunnion, he locked himself up with his sister Julia, whom he admonished to cultivate her aunt with the most complaisant and respectful attention, without stooping to any circumstance of submission that she should judge unworthy of her practice; he protested, that his chief study should be to make her amends for the privilege she had forfeited by her affection for him; entreated her to enter into no engagement without his knowledge and approbation; put into her hand the purse which he had received from his aunt, to defray her pocket expenses in his absence, and parted from her, not without tears, after she had for some minutes hung about his neck, kissing him, and weeping in the most pathetic silence.

Having performed these duties of affection and consanguinity overnight, he went to bed, and was, by his own direction, called at four o'clock in the morning, when he found the post-chaise, coach, and riding-horses ready at the gate, his friends Gauntlet and Hatchway on foot, the commodore himself almost dressed, and every servant in the garrison assembled in the yard to wish him a good journey. Our hero shook each of these humble friends by the hand, tipping them at the same time with marks of his bounty; and was very much surprised when he could not perceive his old attendant Pipes among the number. When he expressed his wonder at this disrespectful omission of Tom, some of those present ran to his chamber, in order to give him a call, but his hammock and room were both deserted; and they soon returned with an account of his having eloped. Peregrine was disturbed at this information, believing that the fellow had taken some desperate course in consequence of his being dismissed from his service, and began to wish that he had indulged his inclination by retaining him still about his person. However, as there was now no other remedy, he recommended him strenuously to the particular favour and distinction of his uncle and Hatchway, in case he should appear again; and, as he went out of the gate, was saluted by three cheers by all the domestics in the family.

The commodore, Gauntlet, lieutenant, Peregrine, and Jolter went into the coach together, that they might enjoy each other's conversation as much as possible, resolving to breakfast at an inn upon the road, where Trunnion and Hatchway intended to bid our adventurer farewell; the valet-de-chambre got into the post-chaise, the French lacquey rode one horse and led another; one of the valets of the garrison mounted at the back of the coach, and thus the cavalcade set out on the road to Dover. As the commodore could not bear the fatigue of jolting, they travelled at an easy pace during the first stage, so that the old gentleman had an opportunity of communicating his exhortations to his godson, with regard to his conduct abroad; he advised him, now that he was going into foreign parts, to be upon his guard against the fair weather of the French politesse, which was no more to be trusted than a whirlpool at sea. He observed, that many young men had gone to Paris with good cargoes of sense, and returned with a great deal of canvas, and no ballast at all; whereby they became crank all the days of their lives, and sometimes carried their keels above water. He desired Mr. Jolter to keep his pupil out of the clutches of those sharking priests, who lie in wait to make converts of all young strangers;

and, in a particular manner, cautioned the youth against carnal conversation with the Parisian dames, who, he understood, were no better than gaudy fireships, ready primed with death and destruction.

Peregrine listened with great respect, thanking him for his kind admonitions, which he faithfully promised to observe. They halted and breakfasted at the end of the stage, where Jolter provided himself with a horse; and the commodore settled the method of corresponding with his nephew. The minute of parting being arrived, the old commander wrung his godson by the hand, saying, "I wish thee a prosperous voyage, and good cheer, my lad; my timbers are now a little crazy, d'ye see; and God knows if I shall keep afloat till such time as I see thee again; but howsomever, hap what will, thou wilt find thyself in a condition to keep in the line with the best of thy fellows." He then reminded Gauntlet of his promise to call at the garrison in his return from Dover, and imparted something in a whisper to the governor, while Jack Hatchway, unable to speak, pulled his hat over his eyes, and, squeezing Peregrine by the hand, gave him an iron pistol of curious workmanship, as a memorial of his friendship. Our youth, who was not unmoved on this occasion, received the pledge, which he acknowledged with the present of a silver tobacco-box, bought for that purpose; and the two lads of the castle getting into the coach, were driven homewards in a state of silent dejection.

Godfrey and Peregrine seated themselves in the post-chaise, and Jolter, the valet-de-chambre, and lacquey bestriding their beasts, they proceeded for the place of their destination, at which they arrived in safety that same night, and bespoke a passage in the packet-boat, which was to sail next day.

CHAPTER XXXIV

He adjusts the Method of his Correspondence with Gauntlet—Meets by Accident with an Italian Charlatan, and a certain Apothecary, who proves to be a noted Character.

THERE the two friends adjusted the articles of their future correspondence; and Peregrine having written a letter to his mistress, wherein he renewed his former vows of eternal fidelity, it was entrusted to the care of her brother; while Mr. Jolter, at the desire of his pupil, provided an elegant supper, and some excellent burgundy, that they might spend this eve of his departure with the greater enjoyment.

Things being thus disposed, and a servant employed in laying the cloth, their ears were all of a sudden invaded by a strange tumultuous noise in the next room, occasioned by the overthrow of tables, chairs, and glasses, with odd unintelligible exclamations in broken French, and a jargon of threats in the Welsh dialect. Our young gentlemen ran immediately into the apartment from whence this clamour seemed to proceed, and found a thin, meagre, swarthy figure, gasping in all the agony of fear, under the hands of a squat, thick, hard-featured man, who collared him with great demonstrations of wrath, saying, "If you was as mighty a magician as Owen Glendower, or the witch of Entor, look you, ay, or as Paul Beor himself, I will meke pold, by the assistance of Cot, and in his Majesty's naam, to seize and secure, and confine and confront you, until such time as you suffer and endure and undergo the pains and penalties of the law, for your diabolical practices. Shentlements," added he, turning to our adventurers, "I take you to witness that I protest and assert and avow, that this person is as pig a necromancer as you would desire to behold; and I supplicate and beseech and entreat of you, that he may be prought pefore his petters, and compelled to give an account of his compact and commerce with the imps of darkness, look you; for as I am a Christian soul, and hope for joyful resurrection, I have this plessed evening seen him perform such things as could not be done without the aid and instruction and connivance of the tevil."

Gauntlet seemed to enter into the sentiments of this Welsh reformer, and actually laid hold on the delinquent's shoulder, crying, "D—n the rascal! I'll lay any wager that he's a Jesuit, for none of his order travel without a familiar." But Peregrine, who looked upon the affair in another point of view, interposed in behalf of the stranger, whom he freed from his aggressors, observing that there was no occasion to use violence, and asked in French what he had done to incur the censure of the informer. The poor foreigner, more dead than alive, answered that he was an Italian charlatan, who had practised with some reputation in Padua, until he had the misfortune to attract the notice of the Inquisition, by exhibiting certain wonderful performances by his skill in natural knowledge, which that tribunal considered as the effects of sorcery, and persecuted him accordingly; so that he had been fain to make a precipitate retreat into France, where not finding his account in his talents, he was now arrived in England, with a view of practising his art in London; and that, in consequence of a specimen which he had given to a company below, the choleric gentleman had followed him upstairs to his own apartment, and assaulted him in that inhospitable manner. He therefore earnestly begged that our hero would take him under his protection; and if he entertained the least suspicion of his employing preternatural means in the operations of his art, he would freely communicate all the secrets in his possession.

The youth dispelled his apprehension, by assuring him that he was in no danger of suffering for his art in England, where, if ever he should be questioned by the zeal of superstitious individuals, he had nothing to do but to appeal to the next justice of the peace, who would immediately quit him of the charge, and punish his accusers for their impertinence and discretion.

He then told Gauntlet and the Welshman that the stranger had a good action against them for an assault, by virtue of an act of parliament, which makes it criminal for any person to accuse another of sorcery and witchcraft, these idle notions being now justly exploded by all sensible men. Mr. Jolter, who had by this time joined the company, could not help signifying his dissent from this opinion of his pupil, which he endeavoured to invalidate by the authority of Scripture, quotations from the fathers, and the confession of many wretches who suffered death for having carried on correspondence with evil spirits, together with the evidence of *Satan's Invisable World*, and Moreton's *History of Witchcraft*.

The soldier corroborated these testimonies by facts that had happened within the sphere of his own knowledge; and, in particular, mentioned the case of an old woman in the parish in which he was born, who used to transform herself into the shapes of sundry animals, and was at last killed by small shot in the character of a hare. The Welshman thus supported, expressed his surprise at hearing that the legislature had shown such tenderness for criminals of so dark a hue; and offered to prove, by undeniable instances, that there was not a mountain in Wales which had not been in his memory the scene of necromancy and witchcraft. "Wherefore," said he, "I am assuredly more than apove astonished and confounded and concerned, that the parliament of Great Pritain should in their great wisdoms, and their prudence, and their penetration, give countenance and encouragement, look you, to the works of darkness and the empire of Pelzepup; ofer and apove the evidence of holy writ, and those writers who have been quoted by that aggurate and learned shentleman, we are informed by profane history of the pribbles and pranks of the old serpent, in the bortents and oracles of antiquity; as you will find in that most excellent historian Bolypius, and Titus Lisius; ay, and moreofer, in the Commentaries of Julius Cæsar himself, who, as the 'ole world knows, was a most famous, and a most faliant, and a most wise, and a most prudent, and a most fortunate chiftan, and a most renowned orator; ay, and a most elegant writer to boot."

Peregrine did not think proper to enter the lists of dispute with three such obstinate antagonists; but contented himself with saying, that he believed it would be no difficult matter to impugn the arguments they had advanced, though he did not find himself at all disposed to undertake the task, which must of course break in upon the evening's entertainment. He therefore invited the Italian to supper, and asked the same favour of his accuser, who seemed to have something curious and characteristic in his manner and disposition, resolving to make himself an eye-witness of those surprising feats, which had given offence to the choleric Briton. This scrupulous gentleman thanked our hero for his courtesy, but declined communicating with the stranger, until his character should be further explained; upon which his inviter, after some conversation with the charlatan, assured him that he would himself undertake for the innocence of his art; and then he was prevailed upon to favour them with his company.

In the course of the conversation, Peregrine learnt that the Welshman was a surgeon of Canterbury, who had been called into a consultation at Dover, and, understanding that his name was Morgan, took the liberty of asking if he was not the person so respectfully mentioned in the *Adventures of Roderick Random*. Mr. Morgan assumed a look of gravity and importance at this interrogation, and, screwing up his mouth, answered, "Mr. Random, my goot sir, I believe upon my conscience and salfation, is my very goot frient and well-wisher; and he and I have been companions, and messmates, and fellow-sufferers, look you; but nevertheless, for all that, peradventure he hath not pehaved with so much complaisance, and affability, and respect, as I might have expected from him; pecause he hath revealed, and tivulged, and published our private affairs, without my knowledge, and privity, and consent; but as Cot is my Saviour, I think he had no evil intention in his pelly: and though there be certain persons, look you, who, as I am told, take upon them to laugh at his descriptions of my person, deportment and conversation,

I do affirm and maintain, and insist with my heart, and my ploot, and my soul, that those persons are no petter than ignorant asses, and that they know not how to discern, and distinguish, and define true ridicule, or, as Aristotle calls it, the *to geloion*, no more, look you, than a herd of mountain goats; for I will make pold to observe, and I hope this goot company will be of the same opinion, that there is nothing said of me in that performance which is unworthy of a Christian and a shentleman."

Our young gentleman and his friends acquiesced in the justness of his observation. Peregrine particularly assured him, that, from reading the book, he had conceived the utmost regard and veneration for his character; and that he thought himself extremely fortunate in having this opportunity of enjoying his conversation. Morgan, not a little proud of such advances from a person of Peregrine's appearance, returned the compliment with a profusion of civility, and, in the warmth of acknowledgment, expressed a desire of seeing him and his company at his house in Canterbury: "I will not pretend or presume, kind sir," said he, "to entertain you according to your merits and deserts; but you shall be as welcome to my poor cottage, and my wife and family, as the Prince of Wales himself; and it shall go hard, if, one way or other, I do not find ways and means of making you confess that there is some goot fellowship in an ancient Priton. For, though I am no better than a simple apothecary, I have as goot ploot circulating in my veins as any he in the country (and I can describe and delineate and demonstrate my pedigree to the satisfaction of the 'ole 'orld); and moreover, by Cot's goot providence and assistance, I can afford to treat my friend with a joint of goot mutton, and a pottle of excellent wine, and no tradesman can peard me with a bill." He was congratulated on his happy situation, and assured that our youth would visit him on his return from France, provided he should take Canterbury on his route.

As Peregrine manifested an inclination of being acquainted with the state of his affairs, he very complaisantly satisfied his curiosity, by giving him to know, that his spouse had left off breeding, after having blessed him with two boys and a girl, who were still alive and well; that he lived in good esteem with his neighbours, and by his practice, which was considerably extended immediately after the publication of *Roderick Random*, had saved some thousand pounds. He had begun to think of retiring among his own relations in Glamorganshire, though his wife had made objections to this proposal, and opposed the execution of it with such obstinacy, that he had been at infinite pains in asserting his own prerogative, by convincing her, both from reason and example, that he was king and priest in his own family, and that she owed the most implicit submission to his will. He likewise informed the company, that he had lately seen his friend Roderick, who had come from London on purpose to visit him, after having gained his law-suit with Mr. Tophall, who was obliged to pay Narcissa's fortune; that Mr. Random, in all appearance, led a very happy life in the conversation of his father and bedfellow, by whom he enjoyed a son and daughter; and that Morgan had received, in a present from him, a piece of very fine linen, of his wife's own making, several kits of salmon and two casks of pickled pork, the most delicate he had ever tasted, together with a barrel of excellent herrings for salma-gundy, which he knew to be his favourite dish

This topic of conversation being discussed, the Italian was desired to exhibit a specimen of his art, and in a few minutes conducted the company into the next room, where, to their great astonishment and affright, they beheld a thousand ser-pents winding along the ceiling. Morgan, struck with this phenomenon, which he had not seen before, began to utter exorcisms with great devotion, Mr. Jolter ran terrified out of the room, Gauntlet drew his hanger, and Peregrine himself was disconcerted. The operator, perceiving their confusion, desired them to retire, and calling them back in an instant, there was not a viper to be seen. He raised their admiration by sundry other performances, and the Welshman's former opinion and abhorrence of his character began to recur, when, in consideration of the civility with which he had been treated, this Italian imparted to them all the methods by which he had acted such wonders, that were no other than the effects of natural causes curiously combined; so that Morgan became a convert to his skill, asked pardon for the suspicion he had entertained, and invited the stranger to pass a few days with him at Canterbury. The scruples of Godfrey and Jolter were removed at the same time, and Peregrine testified his approbation by a handsome gratuity which he bestowed upon their entertainer.

The evening being spent in this sociable manner, every man retired to his respective chamber, and next morning they break-fasted together, when Morgan declared he would stay till he should see our hero fairly embarked, that he might have the pleasure of Mr. Gauntlet's company to his own habitation. Meanwhile, by the skipper's advice, the servants were ordered to carry a store of wine and provision on board, in case of accident; and, as the packet-boat could not sail before one o'clock, the company walked up hill to visit the castle, where they saw the sword of Julius Cæsar, and Queen Elizabeth's pocket-pistol, repeated Shakespeare's description, while they surveyed the chalky cliffs on each side, and cast their eyes towards the city of Calais, that was obscured by a thick cloud, which did not much regale their eyesight, because it seemed to portend foul weather.

Having viewed everything remarkable in this place, they returned to the pier, where, after the compliments of parting, and an affectionate embrace between the two young gentlemen, Peregrine and his governor stepped aboard, the sails were hoisted, and they went to sea with a fair wind, while Godfrey, Morgan, and the conjuror walked back to the inn, from whence they set out for Canterbury before dinner.

CHAPTER XXXV

He embarks for France—Is overtaken by a Storm—Is surprised with the Appearance of Pipes—Lands at Calais, and has an Affray with the Officers of the Custom-house.

SCARCE had the vessel proceeded two leagues on the passage, when the wind shifting, blew directly in their teeth; so that they were obliged to haul upon a wind, and alter their course. The sea running pretty high at the same time, our hero, who was below in his cabin, began to be squeamish, and, in consequence of the skipper's advice, went upon the deck for the comfort of his stomach; while the governor, experienced in these disasters, slipt into bed, where he lay at his ease, amusing himself with a treatise on the cycloid, with algebraical demonstrations, which never failed to engage his imagination in the most agreeable manner.

In the meantime the wind increased to a very hard gale, the vessel pitched with great violence, the sea washed over the decks, the master was alarmed, the crew were confounded, the passengers were overwhelmed with sickness and fear, and universal distraction ensued. In the midst of this uproar, Peregrine holding fast by the taffrill, and looking ruefully ahead, the countenance of Pipes presented itself to his astonished view, rising as it were from the hold of the ship. At first he imagined it was a fear-formed shadow of his own brain, though he did not remain long in this terror, but plainly perceived that it was no other than the real person of Thomas, who, jumping on the quarter-deck, took charge of the helm, and dictated to the sailors, with as much authority as if he had been commander of the ship. The skipper looked upon him as an angel sent to his assistance, and the crew, soon discovering him to be a thorough-bred seaman, notwithstanding his livery frock, obeyed his orders with such alacrity, that in a little time the confusion vanished, and every necessary step was taken to weather the gale.

Our young gentleman immediately conceived the meaning of Tom's appearance on board, and, when the tumult was a little subsided, went up, and encouraged him to exert himself for the preservation of the ship, promising to take him again into his service, from which he should never be dismissed, except at his own desire. This assurance had a surprising effect upon Pipes, who, though he made no manner of reply, thrust the helm into the master's hand, saying, "Here, you old bumboat woman, take hold of the tiller, and keep her thus, boy, thus"; and skipped about the vessel, trimming the sails, and managing the ropes with such agility and skill, that everybody on deck stood amazed at his dexterity.

Mr. Jolter was far from being unconcerned at the uncommon motion of the vessel, the singing of the wind, and the uproar which he heard above him; he looked towards the cabin door with the most fearful expectation, in hope of seeing some person who could give some account of the weather, and what was doing upon deck; but not a soul appeared, and he was too well acquainted with the disposition of his own bowels to make the least alteration in his attitude. When he had lain a good while in all the agony of suspense, the boy tumbled headlong into his apartment with such noise, that he believed the mast had gone by the board, and starting upright in his bed, asked, with all the symptoms of horror, what was the cause of that disturbance? The boy, half-stunned by his fall, answered in a dolorous tone, "I'm come to put up the dead-lights." At the mention of dead-lights, the meaning of which he did not understand, the poor governor's heart died within him, and he shivered with despair. His recollection forsaking him, he fell upon his knees in the bed, and fixing his eyes upon the book which was in his hand, began to pronounce aloud with great fervour, "The time of a complete oscillation in the cycloid, is to the time in which a body would fall through the axis of the cycloid DV, as the circumference of a circle to its diameter."

He would in all likelihood have proceeded with the demonstration of this proposition, had he not been seized with such a qualm, as compelled him to drop the book, and accommodate himself to the emergency of his distemper; he therefore stretched himself at full length, and, putting up ejaculations to heaven, began to prepare himself for his latter end, when all of a sudden the noise above was intermitted; and, as he could not conceive the cause of this tremendous silence, he imagined that either the men were washed overboard, or that, despairing of safety, they had ceased to oppose the tempest. While he was harrowed by this miserable uncertainty, which, however, was not altogether unenlightened by some scattered rays of hope, the master entered the cabin; then he asked, with a voice half extinguished by fear, how matters went upon deck? and the skipper, with a large bottle of brandy applied to his mouth, answered in a hollow tone, "All's over now, master." Upon which, Mr. Jolter, giving himself over for lost, exclaimed with the utmost horror, "Lord have mercy upon us! Christ have mercy upon us!" and repeated this supplication as it were mechanically, until the master undeceived him, by explaining the meaning of what he had said, and assuring him that the squall was over.

Such a sudden transition from fear to joy occasioned a violent agitation both in his mind and body; and it was a full quarter of an hour before he recovered the right use of his organs. By this time the weather cleared up, the wind began to blow again from the right corner, and the spires of Calais appeared at the distance of five leagues; so that the countenances of all on board were lighted up with joyous expectation; and Peregrine, venturing to go down into the cabin, comforted his governor with an account of the happy turn in their affairs.

Jolter, transported with the thoughts of a speedy landing, began to launch out in praise of that country for which they were bound. He observed, that France was the land of politeness and hospitality, which were conspicuous in the behaviour of all ranks and degrees, from the peer to the peasant; that a gentleman and a foreigner, far from being insulted and imposed upon by the lower class of people, as in England, was treated with the utmost reverence, candour, and respect; that their fields were fertile, their climate pure and healthy, their farmers rich and industrious, and the subjects in general the happiest of men. He would have prosecuted this favourite theme still farther, had not his pupil been obliged to run on deck, in consequence of certain warnings he received from his stomach.

The skipper seeing his condition, very honestly reminded him of the cold ham and fowls, with a basket of wine, which he had ordered to be sent on board, and asked if he would have the cloth laid below. He could not have chosen a more seasonable opportunity of manifesting his own disinterestedness. Peregrine made wry faces at the mention of food, bidding him, for Christ's sake, talk no more on that subject. He then descended into the cabin, and put the same question to Mr. Jolter, who, he knew, entertained the same abhorrence for his proposal; and, meeting with the like reception from him, went between decks, and repeated his courteous proffer to the valet-de-chambre and lacquey, who lay sprawling in all the pangs of a double evacuation, and rejected his civility with the most horrible loathing. Thus baffled in all his kind endeavours, he ordered his boy to secure the provision in one of his own lockers, according to the custom of the ship.

It being low water when they arrived on the French coast, the vessel could not enter the harbour, and they were obliged to bring to, and wait for a boat, which in less than half an hour came alongside from the shore. Mr. Jolter now came upon deck, and snuffing up the French air with symptoms of infinite satisfaction, asked of the boatmen (with the friendly appellation of *mes enfans*) what they demanded for transporting him and his pupil, with their baggage, to the pier. But how was he disconcerted, when those polite, candid, reasonable watermen demanded a louis d'or for that service! Peregrine, with a sarcastic sneer, observed, that he already began to perceive the justice of his encomiums on the French; and the disappointed governor could say nothing in his own vindication, but that they were debauched by their intercourse with the inhabitants of Dover. His pupil, however, was so much offended at their extortion, that he absolutely refused to employ them, even when they abated one-half in their demand, and swore he would stay on board till the packet should be able to enter the harbour, rather than encourage such imposition.

The master, who in all probability had some sort of fellow-feeling with the boatmen, in vain represented, that he could not with safety lie to, or anchor upon a lee-shore; our hero, having consulted Pipes, answered, that he had hired his vessel to transport him to Calais, and that he would oblige him to perform what he had undertaken.

The skipper, very much mortified at this peremptory reply, which was not over and above agreeable to Mr. Jolter, dismissed the boat, notwithstanding the solicitations and condescension of the watermen. Running a little farther in shore, they came to an anchor, and waited till there was water enough to float them over the bar. Then they stood into the harbour, and our gentleman, with his attendants and baggage, were landed on the pier by the sailors, whom he liberally rewarded for their trouble.

He was immediately plied by a great number of porters, who, like so many hungry wolves, laid hold on his luggage, and began to carry it off piecemeal, without his order or direction. Incensed at this officious insolence, he commanded them to desist with many oaths and opprobrious terms that his anger suggested; and, perceiving that one of them did not seem to pay any regard to what he said, but marched off with his burden, he snatched a cudgel out of his lacquey's hand, and, overtaking the fellow in a twinkling, brought him to the ground with one blow. He was instantly surrounded by the whole congregation of this *canaille*, who resented the injury which their brother had sustained, and would have taken immediate satisfaction of the aggressor, had not Pipes, seeing his master involved, brought the whole crew to his assistance, and exerted himself so manfully, that the enemy were obliged to retreat, with many marks of defeat, and menaces of interesting the commandant in their quarrel. Jolter, who knew and dreaded the power of the French governor, began to shake with apprehension, when he heard their repeated threats; but they durst not apply to this magistrate, who, upon a fair representation of the case, would have punished them severely for their rapacious and insolent behaviour. Peregrine, without further molestation, availed himself of his own attendants, who shouldered his baggage, and followed him to the gate, where they were stopped by the sentinels, until their names should be registered.

Mr. Jolter, who had undergone this examination before, resolved to profit by his experience, and cunningly represented his pupil as a young English lord. This intimation, supported by the appearance of his equipage, was no sooner communicated to the officer, than he turned out the guard, and ordered his soldiers to rest upon their arms, while his lordship passed in great state to the "Lion d'Argent," where he took up his lodgings for the night, resolving to set out for Paris next morning in a post-chaise.

The governor triumphed greatly in this piece of complaisance and respect with which they had been honoured, and resumed his beloved topic of discourse, in applauding the method and subordination of the French government, which was better calculated for maintaining order, and protecting the people, than any constitution upon earth. Of their courteous attention to strangers, there needed no other proof than the compliment which had been paid to them, together with the governor's connivance at Peregrine's employing his own servants in carrying the baggage to the inn, contrary to the privilege of the inhabitants.

While he expatiated with a remarkable degree of self-indulgence on this subject, the valet-de-chambre coming into the room, interrupted his harangue, by telling his master that their trunks and portmanteaus must be carried to the custom-house, in order to be searched and sealed with lead, which must remain untouched until their arrival at Paris.

Peregrine made no objection to this practice, which was in itself reasonable enough; but when he understood that the gate was besieged by another multitude of porters, who insisted upon their right of carrying the goods, and also of fixing their own price, he absolutely refused to comply with their demand. Nay, he chastised some of the most clamorous among them with his foot, and told them, that if their custom-house officers had a mind to examine his baggage, they might come to the inn for that purpose. The valet-de-chambre was abashed at this boldness of his master's behaviour, which the lacquey, shrugging up his shoulders, observed was *bien à l'Angloise;* while the governor represented it as an indignity to the whole nation, and endeavoured to persuade his pupil to comply with the custom of the place. But Peregrine's natural haughtiness of disposition hindered him from giving ear to Jolter's wholesome advice; and, in less than half an hour, they observed a file of musketeers marching up to the gate. At sight of this detachment the tutor trembled, the valet grew pale, and the lacquey crossed himself; but our hero, without exhibiting any other symptoms than those of indignation, met them on the threshold, and, with a ferocious air, demanded their business. The corporal, who commanded the file, answered with great deliberation, that he had orders to convey his baggage to the custom-house; and seeing the trunks standing in the entry, placed his men between them and the owner, while the porters that followed took them up, and proceeded to the Douane without opposition.

Pickle was not mad enough to dispute the authority of this message; but, in order to gall, and specify his contempt for those who brought it, he called aloud to his valet, desiring him, in

French, to accompany his things, and see that none of his linens and effects should be stolen by the searchers. The corporal, mortified at this satirical insinuation, darted a look of resentment at the author, as if he had been interested for the glory of his nation, and told him, that he could perceive he was a stranger in France, or else he would have saved himself the trouble of such a needless precaution.

CHAPTER XXXVI

He makes a fruitless Attempt in Gallantry—Departs for Boulogne, where he spends the Evening with certain English Exiles.

HAVING thus yielded to the hand of power, he inquired if there was any other English company in the house; when, understanding that a gentleman and lady lodged in the next apartment, and had bespoke a post-chaise for Paris, he ordered Pipes to ingratiate himself with their footman, and, if possible, learn their names and condition, while he and Mr. Jolter, attended by the lacquey, took a turn round the ramparts, and viewed the particulars of the fortification.

Tom was so very successful in his inquiry, that when his master returned, he was able to give him a satisfactory account of his fellow-lodgers, in consequence of having treated his brother with a bottle of wine. The people in question were a gentleman and his lady lately arrived from England in their way to Paris. The husband was a man of good fortune, who had been a libertine in his youth, and a professed declaimer against matrimony. He wanted neither sense nor experience, and piqued himself in particular upon his art of avoiding the snares of the female sex, in which he pretended to be deeply versed. But, notwithstanding all his caution and skill, he had lately fallen a sacrifice to the attractions of an oyster wench, who had found means to decoy him into the bands of wedlock; and, in order to evade the compliments and congratulations of his friends and acquaintance, he had come so far on a tour to Paris, where he intended to initiate his spouse in the beau monde. In the meantime he chose to live upon the reserve, because her natural talents had as yet received but little cultivation; and he had not the most implicit confidence in her virtue and discretion, which, it seems, had like to have yielded to the addresses of an officer at Canterbury, who had made shift to insinuate himself into her acquaintance and favour.

Peregrine's curiosity being inflamed by this information, he lounged about the yard, in hopes of seeing the Dulcinea who had captivated the old bachelor; and at length, observing her at a window, took the liberty of bowing to her with great respect. She returned the compliment with a curtsey, and appeared so decent in her dress and manner, that, unless he had been previously informed of her former life and conversation, he never would have dreamed that her education was different from that of other ladies of fashion; so easy is it to acquire that external deportment on which people of condition value themselves so much. Not but that Mr. Pickle pretended to distinguish a certain vulgar audacity in her countenance, which, in a lady of birth and fortune, would have passed for an agreeable vivacity that enlivens the aspect, and gives poignancy to every feature; but as she possessed a pair of fine eyes, and a clear complexion overspread with the glow of health, which never fails of recommending the owner, he could not help gazing at her with desire, and forming the design of making a conquest of her heart. With this view he sent his compliments to her husband, whose name was Hornbeck, with an intimation, that he proposed to set out next day for Paris, and as he understood that he was resolved upon the same journey, he should be extremely glad of his company on the road, if he was not better engaged. Hornbeck, who in all probability did not choose to accommodate his wife with a squire of our hero's appearance, sent a civil answer to his message, professing infinite mortification at his being unable to embrace the favour of this kind offer, by reason of the indisposition of his wife, who, he was afraid, would not be in a condition for some days to bear the fatigue of travelling.

This rebuff, which Peregrine ascribed to the husband's jealousy, stifled his project in embryo; he ordered his French servant to take a place for himself in the diligence, where all his luggage was stowed, except a small trunk with some linen and other necessaries, that was fixed upon the post-chaise which they hired of the landlord; and early next morning he and Mr. Jolter departed from Calais, attended by his valet-de-chambre and Pipes on horseback. They proceeded without any accident as far as Boulogne, where they breakfasted, and visited old Father Graham, a Scottish gentleman of the governor's acquaintance, who had lived as a Capuchin in that place for the space of three score years, and during that period conformed to all the austerities of the order with the most rigorous exactness; being equally remarkable for the frankness of his conversation, the humanity of his disposition, and the simplicity of his manners. From Boulogne they took their departure about noon, and, as they proposed to sleep at Abbeville, commanded the postillion to drive with extraordinary speed. Perhaps it was well for his cattle that the axle-tree gave way, and the chaise of course overturned, before they had travelled one-third part of the stage.

This accident compelled them to return to the place from whence they had set out, and as they could not procure another convenience, they found themselves under the necessity of staying till their chaise could be refitted. Understanding that this operation would detain them a whole day, our young gentleman had recourse to his patience, and demanded to know what they would have for dinner; the garçon or waiter thus questioned, vanished in a moment, and immediately they were surprised with the appearance of a strange figure, which, from the extravagance of its dress and gesticulation, Peregrine mistook for a madman of the growth of France. This phantom, which, by the bye, happened to be no other than the cook, was a tall, long-legged, meagre, swarthy fellow, that stooped very much; his cheek-bones were remarkably raised, his nose bent into the shape and size of a powder-horn, and the sockets of his eyes as raw round the edges, as if the skin had been pared off. On his head he wore an handkerchief, which had once been white, and now served to cover the upper part of a black periwig, to which was attached a bag, at least a foot square, with a solitaire and rose that stuck up on each side to his ear; so that he looked like a criminal on the pillory. His back was accommodated with a linen waistcoat, his hands adorned with long ruffles of the same piece, his middle was girded by an apron tucked up, that it might not conceal his white silk stockings rolled; and at his entrance he brandished a bloody weapon full three feet in length.

Peregrine, when he first saw him approach in this menacing attitude, put himself upon his guard; but, being informed of his quality, perused his bill of fare, and having bespoke three or four things for dinner, walked out with Mr. Jolter to view both towns, which they had not leisure to consider minutely before. In their return from the harbour, they met with four or five gentlemen, all of whom seemed to look with an air of dejection, and, perceiving our hero and his governor to be English by their dress, bowed with great respect as they passed. Pickle, who was naturally compassionate, felt an emotion of sympathy; and seeing a person, who by his habit he judged to be one of their servants, accosted him in English, and asked who the gentlemen were. The lacquey gave him to understand that they were his own countrymen, exiled from their native homes, in consequence of their adherence to an unfortunate and ruined cause; and that they were gone to the seaside, according to their daily practice, in order to indulge their longing eyes with a prospect of the white cliffs of Albion, which they must never more approach.

Though our young gentleman differed widely from them in point of political principles, he was not one of those enthusiasts who look upon every schism from the established articles of faith as d—nable, and exclude the sceptic from every benefit of humanity and Christian forgiveness. He could easily comprehend how a man of the most unblemished morals might, by the prejudice of education, or indispensable attachments, be engaged in such a blameworthy and pernicious undertaking; and thought that they already suffered severely for their imprudence. He was affected with the account of their diurnal pilgrimage to the seaside, which he considered as a pathetic proof of their affliction, and invested Mr. Jolter with the agreeable office of going to them with a compliment in his name, and begging the honour of drinking a glass with them in the evening. They accepted the proposal with great satisfaction and respectful acknowledgment, and in the afternoon waited upon the kind inviter, who treated them with coffee, and would have detained them to supper; but they entreated the favour of his company at the house which they frequented, so earnestly, that he yielded to their solicitations, and with his governor was conducted by them to the place, where they had provided an elegant repast, and regaled them with some of the best claret in France.

It was easy for them to perceive that their principal guest was no favourer of their state maxims, and therefore they industriously avoided every subject of conversation which could give the least offence; not but that they lamented their own situation, which cut them off from all their dearest connexions, and doomed them to perpetual banishment from their families and friends; but they did not, even by the most distant hint, impeach the justice of that sentence by which they were condemned; although one of them, who seemed to be about the age of thirty, wept bitterly over his misfortune, which had involved a beloved wife and three children in misery and distress, and, in the impatience of his grief, cursed his own fate with frantic imprecations. His companions, with a view of beguiling his sorrow, and manifesting their own hospitality at the same time, changed the topic of discourse, and circulated the bumpers with great assiduity; so that all their cares were overwhelmed and forgotten, several drinking French catches were sung, and mirth and good-fellowship prevailed.

In the midst of this elevation, which commonly unlocks the most hidden sentiment, and dispels every consideration of caution and constraint, one of the entertainers, being more intoxicated than his fellows, proposed a toast, to which Peregrine with some warmth excepted, as an unmannerly insult. The other maintained his proposition with indecent heat; and the dispute beginning to grow very serious, the company interposed, and gave judgment against their friend, who was so keenly reproached and rebuked for this impolite behaviour, that he retired in high dudgeon, threatening to relinquish their society, and branding them with the appellation of apostates from the common cause. Mortified at the behaviour of their companion, those that remained were earnest in their apologies to their guests, whom they besought to forgive his intemperance, assuring them with great confidence, that he would, upon the recovery of his reflection, wait upon them in person, and ask pardon for the umbrage he had given. Pickle was satisfied with their remonstrances, resumed his good-humour, and the night being pretty far advanced, resisted all their importunities with which he was entreated to see another bottle go round, and was escorted to his own lodgings more than half-seas-over. Next morning, about eight o'clock, he was waked by his valet-de-chambre, who told him that two of the gentlemen with whom he had spent the evening were in the house, and desired the favour of being admitted into his chamber. He could not conceive the meaning of this extraordinary visit, and, ordering his man to show them into his apartment, beheld the person who had affronted him enter, with the gentleman who had reprehended his rudeness.

He who had given the offence, after having made an apology for disturbing Mr. Pickle, told him that his friend there present had been with him early that morning, and proposed the alternative of either fighting with him immediately, or coming to beg pardon for his unmannerly deportment overnight; that, though he had courage enough to face any man in the field in a righteous cause, he was not so brutal as to disobey the dictates of his own duty and reflection, in consequence of which, and not out of any regard to the other's menaces, which he despised, he had now taken the liberty of interrupting his repose, that he might, as soon as possible, atone for the injury he had done him, which he protested was the effect of intoxication alone, and begged his

forgiveness accordingly. Our hero accepted of this acknowledgment very graciously, thanked the other gentleman for the gallant
part he had acted in his behalf; and, perceiving that his
companion was a little irritated at his officious interposition,
effected a reconciliation, by convincing him that what he had
done was for the honour of the company. He then kept them to
breakfast, expressed a desire of seeing their situation altered
for the better; and, the chaise being repaired, took leave of his
entertainers, who came to wish him a good journey, and with his
attendants left Boulogne for the second time.

CHAPTER XXXVII

Proceeds for the Capital—Takes up his Lodgings at Bernay, where he is
overtaken by Mr. Hornbeck, whose Head he longs to fortify.

DURING this day's expedition, Mr. Jolter took an opportunity
of imparting to his pupil the remarks he had made upon the
industry of the French, as an undeniable proof of which he bade
him cast his eyes around, and observe with what care every
spot of ground was cultivated; and, from the fertility of that
province, which is reckoned the poorest in France, conceive
the wealth and affluence of the nation in general. Peregrine,
amazed as well as disgusted at this infatuation, answered, that
what he ascribed to industry was the effect of mere wretchedness;
the miserable peasants being obliged to plough up every inch of
ground to satisfy their oppressive landlords, while they themselves and their cattle looked like so many images of famine;
that their extreme poverty was evident from the face of the
country, on which there was not one enclosure to be seen, or any
other object, except scanty crops of barley and oats, which could
never reward the toil of the husbandman; that their habitations
were no better than paltry huts; that, in twenty miles of extent,
not one gentleman's house appeared; that nothing was more
abject and forlorn than the attire of their country people; that
the equipage of their travelling chaises was infinitely inferior to
that of a dung-cart in England; and that the postillion, who then
drove their carriage, had neither stockings to his legs, nor a shirt
to his back.

The governor, finding his charge so untractable, resolved to
leave him in the midst of his own ignorance and prejudice, and
reserve his observations for those who would pay more deference

to his opinion. And indeed this resolution he had often made, and as often broke, in the transports of his zeal, that frequently hurried him out of the plan of conduct which in his cooler moments he had laid down. They halted for a refreshment at Montreuil, and about seven in the evening arrived at a village called Bernay, where, while they waited for fresh horses, they were informed by the landlord, that the gates of Abbeville were shut every night punctually at eight o'clock, so that it would be impossible for them to get admittance. He said, there was not another place of entertainment on the road where they could pass the night; and therefore, as a friend, he advised them to stay at his house, where they would find the best of accommodation, and proceed upon their journey betimes in the morning.

Mr. Jolter, though he had travelled on that road before, could not recollect whether or not mine host spoke truth; but his remonstrance being very plausible, our hero determined to follow his advice, and, being conducted into an apartment, asked what they could have for supper. The landlord mentioned everything that was eatable in the house, and the whole being engrossed for the use of him and his attendants, he amused himself till such time as it should be dressed, in strolling about the house, which stands in a very rural situation. While he thus loitered away the time that hung heavy on his hands, another chaise arrived at the inn; and, upon inquiry, he found that the new-comers were Mr. Hornbeck and his lady. The landlord, conscious of his inability to entertain this second company, came and begged with great humiliation, that Mr. Pickle would spare them some part of the victuals he had bespoke; but he refused to part with so much as the wing of a partridge, though at the same time he sent his compliments to the strangers, and, giving them to understand how ill the house was provided for their reception, invited them to partake of his supper. Mr. Hornbeck, who was not deficient in point of politeness, and extremely well disposed for a relishing meal, which he had reason to expect from the savoury steam that issued from the kitchen, could not resist this second instance of our young gentleman's civility, which he acknowledged by a message, importing that he and his wife would do themselves the pleasure of profiting by his courteous offer. Peregrine's cheeks glowed when he found himself on the eve of being acquainted with Mrs. Hornbeck, of whose heart he had already made a conquest in imagination; and he forthwith set his invention at work to contrive some means of defeating her husband's vigilance.

When supper was ready, he in person gave notice to his guests, and leading the lady into his apartment, seated her in an elbow-chair at the upper end of the table, squeezing her hand, and darting a most insidious glance at the same time. This abrupt behaviour he practised, on the presumption that a lady of her breeding was not to be addressed with the tedious forms that must be observed in one's advances to a person of birth and genteel education. In all probability his calculation was just; for Mrs. Hornbeck gave no signs of discontent at this sort of treatment, but, on the contrary, seemed to consider it as a proof of the young gentleman's regard; and though she did not venture to open her mouth three times during the whole repast, she showed herself particularly well satisfied with her entertainer, by sundry sly and significant looks, while her husband's eyes were directed another way, and divers loud peals of laughter, signifying her approbation of the sallies which he uttered in the course of their conversation.

Her spouse began to be very uneasy at the frank demeanour of his yoke-fellow, whom he endeavoured to check in her vivacity, by assuming a severity of aspect; but whether she obeyed the dictates of her own disposition, which perhaps was merry and unreserved, or wanted to punish Mr. Hornbeck for his jealousy of temper, certain it is, her gaiety increased to such a degree, that her husband was grievously alarmed and incensed at her conduct, and resolved to make her sensible of his displeasure, by treading in secret upon her toes. He was, however, so disconcerted by his indignation, that he mistook his mark, and applied the sharp heel of his shoe to the side of Mr. Jolter's foot, comprehending his little toe that was studded with an angry corn, which he invaded with such a sudden jerk, that the governor, unable to endure the torture in silence, started up, and, dancing on the floor, roared hideously with repeated bellowings, to the unspeakable enjoyment of Peregrine and the lady, who laughed themselves almost into convulsions at the joke. Hornbeck, confounded at the mistake he had committed, begged pardon of the injured tutor with great contrition, protesting that the blow he had so unfortunately received was intended for an ugly cur which he thought had posted himself under the table. It was lucky for him that there was actually a dog in the room, to justify this excuse, which Jolter admitted with the tears running over his cheeks; and the economy of the table was recomposed.

As soon, however, as the strangers could with decency withdraw, this suspicious husband took his leave of the youth, on pretence of being fatigued with his journey, after having, by way of compliment, proposed that they should travel together next day; and Peregrine handed the lady to her chamber, where he wished her good-night with another warm squeeze, which she returned. This favourable hint made his heart bound with a transport of joy; he lay in wait for an opportunity of declaring himself, and seeing the husband go down into the yard with a candle, glided softly into his apartment, where he found her almost undressed. Impelled by the impetuosity of his passion, which was still more inflamed by her present luscious appearance, and encouraged by the approbation she had already expressed, he ran towards her with eagerness, crying, "Zounds! madam, your charms are irresistible!" and without further ceremony, would have clasped her in his arms, had she not begged him, for the love of God, to retire, for should Mr. Hornbeck return and find him there, she would be undone for ever. He was not so blinded by his passion, but that he saw the reasonableness of her fear, and as he could not pretend to crown his wishes at that interview, he avowed himself her lover, assured her that he would exhaust his whole invention in finding a proper opportunity for throwing himself at her feet; and in the meantime he ravished sundry small favours, which she, in the hurry of her fright, could not withhold from his impudence of address. Having thus happily settled the preliminaries, he withdrew to his own chamber, and spent the whole night in contriving stratagems to elude the jealous caution of his fellow-traveller.

CHAPTER XXXVIII

They set out in Company, breakfast at Abbeville, dine at Amiens, and about eleven o'clock arrive at Chantilly, where Peregrine executes a Plan which he had concerted upon Hornbeck.

THE whole company, by agreement, rose and departed before day, and breakfasted at Abbeville, where they became acquainted with the finesse of their Bernay landlord, who had imposed upon them, in affirming that they would not have been admitted after the gates were shut. From thence they proceeded to Amiens, where they dined, and were pestered by begging friars; and the roads being deep, it was eleven o'clock at night before they reached Chantilly, where they found supper already dressed, in consequence of having despatched the valet-de-chambre before them on horseback.

The constitution of Hornbeck being very much impaired by a life of irregularity, he found himself so fatigued with his day's journey, which amounted to upwards of an hundred miles, that, when he sat down at table, he could scarcely sit upright, and in less than three minutes, began to nod in his chair. Peregrine, who had foreseen and provided for this occasion, advised him to exhilarate his spirits with a glass of wine; and the proposal being embraced, tipped his valet-de-chambre the wink, who, according to the instructions he had received, qualified the burgundy with thirty drops of laudanum, which this unfortunate husband swallowed in one glass. The dose co-operating with his former drowsiness, lulled him so fast asleep, as it were instantaneously, that it was found necessary to convey him to his own chamber, where his footman undressed and put him to bed. Nor was Jolter, naturally of a sluggish disposition, able to resist his propensity to sleep, without suffering divers dreadful yawns, which encouraged his pupil to administer the same dose to him, which had operated so successfully upon the other Argus. This cordial had not such a gentle effect upon the rugged organs of Jolter, as upon the more delicate nerves of Hornbeck; but discovered itself in certain involuntary startings, and convulsive motions in the muscles of his face; and when his nature at length yielded to the power of this medicine, he sounded the trumpet so loud through his nostrils, that our adventurer was afraid the noise would wake his other patient, and consequently prevent the accomplishment of his aim. The governor was therefore committed to the care of Pipes, who lugged him into the next room, and having stripped off his clothes, tumbled him into his nest, while the two lovers remained at full liberty to indulge their mutual passion.

Peregrine in the impatience of his inclination, would have finished the fate of Hornbeck immediately; but his inamorata disapproved of his intention, and represented that their being together by themselves for any length of time, would be observed by her servant, who was kept as a spy upon her actions; so that they had recourse to another scheme, which was executed in this manner:—He conducted her into her own apartment, in presence of her footman, who lighted them thither, and, wishing her good rest, returned to his own chamber, where he waited till everything was quiet in the house; then, stealing softly to her door, which had been left open for his admission in the dark, found the husband still secure in the embraces of sleep, and the lady in a loose gown, ready to seal his happiness. He conveyed her to his own chamber, but his guilty passion was not gratified.

The opium which had been given to Jolter, together with the wine he had drank, produced such a perturbation in his fancy, that he was visited with horrible dreams, and, among other miserable situations, imagined himself in danger of perishing in the flames, which he thought had taken hold on his apartment. This vision made such an impression upon his faculties, that he alarmed the whole house with the repeated cries of *fire!—fire!—* and even leaped out of his bed, though he still continued fast asleep. The lovers were very disagreeably disturbed by this dreadful exclamation, and Mrs. Hornbeck, running in great confusion to the door, had the mortification to see the footman, with a light in his hand, enter her husband's chamber, in order to give him notice of this accident. She knew that she would be instantly missed, and could easily divine the consequence, unless her invention could immediately trump up some plausible excuse for her absence.

Women are naturally fruitful of expedients in cases of such emergency: she employed but a few seconds in recollection, and rushing directly towards the apartment of the governor, who still continued to hollow in the same note, exclaimed in a screaming tone, "Lord have mercy upon us!—where?—where?" By this time all the servants were assembled in strange attire; Peregrine burst into Jolter's room, and seeing him stalking in his shirt, with his eyes shut, bestowed such a slap upon his back, as in a moment dissolved his dream, and restored him to the use of his senses. He was astonished and ashamed at being discovered in such an indecent attitude; and taking refuge under the clothes, asked pardon of all present for the disturbance he had occasioned; soliciting, with great humility, the forgiveness of the lady, who, to a miracle, counterfeited the utmost agitation of terror and surprise. Meanwhile, Hornbeck being awakened by the repeated efforts of his man, no sooner understood that his wife was missing, than all the chimeras of jealousy taking possession of his imagination, he started up in a sort of frenzy, and snatching his sword, flew straight to Peregrine's chamber; where, though he found not that which he looked for, he unluckily perceived an under-petticoat, which his wife had forgot in the hurry of her retreat. This discovery added fuel to the flame of his resentment. He seized the fatal proof of his dishonour, and meeting his spouse in her return to bed, presented it to her view, saying with a most expressive countenance,

"Madam, you have dropped your under-petticoat in the next room." Mrs. Hornbeck, who inherited from nature a most admirable presence of mind, looking earnestly at the object in question, and with incredible serenity of countenance, affirmed that the petticoat must belong to the house, for she had none such in her possession.

Peregrine, who walked behind her, hearing this asseveration, immediately interposed, and pulling Hornbeck by the sleeve into his chamber, "Gads zooks!" said he, "what business had you with that petticoat? Can't you let a young fellow enjoy a little amour with an innkeeper's daughter, without exposing his infirmities to your wife? Pshaw! that's so malicious, because you have quitted these adventures yourself, to spoil the sport of other people." The poor husband was so confounded at the effrontery of his wife, and this cavalier declaration of the young man, that his faith began to waver; he distrusted his own conscious diffidence of temper, which, that he might not expose, he expressed no doubts of Peregrine's veracity, but, asking pardon for the mistake he had committed, retired. He was not yet satisfied with the behaviour of his ingenious helpmate, but, on the contrary, determined to inquire more minutely into the circumstances of this adventure, which turned out so little to his satisfaction, that he ordered his servant to get everything ready for his departure by break of day; and when our adventurer rose next morning, he found that his fellow-travellers were gone above three hours, though they had agreed to stay all the forenoon, with a view of seeing the Prince of Condé's palace, and to proceed all together for Paris in the afternoon.

Peregrine was a little chagrined when he understood that he was so suddenly deprived of this untasted morsel; and Jolter could not conceive the meaning of their abrupt and uncivil disappearance, which, after many profound conjectures, he accounted for, by supposing that Hornbeck was some sharper who had run away with an heiress, whom he found it necessary to conceal from the inquiry of her friends.

The pupil, who was well assured of the true motive, allowed his governor to enjoy the triumph of his own penetration, and consoled himself with the hope of seeing his Dulcinea again at some of the public places in Paris, which he proposed to frequent. Thus comforted, he visited the magnificent stables and palace of Chantilly, and immediately after dinner they set out for Paris, where they arrived in the evening, and hired apartments at an hotel in the Fauxbourg St. Germaine, not far from the playhouse

CHAPTER XXXIX

He is involved in an Adventure at Paris, and taken Prisoner by the City-guard—Becomes acquainted with a French Nobleman, who introduces him in the Beau Monde.

THEY were no sooner settled in these lodgings than our hero wrote to his uncle an account of their safe arrival, and sent another letter to his friend Gauntlet, with a very tender billet enclosed for his dear Emilia, to whom he repeated all his former vows of constancy and love.

The next care that engrossed him was that of bespeaking several suits of clothes suitable to the French mode; and, in the meantime, he never appeared abroad, except in the English coffee-house, where he soon became acquainted with some of his own countrymen, who were at Paris on the same footing with himself. The third evening after his journey, he was engaged in a party of those young sparks at the house of a noted *traiteur*, whose wife was remarkably handsome, and otherwise extremely well qualified for alluring customers to her house. To this lady our young gentleman was introduced as a stranger fresh from England; and he was charmed with her personal accomplishment, as well as with the freedom and gaiety of her conversation. Her frank deportment persuaded him that she was one of those kind creatures who granted favours to the best bidder; on this supposition he began to be so importunate in his addresses, that the fair bourgeoise was compelled to cry aloud in defence of her own virtue. Her husband ran immediately to her assistance, and, finding her in a very alarming situation, flew upon her ravisher with such fury, that he was fain to quit his prey, and turn against the exasperated *traiteur*, whom he punished without mercy for his impudent intrusion. The lady, seeing her yoke-fellow treated with so little respect, espoused his cause, and fixing her nails in his antagonist's face, scarified all one side of his nose. The noise of this encounter brought all the servants of the house to the rescue of their master, and Peregrine's company opposing them, a general battle ensued, in which the French were totally routed, the wife insulted, and the husband kicked downstairs.

The publican, enraged at the indignity which had been offered to him and his family, went out into the street, and implored the protection of the guet or city-guard, which, having heard his complaint, fixed their bayonets, and surrounded the door, to the number of twelve or fourteen. The young gentlemen, flushed with their success, and considering the soldiers as so many London watchmen, whom they had often put to flight, drew their swords, and sallied out, with Peregrine at their head. Whether the guard respected them as foreigners, or inexperienced youths intoxicated with liquor, they opened to right and left, and gave them room to pass without opposition. This complaisance, which was the effect of compassion, being misinterpreted by the English leader, he out of mere wantonness attempted to trip up the heels of the soldier that stood next him, but failed in the execution, and received a blow on his breast with the butt-end of his fusil, that made him stagger several paces backward. Incensed at this audacious application, the whole company charged the detachment sword in hand, and, after an obstinate engagement, in which divers wounds were given and received, every soul of them was taken, and conveyed to the main-guard. The commanding officer, being made acquainted with the circumstances of the quarrel, in consideration of their youth, and national ferocity, for which the French made large allowances, set them all at liberty, after having gently rebuked them for the irregularity and insolence of their conduct; so that all our hero acquired by his gallantry and courage, was a number of scandalous marks upon his visage, that confined him a whole week to his chamber. It was impossible to conceal this disaster from Mr. Jolter who, having obtained intelligence of the particulars, did not fail to remonstrate against the rashness of the adventure, which, he observed, must have been fatal to them, had their enemies been other than Frenchmen, who, of all people under the sun, most rigorously observed the laws of hospitality.

As the governor's acquaintance lay chiefly among Irish and English priests, and a set of low people who live by making themselves necessary to strangers, either in teaching the French language, or executing small commissions with which they are entrusted, he was not the most proper person in the world for regulating the taste of a young gentleman who travelled for improvement in expectation of making a figure one day in his own country. Being conscious of his own incapacity, he contented himself with the office of a steward, and kept a faithful account of all the money that was disbursed in the course of their family expense; not but that he was acquainted with all the places which were visited by strangers on their first arrival at Paris; and he knew to a liard what was commonly given to the Swiss of each remarkable hotel: though, with respect to the curious painting and statuary that everywhere abound in that metropolis, he was more ignorant than the domestic that attends for a livre a day.

In short, Mr. Jolter could give a very good account of the stages on the road, and save the expense of Antonini's detail of the curiosities in Paris; he was a connoisseur in ordinaries, from twelve to five-and-thirty livres, knew all the rates of a fiacre and a remise, could dispute with a tail[l]eur or a traiteur upon the articles of his bill, and scold the servants in tolerable French. But the laws, customs, and genius of the people, the characters of individuals, and scenes of polished life, were subjects which he had neither opportunities to observe, inclination to consider, nor discernment to distinguish. All his maxims were the suggestions of pedantry and prejudice; so that his perception was obscured, his judgment biassed, his address awkward, and his conversation absurd and unentertaining; yet such as I have represented this tutor, is the greatest part of those animals who lead raw boys about the world, under the denomination of travelling governors. Peregrine, therefore, being perfectly well acquainted with the extent of Mr. Jolter's abilities, never dreamed of consulting him in the disposition of his conduct, but parcelled out his time according to the dictates of his own reflection, and the information and direction of his companions, who had lived longer in France, and consequently were better acquainted with the pleasures of the place.

As soon as he was in a condition to appear à la Française, he hired a genteel chariot by the month, made the tour of the Luxembourg gallery, Palais Royal, all the remarkable hotels, churches, and celebrated places in Paris; visited St. Cloud, Marli, Versailles, Trianon, St. Germaine, and Fontainebleau; enjoyed the opera, masquerades, Italian and French comedy; and seldom failed of appearing in the public walks, in hopes of meeting with Mrs. Hornbeck, or some adventure suited to his romantic disposition. He never doubted that his person would attract the notice of some distinguished inamorata, and was vain enough to believe that few female hearts were able to resist the artillery of his accomplishments, should he once find an opportunity of planting it to advantage. He presented himself, however, at all the spectacles for many weeks, without reaping the fruits of his expectation; and began to entertain a very indifferent idea of French discernment, which had overlooked him so long, when one day, in his way to the opera, his chariot was stopped by an embarras in the street, occasioned by two peasants, who, having driven their carts against each other, quarrelled, and went to loggerheads on the spot. Such a rencontre is so uncommon in France, that the people shut up their shops, and from their windows threw cold water upon the combatants, with a view of putting an end to the battle, which was maintained with great fury and very little skill, until one of them receiving an accidental fall, the other took the advantage of this misfortune, and fastening upon him as he lay, began to thump the pavement with his head. Our hero's equipage being detained close by the field of this contention, Pipes could not bear to see the laws of boxing so scandalously transgressed, and, leaping from his station, pulled the offender from his antagonist, whom he raised up, and, in the English language, encouraged to a second essay, instructing him at the same time, by clenching his fists according to art, and putting himself in a proper attitude.

Thus confirmed, the enraged carman sprang upon his foe, and in all appearance would have effectually revenged the injury he had sustained, if he had not been prevented by the interposition of a lacquey belonging to a nobleman, whose coach was obliged to halt in consequence of the dispute. This footman, who was distinguished by a cane, descending from his post, without the least ceremony or expostulation, began to employ his weapon upon the head and shoulders of the peasant who had been patronised by Pipes; upon which Thomas, resenting such ungenerous behaviour, bestowed such a stomacher upon the officious intermeddler, as discomposed the whole economy of his entrails, and obliged him to discharge the interjection, Ah! with demonstrations of great anguish and amazement. The other two footmen who stood behind the coach, seeing their fellow-servant so insolently assaulted, flew to his assistance, and rained a most disagreeable shower upon the head of his aggressor, who had no means of diversion or defence. Peregrine, though he did not approve of Tom's conduct, could not bear to see him so roughly handled, especially as he thought his own honour concerned in the fray, and therefore quitting his machine, came to the rescue of his attendant, and charged his adversaries sword in hand. Two of them no sooner perceived this reinforcement, than they betook themselves to flight; and Pipes, having twisted the cane out of the hands of the third, belaboured him so unmercifully, that our hero thought proper to interpose his authority in his behalf. The common people stood aghast at this unprecedented boldness of Pickle, who, understanding that the person whose servants he had disciplined was a general and prince of the blood, went up to the coach, and asked pardon for what he had done, imputing his own behaviour to the ignorance of the other's quality. The old nobleman accepted of his apology with great politeness, thanking him for the trouble he had taken to reform the manners of his domestics; and guessing from our youth's appearance, that he was some stranger of condition, very courteously invited him into the coach, on the supposition that they were both going to the opera. Pickle gladly embraced this opportunity of becoming acquainted with a person of such rank, and, ordering his own chariot to follow, accompanied the count to his loge, where he conversed with him during the whole entertainment.

He soon perceived that Peregrine was not deficient in spirit or sense, and seemed particularly pleased with his engaging manner and easy deportment, qualifications for which the English nation is by no means remarkable in France, and therefore the more conspicuous and agreeable in the character of our hero, whom the nobleman carried home that same evening, and introduced to his lady and several persons of fashion, who supped at his house. Peregrine was quite captivated by their affable behaviour and the vivacity of their discourse; and, after having been honoured with particular marks of consideration, took his leave, fully determined to cultivate such a valuable acquaintance.

His vanity suggested, that now the time was come when he should profit by his talents among the fair sex, on whom he resolved to employ his utmost art and address. With this view he assiduously engaged in all parties to which he had access by means of his noble friend, who let slip no opportunity of gratifying his ambition. He, for some time, shared in all his amusements, and was entertained in many of the best families of France; but he did not long enjoy that elevation of hope, which had flattered his imagination. He soon perceived that it would be impossible to maintain the honourable connexions he had made, without engaging every day at quadrille, or, in other words, losing his money; for every person of rank, whether male or female, was a professed gamester, who knew and practised all the finesse of the art, of which he was entirely ignorant. Besides, he began to find himself a mere novice in French gallantry, which is supported by an amazing volubility of tongue, an obsequious and incredible attention to trifles, a surprising facility of laughing out of pure complaisance, and a nothingness of conversation, which he could never attain. In short, our hero,

who, among his own countrymen, would have passed for a
sprightly entertaining fellow, was considered in the brilliant
assemblies of France as a youth of a very phlegmatic disposition.
No wonder then that his pride was mortified at his own want of
importance, which he did not fail to ascribe to their defect in
point of judgment and taste.   He conceived a disgust at the
mercenary conduct, as well as the shallow intellects of the
ladies; and, after he had spent some months, and a round sum of
money, in fruitless attendance and addresses, he fairly quitted
the pursuit, and consoled himself with the conversation of a
merry *fille de joie*, whose good graces he acquired by an allowance
of twenty louis per month.   That he might the more easily
afford this expense, he dismissed his chariot and French lacquey
at the same time.

He then entered himself in a noted academy, in order to finish
his exercises, and contracted an acquaintance with a few sensible
people, whom he distinguished at the coffee-house and ordinary
to which he resorted, and who contributed not a little to the
improvement of his knowledge and taste.   For, prejudice apart,
it must be owned that France abounds with men of consummate
honour, profound sagacity, and the most liberal education.
From the conversation of such, he obtained a distinct idea of
their government and constitution; and though he could not
help admiring the excellent order and economy of their police,
the result of all his inquiries was a self-congratulation on his title
to the privileges of a British subject.   Indeed this invaluable
birthright was rendered conspicuous by such flagrant occurrences, which fell every day almost under his observation, that
nothing but the grossest prejudice could dispute its existence.

CHAPTER XL

Acquires a distinct Idea of the French Government—Quarrels with a
Mousquetaire, whom he afterwards fights and vanquishes, after having
punished him for interfering in his amorous Recreations.

AMONG many other instances of the same nature, I believe it will
not be amiss to exhibit a few specimens of their administration,
which happened during his abode at Paris, that those who have
not the opportunity of observing for themselves, or are in danger
of being influenced by misrepresentation, may compare their
own condition with that of their neighbours, and do justice to
the constitution under which they live.

A lady of distinguished character having been lampooned by some obscure scribbler, who could not be discovered, the ministry in consequence of her complaint, ordered no fewer than five-and-twenty abbés to be apprehended and sent to the Bastile, on the maxim of Herod, when he commanded the innocents to be murdered, hoping that the principal object of his cruelty would not escape in the general calamity; and the friends of those unhappy prisoners durst not even complain of the unjust persecution, but shrugged up their shoulders, and, in silence, deplored their misfortune, uncertain whether or not they should ever set eyes on them again.

About the same time a gentleman of family, who had been oppressed by a certain powerful duke that lived in the neighbourhood, found means to be introduced to the king, who, receiving his petition very graciously, asked him in what regiment he served; and, when the memorialist answered, that he had not the honour of being in the service, returned the paper unopened, and refused to hear one circumstance of his complaint; so that, far from being redressed, he remained more than ever exposed to the tyranny of his oppressor. Nay, so notorious is the discouragement of all those who presume to live independent of court favour and connexions, that one of the gentlemen, whose friendship Peregrine cultivated, frankly owned he was in possession of a most romantic place in one of the provinces, and deeply enamoured of a country life; and yet he durst not reside upon his own estate, lest, by slackening in his attendance upon the great, who honoured him with their protection, he should fall a prey to some rapacious intendant.

As for the common people, they are so much inured to the scourge and insolence of power, that every shabby subaltern, every beggarly cadet of the noblesse, every low retainer to the court, insults and injures them with impunity. A certain écuyer, or horse-dealer, belonging to the king, being one day under the hands of a barber, who happened to cut the head of a pimple on his face, he started up, and drawing his sword, wounded him desperately in the shoulder. The poor tradesman, hurt as he was, made an effort to retire, and was followed by this barbarous assassin, who, not contented with the vengeance he had taken, plunged his sword a second time into his body, and killed him on the spot. Having performed this inhuman exploit, he dressed himself with great deliberation, and, going to Versailles, immediately obtained a pardon for what he had done, triumphing in his brutality with such insolence, that the very next time he had occasion to be shaved, he sat with his sword ready drawn, in order to repeat the murder, in case the barber should commit the same mistake. Yet so tamed are those poor people to subjection, that when Peregrine mentioned this assassination to his own trimmer, with expressions of horror and detestation, the infatuated wretch replied, that without all doubt it was a misfortune, but it proceeded from the gentleman's passion; and observed, by way of encomium on the government, that such vivacity is never punished in France.

A few days after this outrage was committed, our youth, who was a professed enemy to all oppression, being in one of the first loges at the comedy, was eye-witness of an adventure, which filled him with indignation. A tall ferocious fellow, in the parterre, without the least provocation, but prompted by the mere wantonness of pride, took hold of the hat of a very decent young man, who happened to stand before him, and twirled it round upon his head. The party thus offended turned to the aggressor, and civilly asked the reason of such treatment, but he received no answer; and when he looked the other way, the insult was repeated. Upon which he expressed his resentment as became a man of spirit, and desired the offender to walk out with him. No sooner did he thus signify his intention, than his adversary, swelling with rage, cocked his hat fiercely in his face, and, fixing his hands in his sides, pronounced with the most imperious tone, "Hark ye, Mr. Round Periwig, you must know that I am a mousquetaire." Scarce had this awful word escaped from his lips, when the blood forsook the lips of the poor challenger, who, with the most abject submission, begged pardon for his presumption, and with difficulty obtained it, on condition that he should immediately quit the place. Having thus exercised his authority, he turned to one of his companions, and with an air of disdainful ridicule, told him he was like to have had an affair with a bourgeois; adding, by way of heightening the irony, "Egad! I believe he's a physician."

Our hero was so much shocked and irritated at this licentious behaviour, that he could not suppress his resentment, which he manifested, by saying to this Hector, "Sir, a physician may be a man of honour." To this remonstrance, which was delivered in a very significant countenance, the mousquetaire made no other reply, but that of echoing his assertion with a loud laugh, in which he was joined by his confederates. Peregrine, glowing with resentment, called him a *Fanfaron*, and withdrew in expectation of being followed into the street. The other understood the hint, and a rencontre must have ensued, had not the officer of the guard, who overheard what passed, prevented their meeting, by putting the mousquetaire immediately under arrest. Our young gentleman waited at the door of the parterre, until he was informed of this interposition, and then went home very much chagrined at his disappointment; for he was an utter stranger to fear and diffidence on those occasions, and had set his heart upon chastising the insolence of this bully, who had treated him with such disrespect.

This adventure was not so private but that it reached the ears of Mr. Jolter, by the canal of some English gentlemen who were present when it happened; and the governor, who entertained a most dreadful idea of the mousquetaires, being alarmed at a quarrel, the consequence of which might be fatal to his charge, waited on the British ambassador, and begged he would take Peregrine under his immediate protection. His excellency having heard the circumstances of the dispute, sent one of his gentlemen to invite the youth to dinner; and, after having assured him that he might depend upon his countenance and regard, represented the rashness and impetuosity of his conduct so much to his conviction, that he promised to act more circumspectly for the future, and drop all thoughts of the mousquetaire from that moment.

A few days after he had taken this laudable resolution, Pipes, who had carried a billet to his mistress, informed him that he had perceived a laced hat lying upon a marble slab in her apartment; and that, when she came out of her own chamber to receive the letter, she appeared in manifest disorder.

From these hints of intelligence, our young gentleman suspected, or rather made no doubt of her infidelity; and, being by this time well-nigh cloyed with possession, was not sorry to find that she had given him cause to renounce her correspondence. That he might therefore detect her in the very breach of duty, and at the same time punish the gallant who had the presumption to invade his territories, he concerted with himself a plan, which was executed in this manner. During his next interview with his Dulcinea, far from discovering the least sign of jealousy or discontent, he affected the appearance of extraordinary fondness; and, after having spent the afternoon with the show of uncommon satisfaction, told her he was engaged in a party for Fontainebleau, and would set out from Paris that same evening; so that he should not have the pleasure of seeing her again for some days.

The lady, who was very well versed in the arts of her

occupation, pretended to receive this piece of news with great affliction, and conjured him, with such marks of real tenderness, to return as soon as possible to her longing arms, that he went away almost convinced of her sincerity. Determined, however, to prosecute his scheme, he actually departed from Paris with two or three gentlemen of his acquaintance, who had hired a remise for a jaunt to Versailles; and, having accompanied them as far as the village of Passe, returned in the dusk of the evening on foot.

He waited patiently till midnight, and then arming himself with a case of pocket-pistols, and attended by trusty Tom, with a cudgel in his hand, repaired to the lodgings of his suspected inamorata. Having given Pipes his cue, he knocked gently at the door, which was no sooner opened by the lacquey, than he bolted in, before the fellow could recollect himself from the confusion occasioned by this unexpected appearance; and, leaving Tom to guard the door, ordered the trembling valet to light him upstairs into his lady's apartment. The first object that presented itself to his view, when he entered the ante-chamber was a sword upon the table, which he immediately seized, exclaiming in a loud and menacing voice, that his mistress was false, and then in bed with another gallant. whom he would instantly put to death. This declaration, confirmed by many terrible oaths, he calculated for the hearing of his rival, who, understanding his sanguinary purpose, started up in great trepidation, and, naked as he was, dropped from the balcony into the street, while Peregrine thundered at the door for admittance; and guessing his design, gave him an opportunity of making this precipitate retreat. Pipes, who stood sentinel at the door, observing the fugitive descend, attacked him with his cudgel, and sweating him from one end of the street to the other, at last committed him to the guet, by whom he was conveyed to the officer on duty in a most disgraceful and deplorable condition.

Meanwhile, Peregrine having burst open the chamber door, found the lady in the utmost dread and consternation, and the spoils of her favourite scattered about the room; but his resentment was doubly gratified, when he learned upon inquiry, that the person who had been so disagreeably interrupted was no other than that individual mousquetaire with whom he had quarrelled at the comedy. He upbraided the nymph with her perfidy and ingratitude, and, telling her that she must not expect the continuance of his regard, or the appointments which she had hitherto enjoyed from his bounty, went home to his own lodgings, overjoyed at the issue of the adventure.

The soldier, exasperated at the disgrace he had undergone, as well as at the outrageous insult of the English valet, whom he believed his master had tutored for that purpose, no sooner extricated himself from the opprobrious situation he had incurred, than, breathing vengeance against the author of the affront, he came to Peregrine's apartment, and demanded satisfaction upon the ramparts next morning before sunrise. Our hero assured him, he would not fail to pay his respects to him at the time and place appointed; and, foreseeing that he might be prevented from keeping this engagement by the officious care of his governor, who saw the mousquetaire come in, he told Mr. Jolter that the Frenchman had visited him in consequence of an order he had received from his superiors, to make an apology for his rude behaviour to him in the playhouse, and that they had parted good friends. This assurance, together with Pickle's very tranquil and unconcerned behaviour through the day, quieted the terrors which had begun to take possession of his tutor's imagination; so that the youth had an opportunity of giving him the slip at night, when he betook himself to the lodgings of a friend, whom he engaged as his second, and with whom he immediately took the field, in order to avoid the search which Jolter, upon missing him, might set on foot.

This was a necessary precaution; for, as he did not appear at supper, and Pipes, who usually attended him in his excursions, could give no account of his motions, the governor was dreadfully alarmed at his absence, and ordered his man to run in quest of his master to all the places which he used to frequent, while he himself went to the commissaire, and communicating his suspicions, was accommodated with a party of the horse-guards, who patrolled round all the environs of the city, with a view of preventing the rencontre. Pipes might have directed them to the lady, by whose information they could have learnt the name and lodging of the mousquetaire, and, if he had been apprehended, the duel would not have happened; but he did not choose to run the risk of disobliging his master, by intermeddling in the affair, and was moreover very desirous that the Frenchman should be humbled; for he never doubted that Peregrine was more than a match for any two men in France. In this confidence, therefore, he sought his master with great diligence, not with a view of disappointing his intention, but in order to attend him to the battle, that he might stand by him and see justice done.

While this inquiry was carried on, our hero and his companion concealed themselves among some weeds that grew on the edge of the parapet, a few yards from the spot where he had agreed to meet the mousquetaire; and scarce had the morning rendered objects distinguishable, when they perceived their men advancing boldly to the place. Peregrine, seeing them approach, sprung forward to the ground, that he might have the glory of anticipating his antagonist; and, swords being drawn, all four were engaged in a twinkling. Pickle's eagerness had well-nigh cost him his life; for, without minding his footing, he flew directly to his opposite, and, stumbling over a stone, was wounded on one side of his head, before he could recover his attitude. Far from being dispirited at this check, it served only to animate him the more. Being endowed with uncommon agility, he retrieved his posture in a moment, and, having parried a second thrust, returned the longe with such incredible speed, that the soldier had not time to resume his guard, but was immediately run through the bend of his right arm, and, the sword dropping out of his hand, our hero's victory was complete.

Having despatched his own business, and received the acknowledgment of his adversary, who, with a look of infinite mortification, observed, that his was the fortune of the day, he ran to part the seconds, just as the weapon was twisted out of his companion's hand; upon which he took his place, and, in all likelihood, an obstinate dispute would have ensued, had they not been interrupted by the guard, at sight of whom the two Frenchmen scampered off. Our young gentleman and his friend allowed themselves to be taken prisoners by the detachment which had been sent out for that purpose, and were carried before the magistrate, who, having sharply reprimanded them for presuming to act in contempt of the laws, set them at liberty, in consideration of their being strangers; cautioning them, at the same time, to beware of such exploits for the future.

When Peregrine returned to his own lodgings, Pipes, seeing the blood trickling down upon his master's neckcloth and solitaire, gave evident tokens of surprise and concern, not for the consequences of the wound, which he did not suppose dangerous, but for the glory of old England, which he was afraid had suffered in the engagement; for he could not help saying, with an air of chagrin, as he followed the youth into his chamber, "I do suppose as how you gave that lubberly Frenchman as good as he brought."

CHAPTER XLI

Mr. Jolter threatens to leave him on account of his Misconduct, which he promises to rectify; but his Resolution is defeated by the Impetuosity of his Passions—He meets accidentally with Mrs. Hornbeck, who elopes with him from her Husband, but is restored by the Interposition of the British Ambassador.

THOUGH Mr. Jolter was extremely well pleased at the safety of his pupil, he could not forgive him for the terror and anxiety he had undergone on his account; and roundly told him, that, notwithstanding the inclination and attachment he had to his person, he would immediately depart for England, if ever he should hear of his being involved in such another adventure; for it could not be expected that he would sacrifice his own quiet to an unrequited regard for one who seemed determined to keep him in continued uneasiness and apprehension.

To this declaration Pickle made answer, that Mr. Jolter, by this time, ought to be convinced of the attention he had always paid to his ease and satisfaction; since he well knew that he had ever looked upon him in the light of a friend, rather than as a counsellor or tutor, and desired his company in France, with a view of promoting his interest, not from any emolument he could expect from his instruction. This being the case, he was at liberty to consult his own inclinations, with regard to going or staying; though he could not help owning himself obliged by the concern he expressed for his safety, and would endeavour, for his own sake, to avoid giving him any cause of disturbance in time to come.

No man was more capable of moralising upon Peregrine's misconduct than himself; his reflections were extremely just and sagacious, and attended with no other disadvantage but that of occurring too late. He projected a thousand salutary schemes of deportment, but, like other projectors, he never had interest enough with the ministry of his passions to bring any one of them to bear. He had, in the heyday of his gallantry, received a letter from his friend Gauntlet, with a kind postscript from his charming Emilia; but it arrived at a very unseasonable juncture, when his imagination was engrossed by conquests that more agreeably flattered his ambition; so that he could not find leisure and inclination from that day to honour the correspondence which he himself had solicited. His vanity had, by this time, disapproved of the engagement he had contracted in the rawness and inexperience of youth, suggesting that he was born to make such an important figure in life as ought to raise his ideas above the consideration of any such middling connexions, and fix his attention upon objects of the most sublime attraction. These dictates of ridiculous pride had almost effaced the remembrance of his amiable mistress—or, at least, so far warped his morals and integrity, that he actually began to conceive hopes of her altogether unworthy of his own character, and her deserts.

Meanwhile, being destitute of a toy for the dalliance of his idle hours, he employed several spies, and almost every day made a tour of the public places in person, with a view of procuring intelligence of Mr. Hornbeck, with whose wife he longed to have another interview. In this course of expectation had he exercised himself a whole fortnight, when chancing to be at the Hospital of Invalids with a gentleman lately arrived from England, he no sooner entered the church, than he perceived this lady, attended by her spouse who, at sight of our hero, changed colour, and looked another way, in order to discourage any communication between them. But the young man, who was not so easily repulsed, advanced with great assurance to his fellow-traveller, and, taking him by the hand, expressed his satisfaction at this unexpected meeting, kindly upbraiding him for his precipitate retreat from Chantilly. Before Hornbeck could make any reply, he went up to his wife, whom he complimented in the same manner, assuring her, with some significant glances, he was extremely mortified that she had put it out of his power to pay his respects to her on his first arrival at Paris; and then, turning to her husband, who thought proper to keep close to him in this conference, begged to know where he could have the honour of waiting upon him; observing, at the same time, that he himself lived à l'Académie de Palfrenier.

Mr. Hornbeck, without making any apology for his elopement on the road, thanked Mr. Pickle for his complaisance in a very cool and disobliging manner, saying, that, as he intended to shift his lodgings in a day or two, he could not expect the pleasure of seeing him until he should be settled, when he would call at the academy, and conduct him to his new habitation.

Pickle, who was not unacquainted with the sentiments of this jealous gentleman, did not put much confidence in his promise, and therefore made divers efforts to enjoy a little private conversation with his wife; but he was baffled in all his attempts by the indefatigable vigilance of her keeper, and reaped no other immediate pleasure from this accidental meeting than that of a kind squeeze while he handed her into the coach. However, as he had been witness to some instances of her invention, and was no stranger to the favourable disposition of her heart, he entertained some faint hopes of profiting by her understanding, and was not deceived in his expectations; for, the very next afternoon, a Savoyard called at the academy, and put the following billet into his hand:

COIND SUR,—Heaving the playsure of meating with you at the osspital of anvilheads. I take this lubbertea of latin you know, that I lotch at the Hottail de May cong dangle rouy Doghouseten, with two postis at the gait, naytheir of um very hole, ware I shall be at the windore, if in kais you will be so good as to pass that way at sicks a cloak in the heavening, when Mr. Hornbeck goes to the Calf hay de Contea. Prey for the loaf of Geesus keep this from the nolegs of my hussban, ells he will make me leed a hell upon urth. Being all from, deer Sur, Your most umbel servan wile

DEBORAH HORNBECK.

Our young gentleman was ravished at the receipt of this elegant epistle, which was directed, "A Monsr. Monsr. Pickhell, a la Gaddamme de Paul Freny," and did not fail to obey the summons at the hour of assignation; when the lady, true to her appointment, beckoned him upstairs, and he had the good fortune to be admitted unseen.

After the first transports of their mutual joy at meeting, she told him that her husband had been very surly and cross ever since the adventure at Chantilly, which he had not yet digested; that he had laid severe injunctions upon her to avoid all commerce with Pickle, and even threatened to shut her up in a convent for life, if ever she should discover the least inclination to renew that acquaintance; that she had been cooped up in her chamber since her arrival at Paris, without being permitted to see the place, or, indeed, any company, except that of her landlady, whose language she did not understand; so that, her spirit being broke, and her health impaired, he was prevailed upon, some days ago, to indulge her in a few airings, during which she had seen the gardens of the Luxembourg, the Tuilleries, and Palais Royal, though at those times when there was no company in the walks; and that it was in one of those excursions she had the happiness of meeting with him. Finally, she gave him to understand that, rather than continue longer under such confinement with the man whom she could not love, she would instantly give him the slip, and put herself under the protection of her lover.

Rash and unthinking as this declaration might be, the young gentleman was so much of a gallant, that he would not balk the lady's inclinations, and too infatuated by his passion to foresee the consequences of such a dangerous step. He therefore, without hesitation, embraced the proposal, and, the coast being clear, they sallied into the street, where Peregrine called a fiacre, and ordered the coachman to drive them to a tavern. But, knowing it would not be in his power to conceal her from the search of the lieutenant de police, if she should remain within the walls of Paris, he hired a remise, and carried her that same evening to Villejuif, about four leagues from town, where he staid with her all night; and having boarded her on a genteel pension, and settled the economy of his future visits, returned next day to his own lodgings.

While he thus enjoyed his success, her husband endured the tortures of the damned. When he returned from the coffee-house, and understood that his wife had eloped, without being perceived by any person in the family, he began to rave and foam with rage and jealousy, and, in the fury of distraction, accused the landlady of being an accomplice in her escape, threatening to complain of her to the commissaire. The woman could not conceive how Mrs. Hornbeck, who she knew was an utter stranger to the French language, and kept no sort of company, could elude the caution of her husband, and find any refuge in a place where she had no acquaintance; and began to suspect the lodger's emotion was no other than an affected passion to conceal his own practices upon his wife, who had perhaps fallen a sacrifice to his jealous disposition. She therefore spared him the trouble of putting his menaces into execution, by going to the magistrate without any further deliberation, and giving an account of what she knew concerning this mysterious affair, with certain insinuations against Hornbeck's character, which she represented as peevish and capricious to the last degree.

While she thus anticipated the purpose of the plaintiff, her information was interrupted by the arrival of the party himself, who exhibited his complaint with such evident marks of per-turbation, anger, and impatience, that the commissaire could easily perceive that he had no share in the disappearance of his wife; and directed him to the lieutenant de police, whose province it is to take cognisance of such occurrences. This gentleman, who presides over the city of Paris, having heard the particulars of Hornbeck's misfortune, asked if he suspected any individual person as the seducer of his yoke-fellow; and, when he mentioned Peregrine as the object of his suspicion, granted a warrant, and a detachment of soldiers, to search for and retrieve the fugitive.

The husband conducted them immediately to the academy, where our hero lodged, and having rummaged the whole place, to the astonishment of Mr. Jolter, without finding either his wife or the supposed ravisher, accompanied them to all the public-houses in the Fauxbourg; which having examined also without success, he returned to the magistrate in a state of despair, and obtained a promise of his making such an effectual inquiry, that, in three days, he should have an account of her, provided she was alive, and within the walls of Paris.

Our adventurer, who had foreseen all this disturbance, was not at all surprised when his governor told him what had happened; and conjured him to restore the woman to the right owner, with many pathetic remonstrances touching the heinous sin of adultery, the distraction of the unfortunate husband, and the danger of incurring the resentment of an arbitrary government, which, upon application being made, would not fail of espousing the cause of the injured. He denied, with great effrontery, that he had the least concern in the matter, pretended to resent the deportment of Hornbeck, whom he threatened to chastise for his scandalous suspicion, and expressed his displeasure at the credulity of Jolter, who seemed to doubt the veracity of his asseveration.

Notwithstanding this confident behaviour, Jolter could not help entertaining doubts of his sincerity; and, visiting the disconsolate swain, begged he would, for the honour of his country, as well as for the sake of his own reputation, discontinue his addresses to the lieutenant de police, and apply to the British ambassador, who, by dint of friendly admonitions, would certainly prevail upon Mr. Pickle to do him all the justice in his power, if he was really the author of the injury he had sustained. The governor urged this advice with the appearance of so much sympathy and concern, promising to co-operate with all his influence in his behalf, that Hornbeck embraced the proposal, communicated his purpose to the magistrate, who commended the resolution as the most decent and desirable expedient he could use, and then waited upon his excellency, who readily espoused his cause, and, sending for the young gentleman that same evening, read him such a lecture in private, as extorted a confession of the whole affair. Not that he assailed him with sour and supercilious maxims, or severe rebuke, because he had penetration enough to discern that Peregrine's disposition was impregnable to all such attacks; but he first of all rallied him upon his intriguing genius, then in an humorous manner described the distraction of the poor cuckold, who, he owned, was justly punished for the absurdity of his conduct; and, lastly, upon the supposition that it would be no great effort in Pickle to part with such a conquest, especially after it had been for some time possessed, he represented the necessity and expediency of restoring her, not only out of regard to his own character, and that of his nation, but also with a view to his ease, which would in a little time be very much invaded by such an incumbrance, that in all probability would involve him in a thousand difficulties and disgusts. Besides, he assured him, that he was already, by order of the lieutenant de police, surrounded with spies, who would watch all his motions, and immediately discover the retreat in which he had disposed of his prize.

These arguments, and the frank, familiar manner in which they were delivered, but, above all, the last consideration, induced the young gentleman to disclose the whole of his proceedings to the ambassador, and promised to be governed by his direction, provided the lady should not suffer for the step she had taken, but be received by her husband with due reverence and respect. These stipulations being agreed to, he undertook to produce her in eight-and-forty hours; and, taking coach immediately, drove to the place of her residence, where he spent a whole day and night in convincing her of the impossibility of their enjoying each other in that manner. Then, returning to Paris, he delivered her into the hands of the ambassador, who, having assured her that she might depend upon his friendship and protection, in case she should find herself aggrieved by the jealous temper of Mr. Hornbeck, restored her to her legitimate lord, whom he counselled to exempt her from that restraint which in all probability had been the cause of her elopement, and endeavour to conciliate her affection by tender and respectful usage.

The husband behaved with great humility and compliance, protesting that his chief study should be to contrive parties for her pleasure and satisfaction. But no sooner did he regain possession of his stray sheep, than he locked her up more closely than ever; and, after having revolved various schemes for her reformation, determined to board her in a convent, under the inspection of a prudent abbess, who should superintend her morals, and recal her to the paths of virtue, which she had forsaken. With this view he consulted an English priest of his acquaintance, who advised him to settle her in a monastery at Lisle, that she might be as far as possible from the machinations of her lover; and gave him a letter of recommendation to the superior of a certain convent in that place, for which Mr. Hornbeck set out in a few days with his troublesome charge.

CHAPTER XLII

Peregrine resolves to return to England—Is diverted with the odd Characters of two of his Countrymen, with whom he contracts an Acquaintance in the Apartments of the Palais Royal.

IN the meantime our hero received a letter from his aunt, importing that the commodore was in a very declining way, and longed much to see him at the garrison; and, at the same time, he heard from his sister, who gave him to understand, that the young gentleman who had for some time made his addresses to her, was become very pressing in his solicitations; so that she wanted to know in what manner she should answer his repeated entreaties. These two considerations determined the young gentleman to return to his native country, a resolution that was far from being disagreeable to Jolter, who knew that the incumbent on a living which was in the gift of Trunnion, was extremely old, and that it would be his interest to be upon the spot at the said incumbent's decease.

Peregrine, who had resided about fifteen months in France, thought he was now sufficiently qualified for eclipsing most of his cotemporaries in England, and therefore prepared for his departure, with infinite alacrity, being moreover inflamed with the most ardent desire of revisiting his friends, and renewing his connexions, particularly with Emilia, whose heart he, by this time, thought he was able to reduce on his own terms.

As he proposed to make the tour of Flanders and Holland in his return to England, he resolved to stay at Paris a week or two after his affairs were settled, in hope of finding some agreeable companion, disposed for the same journey, and, in order to refresh his memory, made a second circuit round all the places in that capital, where any curious production of art is to be seen. In the course of this second examination, he chanced to enter the Palais Royal just as two gentlemen alighted from a fiacre at the gate, and all three being admitted at the same time, he soon perceived that the strangers were of his own country. One of them was a young man, in whose air and countenance appeared all the uncouth gravity and supercilious self-conceit of a physician piping hot from his studies; while the other, to whom his companion spoke by the appellation of Mr. Pallet, displayed at first sight a strange composition of levity and assurance. Indeed, their characters, dress, and address were strongly contrasted. The doctor wore a suit of black, and a huge tie-wig, neither suitable to his own age, nor the fashion of the country where he then lived; whereas the other, though seemingly turned of fifty, strutted in a gay dress of the Parisian cut, with a bag to his own grey hair, and a red feather in his hat, which he carried under his arm. As these figures seemed to promise something entertaining, Pickle entered into conversation with them immediately, and soon discovered that the old gentleman was a painter from London, who had stole a fortnight from his occupation, in order to visit the remarkable paintings of France and Flanders; and that the doctor had taken the opportunity of accompanying him in his tour. Being extremely talkative, he not only communicated these particulars to our hero in a very few minutes after their meeting, but also took occasion to whisper in his ear, that his fellow-traveller was a man of vast learning, and, beyond all doubt, the greatest poet of the age. As for himself, he was under no necessity of making his own eulogium; for he soon gave such specimens of his taste and talent, as left Pickle no room to doubt of his capacity.

While they stood considering the pictures in one of the first apartments, which are by no means the most masterly compositions, the Swiss, who sets up for a connoisseur, looking at a certain piece, pronounced the word *magnifique!* with a note of admiration; upon which Mr. Pallet, who was not at all a critic in the French language, replied with great vivacity, "*Manufac*, you mean, and a very indifferent piece of manufacture it is; pray, gentlemen, take notice, there is no keeping in those heads upon the background, nor no relief in the principal figure. Then you'll observe the shadings are harsh to the last degree; and— come a little closer this way—don't you perceive that the fore-shortening of that arm is monstrous—egad, sir, there is an absolute fracture in the limb—Doctor, you understand anatomy; don't you think that muscle evidently misplaced? Hark ye, Mr. what d'ye call um," turning to the attendant, "what is the name of the dauber who painted that miserable performance?" The Swiss, imagining that he was all this time expressing his satisfaction, sanctioned his supposed commendation, by exclaiming "*Sans prix!*" "Right," cried Pallet, "I could not recollect his name, though his manner is quite familiar to me. We have a few pieces in England done by that same Sangpree; but there they are in no estimation; we have more taste among us, than to relish the productions of such a miserable gout. A'n't he an ignorant coxcomb, doctor?" The physician, ashamed of his companion's blunder, thought it was necessary, for the honour of his own character, to take notice of it before the stranger, and therefore answered his question, by repeating this line from Horace—

Mutato nomine, de te fabula narratur.

The painter, who was rather more ignorant of Latin than of French, taking it for granted that this quotation of his friend conveyed an assent to his opinion, "Very true," said he, "*Potatoe domine date*, this piece is not worth a single potatoe." Peregrine was astonished at this surprising perversion of the words and meaning of a Latin line, which, at first, he could not help thinking was a premeditated joke; but, upon second thoughts, he saw no reason to doubt that it was the extemporaneous effect of sheer pertness and ignorance, at which he broke out into an immoderate fit of laughter. Pallet, believing that the gentleman's mirth was occasioned by his arch animadversion upon the works of Sangpree, underwent the same emotion in a much louder strain, and endeavoured to heighten the jest by more observations of the same nature; while the doctor, confounded at his impudence and want of knowledge, reprimanded him in these words of Homer—

Siga me tis allos Achaion touton akouse muthon.

This rebuke, the reader will easily perceive, was not calculated for the meridian of his friend's intellects, but uttered with a view of raising his own character in the opinion of Mr. Pickle, who retorted this parade of learning in three verses from the same author, being part of the speech of Polydamas to Hector, importing that it is impossible for one man to excel in everything. The self-sufficient physician, who did not expect such a repartee from a youth of Peregrine's appearance, looked upon his reply as a fair challenge, and instantly rehearsed forty or fifty lines of the Iliad in a breath. Observing that the stranger made no effort to match this effusion, he interpreted his silence into submission; then, in order to ascertain his victory, insulted him with divers fragments of authors, whom his supposed competitor did not even know by name; while Mr. Pallet stared with admiration at the profound scholarship of his companion. Our young gentleman, far from repining at this superiority, laughed within himself at the ridiculous ambition of the pedantic doctor. He rated him in his own mind as a mere index-hunter, who held the eel of science by the tail, and foresaw an infinite fund of diversion in his solemnity and pride, if properly extracted by means of his fellow-traveller's vanity and assurance. Prompted by these considerations, he resolved to cultivate their acquaintance, and, if possible, amuse himself at their expense in his journey through Flanders, understanding that they were determined upon the same route. In this view he treated them with extraordinary attention, and seemed to pay particular deference to the remarks of the painter, who with great intrepidity pronounced judgment upon every picture in the palace, or in other words, exposed his own nakedness, in every sentence that proceeded from his mouth.

When they came to consider the Murder of the Innocents, by Le Brun, the Swiss observed, that it was *un beau morceau*; and Mr. Pallet replied, "Yes, yes, one may see with half an eye, that it can be the production of no other; for Bomorso's style, both in colouring and drapery, is altogether peculiar; then his design is tame, and his expression antic and unnatural. Doctor, you have seen my Judgment of Solomon; I think I may without presumption—but I don't choose to make comparisons; I leave that odious task to other people, and let my works speak for themselves. France, to be sure, is rich in the arts; but what is the reason? The King encourages men of genius with honour and rewards; whereas, in England, we are obliged to stand upon our own feet, and combat the envy and malice of our brethren—egad! I have a good mind to come and settle here in Paris; I should like to have an apartment in the Louvre, with a snug pension of so many thousand livres."

In this manner did Pallet proceed with an eternal rotation of tongue, floundering from one mistake to another, until it was the turn of Poussin's Seven Sacraments to be examined. Here again the Swiss, out of the abundance of his zeal, expressed his admiration, by saying these pieces were *impayable*; when the painter turning to him with an air of exultation, "Pardon me, friend, there you happen to be mistaken; these are none of Impayable's, but done by Nicholas Pouseen. I have seen prints of them in England; so that none of your tricks upon travellers, Mr. Swiss, or Swash, or what's your name." He was very much elated by this imaginary triumph of his understanding, which animated him to persevere in his curious observations upon all the other pieces of that celebrated collection; but, perceiving that the doctor manifested no signs of pleasure and satisfaction, but rather beheld them with a silent air of disdain, he could not digest his indifference, and asked, with a waggish sneer, if ever he had seen such a number of masterpieces before? The physician, eyeing him with a look of compassion, mingled with contempt, observed, that there was nothing there which deserved the attention of any person acquainted with the ideas of the ancients; and that the author of the finest piece now in being was unworthy to clean the brushes of one of those great masters who are celebrated by the Greek and Roman writers.

"O lud! O lud!" exclaimed the painter, with a loud laugh, "you have fairly brought yourself into a dilemma at last, dear doctor, for it is well known that your ancient Greek and Roman artists knew nothing at all of the matter, in comparison with our modern masters; for this good reason, because they had but three or four colours, and knew not how to paint with oil. Besides, which of all your old fusty Grecians would you put upon a footing with the divine Raphael, the most excellent Michael Angelo, Bona Roti, the graceful Guido, the bewitching Titian, and, above all others, the sublime Rubens, the"—he would have proceeded with a long catalogue of names which he had got by heart for the purpose, without retaining the least idea of their several qualifications, had not he been interrupted by his friend, whose indignation being kindled by the irreverence with which he mentioned the Greeks, he called him blasphemer, Goth, Bœotian, and, in his turn, asked with great vehemence which of those puny moderns could match with Panænus of Athens, and his brother Phidias, Polycletus of Sicyon, Polygnotus the Thasian, Parrhasius of Ephesus, surnamed Abrodiaitos, or *the Beau*, and Apelles, the prince of painters? He challenged him to show any portrait of these days that could vie with the Helen of Xeuxis the Heraclean, or any composition equal to the Sacrifice of Iphigenia, by Timanthes the Sicyonian; not to mention the twelve gods of Asclepiadorus the Athenian, for which Mnason, tyrant of Elatea, gave him about three hundred pounds a-piece; or Homer's Hell, by Nicias, who refused sixty talents, amounting to upwards of eleven thousand pounds, and generously made a present of it to his own country. He desired him to produce a collection equal to that in the Temple of Delphos, mentioned in the *Ion* of Euripides, where Hercules and his companion Iolaus are represented in the act of killing the

Lernæan hydra, with golden sickles, *kruseais harpais*, where Bellerophon appears on his winged steed, vanquishing the fire-breathing chimera, *tan puripneousan*, and the War of the Giants is described—here Jupiter stands wielding the red-hot thunder-bolt, *Keraunon amphipuron*; there Pallas, dreadful to the view, *Gorgopon*, brandisheth her spear against the huge Enceladus; and Bacchus, with slender ivory rods, defeats and slays the *gas teknon*, or mighty son of earth.

The painter was astonished and confounded at this rhapsody of names and instances, which was uttered with surprising eagerness and rapidity, and suspected at first that the whole was the creation of his own brain. But when Pickle, with a view of flattering the doctor's self-conceit, espoused his side of the question, and confirmed the truth of everything he advanced, Mr. Pallet changed his opinion, and in emphatic silence adored the immensity of his friend's understanding. In short, Peregrine easily perceived that they were false enthusiasts, without the smallest pretensions to taste and sensibility, and pretended to be in raptures with they knew not what, the one thinking it was incumbent upon him to express transports on seeing the works of those who had been most eminent in his profession, whether they did or did not really raise his admiration; and the other, as a scholar, deeming it his duty to magnify the ancients above all competition, with an affected fervour, which the knowledge of their excellences never inspired. Indeed, our young gentle-man so successfully accommodated himself to the dispositions of each, that, long before their review was finished, he was become a particular favourite with both.

From the Palais Royal he accompanied them to the cloisters of the Carthusians, where they considered the history of St. Bruno, by Le Sueur, whose name being unknown to the painter, he gave judgment against the whole composition, as pitiful and paltry, though, in the opinion of all good judges, it is a most masterly performance.

Having satisfied their curiosity in this place, Peregrine asked them to favour him with their company at dinner; but, whether out of caution against the insinuations of one whose character they did not know, or by reason of a prior engagement, they declined his invitation, on pretence of having an appointment at a certain ordinary, though they expressed a desire of being far-ther acquainted with him; and Mr. Pallet took the freedom of asking his name, which he not only declared, but promised, as they were strangers in Paris, to wait upon them next day in the forenoon, in order to conduct them to the Hôtel de Toulouse, and the houses of several other noblemen, remarkable for paintings or curious furniture. They thankfully embraced his proposal, and that same day made inquiry among the English gentlemen about the character of our hero, which they found so much to their satisfaction, that, upon their second meeting, they courted his good graces without reserve; and, as they had heard of his intended departure, begged earnestly to have the honour of accompanying him through the Low Countries. He assured them, that nothing could be more agreeable to him than the prospect of having such fellow-travellers; and they immediately appointed a day for setting out on that tour.

CHAPTER XLIII

He introduces his new Friends to Mr. Jolter, with whom the Doctor enters into a Dispute upon Government, which had well-nigh terminated in open War.

MEANWHILE, he not only made them acquainted with everything worth seeing in town, but attended them in their excursions to all the King's houses within a day's journey of Paris; and, in course of these parties, treated them with an elegant dinner at his own apartments, where a dispute arose between the doctor and Mr. Jolter, which had well-nigh terminated in an irreconcilable animosity. These gentlemen, with an equal share of pride, pedantry, and saturnine disposition, were, by the accidents of education and company, diametrically opposite in political maxims; the one, as we have already observed, being a bigoted high churchman, and the other a rank republican. It was an article of the governor's creed, that the people could not be happy, nor the earth yield its fruits in abundance, under a restricted clergy and limited government; whereas, in the doctor's opinion, it was an eternal truth, that no constitution was so perfect as the democracy, and that no country could flourish, but under the administration of the mob.

These considerations being premised, no wonder that they happened to disagree in the freedom of an unreserved conversation, especially as their entertainer took all opportunities of encouraging and inflaming the contention. The first source of their difference was an unlucky remark of the painter, who observed that the partridge, of which he was then eating, had the finest relish of any he had ever tasted. His friend owned that the birds were the best of the kind he had seen in France; but affirmed that they were neither so plump nor delicious as those that were caught in England.—The governor, considering this observation as the effect of prejudice and inexperience, said, with a sarcastical smile, "I believe, sir, you are very well disposed to find everything here inferior to the productions of your own country." "True, sir," answered the physician, with a certain solemnity of aspect, "and not without good reason, I hope." "And pray," resumed the tutor, "why may not the partridges of France be as good as those of England?" "For a very plain reason," replied the other, "because they are not so well fed. The iron hand of oppression is extended to all animals within the French dominions, even to the beasts of the field and the fowls of the air. *Kunessin oionoisi te pasi.*" "Egad!" cried the painter, "that is a truth not to be controverted; for my own part, I am none of your tit-bits, one would think, but yet there's a freshness in the English complexion, a *ginseekye*, I think you call it, so inviting to a hungry Frenchman, that I have caught several in the very act of viewing me with an eye of extreme appetite as I passed; and as for their curs, or rather their wolves, whenever I set eyes on one of 'em, Ah! your humble servant, Mr. Son of a bitch; I am upon my guard in an instant. The doctor can testify that their very horses, or more properly their live carrion, that drew our chaise, used to reach back their long necks, and smell at us, as a couple of delicious morsels."

This sally of Mr. Pallet, which was received with a general laugh of approbation, would, in all probability, have stifled the dispute in embryo, had not Mr. Jolter, with a self-applauding simper, ironically complimented the strangers on their talking like true Englishmen. The doctor, affronted at the insinuation, told him, with some warmth, that he was mistaken in his conjecture, his affections and ideas being confined to no particular country; for he considered himself as a citizen of the world. He owned himself more attached to England than to any other kingdom, but this preference was the effect of reflection, and not of prejudice; because the British constitution approached nearer than any other to that perfection of government, the democracy of Athens, which he hoped one day to see revived. He mentioned the death of Charles the First, and the expulsion of his son, with raptures of applause; inveighed with great acrimony against the kingly name; and, in order to strengthen his opinion, repeated forty or fifty lines from one of the Philippics of Demosthenes.

Jolter, hearing him speak so disrespectfully of the higher powers, glowed with indignation. He said his doctrines were detestable, and destructive of all right, order, and society; that monarchy was of divine institution, therefore indefeasible by any human power; and, of consequence, those events in the English history, which he had so liberally commended, were no other than flagrant instances of sacrilege, perfidy, and sedition; that the democracy of Athens was a most absurd constitution, productive of anarchy and mischief, which must always happen when the government of a nation depends upon the caprice of the ignorant hair-brained vulgar; that it was in the power of the most profligate member of the commonwealth, provided he was endowed with eloquence, to ruin the most deserving, by a desperate exertion of his talents upon the populace, who had been often persuaded to act in the most ungrateful and imprudent manner against the greatest patriots that their country had produced; and, finally, he averred, that the liberal arts and sciences had never flourished so much in a republic as under the encouragement and protection of absolute power; witness the Augustan age, and the reign of Lewis the Fourteenth, nor was it to be supposed that genius and merit could ever be so amply recompensed by individuals, or distracted councils of a commonwealth, as by the generosity and magnificence of one who had the whole treasures at his own command.

Peregrine, who was pleased to find the contest grow warm, observed that there seemed to be a good deal of truth in what Mr. Jolter advanced; and the painter, whose opinion began to waver, looked with a face of expectation at his friend, who, modelling his features into an expression of exulting disdain, asked of his antagonist, if he did not think that very power of rewarding merit enabled an absolute prince to indulge himself in the most arbitrary licence over the lives and fortunes of his people? Before the governor had time to answer this question, Pallet broke forth into an exclamation of "By the Lord! that is certainly a fact, egad! that was a home-thrust, doctor." When Mr. Jolter, chastising this shallow intruder with a contemptuous look, affirmed, that though supreme power furnished a good prince with the means of exerting his virtues, it would not support a tyrant in the exercise of cruelty and oppression; because in all nations the genius of the people must be consulted by their governors, and the burden proportioned to the shoulders on which it is laid.—"Else, what follows?" said the physician. "The consequence is plain," replied the governor, "insurrection, revolt, and his own destruction; for it is not to be supposed that the subjects of any nation would be so abject and pusillanimous as to neglect the means which Heaven had put in their power for their own preservation." "Gadzooks, you're in the right, sir," cried Pallet, "that I grant you must be confessed. Doctor, I'm afraid we have got into the wrong box." This son of Pæan, however, far from being of his friend's opinion, observed with an air of triumph, that he would not only demonstrate the sophistry of the gentleman's last allegation by arguments and facts, but even confute him with his own words. Jolter's eyes kindling at this presumptuous declaration, he told his antagonist, while his lip quivered with resentment, that, if his arguments were no better than his breeding, he was sure he would make very few converts to his opinion; and the doctor, with all the insolence of triumph, advised him to beware of disputes for the future, until he should have made himself more master of his subject.

Peregrine both wished and hoped to see the disputants proceed to arguments of more weight and conviction; and the painter, dreading the same issue, interposed with the usual exclamation of "For God's sake, gentlemen!" when the governor rose from table in great dudgeon, and left the room, muttering some ejaculation, of which the word coxcomb only could be distinctly heard. The physician, being thus left master of the field of battle, was complimented on his victory by Peregrine, and so elevated by his success, that he declaimed a full hour on the absurdity of Jolter's proposition, and the beauty of the democratic administration; canvassed the whole scheme of Plato's republic, with many quotations from that ideal author touching the *to kalon*; from thence he made a transition to the moral sense of Shaftesbury, and concluded his harangue with the greatest part of that frothy writer's rhapsody, which he repeated with all the violence of enthusiastic agitation, to the unspeakable satisfaction of his entertainer, and the unutterable admiration of Pallet, who looked upon him as something supernatural and divine.

So intoxicated was this vain young man with the ironical praises of Pickle, that he forthwith shook off all reserve, and, having professed a friendship for our hero, whose taste and learning he did not fail to extol, intimated, in plain terms, that he was the only person in these latter ages who possessed that sublime genius, that portion of the divinity of *Ti Theion*, which immortalised the Grecian poets; that as Pythagoras affirmed the spirit of Euphorbus had transmigrated into his body, he, the doctor, was strangely possessed with the opinion that he himself was inspired by the soul of Pindar; because, making allowance for the difference of languages in which they wrote, there was a surprising affinity between his own works and those of that celebrated Theban; and, as a confirmation of this truth, he immediately produced a sample of each, which, though in spirit and versification as different as the Odes of Horace, and our present Poet Laureate, Peregrine did not scruple to pronounce altogether congenial, notwithstanding the violence he by this sentence offered to his own conscience, and a certain alarm of his pride, that was weak enough to be disturbed by the physician's ridiculous vanity and presumption, which, not contented with displaying his importance in the world of taste and polite literature, manifested itself in arrogating certain material discoveries in the province of physic, which could not fail to advance him to the highest pinnacle of that profession, considering the recommendation of his other talents, together with a liberal fortune which he inherited from his father.

CHAPTER XLIV

The Doctor prepares an Entertainment in the Manner of the Ancients, which is attended with divers ridiculous Circumstances.

In a word, our young gentleman, by his insinuating behaviour, acquired the full confidence of the doctor, who invited him to an entertainment, which he intended to prepare in the manner of the ancients. Pickle, struck with this idea, eagerly embraced the proposal, which he honoured with many encomiums, as a plan in all respects worthy of his genius and apprehension; and the day was appointed at some distance of time, that the treater might have leisure to compose certain pickles and confections, which were not to be found among the culinary preparations of these degenerate days.

With a view of rendering the physician's taste more conspicuous, and extracting from it the more diversion, Peregrine proposed that some foreigners should partake of the banquet; and the task being left to his care and discretion, he actually bespoke the company of a French marquis, an Italian count, and a German baron, whom he knew to be egregious coxcombs, and therefore more likely to enhance the joy of the entertainment.

Accordingly, the hour being arrived, he conducted them to the hotel where the physician lodged, after having regaled their expectations with an elegant meal in the genuine old Roman taste; and they were received by Mr. Pallet, who did the honours of the house, while his friend superintended the cook below. By this communicative painter, the guests understood that the doctor had met with numerous difficulties in the execution of his design; that no fewer than five cooks had been dismissed, because they could not prevail upon their own consciences to obey his directions in things that were contrary to the present practice of their art; and that although he had at last engaged a person, by an extraordinary premium, to comply with his orders, the fellow was so astonished, mortified, and incensed at the commands he had received, that his hair stood on end, and he begged, on his knees, to be released from the agreement he had made; but finding that his employer insisted upon the performance of his contract, and threatened to introduce him to the commissaire, if he should flinch from the bargain, he had, in the discharge of his office, wept, sung, cursed, and capered, for two whole hours without intermission.

While the company listened to this odd information, by which they were prepossessed with strange notions of the dinner, their ears were invaded by a piteous voice, that exclaimed in French, "For the love of God! dear sir! for the passion of Jesus Christ! spare me the mortification of the honey and oil!" Their ears still vibrated with the sound, when the doctor entering, was by Peregrine made acquainted with the strangers, to whom he, in the transports of his wrath, could not help complaining of the want of complaisance he had found in the Parisian vulgar, by which his plan had been almost entirely ruined and set aside. The French marquis, who thought the honour of his nation was concerned at this declaration, professed his sorrow for what had happened, so contrary to the established character of the people, and undertook to see the delinquents severely punished, provided he could be informed of their names or places of abode.

The mutual compliments that passed on this occasion were scarce finished, when a servant, coming into the room, announced dinner; and the entertainer led the way into another apartment, where they found a long table, or rather two boards joined together, and furnished with a variety of dishes, the steams of which had such evident effect upon the nerves of the company, that the marquis, made frightful grimaces, under pretence of taking snuff; the Italian's eyes watered; the German's visage underwent several distortions of feature; our hero found means to exclude the odour from his sense of smelling, by breathing only through his mouth; and the poor painter, running into another room, plugged his nostrils with tobacco. The doctor himself, who was the only person then present whose organs were not discomposed, pointing to a couple of couches placed on each side of the table, told his guests that he was sorry he could not procure the exact triclinia of the ancients, which were somewhat different from these conveniences, and desired they would have the goodness to repose themselves without ceremony, each in his respective couchette, while he and his friend Mr. Pallet would place themselves upright at the ends, that they might have the pleasure of serving those that lay along. This disposition, of which the strangers had no previous idea, disconcerted and perplexed them in a most ridiculous manner; the marquis and baron stood bowing to each other, on pretence of disputing the lower seat, but in reality with a view of profiting by the example of each other, for neither of them understood the manner in which they were to loll; and Peregrine, who enjoyed their confusion, handed the count to the other side, where, with the most mischievous politeness, he insisted upon his taking possession of the upper place.

In this disagreeable and ludicrous suspense, they continued acting a pantomime of gesticulations, until the doctor earnestly entreated them to waive all compliment and form, lest the dinner should be spoiled before the ceremonial could be adjusted. Thus conjured, Peregrine took the lower couch on the left-hand side, laying himself gently down, with his face towards the table. The marquis, in imitation of this pattern, though he would have much rather fasted three days than run the risk of discomposing his dress by such an attitude, stretched himself upon the opposite place, reclining upon his elbow in a most painful and awkward situation, with his head raised above the end of the couch, that the economy of his hair might not suffer by the projection of his body. The Italian, being a thin limber creature, planted himself next to Pickle, without sustaining any misfortune, but that of his stocking being torn by a ragged nail of the seat, as he raised his legs on a level with the rest of his limbs. But the baron, who was neither so wieldy nor supple in his joints as his companions, flounced himself down with such precipitation, that his feet, suddenly tilting up, came in furious contact with the head of the marquis, and demolished every curl in a twinkling, while his own skull, at the same instant, descended upon the side of his couch with such violence, that his periwig was struck off, and the whole room filled with pulvilio.

The drollery of distress that attended this disaster entirely vanquished the affected gravity of our young gentleman, who was obliged to suppress his laughter by cramming his handkerchief in his mouth; for the bareheaded German asked pardon with such ridiculous confusion, and the marquis admitted his apology with such rueful complaisance, as were sufficient to awake the mirth of a Quietist.

This misfortune being repaired as well as the circumstances of the occasion would permit, and every one settled according to the arrangement already described, the doctor graciously undertook to give some account of the dishes as they occurred, that the company might be directed in their choice; and, with an air of infinite satisfaction, thus began, "This here, gentlemen, is a boiled goose, served up in a sauce composed of pepper, lovage, coriander, mint, rue, anchovies, and oil! I wish, for your sakes, gentlemen, it was one of the geese of Ferrara, so much celebrated among the ancients for the magnitude of their livers, one of which is said to have weighed upwards of two pounds; with this food, exquisite as it was, did the tyrant Heliogabalus regale his hounds. But I beg pardon, I had almost forgot the soup, which I hear is so necessary an article at all the tables in France. At each end there are dishes of the salacacabia of the Romans; one is made of parsley, pennyroyal, cheese, pinetops, honey, vinegar, brine, eggs, cucumbers, onions, and hen livers; the other is much the same as the soup-maigre of this country. Then there is a loin of boiled veal with fennel and carraway seed, on a pottage composed of pickle, oil, honey, and flour, and a curious hashis of the lights, liver, and blood of a hare, together with a dish of roasted pigeons. Monsieur le baron, shall I help you to a plate of this soup?" The German, who did not at all disapprove of the ingredients, assented to the proposal, and seemed to relish the composition; while the marquis being asked by the painter which of the silly-kickabys he chose, was, in consequence of his desire, accommodated with a portion of the soup-maigre; and the count, in lieu of spoon meat, of which he said he was no great admirer, supplied himself with a pigeon, therein conforming to the choice of our young gentleman, whose example he determined to follow through the whole course of the entertainment.

The Frenchman having swallowed the first spoonful, made a full pause, his throat swelled as if an egg had stuck in his gullet, his eyes rolled, and his mouth underwent a series of involuntary contractions and dilatations. Pallet, who looked stedfastly at this connoisseur, with a view of consulting his taste, before he himself would venture upon the soup, began to be disturbed at these emotions, and observed, with some concern, that the poor gentleman seemed to be going into a fit; when Peregrine assured him, that these were symptoms of ecstasy, and, for further confirmation, asked the marquis how he found the soup. It was with infinite difficulty that his complaisance could so far master his disgust, as to enable him to answer, "Altogether excellent, upon my honour!" And the painter being certified of his approbation, lifted the spoon to his mouth without scruple; but far from justifying the eulogium of his taster, when this precious composition diffused itself upon his palate, he seemed to be deprived of all sense and motion, and sat like the leaden statue of some river god, with the liquor flowing out at both sides of his mouth.

The doctor, alarmed at this indecent phenomenon, earnestly inquired into the cause of it; and when Pallet recovered his recollection, and swore that he would rather swallow porridge made of burning brimstone, than such an infernal mess as that which he had tasted, the physician, in his own vindication, assured the company, that, except the usual ingredients, he had mixed nothing in the soup but some sal-ammoniac, instead of the ancient nitrum, which could not now be procured; and appealed to the marquis, whether such a succedaneum was not an improvement on the whole. The unfortunate petit-maître, driven to the extremity of his condescension, acknowledged it to be a masterly refinement; and deeming himself obliged, in point of honour, to evince his sentiments by his practice, forced a few more mouthfuls of this disagreeable potion down his throat, till his stomach was so much offended, that he was compelled to start up of a sudden, and, in the hurry of his elevation, over-turned his plate into the bosom of the baron. The emergency of his occasions would not permit him to stay and make apologies for this abrupt behaviour; so that he flew into another apart-ment, where Pickle found him puking, and crossing himself with great devotion; and a chair, at his desire, being brought to the door, he slipped into it more dead than alive, conjuring his friend Pickle to make his peace with the company, and, in par-ticular, excuse him to the baron, on account of the violent fit of illness with which he had been seized. It was not without reason that he employed a mediator; for when our hero returned to the

dining-room, the German got up, and was under the hands of
his own lacquey, who wiped the grease from a rich embroidered
waistcoat, while he, almost frantic with his misfortune, stamped
upon the ground, and, in High Dutch, cursed the unlucky banquet, and the impertinent entertainer, who all this time, with
great deliberation, consoled him for the disaster, by assuring him,
that the damage might be repaired with some oil of turpentine
and a hot iron.   Peregrine, who could scarce refrain from laughing in his face, appeased his indignation, by telling him how
much the whole company, and especially the marquis, was
mortified at the accident; and the unhappy salacacabia being
removed, the places were filled with two pies—one of dormice,
liquored with syrup of white poppies, which the doctor had
substituted in the room of toasted poppy-seed, formerly eaten
with honey, as a dessert; and the other composed of an hock of
pork baked in honey.

Pallet hearing the first of these dishes described, lifted up his
hands and eyes, and, with signs of loathing and amazement,
pronounced, "A pie made of dormice and syrup of poppies!—
Lord in heaven! what beastly fellows those Romans were!"
His friend checked him for his irreverent exclamation with a
severe look, and recommended the veal, of which he himself
cheerfully ate, with such encomiums to the company, that the
baron resolved to imitate his example, after having called for a
bumper of burgundy, which the physician, for his sake, wished
to have been the true wine of Falernum.   The painter, seeing
nothing else upon the table which he would venture to touch,
made a merit of necessity, and had recourse to the veal also;
although he could not help saying, that he would not give one
slice of the roast beef of Old England for all the dainties of a
Roman emperor's table.   But all the doctor's invitations and
assurances could not prevail upon his guests to honour the hashis
and the goose; and that course was succeeded by another, in
which he told them were divers of those dishes, which, among
the ancients, had obtained the appellation of *politeles*, or
magnificent.   "That which smokes in the middle," said he,
"is a sow's stomach, filled with a composition of minced pork,
hog's brains, eggs, pepper, cloves, garlic, aniseed, rue, ginger,
oil, wine, and pickle.   On the right-hand side are the teats
and belly of a sow, just farrowed, fried with sweet wine,
oil, flour, lovage, and pepper.   On the left is a fricassee of
snails, fed, or rather purged, with milk.   At that end, next
Mr. Pallet, are fritters of pompions, lovage, origanum, and oil;

and here are a couple of pullets, roasted and stuffed in the manner of Apicius."

The painter, who had, by wry faces, testified his abhorrence of the sow's stomach, which he compared to a bagpipe, and the snails, which had undergone purgation, no sooner heard him mention the roasted pullets, than he eagerly solicited a wing of the fowl; upon which the doctor desired he would take the trouble of cutting them up, and accordingly sent them round, while Mr. Pallet tucked the tablecloth under his chin, and brandished his knife and fork with singular address; but scarce were they set down before him, when the tears ran down his cheeks, and he called aloud in a manifest disorder, "Zounds! this is the essence of a whole bed of garlic!" That he might not, however, disappoint or disgrace the entertainer, he applied his instruments to one of the birds; and, when he opened up the cavity, was assaulted by such an irruption of intolerable smells, that, without staying to disengage himself from the cloth, he sprung away, with an exclamation of "Lord Jesus!" and involved the whole table in havoc, ruin, and confusion.

Before Pickle could accomplish his escape, he was sauced with a syrup of the dormice pie, which went to pieces in the general wreck. And as for the Italian count, he was overwhelmed by the sow's stomach, which, bursting in the fall, discharged its contents upon his leg and thigh, and scalded him so miserably, that he shrieked with anguish, and grinned with a most ghastly and horrible aspect.

The baron, who sat secure without the vortex of this tumult, was not at all displeased at seeing his companions involved in such a calamity as that which he had already shared; but the doctor was confounded with shame and vexation. After having prescribed an application of oil to the count's leg, he expressed his sorrow for the misadventure, which he openly ascribed to want of taste and prudence in the painter, who did not think proper to return, and make an apology in person; and protested that there was nothing in the fowls which could give offence to a sensible nose, the stuffing being a mixture of pepper, lovage, and *assafœtida*, and the sauce consisting of wine and herring-pickle, which he had used instead of the celebrated *garum* of the Romans; that famous pickle having been prepared sometimes of the *scombri*, which were a sort of tunny-fish, and sometimes of the *silurus* or shad-fish; nay, he observed that there was a third kind, called *garum hœmation*, made of the guts, gills, and blood of the *thynnus*.

The physician, finding it would be impracticable to re-establish the order of the banquet, by presenting again the dishes which had been discomposed, ordered everything to be removed, a clean cloth to be laid, and the dessert to be brought in.

Meanwhile, he regretted his incapacity to give them a specimen of the *alieus*, or fish-meals of the ancients—such as the *jus diabaton*, the conger-eel; which, in Galen's opinion, is hard of digestion; the *cornuta*, or gurnard, described by Pliny, in his *Natural History*, who says, the horns of many of them were a foot and a half in length; the mullet and lamprey, that were in the highest estimation of old, of which last Julius Cæsar borrowed six thousand for one triumphal supper. He observed, that the manner of dressing them was described by Horace, in the account he gives of the entertainment to which Mæcenas was invited by the epicure Nasidienus—

Affertur squillos inter murena natantes, etc.

and told them, that they were commonly eaten with the *thus Syriacum*, a certain anodyne and astringent seed, which qualified the purgative nature of the fish. Finally, this learned physician gave them to understand, that, though this was reckoned a luxurious dish in the zenith of the Roman taste, it was by no means comparable, in point of expense, to some preparations in vogue about the time of that absurd voluptuary Heliogabalus, who ordered the brains of six hundred ostriches to be compounded in one mess.

By this time the dessert appeared; and the company were not a little rejoiced to see plain olives, in salt and water. But what the master of the feast valued himself upon was, a sort of jelly, which he affirmed to be preferable to the *hypotrimma* of Hesychius, being a mixture of vinegar, pickle, and honey, boiled to a proper consistence, and candied *assafœtida*, which he asserted, in contradiction to Aumelbergius and Lister, was no other than the *laser Syriacum*, so precious as to be sold among the ancients to the weight of a silver penny. The gentlemen took his word for the excellency of this gum, but contented themselves with the olives, which gave such an agreeable relish to the wine that they seemed very well disposed to console themselves for the disgraces they had endured; and Pickle, unwilling to lose the least circumstance of entertainment that could be enjoyed in their company, went in quest of the painter, who remained in his penitentials in another apartment, and could not be persuaded to re-enter the banqueting-room, until Peregrine undertook to procure his pardon from those whom he had injured. Having assured him of this indulgence, our young gentleman led him in like a criminal, bowing on all hands with an air of humility and contrition; and particularly addressing himself to the count, to whom he swore in English, as God was his Saviour, he had no intent to affront man, woman, or child; but was fain to make the best of his way, that he might not give the honourable company cause of offence, by obeying the dictates of nature in their presence.

When Pickle interpreted this apology to the Italian, Pallet was forgiven in very polite terms, and even received into favour by his friend the doctor, in consequence of our hero's intercession; so that all the guests forgot their chagrin, and paid their respects so piously to the bottle, that, in a short time, the champagne produced very evident effects in the behaviour of all present.

CHAPTER XLV

The Painter is persuaded to accompany Pickle to a Masquerade in Woman's Apparel—Is engaged in a troublesome Adventure, and, with his Companion, conveyed to the Bastile.

THE painter, at the request of Pickle, who had a design upon the count's sense of hearing, favoured the company with the song of *Bumper Squire Jones*, which yielded infinite satisfaction to the baron; but affected the delicate ears of the Italian in such a manner, that his features expressed astonishment and disquiet; and, by his sudden and repeated journeys to the door, it plainly appeared that he was in the same predicament with those who, as Shakespeare observes, when the bagpipe sings in the nose, cannot contain their urine for affection.

With a view, therefore, of vindicating music from such a barbarous taste, Mr. Pallet had no sooner performed his task, than the count honoured his friends with some favourite airs of his own country, which he warbled with infinite grace and expression, though they had not energy sufficient to engage the attention of the German, who fell fast asleep upon his couch, and snored so loud as to interrupt and totally annul this ravishing entertainment; so that they were fain to have recourse again to the glass, which made such innovation upon the brain of the physician, that he sung divers odes of Anacreon, to a tune of his own composing, and held forth upon the music and recitative of the ancients with great erudition; while Pallet, having found means to make the Italian acquainted with the nature of his profession, harangued upon painting with wonderful volubility, in a language which it was well for his own credit the stranger did not understand.

At length the doctor was seized with such a qualm, that he begged Peregrine to lead him to his chamber; and the baron being waked, retired with the count.

Peregrine, being rendered frolicsome by the wine he had drank, proposed that he and Pallet should go to a masquerade, which he recollected was to be given that night. The painter did not want curiosity and inclination to accompany him, but expressed his apprehension of losing him in the ball, an accident which could not fail to be very disagreeable, as he was an utter stranger to the language and the town. To obviate this objection, the landlady, who was of their counsel, advised him to appear in a woman's dress, which would lay his companion under the necessity of attending him with more care, as he could not with decency detach himself from the lady whom he should introduce: besides, such a supposed connexion would hinder the ladies of pleasure from accosting and employing their seducing arts upon a person already engaged.

Our young gentleman, foreseeing the abundance of diversion in the execution of this project, seconded the proposal with such importunity and address, that the painter allowed himself to be habited in a suit belonging to the landlady, who also procured for him a mask and domino, while Pickle provided himself with a Spanish dress. In this disguise, which they put on about eleven o'clock, did they, attended by Pipes, set out in a fiacre for the ballroom, into which Pickle led this supposititious female, to the astonishment of the whole company, who had never seen such an uncouth figure in the appearance of a woman.

After they had taken a view of all the remarkable masks, and the painter had been treated with a glass of liquor, his mischievous companion gave him the slip, and vanishing in an instant, returned with another mask and domino over his habit, that he might enjoy Pallet's perplexity, and be at hand to protect him from insult.

The poor painter, having lost his guide, was almost distracted with anxiety, and stalked about the room in quest of him, with such huge strides and oddity of gesture, that he was followed by a whole multitude, who gazed at him, as a preternatural phenomenon. This attendance increased his uneasiness to such a degree, that he could not help uttering a soliloquy aloud, in which he cursed his fate for having depended upon the promise of such a wag; and swore, that, if once he was clear of this scrape, he would not bring himself into such a premunire again for the whole kingdom of France.

Divers petit-maîtres, understanding the mask was a foreigner, who, in all probability, could not speak French, made up to him in their turns, in order to display their wit and address, and teased him with several arch questions, to which he made no other answer than, "No *parly Francy*. D—n your chattering! —Go about your business, can't ye?" Among the masks was a nobleman, who began to be very free with the supposed lady, and attempted to plunge his hand into her bosom. But the painter was too modest to suffer such indecent treatment; and, when the gallant repeated his efforts in a manner still more indelicate, lent him such a box on the ear, as made the lights dance before him, and created such a suspicion of Pallet's sex, that the Frenchman swore that he was either a male or herma-phrodite, and insisted upon a scrutiny, for the sake of his own honour, with such obstinacy of resentment, that the fictitious nymph was in imminent danger, not only of being exposed, but also of undergoing severe chastisement, for having made so free with the prince's ear; when Peregrine, who saw and overheard everything that passed, thought it was high time to interpose; and accordingly asserted his pretensions to the insulted lady, who was overjoyed at this proof of his protection.

The affronted gallant persevered in demanding to know who she was, and our hero as strenuously refused to give him that satisfaction; so that high words ensued; and the prince threat-ening to punish his insolence, the young gentleman, who was not supposed to know his quality, pointed to the place where his own sword used to hang; and snapping his fingers in his face, laid hold on the painter's arm, and led him to another part of the room, leaving his antagonist to the meditations of his own revenge.

Pallet, having chid his conductor for his barbarous desertion, made him acquainted with the difficulty in which he had been involved, and flatly telling him he would not put it in his power to give him the slip again, held fast by his arm during the remaining part of the entertainment, to the no small diver-sion of the company, whose attention was altogether engrossed in the contemplation of such an awkward, ungainly, stalking apparition. At last, Pickle being tired of exhibiting this raree-show, complied with the repeated desires of his companion, and handed her into the coach; which he himself had no sooner entered, than they were surrounded by a file of musketeers, commanded by an exempt, who, ordering the coach-door to be opened, took his place with great deliberation, while one of his detachment mounted the box, in order to direct the driver.

Peregrine at once conceived the meaning of this arrest, and it was well for him that he had no weapon wherewith to stand upon his defence; for such was the impetuosity and rashness of his temper, that, had he been armed, he would have run all risks rather than surrender himself to any odds whatever; but Pallet imagining that the officer was some gentleman who had mistaken their carriage for his own, desired his friend to undeceive the stranger; and, when he was informed of the real state of their condition, his knees began to shake, his teeth to chatter, and he uttered a most doleful lamentation, importing his fear of being carried to some hideous dungeon of the Bastile, where he should spend the rest of his days in misery and horror, and never see the light of God's sun, nor the face of a friend, but perish in a foreign land, far removed from his family and connexions. Pickle d—ned him for his pusillanimity; and the exempt hearing a lady bemoan herself so piteously, expressed his mortification at being the instrument of giving her such pain, and endeavoured to console them, by representing the lenity of the French government, and the singular generosity of the prince, by whose order they were apprehended.

Peregrine, whose discretion seemed to forsake him on all such occasions, exclaimed with great bitterness against the arbitrary administration of France, and inveighed, with many expressions of contempt, against the character of the offended prince, whose resentment (far from being noble, he said) was pitiful, ungenerous, and unjust. To this remonstrance, the officer made no reply, but shrugged up his shoulders in silent astonishment at the hardiesse of the prisoner, and the fiacre was just on the point of setting out, when they heard the noise of a scuffle at the back of the coach, and the voice of Tom Pipes pronouncing, "I'll be d—ned if I do." This trusty attendant had been desired by one of the guard to descend from his station in the rear, but, as he resolved to share his master's fate, he took no notice of their entreaties, until they were seconded by force; and that he endeavoured to repel with his heel, which he applied with such energy to the jaws of the soldier who first came in contact with him, that they emitted a crashing sound like a dried walnut between

the grinders of a templar in the pit. Exasperated at this outrage, the other saluted Tom's posteriors with his bayonet, which
incommoded him so much, that he could no longer keep his post,
but, leaping upon the ground, gave his antagonist a chuck under
the chin, which laid him upon his back, and then skipping over
him with infinite agility, absconded among the crowd of coaches,
till he saw the guard mount before and behind upon his master's
fiacre, which no sooner set forward than he followed at a small
distance, to reconnoitre the place where Peregrine should be
confined.

After having proceeded slowly through many windings and
turnings, to a part of Paris in which Pipes was an utter stranger,
the coach stopped at a great gate, with a wicket in the middle,
which being opened at the approach of the carriage, the prisoners
were admitted; and, the guard returning with the fiacre, Tom
determined to watch in that place all night, that in the morning
he might make such observations as might be conducive to the
enlargement of his master.

CHAPTER XLVI

By the Fidelity of Pipes, Jolter is informed of his Pupil's Fate—Confers
with the Physician—Applies to the Ambassador, who, with great Difficulty,
obtains the Discharge of the Prisoners, on certain Conditions.

THIS plan he executed, notwithstanding the pain of his wound,
and the questions of the city-guard both horse and foot, to which
he could make no other answer than "*Anglois, Anglois*"; and as
soon as it was light, taking an accurate survey of the castle (for
such it seemed to be) into which Peregrine and Pallet had been
conveyed, together with its situation in respect to the river, he
went home to their lodgings, and waking Mr. Jolter, gave him an
account of the adventure. The governor wrung his hands in the
utmost grief and consternation, when he heard this unfortunate
piece of news; he did not doubt that his pupil was imprisoned in
the Bastile for life; and, in the anguish of his apprehension,
cursed the day on which he had undertaken to superintend the
conduct of such an imprudent young man, who had, by reiter-
ated insults, provoked the vengeance of such a mild forbearing
administration.

That he might not, however, neglect any means in his power
to extricate him from his present misfortune, he despatched

Thomas to the doctor, with an account of his companion's fate, that they might join their interest in behalf of the captives; and the physician, being informed of what had happened, immediately dressed himself and repaired to Jolter, whom he accosted in these words: "Now, sir, I hope you are convinced in your error, in asserting that oppression can never be the effect of arbitrary power. Such a calamity as this could never have happened under the Athenian democracy. Nay, even when the tyrant Pisistratus got possession of the commonwealth, he durst not venture to rule with such absolute and unjust dominion. You shall see now that Mr. Pickle and my friend Pallet will fall a sacrifice to the tyranny of lawless power; and, in my opinion, we shall be accessary to the ruin of this poor enslaved people, if we bestir ourselves in demanding or imploring the release of our unhappy countrymen; as we may thereby prevent the commission of a flagrant crime, which would fill up the vengeance of Heaven against the perpetrators, and perhaps be the means of restoring a whole nation to the unspeakable fruition of freedom. For my own part, I should rejoice to see the blood of my father spilt in such a glorious cause, provided such a victim would furnish me with the opportunity of dissolving the chains of slavery, and vindicating that liberty which is the birthright of man. Then would my name be immortalised among the patriot heroes of antiquity, and my memory, like that of Harmodius and Aristogiton, be honoured by statues erected at the public expense." This rhapsody, which was delivered with great emphasis and agitation, gave so much offence to Jolter, that, without speaking one word, he retired in great wrath to his own chamber, and the republican returned to his lodging, in full hope of his prognostic being verified in the death and destruction of Peregrine and the painter, which must give rise to some renowned revolution, wherein he himself would act a principal part. But the governor, whose imagination was not quite so warm and prolific, went directly to the ambassador, whom he informed of his pupil's situation, and besought to interpose with the French ministry, that he and the other British subject might obtain their liberty.

His excellency asked if Jolter could guess at the cause of his imprisonment, that he might be the better prepared to vindicate or excuse his conduct; but neither he nor Pipes could give the smallest hint of intelligence on that subject; though he furnished himself from Tom's own mouth with a circumstantial account of the manner in which his master had been arrested, as well as of his own behaviour, and the disaster he had received on that occasion. His lordship never doubted that Pickle had brought this calamity upon himself by some unlucky prank he had played at the masquerade; especially when he understood that the young gentleman had drank freely in the afternoon, and been so whimsical as to go thither with a man in woman's apparel; and he, that same day, waited on the French minister, in full confidence of obtaining his discharge; but met with more difficulty than he expected, the court of France being extremely punctilious in everything that concerns a prince of the blood. The ambassador was therefore obliged to talk in very high terms; and, though the present circumstances of the French politics would not allow them to fall out with the British administration for trifles, all the favour he could procure, was a promise that Pickle should be set at liberty, provided he would ask pardon of the prince to whom he had given offence. His excellency thought this was but a reasonable condescension, supposing Peregrine to have been in the wrong; and Jolter was admitted to him, in order to communicate and reinforce his lordship's advice, which was, that he should comply with the terms proposed.

The governor, who did not enter this gloomy fortress without fear and trembling, found his pupil in a dismal apartment, void of all furniture but a stool and truckle-bed; the moment he was admitted, he perceived the youth whistling with great unconcern, and working with his pencil at the bare wall, on which he had delineated a ludicrous figure, labelled with the name of the nobleman whom he had affronted, and an English mastiff with his leg lifted up, in the attitude of making water in his shoe. He had been even so presumptuous as to explain the device with satirical inscriptions in the French language, which when Jolter perused, his hair stood on end with affright. The very turnkey was confounded and overawed by the boldness of his behaviour, which he had never seen matched by any inhabitant of that place; and actually joined his friend in persuading him to submit to the easy demand of the minister. But our hero, far from embracing the counsel of this advocate, handed him to the door with great ceremony, and dismissed him with a kick on the breech; and to all the supplications and even tears of Jolter, made no other reply than that he would stoop to no condescension, because he had committed no crime; but would leave his case to the cognisance and exertion of the British court, whose duty it was to see justice done to its own subjects. He desired, however, that Pallet, who was confined in another place, might avail himself of his own disposition, which was sufficiently pliable. But when the governor desired to see his fellow-prisoner, the turnkey gave him to understand, that he had received no orders relating to the lady, and therefore could not admit him into her apartment; though he was complaisant enough to tell him that she seemed very much mortified at her confinement, and at certain times behaved as if her brain was not a little disordered.

Jolter, thus baffled in all his endeavours, quitted the Bastile with a heavy heart, and reported his fruitless negotiation to the ambassador, who could not help breaking forth into some acrimonious expressions against the obstinacy and insolence of the young man, who, he said, deserved to suffer for his folly. Nevertheless, he did not desist from his representations to the French ministry, which he found so unyielding, that he was obliged to threaten in plain terms to make it a national concern; and not only write to his court for instructions, but even advise the council to make reprisals, and send some French gentlemen in London to the Tower. This intimation had an effect upon the ministry at Versailles, who, rather than run the risk of incensing a people, whom it was neither their interest nor inclination to disoblige, consented to discharge the offenders, on condition that they should leave Paris in three days after their enlargement. This proposal was readily agreed to by Peregrine, who was now a little more tractable, and heartily tired of being cooped up in such an uncomfortable abode, for the space of three long days, without any sort of communication or entertainment, but that which his own imagination suggested.

CHAPTER XLVII

Peregrine makes himself merry at the Expense of the Painter, who curses his Landlady, and breaks with the Doctor.

As he could easily conceive the situation of his companion in adversity, he was unwilling to leave the place, until he had reaped some diversion from his distress, and with that view repaired to the dungeon of the afflicted painter, to which he had by this time free access. When he entered, the first object that presented itself to his eye was so uncommonly ridiculous, that he could scarce preserve that gravity of countenance which he had affected in order to execute the joke he had planned.

The forlorn Pallet sat upright in his bed, in a dishabille that was altogether extraordinary. He had laid aside his monstrous hoop, together with his stays, gown, and petticoat, wrapped his lappets about his head by way of night-cap, and wore his domino as a loose morning-dress; his grizzled locks hung down about his lack-lustre eyes, and tawny neck, in all the disorder of negligence; his grey beard bristled about half an inch through the remains of the paint with which his visage had been daubed, and every feature of his face was lengthened to the most ridiculous expression of grief and dismay. Seeing Peregrine come in, he started up in a sort of frantic ecstasy, and, running towards him with open arms, no sooner perceived the woeful appearance into which our hero had modelled his physiognomy, than he stopped short all of a sudden, and the joy which had begun to take possession of his heart was in a moment dispelled by the most rueful presages; so that he stood in a most ludicrous posture of dejection, like a malefactor at the Old Bailey, when sentence is about to be pronounced. Pickle, taking him by the hand, heaved a profound sigh, and after having protested that he was extremely mortified at being pitched upon as the messenger of bad news, told him, with an air of sympathy and infinite concern, that the French court having discovered his sex, had resolved, in consideration of the outrageous indignity he offered in public to a prince of the blood, to detain him in the Bastile a prisoner for life; and that this sentence was a mitigation obtained by the importunities of the British ambassador, the punishment ordained by law being no other than breaking alive on the wheel.

These tidings aggravated the horrors of the painter to such a degree, that he roared aloud, and skipped about the room in all the extravagance of distraction; taking God and man to witness that he would rather suffer immediate death, than endure one year's imprisonment in such a hideous place; and cursing the hour of his birth, and the moment on which he departed from his own country. "For my own part," said his tormentor, in a hypocritical tone, "I was obliged to swallow the bitter pill of making submission to the prince, who, as I had not presumed to strike him, received acknowledgments, in consequence of which I shall be this day set at liberty; and there is even one expedient left for the recovery of your freedom. It is, I own, a disagreeable remedy; but one had better undergo a little mortification, than be for ever wretched. Besides, upon second thoughts, I begin to imagine that you will not for such a trifle sacrifice yourself to the unceasing horrors of a solitary dungeon, especially as your condescension will in all probability be attended with advantages which you could not otherwise enjoy." Pallet, interrupting him with great eagerness, begged for the love of God that he would no longer keep him in the torture of suspense, but mention that same remedy, which he was resolved to swallow let it be never so unpalatable.

Peregrine, having thus played upon his passions of fear and hope, answered, that, as the offence was committed in the habit of a woman, which was a disguise unworthy of the other sex, the French court was of opinion that the delinquent should be reduced to the neuter gender; so that there was an alternative at his own option, by which he had it in his power to regain immediate freedom. "What!" cried the painter in despair, "become a singer? Gadzooks! and the devil and all that, I'll rather lie still where I am, and let myself be devoured by vermin." Then thrusting out his throat, "Here is my windpipe," said he, "be so good, my dear friend, as to give it a slice or two; if you don't, I shall one of these days be found dangling in my garters. What an unfortunate rascal I am! What a blockhead, and a beast, and a fool was I to trust myself among such a barbarous ruffian race! Lord forgive you, Mr. Pickle, for having been the immediate cause of my disaster; if you had stood by me from the beginning, according to your promise, I should not have been teased by that coxcomb who has brought me to this pass. And why did I put on this d—ned unlucky dress? Lard curse that chattering Jezebel of a landlady, who advised such a preposterous disguise; a disguise which hath not only brought me to this pass, but also rendered me abominable to myself and frightful to others; for when I this morning signified to the turnkey, that I wanted to be shaved, he looked at my beard with astonishment, and, crossing himself, muttered his paternoster, believing me, I suppose, to be a witch, or something worse. And Heaven confound that loathsome banquet of the ancients, which provoked me to drink too freely, that I might wash away the taste of that accursed silly-kickaby."

Our young gentleman, having heard his lamentation to an end, excused himself for his conduct, by representing, that he could not possibly foresee the disagreeable consequences that attended it; and, in the meantime, strenuously counselled him to submit to the terms of his enlargement. He observed, that he was now arrived at that time of life, when the lusts of the flesh should be entirely mortified within him, and his greatest concern ought to be the health of his soul, to which nothing could more effectually contribute than the amputation which was proposed; that his body, as well as his mind, would profit by the change, because he would have no dangerous appetite to gratify, and no carnal thoughts to divert him from the duties of his profession; and his voice, which was naturally sweet, would improve to such a degree, that he would captivate the ears of all the people of fashion and taste, and in a little time be celebrated under the appellation of the English Senesino.

These arguments did not fail to make an impression upon the painter, who, nevertheless, started two objections to his compliance; namely, the disgrace of the punishment, and the dread of his wife. Pickle undertook to obviate these difficulties, by assuring him, that the sentence would be executed so privately as never to transpire; and that his wife could not be so unconscionable, after so many years of cohabitation, as to take exceptions to an expedient, by which she would not only enjoy the conversation of her husband, but even the fruits of those talents which the knife would so remarkably refine.

Pallet shook his head at this last remonstrance, as if he thought it would not be altogether convincing to his spouse; but yielded to the proposal, provided her consent could be obtained. Just as he signified this condescension, the gaoler entered, and, addressing himself to the supposed lady, expressed his satisfaction in having the honour to tell her, that she was no longer a prisoner. As the painter did not understand one word of what he said, Peregrine undertook the office of interpreter, and made his friend believe the gaoler's speech was no other than an intimation, that the ministry had sent a surgeon to execute what was proposed, and that the instruments and dressings were prepared in the next room. Alarmed and terrified at this sudden appointment, he flew to the other end of the room, and, snatching up an earthen chamber-pot, which was the only offensive weapon in the place, put himself in a posture of defence, and, with many oaths, threatened to try the temper of the barber's skull, if he should presume to set his nose within the apartment.

The gaoler, who little expected such a reception, concluded that the poor gentlewoman had actually lost her wits, and retreated with precipitation, leaving the door open as he went out. Upon which Pickle, gathering up the particulars of his dress with great despatch, crammed them into Pallet's arms, and, taking notice that now the coast was clear, exhorted him to follow his footsteps to the gate, where a hackney-coach stood for his reception. There being no time for hesitation, the painter took his advice, and, without quitting the utensil, which in his hurry he forgot to lay down, sallied out in the rear of our hero, with all that wildness of terror and impatience which may be reasonably supposed to take possession of a man who flies from perpetual imprisonment. Such was the tumult of his agitation, tha this faculty of thinking was for the present utterly overwhelmed, and he saw no object but his conductor, whom he followed by a sort of instinctive impulse, without regarding the keepers and sentinels, who, as he passed, with his clothes under one arm, and his chamber-pot brandished above his head, were confounded, and even dismayed at the strange apparition.

During the whole course of this irruption, he ceased not to cry with great vociferation, "Drive, coachman, drive, in the name of God!" And the carriage had proceeded the length of a whole street before he manifested the least sign of reflection, but stared like the Gorgon's head, with his mouth wide open, and each particular hair crawling and twining like an animated serpent. At length, however, he began to recover the use of his senses, and asked if Peregrine thought him out of all danger of being retaken. This unrelenting wag, not yet satisfied with the affliction he had imposed upon the sufferer, answered, with an air of doubt and concern, that he hoped they would not be overtaken, and prayed to God that they might not be retarded by a stop of carriages. Pallet fervently joined in this supplication, and they advanced a few yards farther, when the noise of a coach at full speed behind them invaded their ears; and Pickle having looked out of the window, withdrew his head in a seeming confusion, and exclaimed, "Lord have mercy upon us! I wish that may not be a guard sent after us. Methinks I saw the muzzle of a fusil sticking out of the coach." The painter, hearing these tidings, that instant thrust himself half out at the window, with his helmet still in his hand, bellowing to the coachman, as loud as he could roar, "Drive, d—n ye, drive! to the gates of Jericho and ends of the earth! Drive, you ragamuffin, you rascallion, you hell-hound! drive us to the pit of hell, rather than we should be taken."

Such a phantom could not pass without attracting the curiosity of the people, who ran to the doors and windows, in order to behold this object of admiration. With the same view, that coach, which was supposed to be in pursuit of him, stopped just as the windows of each happened to be opposite; and Pallet looking behind, and seeing three men standing upon the footboard, armed with canes, which his fear converted into fusils, never doubted that his friend's suspicion was just, but, shaking his jordan at the imaginary guard, swore he would sooner die than part with his precious ware. The owner of the coach, who was a nobleman of the first quality, mistook him for some unhappy woman deprived of her senses; and, ordering his coachman to proceed, convinced the fugitive, to his infinite joy, that it was no more than a false alarm. He was not, for all that, freed from anxiety and trepidation; but our young gentleman, fearing his brain would not bear a repetition of the same joke, permitted him to gain his own lodgings without further molestation.

His landlady, meeting him on the stair, was so affected at his appearance, that she screamed aloud, and betook herself to flight; while he, cursing her with great bitterness, rushed into the apartment of the doctor, who, instead of receiving him with cordial embraces, and congratulating him upon his deliverance, gave evident tokens of umbrage and discontent; and even plainly told him, he hoped to have heard that he and Mr. Pickle had acted the glorious part of Cato—an event which would have laid the foundation of such noble struggles, as could not fail to end in happiness and freedom; and that he had already made some progress in an ode that would have immortalised their names, and inspired the flame of liberty in every honest breast.— "There," said he, "I would have proved, that great talents, and high sentiments of liberty, do reciprocally produce and assist each other; and illustrated my assertions with such notes and quotations from the Greek writers, as would have opened the eyes of the most blind and unthinking, and touched the most callous and obdurate heart. *O fool! to think the man, whose ample mind must grasp whatever yonder stars survey*—Pray, Mr. Pallet, what is your opinion of that image of the mind's grasping the whole universe? For my own part, I can't help thinking it the most happy conception that ever entered my imagination."

The painter, who was not such a flaming enthusiast in the cause of liberty, could not brook the doctor's reflections, which he thought savoured a little too much of indifference and deficiency in point of private friendship; and therefore seized the present opportunity of mortifying his pride, by observing, that the image was, without all doubt, very grand and magnificent; but that he had been obliged for the idea to Mr. Bayes, in the *Rehearsal*, who values himself upon the same figure, conveyed in these words, *But all these clouds, when by the eye of reason grasp'd*, etc. Upon any other occasion, the painter would have triumphed greatly in this detection; but such was the flutter and confusion of his spirits, under the apprehension of being retaken, that, without further communication, he retreated to his own room, in order to resume his own dress, which he hoped would alter his appearance in such a manner as to baffle all search and examination; while the physician remained ashamed and abashed; to find himself convicted of bombast by a person of such contemptible talents. He was offended at this proof of his memory, and so much enraged at his presumption in exhibiting it, that he could never forgive his want of reverence, and took every opportunity of exposing his ignorance and folly in the sequel. Indeed, the ties of private affection were too weak to engage the heart of this republican, whose zeal for the community had entirely swallowed up his concern for individuals. He looked upon particular friendship as a passion unworthy of his ample soul, and was a professed admirer of L. Manlius, Junius Brutus, and those later patriots of the same name, who shut their ears against the cries of nature, and resisted all the dictates of gratitude and humanity.

CHAPTER XLVIII

Pallet conceives a hearty Contempt of his Fellow-Traveller, and attaches himself to Pickle, who, nevertheless, persecutes him with his mischievous Talent upon the Road to Flanders.

In the meantime, his companion, having employed divers pails full of water in cleansing himself from the squalor of the jail, submitted his face to the barber, tinged his eyebrows with a sable hue, and, being dressed in his own clothes, ventured to visit Peregrine, who was still under the hands of his valet-de-chambre, and who gave him to understand, that his escape had been connived at, and that the condition of their deliverance was their departure from Paris in three days.

The painter was transported with joy, when he learnt that he ran no risk of being retaken; and, far from repining at the terms of his enlargement, would have willingly set out on his return to England that same afternoon; for the Bastile had made such an impression upon him, that he started at the sound of every coach, and turned pale at sight of a French soldier. In the fulness of his heart, he complained of the doctor's indifference, and related what had passed at their meeting with evident marks of resentment and disrespect; which were not at all diminished,

when Jolter informed him of the physician's behaviour, when
he sent for him to confer about the means of abridging their
confinement. Pickle himself was incensed at his want of bowels;
and, perceiving how much he had sunk in the opinion of his
fellow-traveller, resolved to encourage these sentiments of disgust, and occasionally foment the division to a downright quarrel,
which he foresaw would produce some diversion, and perhaps
expose the poet's character in such a light as would effectually
punish him for his arrogance and barbarity. With this view,
he levelled several satirical jokes at the doctor's pedantry and
taste, which had appeared so conspicuous in the quotations he
had got by heart from ancient authors; in his affected disdain
of the best pictures in the world, which, had he been endowed
with the least share of discernment, he could not have beheld
with such insensibility; and, lastly, in his ridiculous banquet,
which none but an egregious coxcomb, devoid of all elegance
and sense, would have prepared, or presented to rational beings.
In a word, our young gentleman played the artillery of his wit
against him with such success, that the painter seemed to wake
from a dream, and went home with the most hearty contempt for
the person he had formerly adored.

Instead of using the privilege of a friend, to enter his apartment without ceremony, he sent in his servant with a message,
importing, that he intended to set out from Paris next day, in
company with Mr. Pickle, and desiring to know whether or not
he was or would be prepared for the journey. The doctor, struck
with the manner, as well as the matter of this intimation, went
immediately to Pallet's room, and demanded to know the cause
of such a sudden determination, without his privity or concurrence; and, when he understood the necessity of their affairs,
rather than travel by himself, he ordered his baggage to be packed
up, and signified his readiness to conform to the emergency of
the case; though he was not at all pleased with the cavalier
behaviour of Pallet, to whom he threw out some hints of his
own importance, and the immensity of his condescension, in
favouring him with such marks of regard. But by this time
these insinuations had lost their effect upon the painter, who
told him, with an arch sneer, that he did not at all question
his learning and abilities, and particularly his skill in cookery,
which he should never forget while his palate retained its
function; but nevertheless advised him, for the sake of the
degenerate eaters of these days, to spare a little of the sal-
ammoniac in the next silly-kickaby he should prepare; and bate

somewhat of the devil's dung, which he had so plentifully crammed into the roasted fowls, unless he had a mind to convert his guests into patients, with a view of licking himself whole for the expense of the entertainment.

The physician, nettled at these sarcasms, eyed him with a look of indignation and disdain; and, being unwilling to express himself in English, lest, in the course of the altercation, Pallet should be so much irritated as to depart without him, he vented his anger in Greek. The painter, though, by the sound, he supposed this quotation to be Greek, complimented his friend upon his knowledge in the Welsh language, and found means to rally him quite out of temper; so that he retired to his own chamber in the utmost wrath and mortification, and left his antagonist exulting over the victory he had won.

While those things passed between these originals, Peregrine waited upon the ambassador, whom he thanked for his kind interposition, acknowledging the indiscretion of his own conduct, with such appearance of conviction, and promises of reformation, that his excellency freely forgave him for all the trouble he had been put to on his account, fortified him with sensible advices, and, assuring him of his continual favour and friendship, gave him, at parting, letters of introduction to several persons of quality belonging to the British court.

Thus distinguished, our young gentleman took leave of all his French acquaintance, and spent the evening with some of those who had enjoyed the greatest share of his intimacy and confidence; while Jolter superintended his domestic concerns, and, with infinite joy, bespoke a post-chaise and horses, in order to convey him from a place where he lived in continual apprehension of suffering by the dangerous disposition of his pupil. Everything being adjusted according to their plan, they and their fellow-travellers next day dined together, and, about four in the afternoon, took their departure in two chaises, escorted by the valet-de-chambre, Pipes, and the doctor's lacquey, on horseback, well furnished with arms and ammunition, in case of being attacked by robbers on the road.

It was about eleven o'clock at night when they arrived at Senlis, which was the place at which they proposed to lodge, and where they were obliged to knock up the people of the inn, before they could have their supper prepared. All the provision in the house was but barely sufficient to furnish one indifferent meal. However, the painter consoled himself for the quantity with the quality of the dishes, one of which was a fricassee of rabbit, a preparation which he valued above all the dainties that ever smoked upon the table of the sumptuous Heliogabalus.

He had no sooner expressed himself to this effect than our hero, who was almost incessantly laying traps for diversion at his neighbour's expense, laid hold on the declaration; and, recollecting the story of Scipio and the muleteer in *Gil Blas*, resolved to perpetrate a joke upon the stomach of Pallet, which seemed particularly well disposed to an hearty supper. He accordingly digested his plan; and, the company being seated at table, affected to gaze with peculiar eagerness at the painter, who had helped himself to a large portion of the fricassee, and began to swallow it with infinite relish. Pallet, notwithstanding the keenness of his appetite, could not help taking notice of Pickle's demeanour; and, making a short pause in the exercise of his grinders, "You are surprised," said he, "to see me make so much despatch; but I was extremely hungry, and this is one of the best fricassees I ever tasted. The French are very expert in these dishes, that I must allow; and, upon my conscience, I would never desire to eat a more delicate rabbit than this that lies upon my plate."

Peregrine made no other reply to this encomium, than the repetition of the word "rabbit!" with a note of admiration, and such a significant shake of the head, as effectually alarmed the other, who instantly suspended the action of his jaws, and, with the morsel half chewed in his mouth, stared round him with a certain solidity of apprehension, which is easier conceived than described, until his eyes encountered the countenance of Thomas Pipes, who being instructed, and posted opposite to him for the occasion, exhibited an arch grin, that completed the painter's disorder. Afraid of swallowing his mouthful, and ashamed to dispose of it any other way, he sat some time in a most distressed state of suspense; and, being questioned by Mr. Jolter touching his calamity, made a violent effort of the muscles of his gullet, which with difficulty performed their office, and then, with great confusion and concern, asked if Mr. Pickle suspected the rabbit's identity. The young gentleman, assuming a mysterious air, pretended ignorance of the matter, observing, that he was apt to suspect all dishes of that kind, since he had been informed of the tricks which were commonly played at inns in France, Italy, and Spain, and recounted that passage in *Gil Blas*, which we have hinted at above, saying, he did not pretend to be a connoisseur in animals, but the legs of the creature which composed that fricassee did not, in his opinion, resemble those of the rabbits he had usually seen. This observation had an evident effect upon the features of the painter, who, with certain signs of loathing and astonishment, exclaimed, "Lord Jesus!" and appealed to Pipes for a discovery of the truth, by asking if he knew anything of the affair. Tom very gravely replied, that he did suppose the food was wholesome enough, for he had seen the skin and feet of a special ram-cat, new flayed, hanging upon the door of a small pantry adjoining to the kitchen.

Before this sentence was uttered, Pallet's belly seemed to move in contact with his backbone, his colour changed, no part but the whites of his eyes were to be seen, he dropped his lower jaw, and fixing his hands in his sides, retched with such convulsive agonies, as amazed and disconcerted the whole company; and what augmented his disorder, was the tenacious retention of his stomach, which absolutely refused to part with its contents, notwithstanding all the energy of his abhorrence, which threw him into a cold sweat, and almost into a swoon.

Pickle, alarmed at his condition, assured him it was a genuine rabbit, and that he had tutored Pipes to say otherwise for the joke's sake. But this confession he considered as a friendly artifice of Pickle's compassion, and, therefore, it had little effect upon his constitution. By the assistance, however, of a large bumper of brandy, his spirits were recruited, and his recollection so far recovered, that he was able to declare, with divers contortions of face, that the dish had a particular rankness of taste, which he had imputed partly to the nature of the French coney, and partly to the composition of their sauces. Then he inveighed against the infamous practices of French publicans, attributing such imposition to their oppressive government, which kept them so necessitous, that they were tempted to exercise all manner of knavery upon their unwary guests.

Jolter, who could not find in his heart to let slip any opportunity of speaking in favour of the French, told him "that he was a very great stranger to their police, else he would know, that if, upon information to the magistrate, it should appear, that any traveller, native or foreigner, had been imposed upon or ill-treated by a publican, the offender would be immediately obliged to shut up his house; and, if his behaviour had been notorious, he himself would be sent to the galleys without the least hesitation. And as for the dish which has been made the occasion of your present disorder," said he, "I will take upon me to affirm it was prepared of a genuine rabbit, which was skinned in my presence; and, in confirmation of what I assert, though such fricassees are not the favourites of my taste, I will eat a part of this without scruple." So saying, he swallowed several mouthfuls of the questioned coney, and Pallet seemed to eye it again with inclination; nay, he even resumed his knife and fork, and, being just on the point of applying them, was seized with another qualm of apprehension, that broke out in an exclamation of, "After all, Mr. Jolter, if it should be a real ram-cat—Lord have mercy upon me! here is one of the claws!"

With these words, he presented the tip of a toe, of which Pipes had snipped off five or six from a duck that was roasted, and purposely scattered them in the fricassee; and the governor could not behold this testimonial without symptoms of uneasiness and remorse; so that he and the painter sat silent and abashed, and made faces at each other, while the physician, who hated them both, exulted over their affliction, bidding them be of good cheer, and proceed with their meal; for he was ready to demonstrate, that the flesh of a cat was as nourishing and delicious as veal or mutton, provided they could prove that the said cat was not of the boar kind, and had fed chiefly on vegetable diet, or even confined its carnivorous appetite to rats and mice, which he affirmed to be dainties of exquisite taste and flavour. He said it was a vulgar mistake to think that all flesh-devouring creatures were unfit to be eaten; witness the consumption of swine and ducks, animals that delight in carnage, as well as fish, which prey upon each other, and feed on bait and carrion; together with the demand for bear, of which the best hams in the world are made. He then observed, that the negroes on the coast of Guinea, who are healthy and vigorous people, prefer cats and dogs to all other fare; and mentioned from history several sieges, during which the inhabitants, who were blocked up, lived upon these animals, and had recourse even to human flesh, which, to his certain knowledge, was in all respects preferable to pork; for, in the course of his studies, he had, for the experiment's sake, eaten a steak cut from the buttock of a person who had been hanged.

This dissertation, far from composing, increased the disquiet in the stomachs of the governor and painter, who, hearing the last illustration, turned their eyes upon the orator at the same instant with looks of horror and disgust; and, the one muttering the term *cannibal*, and the other pronouncing the word *abomination*, they rose from the table in a great hurry, and, running towards another apartment, jostled with such violence in the passage, that both were overturned by the shock, which also contributed to the effect of their nausea, that mutually defiled them as they lay.

CHAPTER XLIX

Nor is the Physician sacred from his Ridicule—They reach Arras, where our Adventurer engages in Play with two French Officers, who next Morning give the Landlord an interesting Proof of their Importance.

THE doctor remained sullen and dejected during the whole journey; not but that he attempted to recover his importance, by haranguing upon the Roman highways, when Mr. Jolter desired the company to take notice of the fine pavement upon which they travelled from Paris into Flanders; but Pallet, who thought he had now gained the ascendency over the physician, exerted himself in maintaining the superiority he had acquired, by venting various sarcasms upon his self-conceit and affectation of learning, and even uttering puns and conundrums upon the remarks which the republican retailed. When he talked of the Flaminian Way, the painter questioned if it was a better pavement than the Fleminian way on which they travelled. And the doctor having observed, that this road was made for the convenience of drawing the French artillery into Flanders, which was often the seat of war, his competitor in wit replied, with infinite vivacity, "There are more great guns than the French King knows of, drawn along this causeway, doctor!"

Encouraged by the success of these efforts, which tickled the imagination of Jolter, and drew smiles, as he imagined, of approbation from our hero, he sported in many other equivoques of the same nature, and, at dinner, told the physician that he was like the root of the tongue, as being cursedly down in the mouth.

By this time, such was the animosity subsisting between these quondam friends, that they never conversed together, except with a view of exposing each other to the ridicule or contempt of their fellow-travellers. The doctor was at great pains to point out the folly and ignorance of Pallet in private to Peregrine, who was often conjured in the same manner by the painter to take notice of the physician's want of manners and taste. Pickle pretended to acquiesce in the truth of their mutual severity, which, indeed, was extremely just; and, by malicious insinuations, blew up their contention, with a view of bringing it to open hostility. But both seemed so averse to deeds of mortal purpose, that, for a long time, his arts were baffled, and he could not spirit them up to any pitch of resentment higher than scurrilous repartee.

Before they reached Arras, the city gates were shut, so that they were obliged to take up their lodging at an indifferent house in the suburbs, where they found a couple of French officers, who had also rode post from Paris so far on their way to Lisle. These gentlemen were about the age of thirty, and their deportment distinguished by such an air of insolence, as disgusted our hero, who, nevertheless, accosted them politely in the yard, and proposed that they should sup together. They thanked him for the honour of his invitation, which, however, they declined, upon pretence of having ordered something for themselves, but promised to wait upon him, and his company, immediately after their repast.

This they accordingly performed; and, after having drank a few glasses of burgundy, one of them asked if the young gentleman would, for pastime, take a hand at quadrille. Peregrine easily divined the meaning of this proposal, which was made with no other view than that of fleecing him and his fellow-travellers; for he well knew to what shifts a subaltern in the French service is reduced, in order to maintain the appearance of a gentleman, and had reason to believe that most of them were sharpers from their youth; but, as he depended a good deal upon his own penetration and address, he gratified the stranger's desire, and a party was instantly formed of the painter, the physician, the proposer, and himself, the other officer having professed himself utterly ignorant of the game; yet, in the course of the play, he took his station at the back of Pickle's chair, which was opposite to his friend, on pretence of amusing himself with seeing his manner of conducting the cards. The youth was not such a novice but that he perceived the design of this palpable piece of behaviour, which notwithstanding he overlooked for the present, with a view of flattering their hopes in the beginning, that they might be the more effectually punished by their disappointment in the end.

The game was scarce begun, when, by the reflection of a glass, he discerned the officer at his back making signs to his companion, who, by these preconcerted gestures, was perfectly informed of the contents of Peregrine's hand, and of consequence fortunate in the course of the play.

Thus they were allowed to enjoy the fruits of their dexterity, until their money amounted to some louis, when our young gentleman, thinking it high time to do himself justice, signified in very polite terms to the gentleman who stood behind him, that he could never play with ease and deliberation when he was overlooked by any bystander, and begged that he would have the goodness to be seated.

As this was a remonstrance which the stranger could not with any show of breeding resist, he asked pardon, and retired to the chair of the physician, who frankly told him, that it was not the fashion of his country for one to submit his hand to the perusal of a spectator; and when, in consequence of this rebuff, he wanted to quarter himself upon the painter, he was refused by a wave of the hand, and shake of the head, with an exclamation of *Pardonnez moi!* which was repeated with such emphasis, as discomposed his effrontery, and he found himself obliged to sit down in a state of mortification.

The odds being thus removed, fortune proceeded in her usual channel; and though the Frenchman, deprived of his ally, endeavoured to practise divers strokes of finesse, the rest of the company observed him with such vigilance and caution, as baffled all his attempts, and in a very little time he was compelled to part with his winning. But having engaged in the match with an intention of taking all advantages, whether fair or unfair, that his superior skill should give him over the Englishman, the money was not refunded without a thousand disputes, in the course of which he essayed to intimidate his antagonist with high words, which were retorted by our hero with such interest, as convinced him that he had mistaken his man, and persuaded him to make his retreat in quiet. Indeed, it was not without cause that they repined at the bad success of their enterprise; because, in all likelihood, they had nothing to depend upon for the present but their own industry, and knew not how to defray their expenses on the road, except by some acquisition of this kind.

Next morning they rose at daybreak, and resolving to anticipate their fellow-lodgers, bespoke post-horses as soon as they could be admitted into the city; so that, when our company appeared, their beasts were ready in the yard; and they only waited to discuss the bill, which they had ordered to be made out. The landlord of the inn presented his carte with fear and trembling to one of those ferocious cavaliers, who no sooner cast his eye upon the sum-total, than he discharged a volley of dreadful oaths, and asked if the King's officers were to be treated in that manner? The poor publican protested, with great humility, that he had the utmost respect for his Majesty, and everything that belonged to him; and that far from consulting his own interest, all that he desired was to be barely indemnified for the expense of their lodging.

This condescension seemed to have no other effect than that of encouraging their arrogance. They swore his extortion should be explained to the commandant of the town, who would, by making him a public example, teach other innkeepers how to behave towards men of honour; and threatened with such confidence of indignation, that the wretched landlord, dreading the consequence of their wrath, implored pardon in the most abject manner, begging, with many supplications, that he might have the pleasure of lodging them at his own charge. This was a favour which he with great difficulty obtained; they chid him severely for his imposition, exhorted him to have more regard for his own conscience, as well as for the convenience of his guests; and cautioning him in particular touching his behaviour to the gentlemen of the army, mounted their horses, and rode off in great state, leaving him very thankful for having so successfully appeased the choler of two officers, who wanted either inclination or ability to pay their bill; for experience had taught him to be apprehensive of all such travellers, who commonly lay the landlord under contribution, by way of atonement for the extravagance of his demands, even after he has professed his willingness to entertain them on their own terms.

CHAPTER L

Peregrine moralises upon their Behaviour, which is condemned by the Doctor, and defended by the Governor—They arrive in safety at Lisle—Dine at an Ordinary—Visit the Citadel—The Physician quarrels with a North Briton, who is put in Arrest.

THESE honourable adventurers being gone, Peregrine, who was present during the transaction, informed himself of the particulars from the mouth of the innkeeper himself, who took God and the saints to witness, that he should have been a loser by their custom, even if the bill had been paid; because he was on his guard against their objections, and had charged every article at an under price. But such was the authority of officers in France, that he durst not dispute the least circumstance of their will; for, had the case come under the cognisance of the magistrate, he must in course have suffered by the maxims of their government, which never fail to abet the oppression of the army; and besides run the risk of incurring their future resentment, which would be sufficient to ruin him from top to bottom.

Our hero boiled with indignation at this instance of injustice and arbitrary power; and, turning to his governor, asked if this too was a proof of the happiness enjoyed by the French people. Jolter replied, that every human constitution must in some things be imperfect; and owned, that in this kingdom gentlemen were more countenanced than the vulgar, because it was to be presumed that their own sentiments of honour and superior qualifications would entitle them to this pre-eminence, which had also a retrospective view to the merit of their ancestors, in consideration of which they were at first ennobled. But he affirmed, that the innkeeper had misrepresented the magistracy, which in France never failed to punish flagrant outrages and abuse, without respect of persons.

The painter approved of the wisdom of the French government, in bridling the insolence of the mob, by which, he assured them, he had often suffered in his own person; having been often bespattered by hackney-coachmen, jostled by draymen and porters, and reviled in the most opprobrious terms by the watermen of London, where he had once lost his bag and a considerable quantity of hair, which had been cut off by some rascal in his passage through Ludgate, during the Lord Mayor's procession. On the other hand, the doctor, with great warmth, alleged, that those officers ought to suffer death, or banishment at least, for having plundered the people in this manner, which was so impudent and barefaced, as plainly to prove they were certain of escaping with impunity, and that they were old offenders in the same degree of delinquency. He said, that the greatest man in Athens would have been condemned to perpetual exile, and seen his estate confiscated for public use, had he dared in such a licentious manner to violate the rights of a fellow-citizen; and as for the little affronts to which a man may be subject from the petulance of the multitude, he looked upon them as glorious indications of liberty, which ought not to be repressed, and would at any time rejoice to find himself overthrown in a kennel by the insolence of a son of freedom, even though the fall should cost him a limb; adding, by way of illustration, that the greatest pleasure he ever enjoyed was in seeing a dustman wilfully overturn a gentleman's coach, in which two ladies were bruised, even to the danger of their lives. Pallet, shocked at the extravagance of this declaration, "If that be the case," said he, "I wish you may see every bone in your body broke by the first carman you meet in the streets of London."

This argument being discussed, and the reckoning discharged without any deduction, although the landlord, in stating the articles, had an eye to the loss he had sustained by his own countrymen, they departed from Arras, and arrived in safety at Lisle, about two o'clock in the afternoon.

They had scarce taken possession of their lodgings, in a large hotel in the Grande Place, when the innkeeper gave them to understand, that he kept an ordinary below, which was frequented by several English gentlemen who resided in town, and that dinner was then set upon the table. Peregrine, who seized all opportunities of observing new characters, persuaded his company to dine in public; and they were accordingly conducted to the place, where they found a mixture of Scotch and Dutch officers, who had come from Holland to learn their exercises at the academy, and some gentlemen in the French service, who were upon garrison duty in the citadel. Among these last was a person about the age of fifty, of a remarkably genteel air and polite address, dignified with a Maltese cross, and distinguished by the particular veneration of all those who knew him. When he understood that Pickle and his friends were travellers, he accosted the youth in English, which he spoke tolerably well; and, as they were strangers, offered to attend them in the afternoon to all the places worth seeing in Lisle. Our hero thanked him for his excess of politeness, which, he said, was peculiar to the French nation; and, struck with his engaging appearance, industriously courted his conversation, in the course of which he learnt that this chevalier was a man of good sense and great experience, that he was perfectly well acquainted with the greatest part of Europe, had lived some years in England, and was no stranger to the constitution and genius of that people.

Having dined, and drank to the healths of the English and French Kings, two fiacres were called, in one of which the knight, with one of his companions, the governor, and Peregrine seated themselves, the other being occupied by the physician, Pallet, and two Scottish officers, who proposed to accompany them in their circuit. The first place they visited was the citadel, round the ramparts of which they walked, under the conduct of the knight, who explained with great accuracy the intention of every particular fortification belonging to that seemingly impregnable fortress; and, when they had satisfied their curiosity, took coach again, in order to view the arsenal, which stands in another quarter of the town; but, just as Pickle's carriage had crossed the promenade, he heard his own name bawled aloud by the painter; and, ordering the fiacre to stop, saw Pallet with one half of his body thrust out at the window of the other coach, crying with a terrified look, "Mr. Pickle, Mr. Pickle, for the love of God! halt and prevent bloodshed, else here will be carnage and cutting of throats." Peregrine, surprised at this exclamation, immediately alighted, and, advancing to the other vehicle, found one of their military companions standing upon the ground at the further side of the coach, with his sword drawn, and fury in his countenance; and the physician, with a quivering lip and haggard aspect, struggling with the other, who had interposed in the quarrel, and detained him in his place.

Our young gentleman, upon inquiry, found that this animosity had sprung from a dispute that happened upon the ramparts, touching the strength of the fortification, which the doctor, according to custom, undervalued, because it was a modern work; saying, that, by the help of the military engines used among the ancients, and a few thousands of pioneers, he would engage to take it in less than ten days after he should sit down before it. The North Briton, who was as great a pedant as the physician, having studied fortification, and made himself master of Cæsar's Commentaries and Polybius, with the observations of Folard, affirmed, that all the methods of besieging practised by the ancients would be utterly ineffectual against such a plan as that of the citadel of Lisle; and began to compare the *vineæ, aggeres, arietes, scorpiones,* and *catapultæ* of the Romans, with the trenches, mines, batteries, and mortars used in the present art of war. The republican, finding himself attacked upon what he thought his strong side, summoned all his learning to his aid; and, describing the famous siege of Platæa, happened to misquote a passage of Thucydides, in which he was corrected by the other, who, having been educated for the church, was also a connoisseur in the Greek language. The doctor, incensed at being detected in such a blunder in presence of Pallet, who, he knew, would promulgate his shame, told the officer, with great arrogance, that his objection was frivolous, and that he must not pretend to dispute on these matters with one who had considered them with the utmost accuracy and care. His antagonist, piqued at this supercilious insinuation, replied with great heat, that, for aught he knew, the doctor might be a very expert apothecary, but that, in the art of war, and knowledge in the Greek tongue, he was no other than an ignorant pretender.

This asseveration produced an answer full of virulence, including a national reflection upon the soldier's country; and the contention rose to mutual abuse, when it was suppressed by the admonitions of the other two, who begged they would not expose themselves in a strange place, but behave themselves like fellow-subjects and friends. They accordingly ceased reviling each other, and the affair was seemingly forgot; but after they had resumed their places in the coach, the painter unfortunately asked the meaning of the word tortoise, which he had heard them mention among the Roman implements of war. This question was answered by the physician, who described the nature of this expedient so little to the satisfaction of the officer, that he contradicted him flatly, in the midst of his explanation; a circumstance which provoked the republican to such a degree, that, in the temerity of his passion, he uttered the epithet *impertinent scoundrel*; which was no sooner pronounced than the Caledonian made manual application to his nose, and, leaping out of the coach, stood waiting for him on the plain; while he, the physician, made feeble efforts to join him, being easily retained by the other soldier; and Pallet, dreading the consequence in which he himself might be involved, bellowed aloud for prevention.

Our hero endeavoured to quiet the commotion, by representing to the Scot, that he had already taken satisfaction for the injury he had received, and telling the doctor that he had deserved the chastisement which was inflicted upon him. But the officer, encouraged perhaps by the confusion of his antagonist, insisted upon his asking pardon for what he had said; and the doctor, believing himself under the protection of his friend Pickle, far from agreeing to such concession, breathed nothing but defiance and revenge. So that the chevalier, in order to prevent mischief, put the soldier under arrest, and sent him to his lodgings, under the care of the other French gentleman and his own companion; they being also accompanied by Mr. Jolter, who, having formerly seen all the curiosities of Lisle, willingly surrendered his place to the physician.

CHAPTER LI

Pickle engages with a Knight of Malta in a Conversation upon the English Stage, which is followed by a Dissertation on the Theatres of the Ancients, by the Doctor.

THE rest of the company proceeded to the arsenal, which having viewed, together with some remarkable churches, they, in their return, went to the comedy, and saw the *Cid* of Corneille tolerably well represented. In consequence of this entertainment, the discourse at supper turned upon dramatic performances; and all the objections of Mons. de Scudéry to the piece they had seen acted, together with the decision of the French Academy, were canvassed and discussed. The knight was a man of letters and taste, and particularly well acquainted with the state of the English stage; so that, when the painter boldly pronounced sentence against the French manner of acting, on the strength of having frequented a Covent Garden club of critics, and been often admitted, by virtue of an order, into the pit, a comparison immediately ensued, not between the authors, but the actors of both nations, to whom the chevalier and Peregrine were no strangers. Our hero, like a good Englishman, made no scruple of giving the preference to the performers of his own country, who, he alleged, obeyed the genuine impulses of nature, in exhibiting the passions of the human mind; and entered so warmly into the spirit of their several parts, that they often fancied themselves the very heroes they represented; whereas the action of the Parisian players, even in their most interesting characters, was generally such an extravagance in voice and gesture, as is nowhere to be observed but on the stage. To illustrate this assertion, he availed himself of his talent, and mimicked the manner and voice of all the principal performers, male and female, belonging to the French comedy, to the admiration of the chevalier, who, having complimented him upon this surprising modulation, begged leave to dissent in some particulars from the opinion he had avowed.

"That you have good actors in England," said he, "it would be unjust and absurd in me to deny; your theatre is adorned by one woman, whose sensibility and sweetness of voice is such as I have never observed on any other stage; she has, besides, an elegance of person and expression of features, that wonderfully adapt her for the most engaging characters of your best plays; and I must freely own that I have been as highly delighted and as deeply affected by a Monimia and Belvidera at London, as ever I was by a Cornelia and Cleopatra at Paris. Your favourite actor is a surprising genius. You can, moreover, boast of several comic actors, who are perfect masters of buffoonery and grimace; though, to be free with you, I think, in these qualifications, you are excelled by the players of Amsterdam. Yet one of your gratiosos I cannot admire, in all the characters he assumes. His utterance is a continual sing-song, like the chanting of vespers, and his action resembles that of heaving ballast into the hold of a ship. In his outward deportment, he seems to have confounded the ideas of dignity and insolence of mien; acts the crafty, cool, designing Crookback, as a loud, shallow, blustering Hector; in the character of the mild patriot Brutus, he loses all temper and decorum; nay, so ridiculous is the behaviour of him and Cassius at their interview, that, setting foot to foot, and grinning at each other, with the aspect of two cobblers enraged, they thrust their left sides together with repeated shocks, that the hilts of their swords may clash for the entertainment of the audience, as if they were a couple of merry-andrews, endeavouring to raise the laugh of the vulgar, on some scaffold at Bartholomew Fair. The despair of a great man, who falls a sacrifice to the infernal practices of a subtle traitor, that enjoyed his confidence, this English Æsopus represents, by beating his own forehead, and bellowing like a bull; and, indeed, in almost all his most interesting scenes, performs such strange shakings of the head, and other antic gesticulations, that, when I first saw him act, I imagined the poor man laboured under that paralytical disorder, which is known by the name of St. Vitus's dance. In short, he seems to be a stranger to the more refined sensations of the soul; consequently his expression is of the vulgar kind, and he must often sink under the idea of the poet; so that he has recourse to such violence of affected agitation, as imposes upon the undiscerning spectator, but, to the eye of taste, evinces him a mere player of that class whom your admired Shakespeare justly compares to nature's journeyman tearing a passion to rags. Yet this man, in spite of all these absurdities, is an admirable Falstaff, exhibits the character of the Eighth Henry to the life, is reasonably applauded in the Plain Dealer, excels in the part of Sir John Brute, and would be equal to many humorous situations in low comedy, which his pride will not allow him to undertake. I should not have been so severe upon this actor, had I not seen him extolled by his partisans with the most ridiculous and fulsome manifestations of praise, even in those very circumstances wherein, as I have observed, he chiefly failed.''

Pickle, not a little piqued to hear the qualifications of such a celebrated actor in England treated with such freedom and disrespect, answered with some asperity, that the chevalier was a true critic, more industrious in observing the blemishes, than in acknowledging the excellence of those who fell under his examination.   It was not to be supposed that one actor could shine equally in all characters; and, though his observations were undoubtedly very judicious, he himself could not help wondering that some of them had always escaped his notice, though he had been an assiduous frequenter of the playhouse.

"The player in question," said he, "has, in your own opinion, considerable share of merit in the characters of comic life; and as to the manners of the great personages in tragedy, and the operation of the grand passions of the soul, I apprehend they may be variously represented, according to the various complexion and cultivation of different men. A Spaniard, for example, though impelled by the same passion, will express it very differently from a Frenchman; and what is looked upon as graceful vivacity and address by the one, would be considered as impertinence and foppery by the other. Nay, so opposite is your common deportment from that of some other nations, that one of your own countrymen, in the relation of his travels, observes, that the Persians, even of this age, when they see any man perform unnecessary gestures, say he is either a fool or a Frenchman. The standard of demeanour being thus unsettled, a Turk, a Moor, an Indian, or inhabitant of any country, whose customs and dress are widely different from ours, may, in his sentiments, possess all the dignity of the human heart, and be inspired by the noblest passion that animates the soul, and yet excite the laughter rather than the respect of an European spectator.   When I first beheld your famous Parisian stage heroine in one of her principal parts, her attitudes seemed so violent, and she tossed her arms around with such extravagance, that she put me in mind of a windmill under the agitation of a hard gale; while her voice and features exhibited the lively representation of an English scold.   The action of your favourite male performer was, in my opinion, equally unnatural; he appeared with the affected airs of a dancing-master; at the most pathetic junctures of his fate, he lifted up his hands above his head, like a tumbler going to vault, and spoke as if his throat had been obstructed by an hairbrush; yet, when I compared their manners with those of the people before whom they performed, and made allowance for that exaggeration which obtains on all theatres, I was insensibly reconciled to their method of performance, and I could distinguish abundance of merit beneath that oddity of appearance."

The chevalier, perceiving Peregrine a little irritated at what he had said, asked pardon for the liberty he had taken in censuring the English players, assuring him that he had an infinite veneration for the British learning, genius, and taste, which were so justly distinguished in the world of letters, and that, notwithstanding the severity of his criticism, he thought the theatre of London much better supplied with actors than that of Paris. The young gentleman thanked him for his polite condescension, at which Pallet exulted, saying with a shake of the head, "I believe so, too, Monsieur"; and the physician, impatient of the dispute in which he had borne no share, observed with a supercilious air, that the modern stage was altogether beneath the notice of one who had an idea of ancient magnificence and execution; that plays ought to be exhibited at the expense of the state, as those of Sophocles were by the Athenians; and that proper judges should be appointed for receiving or rejecting all such performances as are offered to the public.

He then described the theatre at Rome, which contained eighty thousand spectators, [and] gave them a learned disquisition into the nature of the *persona*, or mask, worn by the Roman actors, which, he said, was a machine that covered the whole head, furnished on the inside with a brazen concavity, that, by reverberating the sound, as it issued from the mouth, raised the voice, so as to render it audible to such an extended audience. He explained the difference between the *saltator* and *declamator*, one of whom acted, while the other rehearsed the part; and from thence took occasion to mention the perfections of their pantomimes, who were so amazingly distinct in the exercise of their art, that a certain prince of Pontus, being at the court of Nero, and seeing one of them represent a story, begged him of the emperor, in order to employ him as an interpreter among barbarous nations, whose language he did not understand. Nay, divers cynic philosophers, who had condemned this entertainment unseen, when they chanced to be eye-witnesses of their admirable dexterity, expressed their sorrow for having so long debarred themselves of such rational enjoyment.

He dissented, however, from the opinion of Peregrine, who, as a proof of their excellence, had advanced, that some of the

English actors fancied themselves the very thing they represented, and recounted a story from Lucian, of a certain celebrated pantomime, who, in acting the part of Ajax, in his frenzy was transported into a real fit of delirium, during which he tore to pieces the clothes of the actor who stalked before him, beating the stage with iron shoes, in order to increase the noise, snatched an instrument from one of the musicians, and broke it over the head of him who represented Ulysses; and, running to the consular bench, mistook a couple of senators for the sheep which were to be slain. The audience applauded him to the skies; but so conscious was the mimic of his own extravagance, when he recovered the use of his reason, that he actually fell sick with mortification; and, being afterwards desired to react the piece, flatly refused to appear in any such character, saying, that the shortest follies were the best, and that it was sufficient for him to have been a madman once in his life.

CHAPTER LII

An Adventure happens to Pipes, in consequence of which he is dismissed from Peregrine's Service—The whole Company set out for Ghent in the Diligence—Our Hero is captivated by a Lady in that Carriage—Interests her Spiritual Director in his behalf.

THE doctor, being fairly engaged on the subject of the ancients, would have proceeded the Lord knows how far, without hesitation, had not he been interrupted by the arrival of Mr. Jolter who, in great confusion, told them, that Pipes, having affronted a soldier, was then surrounded in the street, and would certainly be put to death, if some person of authority did not immediately interpose in his behalf.

Peregrine no sooner learned the danger of his trusty squire, than, snatching up his sword, he ran downstairs, and was followed by the chevalier, intreating him to leave the affair to his management. Within ten yards of the door they found Tom with his back to a wall, defending himself manfully with a mopstick against the assault of three or four soldiers, who, at sight of the Maltese cross, desisted from the attack, and were taken into custody by order of the knight. One of the aggressors, being an Irishman, begged to be heard with great importunity, before he should be sent to the guard; and, by the mediation of Pickle, was accordingly brought into the hotel with his companions, all three bearing upon their heads and faces evident marks of their adversary's prowess and dexterity. The spokesman being confronted with Pipes, informed the company, that, having by accident met with Mr. Pipes, whom he considered as his countryman, though fortune had disposed of them in different services, he invited him to drink a glass of wine, and accordingly carried him to a cabaret, where he introduced him to his comrades; but, in the course of the conversation, which turned upon the power and greatness of the Kings of France and England, Mr. Pipes had been pleased to treat his most Christian Majesty with great disrespect; and when he, the entertainer, expostulated with him in a friendly manner about his impolite behaviour, observing, that he being in the French service, would be under the necessity of resenting his abuse, if he did not put a stop to it before the other gentlemen of the cloth should comprehend his meaning, he had set them all three at defiance, dishonoured him in particular with the opprobrious epithet of *rebel to his native King and country*, and even drank, in broken French, to the perdition of Louis and all his adherents! that, compelled by this outrageous conduct, he, as the person who had recommended him to their society, had, in vindication of his own character, demanded satisfaction of the delinquent, who, on pretence of fetching his sword, had gone to his lodging, from whence he all of a sudden sallied upon them with the mopstick, which he employed in the annoyance of them all without distinction, so that they were obliged to draw in their own defence.

Pipes, being questioned by his master with regard to the truth of this account, owned that every circumstance was justly represented; saying, he did not value their cheese-toasters a pinch of oakum; and, that, if the gentleman had not shot in betwixt them, he would have trimmed them to such a tune, that they should not have had a whole yard to square. Peregrine reprimanded him sharply for his unmannerly behaviour, and insisted upon his asking pardon of those he had injured upon the spot. But no consideration was efficacious enough to produce such concession; to this command he was both deaf and dumb, and the repeated threats of his master had no more effect than if they had been addressed to a marble statue. At length our hero, incensed at his obstinacy, started up, and would have chastised him with manual operation, had not he been prevented by the chevalier, who found means to moderate his indignation so far, that he contented himself with dismissing the offender from his service; and after having obtained the discharge of the prisoners, gave them a louis to drink by way of recompense for the disgrace and damage they had sustained.

The knight, perceiving our young gentleman very much ruffled at this accident, and reflecting upon the extraordinary deportment and appearance of his valet, whose hair had by this time adopted a grizzled hue, imagined he was some favourite domestic, who had grown grey in the service of his master's family, and that of consequence he was uneasy at the sacrifice he had made. Swayed by this conjecture, he earnestly solicited in his behalf; but all he could obtain was a promise of re-admitting him into favour on the terms already proposed, or at least on condition that he should make his acknowledgment to the chevalier, for his want of reverence and respect for the French monarch.

Upon this condescension, the culprit was called upstairs, and made acquainted with the mitigation of his fate; upon which he said, he would down on his marrow-bones to his own master, but would be d—ned before he would ask pardon of e'er a Frenchman in Christendom. Pickle, exasperated at this blunt declaration, ordered him out of his presence, and charged him never to appear before his face again; while the officer in vain employed all his influence and address to appease his resentment, and about midnight took his leave with marks of mortification at his want of success.

Next day the company agreed to travel through Flanders in the diligence, by the advice of Peregrine, who was not without hope of meeting with some adventure or amusement in that carriage; and Jolter took care to secure places for them all;—it being resolved that the valet-de-chambre and the doctor's man should attend the vehicle on horseback; and as for the forlorn Pipes, he was left to reap the fruits of his own stubborn disposition, notwithstanding the united efforts of the whole triumvirate, who endeavoured to procure his pardon.

Every previous measure being thus taken, they set out from Lisle about six in the morning, and found themselves in the company of a female adventurer, a very handsome young lady, a Capuchin, and a Rotterdam Jew. Our young gentleman, being the first of this society that entered, surveyed the strangers with an attentive eye, and seated himself immediately behind the beautiful unknown, who at once attracted his attention. Pallet, seeing another lady unengaged, in imitation of his friend, took possession of her neighbourhood; the physician paired with the priest, and Jolter sat down by the Jew.

The machine had not proceeded many furlongs, when Pickle,

accosting the fair incognita, congratulated himself upon his happiness in being a fellow-traveller of so charming a lady. She, without the least reserve or affectation, thanked him for his compliment, and replied with a sprightly air, that now they were embarked in one common bottom, they must club their endeavours to make one another as happy as the nature of their situation would permit them to be. Encouraged by this frank intimation, and captivated by her fine black eyes and easy behaviour, he attached himself to her from that moment; and, in a little time, the conversation became so particular, that the Capuchin thought proper to interfere in the discourse, in such a manner as gave the youth to understand that he was there on purpose to superintend her conduct. He was doubly rejoiced at this discovery, in consequence of which he hoped to profit in his addresses, not only by the young lady's restraint, that never fails to operate in behalf of the lover, but also by the corruptibility of her guardian, whom he did not doubt of rendering propitious to his cause. Flushed with these expectations, he behaved with uncommon complacency to the father, who was charmed with the affability of his carriage, and on the faith of his generosity, abated of his vigilance so much, that our hero carried on his suit without further molestation; while the painter, in signs and loud bursts of laughter, conversed with his Dulcinea, who was perfectly well versed in these simple expressions of satisfaction, and had already found means to make a dangerous invasion upon his heart.

Nor were the governor and physician unemployed, while their friends interested themselves in this agreeable manner. Jolter no sooner perceived the Hollander was a Jew, than he entered into an investigation of the Hebrew tongue, in which he was a connoisseur; and the doctor at the same time attacked the mendicant on the ridiculous maxims of his order, together with the impositions of priestcraft in general, which, he observed, prevailed so much among those who profess the Roman Catholic religion.

Thus coupled, each committee enjoyed their own conversation apart, without any danger of encroachment, and all were so intent upon their several topics, that they scarce allowed themselves a small interval in viewing the desolation of Menin, as they passed through that ruined frontier. About twelve o'clock they arrived at Courtray, where the horses are always changed, and the company halt an hour for refreshment. Here Peregrine handed his charmer into an apartment, where she was joined by the other lady; and, on pretence of seeing some of the churches in town, put himself under the direction of the Capuchin, from whom he learned that the young lady was wife to a French gentleman, to whom she had been married about a year, and that she was now on her journey to visit her mother, who lived in Brussels, and who at that time laboured under a lingering distemper, which, in all probability, would soon put a period to her life. He then launched out in praise of her daughter's virtue and conjugal affection; and lastly told him, that he was her father confessor, and pitched upon to be her conductor through Flanders, by her husband, who, as well as his wife, placed the utmost confidence in his prudence and integrity.

Pickle easily comprehended the meaning of this insinuation, and took the hint accordingly. He tickled the priest's vanity, with extraordinary encomiums upon the disinterested principles of his order, which were detached from all worldly pursuits, and altogether devoted to the eternal salvation of mankind. He applauded their patience, humanity, and learning, and lavished a world of praise upon their talent in preaching, which, he said, had more than once operated so powerfully upon him, that, had he not been restrained by certain considerations which he could not possibly waive, he should have embraced their tenets, and begged admission into their fraternity. But, as the circumstances of his fate would not permit him to take such a salutary measure for the present, he entreated the good father to accept a small token of his love and respect, for the benefit of that convent to which he belonged. So saying, he pulled out a purse of ten guineas, which the Capuchin observing, turned his head another way, and, lifting up his arm, displayed a pocket almost as high as his collar-bone, in which he deposited the money.

This proof of affection for the order produced a sudden and surprising effect upon the friar. In the transport of his zeal he wrung this semi-convert's hand, showered a thousand benedictions upon his head, and exhorted him, with the tears flowing from his eyes, to perfect the great work which the finger of God had begun in his heart; and, as an instance of his concern for the welfare of his precious soul, the holy brother promised to recommend him strenuously to the pious admonitions of the young woman under his care, who was a perfect saint upon earth, and endowed with a peculiar gift of mollifying the hearts of obdurate sinners. "O father!" cried the hypocritical projector, who by this time perceived that his money was not thrown away, "if I could be favoured but for one half hour with the private instruction of that inspired devotee, my mind presages, that I should be a strayed sheep brought back into the fold, and that I should find easy entrance at the gates of heaven! There is something supernatural in her aspect; I gaze upon her with the most pious fervour, and my whole soul is agitated with tumults of hope and despair!" Having pronounced this rhapsody with transport half natural and half affected, the priest assured him, that these were the operations of the Spirit, which must not be repressed; and comforted him with the hope of enjoying the blessed interview which he desired, protesting, that, as far as his influence extended, his wish should be that very evening indulged. The gracious pupil thanked him for his benevolent concern, which he swore should not be squandered upon an ungrateful object; and the rest of the company interrupting the conversation, they returned in a body to the inn, where they dined all together, and the ladies were persuaded to be our hero's guests.

As the subjects on which they had been engaged before dinner were not exhausted, each brace resumed their former theme when they were replaced in the diligence. The painter's mistress finished her conquest, by exerting her skill in the art of ogling, accompanied by frequent bewitching sighs, and some tender French songs, that she sung with such pathetic expression, as quite melted the resolution of Pallet, and utterly subdued his affection. And he, to convince her of the importance of her victory, gave a specimen of his own talents, by entertaining her with that celebrated English ditty, the burden of which begins with, *The pigs they lie with their a—es bare.*

CHAPTER LIII

He makes some Progress in her Affections—Is interrupted by a Dispute between Jolter and the Jew—Appeases the Wrath of the Capuchin, who procures for him an Interview with his fair Enslaver, in which he finds himself deceived.

PEREGRINE, meanwhile, employed all his insinuation and address in practising upon the heart of the Capuchin's fair charge. He had long ago declared his passion, not in the superficial manner of a French gallant, but with all the ardour of an enthusiast. He had languished, vowed, flattered, kissed her hand by stealth, and had no reason to complain of his reception. Though by a man of a less sanguine disposition, her particular complaisance would have been deemed equivocal, and perhaps nothing more than the effect of French breeding and constitutional vivacity, he gave his own qualifications credit for the whole, and with these sentiments carried on the attack with such unabating vigour, that she was actually prevailed upon to accept a ring which he presented as a token of his esteem; and everything proceeded in a most prosperous train, when they were disturbed by the governor and Israelite, who in the heat of disputation, raised their voices, and poured forth such effusions of gutturals, as set our lover's teeth on edge. As they spoke in a language unknown to every one in the carriage but themselves, and looked at each other with mutual animosity and rancour, Peregrine desired to know the cause of their contention. Upon which Jolter exclaimed in a furious tone, "This learned Levite, forsooth, has the impudence to tell me that I don't understand Hebrew; and affirms, that the word *Benoni* signifies *child of joy*; whereas I can prove, and indeed have already said enough to convince any reasonable man, that in the Septuagint it is rightly translated into *son of my sorrow*." Having thus explained himself to his pupil, he turned to the priest, with intention to appeal to his determination; but the Jew pulled him by the sleeve with great eagerness, saying, "For the love of God be quiet, the Capuchin will discover who we are!" Jolter, offended at this conjunction, echoed "Who we are!" with great emphasis; and repeating *Nos poma natamus*, asked ironically to which of the tribes the Jew thought he belonged. The Levite, affronted at his comparing him to a ball of horse-dung, replied with a most significant grin, "To the tribe of Issachar." His antagonist, taking the advantage of his unwillingness to be known by the friar, and prompted by revenge for the freedom he had used, answered in the French language, that the judgment of God was still manifest upon their whole race, not only in their being in the state of exiles from their native land, but also in the spite of their hearts and pravity of their dispositions, which demonstrate them to be the genuine offspring of those who crucified the Saviour of the world.

His expectation was, however, defeated; the priest himself was too deeply engaged to attend to the debates of other people. The physician, in the pride and insolence of his learning, had undertaken to display the absurdity of the Christian faith; having already, as he thought, confuted the Capuchin, touching the points of belief in which the Roman Catholics differ from the rest of the world.   But not contented with the imagined victory he had gained, he began to strike at the fundamentals of religion; and the father, with incredible forbearance, suffered him to make very free with the doctrine of the Trinity.   But, when he levelled the shafts of his ridicule at the immaculate conception of the Blessed Virgin, the good man's patience forsook him, his eyes seemed to kindle with indignation, he trembled in every joint, and uttered with a loud voice, "You are an abominable—I will not call thee heretic, for thou art worse, if possible, than a Jew; you deserve to be enclosed in a furnace seven times heated, and I have a good mind to lodge an information against you with the Governor of Ghent, that you may be apprehended and punished as an impious blasphemer."

This menace operated like a charm on all present.   The doctor was confounded, the governor dismayed, the Levite's teeth chattered, the painter was astonished at the general confusion, the cause of which he could not comprehend; and Pickle himself, not a little alarmed, was obliged to use all his interest and assiduity in appeasing this son of the church, who at length, in consideration of the friendship he professed for the young gentleman, consented to forgive what had passed, but absolutely refused to sit in contact with such a profane wretch, whom he looked upon as a fiend of darkness sent by the enemy of mankind to poison the minds of weak people; so that after having crossed himself, and muttered certain exorcisms, he insisted upon the doctor's changing places with the Jew, who approached the offended ecclesiastic in an agony of fear.

Matters being thus compromised, the conversations flowed in a more general channel; and without the intervention of any other accident, or bone of contention, the carriage arrived at the city of Ghent about seven in the evening.   Supper being bespoke for the whole company, our adventurer and his friends went out to take a superficial view of the place, leaving his new mistress to the pious exhortations of her confessor, whom, as we have already observed, he had secured in his interest. This zealous mediator spoke so warmly in his commendation, and interested her conscience so much in the affair, that she could not refuse her helping-hand to the great work of his conversion, and promised to grant the interview he desired.

This agreeable piece of intelligence, which the Capuchin communicated to Peregrine at his return, elevated his spirits to such a degree, that he shone at supper with uncommon brilliance, in a thousand sallies of wit and pleasantry, to the admiration and delight of all present, especially of his fair Fleming, who seemed quite captivated by his person and behaviour.

The evening being thus spent to the satisfaction of all parties, the company broke up, and retired to their several apartments, when our lover, to his unspeakable mortification, learned that the two ladies were obliged to lie in the same room, all the other chambers of the inn being preoccupied. When he imparted this difficulty to the priest, that charitable father, who was very fruitful in expedients, assured him, that his spiritual concerns should not be obstructed by such a slender impediment; and accordingly availed himself of his prerogative, by going into his daughter's chamber when she was almost undressed, and leading her into his own, on pretence of administering salutary food for her soul. Having brought the two votaries together, he prayed for success to the operations of grace, and left them to their mutual meditations, after having conjured them in the most solemn manner to let no impure sentiments or temptations of the flesh, interfere with the hallowed design of their meeting.

The reverend intercessor being gone, and the door fastened on the inside, the pseudo-convert, transported with his passion, threw himself at Amanda's feet; and begging she would spare him the tedious form of addresses, which the nature of their interview would not permit him to observe, began with all the impetuosity of love to make the most of the occasion. But whether she was displeased by the intrepidity and assurance of his behaviour, thinking herself entitled to more courtship and respect, or was really better fortified with chastity than he or his procurer had supposed her to be, certain it is, she expressed resentment and surprise at his boldness and presumption, and upbraided him with having imposed upon the charity of the friar. The young gentleman was really as much astonished at this rebuff, as she pretended to be at his declaration, and earnestly entreated her to consider how precious the moments were, and for once sacrifice superfluous ceremony to the happiness of one who adored her with such a flame, as could not fail to consume his vitals, if she would not deign to bless him with her favour. Notwithstanding all his tears, vows, and supplications, his personal accomplishments, and the tempting opportunity, all that he could obtain was an acknowledgment of his having made an impression upon her heart, which she hoped the dictates of her duty would enable her to erase. This confession he considered as a delicate consent; and, obeying the impulse of his love, snatched her up in his arms, with an intention of seizing that which she declined to give; when this French Lucretia, unable to defend her virtue any other way, screamed aloud; and the Capuchin, setting his shoulder to the door, forced it open, and entered in an affected ecstasy of amazement. He lifted up his hands and eyes, and pretended to be thunderstruck at the discovery he had made; then, in broken exclamations, professed his horror at the wicked intention of our hero, who had covered such a damnable scheme with the mask of religion.

In short, he performed his cue with such dexterity, that the lady, believing him in earnest, begged he would forgive the stranger, on account of his youth and education, which had been tainted by the errors of heresy; and he was on these considerations content to accept the submission of our hero, who, far from renouncing his expectations, notwithstanding this mortifying repulse, confided so much in his own talents, and the confession which his mistress had made, that he resolved to make another effort, to which nothing could have prompted him but the utmost turbulence of unruly desire.

CHAPTER LIV

He makes another Effort towards the Accomplishment of his Wish, which is postponed by a strange Accident.

HE directed his valet-de-chambre, who was a thorough-paced pimp, to kindle some straw in the yard, and then pass by the door of her apartment, crying with a loud voice, that the house was on fire. This alarm brought both ladies out of their chamber in a moment; and Peregrine, taking the advantage of their running to the street door, entered the room, and concealed himself under a large table that stood in an unobserved corner. The nymphs, as soon as they understood the cause of his Mercury's supposed affright, returned to their apartment, and, having said their prayers, undressed themselves, and went to bed. This scene, which fell under the observation of Pickle, did not at all contribute to the cooling of his concupiscence, but, on the contrary, inflamed him to such a degree, that he could scarce restrain his impatience, until by her breathing deep, he concluded the fellow-lodger of his Amanda was asleep.

This welcome note no sooner saluted his ears, than he crept to his charmer's bedside, and, placing himself on his knees, gently laid hold on her white hand, and pressed it to his lips. She had just begun to close her eyes, and enjoy the agreeable oppression of slumber, when she was roused by this rape, at which she started, pronouncing, in a tone of surprise and dismay, "My God! who's that!" The lover, with the most insinuating humility, besought her to hear him; vowing, that his intention in approaching her thus, was not to violate the laws of decency, or that indelible esteem which she had engraven on his heart, but to manifest his sorrow and contrition for the umbrage he had given, to pour forth the overflowings of his soul, and tell her that he neither could nor would survive her displeasure. These, and many other pathetic protestations, accompanied with sighs and tears, and other expressions of grief, which our hero had at command, could not fail to melt the tender heart of the amiable Fleming, already prepossessed in favour of his qualifications. She sympathised so much with his affliction as to weep in her turn, when she represented the impossibility of her rewarding his passion; and he, seizing the favourable moment, reinforced his solicitations with such irresistible transports, that her resolution gave way, she began to breathe quick, expressed her fear of being overheard by the other lady, and, with an ejaculation of "O Heavens! I'm undone," suffered him, after a faint struggle, to make a lodgement upon the covered way of her bed. Her honour, however, was secured for the present, by a strange sort of knocking upon the wainscot, at the other end of the room, hard by the bed in which the female adventurer lay.

Surprised at this circumstance, the lady begged him for heaven's sake to retreat, or her reputation would be ruined for ever. But when he represented to her, that her character would run a much greater risk if he should be detected in withdrawing, she consented with great trepidation to his stay; and they listened in silence to the sequel of the noise that alarmed them. This was no other than an expedient of the painter, to awaken his Dulcinea, with whom he had made an assignation, or at least interchanged such signals as he thought amounted to a firm appointment. His nymph being disturbed in her first sleep, immediately understood the sound, and, true to the agreement, rose, and unbolting the door as softly as possible, gave him admittance, leaving it open for his more commodious retreat.

While this happy gallant was employed in disengaging himself from the dishabille in which he had entered, the Capuchin, suspecting that Peregrine would make another attempt upon his charge, had crept silently to the apartment, in order to reconnoitre, lest the adventure should be achieved without his knowledge; a circumstance that might deprive him of the profits he might expect from his privity and concurrence. Finding the door unlatched, his suspicion was confirmed, and he made no scruple of creeping into the chamber on all four; so that the painter, having stripped himself to the shirt, in groping about for his Dulcinea's bed, chanced to lay his hand upon the shaven crown of the father's head, which, by a circular motion, the priest began to turn round in his grasp, like a ball in a socket, to the surprise and consternation of poor Pallet, who, having neither penetration to comprehend the case, nor resolution to withdraw his fingers from this strange object of his touch, stood sweating in the dark, and venting ejaculations with great devotion. The friar, tired with this exercise, and the painful posture in which he stooped, raised himself gradually upon his feet, heaving up at the same time the hand of the painter, whose terror and amazement increased to such a degree at this unaccountable elevation, that his faculties began to fail; and his palm, in the confusion of his fright, sliding over the priest's forehead, one of his fingers happened to slip into his mouth, and was immediately secured between the Capuchin's teeth, with as firm a fixture as if it had been screwed in a blacksmith's vice. The painter was so much disordered by this sudden snap, which tortured him to the bone, that, forgetting all other considerations, he roared aloud, "Murder! a fire! a trap, a trap! help, Christians, for the love of God, help!"

Our hero, confounded by these exclamations, which he knew would soon fill the room with spectators, and incensed at his own mortifying disappointment, was obliged to quit the untasted banquet, and approaching the cause of his misfortune, just as his tormentor had thought proper to release his finger, discharged such a hearty slap between his shoulders, as brought him to the ground with hideous bellowing; then retiring unperceived to his own chamber, was one of the first who returned with a light, on pretence of having been alarmed with his cries. The Capuchin had taken the same precaution, and followed Peregrine into the room, pronouncing *Benedicite*, and crossing himself with many marks of astonishment. The physician and Jolter, appearing at the same time, the unfortunate painter was found lying naked on the floor, in all the agony of horror and dismay, blowing upon his left hand, that hung dangling from the elbow. The circumstance of his being found in that apartment, and the attitude of his affliction, which was extremely ridiculous, provoked the doctor to a smile, and produced a small relaxation in the severity of the governor's countenance; while Pickle, testifying surprise and concern, lifted him from the ground, and inquired into the cause of his present situation. Having, after some recollection, and fruitless endeavours to speak, recovered the use of his tongue, he told them that the house was certainly haunted by evil spirits, by which he had been conveyed, he knew not how, into that apartment, and afflicted with all the tortures of hell. That one of them had made itself sensible to his feeling, in the shape of a round ball of smooth flesh, which turned round under his hand, like an astronomer's globe, and then rising up to a surprising height, was converted into a machine that laid hold on his finger, by a snap, and having pinned him to the spot, he continued for some moments in unspeakable agony. At last he said the engine seemed to melt away from his finger, and he received a sudden thwack upon his shoulders, as if discharged by the arm of a giant, which overthrew him in an instant upon the floor.

The priest hearing this strange account, pulled out of one of his pouches a piece of consecrated candle, which he lighted immediately, and muttered certain mysterious conjurations. Jolter imagining that Pallet was drunk, shook his head, saying, he believed the spirit was nowhere but in his own brain. The physician for once condescended to be a wag, and looking towards one of the beds, observed that in his opinion, the painter had been misled by the flesh, and not by the spirit. The fair Fleming lay in silent astonishment and affright; and her fellow-lodger, in order to acquit herself of all suspicion, exclaimed with incredible volubility against the author of this uproar, who, she did not doubt, had concealed himself in the apartment, with a view of perpetrating some wicked attempt upon her precious virtue, and was punished and prevented by the immediate interposition of Heaven. At her desire, therefore, and at the earnest solicitation of the other lady, he was conducted to his own bed, and the chamber being evacuated, they locked their door, fully resolved to admit no more visitants for that night; while Peregrine, mad with seeing the delicious morsel snatched, as it were, from his very lip, stalked through the passage like a ghost, in hope of finding some opportunity of re-entering, till the day beginning to break, he was obliged to retire, cursing the idiotical conduct of the painter, which had so unluckily interfered with his delight.

CHAPTER LV

They depart from Ghent—Our Hero engages in a Political Dispute with his Mistress, whom he offends, and pacifies with Submission—He practises an Expedient to detain the Carriage at Alost, and confirms the Priest in his Interest.

NEXT day, about one o'clock, after having seen everything remarkable in town, and been present at the execution of two youths, who were hanged for ravishing a whore, they took their departure from Ghent, in the same carriage which had brought them thither; and the conversation turning upon the punishment they had seen inflicted, the Flemish beauty expressed great sympathy and compassion for the unhappy sufferers, who, as she had been informed, had fallen victims to the malice of the accuser. Her sentiments were espoused by all the company, except the French lady of pleasure, who, thinking the credit of the sisterhood concerned in the affair, bitterly inveighed against the profligacy of the age, and particularly the base and villainous attempts of man upon the chastity of the weaker sex; saying, with a look of indignation, directed to the painter, that, for her own part, she should never be able to manifest the acknowledgment she owed to Providence, for having protected her last night from the wicked aims of unbridled lust. This observation introduced a series of jokes, at the expense of Pallet, who hung his ears, and sat with a silent air of dejection, fearing that, through the malevolence of the physician, his adventure might reach the ears of his wife. Indeed, though we have made shift to explain the whole transaction to the reader, it was an inextricable mystery to every individual in the diligence. Because the part which was acted by the Capuchin was known to himself alone; and even he was utterly ignorant of Pickle's being concerned in the affair; so that the greatest share of the painter's sufferings were supposed to be the exaggerations of his own extravagant imagination.

In the midst of their discourse on this extraordinary subject, the driver told them, that they were now on the very spot where a detachment of the allied army had been intercepted and cut off by the French; and, stopping the vehicle, entertained them with a local description of the battle of Melle. Upon this occasion, the Flemish lady, who, since her marriage, had become a keen partisan for the French, gave a minute detail of all the circumstances, as they had been represented to her by her husband's brother, who was in the action. This account, which sunk the number of the French to sixteen, and raised that of the allies to twenty thousand men, was so disagreeable to truth, as well as to the laudable partiality of Peregrine, that he ventured to contradict her assertions, and a fierce dispute commenced, that not only regarded the present question, but also comprehended all the battles in which the Duke of Marlborough had commanded against Louis the Fourteenth. In the course of these debates, she divested the great general of all the glory he had acquired, by affirming, that every victory he gained was purposely lost by the French generals, in order to bring the schemes of Madame de Maintenon into discredit; and, as a particular instance, alleged, that while the citadel of Lisle was besieged, Louis said, in presence of the Dauphin, that, if the allies should be obliged to raise the siege, he would immediately declare his marriage with that lady; upon which the son sent private orders to Marshal Boufflers to surrender the place. This strange allegation was supported by the asseverations of the priest and the courtesan, and admitted as truth by the governor, who pretended to have heard it from good authority; while the doctor sat neutral, as one who thought it scandalous to know the history of such modern events. The Israelite, being a true Dutchman, lifted himself under the banners of our hero, who, in attempting to demonstrate the absurdity and improbability of what they had advanced, raised such a hue and cry against himself, and being insensibly heated in the altercation, irritated his Amanda to such a degree, that her charming eyes kindled with fury, and he saw great reason to think, that, if he did not fall upon some method to deprecate her wrath, she would in a twinkling sacrifice all her esteem for him to her own zeal for the glory of the French nation. Moved by this apprehension, his ardour cooled by degrees, and he insensibly detached himself from the argument, leaving the whole care of supporting it to the Jew, who, finding himself deserted, was fain to yield at discretion; so that the French remained masters of the field, and their young heroine resumed her good-humour.

Our hero having prudently submitted to the superior intelligence of his fair enslaver, began to be harassed with the fears of losing her for ever, and set his invention at work, to contrive some means of indemnifying himself for his assiduities, presents, and the disappointments he had already undergone. On pretence of enjoying a free air, he mounted the box, and employed his elocution and generosity with such success, that the driver undertook to disable the diligence from proceeding beyond the town of Alost for that day; and, in consequence of his promise, gently overturned it when they were but a mile short of that baiting-place. He had taken his measures so discreetly, that this accident was attended with no other inconvenience than a fit of fear that took possession of the ladies, and the necessity to which they were reduced by the declaration of the coachman, who, upon examining the carriage, assured the company that the axle-tree had given way, and advised them to walk forward to the inn, while he would jog after them at a slow pace, and to his endeavour the damage should be immediately repaired. Peregrine pretended to be very much concerned at what had happened, and even cursed the driver for his inadvertency, expressing infinite impatience to be at Brussels, and wishing that this misfortune might not detain them another night upon the road; but when his understrapper, according to his instructions, came forward to the inn, and gave them to understand, that the workmen he had employed could not possibly refit the machine in less than six hours, the crafty youth affected to lose all temper, stormed at his emissary, whom he reviled in the most opprobrious terms, and threatened to cane for his misconduct. The fellow protested, with great humility, that their being overturned was owing to the failure of the axle-tree, and not to his want of care or dexterity in driving; though rather than be thought the cause of incommoding him, he would inquire for a post-chaise, in which he might depart for Brussels immediately.

This expedient Pickle rejected, unless the whole company could be accommodated in the same manner; and he had been previously informed by the driver that the town could not furnish more than one vehicle of that sort. His governor, who was quite ignorant of his scheme, represented, that one night would soon be passed, and exhorted him to bear this small disappointment with a good grace, especially as the house seemed to be well provided for their entertainment, and the company so much disposed to be sociable. The Capuchin, who had found his account in cultivating the acquaintance of the young stranger, was not ill-pleased at this event, which might, by protracting the term of their intercourse, yield him some opportunity of profiting still further by his liberality. He therefore joined Mr. Jolter in his admonitions, congratulating himself upon the prospect of enjoying his conversation a little longer than he had expected. Our young gentleman received a compliment to the same purpose from the Hebrew, who had that day exercised his gallantry upon the French coquette, and was not without hope of reaping the fruits of his attention; his rival, the painter, being quite disgraced and dejected by the adventure of last night. As for the doctor, he was too much engrossed in the contemplation of his own importance, to interest himself in the affair, or its consequences, further than by observing that the European powers ought to establish public games, like those that were celebrated of old in Greece; in which case, every state would be supplied with such dexterous charioteers, as would drive a machine at full speed, within a hair's breadth of a precipice, without any danger of its being overthrown.

Peregrine could not help yielding to their remonstrances, and united complaisance, for which he thanked them in very polite terms, and his passion seeming to subside, proposed that they should amuse themselves in walking round the ramparts. He hoped to enjoy some private conversation with his admired Fleming, who had this whole day behaved with remarkable reserve. The proposal being embraced, he, as usual, handed her into the street, and took all opportunities of promoting his suit; but they were attended so closely by her father confessor, that he foresaw it would be impracticable to accomplish his aim, without the connivance of that ecclesiastic. This he was obliged to purchase with another purse, which he offered, and was accepted as a charitable atonement for his criminal behaviour during the interview which the friar had procured for the good of his soul. The benefaction was no sooner made, than the pious mendicant edged off by little and little, till he joined the rest of the company, leaving his generous patron at full liberty to prosecute his purpose.

It is not to be doubted that our adventurer made a good use of this occasion. He practised a thousand flowers of rhetoric, and actually exhausted his whole address, in persuading her to have compassion upon his misery, and indulge him with another private audience, without which he should run distracted, and be guilty of extravagances which, in the humanity of her disposition, she would weep to see. But, instead of complying with his request, she chid him severely for his presumption, in persecuting her with his vicious addresses. She assured him, that although she had secured a chamber for herself in this place, because she had no ambition to be better acquainted with the other lady, he would be in the wrong to disturb her with another nocturnal visit; for she was determined to deny him admittance. The lover was comforted by this hint, which he understood in the true acceptation, and his passion being inflamed by the obstacles he had met with, his heart beat high with the prospect of possession. These raptures of expectation produced an inquietude, which disabled him from bearing that share of the conversation for which he used to be distinguished. His behaviour at supper was a vicissitude of startings and reveries. The Capuchin, imputing this disorder to a second repulse from his charge, began to be invaded with the apprehension of being obliged to refund, and, in a whisper, forbade our hero to despair.

CHAPTER LVI

The French Coquette entraps the Heart of the Jew, against whom Pallet enters into a Conspiracy; by which Peregrine is again disappointed, and the Hebrew's Incontinence exposed.

MEANWHILE the French syren, balked in her design upon her English cully, who was so easily disheartened, and hung his ears in manifest despondence, rather than run the risk of making a voyage that should be altogether unprofitable, resolved to practise her charms upon the Dutch merchant. She had already made such innovations upon his heart, that he cultivated her with peculiar complacency, gazed upon her with a most libidinous stare, and unbended his aspect into a grin that was truly Israelitish. The painter saw and was offended at this correspondence, which he considered as an insult upon his misfortune, as well as an evident preference of his rival; and, conscious of his own timidity, swallowed an extraordinary glass, that his invention might be stimulated, and his resolution raised to the contrivance and execution of some scheme of revenge. The wine, however, failed in the expected effect, and, without inspiring him with the plan, served only to quicken his desire of vengeance; so that he communicated his purpose to his friend Peregrine, and begged his assistance. But our young gentleman was too intent upon his own affair, to mind the concerns of any other person; and he declining to be engaged in the project, Pallet had recourse to the genius of Pickle's valet-de-chambre, who readily embarked in the undertaking, and invented a plan, which was executed accordingly.

The evening being pretty far advanced, and the company separated into their respective apartments, Pickle repaired, in all the impatience of youth and desire, to the chamber of his charmer, and finding the door unbolted, entered in a transport of joy. By the light of the moon, which shone through the window, he was conducted to her bed, which he approached in the utmost agitation, and perceiving her to all appearance asleep, essayed to wake her with a gentle kiss; but this method proved ineffectual, because she was determined to save herself the confusion of being an accomplice in his guilt. He repeated the application, murmured a most passionate salutation in her ear, and took such other gentle methods of signifying his presence, as persuaded him that she was resolved to sleep, in spite of all his endeavours. Flushed with this agreeable supposition, he locked the door, in order to prevent interruption, and stealing himself under the clothes, set fortune at defiance, while he held the fair creature circled in his arms.

Nevertheless, near as he seemed to be to the happy accomplishment of his desire, his hope was again frustrated with a frightful noise, which in a moment awaked his Amanda in a fright, and, for the present, engaged all his attention. His valet-de-chambre, whom Pallet had consulted as a confederate in his revenge against the lady of pleasure, and her Jewish gallant, had hired of certain Bohemians, who chanced to lodge at the inn, a jackass, adorned with bells, which, when everybody was retired to rest, and the Hebrew supposed to be bedded with his mistress, they led upstairs into a long thoroughfare, from which the chambers were detached on each side. The painter, perceiving the lady's door ajar, according to his expectation, mounted this animal, with intention to ride into the room, and disturb the lovers in the midst of their mutual endearments; but the ass, true to its kind, finding himself bestrid by an unknown rider, instead of advancing in obedience to his conductor, retreated backwards to the other end of the passage, in spite of all the efforts of the painter, who spurred and kicked, and pommelled to no purpose. It was the noise of this contention between Pallet and the ass which invaded the ears of Peregrine and his mistress, neither of whom could form the least rational conjecture about the cause of such strange disturbance, which increased as the animal approached the apartment. At length, the bourrique's retrograde motion was obstructed by the door, which it forced open in a twinkling, with one kick, and entered with such complication of sound, as terrified the lady almost into a fit, and threw her lover into the utmost perplexity and confusion.

The painter, finding himself thus violently intruded into the bedchamber of he knew not whom, and dreading the resentment of the possessor, who might discharge a pistol at him, as a robber who had broke into his apartment, was overwhelmed with consternation, and redoubled his exertion to accomplish a speedy retreat, sweating all the time with fear, and putting up petitions to Heaven for his safety; but his obstinate companion, regardless of his situation, instead of submitting to his conduct, began to turn round like a millstone, the united sound of his feet and bells producing a most surprising concert. The unfortunate rider, whirling about in this manner, would have quitted his seat, and left the beast to his own amusement, but the rotation was so rapid, that the terror of a severe fall hindered him from attempting to dismount; and, in the desperation of his heart, he seized one of its ears, which he pinched so unmercifully, that the creature set up his throat and brayed aloud. This hideous exclamation was no sooner heard by the fair Fleming, already chilled by panic, and prepared with superstition, than, believing herself visited by the devil, who was permitted to punish her for her infidelity to the marriage-bed, she uttered a scream, and began to repeat her paternoster with a loud voice. Her lover, finding himself under the necessity of retiring, started up, and, stung with the most violent pangs of rage and disappointment, ran directly to the spot whence this diabolical noise seemed to proceed. There, encountering the ass, he discharged such a volley of blows at him and his rider, that the creature carried him off at a round trot, and they roared in unison all the way. Having thus cleared the room of such disagreeable company, he went back to his mistress, and assuring her that this was only some foolish prank of Pallet, took his leave, with a promise of returning after the quiet of the inn should be re-established.

In the meantime, the noise of the bourrique, the cries of the painter, and the lady's scream, had alarmed the whole house; and the ass, in the precipitation of his retreat, seeing people with lights before him, took shelter in the apartment for which he was at first designed, just as the Levite, aroused at the uproar, had quitted his Dulcinea, and was attempting to recover his own chamber unperceived. Seeing himself opposed by such an animal, mounted by a tall, meagre, lantern-jawed figure, half-naked, with a white nightcap upon his head, which added to the natural paleness of his complexion, the Jew was sorely troubled in mind, and believing it to be an apparition of Balaam and his ass, fled backward with a nimble pace, and crept under the bed, where he lay concealed. Mr. Jolter and the priest, who were the foremost of those who had been aroused by the noise, were not unmoved when they saw such a spectacle rushing into the chamber from whence the lady of pleasure began to shriek. The governor made a full halt, and the Capuchin discovered no inclination to proceed. They were, however, by the pressure of the crowd that followed them, thrust forward to the door through which the vision entered; and there Jolter, with great ceremony, complimented his reverence with the pass, beseeching him to walk in. The mendicant was too courteous and humble to accept this pre-eminence, and a very earnest dispute ensued; during which the ass, in the course of his circuit, showed himself and rider, and, in a trice, decided the contest; for, struck with this second glimpse, both at one instant sprung back with such force, as overturned the next men, who communicated the impulse to those that stood behind them, and these again to others; so that the whole passage was strewed with a long file of people, that lay in a line like the sequel and dependence of a pack of cards.

In the midst of this havoc, our hero returned from his own room, with an air of astonishment, asking the cause of this uproar. Receiving such hints of intelligence as Jolter's consternation would permit him to give, he snatched the candle out of his hand, and advanced into the haunted chamber without hesitation, being followed by all present, who broke forth into a long and loud peal of laughter, when they perceived the ludicrous source of their disquiet. The painter himself made an effort to join their mirth; but he had been so harrowed by fear, and smarted so much with the pain of the discipline he had received from Pickle, that he could not, with all his endeavour, vanquish the ruefulness of his countenance. His attempt served only to increase the awkwardness of his situation, which was not at all mended by the behaviour of the coquette, who, furious with her disappointment, slipped on a petticoat and bedgown, and springing upon him like another Hecuba, with her nails deprived all one side of his nose of the skin, and would not have left him an eye to see through, if some of the company had not rescued him from her unmerciful talons. Provoked at this outrage, as well as by her behaviour to him in the diligence, he publicly explained his intention in entering her chamber in this equipage; and, missing the Hebrew among the spectators, assured them that he must have absconded somewhere in the apartment. In pursuance of this intimation, the room was immediately searched, and the mortified Levite pulled by the heels from his lurking-place; so that Pallet had the good fortune at last to transfer the laugh from himself to his rival and the French inamorata, who accordingly underwent the ridicule of the whole audience.

CHAPTER LVII

Pallet, endeavouring to unravel the Mystery of the Treatment he had received, falls out of the Frying-pan into the Fire.

NEVERTHELESS, Pallet was still confounded and chagrined by one consideration, which was no other than that of his having been so roughly handled in the chamber belonging, as he found upon inquiry, to the handsome young lady who was under the Capuchin's direction. He recollected that the door was fast locked when his beast burst it open; and he had no reason to believe that any person followed him in his irruption. On the other hand, he could not imagine that such a gentle creature would either attempt to commit, or be able to execute, such a desperate assault as that which his body had sustained; and her demeanour was so modest and circumspect, that he durst not harbour the least suspicion of her virtue.

These reflections bewildered him in the labyrinth of thought; he rummaged his whole imagination, endeavouring to account for what had happened. At length he concluded, that either Peregrine, or the devil, or both, must have been at the bottom of the whole affair, and determined, for the satisfaction of his curiosity, to watch our hero's motions, during the remaining part of the night, so narrowly, that his conduct, mysterious as it was, should not be able to elude his penetration.

With these sentiments he retired to his own room, after the ass had been restored to the right owners, and the priest had visited and confirmed his fair ward, who had been almost distracted with fear. Silence no sooner prevailed again, than he crawled darkling towards her door, and huddled himself up in an obscure corner, from whence he might observe the ingress or egress of any human creature. He had not long remained in this posture, when, fatigued with this adventure, and that of the preceding night, his faculties were gradually overpowered with slumber; and, falling fast asleep, he began to snore like a whole congregation of Presbyterians. The Flemish beauty, hearing this discordant noise in the passage, began to be afraid of some new alarm, and very prudently bolted her door; so that when her lover wanted to repeat his visit, he was not only surprised and incensed at this disagreeable serenade, the author of which he did not know, but when compelled by his passion, which was by this time wound to the highest pitch, he ventured to approach the entrance, he had the extreme mortification to find himself shut out. He durst not knock to signify his presence in any other manner, on account of the lady's reputation, which would have greatly suffered, had the snorer been awaked by his endeavours. Had he known that the person who thus thwarted his views was the painter, he would have taken some effectual step to remove him; but he could not conceive what should induce Pallet to take up his residence in that corner; nor could he use the assistance of a light to distinguish him, because there was not a candle burning in the house.

It is impossible to describe the rage and vexation of our hero, while he continued thus tantalised upon the brink of bliss, after his desire had been exasperated by the circumstances of his two former disappointments. He ejaculated a thousand execrations against his own fortune, cursed his fellow-travellers without exception, vowed revenge against the painter, who had twice confounded his most interesting scheme, and was tempted to execute immediate vengeance upon the unknown cause of his present miscarriage. In this agony of distraction did he sweat two whole hours in the passage, though not without some faint hopes of being delivered from his tormentor, who, he imagined, upon waking, would undoubtedly shift his quarters, and leave the field free to his designs; but when he heard the cock repeat his salutation to the morn, which began to open on the rear of night, he could no longer restrain his indignation. Going to his own chamber, he filled a basin with cold water, and, standing at some distance, discharged it full in the face of the gaping snorer, who, over and above the surprise occasioned by the application, was almost suffocated by the liquor that entered his mouth and ran down into his windpipe. While he gasped like a person half-drowned, without knowing the nature of his disaster, or remembering the situation in which he fell asleep, Peregrine retired to his own door, and to his no small astonishment, from a long howl that invaded his ears, learned that the patient was no other than Pallet, who had now for the third time balked his good fortune.

Enraged at the complicated trespasses of this unfortunate

offender, he rushed from his apartment with a horsewhip, and encountering the painter in his flight, overturned him in the passage. There he exercised the instrument of his wrath with great severity, on pretence of mistaking him for some presumptuous cur, which had disturbed the repose of the inn; nay, when he called aloud for mercy in a supplicating tone, and his chastiser could no longer pretend to treat him as a quadruped, such was the virulence of the young gentleman's indignation, that he could not help declaring his satisfaction, by telling Pallet he had richly deserved the punishment he had undergone, for his madness, folly, and impertinence, in contriving and executing such idle schemes, as had no other tendency than that of plaguing his neighbours.

Pallet protested, with great vehemence, that he was innocent, as the child unborn, of an intention to give umbrage to any person whatever, except the Israelite and his doxy, who he knew had incurred his displeasure. "But, as God is my Saviour," said he, "I believe I am persecuted with witchcraft, and begin to think that d—ned priest is an agent of the devil; for he hath been but two nights in our company, during which I have not closed an eye, but, on the contrary, have been tormented by all the fiends of hell." Pickle peevishly replied, that his torments had been occasioned by his own foolish imagination; and asked him how he came to howl in that corner. The painter, who did not think proper to own the truth, said, that he had been transported thither by some preternatural conveyance, and soused in water by an invisible hand. The youth, in hope of profiting by his absence, advised him to retire immediately to his bed, and by sleep strive to comfort his brain, which seemed to be not a little disordered by the want of that refreshment. Pallet himself began to be very much of the same way of thinking; and, in compliance with such wholesome counsel, betook himself to rest, muttering prayers all the way for the recovery of his own understanding.

Pickle attended him to his chamber, and, locking him up, put the key in his own pocket, that he might not have it in his power to interrupt him again; but, in his return he was met by Mr. Jolter and the doctor, who had been a second time alarmed by the painter's cries, and come to inquire about this new adventure. Half-frantic with such a series of disappointments, he cursed them in his heart for their unseasonable appearance. When they questioned him about Pallet, he told them he had found him stark staring mad, howling in a corner, and wet to the skin, and conducted him to his room, where he was now abed. The physician, hearing this circumstance, made a merit of his vanity; and, under pretence of concern for the patient's welfare, desired he might have an opportunity of examining the symptoms of his disorder, without loss of time; alleging that many diseases might have been stifled in the birth, which afterwards baffled all the endeavours of the medical art.   The young gentleman accordingly delivered the key, and once more withdrew into his own chamber, with a view of seizing the first occasion that should present itself of renewing his application to his Amanda's door; while the doctor, in his way to Pallet's apartment, hinted to the governor his suspicion that the patient laboured under the dreadful symptom called the *hydrophobia*, which, he observed, had sometimes appeared in persons who were not previously bit by a mad dog.   This conjecture he founded upon the howl he uttered when he was soused with water, and began to recollect certain circumstances of the painter's behaviour for some days past, which now he could plainly perceive had prognosticated some such calamity.   He then ascribed the distemper to the violent frights he had lately undergone; affirmed that the affair of the Bastile had made such a violent encroachment upon his understanding, that his manner of thinking and speaking was entirely altered.   By a theory of his own invention, he explained the effect of fear upon a loose system of nerves, and demonstrated the modus in which the animal spirits operate upon the ideas and power of imagination.

This disquisition, which was communicated at the painter's door, might have lasted till breakfast, had not Jolter reminded him of his own maxim, *Venienti occurrite morbo*; upon which he put the key to immediate use, and they walked softly towards the bed, where the patient lay extended at full length in the arms of sleep.   The physician took notice of his breathing hard, and his mouth being open; and from these diagnostics declared that the *liquidum nervosum* was intimately affected, and the *saliva* impregnated with the spiculated particles of the *virus*, howsoever contracted.   This sentence was still farther confirmed by the state of his pulse, which, being full and slow, indicated an oppressed circulation, from a loss of elasticity in the propelling arteries.   He proposed that he should immediately suffer a second aspersion of water, which would not only contribute to the cure, but also certify them beyond all possibility of doubt, with regard to the state of the disease; for it would evidently appear, from the manner in which he would bear the application, whether or not his horror of water amounted to a confirmed hydrophobia. Mr. Jolter, in compliance with this proposal, began to empty a bottle of water, which he found in the room, in a basin; when he was interrupted by the prescriber, who advised him to use the contents of the chamber-pot, which, being impregnated with salt, would operate more effectually than pure element. Thus directed, the governor lifted up the vessel, which was replete with medicine, and with one turn of his hand discharged the whole healing inundation upon the ill-omen'd patient, who, waking in the utmost distraction of horror, yelled most hideously, just at the time when Peregrine had brought his mistress to a parley, and entertained hopes of being admitted into her chamber.

Terrified at this exclamation, she instantly broke off the treaty, beseeching him to retire from the door, that her honour might receive no injury from his being found in that place; and he had just enough of recollection left to see the necessity of obeying the order; in conformity to which he retreated, well-nigh deprived of his senses, and almost persuaded that so many unaccountable disappointments must have proceeded from some supernatural cause, of which the idiot Pallet was no more than the involuntary instrument.

Meanwhile, the doctor having ascertained the malady of the patient, whose cries, interrupted by frequent sobs and sighs, he interpreted into the barking of a dog, and having no more salt water at hand, resolved to renew the bath with such materials as chance would afford. He actually laid hold of the bottle and basin; but by this time the painter had recovered the use of his senses so well, as to perceive his drift; and, starting up like a frantic bedlamite, ran directly to his sword, swearing with many horrid imprecations, that he would murder them both immediately, if he should be hanged before dinner. They did not choose to wait the issue of his threat, but retired with such precipitation, that the physician had almost dislocated his shoulder, by running against one side of the entry. Jolter, having pulled the door after him, and turned the key, betook himself to flight, roaring aloud for assistance. His colleague, seeing the door secured, valued himself upon his resolution, and exhorted him to return; declaring, that for his own part, he was more afraid of the madman's teeth than of his weapon, and admonishing the governor to re-enter, and execute what they had left undone. "Go in," said he, "without fear or apprehension, and if any accident shall happen to you, either from his slaver or his sword, I will assist you with my advice, which from this station I can more coolly and distinctly administer, than I should be able to supply, if my ideas were disturbed, or my attention engaged in any personal concern."

Jolter, who could make no objection to the justness of the conclusion, frankly owned, that he had no inclination to try the experiment; observing, that self-preservation was the first law of nature; that his connexions with the unhappy lunatic were but slight; and that it could not be reasonably expected that he would run such risks for his service, as were declined by one who had set out with him from England, on the footing of a companion. This insinuation introduced a dispute upon the nature of benevolence, and the moral sense, which, the republican argued, existed independent of any private consideration, and could never be affected by any contingent circumstance of time and fortune; while the other, who abhorred his principles, asserted the duties and excellence of private friendship, with infinite rancour of altercation.

During the hottest of the argument, they were joined by the Capuchin, who, being astonished to see them thus virulently engaged at the door, and to hear the painter bellowing within the chamber, conjured them in the name of God, to tell him the cause of that confusion, which had kept the whole house in continual alarm during the best part of the night, and seemed to be the immediate work of the devil and his angels. When the governor gave him to understand, that Pallet was visited with an evil spirit, he muttered a prayer of St. Antonio de Padua, and undertook to cure the painter, provided he could be secured so as that he might, without danger to himself, burn part of a certain relic under his nose, which he assured them was equal to the miraculous power of Eleazar's ring. They expressed great curiosity to know what this treasure was; and the priest was prevailed upon to tell them in confidence, that it was a collection of the paring of the nails belonging to those two madmen whom Jesus purged of the legion of devils that afterwards entered the swine. So saying, he pulled from one of his pockets a small box, containing about an ounce of the parings of an horse's hoof; at sight of which the governor could not help smiling, on account of the grossness of the imposition. The doctor asked, with a supercilious smile, whether those maniacs whom Jesus cured, were of the sorrel complexion, or dapple grey; for, from the texture of these parings, he could prove, that the original owners were of the quadruped order, and even distinguished, that their feet had been fortified with shoes of iron.

The mendicant, who bore an inveterate grudge against this son of Æsculapius, ever since he had made so free with the Catholic religion, replied, with great bitterness, that he was a wretch, with whom no Christian ought to communicate; that the vengeance of Heaven would one day overtake him, on account of his profanity; and that his heart was shod with a metal much harder than iron, which nothing but hell-fire would be able to melt.

It was now broad day, and all the servants of the inn were afoot. Peregrine, seeing it would be impossible to obtain any sort of indemnification for the time he had lost, and the perturbation of his spirits hindering him from enjoying repose, which was, moreover, obstructed by the noise of Pallet, and his attendants, put on his clothes at once, and, in exceeding ill-humour, arrived at the spot where this triumvirate stood debating about the means of overpowering the furious painter, who still continued his song of oaths and execrations, and made sundry efforts to break open the door. Chagrined as our hero was, he could not help laughing when he heard how the patient had been treated; and his indignation changing into compassion, he called to him through the key-hole, desiring to know the reason of his distracted behaviour. Pallet no sooner recognised his voice, than lowering his own to a whimpering tone, "My dear friend," said he, "I have at last detected the ruffians who have persecuted me so much. I caught them in the fact of suffocating me with cold water; and by the Lord I will be revenged, or may I never live to finish my Cleopatra. For the love of God open the door, and I will make that conceited pagan, that pretender to taste, that false devotee of the ancients, who poisons people with silly-kickabys and devil's dung; I say, I will make him a monument of my wrath, and an example to all the cheats and impostors of the faculty; and, as for that thick-headed, insolent pedant, his confederate, who emptied my own jordan upon me while I slept, he had better been in his beloved Paris, botching schemes for his friend the Pretender, than incur the effects of my resentment. Gadsbodikins! I won't leave him a windpipe for the hangman to stop, at the end of another rebellion."

Pickle told him his conduct had been so extravagant, as to confirm the whole party in the belief that he was actually deprived of his senses; on which supposition Mr. Jolter and the doctor had acted the part of friends, in doing that which they thought most conducive to his recovery; so that their concern merited his thankful acknowledgment, instead of his frantic menaces. That, for his own part, he would be the first to condemn him, as one utterly bereft of his wits, and give orders for his being secured as a madman, unless he would immediately give a proof of his sanity, by laying aside his sword, composing his spirits, and thanking his injured friends for their care of his person.

This alternative quieted his transports in a moment; he was terrified at the apprehension of being treated like a bedlamite, being dubious of the state of his own brain; and, on the other hand, had conceived such a horror and antipathy for his tormentors, that, far from believing himself obliged by what they had done, he could not even think of them without the utmost rage and detestation. He, therefore, in the most tranquil voice he could assume, protested, that he never was less out of his senses than at present, though he did not know how long he might retain them, if he should be considered in the light of a lunatic. That, in order to prove his being *compos mentis*, he was willing to sacrifice the resentment he so justly harboured against those, who, by their malice, had brought him to this pass. But as he apprehended it would be the greatest sign of madness he could exhibit, to thank them for the mischiefs they had brought upon him, he desired to be excused from making any such concession; and swore he would endure everything, rather than be guilty of such mean absurdity.

Peregrine held a consultation upon this reply, when the governor and physician strenuously argued against any capitulation with a maniac, and proposed that some method might be taken to seize, fetter, and convey him into a dark room, where he might be treated according to the rules of art. But the Capuchin, understanding the circumstances of the case, undertook to restore him to his former state, without having recourse to such violent measures. Pickle, who was a better judge of the affair than any person present, opened the door without further hesitation, and displayed the poor painter standing with a woeful countenance, shivering in his shirt, which was as wet as if he had been dragged through the Dender: a spectacle which gave such offence to the chaste eyes of the Hebrew's mistress, who was by this time one of the spectators, that she turned her head another way, and withdrew to her own room, exclaiming against the indecent practices of men.

Pallet, seeing the young gentleman enter, ran to him, and,

shaking him by the hand, called him his best friend, and said he had rescued him from those who had a design against his life. The priest would have produced his parings, and applied them to his nose, but was hindered by Pickle, who advised the patient to shift himself, and put on his clothes. This being done with great order and deliberation, Mr. Jolter, who, with the doctor, had kept a wary distance, in expectation of seeing some strange effects of his distraction, began to believe that he had been guilty of a mistake, and accused the physician of having misled him by his false diagnostic. The doctor still insisted upon his former declaration, assuring him, that although Pallet enjoyed a short interval for the present, the delirium would soon recur, unless they would profit by this momentary calm, and ordered him to be blooded, blistered and purged, with all imaginable despatch.

The governor, however, notwithstanding this caution, advanced to the injured party, and begged pardon for the share he had in giving him such disturbance. He declared, in the most solemn manner, that he had no other intention than that of contributing towards his welfare, and that his behaviour was the result of the physician's prescription, which he affirmed was absolutely necessary for the recovery of his health.

The painter, who had very little gall in his disposition, was satisfied with this apology; but his resentment, which was before divided, now glowed with double fire against his first fellow-traveller, whom he looked upon as the author of all the mischances he had undergone, and marked out for his vengeance accordingly. Yet the doors of reconciliation were not shut against the doctor, who, with great justice, might have transferred this load of offence from himself to Peregrine, who was, without doubt, the source of the painter's misfortune. But, in that case, he must have owned himself mistaken in his medical capacity; and he did not think the friendship of Pallet important enough to be retrieved by such condescension; so that he resolved to neglect him entirely, and gradually forget the former correspondence he had maintained with a person whom he deemed so unworthy of his notice.

CHAPTER LVIII

Peregrine, almost distracted with his Disappointments, conjures the fair Fleming to permit his Visits at Brussels—She withdraws from his Pursuit.

THINGS being thus adjusted, and all the company dressed, they went to breakfast about five in the morning, and in less than an hour after were seated in the diligence, where a profound silence prevailed. Peregrine, who used to be the life of the society, was extremely pensive and melancholy on account of his mishap, the Israelite and his Dulcinea dejected in consequence of their disgrace, the poet absorbed in lofty meditation, the painter in schemes of revenge, while Jolter, rocked by the motion of the carriage, made himself amends for the want of rest he had sustained, and the mendicant, with his fair charge, were infected by the cloudy aspect of our youth, in whose disappointment each of them, for different reasons, bore no inconsiderable share. This general languor and recess from all bodily exercise, disposed them all to receive the gentle yoke of slumber; and, in half an hour after they had embarked, there was not one of them awake, except our hero and his mistress, unless the Capuchin was pleased to counterfeit sleep, in order to indulge our young gentleman with an opportunity of enjoying some private conversation with his beauteous ward. Peregrine did not neglect the occasion; but, on the contrary, seized the first minute, and, in gentle murmurs, lamented his hard hap in being thus the sport of fortune. He assured her, and that with great sincerity, that all the cross accidents of his life had not cost him one half of the vexation and keenness of chagrin which he had suffered last night; and that, now he was on the brink of parting from her, he should be overwhelmed with the blackest despair, if she would not extend her compassion so far as to give him an opportunity of sighing at her feet in Brussels, during the few days his affairs would permit him to spend in that city.

This young lady, with an air of mortification, expressed her sorrow for being the innocent cause of his anxiety; said, she hoped last night's adventure would be a salutary warning to both their souls; for she was persuaded that her virtue was protected by the intervention of Heaven; that whatever impression it might have made upon him, she was enabled by it to adhere to that duty from which her passion had begun to swerve; and, beseeching him to forget her for his own peace, gave him to understand, that neither the plan she had laid down for her own conduct, nor the dictates of her honour, would allow her to receive his visits, or carry on any other correspondence with him, while she was restricted by the articles of her marriage vow.

This explanation produced such a violent effect upon her admirer, that he was for some minutes deprived of the faculty of speech; which he no sooner recovered, than he gave vent to the most unbridled transports of passion. He taxed her with barbarity and indifference; told her, that she had robbed him of his reason and internal peace; that he would follow her to the end of the earth, and cease to live sooner than cease to love her; that he would sacrifice the innocent fool who had been the occasion of all this disquiet, and murder every man whom he considered as an obstruction to his views. In a word, his passions, which had continued so long in a state of the highest fermentation, together with the want of that repose which calms and quiets the perturbation of the spirits, had wrought him up to a pitch of real distraction. While he uttered these delirious expressions, the tears ran down his cheeks; and he underwent such agitation, that the tender heart of the fair Fleming was affected with his condition; and, while her own face was bedewed with the streams of sympathy, she begged him, for Heaven's sake, to be composed; and promised, for his satisfaction, to abate somewhat of the rigour of her purpose. Consoled by this kind declaration, he recollected himself; and, taking out his pencil, gave her his address, when she had assured him that he should hear from her in four-and-twenty hours at farthest after their separation.

Thus soothed, he regained the empire of himself, and, by degrees, recovered his serenity. But this was not the case with his Amanda, who, from this sample of his disposition, dreaded the impetuosity of his youth, and was effectually deterred from entering into any engagements that might subject her peace and reputation to the rash effects of such a violent spirit. Though she was captivated by his person and accomplishments, she had reflection enough to foresee, that the longer she countenanced his passion, her own heart would be more and more irretrievably engaged, and the quiet of her life the more exposed to continual interruption. She therefore profited by these considerations, and a sense of religious honour, which helped her to withstand the suggestions of inclination, and resolved to amuse her lover with false hopes, until she should have it in her power to relinquish his conversation, without running any risk of suffering by the inconsiderate sallies of his love. It was with this view that she desired he would not insist upon attending her to her mother's house, when the diligence arrived at Brussels, and he, cajoled by her artifice, took a formal leave of her, together with the other strangers, fixing his habitation at the inn to which he and his fellow-travellers had been directed, in the impatient expectation of receiving a kind summons from her within the limited time.

Meanwhile, in order to divert his imagination, he went to see the Stadthouse, park, and arsenal, took a superficial view of the bookseller's cabinet of curiosities, and spent the evening at the Italian opera, which was at that time exhibited for the entertainment of Prince Charles of Lorrain, then governor of the Low Countries. In short, the stated period was almost elapsed, when Peregrine received a letter to this purpose—

SIR,—If you knew what violence I do my own heart, in declaring that I have withdrawn myself for ever from your addresses, you would surely applaud the sacrifice I make to virtue, and strive to imitate this example of self-denial. Yes, sir, Heaven hath lent me grace to struggle with my guilty passion, and henceforth to avoid the dangerous sight of him who inspired it. I therefore conjure you, by the regard you ought to have for the eternal welfare of us both, as well as by the esteem and affection you profess, to war with your unruly inclination, and desist from all attempts of frustrating the laudable resolution I have made. Seek not to invade the peace of one who loves you, to disturb the quiet of a family that never did you wrong, and to alienate the thoughts of a weak woman from a deserving man, who, by the most sacred claim, ought to have the full possession of her heart.

This billet, without either date or subscription, banished all remains of discretion from the mind of our hero, who ran instantly to the landlord, in all the ecstasy of madness, and demanded to see the messenger who brought the letter, on pain of putting his whole family to the sword. The innkeeper, terrified by his looks and menaces, fell upon his knees, protesting, in the face of Heaven, that he was utterly ignorant and innocent of anything that could give him offence, and that the billet was brought by a person whom he did not know, and who retired immediately, saying it required no answer. He then gave utterance to his fury in a thousand imprecations and invectives against the writer, whom he dishonoured with the appellations of a coquette, a jilt, an adventurer, who, by means of a pimping priest, had defrauded him of his money. He denounced vengeance against the mendicant, whom he swore he would destroy, if ever he set eyes on him again. The painter unluckily appearing during this paroxysm of rage, he seized him by the throat, saying, he was ruined by his accursed folly; and, in all likelihood, poor Pallet would have been strangled had not Jolter interposed in his behalf, beseeching his pupil to have mercy upon the sufferer, and, with infinite anxiety, desiring to know the cause of this violent assault. He received no answer but a string of incoherent curses. When the painter, with unspeakable astonishment, took God to witness that he had done nothing to disoblige him, the governor began to think, in sad earnest, that Peregrine's vivacity had at length risen to the transports of actual madness, and was himself almost distracted with this supposition. That he might the better judge what remedy ought to be applied, he used his whole influence, and practised all his eloquence upon the youth, in order to learn the immediate cause of his delirium. He employed the most pathetic entreaties, and even shed tears in the course of his supplication; so that Pickle, the first violence of the hurricane being blown over, was ashamed of his own imprudence, and retired to his chamber, in order to recollect his dissipated thoughts.

There he shut himself up, and, for the second time, perusing the fatal epistle, began to waver in his opinion of the author's character and intention. He sometimes considered her as one of those nymphs who, under the mask of innocence and simplicity, practise upon the hearts and purses of unwary and unexperienced youths. This was the suggestion of his wrath, inflamed by disappointment; but, when he reflected upon the circumstances of her behaviour, and recalled her particular charms to his imagination, the severity of his censure gave way, and his heart declared in favour of her sincerity. Yet even this consideration aggravated the sense of his loss, and he was in danger of relapsing into his former distraction, when his passion was a little becalmed by the hope of seeing her again, either by accident, or in the course of a diligent and minute inquiry, which he forthwith resolved to set on foot. He had reason to believe, that her own heart would espouse his cause, in spite of her virtue's determination, and did not despair of meeting with the Capuchin, whose good offices he knew he could at any time command. Comforted with these reflections, the tempest of his soul subsided. In less than two hours he joined his company, with an air of composure, and asked the painter's forgiveness for the freedom he had taken—the cause of which he promised hereafter to explain. Pallet was glad of being reconciled on any terms to one whose countenance supported him in equilibrio with his antagonist the doctor; and Mr. Jolter was rejoiced beyond measure at his pupil's recovery.

CHAPTER LIX

Peregrine meets with Mrs. Hornbeck, and is consoled for his Loss— His Valet-de-Chambre is embroiled with her Duenna, whom, however, he finds Means to appease.

EVERYTHING having thus resumed its natural channel, they dined together in great tranquillity. In the afternoon, Peregrine, on pretence of staying at home to write letters, while his companions were at the coffee-house, ordered a coach to be called, and, with his valet-de-chambre, who was the only person acquainted with the present state of his thoughts, set out for the Promenade, to which all the ladies of fashion resort in the evening during the summer season, in hopes of seeing his fugitive among the rest.

Having made a circuit round the walk, and narrowly observed every female in the place, he perceived at some distance the livery of Hornbeck upon a lacquey that stood at the back of a coach; upon which he ordered his man to reconnoitre the said carriage, while he pulled up his glasses, that he might not be discovered, before he should have received some intelligence, by which he might conduct himself on this unexpected occasion, that already began to interfere with the purpose of his coming thither, though it could not dispute his attention with the idea of his charming unknown.

His Mercury having made his observations, reported, that there was nobody in the coach but Mrs. Hornbeck and an elderly woman, who had all the air of a duenna, and that the servant was not the same footman who had attended them in France. Encouraged by this information, our hero ordered himself to be driven close up to that side of their convenience on which his old mistress sat; and accosted her with the usual salutation. This lady no sooner beheld her gallant, than her cheeks reddened with a double glow; and she exclaimed, "Dear brother, I am overjoyed to see you! Pray come into our coach." He took the hint immediately, and, complying with her request, embraced this new sister with great affection.

Perceiving that her attendant was very much surprised and alarmed at this unexpected meeting, she, in order to banish her suspicion, and at the same time give her lover his cue, told him, that his brother (meaning her husband) was gone to the Spa for a few weeks, by the advice of physicians, on account of his ill state of health; and that, from his last letter, she had the pleasure to tell him, he was in a fair way of doing well. The young gentleman expressed his satisfaction at this piece of news; observing, with an air of fraternal concern, that if his brother had not made too free with his constitution, his friends in England would have had no occasion to repine at his absence and want of health, by which he was banished from his own country and connexions. He then asked, with an affectation of surprise, why she had not accompanied her spouse; and was given to understand, that his tenderness of affection would not suffer him to expose her to the fatigues of the journey, which lay among rocks that were almost inaccessible.

The duenna's doubts being eased by this preamble of conversation, he changed the subject to the pleasures of the place; and among other such questions, inquired if she had as yet visited Versailles? This is a public-house, situated upon the canal at the distance of about two miles from town, and accommodated with tolerable gardens for the entertainment of company. When she replied in the negative, he proposed to accompany her thither immediately; but the governante, who had hitherto sat silent, objected to this proposal; telling them, in broken English, that as the lady was under her care, she could not answer to Mr. Hornbeck for allowing her to visit such a suspicious place. "As for that matter, madam," said the confident gallant, "give yourself no trouble; the consequences shall be at my peril, and I will undertake to ensure you against my brother's resentment." So saying, he directed the coachman to the place, and ordered his own to follow, under the auspices of his valet-de-chambre, while the old gentlewoman, overruled by his assurance, quietly submitted to his authority.

Being arrived at the place, he handed the ladies from the coach, and then for the first time observed that the duenna was lame, a circumstance of which he did not scruple to take the advantage; for they had scarce alighted, and drank a glass of wine, when he advised his sister to enjoy a walk in the garden. And although the attendant made shift to keep them almost always in view, they enjoyed a detached conversation, in which Peregrine learned, that the true cause of her being left at Brussels, whilst her husband proceeded to Spa, was his dread of the company and familiarities of that place, to which his jealousy durst not expose her; and that she had lived three weeks in a convent at Lisle, from which she was delivered by his own free motion, because indeed he could no longer exist without her company; and lastly, our lover understood, that her governante was a mere dragon, who had been recommended to him by a Spanish merchant whose wife she attended to her dying day. But she very much questioned whether or not her fidelity was proof enough against money and strong waters. Peregrine assured her the experiment should be tried before parting; and they agreed to pass the night at Versailles, provided his endeavours should succeed.

Having exercised themselves in this manner until the duenna's spirits were pretty much exhausted, that she might be the better disposed to recruit them with a glass of liquor, they returned to their apartment, and the cordial was recommended and received in a bumper. But as it did not produce such a visible alteration as the sanguine hopes of Pickle had made him expect, and the old gentlewoman observed that it began to be late, and that the gates would be shut in a little time, he filled up a parting glass, and pledged her in equal quantity. Her blood was too much chilled to be warmed even by this extraordinary dose, which made immediate innovation on the brain of our youth, who, in the gaiety of his imagination, overwhelmed this she-Argus with such profusion of gallantry, that she was more intoxicated with his expressions than with the spirits she had drank. When, in the course of toying, he dropped a purse into her bosom, she seemed to forget how the night wore, and, with the approbation of her charge, assented to his proposal of having something for supper.

This was a great point which our adventurer had gained; and yet he plainly perceived that the governante mistook his meaning, by giving herself credit for all the passion he had professed. As this error could be rectified by no other means than those of plying her with the bottle, until her distinguishing faculties should be overpowered, he promoted a quick circulation. She did him justice, without any manifest signs of inebriation; so long, that his own eyes began to reel in their sockets; and he found, that, before his scheme could be accomplished, he should be effectually unfitted for all the purposes of love. He therefore had recourse to his valet-de-chambre, who understood the hint as soon as it was given, and readily undertook to perform the part, of which his master had played the prelude. This affair being settled to his satisfaction, and the night at odds with morning, he took an opportunity of imparting to the ear of this aged Dulcinea a kind whisper, importing a promise of visiting her, when his sister should be retired to her own chamber, and an earnest desire of leaving her door unlocked.

This agreeable intimation being communicated, he conveyed a caution of the same nature to Mrs. Hornbeck, as he led her to her apartment; and darkness and silence no sooner prevailed in the house, than he and his trusty squire set out on their different voyages. Everything would have succeeded according to their wish, had not the valet-de-chambre suffered himself to fall asleep at the side of his inamorata, and, in the agitation of a violent dream, exclaimed in a voice so unlike that of her supposed adorer, that she distinguished the difference at once. Waking him with a pinch and a loud shriek, she threatened to prosecute him for rape, and reviled him with all the epithets her rage and disappointment could suggest.

The Frenchman, finding himself detected, behaved with great temper and address. He begged she would compose herself, on account of her own reputation, which was extremely dear to him; protesting, that he had a most inviolable esteem for her person. His representations had weight with the duenna, who, upon recollection, comprehended the whole affair, and thought it would be her interest to bring matters to an accommodation. She therefore admitted the apologies of her bed-fellow, provided he would promise to atone by marriage for the injury she had sustained; and in this particular, he set her heart at ease by repeated vows, which he uttered with surprising volubility, though without any intention to perform the least tittle of their contents.

Peregrine, who had been alarmed by her exclamation, and run to the door with a view of interposing, according to the emergency of the case, overhearing the affair thus compromised, returned to his mistress, who was highly entertained with an account of what had passed, foreseeing, that, for the future, she should be under no difficulty of restriction from the severity of her guard.

CHAPTER LX

Hornbeck is informed of his Wife's Adventure with Peregrine, for whom he prepares a Stratagem, which is rendered ineffectual by the Information of Pipes—The Husband is ducked for his Intention, and our Hero apprehended by the Patrol.

THERE was another person, however, still ungained; and that was no other than her footman, whose secrecy our hero attempted to secure in the morning by a handsome present, which he received with many expressions of gratitude and devotion to his service; yet this complaisance was nothing but a cloak used to disguise the design he harboured of making his master acquainted with the whole transaction. Indeed, this lacquey had been hired, not only as a spy upon his mistress, but also as a check on the conduct of the governante, with promise of ample reward, if ever he should discover any sinister or suspicious practices in the course of her behaviour. As for the footman whom they had brought from England, he was retained in attendance upon the person of his master, whose confidence he had lost, by advising him to gentle methods of reclaiming his lady, when her irregularities had subjected her to his wrath.

The Flemish valet, in consequence of the office he had undertaken, wrote to Hornbeck by the first post, giving an exact detail of the adventure at Versailles, with such a description of the pretended brother, as left the husband no room to think he could be any other person than his first dishonourer; and exasperated him to such a degree, that he resolved to lay an ambush for this invader, and at once disqualify him from disturbing his repose, by maintaining further correspondence with his wife.

Meanwhile the lovers enjoyed themselves without restraint, and Peregrine's plan of inquiry after his dear unknown was for the present postponed. His fellow-travellers were confounded at his mysterious motions, which filled the heart of Jolter with anxiety and terror. This careful conductor was fraught with such experience of his pupil's disposition, that he trembled with the apprehension of some sudden accident, and lived in continual alarm, like a man that walks under the wall of a nodding tower. Nor did he enjoy any alleviations of his fears, when, upon telling the young gentleman, that the rest of the company were desirous of departing for Antwerp, he answered, that they were at liberty to consult their own inclinations; but, for his own part, he was resolved to stay in Brussels a few days longer.

By this declaration the governor was confirmed in the opinion of his having some intrigue upon the anvil. In the bitterness of his vexation, he took the liberty of signifying his suspicion, and reminding him of the dangerous dilemmas to which he had been reduced by his former precipitation.

Peregrine took his caution in good part, and promised to behave with such circumspection as would screen him from any troublesome consequences for the future; but, nevertheless, behaved that same evening in such a manner, as plainly showed that his prudence was nothing else than vain speculation. He had made an appointment to spend the night, as usual, with Mrs. Hornbeck; and, about nine o'clock, hastened to her lodgings, when he was accosted in the street by his old discarded friend, Thomas Pipes, who, without any other preamble, told him, that, for all he had turned him adrift, he did not choose to see him run full sail into his enemy's harbour, without giving him timely notice of the danger. "I'll tell you what," said he; "mayhap you think I want to curry favour, that I may be taken in tow again; if you do, you have made a mistake in your reckoning. I am old enough to be laid up, and have wherewithal to keep my planks from the weather. But this here is the affair; I have known you since you were no higher than a marlinspike, and shouldn't care to see you deprived of your rigging at these years. Whereby, I am informed by Hornbeck's man, whom I this afternoon fell in with by chance, as how his master has got intelligence of your boarding his wife, and has steered privately into this port, with a large complement of hands, in order, d'ye see, to secure you while you are under the hatches. Now, if so be as how you have a mind to give him a salt eel for his supper, here am I, without hope of fee or reward, ready to stand by you as long as my timbers will stick together; and if I expect any recompense, may I be bound to eat oakum, and drink bilgewater, for life."

Startled at this information, Peregrine examined him upon the particulars of his discourse with the lacquey; and when he understood that Hornbeck's intelligence flowed from the canal of his Flemish footman, he believed every circumstance of Tom's report, thanked him for his warning, and, after having reprimanded him for his misbehaviour at Lisle, assured him that it should be his own fault if ever they should part again. He then deliberated with himself whether or not he should retort the purpose upon his adversary; but when he considered that Hornbeck was not the aggressor, and made that unhappy husband's case his own, he could not help acquitting his intention of revenge, though, in his opinion, it ought to have been executed in a more honourable manner; and therefore he determined to chastise him for his want of spirit. Nothing surely can be more insolent and unjust than this determination, which induced him to punish a person for his want of courage to redress the injury which he himself had done to his reputation and peace; and yet this barbarity of decision is authorised by the opinion and practice of mankind.

With these sentiments he returned to the inn, and, putting a pair of pistols in his pocket, ordered his valet-de-chambre and Pipes to follow him at a small distance, so as that they should be within call in case of necessity, and then posted himself within thirty yards of his Dulcinea's door. There he had not been above half an hour, when he perceived four men take their station on the other side, with a view, as he guessed, to watch for his going in, that he might be taken unaware. But when they had tarried a considerable time in that corner, without reaping the fruits of their expectation, their leader, persuaded that the gallant had gained admittance by some secret means, approached the door with his followers, who, according to the instructions they had received, no sooner saw it opened, than they rushed in, leaving their employer in the street, where he thought his person would be least endangered. Our adventurer, seeing him all alone, advanced with speed, and clapping a pistol to his breast, commanded him to follow his footsteps, without noise, on pain of immediate death.

Terrified at this sudden apparition, Hornbeck obeyed in silence; and, in a few minutes, they arrived at the quay, where Pickle, halting, gave him to understand that he was no stranger to his villainous design; told him, that if he conceived himself injured by any circumstance of his conduct, he would now give him an opportunity of resenting the wrong in a manner becoming a man of honour. "You have a sword about you," said he; "or, if you don't choose to put the affair on that issue, here is a brace of pistols; take which you please." Such an address could not fail to disconcert a man of his character. After some hesitation, he, in a faltering accent, denied that his design was to mutilate Mr. Pickle, but that he thought himself entitled to the benefit of the law, by which he would have obtained a divorce, if he could have procured evidence of his wife's infidelity; and, with that view, he had employed people to take advantage of the information he had received. With regard to this alternative, he declined it entirely, because he could not see what satisfaction he should enjoy in being shot through the head, or run through the lungs, by a person who had already wronged him in an irreparable manner. Lastly, his fear made him propose that the affair should be left to the arbitration of two creditable men, altogether unconcerned in the dispute.

To these remonstrances Peregrine replied, in the style of a hot-headed young man, conscious of his own unjustifiable behaviour, that every gentleman ought to be a judge of his own honour, and therefore he would submit to the decision of no umpire whatsoever; that he would forgive his want of courage, which might be a natural infirmity, but his mean dissimulation he could not pardon. That, as he was certified of the rascally intent of his ambuscade by undoubted intelligence, he would treat him, not with a retaliation of his own treachery, but with such indignity as a scoundrel deserves to suffer, unless he would make one effort to maintain the character he assumed in life. So saying, he again presented his pistols, which being rejected as before, he called his two ministers, and ordered them to duck him in the canal.

This command was pronounced and executed almost in the same breath, to the unspeakable terror and disorder of the poor shivering patient, who, having undergone the immersion, ran about like a drowned rat, squeaking for assistance and revenge. His cries were overheard by the patrol, who, chancing to pass that way, took him under their protection, and, in consequence of his complaint and information, went in pursuit of our adventurer and his attendants, who were soon overtaken and surrounded. Rash and inconsiderate as the young gentleman was, he did not pretend to stand upon the defensive against a file of musketeers, although Pipes had drawn his cutlass at their approach, but surrendered himself without opposition, and was conveyed to the main guard, where the commanding officer, engaged by his appearance and address, treated him with all imaginable respect. Hearing the particulars of his adventure, he assured him that the Prince would consider the whole as a *tour de jeunesse*, and order him to be released without delay.

Next morning, when this gentleman gave in his report, he made such a favourable representation of the prisoner, that our hero was on the point of being discharged, when Hornbeck preferred a complaint, accusing him of a purposed assassination, and praying that such punishment should be inflicted upon him as his highness should think adequate to the nature of the crime.

The Prince, perplexed with this petition, in consequence of which he foresaw that he must disoblige a British subject, sent for the plaintiff, of whom he had some knowledge, and, in person, exhorted him to drop the prosecution, which would only serve to propagate his own shame. But Hornbeck was too much incensed to listen to any proposal of that kind, and peremptorily demanded justice against the prisoner, whom he represented as an obscure adventurer, who had made repeated attempts upon his honour and his life. Prince Charles told him, that what he had advised was in the capacity of a friend; but, since he insisted upon his acting as a magistrate, the affair should be examined, and determined according to the dictates of justice and truth.

The petitioner being dismissed with this promise, the defendant was, in his turn, brought before the judge, whose prepossession in his favour was in a great measure weakened by what his antagonist had said to the prejudice of his birth and reputation.

CHAPTER LXI

Peregrine is released—Jolter confounded at his mysterious Conduct— A Contest happens between the Poet and Painter, who are reconciled by the Mediation of their Fellow-Travellers.

OUR hero, understanding from some expressions which escaped the Prince, that he was considered in the light of a sharper and assassin, begged that he might have the liberty of sending for some vouchers, that would probably vindicate his character from the malicious aspersions of his adversary. This permission being granted, he wrote a letter to his governor, desiring that he would bring to him the letters of recommendation which he had received from the British ambassador at Paris, and such other papers as he thought conducive to evince the importance of his situation.

The billet was given in charge to one of the subaltern officers, on duty, who carried it to the inn, and demanded to speak with Mr. Jolter. Pallet, who happened to be at the door when this messenger arrived, and heard him inquire for the tutor, ran directly to that gentleman's apartment, and in manifest disorder, told him that a huge fellow of a soldier, with a monstrous pair of whiskers, and fur cap as big as a bushel, was asking for him at the door. The poor governor began to shake at this intimation, though he was not conscious of having committed anything that could attract the attention of the state. When the officer appeared at his chamber door, his confusion increased to such a degree, that his perception seemed to vanish, and the subaltern repeated the purport of his errand three times, before he could comprehend his meaning, or venture to receive the letter which he presented. At length he summoned all his fortitude, and having perused the epistle, his terror sunk into anxiety. His ingenuous fear immediately suggested, that Peregrine was confined in a dungeon, for some outrage he had committed. He ran with great agitation to a trunk, and, taking out a bundle of papers, followed his conductor, being attended by the painter, to whom he had hinted his apprehension. When they passed through the guard, which was under arms, the hearts of both died within them; and when they came into the presence, there was such an expression of awful horror on the countenance of Jolter, that the Prince, observing his dismay, was pleased to encourage him with an assurance that he had nothing to fear.

Thus comforted, he recollected himself so well as to understand his pupil, when he desired him to produce the ambassador's letters; some of which being open, were immediately read by his highness, who was personally acquainted with the writer, and knew several of the noblemen to whom they were addressed. These recommendations were so warm, and represented the young gentleman in such an advantageous light, that the Prince, convinced of the injustice his character had suffered by the misrepresentation of Hornbeck, took our hero by the hand, asked pardon for the doubts he had entertained of his honour, declared him from that moment at liberty, ordered his domestics to be enlarged, and offered him his countenance and protection as long as he should remain in the Austrian Netherlands. At the same time, he cautioned him against indiscretion in the course of his gallantries; and took his word of honour, that he should drop all measures of resentment against the person of Hornbeck during his residence in that place.

The delinquent, thus honourably acquitted, thanked the Prince in the most respectful manner, for his generosity and candour, and retired with his two friends, who were amazed and bewildered in their thoughts at what they had seen and heard, the whole adventure still remaining without the sphere of their comprehension, which was not at all enlarged by the unaccountable appearance of Pipes, who, with the valet-de-chambre, joined them at the castle gate. Had Jolter been a man of a luxuriant imagination, his brain would undoubtedly have suffered in the investigation of his pupil's mysterious conduct, which he strove in vain to unravel; but his intellects were too solid to be affected by the miscarriage of his invention; and, as Peregrine did not think proper to make him acquainted with the cause of his being apprehended, he contented himself with supposing that there was a lady in the case.

The painter, whose imagination was of a more flimsy texture, formed a thousand chimerical conjectures, which he communicated to Pickle, in imperfect insinuations, hoping, by his answers and behaviour, to discover the truth; but the youth, in order to tantalise him, eluded all his inquiries, with such appearance of industry and art, as heightened his curiosity, while it disappointed his aim, and inflamed him to such a degree of impatience, that his wits began to be unsettled. Then Peregrine was fain to recompose his brain, by telling him in confidence, that he had been arrested as a spy. This secret he found more intolerable than his former uncertainty. He ran from one apartment to another, like a goose in the agonies of egg-laying, with intention of disburdening this important load; but Jolter being engaged with the pupil, and all the people of the house ignorant of the only language he could speak, he was compelled, with infinite reluctance, to address himself to the doctor, who was at that time shut up in his own chamber.

Having knocked at the door to no purpose, he peeped through the key-hole, and saw the physician sitting at a table, with a pen in one hand, and paper before him, his head reclined upon his other hand, and his eyes fixed upon the ceiling, as if he had been entranced. Pallet, concluding that he was under the power of some convulsion, endeavoured to force the door open, and the noise of his efforts recalled the doctor from his reverie. This poetical republican, being so disagreeably disturbed, started up in a passion, and, opening the door, no sooner perceived who had interrupted him, than he flung it in his face with great fury, and cursed him for his impertinent intrusion, which had deprived him of the most delightful vision that ever regaled the human fancy. He imagined, as he afterwards imparted to Peregrine, that, as he enjoyed himself in walking through the flowery plain that borders on Parnassus, he was met by a venerable sage, whom, by a certain divine vivacity that lightened from his eyes, he instantly knew to be the immortal Pindar. He was immediately struck with reverence and awe, and prostrated himself before the apparition, which, taking him by the hand, lifted him gently from the ground and, with words more sweet than the honey of the Hybla bees, told him, that, of all the moderns, he alone was visited by that celestial impulse by which he himself had been inspired, when he produced his most applauded odes. So saying, he led him up the sacred hill, persuaded him to drink a copious draught of the waters of the Hippocrene, and then presented him to the harmonious Nine, who crowned his temples with a laurel wreath.

No wonder that he was enraged to find himself cut off from such sublime society. He raved in Greek against the invader, who was so big with his own purpose, that, unmindful of the disgrace he had sustained, and disregarding all the symptoms of the physician's displeasure, he applied his mouth to the door, in an eager tone: "I'll hold you any wager," said he, "that I guess the true cause of Mr. Pickle's imprisonment." To this challenge he received no reply, and therefore repeated it, adding, "I suppose you imagine he was taken up for fighting a duel, or affronting a nobleman, or lying with some man's wife, or some such matter; but, egad! you was never more mistaken in your life; and I'll lay my Cleopatra against your Homer's head, that in four-and-twenty hours you shan't light on the true reason."

The favourite of the muses, exasperated at this vexatious perseverance of the painter, who he imagined had come to tease and insult him, "I would," said he, "sacrifice a cock to Æsculapius, were I assured that any person had been taken up for extirpating such a troublesome Goth as you are from the face of the earth. As for your boasted Cleopatra, which you say was drawn from your own wife, I believe the copy has as much of the *to kalon* as the original; but, were it mine, it should be hung up in the Temple of Cloacina, as the picture of that goddess; for any other apartment would be disgraced by its appearance."

"Hark ye, sir," replied Pallet, enraged in his turn at the contemptuous mention of his darling performance, "you may make as free with my wife as you think proper, but 'ware my works; those are the children of my fancy, conceived by the glowing imagination, and formed by the art of my own hands; and you yourself are a Goth, and a Turk, and a Tartar, and an impudent pretending jackanapes, to treat with such disrespect a production which, in the opinion of all the connoisseurs of the age, will, when finished, be a masterpiece in its kind, and do honour to human genius and skill. So I say again and again, and I care not though your friend Playtor heard me, that you have no more taste than a drayman's horse, and that those foolish notions of the ancients ought to be drubbed out of you with a good cudgel, that you might learn to treat men of parts with more veneration. Perhaps you may not always be in the company of one who will halloo for assistance when you are on the brink of being chastised for your insolence, as I did, when you brought upon yourself the resentment of that Scot, who, by the Lard! would have paid you both scot and lot, as Falstaff says, if the French officer had not put him in arrest."

The physician, to this declamation, which was conveyed through the key-hole, answered, that he (the painter) was a fellow so infinitely below his consideration, that his conscience upbraided him with no action of his life, except that of choosing such a wretch for his companion and fellow-traveller. That he had viewed his character through the medium of good-nature and compassion, which had prompted him to give Pallet an opportunity of acquiring some new ideas under his immediate instruction; but he had abused his goodness and condescension in such a flagrant manner, that he was now determined to discard him entirely from his acquaintance; and desired him, for the present, to take himself away, on pain of being kicked for his presumption.

Pallet was too much incensed to be intimidated by this threat, which he retorted with great virulence, defying him to come forth, that it might appear which of them was best skilled in that pedestrian exercise, which he immediately began to practise against the door with such thundering application, as reached the ears of Pickle and his governor, who coming out into the passage, and seeing him thus employed, asked if he had forgot the chamber-pots of Alost, that he ventured to behave in such a manner as entitled him to a second prescription of the same nature?

The doctor, understanding that there was company at hand, opened the door in a twinkling, and, springing upon his antagonist like a tiger, a fierce contention would have ensued, to the infinite satisfaction of our hero, had not Jolter, to the manifest peril of his own person, interposed, and partly by force, and partly by exhortations, put a stop to the engagement before it was fairly begun. After having demonstrated the indecency of such a vulgar rencontre, betwixt two fellow-citizens in a foreign land, he begged to know the cause of their dissension, and offered his good offices towards an accommodation. Peregrine also, seeing the fray was finished, expressed himself to the same purpose; and the painter, for obvious reasons, declining an explanation, his antagonist told the youth what a mortifying interruption he had suffered by the impertinent intrusion of Pallet, and gave him a detail of the particulars of his vision, as above recited. The arbiter owned the provocation was not to be endured; and decreed that the offender should make some atonement for his transgression. Upon which the painter observed, that, however he might have been disposed to make acknowledgments, if the physician had signified his displeasure like a gentleman, the complainant had now forfeited all claim to any such concessions, by the vulgar manner in which he had reviled him and his productions; observing, that, if he (the painter) had been inclined to retort his slanderous insinuations, the republican's own works would have afforded ample subject for his ridicule and censure.

After divers disputes and representations, peace was at length concluded, on condition, that, for the future, the doctor should never mention Cleopatra, unless he could say something in her praise; and that Pallet, in consideration of his having been the first aggressor, should make a sketch of the physician's vision, to be engraved and prefixed to the next edition of his odes.

CHAPTER LXII

The Travellers depart for Antwerp, at which place the Painter gives a loose to his Enthusiasm.

OUR adventurer, baffled in all his efforts to retrieve his lost Amanda, yielded at length to the remonstrances of his governor and fellow-travellers, who, out of pure complaisance to him, had exceeded their intended stay by six days at least; and a couple of post-chaises, with three riding-horses, being hired, they departed from Brussels in the morning, dined at Mechlin, and arrived about eight in the evening at the venerable city of Antwerp. During this day's journey Pallet was elevated to an uncommon flow of spirits, with the prospect of seeing the birthplace of Rubens, for whom he professed an enthusiastic admiration. He swore, that the pleasure he felt was equal to that of a Mussulman, on the last day of his pilgrimage to Mecca; and that he already considered himself a native of Antwerp, being so intimately acquainted with their so justly boasted citizen, from whom, at certain junctures, he could not help believing himself derived, because his own pencil adopted the manner of that great man with surprising facility, and his face wanted nothing but a pair of whiskers and a beard, to exhibit the express image of the Fleming's countenance. He told them he was so proud of this resemblance, that, in order to render it more striking, he had, at one time of his life, resolved to keep his face sacred from the razor; and in that purpose had persevered, notwithstanding the continual reprehensions of Mrs. Pallet, who, being then with child, said, his aspect was so hideous, that she dreaded a miscarriage every hour, until she threatened in plain terms, to dispute the sanity of his intellects, and apply to the chancellor for a committee.

The doctor, on this occasion, observed, that a man who is not proof against the solicitations of a woman, can never expect to make a great figure in life; that painters and poets ought to cultivate no wives but the muses; or, if they are by the accidents of fortune encumbered with families, they should carefully guard against that pernicious weakness, falsely honoured with the appellation of *natural affection*, and pay no manner of regard to the impertinent customs of the world. "Granting that you had been for a short time deemed a lunatic," said he, "you might have acquitted yourself honourably of that imputation, by some performance that would have raised your character above all censure. Sophocles himself, that celebrated tragic poet, who, for the sweetness of his versification, was styled *melitta*, or *the bee*, in his old age, suffered the same accusation from his own children, who, seeing him neglect his family affairs, and devote himself entirely to poetry, carried him before the magistrate, as a man whose intellects were so much impaired by the infirmities of age, that he was no longer fit to manage his domestic concerns; upon which the reverend bard produced his tragedy of *Œdipus epi kolono*, as a work he had just finished; which being perused, instead of being declared unsound of understanding, he was dismissed with admiration and applause. I wish your beard and whiskers had been sanctioned by the like authority; though I am afraid you would have been in the predicament of those disciples of a certain philosopher, who drank decoctions of cummin seeds, that their faces might adopt the paleness of their master's complexion, hoping that, in being as wan, they would be as learned as their teacher." The painter, stung by this sarcasm, replied, "Or like those virtuosi, who, by repeating Greek, eating silly-kickaby, and pretending to see visions, think they equal the ancients in taste and genius." The physician retorted, Pallet rejoined, and the altercation continued until they entered the gates of Antwerp, when the admirer of Rubens broke forth into a rapturous exclamation, which put an end to the dispute and attracted the notice of the inhabitants, many of whom by shrugging up their shoulders and pointing to their foreheads, gave shrewd indications that they believed him a poor gentleman disordered in his brain.

They had no sooner alighted at the inn, than this pseudo-enthusiast proposed to visit the great church, in which he had been informed some of his master's pieces were to be seen; and was remarkably chagrined, when he understood that he could not be admitted till next day. He rose next morning by day-break, and disturbed his fellow-travellers in such a noisy and clamorous manner, that Peregrine determined to punish him with some new infliction; and, while he put on his clothes, actu-ally formed the plan of promoting a duel between him and the doctor; in the management of which, he promised himself store of entertainment, from the behaviour of both.

Being provided with one of those domestics who are always in waiting to offer their services to strangers on their first arrival, they were conducted to the house of a gentleman who had an excellent collection of pictures; and though the greatest part of them were painted by his favourite artist, Pallet condemned them all by the lump, because Pickle had told him beforehand, that there was not one performance of Rubens among the number.

The next place they visited was what is called the Academy of Painting, furnished with a number of paltry pieces, in which our painter recognised the style of Peter Paul, with many expressions of admiration, on the same sort of previous intelligence.

From this repository, they went to the great church; and being led to the tomb of Rubens, the whimsical painter fell upon his knees, and worshipped with such appearance of devotion, that the attendant, scandalised at his superstition, pulled him up, observing, with great warmth, that the person buried in that place was no saint, but as great a sinner as himself; and that, if he was spiritually disposed, there was a chapel of the Blessed Virgin, at the distance of three yards on the right hand, to which he might retire. He thought it was incumbent upon him to manifest some extraordinary inspiration, while he resided on the spot where Rubens was born; and, therefore, his whole behaviour was an affectation of rapture, expressed in distracted exclama-tions, convulsive starts, and uncouth gesticulations. In the midst of this frantic behaviour, he saw an old Capuchin, with a white beard, mount the pulpit, and hold forth to the congrega-tion with such violence of emphasis and gesture, as captivated his fancy; and, bawling aloud, "Zounds! what an excellent Paul preaching at Athens!" he pulled a pencil and a small memorandum book from his pocket, and began to take a sketch of the orator, with great eagerness and agitation, saying, "Egad! friend Raphael, we shall see whether you or I have got the best knack at trumping up an apostle." This appearance of disrespect gave offence to the audience, who began to murmur against this heretic libertine; when one of the priests belonging to the choir, in order to prevent any ill consequence from their displeasure, came and told him in the French language, that such liberties were not permitted in their religion, and advised him to lay aside his implements, lest the people should take umbrage at his design, and be provoked to punish him as a profane scoffer at their worship.

The painter, seeing himself addressed by a friar, who, while he spoke, bowed with great complaisance, imagined that he was a begging brother come to supplicate his charity; and his attention being quite engrossed by the design he was making, he patted the priest's shaven crown with his hand, saying, *Oter tems, oter tems*, and then resumed his pencil with great earnestness. The ecclesiastic, perceiving that the stranger did not comprehend his meaning, pulled him by the sleeve, and explained himself in the Latin tongue; upon which Pallet, provoked at his intrusion, cursed him aloud for an impudent beggarly son of a whore, and, taking out a shilling, flung it upon the pavement, with manifest signs of indignation.

Some of the common people, enraged to see their religion contemned, and their priests insulted at the very altar, rose from their seats, and, surrounding the astonished painter, one of the number snatched his book from his hand, and tore it into a thousand pieces. Frightened as he was, he could not help crying, "Fire and fagots! all my favourite ideas are gone to wreck!" and was in danger of being very roughly handled by the crowd, had not Peregrine stepped in, and assured them, that he was a poor unhappy gentleman, who laboured under a transport of the brain. Those who understood the French language communicated this information to the rest, so that he escaped without any other chastisement than being obliged to retire. And as they could not see the famous Descent from the Cross till after the service was finished, they were conducted by their domestic to the house of a painter, where they found a beggar standing for his picture, and the artist actually employed in representing a huge louse that crawled upon his shoulder. Pallet was wonderfully pleased with this circumstance, which he said was altogether a new thought, and an excellent hint, of which he would make his advantage; and, in the course of his survey of this Fleming's performances, perceiving a piece in which two flies were engaged upon the carcass of a dog half devoured, he ran to his brother brush, and swore he was worthy of being a fellow-citizen of the immortal Rubens. He then lamented, with many expressions of grief and resentment, that he had lost his commonplace book, in which he had preserved a thousand conceptions of the same sort, formed by the accidental objects of his senses and imagination; and took an opportunity of telling his fellow-travellers, that in execution he had equalled, if not excelled, the two ancient painters who had vied with each other in the representation of a curtain and a bunch of grapes; for he had exhibited the image of a certain object so like to nature, that the bare sight of it set a whole hogstye in an uproar.

When he had examined and applauded all the productions of this minute artist, they returned to the great church, and were entertained with the view of that celebrated masterpiece of Rubens, in which he has introduced the portraits of himself and his whole family. The doors that conceal this capital performance were no sooner unfolded, than our enthusiast, debarred the use of speech, by a previous covenant with his friend Pickle, lifted up his hands and eyes, and putting himself in the attitude of Hamlet, when his father's ghost appears, adored in silent ecstasy and awe. He even made a merit of necessity; and, when they had withdrawn from the place, protested that his whole faculties were swallowed up in love and admiration. He now professed himself more than ever enamoured of the Flemish school, raved in extravagant encomiums, and proposed that the whole company should pay homage to the memory of the divine Rubens, by repairing forthwith to the house in which he lived, and prostrating themselves on the floor of his painting-room.

As there was nothing remarkable in the tenement, which had been rebuilt more than once since the death of that great man, Peregrine excused himself from complying with the proposal, on pretence of being fatigued with the circuit they had already performed. Jolter declined it for the same reason; and the question being put to the doctor, he refused his company with an air of disdain. Pallet, piqued at his contemptuous manner, asked, if he would not go and see the habitation of Pindoor, provided he was in the city where that poet lived? and when the physician observed, that there was an infinite difference between the men—"That I'll allow," replied the painter, "for the devil a poet ever lived in Greece or Troy, that was worthy to clean the pencils of our beloved Rubens." The physician could not, with any degree of temper and forbearance, hear this outrageous blasphemy, for which, he said, Pallet's eyes ought to be picked out by owls; and the dispute arose, as usual, to such scurrilities of language, and indecency of behaviour, that passengers began to take notice of their animosity, and Peregrine was obliged to interpose for his own credit.

CHAPTER LXIII

Peregrine artfully foments a Quarrel between Pallet and the Physician, who fight a Duel on the Ramparts.

THE painter betook himself to the house of the Flemish Raphael, and the rest of the company went back to their lodgings; where the young gentleman, taking the advantage of being alone with the physician, recapitulated all the affronts he had sustained from the painter's petulance, aggravating every circumstance of the disgrace, and advising him, in the capacity of a friend, to take care of his honour, which could not fail to suffer in the opinion of the world, if he allowed himself to be insulted with impunity, by one so much his inferior in every degree of consideration.

The physician assured him, that Pallet had hitherto escaped chastisement, by being deemed an object unworthy his resentment, and in consideration of the wretch's family, for which his compassion was interested; but that repeated injuries would inflame the most benevolent disposition. And, though he could find no precedent of duelling among the Greeks and Romans, whom he considered as the patterns of demeanour, Pallet should no longer avail himself of his veneration for the ancients, but be punished for the very next offence he should commit.

Having thus spirited up the doctor to a resolution from which he could not decently swerve, our adventurer acted the incendiary with the other party also; giving him to understand, that the physician treated his character with such contempt, and behaved to him with such insolence, as no gentleman ought to bear. That, for his own part, he was every day put out of countenance by their mutual animosity, which appeared in nothing but vulgar expressions, more becoming shoe-boys and oyster-women than men of honour and education; and therefore he should be obliged, contrary to his inclination, to break off all correspondence with them both, if they would not fall upon some method to retrieve the dignity of their characters.

These representations would have had little effect upon the timidity of the painter, who was likewise too much of a Grecian to approve of single combat, in any other way than that of boxing, an exercise in which he was well skilled, had they not been accompanied with an insinuation, that his antagonist was no Hector, and that he might humble him into any concession, without running the least personal risk. Animated by this assurance, our second Rubens set the trumpet of defiance to his mouth, swore he valued not his life a rush, when his honour was concerned, and entreated Mr. Pickle to be the bearer of a challenge, which he would instantly commit to writing.

The mischievous fomenter highly applauded this manifestation of courage, by which he was at liberty to cultivate his friendship and society, but declined the office of carrying the billet, that his tenderness of Pallet's reputation might not be misinterpreted into an officious desire of promoting quarrels. At the same time, he recommended Tom Pipes, not only as a very proper messenger on this occasion, but also as a trusty second in the field. The magnanimous painter took his advice, and, retiring to his chamber, penned a challenge in these terms:

SIR,—When I am heartily provoked, I fear not the devil himself, much less——I will not call you a pedantic coxcomb, nor an unmannerly fellow, because these are the hippythets of the wulgar. But, remember, such as you are, I nyther love you nor fear you; but, on the contrary, expect satisfaction for your audacious behaviour to me on divers occasions; and will, this evening, in the twilight, meet you on the ramparts with sword and pistol, where the Lord have mercy on the soul of one of us, for your body shall find no favour with your incensed defier, till death,

LAYMAN PALLET.

This resolute defiance, after having been submitted to the perusal, and honoured with the approbation of our youth, was committed to the charge of Pipes, who, according to his orders, delivered it in the afternoon; and brought for answer, that the physician would attend him at the appointed time and place. The challenger was evidently discomposed at the unexpected news of this acceptance, and ran about the house in great disorder, in quest of Peregrine, to beg his further advice and assistance; but understanding that the youth was engaged in private with his adversary, he began to suspect some collusion, and cursed himself for his folly and precipitation. He even entertained some thoughts of retracting his invitation, and submitting to the triumph of his antagonist. But before he would stoop to this opprobrious condescension, he resolved to try another expedient, which might be the means of saving both his character and person. In this hope he visited Mr. Jolter, and very gravely desired he would be so good as to undertake the office of his second in a duel which he was to fight that evening with the physician.

The governor, instead of answering his expectation, in expressing fear and concern, and breaking forth into exclamations of "Good God! gentlemen, what d'ye mean? You shall not murder one another while it is in my power to prevent your purpose. I will go directly to the governor of the place, who shall interpose his authority"; I say, instead of these and other friendly menaces of prevention, Jolter heard the proposal with the most phlegmatic tranquillity, and excused himself from accepting the honour he intended for him, on account of his character and situation, which would not permit him to be concerned in any such rencontres. Indeed, this mortifying reception was owing to a previous hint from Peregrine, who, dreading some sort of interruption from his governor, had made him acquainted with his design, and assured him, that the affair should not be brought to any dangerous issue.

Thus disappointed, the dejected challenger was overwhelmed with perplexity and dismay; and, in the terrors of death or mutilation, resolved to deprecate the wrath of his enemy, and conform to any submission he should propose, when he was accidentally encountered by our adventurer, who, with demonstrations of infinite satisfaction, told him in confidence, that his billet had thrown the doctor into an agony of consternation; that his acceptance of his challenge was a mere effort of despair, calculated to confound the ferocity of the sender, and dispose him to listen to terms of accommodation; that he had imparted the letter to him with fear and trembling, on pretence of engaging him as a second, but, in reality, with a view of obtaining his good offices in promoting a reconciliation; "but, perceiving the situation of his mind," added our hero, "I thought it would be more for your honour to baffle his expectation, and therefore I readily undertook the task of attending him to the field, in full assurance that he will there humble himself before you, even to prostration. In this security, you may go and prepare your arms, and bespeak the assistance of Pipes, who will squire you in the field, while I keep myself up, that our correspondence may not be suspected by the physician." Pallet's spirits, that were sunk to dejection, rose at this encouragement to all the insolence of triumph; he again declared his contempt of danger, and his pistols being loaded and accommodated with new flints, by his trusty armour-bearer, he waited, without flinching, for the hour of battle.

On the first approach of twilight, somebody knocked at his door, and Pipes having opened it at his desire, he heard the voice of his antagonist pronounce, "Tell Mr. Pallet that I am going to the place of appointment." The painter was not a little surprised at this anticipation, which so ill agreed with the information he had received from Pickle; and his concern beginning to recur, he fortified himself with a large bumper of brandy, which, however, did not overcome the anxiety of his thoughts. Nevertheless, he set out on the expedition with his second, betwixt whom and himselft he following dialogue passed, in their way to the ramparts. "Mr. Pipes," said the painter, with disordered accent, "methinks the doctor was in a pestilent hurry with that message of his." "Ey, ey," answered Tom, "I do suppose he longs to be foul of you." "What," replied the other, "d'ye think he thirsts after my blood?" "To be sure a does," said Pipes, thrusting a large quid of tobacco in his cheek with great deliberation. "If that be the case," cried Pallet, beginning to shake, "he is no better than a cannibal, and no Christian ought to fight him on equal footing." Tom observing his emotion, eyed him with a frown of indignation, saying, "You an't afraid, are you?" "God forbid," replied the challenger, stammering with fear. "What should I be afraid of? The worst he can do is to take my life, and then he'll be answerable both to God and man for the murder. Don't you think he will?" "I think no such matter," answered the second; "if so be as how he puts a brace of bullets through your bows, and kills you fairly, it is no more murder than if I was to bring down a noddy from the main top-sail-yard."

By this time Pallet's teeth chattered with such violence, that he could scarce pronounce this reply: "Mr. Thomas, you seem to make very light of a man's life; but I trust in the Almighty. I shall not be so easily brought down. Sure many a man has fought a duel without losing his life. Do you imagine that I run such a hazard of falling by the hand of my adversary?" "You may or you may not," said the unconcerned Pipes, "just as it happens. What then! Death is a debt that every man owes, according to the song; and if you set foot to foot, I think one of you must go to pot." "Foot to foot!" exclaimed the terrified painter, "that's downright butchery; and I'll be d—ned before I fight any man on earth in such a barbarous way. What! d'ye take me to be a savage beast?" This declaration he made while they ascended the ramparts. His attendant perceiving the physician and his second at the distance of an hundred paces before them, gave him notice of their appearance, and advised him to make ready, and behave like a man. Pallet in vain endeavoured to conceal his panic, which discovered itself in an universal trepidation of body, and the lamentable tone in which he answered this exhortation of Pipes, saying, "I do behave like a man; but you would have me act the part of a brute. Are they coming this way?" When Tom told him that they had faced about, and admonished him to advance, the nerves of his arm refused their office, he could not hold out his pistol, and instead of going forward, retreated with an insensibility of motion; till Pipes, placing himself in the rear, set his own back to that of his principal, and swore he should not budge an inch farther in that direction.

While the valet thus tutored the painter, his master enjoyed the terrors of the physician, which were more ridiculous than those of Pallet, because he was more intent upon disguising them. His declaration to Pickle in the morning would not suffer him to start any objections when he received the challenge; and finding that the young gentleman made no offer of mediating the affair, but rather congratulated him on the occasion, when he communicated the painter's billet, all his efforts consisted in oblique hints, and general reflections upon the absurdity of duelling, which was first introduced among civilised nations by the barbarous Huns and Longobards. He likewise pretended to ridicule the use of firearms, which confounded all the distinctions of skill and address, and deprived a combatant of the opportunity of signalising his personal prowess.

Pickle assented to the justness of his observations; but, at the same time, represented the necessity of complying with the customs of this world, ridiculous as they were, on which a man's honour and reputation depend. So that, seeing no hopes of profiting by that artifice, the republican's agitation became more and more remarkable; and he proposed, in plain terms, that they should contend in armour, like the combatants of ancient days; for it was but reasonable that they should practise the manner of fighting, since they adopted the disposition of those iron times.

Nothing could have afforded more diversion to our hero than the sight of two such duellists cased in iron; and he wished that he had promoted the quarrel in Brussels, where he could have hired the armour of Charles the Fifth, and the valiant Duke of Parma, for their accommodation; but as there was no possibility of furnishing them cap-à-pee at Antwerp, he persuaded him to conform to the modern use of the sword, and meet the painter on his own terms; and suspecting that his fear would supply him with other excuses for declining the combat, he comforted him with some distant insinuations, to the prejudice of his adversary's courage, which would, in all probability, evaporate before any mischief could happen.

Notwithstanding this encouragement, he could not suppress the reluctance with which he went to the field, and cast many a wishful look over his left shoulder, to see whether or not his adversary was at his heels. When, by the advice of his second, he took possession of the ground, and turned about with his face to the enemy, it was not so dark, but that Peregrine could perceive the unusual paleness of his countenance, and the sweat standing in large drops upon his forehead; nay, there was a manifest disorder in his speech, when he regretted his want of the *pila* and *parma*, with which he would have made a rattling noise, to astonish his foe, in springing forward, and singing the hymn to battle, in the manner of the ancients.

In the meantime, observing the hesitation of his antagonist, who, far from advancing, seemed to recoil, and even struggle with his second, he guessed the situation of the painter's thoughts, and, collecting all the manhood that he possessed, seized the opportunity of profiting by his enemy's consternation. Striking his sword and pistol together, he advanced in a sort of trot, raising a loud howl, in which he repeated, in lieu of the Spartan song, part of the strophe from one of Pindar's Pythia, beginning with *Ek theon gar makanoi pasai Broteais aretais, etc.* This imitation of the Greeks had all the desired effect upon the painter, who seeing the physician running towards him like a fury, with a pistol in his right hand, which was extended, and hearing the dreadful yell he uttered, and the outlandish words he pronounced, was seized with an universal palsy of his limbs. He would have dropped down upon the ground, had not Pipes supported and encouraged him to stand upon his defence. The doctor, contrary to his expectation, finding that he had not flinched from the spot, though he had now performed one half of his career, put in practice his last effort, by firing his pistol, the noise of which no sooner reached the ears of the affrighted painter, than he recommended his soul to God, and roared for mercy with great vociferation.

The republican, overjoyed at this exclamation, commanded him to yield, and surrender his arms, on pain of immediate death; upon which he threw away his pistols and sword, in spite of all the admonitions and even threats of his second, who left him to his fate, and went up to his master, stopping his nose with signs of loathing and abhorrence.

The victor, having won the *spolia opima*, granted him his life, on condition that he would on his knees supplicate his pardon, acknowledge himself inferior to his conqueror in every virtue and qualification, and promise for the future to merit his favour by submission and respect. These insolent terms were readily embraced by the unfortunate challenger, who fairly owned, that he was not at all calculated for the purposes of war, and that henceforth he would contend with no weapon but his pencil. He begged with great humility, that Mr. Pickle would not think the worse of his morals for this defect of courage, which was a natural infirmity inherited from his father, and suspend his opinion of his talents, until he should have an opportunity of contemplating the charms of his Cleopatra, which would be finished in less than three months.

Our hero observed, with an affected air of displeasure, that no man could be justly condemned for being subject to the impressions of fear; and therefore his cowardice might easily be forgiven; but there was something so presumptuous, dishonest, and disingenuous, in arrogating a quality to which he knew he had not the smallest pretension, that he could not forget his misbehaviour all at once, though he would condescend to communicate with him as formerly, in hopes of seeking a reformation in his conduct. Pallet protested, that there was no dissimulation in the case; for he was ignorant of his own weakness, until his resolution was put to the trial. He faithfully promised to demean himself, during the remaining part of the tour, with that conscious modesty and penitence which became a person in his condition; and, for the present, implored the assistance of Mr. Pipes, in disembarrassing him from the disagreeable consequence of his fear.

CHAPTER LXIV

The Doctor exults in his Victory—They set out for Rotterdam, where they are entertained by two Dutch Gentlemen in a Yacht, which is overturned in the Maese, to the manifest hazard of the Painter's Life—They spend the Evening with their Entertainers, and next Day visit a Cabinet of Curiosities.

Tom was accordingly ordered to administer to his occasions; and the conqueror, elated with his success, which he in a great measure attributed to his manner of attack, and the hymn which he howled, told Peregrine, that he was now convinced of the truth of what Pindar sung in these words, *Ossa de me pephileke Zeus atuzontai Boan Pieridon aionta*; for he had no sooner began to repeat the mellifluent strains of that divine poet, than the wretch his antagonist was confounded, and his nerves unstrung.

On their return to the inn, he expatiated on the prudence and tranquillity of his own behaviour, and ascribed the consternation of Pallet to the remembrance of some crime that lay heavy upon his conscience; for, in his opinion, a man of virtue and common sense could not possibly be afraid of death, which is not only the peaceful harbour that receives him shattered on the tempestuous sea of life, but also the eternal seal of his fame and glory, which it is no longer in his power to forfeit and forego. He lamented his fate, in being doomed to live in such degenerate days, when war is become a mercenary trade; and ardently wished, that the day would come, when he should have such an opportunity of signalising his courage in the cause of liberty, as that of Marathon, where an handful of Athenians, fighting for their freedom, defeated the whole strength of the Persian empire. "Would to heaven!" said he, "my muse were blessed with an occasion to emulate that glorious testimony on the trophy in Cyprus, erected by Cimon, for two great victories gained on the same day over the Persians by sea and land; in which it is very remarkable, that the greatness of the occasion has raised the manner of expression above the usual simplicity and modesty of all other ancient inscriptions." He then repeated it with all the pomp of declamation, and signified his hope, that the French would one day invade us with such an army as that which Xerxes led into Greece, that it might be in his power to devote himself, like Leonidas, to the freedom of his country.

This memorable combat being thus determined, and everything that was remarkable in Antwerp surveyed, they sent their baggage down the Scheldt to Rotterdam, and set out for the same place in a post-waggon, which that same evening brought them in safety to the banks of the Maese. They put up at an English house of entertainment, remarkable for the modesty and moderation of the landlord; and next morning the doctor went in person to deliver letters of recommendation to two Dutch gentlemen from one of his acquaintance at Paris. Neither of them happened to be at home when he called; so that he left a message at their lodgings, with his address; and in the afternoon, they waited upon the company, and, after many hospitable professions, one of the two invited them to spend the evening at his house.

Meanwhile they had provided a pleasure yacht, in which they proposed to treat them with an excursion upon the Maese. This being almost the only diversion that place affords, our young gentleman relished the proposal; and, notwithstanding the remonstrances of Mr. Jolter, who declined the voyage on account of the roughness of the weather, they went on board without hesitation, and found a collation prepared in the cabin. While they tacked to and fro in the river, under the impulse of a mackerel breeze, the physician expressed his satisfaction, and Pallet was ravished with the entertainment. But the wind increasing, to the unspeakable joy of the Dutchmen, who had now an opportunity of showing their dexterity in the management of the vessel, the guests found it inconvenient to stand upon deck, and impossible to sit below, on account of the clouds of tobacco smoke which rolled from the pipes of their entertainers, in such volumes as annoyed them even to the hazard of suffocation. This fumigation, together with the extraordinary motion of the ship, began to affect the head and stomach of the painter, who begged earnestly to be set on shore. But the Dutch gentlemen, who had no idea of his sufferings, insisted, with surprising obstinacy of regard, upon his staying until he should see an instance of the skill of the mariners; and, bringing him on deck, commanded the men to carry the vessel's lee gunwale under water. This nicety of navigation they instantly performed, to the admiration of Pickle, the discomposure of the doctor, and terror of Pallet, who blessed himself from the courtesy of a Dutchman, and prayed to Heaven for his deliverance.

While the Hollanders enjoyed the reputation of this feat, and the distress of the painter, at the same time, the yacht was overtaken by a sudden squall, that overset her in a moment, and flung every man overboard into the Maese, before they could have the least warning of their fate, much less time to provide against the accident. Peregrine, who was an expert swimmer, reached the shore in safety; the physician, in the agonies of despair, laid fast hold on the trunk-breeches of one of the men, who dragged him to the other side; the entertainers landed at the bomb-keys, smoking their pipes all the way with great deliberation; and the poor painter must have gone to the bottom, had not he been encountered by the cable of a ship that lay at anchor near the scene of their disaster. Though his senses had forsaken him, his hands fastened by instinct on this providential occurrence, which he held with such a convulsive grasp, that, when a boat was sent out to bring him on shore, it was with the utmost difficulty that his fingers were disengaged. He was carried into a house, deprived of the use of speech, and bereft of all sensation; and, being suspended by the heels, a vast quantity of water ran out of his mouth. This evacuation being made, he began to utter dreadful groans, which gradually increased to a continued roar; and, after he had regained the use of his senses, he underwent a delirium that lasted several hours. As for the treaters, they never dreamed of expressing the least concern to Pickle or the physician for what had happened, because it was an accident so common as to pass without notice.

Leaving the care of their vessel to the seamen, the company retired to their respective lodgings, in order to shift their clothes; and in the evening our travellers were conducted to the house of their new friend, who, with a view of making his invitation the more agreeable, had assembled, to the number of twenty or thirty, Englishmen of all ranks and degrees, from the merchant to the periwig-maker's prentice.

In the midst of this congregation stood a chafing-dish with live coals, for the convenience of lighting their pipes, and every individual was accommodated with a spitting-box. There was not a mouth in the apartment unfurnished with a tube, so that they resembled a congregation of chimeras breathing fire and smoke; and our gentlemen were fain to imitate their example in their own defence. It is not to be supposed that the conversation was either very sprightly or polite; that the whole entertainment was of the Dutch cast, frowzy and phlegmatic; and our adventurer, as he returned to his lodging, tortured with the headache, and disgusted with every circumstance of his treatment, cursed the hour in which the doctor had saddled them with such troublesome companions.

Next morning by eight o'clock, these polite Hollanders returned the visit, and, after breakfast, attended their English friends to the house of a person that possessed a very curious cabinet of curiosities, to which they had secured our company's admission. The owner of this collection was a cheesemonger, who received them in a woollen nightcap, with straps buttoned under his chin. As he understood no language but his own, he told them, by the canal of one of their conductors, that he did not make a practice of showing his curiosities; but understanding that they were Englishmen, and recommended to his friends, he was content to submit them to their perusal. So saying, he led them up a dark stair, into a small room, decorated with a few paltry figures in plaster of Paris, two or three miserable land-scapes, the skins of an otter, seal, and some fishes stuffed; and in one corner stood a glass case, furnished with newts, frogs, lizards, and serpents, preserved in spirits; a human fœtus, a calf with two heads, and about two dozen of butterflies pinned upon paper.

The virtuoso having exhibited these particulars, eyed the strangers with a look soliciting admiration and applause; and as he could not perceive any symptom of either in their gestures or countenances, withdrew a curtain, and displayed a wainscot chest of drawers, in which, he gave them to understand, was something that would agreeably amuse the imagination. Our travellers, regaled with this notice, imagined that they would be entertained with the sight of some curious medals, or other productions of antiquity; but how were they disappointed, when they saw nothing but a variety of shells, disposed in whim-sical figures, in each drawer! After he had detained them full two hours with a tedious commentary upon the shape, size, and colour of each department, he, with a supercilious simper, desired that the English gentlemen would frankly and candidly declare, whether his cabinet, or that of Mynheer Sloane, at London, was the most valuable. When this request was signi-fied in English to the company, the painter instantly exclaimed, "By the Lard! they are not to be named of a day. And as for that matter, I would not give one corner of Saltero's coffee-house at Chelsea for all the trash he hath shown." Peregrine, un-willing to mortify any person who had done his endeavour to please him, observed, that what he had seen was very curious and entertaining; but that no private collection in Europe was equal to that of Sir Hans Sloane, which, exclusive of presents, had cost an hundred thousand pounds. The two conductors were con-founded at this asseveration, which, being communicated to the cheesemonger, he shook his head with a significant grin; and, though he did not choose to express his incredulity in words, gave our hero to understand, that he did not much depend upon his veracity.

From the house of this Dutch naturalist, they were dragged all round the city by the painful civility of their attendants, who did not quit them till the evening was well advanced, and then not till after they had promised to be with them before ten o'clock next day, in order to conduct them to a country house, situated in a pleasant village on the other side of the river.

Pickle was already so much fatigued with their hospitality, that, for the first time of his life, he suffered a dejection of spirits; and resolved, at any rate, to avoid the threatened persecution of to-morrow. With this view, he ordered his servants to pack up some clothes and linen in a portmanteau; and in the morning embarked, with his governor, in the Treckskuyt, for the Hague, whither he pretended to be called by some urgent occasion, leaving his fellow-travellers to make his apology to their friends, and assuring them, that he would not proceed for Amsterdam without their society. He arrived at the Hague in the forenoon, and dined at an ordinary frequented by officers and people of fashion; where being informed that the Princess would see company in the evening, he dressed himself in a rich suit of the Parisian cut, and went to court, without any introduction. A person of his appearance could not fail to attract the notice of such a small circle. The Prince himself, understanding he was an Englishman and a stranger, went up to him without ceremony, and, having welcomed him to the place, conversed with him for some minutes on the common topics of discourse.

CHAPTER LXV

They proceed to the Hague; from whence they depart for Amsterdam, where they see a Dutch Tragedy—Visit the Music-house, in which Peregrine quarrels with the Captain of a Man-of-War—They pass through Haerlem, in their way to Leyden—Return to Rotterdam, where the Company separates, and our Hero, with his Attendants, arrive in safety at Harwich.

BEING joined by their fellow-travellers in the morning, they made a tour to all the remarkable places in this celebrated village; saw the Foundery, the Stadthouse, the Spinhuys, Vauxhall, and Count Bentincke's gardens, and in the evening went to the French comedy, which was directed by a noted Harlequin, who had found means to flatter the Dutch taste so effectually, that they extolled him as the greatest actor that ever appeared in the province of Holland. This famous company did not represent regular theatrical pieces, but only a sort of impromptus, in which this noted player always performed the greatest part of the entertainment. Among other sallies of wit that escaped him, there was one circumstance so remarkably adapted to the disposition and genius of his audience, that it were a pity to pass it over in silence. A windmill being exhibited on the scene, Harlequin, after having surveyed it with curiosity and admiration, asks one of the millers the use of that machine; and being told that it was a windmill, observes, with some concern, that as there was not the least breath of wind, he could not have the pleasure of seeing it turn round. Urged by this consideration, he puts himself into the attitude of a person wrapt in profound meditation; and, having continued a few seconds in this posture, runs to the miller with great eagerness and joy, and, telling him that he had found an expedient to make his mill work, very fairly unbuttons his breeches. Then presenting his posteriors to the sails of the machine, certain explosions are immediately heard, and the arms of the mill begin to turn round, to the infinite satisfaction of the spectators, who approve the joke with loud peals of applause.

Our travellers stayed a few days at the Hague, during which the young gentleman waited on the British ambassador, to whom he was recommended by his excellency at Paris, and lost about thirty guineas at billiards to a French adventurer, who decoyed him into the snare by keeping up his game. Then they departed in a post-waggon for Amsterdam, being provided with letters of introduction to an English merchant residing in that city, under whose auspices they visited everything worth seeing, and, among other excursions, went to see a Dutch tragedy acted; an entertainment which, of all others, had the strangest effect upon the organs of our hero; the dress of their chief personages was so antic, their manner so awkwardly absurd, and their language so ridiculously unfit for conveying the sentiment of love and honour, that Peregrine's nerves were diuretically affected with the complicated absurdity, and he was compelled to withdraw twenty times before the catastrophe of the piece.

The subject of this performance was the famous story of Scipio's continence and virtue, in restoring the fair captive to her lover. The young Roman hero was represented by a broad-faced Batavian, in a burgomaster's gown and a fur cap, sitting smoking his pipe at a table furnished with a can of beer, a drinking glass, and a plate of tobacco. The lady was such a person as Scipio might well be supposed to give away, without any great effort of generosity; and indeed the Celtiberian prince seemed to be of that opinion; for, upon receiving her from the hand of the victor, he discovered none of those transports of gratitude and joy which Livy describes in recounting this event. The Dutch Scipio, however, was complaisant enough in his way; for he desired her to sit at his right hand, by the appellation of *Ya frow*, and with his own fingers filling a clean pipe, presented it to Mynheer Allucio the lover. The rest of the economy of the piece was in the same taste; which was so agreeable to the audience, that they seemed to have shaken off their natural phlegm, in order to applaud the performance.

From the play our company adjourned to the house of their friend, where they spent the evening; and the conversation turning upon poetry, a Dutchman who was present, and understood the English language, having listened very attentively to the discourse, lifted up with both hands the greatest part of a Cheshire cheese that lay upon the table, saying, "I do know vat is boeter. Mine brotre be a great boet, and ave vrought a book as dick as all dat." Pickle, diverted with this method of estimating an author according to the quantity of his works, inquired about the subjects of this bard's writings; but of these his brother could give no account, or other information, but that there was little market for the commodity, which hung heavy upon his hands, and induced him to wish he had applied himself to another trade.

The only remarkable scene in Amsterdam, which our company had not seen, was the Spuyl or music-houses, which, by the connivance of the magistrates, are maintained for the recreation of those who might attempt the chastity of creditable women, if they were not provided with such conveniences. To one of these night-houses did our travellers repair, under the conduct of the English merchant, and were introduced into such another place as the ever-memorable coffee-house of Moll King; with this difference, that the company here were not so riotous as the bucks of Covent Garden, but formed themselves into a circle, within which some of the number danced to the music of a scurvy organ and a few other instruments, that uttered tunes very suitable to the disposition of the hearers, while the whole apartment was shrouded with clouds of smoke impervious to the view. When our gentlemen entered, the floor was occupied by two females and their gallants, who, in the performance of their exercise, lifted their legs like so many oxen at plough; and the pipe of one of those hoppers happening to be exhausted, in the midst of his saraband, he very deliberately drew forth his tobacco-box, filling and lighting it again, without any interruption to the dance. Peregrine being unchecked by the presence of his governor, who was too tender of his own reputation to attend them in this expedition, made up to a sprightly French girl who sat in seeming expectation of a customer, and prevailing upon her to be his partner, led her into the circle, and in his turn took the opportunity of dancing a minuet, to the admiration of all present. He intended to have exhibited another specimen of his ability in this art, when a captain of a Dutch man-of-war chancing to come in, and seeing a stranger engaged with the lady whom, it seems, he had bespoke for his bedfellow, he advanced without any ceremony, and seizing her by the arm, pulled her to the other side of the room. Our adventurer, who was not a man to put up with such a brutal affront, followed the ravisher with indignation in his eyes; and pushing him on one side, retook the subject of their contest, and led her back to the place from whence she had been dragged. The Dutchman, enraged at the youth's presumption, obeyed the first dictates of his choler, and lent his rival a hearty box on the ear; which was immediately repaid with interest, before our hero could recollect himself sufficiently to lay his hand upon his sword, and beckon the aggressor to the door.

Notwithstanding the confusion and disorder which this affair produced in the room, and the endeavours of Pickle's company, who interposed, in order to prevent bloodshed, the antagonists reached the street; and Peregrine drawing, was surprised to see the captain advance against him with a long knife, which he preferred to the sword that hung by his side. The youth, confounded at this preposterous behaviour, desired him, in the French tongue, to lay aside that vulgar implement, and approach like a gentleman. But the Hollander, who neither understood the proposal, nor would have complied with this demand, had he been made acquainted with his meaning, rushed forward like a desperado, before his adversary could put himself on his guard; and if the young gentleman had not been endued with surprising agility, his nose would have fallen a sacrifice to the fury of the assailant. Finding himself in such imminent jeopardy, he leaped to one side, and the Dutchman passing him, in the force of his career, he with one nimble kick made such application to his enemy's heels, that he flew like lightning into the canal, where he had almost perished by pitching upon one of the posts with which it is faced.

Peregrine having performed this exploit, did not stay for the captain's coming on shore, but retreated with all despatch, by the advice of his conductor; and next day embarked, with his companions, in the skuyt, for Haerlem, where they dined; and in the evening arrived at the ancient city of Leyden, where they met with some English students, who treated them with great hospitality. Not but that the harmony of the conversation was that same night interrupted by a dispute that arose between one of those young gentlemen and the physician, about the cold and hot methods of prescription in the gout and rheumatism; and proceeded to such a degree of mutual reviling, that Pickle, ashamed and incensed at his fellow-traveller's want of urbanity, espoused the other's cause, and openly rebuked him for his unmannerly petulance, which, he said, rendered him unfit for the purposes, and unworthy of the benefit, of society. This unexpected declaration overwhelmed the doctor with amazement and confusion; he was instantaneously deprived of his speech, and, during the remaining part of the party, sat in silent mortification. In all probability, he deliberated with himself, whether or not he should expostulate with the young gentleman on the freedom he had taken with his character in a company of strangers; but as he knew he had not a Pallet to deal with, he very prudently suppressed that suggestion, and, in secret, chewed the cud of resentment.

After they had visited the Physic-Garden, the University, the Anatomical Hall, and every other thing that was recommended to their view, they returned to Rotterdam, and held a consultation upon the method of transporting themselves to England. The doctor, whose grudge against Peregrine was rather inflamed than allayed by our hero's indifference and neglect, had tampered with the simplicity of the painter, who was proud of his advances towards a perfect reconciliation, and now took the opportunity of parting with our adventurer, by declaring that he and his friend Mr. Pallet were resolved to take their passage in a trading sloop, after he had heard Peregrine object against that tedious, disagreeable, and uncertain method of conveyance. Pickle immediately saw his intention, and, without using the least argument to dissuade them from their design, or expressing the smallest degree of concern at their separation, very coolly wished them a prosperous voyage, and ordered his baggage to be sent to Helvoetsluys. There he himself, and his retinue, went on board of the packet next day, and, by the favour of a fair wind, in eighteen hours arrived at Harwich.

CHAPTER LXVI

Peregrine delivers his Letters of Recommendation at London, and returns to the Garrison, to the unspeakable Joy of the Commodore and his whole Family.

Now that our hero found himself on English ground, his heart dilated with the proud recollection of his own improvement since he left his native soil. He began to recognise the interesting ideas of his tender years; he enjoyed, by anticipation, the pleasure of seeing his friends in the garrison, after an absence of eighteen months; and the image of his charming Emily, which other less worthy considerations had depressed, resumed the full possession of his breast. He remembered, with shame, that he had neglected the correspondence with her brother, which he himself had solicited, and in consequence of which he had received a letter from that young gentleman, while he lived at Paris. In spite of these conscientious reflections, he was too self-sufficient to think he should find any difficulty in obtaining forgiveness for such sins of omission; and began to imagine that his passion would be prejudicial to the dignity of his situation, if it should not be gratified upon terms which formerly his imagination durst not conceive.

Sorry I am, that the task I have undertaken, lays me under the necessity of divulging this degeneracy in the sentiment of our imperious youth, who was now in the heyday of his blood, flushed with the consciousness of his own qualifications, vain of his fortune, and elated on the wings of imaginary expectation. Though he was deeply enamoured of Miss Gauntlet, he was far from proposing her heart as the ultimate aim of his gallantry, which, he did not doubt, would triumph over the most illustrious females of the land, and at once regale his appetite and ambition.

Meanwhile, being willing to make his appearance at the garrison equally surprising and agreeable, he cautioned Mr. Jolter against writing to the commodore, who had not heard of them since their departure from Paris, and hired a post-chaise and horses, for London. The governor, going out to give orders about the carriage, inadvertently left a paper book open upon the table; and his pupil, casting his eyes upon the page, chanced to read these words: "Sept. 15. Arrived in safety, by the blessing of God, in this unhappy kingdom of England. And thus concludes the journal of my last peregrination." Peregrine's curiosity being inflamed by this extraordinary conclusion he turned to the beginning, and perused several sheets of a diary such as is commonly kept by that class of people known by the denomination of travelling governors, for the satisfaction of themselves and the parents or guardians of their pupils, and for the edification and entertainment of their friends.

That the reader may have a clear idea of Mr. Jolter's performance, we shall transcribe the transactions of one day, as he had recorded them; and that abstract will be a sufficient specimen of the whole plan and execution of the work.

"May 3.—At eight o'clock, set out from Boulogne in a post-chaise—the morning hazy and cold. Fortified my stomach with a cordial. Recommended ditto to Mr. P. as an antidote against the fog. Mem. He refused it. The hither horse greased in the off-pastern of the hind leg. Arrived at Samers. Mem. This last was a post and a half, i.e. three leagues, or nine English miles. The day clears up. A fine champaign country, well stored with corn. The postillion says his prayers in passing by a wooden crucifix upon the road. Mem. The horses staled in a small brook that runs in a bottom, betwixt two hills. Arrived at Cormont. A common post. A dispute with my pupil, who is obstinate, and swayed by an unlucky prejudice. Proceed to Montreuil, where we dine on choice pigeons. A very moderate charge. No chamber-pot in the room, owing to the negligence of the maid. This is an ordinary post. Set out again for Nampont. Troubled with flatulences and indigestion. Mr. P. is sullen, and seems to mistake an eructation for the breaking of wind backwards. From Nampont depart for Bernay, at which place we arrive in the evening, and propose to stay all night. N.B. The two last a redouble posts, and our cattle very willing, though not strong. Sup on a delicate ragout and excellent partridges, in company with Mr. H. and his spouse. Mem. The said H. trod upon my corn by mistake. Discharge the bill, which is not very reasonable. Dispute with Mr. P. about giving money to the servant. He insists upon my giving a twenty-four sols piece, which is too much by two-thirds, in all conscience. N.B. She was a pert baggage, and did not deserve a liard."

Our hero was so much disobliged with certain circumstances of this amusing and instructing journal, that, by way of punishing the author, he interlined these words betwixt two paragraphs, in a manner that exactly resembled the tutor's handwriting:—"Mem. Had the pleasure of drinking myself into a sweet intoxication, by toasting our lawful king, and his royal family, among some worthy English fathers of the Society of Jesus."

Having taken this revenge, he set out for London, where he waited upon those noblemen to whom he had letters of recommendation from Paris; and was not only graciously received, but even loaded with caresses and proffers of service, because they understood he was a young gentleman of fortune, who, far from standing in need of their countenance or assistance, would make an useful and creditable addition to the number of their adherents. He had the honour of dining at their tables, in consequence of pressing invitations, and of spending several evenings with the ladies, to whom he was particularly agreeable, on account of his person, address, and bleeding freely at play.

Being thus initiated in the beau monde, he thought it was high time to pay his respects to his generous benefactor, the commodore; and, accordingly, departed one morning, with his train, for the garrison, at which he arrived in safety the same night. When he entered the gate, which was opened by a new servant that did not know him, he found his old friend, Hatchway, stalking in the yard, with a night-cap on his head, and a pipe in his mouth; and, advancing to him, took him by the hand before he had any intimation of his approach. The lieutenant, thus saluted by a stranger, stared at him in silent astonishment, till he recollected his features, which were no sooner known, than, dashing his pipe upon the pavement, he exclaimed, "Smite my cross-trees! th'art welcome to port"; and hugged him in his arms with great affection. He then, by a cordial squeeze, expressed his satisfaction at seeing his old shipmate, Tom, who, applying his whistle to his mouth, the whole castle echoed with his performance.

The servants, hearing the well-known sound, poured out in a tumult of joy; and, understanding that their young master was returned, raised such a peal of acclamation, as astonished the commodore and his lady, and inspired Julia with such an interesting presage, that her heart began to throb with violence. Running out in the hurry and perturbation of her hope, she was so much overwhelmed at sight of her brother, that she actually fainted in his arms. But from this trance she soon awaked; and Peregrine, having testified his pleasure and affection, went upstairs, and presented himself before his godfather and aunt. Mrs. Trunnion rose and received him with a gracious embrace, blessing God for his happy return from a land of impiety and vice, in which she hoped his morals had not been corrupted, nor his principles of religion altered or impaired. The old gentleman being confined to his chair, was struck dumb with pleasure at his appearance; and, having made divers ineffectual efforts to get up, at length discharged a volley of curses against his own limbs, and held out his hand to his godson, who kissed it with great respect.

After he had finished his apostrophe to the gout, which was the daily and hourly subject of his execrations, "Well, my lad," said he, "I care not how soon I go to the bottom, now I behold thee safe in harbour again; and yet I tell a d—n'd lie. I would I could keep afloat until I should see a lusty boy of thy begetting. Odds my timbers! I love thee so well, that I believe thou art the spawn of my own body; though I can give no account of thy being put upon the stocks." Then, turning his eyes upon Pipes, who by this time had penetrated into his apartment, and addressed him with the usual salutation of "What cheer?" "Ahey," cried he, "are you there, you herring-faced son of a sea-calf? What a slippery trick you played your old commander! But come, you dog, there's my fist; I forgive you, for the love you bear to my godson. Go, man your tackle, and hoist a cask of strong beer into the yard, knock out the bung, and put a pump in it, for the use of all my servants and neighbours; and, d'ye hear, let the patereroes be fired, and the garrison illuminated, as rejoicings for the safe arrival of your master. By the Lord! if I had the use of these d—n'd shambling shanks, I would dance a hornpipe with the best of you."

The next object of his attention was Mr. Jolter, who was honoured with particular marks of distinction, and the repeated promise of enjoying the living in his gift, as an acknowledgment of the care and discretion with which he had superintended the education and morals of our hero. The governor was so affected by the generosity of his patron, that the tears ran down his cheeks, while he expressed his gratitude, and the infinite satisfaction he felt in contemplating the accomplishments of his pupil.

Meanwhile, Pipes did not neglect the orders he had received. The beer was produced, the gates were thrown open for the admission of all comers, the whole house was lighted up, and the patereroes were discharged in repeated volleys. Such phenomena could not fail to attract the notice of the neighbourhood. The club at Tunley's were astonished at the report of the guns, which produced various conjectures among the members of that sagacious society. The landlord observed, that, in all likelihood, the commodore was visited by hobgoblins, and ordered the guns to be fired in token of distress, as he had acted twenty years before, when he was annoyed by the same grievance. The exciseman, with a waggish sneer, expressed his apprehension of Trunnion's death, in consequence of which the patereroes might be discharged with an equivocal intent, either as signals of his lady's sorrow or rejoicing. The attorney signified a suspicion of Hatchway's being married to Miss Pickle, and that the firing and illuminations were in honour of the nuptials; upon which Gamaliel discovered some faint signs of emotion, and, taking the pipe from his mouth, gave it as his opinion, that his sister was brought to bed.

While they were thus bewildered in the maze of their own imaginations, a company of countrymen, who sat drinking in the kitchen, and whose legs were more ready than their invention, sallied out to know the meaning of these exhibitions. Understanding that there was a butt of strong beer a-broach in the yard, to which they were invited by the servants, they saved themselves the trouble and expense of returning to spend the evening at the public-house, and listed themselves under the banner of Tom Pipes, who presided as director of this festival.

The news of Peregrine's return being communicated to the parish, the parson, and three or four neighbouring gentlemen, who were well-wishers to our hero, immediately repaired to the garrison, in order to pay their compliments on this happy event, and were detained to supper. An elegant entertainment was prepared by the direction of Miss Julia, who was an excellent housewife; and the commodore was so invigorated with joy, that he seemed to have renewed his age.

Among those who honoured the occasion with their presence, was Mr. Clover, the young gentleman that made his addresses to Peregrine's sister. His heart was so big with his passion, that, while the rest of the company were engrossed by their cups, he seized an opportunity of our hero's being detached from the conversation, and, in the impatience of his love, conjured him to consent to his happiness; protesting, that he would comply with any terms of settlement that a man of his fortune could embrace, in favour of a young lady who was absolute mistress of his affection.

Our youth thanked him very politely for his favourable sentiments and honourable intention towards his sister, and told him, that at present he saw no reason to obstruct his desire; that he would consult Julia's own inclinations, and confer with him about the means of gratifying his wish; but, in the meantime, begged to be excused from discussing any point of such importance to them both. Reminding him of the jovial purpose on which they were happily met, he promoted such a quick circulation of the bottle, that their mirth grew noisy and obstreperous; they broke forth into repeated peals of laughter, without any previous incitement except that of claret. These explosions were succeeded by Bacchanalian songs, in which the old gentleman himself attempted to bear a share; the sedate governor snapped time with his fingers, and the parish priest assisted in the chorus with a most expressive nakedness of countenance. Before midnight they were almost all pinned to their chairs, as if they had been fixed by the power of enchantment; and, what rendered the confinement still more unfortunate, every servant in the house was in the same situation; so that they were fain to take their repose as they sat, and nodded at each other like a congregation of Anabaptists.

Next day Peregrine communed with his sister on the subject of her match with Mr. Clover, who, she told him, had offered to settle a jointure of four hundred pounds, and take her to wife without any expectation of a dowry. She moreover gave him to understand, that, in his absence, she had received several messages from her mother, commanding her to return to her father's house; but that she had refused to obey these orders, by the advice and injunction of her aunt and the commodore, which were indeed seconded by her own inclination; because she had all the reason in the world to believe, that her mother only wanted an opportunity of treating her with severity and rancour. The resentment of that lady had been carried to such indecent lengths, that, seeing her daughter at church one day, she rose up, before the parson entered, and reviled her with great bitterness, in the face of the whole congregation.

CHAPTER LXVII

Sees his Sister happily married—Visits Emilia, who receives him according to his Deserts.

HER brother being of opinion, that Mr. Clover's proposal was not to be neglected, especially as Julia's heart was engaged in his favour, communicated the affair to his uncle, who, with the approbation of Mrs. Trunnion, declared himself well satisfied with the young man's addresses, and desired that they might be buckled with all expedition, without the knowledge or concurrence of her parents, to whom (on account of their unnatural barbarity) she was not bound to pay the least regard. Though our adventurer entertained the same sentiments of the matter, and the lover, dreading some obstruction, earnestly begged the immediate condescension of his mistress, she could not be prevailed upon to take such a material step, without having first solicited the permission of her father, resolved, nevertheless, to comply with the dictates of her own heart, should his objections be frivolous or unjust.

Urged by this determination, her admirer waited upon Mr. Gamaliel at the public-house, and, with the appearance of great deference and respect, made him acquainted with his affection for his daughter, communicated the particulars of his fortune, with the terms of settlement he was ready to make; and in conclusion told him, that he would marry her without a portion. This last offer seemed to have some weight with the father, who received it with civility, and promised in a day or two to favour him with a final answer to his demand. He, accordingly, that same evening consulted his wife, who, being exasperated at the prospect of her daughter's independency, argued with the most virulent expostulation against the match, as an impudent scheme of her own planning, with a view of insulting her parents, towards whom she had already been guilty of the most vicious disobedience. In short, she used such remonstrances, as not only averted this weak husband's inclination from the proposal which he had relished before, but even instigated him to apply for a warrant to apprehend his daughter, on the supposition that she was about to bestow herself in marriage without his privity or consent.

The justice of peace to whom this application was made, though he could not refuse the order, yet, being no stranger to the malevolence of the mother, which, together with Gamaliel's simplicity, was notorious in the county, he sent an intimation of what had happened to the garrison; upon which a couple of sentinels were placed on the gate, and at the pressing solicitation of the lover, as well as the desire of the commodore, her brother, and aunt, Julia was wedded without further delay; the ceremony being performed by Mr. Jolter, because the parish priest prudently declined any occasion of giving offence, and the curate was too much in the interest of their enemies to be employed in that office.

This domestic concern being settled to the satisfaction of our hero, he escorted her next day to the house of her husband, who immediately wrote a letter to her father, declaring his reasons for having thus superseded his authority; and Mrs. Pickle's mortification was unspeakable.

That the new-married couple might be guarded against all insult, our young gentleman and his friend Hatchway, with their adherents, lodged in Mr. Clover's house for some weeks; during which they visited their acquaintance in the neighbourhood, according to custom. When the tranquillity of their family was perfectly established, and the contract of the marriage executed in the presence of the old commodore and his lady, who gave her niece five hundred pounds to purchase jewels and clothes, Mr. Peregrine could no longer restrain his impatience to see his dear Emily; and told his uncle, that next day he proposed to ride across the country, in order to visit his friend Gauntlet, whom he had not heard of for a long time.

The old gentleman, looking stedfastly in his face, "Ah! d—n your cunning!" said he, "I find the anchor holds fast! I did suppose as how you would have slipt your cable, and changed your berth; but, I see, when a young fellow is once brought up by a pretty wench, he may man his capstans and viol block, if he wool; but he'll as soon heave up the Pike of Teneriffe, as bring his anchor a-weigh! Odds heartlikins! had I known the young woman was Ned Gauntlet's daughter, I shouldn't have thrown out signal for leaving off chase."

Our adventurer was not a little surprised to hear the commodore talk in this style; and immediately conjectured that his friend Godfrey had informed him of the whole affair. Instead of listening to this approbation of his flame, with those transports of joy which he would have felt, had he retained his former sentiments, he was chagrined at Trunnion's declaration, and offended at the presumption of the young soldier, in presuming to disclose the secret with which he had entrusted him. Reddening with these reflections, he assured the commodore that he never had serious thoughts of matrimony; so that if any person had told him he was under any engagement of that kind, he had abused his ear; for he protested that he would never contract such attachments without his knowledge and express permission.

Trunnion commended him for his prudent resolution, and observed, that, though no person mentioned to him what promises had passed betwixt him and his sweetheart, it was very plain that he had made love to her, and therefore it was to be supposed that his intentions were honourable; for he could not believe he was such a rogue in his heart, as to endeavour to debauch the daughter of a brave officer, who had served his country with credit and reputation. Notwithstanding this remonstrance, which Pickle imputed to the commodore's ignorance of the world, he set out for the habitation of Mrs. Gauntlet, with the unjustifiable sentiments of a man of pleasure, who sacrifices every consideration to the desire of his ruling appetite; and, as Winchester lay in his way, resolved to visit some of his friends who lived in that place. It was in the house of one of these that he was informed of Emilia's being then in town with her mother; upon which he excused himself from staying to drink tea, and immediately repaired to their lodgings, according to the directions he had received.

When he arrived at the door, instead of undergoing that perturbation of spirits, which a lover in his interesting situation might be supposed to feel, he suffered no emotion but that of vanity and pride, favoured with an opportunity of self-gratification, and entered his Emilia's apartment with the air of a conceited petit-maître, rather than that of the respectful admirer, when he visits the object of his passion, after an absence of seventeen months.

The young lady, having been very much disobliged at his mortifying neglect of her brother's letter, had summoned all her own pride and resolution to her aid; and, by means of a happy disposition, so far overcame her chagrin at his indifference, that she was able to behave in his presence with apparent tranquillity and ease. She was even pleased to find he had, by accident, chosen a time for his visit when she was surrounded by two or three young gentlemen, who professed themselves her admirers. Our gallant was no sooner announced, than she collected all her coquetry, put on the gayest air she could assume, and contrived to giggle just as he appeared at the room door. The compliments of salutation being performed, she welcomed him to England in a careless manner, asked the news of Paris, and, before he could make any reply, desired one of the other gentlemen to proceed with the sequel of that comical adventure, in the relation of which he had been interrupted.

Peregrine smiled within himself at this behaviour, which, without all doubt, he believed she had affected to punish him for his unkind silence while he was abroad, being fully persuaded that her heart was absolutely at his devotion. On this supposition, he practised his Parisian improvements on the art of conversation, and uttered a thousand prettinesses in the way of compliment, with such incredible rotation of tongue, that his rivals were struck dumb with astonishment, and Emilia fretted out of all temper, at seeing herself deprived of the prerogative of the sex. He persisted, however, in this surprising loquacity, until the rest of the company thought proper to withdraw, and then contracted his discourse into the focus of love, which now put on a very different appearance from that which it had formerly worn. Instead of awful veneration, which her presence used to inspire, that chastity of sentiment, and delicacy of expression, he now gazed upon her with the eyes of a libertine, he glowed with the impatience of desire, talked in a strain that barely kept within the bounds of decency, and attempted to snatch such favours, as she, in the tenderness of mutual acknowledgments, had once vouchsafed to bestow.

Grieved and offended as she was, at this palpable alteration in his carriage, she disdained to remind him of his former deportment, and, with dissembled good-humour, rallied him on the progress he had made in gallantry and address. But, far from submitting to the liberties he would have taken, she kept her person sacred from his touch, and would not even suffer him to ravish a kiss of her fair hand; so that he reaped no other advantage from the exercise of his talents, during this interview, which lasted a whole hour, than that of knowing he had overrated his own importance, and that Emily's heart was not a garrison likely to surrender at discretion.

At length his addresses were interrupted by the arrival of the mother, who had gone abroad to visit by herself; and the conversation becoming more general, he understood that Godfrey was at London, soliciting for a lieutenancy that had fallen vacant in the regiment to which he belonged; and that Miss Sophy was at home with her father.

Though our adventurer had not met with all the success he expected by his first visit, he did not despair of reducing the fortress, believing that in time there would be a mutiny in his favour, and accordingly carried on the siege for several days, without profiting by his perseverance; till, at length, having attended the ladies to their own house in the country, he began to look upon this adventure as time misspent, and resolved to discontinue his attack, in hopes of meeting with a more favourable occasion; being, in the meantime, ambitious of displaying, in a higher sphere, those qualifications which his vanity told him were at present misapplied.

CHAPTER LXVIII

He attends his Uncle with great Affection during a Fit of Illness—Sets
out again for London—Meets with his Friend Godfrey, who is prevailed
upon to accompany him to Bath; on the Road to which Place they chance
to Dine with a Person who entertains them with a curious Account of a
certain Company of Adventurers.

THUS determined, he took leave of Emilia and her mother, on
pretence of going to London upon some urgent business, and
returned to the garrison, leaving the good old lady very much
concerned, and the daughter incensed at his behaviour, which was
the more unexpected, because Godfrey had told them that the
commodore approved of his nephew's passion.

Our adventurer found his uncle so ill of the gout, which, for
the first time, had taken possession of his stomach, that his life
was in imminent danger, and the whole family in disorder.　He
therefore took the reins of government in his own hands, sent
for all the physicians in the neighbourhood, and attended him
in person with the most affectionate care, during the whole
fit, which lasted a fortnight, and then retired before the strength
of his constitution.

When the old gentleman recovered his health, he was so penetrated with Peregrine's behaviour, that he actually would have
made over to him his whole fortune, and depended upon him for
his own subsistence, had not our youth opposed the execution
of the deed with all his influence and might, and even persuaded
him to make a will, in which his friend Hatchway, and all his
other adherents, were liberally remembered, and his aunt provided for on her own terms.　This material point being settled,
he, with his uncle's permission, departed for London, after having
seen the family affairs established under the direction and
administration of Mr. Jolter and the lieutenant; for, by this
time, Mrs. Trunnion was wholly occupied with her spiritual
concern.

On his first arrival at London, he sent a card to the lodgings
of Gauntlet, in consequence of a direction from his mother; and
that young gentleman waited on him next morning, though not
with that alacrity of countenance and warmth of friendship
which might have been expected from the intimacy of their
former connexion.　Nor was Peregrine himself actuated by the
same unreserved affection for the soldier which he had formerly
entertained.　Godfrey, over and above the offence he had taken
at Pickle's omission in point of corresponding with him, had been

informed, by a letter from his mother, of the youth's cavalier behaviour to Emilia, during his last residence at Winchester; and our young gentleman, as we have already observed, was disgusted at the supposed discovery which the soldier had made in his absence to the commodore. They perceived their mutual umbrage at meeting, and received each other with that civility of reserve which commonly happens between two persons whose friendship is in the wane.

Gauntlet at once divined the cause of the other's displeasure; and, in order to vindicate his own character, after the first compliments were passed, took the opportunity, on inquiring after the health of the commodore, to tell Peregrine, that, while he tarried at the garrison, on his return from Dover, the subject of the conversation, one night, happening to turn on our hero's passion, the old gentleman had expressed his concern about that affair; and, among other observations, said, he supposed the object of his love was some paltry hussy, whom he had picked up when he was a boy at school. Upon which, Mr. Hatchway assured him, that she was a young woman of as good a family as any in the county; and, after having prepossessed him in her favour, ventured, out of the zeal of his friendship, to tell who she was. Wherefore, the discovery was not to be imputed to any other cause; and he hoped Mr. Pickle would acquit him of all share in the transaction.

Peregrine was very well pleased to be thus undeceived; his countenance immediately cleared up, the formality of his behaviour relaxed into his usual familiarity; he asked pardon for his unmannerly neglect of Godfrey's letter, which he protested, was not owing to any disregard, or abatement of friendship, but to a hurry of youthful engagements, in consequence of which he had procrastinated his answer from time to time, until he was ready to return in person.

The young soldier was contented with this apology; and, as Pickle's intention, with respect to his sister, was still dubious and undeclared, he did not think it was incumbent upon him, as yet, to express any resentment on that score; but was wise enough to foresee, that the renewal of his intimacy with our young gentleman might be the means of reviving that flame which had been dissipated by a variety of new ideas. With those sentiments, he laid aside all reserve, and their communication resumed its former channel. Peregrine made him acquainted with all the adventures in which he had been engaged since their parting; and he, with the same confidence, related the remarkable incidents of his own fate; among other things, giving him to understand, that, upon obtaining a commission in the army, the father of his dear Sophy, without once inquiring about the occasion of his promotion, had not only favoured him with his countenance in a much greater degree than heretofore, but also contributed his interest, and even promised the assistance of his purse, in procuring for him a lieutenancy, which he was then soliciting with all his power; whereas, if he had not been enabled, by a most accidental piece of good fortune, to lift himself into the sphere of an officer, he had all the reason in the world to believe that this gentleman, and all the rest of his wealthy relations, would have suffered him to languish in obscurity and distress; and by turning his misfortune into reproach, made it a plea for their want of generosity and friendship.

Peregrine, understanding the situation of his friend's affairs, would have accommodated him upon the instant with a sum to accelerate the passage of his commission through the offices; but, being too well acquainted with his scrupulous disposition, to manifest his benevolence in that manner, he found means to introduce himself to one of the gentlemen of the War Office, who was so well satisfied with the arguments used in behalf of his friend, that Godfrey's business was transacted in a very few days, though he himself knew nothing of his interest being thus reinforced.

By this time, the season at Bath was begun; and our hero, panting with the desire of distinguishing himself at that resort of the fashionable world, communicated his design of going thither to his friend Godfrey, whom he importuned to accompany him in the excursion; and leave of absence from his regiment being obtained by the influence of Peregrine's new quality friends, the two companions departed from London in a post-chaise, attended, as usual, by the valet-de-chambre and Pipes, who were become almost as necessary to our adventurer as any two of his own organs.

At the inn, when they alighted for dinner, Godfrey perceived a person walking by himself in the yard, with a very pensive air, and, upon observing him more narrowly, recognised him to be a professed gamester, whom he had formerly known at Tunbridge. On the strength of this acquaintance, he accosted the peripatetic, who knew him immediately; and, in the fulness of his grief and vexation, told him, that he was now on his return from Bath, where he had been stripped by a company of sharpers, who resented that he should presume to trade upon his own bottom.

Peregrine, who was extremely curious in his inquiries, imagining that he might learn some entertaining and useful anecdotes from this artist, invited him to dinner, and was accordingly fully informed of all the political systems at Bath. He understood that there was at London one great company of adventurers, who employed agents in all the different branches of imposition throughout the whole kingdom of England, allowing these ministers a certain proportion of the profits accruing from their industry and skill, and reserving the greatest share for the benefit of the common stock, which was chargeable with the expense of fitting out individuals in their various pursuits, as well as with the loss sustained in the course of their adventures. Some, whose persons and qualifications are by the company judged adequate to the task, exert their talents in making love to ladies of fortune, being accommodated with money and accoutrements for that purpose, after having given their bonds payable to one or other of the directors, on the day of marriage, for certain sums, proportioned to the dowries they are to receive. Others, versed in the doctrine of chances, and certain secret expediences, frequent all those places where games of hazard are allowed; and such as are masters in the arts of billiards, tennis, and bowls, are continually lying in wait, in all the scenes of these diversions, for the ignorant and unwary. A fourth class attend horse-races, being skilled in those mysterious practices by which the knowing ones are taken in. Nor is this community unfurnished with those who lay wanton wives and old rich widows under contribution, and extort money, by prostituting themselves to the embraces of their own sex, and then threatening their admirers with prosecution. But their most important returns are made by that body of their undertakers who exercise their understandings in the innumerable stratagems of the card table, at which no sharper can be too infamous to be received, and even caressed by persons of the highest rank and distinction. Among other articles of intelligence, our young gentleman learned, that those agents, by whom their guest was broke, and expelled from Bath, had constituted a bank against all sporters, and monopolised the advantage in all sorts of play. He then told Gauntlet, that, if he would put himself under his direction, he would return with them, and lay such a scheme as would infallibly ruin the whole society at billiards, as he knew that Godfrey excelled them all in his knowledge of that game.

The soldier excused himself from engaging in any party of that kind; and after dinner the travellers parted; but, as the conversation between the two friends turned upon the information they had received, Peregrine projected a plan for punishing those villainous pests of society, who prey upon their fellow-creatures; and it was put in execution by Gauntlet in the following manner.

CHAPTER LXIX

Godfrey executes a Scheme at Bath, by which a whole Company of Sharpers is ruined.

On the evening after their arrival at Bath, Godfrey, who had kept himself up all day for that purpose, went in boots to the billiard table; and, two gentlemen being at play, began to bet with so little appearance of judgment, that one of the adventurers then present was inflamed with a desire of profiting by his inexperience; and, when the table was vacant, invited him to take a game for amusement. The soldier, assuming the air of a self-conceited dupe, answered, that he did not choose to throw away his time for nothing, but, if he pleased, would piddle for a crown a game. This declaration was very agreeable to the other, who wanted to be further confirmed in the opinion he had conceived of the stranger, before he would play for anything of consequence. The party being accepted, Gauntlet put off his coat, and, beginning with seeming eagerness, won the first game, because his antagonist kept up his play with a view of encouraging him to wager a greater sum. The soldier purposely bit at the hook, the stakes were doubled, and he was again victorious, by the permission of his competitor. He now began to yawn; and observing, that it was not worth his while to proceed in such a childish manner; the other swore, in an affected passion, that he would play him for twenty guineas. The proposal being embraced, through the connivance of Godfrey, the money was won by the sharper, who exerted his dexterity to the utmost, fearing that otherwise his adversary would decline continuing the game.

Godfrey thus conquered, pretended to lose his temper, cursed his own ill-luck, swore that the table had a cast, and that the balls did not run true, changed his mast, and with great warmth, challenged his enemy to double the sum. The gamester, who feigned reluctance, complied with his desire; and having got the two first hazards, offered to lay one hundred guineas to fifty on the game. The odds were taken; and Godfrey having allowed himself to be overcome, began to rage with great violence, broke the mast to pieces, threw the balls out of the window, and, in the fury of his indignation, defied his antagonist to meet him to-morrow, when he should be refreshed from the fatigue of travelling. This was a very welcome invitation to the gamester, who, imagining that the soldier would turn out a most beneficial prize, assured him, that he would not fail to be there next forenoon, in order to give him his revenge.

Gauntlet went home to his lodgings, fully certified of his own superiority, and took his measures with Peregrine, touching the prosecution of their scheme; while his opponent made a report of his success to the brethren of the gang, who resolved to be present at the decision of the match, with a view of taking advantage of the stranger's passionate disposition.

Affairs being thus concerted on both sides, the players met, according to appointment, and the room was immediately filled with spectators, who either came thither by accident, curiosity, or design. The match was fixed for one hundred pounds a game, the principals chose their instruments, and laid aside their coats, and one of the knights of the order proffered to lay another hundred on the head of his associate. Godfrey took him upon the instant. A second worthy of the same class, seeing him so eager, challenged him to treble the sum; and his proposal met with the same reception, to the astonishment of the company, whose expectation was raised to a very interesting pitch. The game was begun, and the soldier having lost the first hazard, the odds were offered by the confederacy with great vociferation; but nobody would run such a risk in favour of a person who was utterly unknown. The sharper having gained the second also, the noise increased to a surprising clamour, not only of the gang, but likewise of almost all the spectators, who desired to lay two to one against the brother of Emilia.

Peregrine, who was present, perceiving the cupidity of the association sufficiently inflamed, all of a sudden opened his mouth, and answered their bets, to the amount of twelve hundred pounds; which were immediately deposited, on both sides, in money and notes; so that this was, perhaps, the most important game that ever was played at billiards. Gauntlet seeing the agreement settled, struck his antagonist's ball into the pocket in a twinkling, though it was in one of those situations which are

M 838

supposed to be against the striker. The betters were a little discomposed at this event, for which, however, they consoled themselves by imputing the success to accident; but when, at the very next stroke, he sprung it over the table, their countenances underwent an instantaneous distraction of feature, and they waited, in the most dreadful suspense, for the next hazard, which being likewise taken with infinite ease by the soldier, the blood forsook their cheeks, and the interjection *Zounds!* pronounced with a look of consternation, and in a tone of despair, proceeded from every mouth at the same instant of time. They were overwhelmed with horror and astonishment at seeing three hazards taken in as many strokes, from a person of their friend's dexterity; and shrewdly suspected, that the whole was a scheme preconcerted for their destruction. On this supposition, they changed the note, and attempted to hedge for their own indemnification, by proposing to lay the odds in favour of Gauntlet; but so much was the opinion of the company altered by that young gentleman's success, that no one would venture to espouse the cause of his competitor, who, chancing to improve his game by the addition of another lucky hit, diminished the concern, and revived the hopes of his adherents. But this gleam of fortune did not long continue. Godfrey collected his whole art and capacity, and, augmenting his score to number ten, indulged himself with a view of the whole fraternity. The visages of these professors had adopted different shades of complexion at every hazard he had taken; from their natural colour they had shifted into a sallow hue; from thence into pale; from pale into yellow, which degenerated into a mahogany tint; and now they saw seventeen hundred pounds of their stock depending upon a single stroke, they stood like so many swarthy Moors, jaundiced with terror and vexation. The fire which naturally glowed in the cheeks and nose of the player, seemed utterly extinct, and his carbuncles exhibited a livid appearance, as if a gangrene had already made some progress in his face; his hand began to shake, and his whole frame was seized with such trepidation, that he was fain to swallow a bumper of brandy, in order to re-establish the tranquillity of his nerves. This expedient, however, did not produce the desired effect; for he aimed the ball at the lead with such discomposure, that it struck on the wrong side, and came off at an angle which directed it full in the middle hole. This fatal accident was attended with an universal groan, as if the whole universe had gone to wreck; and notwithstanding that tranquillity for which adventurers are so remarkable, this loss made such an impression upon them all, that each in particular manifested his chagrin, by the most violent emotions. One turned up his eyes to heaven, and bit his nether lip; another gnawed his fingers, while he stalked across the room; a third blasphemed with horrid imprecations; and he who played the party sneaked off, grinding his teeth together, with a look that baffles all description, and as he crossed the threshold, exclaiming, "A d—d bite, by G—d!"

The victors, after having insulted them, by asking, if they were disposed for another chance, carried off their winning, with the appearance of great composure, though in their hearts they were transported with unspeakable joy; not so much on account of the booty they had gained, as in consideration of having so effectually destroyed such a nest of pernicious miscreants.

Peregrine, believing that now he had found an opportunity of serving his friend, without giving offence to the delicacy of his honour, told him, upon their arrival at their lodgings, that fortune had at length enabled him to become in a manner independent, or at least make himself easy in his circumstances, by purchasing a company with the money he had won. So saying, he put his share of the success in Gauntlet's hand, as a sum that of right belonged to him, and promised to write in his behalf to a nobleman, who had interest enough to promote such a quick rise in the service.

Godfrey thanked him for his obliging intention, but absolutely refused, with great loftiness of demeanour, to appropriate to his own use any part of the money which Pickle had gained, and seemed affronted at the other's entertaining a sentiment so unworthy of his character. He would not even accept, in the way of loan, such an addition to his own stock, as would amount to the price of a company of foot; but expressed great confidence in the future exertion of that talent which had been blessed with such a prosperous beginning. Our hero finding him thus obstinately deaf to the voice of his own interest, resolved to govern himself in his next endeavours of friendship, by his experience of this ticklish punctilio; and, in the meantime, gave a handsome benefaction to the hospital, out of these first fruits of the success in play, and reserved two hundred pounds for a set of diamond ear-rings and solitaire, which he intended for a present to Miss Emily.

CHAPTER LXX

The two Friends eclipse all their Competitors in Gallantry, and practise
a pleasant Project of Revenge upon the Physicians of the Place.

THE fame of their exploit against the sharpers was immediately
diffused through all the companies at Bath; so that, when our
adventurers appeared in public, they were pointed out by an
hundred extended fingers, and considered as consummate artists
in all the different species of finesse, which they would not fail
to practise with the first opportunity. Nor was this opinion
of their characters any obstacle to their reception into the
fashionable parties in the place; but, on the contrary, such a
recommendation, which, as I have already hinted, never fails
to operate for the advantage of the possessor.

This first adventure, therefore, served them as an introduction
to the company at Bath, who were not a little surprised to find
their expectations baffled by the conduct of the two companions;
because, far from engaging deeply at play, they rather shunned
all occasions of gaming, and directed their attention to gallantry,
in which our hero shone unrivalled. His external qualifications,
exclusive of any other merit, were strong enough to captivate
the common run of the female sex; and these, reinforced with a
sprightliness of conversation, and a most insinuating address,
became irresistible, even by those who were fortified with pride,
caution, or indifference. But, among all the nymphs of this
gay place, he did not meet with one object that disputed the
empire of his heart with Emilia, and therefore he divided his
attachment according to the suggestions of vanity and whim;
so that, before he had resided a fortnight at Bath, he had set all
the ladies by the ears, and furnished all the hundred tongues of
scandal with full employment. The splendour of his appearance
excited the inquiries of envy, which, instead of discovering any
circumstances to his prejudice, was cursed with the information
of his being a young gentleman of a good family, and heir to an
immense fortune.

The countenance of some of his quality friends, who arrived
at Bath, confirmed this piece of intelligence. Upon which his
acquaintance was courted and cultivated with great assiduity;
and he met with such advances from some of the fair sex, as
rendered him extremely fortunate in his amours. Nor was his
friend Godfrey a stranger to favours of the same kind; his accomplishments were exactly calculated for the meridian of female

taste; and, with certain individuals of that sex, his muscular frame, and the robust connexion of his limbs, were more attractive than the delicate proportions of his companion. He accordingly reigned paramount among those inamoratas who were turned of thirty, without being under the necessity of proceeding by tedious addresses, and was thought to have co-operated with the waters in removing the sterility of certain ladies, who had long undergone the reproach and disgust of their husbands; while Peregrine set up his throne among those who laboured under the disease of celibacy, from the pert miss of fifteen, who, with a fluttering heart, tosses her head, bridles up, and giggles involuntarily at sight of an handsome young man, to the staid maid of twenty-eight, who, with a demure aspect, moralises on the vanity of beauty, the folly of youth, and simplicity of woman, and expatiates on friendship, benevolence, and good sense, in the style of a Platonic philosopher.

In such a diversity of dispositions, his conquests were attended with all the heart-burnings, animosities, and turmoils of jealousy and spite. The younger class took all opportunities of mortifying their seniors in public, by treating them with that indignity which, contrary to the general privilege of age, is, by the consent and connivance of mankind, levelled against those who have the misfortune to come under the denomination of old maids; and these last retorted their hostilities in the private machinations of slander, supported by experience and subtilty of invention. Not one day passed in which some new story did not circulate, to the prejudice of one or other of those rivals.

If our hero, in the Long Room, chanced to quit one of the moralists, with whom he had been engaged in conversation, he was immediately accosted by a number of the opposite faction, who, with ironical smiles, upbraided him with cruelty to the poor lady he had left, exhorted him to have compassion on her sufferings; and, turning their eyes towards the object of their intercession, broke forth into an universal peal of laughter. On the other hand, when Peregrine, in consequence of having danced with one of the minors overnight, visited her in the morning, the Platonists immediately laid hold on the occasion, tasked their imaginations, associated ideas, and, with sage insinuations, retailed a thousand circumstances of the interview, which never had any foundation in truth. They observed, that, if girls are determined to behave with such indiscretion, they must lay their accounts with incurring the censure of the world; that she in question was old enough to act more circumspectly; and wondered that her mother would permit any young fellow to approach the chamber while her daughter was naked in bed. As for the servants peeping through the key-hole, to be sure it was an unlucky accident; but people ought to be upon their guard against such curiosity, and give their domestics no cause to employ their penetration. These and other such reflections were occasionally whispered as secrets among those who were known to be communicative; so that, in a few hours, it became the general topic of discourse; and, as it had been divulged under injunctions of secrecy, it was almost impossible to trace the scandal to its origin; because every person concerned must have promulgated her own breach of trust, in discovering her author of the report.

Peregrine, instead of allaying, rather exasperated this contention, by an artful distribution of his attention among the competitors; well knowing, that, should his regard be converged into one point, he would soon forfeit the pleasure he enjoyed in seeing them at variance; for both parties would join against the common enemy, and his favourite would be persecuted by the whole coalition. He perceived, that, among the secret agents of scandal, none were so busy as the physicians, a class of animals who live in this place, like so many ravens hovering about a carcass, and even ply for employment, like scullers at Hungerford Stairs. The greatest part of them have correspondents in London, who make it their business to inquire into the history, character, and distemper of every one that repairs to Bath, for the benefit of the waters, and if they cannot procure interest to recommend their medical friends to these patients before they set out, they at least furnish them with a previous account of what they could collect, that their correspondents may use this intelligence for their own advantage. By these means, and the assistance of flattery and assurance, they often insinuate themselves into the acquaintance of strangers, and, by consulting their dispositions, become necessary and subservient to their prevailing passions. By their connexion with apothecaries and nurses, they are informed of all the private occurrences in each family, and therefore enabled to gratify the rancour of malice, amuse the spleen of peevish indisposition, and entertain the eagerness of impertinent curiosity.

In the course of these occupations, which frequently affected the reputation of our two adventurers, this whole body fell under the displeasure of our hero, who, after divers consultations with his friend, concerted a stratagem, which was practised upon the faculty in this manner.   Among those who frequented the pump-room, was an old officer, whose temper, naturally impatient, was, by repeated attacks of the gout, which had almost deprived him of the use of his limbs, sublimated into a remarkable degree of virulence and perverseness.   He imputed the inveteracy of his distemper to the mal-practice of a surgeon who had administered to him, while he laboured under the consequences of an unfortunate amour; and this supposition had inspired him with an insurmountable antipathy to all the professors of the medical art, which was more and more confirmed by the information of a friend at London, who had told him, that it was the common practice among the physicians at Bath to dissuade their patients from drinking the water, that the cure, and in consequence their attendance, might be longer protracted.

Thus prepossessed, he had come to Bath, and, conformable to a few general instructions he had received, used the waters without any farther direction, taking all occasions of manifesting his hatred and contempt of the sons of Æsculapius, both by speech and gesticulations, and even by pursuing a regimen quite contrary to that which he knew they prescribed to others who seemed to be exactly in his condition.   But he did not find his account in this method, how successful soever it may have been in other cases.   His complaints, instead of vanishing, were every day more and more enraged; and at length he was confined to his bed, where he lay blaspheming from morn to night, and from night to morn, though still more determined than ever to adhere to his former maxims.

In the midst of his torture, which was become the common joke of the town, being circulated through the industry of the physicians, who triumphed in his disaster, Peregrine, by means of Mr. Pipes, employed a country fellow, who had come to market, to run with great haste, early one morning, to the lodgings of all the doctors in town, and desire them to attend the colonel with all imaginable despatch.   In consequence of this summons, the whole faculty put themselves in motion; and three of the foremost arriving at the same instant of time, far from complimenting one another with the door, each separately essayed to enter, and the whole triumvirate stuck in the passage.   While they remained thus wedged together, they descried two of their brethren posting towards the same goal, with all the speed that God had enabled them to exert; upon which they came to a parley, and agreed to stand by one another.   This covenant being made, they disentangled themselves, and, inquiring about the patient, were told by the servant that he had just fallen asleep.

Having received this intelligence, they took possession of his ante-chamber, and shut the door, while the rest of the tribe posted themselves on the outside as they arrived; so that the whole passage was filled, from the top of the staircase to the street door; and the people of the house, together with the colonel's servant, struck dumb with astonishment. The three leaders of this learned gang had no sooner made their lodgment good, than they began to consult about the patient's malady, which every one of them pretended to have considered with great care and assiduity. The first who gave his opinion, said, the distemper was an obstinate arthritis; the second affirmed, that it was no other than a confirmed pox; and the third swore, it was an inveterate scurvy. This diversity of opinions was supported by a variety of quotations from medical authors, ancient as well as modern; but these were not of sufficient authority, or, at least, not explicit enough to decide the dispute; for there are many schisms in medicine, as well as in religion, and each sect can quote the fathers in support of the tenets they profess. In short, the contention rose to such a pitch of clamour, as not only alarmed the brethren on the stair, but also awaked the patient from the first nap he had enjoyed in the space of ten whole days. Had it been simply waking, he would have been obliged to them for the noise that disturbed him; for, in that case, he would have been relieved from the tortures of hell fire, to which, in his dreams, he fancied himself exposed. But this dreadful vision had been the result of that impression which was made upon his brain by the intolerable anguish of his joints; so that, when he awaked, the pain, instead of being allayed, was rather aggravated by a great acuteness of sensation; and the confused vociferation in the next room invading his ears at the same time, he began to think his dream was realised, and, in the pangs of despair, applied himself to a bell that stood by his bedside, which he rung with great violence and perseverance.

This alarm put an immediate stop to the disputation of the three doctors, who, upon this notice of his being awake, rushed into his chamber, without ceremony; and two of them seizing his arms, the third made the like application to one of his temples. Before the patient could recollect himself from the amazement which had laid hold on him at this unexpected irruption, the room was filled by the rest of the faculty, who followed the servant that entered in obedience to his master's call; and the bed was in a moment surrounded by these gaunt ministers of death. The colonel seeing himself beset with such an assemblage of solemn visages and figures, which he had always considered with the utmost detestation and abhorrence, was incensed to a most inexpressible degree of indignation; and so inspirited by his rage, that though his tongue denied its office, his other limbs performed their functions. He disengaged himself from the triumvirate, who had taken possession of his body, sprung out of bed with incredible agility, and, seizing one of his crutches, applied it so effectually to one of the three, just as he stooped to examine the patient's water, that his tie-periwig dropped into the pot, while he himself fell motionless on the floor.

This significant explanation disconcerted the whole fraternity; every man turned his face, as if it were by instinct, towards the door; and the retreat of the community being obstructed by the efforts of individuals, confusion and tumultuous uproar ensued. For the colonel, far from limiting his prowess to the first exploit, handled his weapon with astonishing vigour and dexterity, without respect of persons; so that few or none of them had escaped without marks of his displeasure, when his spirits failed, and he sunk down again quite exhausted on his bed. Favoured by this respite, the discomfited faculty collected their hats and wigs, which had fallen off in the fray; and perceiving the assailant too much enfeebled to renew the attack, set up their throats together, and loudly threatened to prosecute him severely for such an outrageous assault.

By this time the landlord had interposed; and, inquiring into the cause of the disturbance, was informed of what had happened by the complainants, who, at the same time, giving him to understand that they had been severally summoned to attend the colonel that morning, he assured them that they had been imposed upon by some wag, for his lodger had never dreamed of consulting any one of their profession.

Thunderstruck at this declaration, the general clamour instantaneously ceased; and each, in particular, at once comprehending the nature of the joke, they sneaked silently off with the loss they had sustained, in unutterable shame and mortification; while Peregrine and his friend, who took care to be passing that way by accident, made a full stop at sight of such an extraordinary efflux, and enjoyed the countenance and condition of every one as he appeared; nay, even made up to some of those who seemed most affected with their situation, and mischievously tormented them with questions, touching this unusual congregation; then, in consequence of the information they received from the landlord and the colonel's valet, subjected the sufferers to the ridicule of all the company in town. As it would have been impossible for the authors of this farce to keep themselves concealed from the indefatigable inquiries of the physicians, they made no secret of their having directed the whole; though they took care to own it in such an ambiguous manner, as afforded no handle of prosecution.

CHAPTER LXXI

Peregrine humbles a noted Hector, and meets with a strange Character at the House of a certain Lady.

AMONG those who never failed to reside at Bath during the season, was a certain person, who, from the most abject misery, had, by his industry and art at play, amassed about fifteen thousand pounds; and though his character was notorious, insinuated himself so far into the favour of what is called the best company, that very few private parties of pleasure took place in which he was not principally concerned. He was of a gigantic stature, a most intrepid countenance; and his disposition, naturally overbearing, had, in the course of his adventures and success, acquired a most intolerable degree of insolence and vanity. By the ferocity of his features, and audacity of his behaviour, he had obtained a reputation for the most undaunted courage, which had been confirmed by divers adventures, in which he had humbled the most assuming heroes of his own fraternity; so that he now reigned chief Hector of the place with unquestioned authority.

With this son of fortune was Peregrine one evening engaged at play, and so successful, that he could not help informing his friend of his good luck. Godfrey, hearing the description of the loser, immediately recognised the person, whom he had known at Tunbridge; and, assuring Pickle that he was a sharper of the first water, cautioned him against any further connexion with such a dangerous companion, who, he affirmed, had suffered him to win a small sum, that he might be encouraged to lose a much greater sum upon some other occasion.

Our young gentleman treasured up this advice; and though

he did not scruple to give the gamester an opportunity of re-
trieving his loss, when he next day demanded his revenge, he
absolutely refused to proceed after he had refunded his winning.
The other, who considered him as a hot-headed unthinking youth,
endeavoured to inflame his pride to a continuance of the game,
by treating his skill with scorn and contempt; and, among other
sarcastic expressions, advised him to go to school again, before
he pretended to engage with masters of the art. Our hero, incensed at his arrogance, replied with great warmth, that he knew
himself sufficiently qualified for playing with men of honour,
who deal upon the square, and hoped he should always deem it
infamous either to learn or practise the tricks of a professed
gamester. "Blood and thunder! meaning me, sir?" cried this
artist, raising his voice, and curling his visage into a most in-
timidating frown. "Zounds! I'll cut the throat of any scoundrel
who has the presumption to suppose that I don't play as honourably as e'er a nobleman in the kingdom: and I insist upon an
explanation from you, sir; or, by hell and brimstone! I shall expect
other sort of satisfaction." Peregrine (whose blood by this time
boiled within him) answered without hesitation, "Far from
thinking your demand unreasonable, I will immediately explain
myself without reserve, and tell you, that, upon unquestionable
authority, I believe you to be an impudent rascal and common
cheat."

The Hector was so amazed and confounded at the freedom of
this declaration, which he thought no man on earth would venture to make in his presence, that, for some minutes, he could
not recollect himself; but at length whispered a challenge in the
ear of our hero, which was accordingly accepted. When they
arrived next morning upon the field, the gamester, arming his
countenance with all its terrors, advanced with a sword of a
monstrous length, and, putting himself in a posture, called out
aloud in a most terrific voice, "Draw, d—n ye, draw; I will this
instant send you to your fathers." The youth was not slow in
complying with his desire; his weapon was unsheathed in a
moment, and he began the attack with such unexpected spirit
and address, that his adversary, having made shift with great
difficulty to parry the first pass, retreated a few paces, and demanded a parley, in which he endeavoured to persuade the young
man, that to lay a man of his character under the necessity of
chastising his insolence, was the most rash and inconsiderate
step that he could possibly have taken; but that he had compassion upon his youth, and was willing to spare him if he would

surrender his sword, and promise to ask pardon in public for the offence he had given. Pickle was so much exasperated at this unparalleled effrontery, that, without deigning to make the least reply, he flung his own hat in the proposer's face, and renewed the charge with such undaunted agility, that the gamester, finding himself in manifest hazard of his life, betook himself to his heels, and fled homewards with incredible speed, being closely pursued by Peregrine, who, having sheathed his sword, pelted him with stones as he ran, and compelled him to go, that same day, into banishment from Bath, where he had domineered so long.

By this achievement, which was the subject of astonishment to all the company, who had looked upon the fugitive as a person of heroic courage, our adventurer's reputation was rendered formidable in all its circumstances; although he thereby disobliged a good many people of fashion, who had contracted an intimacy of friendship with the exile, and who resented his disgrace, as if it had been the misfortune of a worthy man. These generous patrons, however, bore a very small proportion to those who were pleased with the event of the duel; because, in the course of their residence at Bath, they had either been insulted or defrauded by the challenger. Nor was this instance of our hero's courage unacceptable to the ladies, few of whom could now resist the united force of such accomplishments. Indeed, neither he nor his friend Godfrey would have found much difficulty in picking up an agreeable companion for life; but Gauntlet's heart was pre-engaged to Sophy; and Pickle, exclusive of his attachment to Emily, which was stronger than he himself imagined, possessed such a share of ambition as could not be satisfied with the conquest of any female he beheld at Bath.

His visits were, therefore, promiscuous, without any other view than that of amusement; and though his pride was flattered by the advances of the fair, whom he had captivated, he never harboured one thought of proceeding beyond the limits of common gallantry, and carefully avoided all particular explanations. But, what above all other enjoyments yielded him the most agreeable entertainment, was the secret history of characters, which he learned from a very extraordinary person, with whom he became acquainted in this manner.

Being at the house of a certain lady on a visiting day, he was struck with the appearance of an old man, who no sooner entered the room than the mistress of the house very kindly desired one of the wits present to roast the old put. This petit-maître, proud of the employment, went up to the senior, who had something extremely peculiar and significant in his countenance, and saluting him with divers fashionable congees, accosted him in these words: "Your servant, you old rascal. I hope to have the honour of seeing you hang'd. I vow to Gad! you look extremely shocking, with these gummy eyes, lanthorn jaws, and toothless chaps. What! you squint at the ladies, you old rotten medlar? Yes, yes, we understand your ogling; but you must content yourself with a cookmaid, sink me! I see you want to sit. These wither'd shanks of yours tremble under their burden; but you must have a little patience, old Hirco; indeed you must. I intend to mortify you a little longer, curse me!"

The company was so tickled with this address, which was delivered with much grimace and gesticulation, that they burst out into a loud fit of laughter, which they fathered upon a monkey that was chained in the room; and, when the peal was over, the wit renewed the attack in these words: "I suppose you are fool enough to think this mirth was occasioned by Pug. Ay, there he is; you had best survey him; he is of your own family; switch me. But the laugh was at your expense; and you ought to thank Heaven for making you so ridiculous." While he uttered these ingenious ejaculations, the old gentleman bowed alternately to him and the monkey, that seemed to grin and chatter in imitation of the beau, and, with an arch solemnity of visage, pronounced, "Gentlemen, as I have not the honour to understand your compliments, they will be much better bestowed on each other." So saying, he seated himself, and had the satisfaction to see the laugh returned upon the aggressor, who remained confounded and abashed, and in a few minutes left the room, muttering, as he retired, "The old fellow grows scurrilous, stap my breath!"

While Peregrine wondered in silence at this extraordinary scene, the lady of the house perceiving his surprise, gave him to understand, that the ancient visitant was utterly bereft of the sense of hearing; that his name was Cadwallader Crabtree, his disposition altogether misanthropical; and that he was admitted into company on account of entertainment he afforded by his sarcastic observations, and the pleasant mistakes to which he was subject from his infirmity. Nor did our hero wait a long time for an illustration of this odd character. Every sentence he spoke was replete with gall; nor did his satire consist in general reflections, but a series of remarks, which had been made through the medium of a most whimsical peculiarity of opinion.

Among those who were present at this assembly was a young officer, who having, by dint of interest, obtained a seat in the Lower House, thought it incumbent upon him to talk of affairs of state; and accordingly regaled the company with an account of a secret expedition which the French were busied in preparing; assuring them that he had it from the mouth of the minister, to whom it had been transmitted by one of his agents abroad.   In descanting upon the particulars of the armament, he observed that they had twenty ships of the line ready manned and victualled at Brest, which were destined for Toulon, where they would be joined by as many more; and from thence proceed to the execution of their scheme, which he imparted as a secret not fit to be divulged.

This piece of intelligence being communicated to all the company except Mr. Crabtree, who suffered by his loss of hearing, that cynic was soon after accosted by a lady, who, by means of an artificial alphabet, formed by a certain conjunction and disposition of the fingers, asked if he had heard any extraordinary news of late?   Cadwallader, with his usual complaisance, replied, that he supposed she took him for a courier or spy, by teasing him eternally with that question.   He then expatiated upon the foolish curiosity of mankind, which, he said, must either proceed from idleness or want of ideas; and repeated almost verbatim the officer's information, a vague ridiculous report invented by some ignorant coxcomb, who wanted to give himself airs of importance, and believed only by those who were utterly unacquainted with the politics and strength of the French nation.

In confirmation of what he had advanced, he endeavoured to demonstrate how impossible it must be for that people to fit out even the third part of such a navy, so soon after the losses they had sustained during the war; and confirmed his proof by asserting, that to his certain knowledge, the harbours of Brest and Toulon could not at that time produce a squadron of eight ships of the line.

The member, who was an utter stranger to this misanthrope, hearing his own asseverations treated with such contempt, glowed with confusion and resentment, and, raising his voice, began to defend his own veracity, with great eagerness and trepidation, mingling with his arguments many blustering invectives, against the insolence and ill-manners of his supposed contradictor, who sat with the most mortifying composure of countenance, till the officer's patience was quite exhausted, and then, to the manifest increase of his vexation, he was informed, that his antagonist was so deaf, that in all probability, the last trumpet would make no impression upon him, without a previous renovation of his organs.

CHAPTER LXXII

He cultivates an Acquaintance with the Misanthrope, who favours him with a short Sketch of his own History.

PEREGRINE was extremely well pleased with this occasional rebuke, which occurred so seasonably, that he could scarce believe it accidental. He looked upon Cadwallader as the greatest curiosity he had ever known, and cultivated the old man's acquaintance with such insinuating address, that in less than a fortnight he obtained his confidence. As they one day walked into the fields together, the man-hater disclosed himself in these words:—"Though the term of our communication has been but short, you must have perceived, that I treat you with uncommon marks of regard; which, I assure you, is not owing to your personal accomplishments, nor the pains you take to oblige me; for the first I overlook, and the last I see through. But there is something in your disposition which indicates a rooted contempt for the world, and I understand you have made some successful efforts in exposing one part of it to the ridicule of the other. It is upon this assurance that I offer you my advice and assistance, in prosecuting other schemes of the same nature; and to convince you that such an alliance is not to be rejected, I will now give you a short sketch of my history, which will be published after my death, in forty-seven volumes of my own compiling.

"I was born about forty miles from this place, of parents who, having a very old family name to support, bestowed their whole fortune on my elder brother; so that I inherited of my father little else than a large share of choler, to which I am indebted for a great many adventures that did not always end to my satisfaction. At the age of eighteen I was sent up to town, with a recommendation to a certain peer, who found means to amuse me with the promise of a commission for seven whole years; and 'tis odds but I should have made my fortune by my perseverance, had not I been arrested, and thrown into the Marshalsea by my landlord, on whose credit I had subsisted three years, after my father had renounced me as an idle vagabond. There I remained six months, among those prisoners who have no other support than chance charity; and contracted a very valuable acquaintance, which was of great service to me in the future emergencies of my life.

"I was no sooner discharged, in consequence of an act of parliament for the relief of insolvent debtors, than I went to the house of my creditor, whom I cudgelled without mercy; and, that I might leave nothing undone of those things which I ought to have done, my next stage was to Westminster Hall, where I waited until my patron came forth from the house, and saluted him with a blow that laid him senseless on the pavement. But my retreat was not so fortunate as I could have wished. The chairmen and lacqueys in waiting having surrounded and disarmed me in a trice, I was committed to Newgate, and loaded with chains; and a very sagacious gentleman, who was afterwards hanged, having sat in judgment upon my case, pronounced me guilty of a capital crime, and foretold my condemnation at the Old Bailey. His prognostic, however, was disappointed; for nobody appearing to prosecute me at the next session, I was discharged by order of the court. It would be impossible for me to recount, in the compass of one day's conversation, all the particular exploits of which I bore considerable share. Suffice it to say, I have been, at different times, prisoner in all the jails within the bills of mortality. I have broken from every roundhouse on this side Temple Bar. No bailiff, in the days of my youth and desperation, durst execute a writ upon me without a dozen of followers; and the justices themselves trembled when I was brought before them.

"I was once maimed by a carman, with whom I quarrelled, because he ridiculed my leek on St. David's day; my skull was fractured by a butcher's cleaver on the like occasion. I have been run through the body five times, and lost the tip of my left ear by a pistol bullet. In a rencontre of this kind, having left my antagonist for dead, I was wise enough to make my retreat into France; and a few days after my arrival at Paris, entering into conversation with some officers on the subject of politics, a dispute arose, in which I lost my temper, and spoke so irreverently of the *grand monarque,* that next morning I was sent to the Bastile, by virtue of a *lettre de cachet.* There I remained for some months, deprived of all intercourse with rational creatures; a circumstance for which I was not sorry, as I had the more time to project schemes of revenge against the tyrant who confined me, and the wretch who had betrayed my private conversation. But tired, at length, with these fruitless suggestions, I was fain to unbend the severity of my thoughts by a correspondence with some industrious spiders, who had hung my dungeon with their ingenious labours.

"I considered their work with such attention that I soon became an adept in the mystery of weaving, and furnished myself with as many useful observations and reflections on that art, as will compose a very curious treatise, which I intend to bequeath to the Royal Society, for the benefit of our woollen manufacture; and this with a view to perpetuate my own name, rather than befriend my country. For, thank Heaven! I am weaned from all attachments of that kind, and look upon myself as one very little obliged to any society whatsoever. Although I presided with absolute power over this long-legged community, and distributed punishments and rewards to each, according to his deserts, I grew impatient of my situation; and my natural disposition one day prevailing, like a fire which had long been smothered, I wreaked the fury of my indignation upon my innocent subjects, and in a twinkling destroyed the whole race. While I was employed in this general massacre, the turnkey, who brought me food, opened the door, and perceiving my transport, shrugged up his shoulders, and leaving my allowance, went out, pronouncing, *Le pauvre diable! la tête lui tourne.* My passion no sooner subsided than I resolved to profit by this opinion of the jailor, and from that day counterfeited lunacy with such success, that in less than three months I was delivered from the Bastile, and sent to the galleys, in which they thought my bodily vigour might be of service, although the faculties of my mind were decayed. Before I was chained to the oar, I received three hundred stripes by way of welcome, that I might thereby be rendered more tractable, notwithstanding I used all the arguments in my power to persuade them I was only *mad north-north-west, and, when the wind was southerly, knew a hawk from a hand-saw.*

"In our second cruise we had the good fortune to be overtaken by a tempest, during which the slaves were unbound, that they might contribute the more to the preservation of the galley, and have a chance for their lives, in case of shipwreck. We were no sooner at liberty, than, making ourselves masters of the vessel, we robbed the officers, and ran her on shore among rocks on the coast of Portugal; from whence I hastened to Lisbon, with a view of obtaining my passage in some ship bound for England, where, by this time, I hoped my affair was forgotten.

"But, before this scheme could be accomplished, my evil genius led me into company; and, being intoxicated, I began to broach doctrines on the subject of religion, at which some of the party were scandalised and incensed; and I was next day dragged out of bed by the officers of the Inquisition, and conveyed to a cell in the prison belonging to that tribunal.

"At my first examination, my resentment was strong enough to support me under the torture, which I endured without flinching; but my resolution abated, and my zeal immediately cooled, when I understood from a fellow-prisoner, who groaned on the other side of the partition, that in a short time there would be an *auto da fé*; in consequence of which I should, in all probability, be doomed to the flames, if I would not renounce my heretical errors, and submit to such penance as the church should think fit to prescribe. This miserable wretch was convicted of Judaism, which he had privately practised by connivance for many years, until he had amassed a fortune sufficient to attract the regard of the church. To this he fell a sacrifice, and accordingly prepared himself for the stake; while I, not at all ambitious of the crown of martyrdom, resolved to temporise. So that, when I was brought to the question the second time, I made a solemn recantation. As I had no worldly fortune to obstruct my salvation, I was received into the bosom of the church, and, by way of penance, enjoined to walk barefoot to Rome in the habit of a pilgrim.

"During my peregrination through Spain, I was detained as a spy, until I could procure credentials from the Inquisition at Lisbon; and behaved with such resolution and reserve, that, after being released, I was deemed a proper person to be employed in quality of a secret intelligencer at a certain court. This office I undertook without hesitation; and being furnished with money and bills of credit, crossed the Pyrenees, with intention to revenge myself upon the Spaniards for the severities I had undergone during my captivity.

"Having therefore effectually disguised myself by a change of dress, and a large patch on one eye, I hired an equipage, and appeared at Bologna in quality of an itinerant physician; in which capacity I succeeded tolerably well, till my servants decamped in the night with my baggage, and left me in the condition of Adam. In short, I have travelled over the greatest part of Europe, as a beggar, pilgrim, priest, soldier, gamester, and quack; and felt the extremes of indigence and opulence, with the inclemency of weather in all its vicissitudes. I have learned that the characters of mankind are everywhere the same; that common sense and honesty bear an infinitely small proportion to folly and vice; and that life is at best a paltry province.

"After having suffered innumerable hardships, dangers, and disgraces, I returned to London, where I lived some years in a garret, and picked up a subsistence, such as it was, by vending purges in the streets, from the back of a pied horse; in which situation I used to harangue the mob in broken English, under pretence of being an High German doctor.

"At last an uncle died, by whom I inherited an estate of three hundred pounds per annum, though, in his lifetime, he would not have parted with a sixpence to save my soul and body from perdition.

"I now appear in the world, not as a member of any community, or what is called a social creature, but merely as a spectator, who entertains himself with the grimaces of a Jackpudding, and banquets his spleen in beholding his enemies at loggerheads. That I may enjoy this disposition, abstracted from all interruption, danger, and participation, I feign myself deaf; an expedient by which I not only avoid all disputes and their consequences, but also become master of a thousand little secrets, which are every day whispered in my presence, without any suspicion of their being overheard. You saw how I handled that shallow politician at my Lady Plausible's the other day. The same method I practise upon the crazed Tory, the bigot Whig, the sour, supercilious pedant, the petulant critic, the blustering coward, the fawning tool, the pert imp, sly sharper, and every other species of knaves and fools, with which this kingdom abounds.

"In consequence of my rank and character, I obtain free admission to the ladies, among whom I have acquired the appellation of the Scandalous Chronicle. As I am considered, while silent, in no other light than that of a footstool or elbow-chair, they divest their conversation of all restraint before me, and gratify my sense of hearing with strange things, which, if I could prevail upon myself to give the world that satisfaction, would compose a curious piece of secret history, and exhibit a quite different idea of characters from what is commonly entertained.

"By this time, young gentleman, you may perceive that I have it in my power to be a valuable correspondent, and that it will be to your interest to deserve my confidence."

Here the misanthrope left off speaking, desirous to know the sentiments of our hero, who embraced the proffered alliance in a transport of joy and surprise; and the treaty was no sooner concluded, than Mr. Crabtree began to perform articles, by imparting to him a thousand delicious secrets, from the possession of which he promised himself innumerable scenes of mirth and enjoyment.   By means of this associate, whom he considered as the ring of Gyges, he foresaw, that he should be enabled to penetrate, not only into the chambers, but even to the inmost thoughts of the female sex.   In order to ward off suspicion, they agreed to revile each other in public, and meet at a certain private rendezvous, to communicate their mutual discoveries, and concert their future operations.

In consequence of a letter from Lieutenant Hatchway, representing the dangerous situation of the commodore, Peregrine took a hasty leave of his friends, and departed immediately for the garrison.

CHAPTER LXXIII

Peregrine arrives at the Garrison, where he receives the last Admonitions of Commodore Trunnion, who next Day resigns his Breath, and is buried according to his own Directions—Some Gentlemen in the Country make a fruitless Attempt to accommodate Matters betwixt Mr. Gamaliel Pickle and his eldest Son.

About four o'clock in the morning our hero arrived at the garrison, where he found his generous uncle in extremity, supported in bed by Julia on one side, and Lieutenant Hatchway on the other, while Mr. Jolter administered spiritual consolation to his soul; and between whiles comforted Mrs. Trunnion, who, with her maid, sat by the fire, weeping with great decorum; the physician having just taken his last fee, and retired, after pronouncing the fatal prognostic, in which he anxiously wished he might be mistaken.

Though the commodore's speech was interrupted by a violent hiccup, he still retained the use of his senses; and, when Peregrine approached, stretched out his hand with manifest signs of satisfaction.   The young gentleman, whose heart overflowed with gratitude and affection, could not behold such a spectacle unmoved.   He endeavoured to conceal his tenderness, which, in the wildness of his youth, and the pride of his disposition, he considered as a derogation from his manhood; but, in spite of all his endeavours, the tears gushed from his eyes, while he kissed the old man's hand; and he was so utterly disconcerted by his grief, that, when he attempted to speak, his tongue denied its office;—so that the commodore, perceiving his disorder, made a last effort of strength, and consoled him in these words—

"Swab the spray from your bowsprit, my good lad, and coil up your spirits. You must not let the toplifts of your heart give way, because you see me ready to go down at these years. Many a better man has foundered before he has made half my way; thof I trust, by the mercy of God, I shall be sure in port in a very few glasses, and fast moored in a most blessed riding; for my good friend Jolter hath overhauled the journal of my sins, and, by the observation he hath taken of the state of my soul, I hope I shall happily conclude my voyage, and be brought up in the latitude of heaven. Here has been a doctor that wanted to stow me chock full of physic; but, when a man's hour is come, what signifies his taking his departure with a 'pothecary's shop in his hold? Those fellows come alongside of dying men, like the messengers of the Admiralty with sailing orders; but I told him as how I could slip my cable without his direction or assistance, and so he hauled off in dudgeon. This cursed hiccup makes such a rippling in the current of my speech, that mayhap you don't understand what I say. Now, while the sucker of my wind-pump will go, I would willingly mention a few things, which I hope you will set down in the log-book of your remembrance, when I am stiff, d'ye see. There's your aunt sitting whimpering by the fire; I desire you will keep her tight, warm, and easy in her old age; she's an honest heart in her own way, and, thof she goes a little crank and humoursome, by being often overstowed with Nantz and religion, she has been a faithful shipmate to me, and I daresay she never turned in with another man since we first embarked in the same bottom. Jack Hatchway, you know the trim of her as well as e'er a man in England, and I believe she has a kindness for you; whereby, if you two will grapple in the way of matrimony, when I am gone, I do suppose that my godson, for love of me, will allow you to live in the garrison all the days of your life."

Peregrine assured him, he would with pleasure comply with any request he should make in behalf of two persons whom he esteemed so much. The lieutenant, with a waggish sneer, which even the gravity of the situation could not prevent, thanked them both for their good-will, telling the commodore, he was obliged to him for his friendship, in seeking to promote him to the command of a vessel which he himself had wore out in the service; but that, notwithstanding, he should be content to take charge of her, though he could not help being shy of coming after such an able navigator.

Trunnion, exhausted as he was, smiled at this sally, and, after some pause, resumed his admonitions in this manner:—"I need not talk of Pipes, because I know you'll do for him without any recommendation; the fellow has sailed with me in many a hard gale, and I'll warrant him as stout a seaman as ever set face to the weather. But I hope you'll take care of the rest of my crew, and not disrate them after I am dead, in favour of new followers. As for that young woman, Ned Gauntlet's daughter, I'm informed as how she's an excellent wench, and has a respect for you; whereby, if you run her on board in an unlawful way, I leave my curse upon you, and trust you will never prosper in the voyage of life. But I believe you are more of an honest man, than to behave so much like a pirate. I beg of all love you wool take care of your constitution, and beware of running foul of harlots, who are no better than so many mermaids, that sit upon rocks in the sea, and hang out a fair face for the destruction of passengers; thof I must say, for my own part, I never met with any of those sweet singers, and yet I have gone to sea for the space of thirty years. But howsomever, steer your course clear of all such brimstone b—es. Shun going to law, as you would shun the devil; and look upon all attorneys as devouring sharks, or ravenous fish of prey. As soon as the breath is out of my body, let minute guns be fired, till I am safe under ground. I would also be buried in the red jacket I had on when I boarded and took the *Renummy*. Let my pistols, cutlass, and pocket-compass be laid in the coffin along with me. Let me be carried to the grave by my own men, rigged in the black caps and white shirts which my barge's crew were wont to wear; and they must keep a good lookout, that none of your pilfering rascallions may come and heave me up again, for the lucre of what they can get, until the carcass is belayed by a tombstone. As for the motto, or what you call it, I leave that to you and Mr. Jolter, who are scholars; but I do desire, that it may not be engraved in the Greek or Latin lingos, and much less in the French, which I abominate, but in plain English, that, when the angel comes to pipe all hands, at the great day, he may know that I am a British man, and speak to me in my mother tongue. And now I have no more to say, but God in heaven have mercy upon my soul, and send you all fair weather, wheresoever you are bound."

So saying, he regarded every individual around him with a look of complacency, and closing his eye, composed himself to rest, while the whole audience, Pipes himself not excepted, were melted with sorrow; and Mrs. Trunnion consented to quit the room, that she might not be exposed to the unspeakable anguish of seeing him expire.

His last moments, however, were not so near as they imagined. He began to doze, and enjoyed small intervals of ease, till next day in the afternoon; during which remissions, he was heard to pour forth many pious ejaculations, expressing his hope, that, for all the heavy cargo of his sins, he should be able to surmount the puttock-shrouds of despair, and get aloft to the cross-trees of God's good favour. At last his voice sunk so low as not to be distinguished; and, having lain about an hour, almost without any perceptible signs of life, he gave up the ghost with a groan which announced his decease.

Julia was no sooner certified of this melancholy event, than she ran to her aunt's chamber, weeping aloud; and immediately a very decent concert was performed by the good widow and her attendants. Peregrine and Hatchway retired till the corpse should be laid out; and Pipes having surveyed the body, with a face of rueful attention,—"Well fare thy soul! old Hawser Trunnion," said he; "man and boy I have known thee these five-and-thirty years, and sure a truer heart never broke biscuit. Many a hard gale hast thou weathered; but now thy spells are all over, and thy hull fairly laid up. A better commander I'd never desire to serve; and who knows but I may help to set up thy standing rigging in another world?"

All the servants of the house were affected with the loss of their old master; and the poor people in the neighbourhood assembled at the gate, and, by repeated howlings, expressed their sorrow for the death of their charitable benefactor. Peregrine, though he felt everything which love and gratitude could inspire on this occasion, was not so much overwhelmed with affliction, as to be incapable of taking the management of the family into his own hands. He gave directions about the funeral with great discretion, after having paid the compliments of condolence to his aunt, whom he consoled with the assurance of his inviolable esteem and affection. He ordered a suit of mourning to be made for every person in the garrison, and invited all the neighbouring gentlemen to the burial, not even excepting his father and brother Gam, who did not, however, honour the ceremony with their presence; nor was his mother humane enough to visit her sister-in-law in her distress.

In the method of interment, the commodore's injunctions

were obeyed to a tittle; and at the same time our hero made a donation of fifty pounds to the poor of the parish, as a benefaction which his uncle had forgot to bequeath.

Having performed these obsequies with the most pious punctuality, he examined the will, to which there was no addition since it had first been executed, adjusted the payment of all the legacies, and, being sole executor, took an account of the estate to which he had succeeded, which, after all deductions, amounted to thirty thousand pounds. The possession of such a fortune, of which he was absolute master, did not at all contribute to the humiliation of his spirit, but inspired him with new ideas of grandeur and magnificence, and elevated his hope to the highest pinnacle of expectation.

His domestic affairs being settled, he was visited by almost all the gentlemen of the county, who came to pay their compliments of congratulation on his accession to the estate; and some of them offered their good offices towards a reconciliation betwixt his father and him, induced by the general detestation which was entertained for his brother Gam, who was by this time looked upon by his neighbours as a prodigy of insolence and malice. Our young squire thanked them for their kind proposal, which he accepted; and old Gamaliel, at their entreaties, seemed very well disposed to any accommodation; but as he would not venture to declare himself before he had consulted his wife, his favourable disposition was rendered altogether ineffectual, by the instigations of that implacable woman; and our hero resigned all expectation of being reunited to his father's house. His brother, as usual, took all opportunities of injuring his character, by false aspersions, and stories misrepresented, in order to prejudice his reputation; nor was his sister Julia suffered to enjoy her good fortune in peace. Had he undergone such persecution from an alien to his blood, the world would have heard of his revenge; but, notwithstanding his indignation, he was too much tinctured by the prejudices of consanguinity, to lift his arm in judgment against the son of his own parents; and this consideration abridged the term of his residence at the garrison, where he had proposed to stay for some months.

CHAPTER LXXIV

The young Gentleman having settled his domestic Affairs, arrives in London, and sets up a gay Equipage—He meets with Emilia, and is introduced to her Uncle.

HIS aunt, at the earnest solicitations of Julia and her husband, took up her quarters at the house of that affectionate kinswoman, who made it her chief study to comfort and cherish the disconsolate widow; and Jolter, in expectation of the living, which was not yet vacant, remained in garrison, in quality of land-steward upon our hero's country estate. As for the lieutenant, our young gentleman communed with him in a serious manner, about the commodore's proposal of taking Mrs. Trunnion to wife; and Jack, being quite tired of the solitary situation of a bachelor, which nothing but the company of his old commander could have enabled him to support so long, far from discovering aversion from the match, observed with an arch smile, that it was not the first time he had commanded a vessel in the absence of Captain Trunnion; and therefore, if the widow was willing, he would cheerfully stand by her helm, and, as he hoped the duty would not be of long continuance, do his endeavour to steer her safe into port, where the commodore might come on board, and take charge of her again.

In consequence of this declaration, it was determined that Mr. Hatchway should make his addresses to Mrs. Trunnion as soon as decency would permit her to receive them; and Mr. Clover and his wife promised to exert their influence on his behalf. Meanwhile Jack was desired to live at the castle as usual, and assured, that it should be put wholly in his possession, as soon as he should be able to accomplish this matrimonial scheme.

When Peregrine had settled all these points to his own satisfaction, he took leave of all his friends, and, repairing to the great city, purchased a new chariot and horses, put Pipes and another lacquey into rich liveries, took elegant lodgings in Pall Mall, and made a most remarkable appearance among the people of fashion. It was owing to this equipage, and the gaiety of his personal deportment, that common fame, which is always a common liar, represented him as a young gentleman who had just succeeded to an estate of five thousand pounds *per annum*, by the death of an uncle; that he was entitled to an equal fortune at the decease of his own father, exclusive of two considerable jointures, which would devolve upon him at the demise of his mother and aunt.

This report, false and ridiculous as it was, he could not find in his heart to contradict. Not but that he was sorry to find himself so misrepresented; but his vanity would not allow him to take any step that might diminish his importance in the opinion of those who courted his acquaintance, on the supposition that his circumstances were actually as affluent as they were said to be. Nay, so much was he infatuated by this weakness, that he resolved to encourage the deception, by living up to the report; and accordingly engaged in the most expensive parties of pleasure, believing that, before his present finances should be exhausted, his fortune would be effectually made, by the personal accomplishments he should have occasion to display to the beau monde in the course of his extravagance. In a word, vanity and pride were the ruling foibles of our adventurer, who imagined himself sufficiently qualified to retrieve his fortune in various shapes, long before he could have any idea of want or difficulty. He thought he should have it in his power, at any time, to make a prize of a rich heiress, or opulent widow; his ambition had already aspired to the heart of a young handsome duchess dowager, to whose acquaintance he had found means to be introduced; or, should matrimony chance to be unsuitable to his inclinations, he never doubted, that, by the interest he might acquire among the nobility, he should be favoured with some lucrative post, that would amply recompense him for the liberality of his disposition. There are many young men who entertain the same expectations, with half the reason he had to be so presumptuous.

In the midst of these chimerical calculations, his passion for Emilia did not subside; but, on the contrary, began to rage with such an inflammation of desire, that her idea interfered with every other reflection, and absolutely disabled him from prosecuting the other lofty schemes which his imagination had projected. He therefore laid down the honest resolution of visiting her in all the splendour of his situation, in order to practise upon her virtue with all his art and address, to the utmost extent of his affluence and fortune. Nay, so effectually had his guilty passion absorbed his principles of honour, conscience, humanity, and regard for the commodore's last words, that he was base enough to rejoice at the absence of his friend Godfrey, who, being then with his regiment in Ireland, could not dive into his purpose, or take measures for frustrating his vicious design.

Fraught with these heroic sentiments, he determined to set out for Sussex in his chariot and six, attended by his valet-de-chambre and two footmen; and as he was now sensible, that in his last essay he had mistaken his cue, he determined to change his battery, and sap the fortress, by the most submissive, soft, and insinuating behaviour.

On the evening that preceded this proposed expedition, he went into one of the boxes at the playhouse, as usual, to show himself to the ladies; and reconnoitring the company through a glass, for no other reason but because it was fashionable to be purblind, perceived his mistress very plainly dressed, in one of the seats above the stage, talking to another young woman of a very homely appearance. Though his heart beat the alarm with the utmost impatience at sight of his Emilia, he was for some minutes deterred from obeying the impulse of his love, by the presence of some ladies of fashion, who, he feared, would think the worse of him, should they see him make his compliment in public to a person of her figure. Nor would the violence of his inclination have so far prevailed over his pride, as to lead him thither, had he not recollected, that his quality friends would look upon her as some handsome Abigail, with whom he had an affair of gallantry, and of consequence give him credit for the intrigue.

Encouraged by this suggestion, he complied with the dictates of love, and flew to the place where his charmer sat. His air and dress were so remarkable, that it was almost impossible he should have escaped the eyes of a curious observer, especially as he had chosen a time for coming in, when his entrance could not fail to attract the notice of the spectators; I mean, when the whole house was hushed in attention to the performance on the stage. Emilia, therefore, perceived him at his first approach; she found herself discovered by the direction of his glass, and, guessing his intention by his abrupt retreat from the box, summoned all her fortitude to her aid, and prepared for his reception. He advanced to her with an air of eagerness and joy, tempered with modesty and respect, and expressed his satisfaction at seeing her, with a seeming reverence of regard. Though she was extremely well pleased at this unexpected behaviour, she suppressed the emotions of her heart, and answered his compliments with affected ease and unconcern, such as might denote the good humour of a person who meets by accident with an indifferent acquaintance. After having certified himself of her own good health, he very kindly inquired about her mother and Miss Sophy, gave her to understand that he had lately been favoured with a letter from Godfrey; that he had actually intended to set out next morning on a visit to Mrs. Gauntlet, which, now that he was so happy as to meet with her, he would postpone, until he should have the pleasure of attending her to the country. After having thanked him for his polite intention, she told him, that her mother was expected in town in a few days, and that she herself had come to London some weeks ago, to give attendance upon her aunt, who had been dangerously ill, but was now pretty well recovered.

Although the conversation of course turned upon general topics, during the entertainment he took all opportunities of being particular with his eyes, through which he conveyed a thousand tender protestations. She saw and inwardly rejoiced at the humility of his looks; but, far from rewarding it with one approving glance, she industriously avoided this ocular intercourse, and rather coquetted with a young gentleman that ogled her from the opposite box. Peregrine's penetration easily detected her sentiments, and he was nettled at her dissimulation, which served to confirm him in his unwarrantable designs upon her person. He persisted in his assiduities with indefatigable perseverance; when the play was concluded, handed her and her companion into an hackney-coach, and with difficulty was permitted to escort them to the house of Emilia's uncle, to whom our hero was introduced by the young lady, as an intimate friend of her brother Godfrey.

The old gentleman, who was no stranger to the nature of Peregrine's connexion with his sister's family, prevailed upon him to stay supper, and seemed particularly well pleased with his conversation and deportment, which, by the help of his natural sagacity, he wonderfully adapted to the humour of his entertainer. After supper, when the ladies were withdrawn, and the citizen called for his pipe, our sly adventurer followed his example. Though he abhorred the plant, he smoked with an air of infinite satisfaction, and expatiated upon the virtues of tobacco, as if he had been deeply concerned in the Virginia trade. In the progress of the discourse, he consulted the merchant's disposition; and the national debt coming upon the carpet, held forth upon the funds like a professed broker. When the alderman complained of the restrictions and discouragements of trade, his guest inveighed against exorbitant duties, with the nature of which he seemed as well acquainted as any commissioner of the customs; so that the uncle was astonished at the extent of his knowledge, and expressed his surprise that a gay young gentleman like him should have found either leisure or inclination to consider subjects so foreign to the fashionable amusements of youth.

Pickle laid hold on this opportunity to tell him, that he was descended from a race of merchants; and that, early in life, he had made it his business to instruct himself in the different branches of trade, which he not only studied as his family profession, but also as the source of all our national riches and power. He then launched out in praise of commerce, and the promoters thereof; and, by way of contrast, employed all his ridicule in drawing such ludicrous pictures of the manners and education of what is called high life, that the trader's sides were shaken by laughter, even to the danger of his life; and he looked upon our adventurer as a miracle of sobriety and good sense.

Having thus ingratiated himself with the uncle, Peregrine took his leave, and next day, in the forenoon, visited the niece in his chariot, after she had been admonished by her kinsman to behave with circumspection, and cautioned against neglecting or discouraging the addresses of such a valuable admirer.

END OF VOL.

Mensaje a la Iglesia de Latinoamérica

Juan Pablo II

MENSAJE A LA IGLESIA DE LATINOAMERICA

BIBLIOTECA DE AUTORES CRISTIANOS

MADRID ● MCMLXXIX

INDICE GENERAL

ACABOSE DE IMPRIMIR ESTE VOLUMEN DE «MEN-
SAJE A LA IGLESIA DE LATINOAMERICA», DE
LA BIBLIOTECA DE AUTORES CRISTIANOS,
EL DIA 5 DE MARZO DE 1979, FESTIVI-
DAD DE NUESTRA SEÑORA DE
AFRICA, EN LOS TALLERES DE
MATEU CROMO, S. A.
(PINTO), MADRID.

LAUS   DEO   VIRGINIQUE   MATRI

ORACION A LA VIRGEN
DE GUADALUPE

¡Oh Virgen Inmaculada,
Madre del verdadero Dios y Madre
de la Iglesia!
Tú, que desde este lugar manifiestas
tu clemencia y tu compasión
a todos los que solicitan tu amparo;
escucha la oración que con filial confianza
te dirigimos, y preséntala ante tu Hijo Jesús,
único Redentor nuestro.

Madre de misericordia, Maestra del sacrificio
escondido y silencioso,
a Ti, que sales al encuentro de nosotros,
los pecadores,
te consagramos en este día todo nuestro ser
y todo nuestro amor.
Te consagramos también nuestra vida,
nuestros trabajos, nuestras alegrías,
nuestras enfermedades y nuestro dolores.

Da la paz, la justicia y la prosperidad
a nuestros pueblos;
ya que todo lo que tenemos y somos
lo ponemos bajo tu cuidado,
Señora y Madre nuestra.

Queremos ser totalmente tuyos
y recorrer contigo el camino de una plena

fidelidad a Jesucristo en su Iglesia:
no nos sueltes de tu mano amorosa.

Virgen de Guadalupe,
Madre de las Américas,
te pedimos por todos los Obispos,
para que conduzcan a los fieles por senderos
de intensa vida cristiana, de amor
y de humilde servicio a Dios y a las almas.

Contempla esta inmensa mies,
e intercede para que el Señor infunda
hambre de santidad en todo el Pueblo de Dios,
y otorgue abundantes vocaciones
de sacerdotes y religiosos,
fuertes en la fe y celosos dispensadores
de los misterios de Dios.

Concede a nuestros hogares la gracia
de amar y de respetar la vida que comienza,
con el mismo amor con el que concebiste
en tu seno la vida del Hijo de Dios.
Virgen Santa María, Madre del Amor Hermoso,
protege a nuestras familias,
para que estén siempre muy unidas,
y bendice la educación de nuestros hijos.

Esperanza nuestra, míranos con compasión,
enséñanos a ir continuamente a Jesús
y, si caemos, ayúdanos a levantarnos,
a volver a El, mediante la confesión
de nuestras culpas y pecados
en el sacramento de la Penitencia,
que trae sosiego al alma.

Te suplicamos que nos concedas un amor
muy grande a todos los santos sacramentos,
que son como las huellas
que tu Hijo nos dejó en la tierra.

Así, Madre Santísima,
con la paz de Dios en la conciencia,
con nuestros corazones libres de mal y de odios,
podremos llevar a todos la verdadera alegría
y la verdadera paz, que vienen de tu Hijo,
nuestro Señor Jesucristo,
que, con Dios Padre y con el Espíritu Santo,
vive y reina por los siglos de los siglos.
Amén.

Joannes Paulus PP. II

México, enero de 1979.

SANTO DOMINGO

MENSAJERO DEL EVANGELIO

Palabras de despedida en el aeropuerto de Fiumicino, 26 de enero.

Os expreso de corazón mi sincero agradecimiento por vuestra presencia en este lugar, en el momento en que me alejo por algunos días de mi amada diócesis y de Italia, para trasladarme a América Latina.

Ese gesto vuestro, tan delicado y solícito, me llena de consuelo y es un sereno augurio del éxito feliz del viaje, el cual —como sabéis— quiere ser, ante todo, una *peregrinación de fe:* el Papa va a arrodillarse ante la prodigiosa imagen de la Virgen de Guadalupe, en México, para invocar su maternal asistencia y protección sobre su servicio pontifical; para decirle otra vez, con una fuerza que los nuevos e inmensos compromisos acrecientan: «Totus tuus sum ego», y para poner en sus manos el porvenir de la evangelización en América Latina.

El Papa, además, visita algunas zonas del Nuevo Mundo como *mensajero del Evangelio* para millones de hermanos y hermanas que creen en Cristo. El Papa quiere conocerles, abrazarles, decir a todos —niños, jóvenes, hombres, mujeres, obreros, campesinos, profesionales— que Dios les ama, que la Iglesia les ama, que el Papa les ama. Quiere también recibir el aliento y el ejemplo de su bondad, de su fe. El Papa, por tanto, sigue idealmente las huellas de los misioneros, de los sacerdotes, de todos aquellos que, desde el descubrimiento del *Nuevo Mundo,* han difundido en aquellas inmensas tierras, con sacrificio, abnegación y generosidad, el mensaje de Jesús, predicando el amor y la paz entre los hombres.

El Papa, en fin, realiza este viaje para participar, junto con sus hermanos obispos, en la III Conferencia General del Episcopado Latinoamericano, que tendrá lugar en Puebla. En esta sede se tratarán importantes problemas en torno a la acción pastoral del Pueblo de Dios, la cual debe tener presente, a la luz del concilio Vaticano II, las complejas situaciones sociopolíticas locales para introducir en ellas el fermento fecundo del anuncio evangélico. El Papa irá a Puebla para ayudar, para «confirmar» (cf. Lc 22,32) a sus hermanos obispos.

En el momento en que me dispongo a emprender el vuelo, después de haber saludado al cardenal secretario de Estado y a los otros cardenales que le acompañan, expreso mi cordial estima al Presidente del Consejo del Gobierno italiano y a las autoridades civiles y militares; saludo al señor decano del Cuerpo Diplomático ante la Santa Sede y a los embajadores de América Latina, y a cuantos han venido a desearme feliz viaje. A todos bendigo de corazón.

LA VISITA DEL PAPA, EMPRESA DE EVANGELIZACION

Discurso del Santo Padre a su llegada a la República Dominicana, 25 de enero.

Señor Presidente, hermanos en el Episcopado, hermanos y hermanas:

Doy gracias a Dios, que me permite llegar a este pedazo de tierra americana, tierra amada de Colón, en la primera etapa de mi visita a un continente al que tantas veces ha volado mi pensamiento, lleno de estima y confianza, sobre todo en este período inicial de mi ministerio de Supremo Pastor de la Iglesia.

El anhelo del pasado se hace realidad con este encuentro, en el que con afecto entusiasta participan —y tantos otros lo habrán deseado— tan numerosos hijos de esta querida tierra dominicana, en cuyo nombre y en el suyo propio usted, señor Presidente, ha querido darme una cordial bienvenida con significativas y nobles palabras. A ellas correspondo con sentimientos de sincero aprecio y honda gratitud, testimonio del amor del Papa para con los hijos de esta hospitalaria nación.

Testimonio de luz y de esperanza

Pero en las palabras escuchadas y en la acogida jubilosa que me tributa hoy el pueblo dominicano siento también la voz, lejana pero presente, de tantísimos otros hijos de todos los países de América Latina, que desde las tierras mexicanas hasta el extremo sur del continente se sienten unidos al Papa por vínculos singulares, que tocan los ámbitos más recónditos de su ser de hombres y de cristianos. A todos y a cada uno de estos países y a sus hijos, llegue el saludo más cordial, el homenaje de respeto y afecto del Papa, su admiración y aprecio por los estupendos valores de historia y cultura que guardan, el deseo de una vida individual, familiar y comunitaria de creciente bienestar humano, en un clima social de moralidad, de justicia para todos, de cultivo intenso de los bienes del espíritu.

Me trae a estas tierras un acontecimiento de grandísima importancia eclesial. Llego a un continente donde la Iglesia ha ido dejando huellas profundas, que penetran muy adentro en la historia y carácter de cada pueblo. Vengo a esta porción viva eclesial, la más numerosa, parte vital para el futuro de la Iglesia católica, que entre hermosas realizaciones no exentas de sombras, entre dificultades y sacrificios, da testimonio de Cristo y quiere hoy responder al reto del momento actual, proponiendo una luz de esperanza, para el aquí y para el más allá, a través de su obra de anuncio de la Buena Nueva, que se concreta en el Cristo Salvador, Hijo de Dios y Hermano mayor de los hombres.

Evangelizar a los pobres

El Papa quiere estar cercano a esta Iglesia evangelizadora para alentar su esfuerzo, para traerle nueva esperanza en su esperanza, para ayudarle a mejor discernir sus caminos, potenciando o modificando lo que convenga, para que sea cada vez más fiel a su misión: la recibida de Jesús, la de Pedro y sus sucesores, la de los apóstoles y los continuadores suyos.

Y puesto que la visita del Papa quiere ser una empresa de evangelización, he deseado llegar aquí siguiendo la ruta que, en el momento del descubrimiento del continente, trazaron los primeros evangelizadores. Aquellos religiosos que vinieron a anunciar a Cristo Salvador, a defender la dignidad de los indígenas, a proclamar sus derechos inviolables, a favorecer su promoción integral, a enseñar la hermandad como hombres y como hijos del mismo Señor y Padre, Dios.

Es éste un testimonio de reconocimiento que quiero tributar a los artífices de aquella admirable gesta evangelizadora, en esta misma tierra del Nuevo Mundo donde se plantó la primera cruz, se celebró la primera misa, se recitó la primera avemaría y de donde, entre diversas vicisitudes, partió la irradiación de la fe a las otras islas cercanas y de allí a la tierra firme.

Desde este evocador lugar del continente, tierra de férvido amor a la Virgen María y de ininterrumpida devoción al Sucesor de Pedro, el Papa quiere reservar su recuerdo y saludo más entrañable a los pobres, a los campesinos, a los enfermos y marginados, que sienten cercana a la Iglesia, que la aman, que siguen a Cristo aun en medio de obstáculos y que con admirable sentido humano ponen en práctica la solidaridad, la hospitalidad, la alegría honesta y esperanzada, a la que Dios prepara su premio.

Pensando en el mayor bien de estos pueblos buenos y generosos, abrigo la confianza de que los responsables, los católicos y hombres de buena voluntad de la República Dominicana y de toda América Latina comprometerán sus mejores energías, ensancharán las fronteras de su creatividad, para edificar un mundo más humano y a la vez más cristiano. Es el llamado que el Papa os hace en este primer encuentro en vuestra tierra.

CRECED EN LA FE

Saludo del Papa al Episcopado y fieles en la catedral de Santo Domingo, 25 de enero.

Señor cardenal, hermanos en el Episcopado, amadísimos hijos:

Hace pocos momentos que he tenido la dicha de llegar a vuestro país, y ahora siento una nueva alegría al encontrarme con vosotros en esta catedral dedicada a la Anunciación —la catedral primada, situada al lado de la que fue la primera sede arzobispal en América— donde tantos habéis querido venir para ver al Papa.

Gracias, ante todo a usted, señor cardenal, por sus bondadosas palabras, que han llenado mi espíritu de satisfacción, de admiración y esperanza.

Deseo deciros que el Papa también anhela estar con vosotros, para conoceros y quereros más todavía. Mi única pena es no poder encontrar y hablar a cada uno en particular.

Pero aunque ello no es posible, sabed que ninguno queda fuera del afecto, fuera del recuerdo del Padre común, que aun estando lejos piensa en vosotros y ruega por vuestras intenciones.

Para que este encuentro sea más íntimo, ha-gamos un instante de oración y pidamos al Señor, por intercesión de Nuestra Señora de la Altagracia, cuya imagen está aquí presente, que os conceda ser siempre buenos hijos de la Iglesia, que crezcáis en la fe y sea la vuestra una vida digna de cristianos.

A vosotros, a vuestros connacionales y familiares, sobre todo a los enfermos y a los que sufren, os concedo muy gustoso mi bendición.

Y rezad también vosotros por el Papa.

APERTURA A DIOS
Y PROMOCION HUMANA

Homilía del Santo Padre en la misa concelebrada en la plaza de la Independencia de Santo Domingo, 25 de enero.

Hermanos en el Episcopado, amadísimos hijos:

1. En esta Eucaristía en la que compartimos la misma fe en Cristo, el Obispo de Roma y de la Iglesia universal, presente entre vosotros, os da su saludo de paz: «La gracia y la paz sea con vosotros de parte de Dios Padre y de Nuestro Señor Jesucristo» (Gál 1,3).

La evangelización, exigencia esencial de la Iglesia

Vengo hasta estas tierras americanas como peregrino de paz y esperanza, para participar en un acontecimiento eclesial de evangelización, acuciado a mi vez por las palabras del apóstol Pablo: «Si evangelizo, no es para mí motivo de gloria, sino que se me impone por necesidad. ¡Ay de mí si no evangelizara!» (1 Cor 9,16).

El actual período de la historia de la humanidad requiere una transmisión reavivada de la fe, para comunicar al hombre de hoy el mensaje perenne de Cristo, adaptado a sus condiciones concretas de vida.

Esa evangelización es una constante y exigencia esencial de la dinámica eclesial. Pablo VI en su encíclica *Evangelii nuntiandi* afirmaba que «evangelizar constituye la dicha y la vocación de la Iglesia, su identidad más profunda. Ella existe para evangelizar» (n.14).

Y el mismo Pontífice precisa que «Cristo, en cuanto evangelizador, anuncia ante todo un reino, el reino de Dios.» «Como núcleo y centro de su Buena Nueva, Jesús anuncia la salvación, ese gran don de Dios que es liberación de todo lo que oprime al hombre, pero que es, sobre todo, liberación del pecado y del Maligno» (n.8-9).

Las órdenes religiosas encarnadas en el pueblo

2. La Iglesia, fiel a su misión, continúa presentando a los hombres de cada tiempo, con la ayuda del Espíritu Santo y bajo la guía del Papa, el mensaje de salvación de su divino Fundador.

Esta tierra dominicana fue un día la primera destinataria, y luego propulsora, de una gran empresa de evangelización, que merece gran admiración y gratitud.

Desde finales del siglo XV esta querida nación se abre a la fe de Jesucristo, a la que ha permanecido fiel hasta hoy. La Santa Sede, por su parte, crea las primeras sedes episcopales de América, precisamente en esta isla, y posteriormente la sede arzobispal y primada de Santo Domingo.

En un período relativamente corto, los senderos de la fe van surcando la geografía dominicana y continental, poniendo los fundamentos del legado hecho vida que hoy contemplamos en lo que fue llamado el Nuevo Mundo.

Desde los primeros momentos del descubrimiento, la preocupación de la Iglesia se pone de manifiesto, para hacer presente el reino de Dios en el corazón de los nuevos pueblos, razas y culturas, y en primer lugar entre vuestros antepasados.

Si queremos tributar un merecido agradecimiento a quienes transplantaron las semillas de la fe, ese homenaje hay que rendirlo en primer lugar a las órdenes religiosas, que se destacaron, aun a costa de ofrendar sus mártires, en la tarea evangelizadora; sobre todo los religiosos dominicos, franciscanos, agustinos, mercedarios y luego los jesuitas, que hicieron árbol frondoso lo que había brotado de tenues raíces. Y es que el suelo de América estaba preparado por corrientes de espiritualidad propia para recibir la nueva sementera cristiana.

No se trata, por otra parte, de una difusión de la fe, desencarnada de la vida de sus destinatarios, aunque siempre debe mantener su esencial referencia a Dios. Por ello la Iglesia en esta isla fue la primera en reivindicar la justicia y en promover la defensa de los derechos humanos en las tierras que se abrían a la evangelización.

Son lecciones de humanismo, de espiritualidad y de afán por dignificar al hombre, las que nos enseñan Antonio Montesinos, Córdoba, Bartolomé de las Casas, a quienes harán eco también en otras partes Juan de Zumárraga, Motolinia, Vasco de Quiroga, José de Anchieta, Toribio de Mogrovejo, Nóbrega y tantos otros. Son hombres en los que late la preocupación por el débil, por el indefenso, por el indígena, sujetos dignos de todo respeto como personas y como portadores de la imagen de Dios, destinados a una vocación transcendente. De ahí nacerá el primer Derecho internacional con Francisco de Vitoria.

Un mundo más digno del hombre

3. Y es que no pueden disociarse —es la gran lección válida hoy también— anuncio del Evangelio y promoción humana; pero para la Iglesia, aquél no puede confundirse ni agotarse —como algunos pretenden— en ésta última. Sería cerrar al hombre espacios infinitos que Dios le ha abierto. Y sería falsear el significado profundo y completo de la evangelización, que es ante todo anuncio de la Buena Nueva del Cristo Salvador.

La Iglesia, experta en humanidad, fiel a los signos de los tiempos, y en obediencia a la invitación apremiante del último Concilio, quiere hoy continuar su misión de fe y de defensa de los derechos humanos. Invitando a los cristianos a comprometerse en la construcción de un mundo más justo, humano y habitable, que no se cierra en sí mismo, sino que se abre a Dios.

Hacer ese mundo más justo significa, entre otras cosas, esforzarse por que no haya niños sin nutrición suficiente, sin educación, sin instrucción; que no haya jóvenes sin la preparación conveniente; que no haya campesinos sin tierra para vivir y desenvolverse dignamente; que no haya trabajadores maltratados ni disminuidos en sus derechos; que no haya sistemas que permitan la explotación del hombre por el hombre o por el Estado; que no haya corrupción; que no haya a quien le sobra mucho, mientras a otros inculpablemente les falte todo; que no haya tanta familia mal constituida, rota, desunida, insuficientemente atendida; que no haya nadie sin amparo de la ley y que la ley ampare a todos por igual; que no prevalezca la fuerza sobre la verdad y el derecho, sino la verdad y el derecho sobre la fuerza; y que no prevalezca jamás lo económico ni lo político sobre lo humano.

La dimensión escatológica del amor

4.   Pero no os contentéis con ese mundo más humano. Haced un mundo explícitamente más divino, más según Dios, regido por la fe y en el que ésta inspire el progreso moral, religioso y social del hombre. No perdáis de vista la orien-

tación vertical de la evangelización. Ella tiene fuerza para liberar al hombre, porque es la revelación del amor. El amor del Padre por los hombres, por todos y cada uno de los hombres, amor revelado en Jesucristo. «Porque tanto amó Dios al mundo, que le dio su unigénito Hijo, para que todo el que crea en El no perezca, sino que tenga la vida eterna» (Jn 3,16).

Jesucristo ha manifestado ese amor ante todo en su vida oculta —«Todo lo ha hecho bien» (Mc 7,37)— y anunciando el Evangelio; después, con su muerte y resurrección, el misterio pascual en el que el hombre encuentra su vocación definitiva a la vida eterna, a la unión con Dios. Es la dimensión escatológica del amor.

Amados hijos: Termino exhortándoos a ser siempre dignos de la fe recibida. Amad a Cristo, amad al hombre por El y vivid la devoción a nuestra querida Madre del cielo, a quien invocáis con el hermoso nombre de Nuestra Señora de la Altagracia, a la que el Papa quiere dejar como homenaje de devoción una diadema. Ella os ayude a caminar hacia Cristo, conservando y desarrollando en plenitud la semilla plantada por vuestros primeros evangelizadores. Es lo que el Papa espera de todos vosotros. De vosotros, hijos de Cuba aquí presentes, de Jamaica, de Curaçao y Antillas, de Haití, de Venezuela y Estados Unidos. Sobre todo de vosotros, hijos de la tierra dominicana. Así sea.

SERVICIO AL BIEN COMUN

Encuentro del Papa con el Cuerpo Diplomático en Santo Domingo, 25 de enero.

Excelencias, señoras y señores:

No quería que en mi breve visita a este país faltase este encuentro con vosotros, que por múltiples y variados motivos sois acreedores de una muestra de especial atención por parte del Papa.

Habéis querido venir a rendirme vuestro homenaje de respeto y adhesión como representantes de vuestros respectivos países, como detentores a diversos niveles de la autoridad en la nación dominicana, como personas vinculadas a la Santa Sede por lazos particulares o como exponentes del mundo cultural.

A todos expreso mi sentido reconocimiento por vuestra presencia benévola, así como mi aprecio profundo por vuestras respectivas funciones. Os deseo todo bien en vuestras tareas, que pueden y deben tener una clara orientación de servicio al bien común, a la causa de la convivencia humana, al bienestar de la sociedad civil y, para muchos, también de la Iglesia. Muchas gracias.

SI HAS ENCONTRADO A CRISTO, ANUNCIALO A LOS DEMAS

Homilía del Santo Padre en la catedral de Santo Domingo durante la misa para el clero, religiosos y seminaristas, 26 de enero.

Amadísimos hermanos y hermanas:

Bendito sea el Señor que me ha traído aquí, a este suelo de la República Dominicana, donde venturosamente, para gloria y alabanza de Dios en este Nuevo Continente, amaneció también el día de la salvación. Y he querido venir a esta catedral de Santo Domingo para estar entre vosotros, amadísimos sacerdotes, diáconos, religiosos, religiosas y seminaristas, para manifestaros mi especial afecto a vosotros en los que el Papa y la Iglesia depositan sus mejores esperanzas, para que os sintáis más alegres en la fe, de modo que vuestro orgullo de ser lo que sois rebose por causa mía (cf. Flp 1,25).

Pero sobre todo quiero unirme a vosotros en la acción de gracias a Dios. Gracias por el crecimiento y celo de esta Iglesia, que tiene en su haber tantas y tan bellas iniciativas y que muestra tanta entrega en el servicio de Dios y de los

hombres. Doy gracias con inmensa alegría
—para decirlo con palabras del Apóstol— «por
la parte que habéis tomado en anunciar la Buena
Nueva desde el primer día hasta hoy; seguro
además de una cosa: de que aquel que dio principio a la buena empresa, le irá dando remate
hasta el día del Mesías, Jesús» (Flp 1,3ss).

Vivencia gozosa del Evangelio

Me gustaría de verdad disponer de mucho
tiempo para estar con vosotros, aprender vuestros nombres y escuchar de vuestros labios «lo
que rebosa del corazón» (Mt 12,34), lo que de
maravilloso habéis experimentado en vuestro interior —*fecit mihi magna qui potens est...* (Lc
1,49)—, habiendo sido fieles al encuentro con el
Señor. Un encuentro de preferencia por su
parte.

Es esto precisamente: el encuentro pascual
con el Señor, lo que deseo proponer a vuestra
reflexión para reavivar más vuestra fe y entusiasmo en esta Eucaristía; un encuentro personal, vivo, de ojos abiertos y corazón palpitante,
con Cristo resucitado (cf. Lc 24,30), el objetivo
de vuestro amor y de toda vuestra vida.

Sucede a veces que nuestra sintonía de fe con
Jesús permanece débil o se hace tenue —cosa
que el pueblo fiel nota en seguida, contagián-
dose por ello de tristeza—, porque lo llevamos
dentro, sí, pero confundido a la vez con nuestras
propensiones y razonamientos humanos (cf.

ibíd., 15), sin hacer brillar toda la grandiosa luz
que El encierra para nosotros. En alguna ocasión hablamos quizá de El amparados en alguna
premisa cambiante o en datos de sabor socioló-
gico, político, psicológico, lingüístico, en vez de
hacer derivar los criterios básicos de nuestra
vida y actividad de un Evangelio vivido con integridad, con gozo, con la confianza y esperanza
inmensas que encierra la cruz de Cristo.

Entrega total al Señor

Una cosa es clara, amadísimos hermanos: la
fe en Cristo resucitado no es resultado de un saber técnico o fruto de un bagaje científico (cf.
1 Cor 1,26). Lo que se nos pide es que anuncie-
mos la muerte de Jesús y proclamemos su resurrección (S. Liturgia). Jesús vive. «Dios lo resucitó rompiendo las ataduras de la muerte» (Act
2,24). Lo que fue un trémulo murmullo entre los
primeros testigos, se convirtió pronto en gozosa
experiencia de la realidad de aquel «con el que
hemos comido y bebido... después que resucitó
de la muerte» (Act 10,41-42). Sí, Cristo vive en
la Iglesia, está en nosotros, portadores de esperanza e inmortalidad.

Si habéis encontrado, pues, a Cristo, ¡vivid a
Cristo, vivid con Cristo! Y anunciadlo en primera persona, como auténticos testigos: «para
mí la vida es Cristo» (Flp 1,21). He ahí también
la verdadera liberación: proclamar a Jesús libre
de ataduras, presente en unos hombres trans-

VEO EN VOSOTROS LA PRESENCIA DEL SEÑOR QUE SUFRE

Saludo del Papa a los habitantes del barrio pobre «Los Minas» de Santo Domingo, 26 de enero.

Desde el primer momento de la preparación de mi viaje a vuestro país, he colocado en puesto prioritario una visita a este barrio, a fin de poder encontrarme con vosotros.

Y he querido venir aquí precisamente porque se trata de una zona pobre, para que tuvierais la oportunidad —diría por título más alto— de estar con el Papa. El ve en vosotros una presencia más viva del Señor, que sufre en los hermanos más necesitados, que sigue proclamando bienaventurados a los pobres de espíritu, a quienes padecen por la justicia y son puros de corazón, trabajan por la paz, son compasivos y mantienen la esperanza en el Cristo Salvador.

Pero al invitaros a cultivar esos valores espirituales y evangélicos, deseo haceros pensar en vuestra dignidad de hombres y de hijos de Dios. Quiero alentaros a ser ricos en humanidad, en amor a la familia, en solidaridad con los demás. A la vez, os animo a desarrollar cada vez más las posibilidades que tenéis de lograr una mayor dignificación humana y cristiana.

Mas no acaba aquí mi discurso. La vista de vuestra realidad debe hacer pensar a tantos en la acción que pueda ser llevada a cabo para remediar eficazmente vuestra condición.

En nombre de estos hermanos nuestros, pido a cuantos puedan hacerlo que les ayuden a vencer su actual situación, para que, sobre todo con una mejor educación, perfeccionen sus mentes y corazones, y sean artífices de su propia elevación y de una más profunda inserción en la sociedad.

Con esta urgente llamada a las conciencias, el Papa alienta vuestros deseos de superación y bendice con gran afecto a vosotros, a vuestros hijos y familiares, a todos los habitantes del barrio.

RELIGIOSIDAD
DEL PUEBLO DOMINICANO

Despedida del Papa al dejar la República Dominicana, 26 de enero.

Señor Presidente:

Con hondo sentimiento por mi parte, llega el momento de tener que dejar esta querida tierra de la República Dominicana, donde la brevedad de mi permanencia se ha visto compensada con una gran abundancia de intensas vivencias religiosas y humanas.

He podido admirar algunas de las bellezas del país, de sus monumentos histórico-religiosos y sobre todo he podido constatar con profunda satisfacción el sentido religioso y humano de sus habitantes.

Son recuerdos imborrables que me acompañan y continuarán haciéndome presente las hermosas jornadas vividas en esta cuna del catolicismo en el Nuevo Mundo.

Gracias, señor Presidente, por las innumerables atenciones que se me han prestado y por su presencia en este momento. Gracias a todo el querido pueblo dominicano por su entusiasta recibimiento, por sus constantes pruebas de amor al Papa y por su fidelidad a la fe cristiana.

MEXICO

Camino de América, Juan Pablo II reza.

Desde el avión, el Papa habla por radioteléfono.

formados, hechos nueva creatura. ¿Por qué nuestro testimonio resulta a veces vano? Porque presentamos a un Jesús sin toda la fuerza seductora que su persona ofrece; sin hacer patentes las riquezas del ideal sublime que su seguimiento comporta; porque no siempre llegamos a mostrar una convicción hecha vida acerca del valor estupendo de nuestra entrega a la gran causa eclesial que servimos.

Hermanos y hermanas: Es preciso que los hombres vean en nosotros a los dispensadores de los misterios de Dios (cf. 1 Cor 4,1), testigos creíbles de su presencia en el mundo. Pensemos frecuentemente que Dios no nos pide, al llamarnos, parte de nuestra persona, sino toda nuestra persona y energías vitales, para anunciar a los hombres la alegría y la paz de la nueva vida en Cristo y guiarlos a su encuentro. Para ello sea nuestro afán primero buscar al Señor, y una vez encontrado, comprobar dónde y cómo vive, quedándonos con El todo el día (cf. Jn 1,39). Quedándonos con El de manera especial en la Eucaristía, donde Cristo se nos da, y en la oración, mediante la cual nos damos a El. La Eucaristía ha de complementarse y prolongarse a través de la oración en nuestro quehacer cotidiano como un «sacrificio de alabanza» (*Misal Romano,* Plegaria eucarística I).

En la oración, en el trato confiado con Dios nuestro Padre, discernimos mejor dónde está nuestra fuerza y dónde está nuestra debilidad, porque el Espíritu viene en nuestra ayuda (cf. Rom 8,26). El mismo Espíritu nos habla y nos va sumergiendo poco a poco en los misterios divinos, en los designios de amor a los hombres que Dios realiza mediante nuestra ofrenda a su servicio.

Lo mismo que Pablo, durante una reunión en Tróade para partir el pan, seguiría hablando con vosotros hasta la medianoche (cf. Act 20,6ss). Tendría muchas cosas que deciros, y que no puedo hacer ahora. Entretanto os recomiendo que leáis atentamente lo que he dicho recientemente al clero, a los religiosos, religiosas y seminaristas en Roma. Ello alargará este encuentro, que continuará espiritualmente con otros semejantes en los próximos días. Que el Señor y nuestra dulce Madre, María Santísima, os acompañen siempre y llenen vuestra vida de un gran entusiasmo en el servicio de vuestra altísima vocación eclesial.

Vamos a continuar la misa, poniendo en la mesa de las ofrendas nuestros anhelos de vivir la nueva vida, nuestras necesidades y nuestras súplicas, las necesidades y súplicas de la Iglesia y Nación Dominicana. Pongamos también los trabajos y los frutos de la III Conferencia General del Episcopado Latinoamericano en Puebla.

El Presidente de la República Dominicana recibe al Papa.

Rodeado por la muchedumbre, Ju

...blo II llega a la basílica de Guadalupe.

Concelebración en la basílica de Guadalupe.

Virgen de Guadalupe, Madre de las Américas.

Interior de la basílica nueva de Guadalupe.

MEXICO, «SIEMPRE FIEL»

Homilía del Santo Padre en la catedral metropolitana de Ciudad de México, 26 de enero.

Queridos señores cardenales, hermanos en el Episcopado y amadísimos hijos:

Hace apenas unas horas que pisé por vez primera, con honda conmoción, esta bendita tierra. Y ahora tengo la dicha de este encuentro con vosotros, con la Iglesia y el pueblo mexicanos, en este que quiere ser el *día de México*.

Es un encuentro que se inició con mi llegada —un espectáculo conmovedor— a esta hermosa ciudad; se extendió mientras atravesaba las calles y plazas, se ha intensificado al ingresar en esta catedral. Pero es aquí, en la celebración del sacrificio eucarístico, donde halla su culminación.

Pongamos este encuentro bajo la protección de la Madre de Dios, la Virgen de Guadalupe, a la que el pueblo mexicano ama con la más arraigada devoción.

A vosotros, señores cardenales, obispos de esta Iglesia; a vosotros, sacerdotes, religiosos, religiosas, seminaristas, miembros de los institutos seculares, laicos de los movimientos católicos y de apostolado; a vosotros niños, jóvenes, adultos, ancianos; a vosotros todos, mexicanos, que tenéis un pasado espléndido de amor a Cristo, aun en medio de las pruebas; a vosotros que lleváis en lo hondo del corazón la devoción a la Virgen de Guadalupe, el Papa quiere hablaros hoy de algo que es, y debe ser más, una esencia vuestra, cristiana y mariana: la fidelidad a la Iglesia.

Buscar el rostro del Señor

De entre tantos títulos atribuidos a la Virgen, a lo largo de los siglos, por el amor filial de los cristianos, hay uno de profundísimo significado: *Virgo fidelis,* Virgen fiel. ¿Qué significa esta fidelidad de María? ¿Cuáles son las dimensiones de esa fidelidad?

La primera dimensión se llama búsqueda. María fue fiel ante todo cuando con amor se puso a buscar el sentido profundo del designio de Dios en Ella y para el mundo. *«Quomodo fiet? ¿Cómo sucederá esto?»,* preguntaba Ella al ángel de la Anunciación. Ya en el Antiguo Testamento el sentido de esta búsqueda se traduce en una expresión de rara belleza y extraordinario contenido espiritual: «buscar el rostro del Señor». No habrá fidelidad si no hubiere en la raíz esta ardiente, paciente y generosa búsqueda; si no se encontrara en el corazón del hombre una pregunta, para la cual sólo Dios tiene respuesta, mejor dicho, para la cual sólo Dios es la respuesta.

Aceptación del misterio

La segunda dimensión de la fidelidad se llama acogida, aceptación. El *quomodo fiet* se transforma, en los labios de María, en un *fiat*. Que se haga, estoy pronta, acepto: éste es el momento crucial de la fidelidad, momento en el cual el hombre percibe que jamás comprenderá totalmente el cómo; que hay en el designio de Dios más zonas de misterio que de evidencia; que, por más que haga, jamás logrará captarlo todo. Es entonces cuando el hombre acepta el misterio, le da un lugar en su corazón así como «María conservaba todas estas cosas, meditándolas en su corazón» (Lc 2,19; cf. ibíd., 3,15). Es el momento en el que el hombre se abandona al misterio, no con la resignación de alguien que capitula frente a un enigma, a un absurdo, sino más bien con la disponibilidad de quien se abre para ser habitado por algo —¡por Alguien!— más grande que el propio corazón. Esa aceptación se cumple en definitiva por la fe, que es la adhesión de todo el ser al misterio que se revela.

Coherencia

Coherencia es la tercera dimensión de la fidelidad. Vivir de acuerdo con lo que se cree. Ajustar la propia vida al objeto de la propia adhesión. Aceptar incomprensiones, persecuciones antes que permitir rupturas entre lo que se vive y lo que se cree: ésta es la coherencia. Aquí se encuentra, quizá, el núcleo más íntimo de la fidelidad.

Constancia

Pero toda fidelidad debe pasar por la prueba más exigente: la de la duración. Por eso la cuarta dimensión de la fidelidad es la constancia. Es fácil ser coherente por un día o algunos días. Difícil e importante es ser coherente toda la vida. Es fácil ser coherente en la hora de la exaltación, difícil serlo en la hora de la tribulación. Y sólo puede llamarse fidelidad una coherencia que dura a lo largo de toda la vida. El *fiat* de María en la Anunciación encuentra su plenitud en el *fiat* silencioso que repite al pie de la cruz. Ser fiel es no traicionar en las tinieblas lo que se aceptó en público.

De todas las enseñanzas que la Virgen da a sus hijos de México, quizá la más bella e importante es esta lección de fidelidad. Esa fidelidad que el Papa se complace en descubrir y que espera del pueblo mexicano.

De mi patria se suele decir: «*Polonia semper fidelis*». Yo quiero poder decir también: *Mexicum semper fidele!:* ¡México siempre fiel!

De hecho la historia religiosa de esta nación es una historia de fidelidad; fidelidad a las semillas de fe sembradas por los primeros misioneros; fidelidad a una religiosidad sencilla pero arraigada, sincera hasta el sacrificio; fidelidad a la devoción mariana; fidelidad ejemplar al Papa. Yo no tenía necesidad de venir hasta México

para conocer esta fidelidad al Vicario de Jesucristo, pues desde hace mucho lo sabía; pero
agradezco al Señor poder experimentarla en el
fervor de vuestra acogida.

En esta hora solemne querría invitaros a consolidar esa fidelidad, a robustecerla. Querría invitaros a traducirla en inteligente y fuerte fidelidad a la Iglesia hoy. ¿Y cuáles serán las dimensiones de esta fidelidad sino las mismas de la fidelidad de María?

Aceptación leal, coherente
y perseverante de la Iglesia

El Papa que os visita espera de vosotros un
generoso y noble esfuerzo por conocer siempre
mejor a la Iglesia. El concilio Vaticano II ha
querido ser por encima de todo un concilio sobre la Iglesia. Tomad en vuestras manos los documentos conciliares, especialmente la *Lumen
gentium,* estudiadlos con amorosa atención, en
espíritu de oración, para ver lo que el Espíritu
ha querido decir sobre la Iglesia. Así podréis da-
ros cuenta de que no hay —como algunos pretenden— una «nueva Iglesia» diversa u opuesta
a la «vieja Iglesia», sino que el Concilio ha querido revelar con más claridad la única Iglesia de
Jesucristo, con aspectos nuevos, pero siempre la
misma en su esencia.

El Papa espera de vosotros, además, una leal
aceptación de la Iglesia. No serían fieles en este
sentido quienes quedasen apegados a aspectos
accidentales de la Iglesia, válidos en el pasado,

pero ya superados. Ni serían tampoco fieles quienes, en nombre de un profetismo poco esclarecido, se lanzaran a la aventurosa y utópica construcción de una Iglesia así llamada del futuro, desencarnada de la presente. Debemos ser fieles a la Iglesia que nacida, una vez por todas, del designio de Dios, de la cruz, del sepulcro abierto del Resucitado y de la gracia de Pentecostés, nace de nuevo cada día, no del pueblo o de otras categorías racionales, sino de las mismas fuentes de las cuales nació en su origen. Ella nace hoy para construir con todas las gentes un pueblo deseoso de crecer en la fe, en la esperanza, en el amor fraterno.

El Papa espera asimismo de vosotros la plena coherencia de vuestra vida con vuestra pertenencia a la Iglesia. Esa coherencia significa tener conciencia de la propia identidad de católicos y manifestarla, con total respeto, pero sin vacilaciones ni temores. La Iglesia tiene hoy necesidad de cristianos dispuestos a dar claro testimonio de su condición y que asuman su parte en la misión de la Iglesia en el mundo, siendo fermento de religiosidad, de justicia, de promoción de la dignidad del hombre, en todos los ambientes sociales, y tratando de dar al mundo un suplemento de alma, para que sea un mundo más humano y fraterno, desde el que se mira hacia Dios.

El Papa espera a la vez que vuestra coherencia no sea efímera, sino constante y perseverante. Pertenecer a la Iglesia, vivir en la Iglesia, ser Iglesia es hoy algo muy exigente. Tal vez no cueste la persecución clara y directa, pero podrá costar el desprecio, la indiferencia, la marginación. Es entonces fácil y frecuente el peligro del miedo, del cansancio, de la inseguridad. No os dejéis vencer por estas tentaciones. No dejéis desvanecerse por alguno de estos sentimientos el vigor y la energía espiritual de vuestro «ser Iglesia», esa gracia que hay que pedir y estar prontos a recibirla con una gran pobreza interior, y que hay que comenzar a vivirla cada mañana. Y cada día con mayor fervor e intensidad.

Compromiso solemne

Queridos hermanos e hijos: En esta Eucaristía que sella un encuentro del siervo de los siervos de Dios con el alma y la conciencia del pueblo mexicano, el nuevo Papa quisiera recoger de vuestros labios, de vuestras manos y de vuestras vidas un compromiso solemne para brindarlo al Señor. Compromiso de las almas consagradas, de los niños, jóvenes, adultos y ancianos, de personas cultivadas, de gente sencilla, de hombres y mujeres, de todos: el compromiso de la fidelidad a Cristo, a la Iglesia de hoy. Pongamos sobre el altar esta intención y compromiso.

La Virgen fiel, la Madre de Guadalupe, de quien aprendemos a conocer el designio de Dios, su promesa y alianza, nos ayude con su intercesión a firmar este compromiso y a cumplirlo hasta el final de nuestra vida, hasta el día en que la voz del Señor nos diga: «Ven, siervo bueno y fiel; entra en el gozo de tu Señor» (Mt 25,21-23). Así sea.

SALUDO DEL PAPA A LOS FIELES

A la salida de la catedral de Ciudad de México, 26 de enero.

Amadísimos hijos:

Después de recibir el saludo de bienvenida del señor cardenal José Salazar y del señor arzobispo de esta ciudad, Mons. Ernesto Corripio, acabo de terminar la celebración de mi primera misa en tierra mexicana, ofrecida en esta catedral metropolitana.

Estoy muy contento de vuestro extraordinario entusiasmo y de encontrarme aquí con vosotros y saludo a todos y cada uno, a los sacerdotes, religiosos y religiosas, seminaristas, personas adultas, padres y madres de familia. Pero llegue mi saludo especialmente cordial a los jóvenes, a los niños, a los ancianos y enfermos.

Sabed que el Papa ha rezado en la misa por todas vuestras intenciones, pidiendo al Señor que os conduzca por el camino de la rectitud moral, del amor a Cristo y a la Iglesia, que os dé su consuelo si tenéis algún motivo de tristeza o dolor, y os conceda vivir con autenticidad vuestra vida cristiana.

Sobre todo en estos días en que estaremos

cercanos, rezad también vosotros por el Papa y
por la Iglesia. Y pidamos con fervor a la Virgen
de Guadalupe que Ella nos ayude en nuestro
camino y sea nuestra guía hacia su Hijo y Hermano nuestro, Jesús.

A todos el Papa os da con gran afecto su bendición.

ARTIFICES DE LA PAZ

Encuentro del Santo Padre con el Cuerpo Diplomático en México, 26 de enero.

Excelencias, ilustrísimos miembros del Cuerpo Diplomático:

Me complace de veras que en medio del programa tan apretado de mi visita a México, esté colocado este encuentro de saludo a un grupo tan distinguido de personas, como es el Cuerpo Diplomático acreditado en Ciudad de México.

Son muchas las ocasiones en las que la Santa Sede ha demostrado su alta estima y aprecio por la función de los representantes diplomáticos. Lo he hecho yo también al principio de mi pontificado. Y gustoso reitero hoy ante ustedes mi positiva valoración de esta noble tarea, cuando es puesta al servicio de la gran causa de la paz, del entendimiento entre las naciones, del acercamiento entre los pueblos y de un intercambio mutuamente provechoso en tantos campos de la interdependencia en la comunidad internacional.

Vosotros y yo, señores, sentimos también una preocupación común: el bien de la humanidad y el porvenir de los pueblos y de todos los hombres. Si vuestra misión es, en primer lugar, la defensa y promoción de los legítimos intereses de vuestras respectivas naciones, la interdependencia ineludible que vincula cada vez más en nuestros días a todos los pueblos del mundo, invita a todos los diplomáticos a hacerse, con espíritu siempre renovado y original, los artífices del entendimiento entre los pueblos, de la seguridad internacional y de la paz entre las naciones.

Promover las relaciones fraternas

Vosotros sabéis muy bien que todas las sociedades humanas serán juzgadas en este campo de la paz por la aportación que hayan dado al desarrollo del hombre y al respeto de sus derechos fundamentales. Si la sociedad debe garantizar, en primer lugar, el disfrute de un derecho verdadero a la existencia y a una existencia digna, no se podrá desligar de este derecho otra exigencia también fundamental y que podríamos llamar el derecho a la paz y a la seguridad.

En efecto, todo ser humano aspira a las condiciones de la paz que permitirán un desarrollo armonioso de las generaciones futuras, al abrigo del azote terrible que será siempre la guerra, al abrigo del recurso a la fuerza o de otra forma de violencia.

Garantizar la paz a todos los habitantes de nuestro planeta quiere decir buscar, con toda la generosidad y dedicación, con todo el dinamismo y perseverancia de que son capaces los hombres de buena voluntad, todos los medios concretos aptos a promover las relaciones pacíficas y fraternas, no sólo en el plano internacional, sino también en el plano de los distintos continentes y regiones, donde será a veces más fácil conseguir resultados que, no por ser limitados, serán menos importantes. Las realizaciones de paz en el plano regional constituyen, en efecto, un ejemplo y una invitación para la entera comunidad internacional.

Yo quisiera exhortar a cada uno de vosotros y, a través de vosotros, a todos los responsables de las naciones que representáis, a eliminar el miedo y la desconfianza, y a sustituirlos por la confianza mutua, por la vigilancia acogedora y por la colaboración fraterna. Este nuevo clima en las relaciones entre las naciones hará posible el descubrimiento de campos de entendimiento frecuentemente insospechados.

Acogida a los refugiados

Permitid al Papa, a este humilde peregrino de la paz que soy yo, reiterar a vuestra atención el llamamiento que hice a todos los responsables de la suerte de las naciones en mi Mensaje para la Jornada de la Paz: no dudéis en comprometeros personalmente por la paz mediante gestos de paz, cada uno en su ámbito y en su esfera de responsabilidad. Dad vida a gestos nuevos y audaces, que sean manifestaciones de respeto, de fraternidad, de confianza y de acogida. Por medio de estos gestos empeñaréis todas vuestras capacidades personales y profesionales al servicio de la gran causa de la paz. Y yo os prometo que, por el camino de la paz, encontraréis siempre a Dios que os acompaña.

En el contexto de este llamamiento, yo quisiera compartir también con vosotros un deseo particular. Me refiero al número creciente de refugiados por todo el mundo y a la situación trágica en que se hallan los refugiados en el sudeste asiático. Expuestos no solamente a los riesgos de un viaje no sin peligros, éstos últimos están expuestos además a que sea rechazada su petición de asilo o, al menos, a una larga espera antes de recibir la posibilidad de comenzar una nueva existencia en un país dispuesto a acogerlos. La solución de este problema trágico es responsabilidad de todas las naciones, y yo deseo que las Organizaciones internacionales apropiadas puedan contar con la comprensión y la ayuda de los países de todos los continentes, especialmente de un continente como América Latina, que ha hecho siempre honor a su tradición secular de hospitalidad, para afrontar abiertamente este problema humanitario.

Permítanme, pues, alentarlos en este cometido, conscientes como son del profundo sentido de ética profesional que debe acompañar este servicio sacrificado, a veces incomprendido, a la sociedad.

Para que Dios bendiga vuestros esfuerzos, vuestras personas y familias, invoco la protección del Todopoderoso.

EL PAPA SE DEBE A TODOS

*Saludo de Juan Pablo II a la co-
lonia polaca de México, 27 de
enero.*

¡Alabado sea Jesucristo!

Querría deciros ante todo que el Papa es
siempre católico, además de que en esta ocasión
es polaco, y me alegro mucho de que este Papa
católico sea polaco.

No necesito explicaros ampliamente por qué
me alegro de esto. Actualmente, el hecho de que
el Papa católico provenga de Polonia, o, como
vosotros decís, el «Papa-polaco», me impone
primero a mí y también a vosotros, a los polacos
en todas las partes del mundo, deberes particulares; no es sólo una fuente de alegría el que po-
damos encontrar de este modo el sitio en el corazón de la Iglesia, sino que comporta además
las obligaciones con que se enfrenta la Iglesia en
Polonia y los polacos esparcidos por el mundo,
porque los polacos, en cualquier parte del
mundo en que se hallen, mantienen vínculos con
la patria a través de la Iglesia, a través del recuerdo de la Madre de Dios de Jasna Gora, a
través de nuestros santos patronos, a través de
los lazos mantenidos gracias a las tradiciones re-

ligiosas en las que ha vivido el pueblo durante mil años y vive todavía. Por esto nuestro sitio en la Iglesia —en ella tienen sitio numerosos pueblos y naciones—, el sitio de Palonia en la Iglesia, se ha puesto de relieve especialmente hoy, pero con él se nos ha impuesto el nuevo deber de ser todavía más «la Iglesia», y de estar más con la Iglesia. Diría, mirad aún más a la Iglesia como a nuestra patria espiritual.

Queridos compatriotas, os deseo esto de corazón con motivo de nuestro encuentro en tierra mexicana.

Guadalupe, evocación de Czestochowa

Ayer en la catedral hice alusión a la frase que ya tiene derecho de ciudadanía en la historia de la Iglesia y de Polonia: «*Polonia semper fidelis* (Polonia, siempre fiel)», y dije también: «*Mexicum semper fidele* (México, siempre fiel)». Considero un hecho providencial el que mis primeros pasos, fuera de Italia, fuera de Roma, durante mi pontificado, me han traído precisamente aquí, a esta tierra donde sus habitantes, ciudadanos cristianos y católicos, han sufrido tanto por Cristo; esto nos une con ellos; también ellos lo sienten y lo manifiestan. Sin duda, la mayor parte de ellos no conocen la historia de Polonia, como nosotros no conocemos la de México, que es más breve —vosotros sois una excepción—, pero sien-

ten que entre ellos y nosotros hay un vínculo espiritual, y como una semejanza de destino
espiritual; y la Madre de Dios del santuario
de Guadalupe nos recuerda vivamente a nuestra
Madre de Dios de Jasna Gora. Y por eso hoy,
esperando peregrinar al santuario de la Madre
de Dios de Guadalupe, vivo los mismos sentimientos que cuando iba —y espero que en un
futuro no lejano podré ir todavía— al santuario
de la Madre de Dios de Jasna Gora en Czesto-
chowa.

Os diré además que, si tuve el valor de emprender este viaje a México, ya en los primeros
meses de mi pontificado, para participar en una
labor tan difícil como es la Conferencia de los
Obispos Latinoamericanos en Puebla, lo hice
guiado por la confianza en la Madre de Dios, por
su ayuda; como me ayudó en Polonia, en Cracovia, así me ayudará también aquí en México,
aunque éste es un mundo distinto, el Nuevo
Mundo; gente distinta, pero tan cercana.

Debo confesaros que estoy profundamente
emocionado por el recibimiento con que me ha
acogido toda la sociedad y la nación mexicana,
sobre todo en esta gran ciudad con 12 millones
de habitantes.

Tengo confianza en que la Madre Santísima
me ayudará en el trabajo que se presenta ante
nosotros, ante mí. Creo que la experiencia ad-
quirida durante veinte años como obispo en Polonia me ayudará a ver tantos problemas que
aún atormentan como nuevos, como no concre-
tados en la mentalidad del pueblo, y quizá tam-

poco en la mentalidad de los sacerdotes de este continente, y me ayudarán a encontrar la respuesta sencilla y clara esperada por todos, porque éste es el deber del Papa: hablar de manera sencilla y clara, y así confirmar a sus hermanos.

Espero que veléis en oración

Me parece que he terminado. Espero que vosotros, mis compatriotas, unidos de modo particular al Papa, velaréis con vuestras oraciones, con vuestros pensamientos, con vuestra entrega, para que en el continente latinoamericano, en el centro de América, que está en México, este vuestro Papa-polaco, como decís, apruebe el examen de Papa verdaderamente católico.

Y esto es todo, no hablaré más. Mejor hubiera querido escuchar todo lo que me dijerais de vosotros mismos. Es verdad que se pueden encontrar polacos en todos los continentes y probablemente en todos los países. Se puede decir que éste es nuestro destino, vale decir, nuestra misión de estar presentes en los diversos pueblos de la tierra.

Querría saber de vosotros cómo habéis venido aquí. Supongo que a la mayoría os han traído las vicisitudes de la segunda guerra mundial. De todos modos, os agradezco mucho este encuentro.

Debéis excusarme por haber llegado con retraso, pero el Papa jamás llega tarde. Nunca llega tarde porque siempre tiene mucho que hacer, y además porque le vigila siempre su secretario, y entonces, aunque haya llegado con retraso, no ha llegado tarde.

Deseo abrazaros una vez más a todos con el corazón y bendeciros en este nuestro camino polaco y católico.

CON MARIA, MADRE DE JESUS Y DE LA IGLESIA

Homilía del Santo Padre en la basílica de Nuestra Señora de Guadalupe, al inaugurar, el 27 de enero, la III Conferencia General del Episcopado Latinoamericano.

¡Salve María!

1. Cuán profundo es mi gozo, queridos hermanos en el Episcopado y amadísimos hijos, porque los primeros pasos de mi peregrinaje, como sucesor de Pablo VI y de Juan Pablo I, me traen precisamente aquí. Me traen a Ti, María, en este santuario del pueblo de México y de toda América Latina, en el que desde hace tantos siglos se ha manifestado tu maternidad.

¡Salve, María!

Pronuncio con inmenso amor y reverencia estas palabras, tan sencillas y a la vez tan maravillosas. Nadie podrá saludarte nunca de un modo más estupendo que como lo hizo un día el arcángel en el momento de la Anunciación. *Ave Maria, gratia plena, Dominus tecum.* Repito estas palabras que tantos corazones guardan y tantos labios pronuncian en todo el mundo. Nosotros aquí presentes las repetimos juntos, conscientes de que éstas son las palabras con las que Dios mismo, a través de su mensajero, ha saludado a Ti, la Mujer prometida en el Edén, y desde la eternidad elegida como Madre del Verbo, Madre de la divina Sabiduría, Madre del Hijo de Dios.

¡Salve, Madre de Dios!

Evangelización con raíz mariana

2. Tu Hijo Jesucristo es nuestro Redentor y Señor. Es nuestro Maestro. Todos nosotros aquí reunidos somos sus discípulos. Somos los sucesores de los apóstoles, de aquellos a quienes el Señor dijo: «Id, pues; enseñad a todas las gentes, bautizándolas en el nombre del Padre y del Hijo y del Espíritu Santo, enseñándoles a observar todo cuanto yo os he mandado. Yo estaré con vosotros hasta la consumación del mundo» (Mt 28,19-20).

Congregados aquí el sucesor de Pedro y los sucesores de los apóstoles, nos damos cuenta de cómo esas palabras se han cumplido, de manera admirable, en esta tierra.

En efecto, desde que en 1492 comienza la gesta evangelizadora en el Nuevo Mundo, apenas una veintena de años después llega la fe a México. Poco más tarde se crea la primera sede arzobispal regida por Juan de Zumárraga, a quien secundarán otras grandes figuras de evangelizadores, que extenderán el cristianismo en muy amplias zonas.

Otras epopeyas religiosas no menos gloriosas escribirán en el hemisferio sur hombres como Santo Toribio de Mogrovejo y otros muchos que merecerían ser citados en larga lista. Los caminos de la fe van alargándose sin cesar, y a finales del primer siglo de evangelización la Jerarquía católica estaba presente en el Nuevo Continente con unos cuatro millones de cristianos. Una empresa singular que continuará por largo tiempo, hasta abarcar hoy en día, tras cinco siglos de evangelización, casi la mitad de la entera Iglesia católica, arraigada en la cultura del pueblo latinoamericano y formando parte de su identidad propia.

Y a medida que sobre estas tierras se realizaba el mandato de Cristo, a medida que con la gracia del bautismo se multiplicaban por doquier los hijos de la adopción divina, aparece también la Madre. En efecto, a Ti, María, el Hijo de Dios y a la vez Hijo tuyo, desde lo alto de la cruz indicó a un hombre y dijo: «He ahí a tu hijo» (Jn 19,26). Y en aquel hombre te ha confiado a cada hombre, te ha confiado a todos. Y Tú, que en el momento de la Anunciación, en estas sencillas palabras: «He aquí la sierva del Señor; hágase en mí según tu palabra» (Lc 1,38), has concentrado todo el programa de tu vida, abrazas a todos, te acercas a todos, buscas maternalmente a todos. De esta manera se cumple lo que el último Concilio ha declarado acerca de tu presencia en el misterio de Cristo y de la Iglesia. Per-

severas de manera admirable en el misterio de
Cristo, tu Hijo unigénito, porque estás siempre
dondequiera están los hombres sus hermanos,
dondequiera está la Iglesia.

Devoción a la Virgen en
América Latina

2a. De hecho, los primeros misioneros llega-
dos a América, provenientes de tierras de eminente tradición mariana, junto con los rudimen-
tos de la fe cristiana van enseñando el amor a
Ti, Madre de Jesús y de todos los hombres. Y
desde que el indio Juan Diego hablara de la
dulce Señora del Tepeyac, Tú, Madre de Guadalupe, entras de modo determinante en la vida
cristiana del pueblo de México. No menor ha
sido tu presencia en otras partes, donde tus hijos
te invocan con tiernos nombres, como Nuestra
Señora de la Altagracia, de la Aparecida, de Lu-
ján y tantos otros no menos entrañables, para no
hacer una lista interminable, con los que en cada
nación, y aun en cada zona, los pueblos latinoamericanos te expresan su devoción más profunda y Tú les proteges en su peregrinar de fe.
El Papa —que proviene de un país en el que
tus imágenes, especialmente una: la de Jasna
Gora, son también signo de tu presencia en la
vida de la nación, en su azarosa historia— es
particularmente sensible a este signo de tu presencia aquí, en la vida del Pueblo de Dios en
México, en su historia, también ella no fácil y a

veces hasta dramática. Pero estás igualmente presente en la vida de tantos otros pueblos y naciones de América Latina, presidiendo y guiando no sólo su pasado remoto o reciente, sino también el momento actual, con sus incertidumbres y sombras. Este Papa percibe en lo hondo de su corazón los vínculos particulares que te unen a Ti con este pueblo y a este pueblo contigo. Este pueblo, que afectuosamente te llama «La Morenita». Este pueblo —e indirectamente todo este inmenso continente— vive su unidad espiritual gracias al hecho de que Tú eres la Madre. Una Madre que, con su amor, crea, conserva, acrecienta espacios de cercanía entre sus hijos.

¡Salve, Madre de México!

¡Madre de América Latina!

3. Nos encontramos aquí en esta hora insólita y estupenda de la historia del mundo. Llegamos a este lugar, conscientes de hallarnos en un momento crucial. Con esta reunión de obispos deseamos entroncar con la precedente Conferencia del Episcopado Latinoamericano que tuvo lugar hace diez años en Medellín, en coincidencia con el Congreso Eucarístico de Bogotá, y en la que participó el papa Pablo VI, de imborrable memoria. Hemos venido aquí no tanto para volver a examinar, al cabo de diez años, el mismo problema, cuanto para revisarlo en modo nuevo, en lugar nuevo y en nuevo momento histórico.

Medellín, impulso de renovación en plena fidelidad eclesial

Queremos tomar como punto de partida lo que se contiene en los documentos y resoluciones de aquella Conferencia. Y queremos a la vez, sobre la base de las experiencias de estos diez años, del desarrollo del pensamiento y a la luz de las experiencias de toda la Iglesia, dar un justo y necesario paso adelante.

La Conferencia de Medellín tuvo lugar poco después de la clausura del Vaticano II, el Concilio de nuestro siglo, y ha tenido por objetivo recoger los planteamientos y contenido esenciales del Concilio, para aplicarlos y hacerlos fuerza orientadora en la situación concreta de la Iglesia Latinoamericana.

Sin el Concilio no hubiera sido posible la reunión de Medellín, que quiso ser un impulso de renovación pastoral, un nuevo «espíritu» de cara al futuro, en plena fidelidad eclesial en la interpretación de los signos de los tiempos en América Latina. La intencionalidad evangelizadora era bien clara y queda patente en los dieciséis temas afrontados, reunidos en torno a tres grandes áreas, mutuamente complementarias: promoción humana, evangelización y crecimiento en la fe, Iglesia visible y sus estructuras.

Con su opción por el hombre latinoamericano visto en su integridad, con su amor preferencial pero no exclusivo por los pobres, con su aliento a una liberación integral de los hombres y de los pueblos, Medellín, la Iglesia allí presente, fue una llamada de esperanza hacia metas más cristianas y más humanas.

Pero han pasado diez años. Y se han hecho interpretaciones, a veces contradictorias, no siempre correctas, no siempre beneficiosas para la Iglesia. Por ello, la Iglesia busca los caminos que le permitan comprender más profundamente y cumplir con mayor empeño la misión recibida de Cristo Jesús.

Gran importancia han tenido a tal respecto las sesiones del Sínodo de los Obispos que se han celebrado en estos años, y sobre todo la del año 1974, centrada sobre la evangelización, cuyas conclusiones ha recogido después, de modo vivo y alentador, la exhortación apostólica *Evangelii nuntiandi* de Pablo VI.

Este es el tema que colocamos hoy sobre nuestra mesa de trabajo, al proponernos estudiar «La evangelización en el presente y en el futuro de América Latina».

Encontrándonos en este lugar santo para iniciar nuestros trabajos, se nos presenta ante los ojos el cenáculo de Jerusalén, lugar de la institución de la Eucaristía. Al mismo cenáculo volvieron los apóstoles después de la ascensión del Señor, para que, permaneciendo en oración con María, la Madre de Cristo, pudieran preparar sus corazones para recibir al Espíritu Santo, en el momento del nacimiento de la Iglesia.

También nosotros venimos aquí para ello, también nosotros esperamos el descenso del Espíritu Santo, que nos hará ver los caminos de la evangelización, a través de los cuales la Iglesia debe continuar y renacer en nuestro gran continente. También nosotros hoy, y en los próximos días, deseamos perseverar en la oración con María, Madre de nuestro Señor y Maestro: contigo, Madre de la esperanza, Madre de Guadalupe.

Ayúdanos a enseñar la verdad

4. Permite, pues, que yo, Juan Pablo II, Obispo de Roma y Papa, junto con mis hermanos en el episcopado que representan a la Iglesia de México y de toda América Latina, en este solemne momento, confiemos y ofrezcamos a Ti, Sierva del Señor, todo el patrimonio del Evangelio, de la cruz, de la resurrección, de los que todos nosotros somos testigos, apóstoles, maestros y obispos.

¡Oh Madre! Ayúdanos a ser fieles dispensadores de los grandes misterios de Dios. Ayúdanos a enseñar la verdad que tu Hijo ha anunciado y a extender el amor, que es el principal mandamiento y el primer fruto del Espíritu Santo. Ayúdanos a confirmar a nuestros hermanos en la fe, ayúdanos a despertar la esperanza en la vida eterna. Ayúdanos a guardar los grandes tesoros encerrados en las almas del Pueblo de Dios que nos ha sido encomendado.

Te ofrecemos todo este Pueblo de Dios. Te ofrecemos la Iglesia de México y de todo el Continente. Te la ofrecemos como propiedad tuya. Tú que has entrado tan adentro en los corazones de los fieles a través de la señal de tu presencia, que es tu imagen en el santuario de Guadalupe, vive como en tu casa en estos corazones, también en el futuro. Sé uno de casa en nuestras familias, en nuestras parroquias, misiones, diócesis y en todos los pueblos.

Y hazlo por medio de la Iglesia santa, la cual, imitándote a Ti, Madre, desea ser a su vez una buena madre, cuidar a las almas en todas sus necesidades, anunciando el Evangelio, administrando los sacramentos, salvaguardando la vida de las familias mediante el sacramento del matrimonio, reuniendo a todos en la comunidad eucarística por medio del santo sacramento del altar, acompañándolos amorosamente desde la cuna hasta la entrada en la eternidad.

¡Oh Madre! Despierta en las jóvenes generaciones la disponibilidad al exclusivo servicio a Dios. Implora para nosotros abundantes vocaciones locales al sacerdocio y a la vida consagrada.

¡Oh Madre! Corrobora la fe de todos nuestros hermanos y hermanas laicos, para que en cada campo de la vida social, profesional, cultural y política, actúen de acuerdo con la verdad y la ley que tu Hijo ha traído a la humanidad, para conducir a todos a la salvación eterna y, al mismo tiempo, para hacer la vida sobre la tierra más humana, más digna del hombre.

Puebla, cauce de evangelización
en la verdad y en la justicia

La Iglesia que desarrolla su labor entre las naciones americanas, la Iglesia en México, quiere servir con todas sus fuerzas a esta causa sublime con un renovado espíritu misionero. ¡Oh Madre! Haz que sepamos servirla en la verdad y en la justicia. Haz que nosotros mismos sigamos este camino y conduzcamos a los demás, sin desviarnos jamás por senderos tortuosos, arrastrando a los otros.

Te ofrecemos y confiamos todos aquellos y todo aquello que es objeto de nuestra responsabilidad pastoral, confiando que Tú estarás con nosotros, y nos ayudarás a realizar lo que tu Hijo nos ha mandado (cf. Jn 2,5). Te traemos esta confianza ilimitada y con ella, yo, Juan Pablo II, con todos mis hermanos en el episcopado de México y de América Latina, queremos vincularte de modo todavía más fuerte a nuestro ministerio, a la Iglesia y a la vida de nuestras naciones. Deseamos poner en tus manos nuestro entero porvenir, el porvenir de la evangelización de América Latina.

¡Reina de los apóstoles! Acepta nuestra prontitud a servir sin reserva la causa de tu Hijo, la causa del Evangelio y la causa de la paz, basada sobre la justicia y el amor entre los hombres y entre los pueblos.

¡Reina de la paz! Salva a las naciones y a los pueblos de todo el Continente, que tanto confían en Ti, de las guerras, del odio y de la subversión.

Haz que todos, gobernantes y súbditos, aprendan a vivir en paz, se eduquen para la paz, hagan cuanto exige la justicia y el respeto de los derechos de todo hombre, para que se consolide la paz.

Acepta esta nuestra confiada entrega, ¡oh Sierva del Señor! Que tu maternal presencia en el misterio de Cristo y de la Iglesia se convierta en fuente de alegría y de libertad para cada uno y para todos; fuente de aquella libertad por medio de la cual «Cristo nos ha liberado» (Gál 5,1), y, finalmente, fuente de aquella paz que el mundo no puede dar, sino que sólo la da El, Cristo (cf. Jn 14,27).

Finalmente, ¡oh Madre!, recordando y confirmando el gesto de mis predecesores Benedicto XIV y Pío X, quienes te proclamaron Patrona de México y de toda la América Latina, te presento una diadema en nombre de todos tus hijos mexicanos y latinoamericanos, para que los conserves bajo tu protección, guardes su concordia en la fe y su fidelidad a Cristo, tu Hijo. Amén.

TESTIGOS Y ARTIFICES DE UNIDAD Y FRATERNIDAD

Encuentro del Santo Padre con los sacerdotes y religiosos de México en la basílica de Guadalupe, 27 de enero.

Amadísimos sacerdotes, diocesanos y religiosos:

Uno de los encuentros que con mayor ilusión esperaba durante mi visita a México, es el que tengo con vosotros aquí en el santuario de nuestra venerada y querida Madre de Guadalupe.

Servidores de una causa sublime

Ved en ello una prueba del afecto y solicitud del Papa. El, como obispo de toda la Iglesia, es consciente de vuestro papel insustituible y se siente muy cercano a quienes son piezas centrales en la tarea eclesial, como principales colaboradores de los obispos, como participantes de los poderes salvadores de Cristo, testigos, anunciadores de su Evangelio, alentadores de la fe y vocación apostólica del Pueblo de Dios. Y no quiero aquí olvidar a tantas otras almas consagradas, colaboradores preciosos, aun sin el carácter sacerdotal, en muchos e importantes sectores del apostolado de la Iglesia.

Pero no sólo tenéis una presencia cualificada en el apostolado eclesial, sino que vuestro amor al hombre por Dios es bien notable entre los estudiantes de los diversos grados, entre los enfermos y necesitados de asistencia, entre los hombres de cultura, entre los pobres que reclaman comprensión y apoyo, entre tantas personas que a vosotros acuden en búsqueda de consejo y aliento.

Por vuestra sacrificada entrega al Señor y a la Iglesia, por vuestra cercanía al hombre, recibid mi agradecimiento en nombre de Cristo.

Servidores de una causa sublime, de vosotros depende en buena parte la suerte de la Iglesia en los sectores confiados a vuestro cuidado pastoral. Ello os impone una profunda conciencia de la grandeza de la misión recibida y de la necesidad de adecuarse cada vez más a ella.

Se trata, en efecto, queridos hermanos e hijos, de la Iglesia de Cristo —¡qué respeto y amor debe esto infundirnos!—, a la que habéis de servir gozosamente en santidad de vida (cf. Ef 4,13).

Mirad al modelo, Cristo

Este servicio alto y exigente no podrá ser prestado sin una clara y arraigada convicción acerca de vuestra identidad como sacerdotes de Cristo, depositarios y administradores de los misterios de Dios, instrumentos de salvación para los hombres, testigos de un reino que se inicia en este mundo, pero que se completa en el más allá. Ante estas certezas de la fe, ¿por qué dudar sobre la propia identidad? ¿Por qué titubear acerca del valor de la propia vida? ¿Por qué la hesitación frente al camino emprendido?

Para conservar o reforzar esta convicción firme y perseverante, mirad al modelo, Cristo, avivad los valores sobrenaturales en vuestra existencia, pedid la fuerza corroborante de lo alto, en el coloquio asiduo y confiado de la oración. Hoy como ayer os es imprescindible. Y sed también fieles a la práctica frecuente del sacramento de la reconciliación, a la meditación cotidiana, a la devoción a la Virgen mediante el rezo del rosario. Cultivad, en una palabra, la unión con Dios mediante una profunda vida interior. Sea éste vuestro primer empeño. No temáis que el tiempo consagrado al Señor quite algo a vuestro apostolado. Muy al contrario, ello será fuente de fecundidad en el ministerio.

Sois personas que habéis hecho del Evangelio una profesión de vida. Del Evangelio deberéis sacar los criterios esenciales de fe —no meros criterios psicológicos o sociológicos— que produzcan una síntesis armónica entre espiritualidad y ministerio. Sin permitir una «profesionalización» del mismo, sin rebajar la estima que debe mereceros vuestro celibato o castidad consagrada, aceptadas por amor del Reino, en una ilimitada paternidad espiritual (cf. 1 Cor 4,15): «A ellos (los sacerdotes) debemos nuestra regeneración bienaventurada —afirma San Juan Crisóstomo— y el conocer una verdadera libertad» *(Sobre el sacerdocio* 4-6).

Comunión con los obispos

Sois participantes del sacerdocio ministerial de Cristo para el servicio de la unidad de la comunidad. Un servicio que se realiza en virtud de la potestad recibida para dirigir al Pueblo de Dios, perdonar los pecados y ofrecer el sacrificio eucarístico (cf. *Lumen gentium* 10; *Presbyterorum ordinis* 2). Un servicio sacerdotal específico, que no puede ser reemplazado en la comunidad cristiana por el sacerdocio común de los fieles, esencialmente diverso del primero (cf. *Lumen gentium* 10).

Sois miembros de una Iglesia particular, cuyo centro de unidad es el obispo (cf. *Christus Dominus* 28), con quien todo sacerdote ha de observar una actitud de comunión y obediencia. Por su parte, los religiosos, en lo referente a las actividades pastorales, no pueden negar su leal colaboración y obediencia a la jerarquía local, alegando una exclusiva dependencia respecto de la Iglesia universal (cf. ibíd., 34; y documento común de la Sagrada Congregación para los Religiosos e Institutos Seculares y de la Sagrada Congregación para los Obispos, 14 de mayo de 1978). Mucho menos sería admisible en sacerdotes o religiosos una práctica de magisterios paralelos respecto de los obispos —auténticos y solos maestros en la fe— o de las Conferencias Episcopales.

Sois servidores del Pueblo de Dios, servidores de la fe, administradores y testigos del amor de Cristo a los hombres; amor que no es partidista, que a nadie excluye, aunque se dirija con preferencia al más pobre. A este respecto, quiero recordaros lo que dije hace poco a los superiores generales de los religiosos en Roma: «El alma que vive en contacto habitual con Dios y se mueve dentro del ardiente rayo de su amor, sabe defenderse con facilidad de la tentación de particularismos y antítesis, que crean el riesgo de dolorosas divisiones; sabe interpretar a la justa luz del Evangelio las opciones por los más pobres y por cada una de las víctimas del egoísmo humano, sin ceder a radicalismos socio-políticos que a la larga se manifiestan inoportunos, contraproducentes» (24 de noviembre de 1978).

Guías espirituales

Sois guías espirituales que se esfuerzan por orientar y mejorar los corazones de los fieles para que, convertidos, vivan el amor a Dios y al prójimo y se comprometan en la promoción y dignificación del hombre.

Sois sacerdotes y religiosos; no sois dirigentes sociales, líderes políticos o funcionarios de un poder temporal. Por eso os repito: «No nos ha-

gamos la ilusión de servir al Evangelio si trata-
mos de "diluir" nuestro carisma a través de un
interés exagerado hacia el amplio campo de los
problemas temporales» (Discurso al clero de
Roma). No olvidéis que el liderazgo temporal
puede fácilmente ser fuente de división, mientras que el sacerdote debe ser signo y factor de
unidad, de fraternidad. Las funciones seculares
son el campo propio de acción de los laicos, que
han de perfeccionar las cosas temporales con
el espíritu cristiano (cf. *Apostolicam actuositatem* 4).

Amadísimos sacerdotes y religiosos: Os diría
muchas otras cosas, pero no quiero alargar de-
masiado este encuentro. Algunas las diré en otra
sede y a ellas os remito.

Termino repitiéndoos mi gran confianza en
vosotros. ¡Espero tanto de vuestro amor a
Cristo y a los hombres! Mucho hay que hacer.
Emprendamos el camino con nuevo entusiasmo.
Unidos a Cristo, bajo la mirada materna de la
Virgen, Nuestra Señora de Guadalupe, dulce
Madre de los sacerdotes y religiosos. Con la
afectuosa bendición del Papa, para vosotros
y para todos los sacerdotes y religiosos de
México.

EXPERTAS EN EL SUBLIME CONOCIMIENTO DE CRISTO

Encuentro del Santo Padre en el Colegio «Miguel Angel» con las religiosas de México, 27 de enero.

Queridas hijas religiosas de México:

Este encuentro del Papa con las religiosas mexicanas que había de celebrarse en la basílica de nuestra Madre de Guadalupe, tiene lugar aquí en su presencia espiritual. Ante Ella, modelo perfecto de mujer, el ejemplo mejor de vida dedicada enteramente a su Hijo el Salvador, en una constante actitud interna de fe, esperanza, de entrega amorosa a una misión sobrenatural.

Fidelidad a vuestro compromiso

En este lugar privilegiado y ante esta figura de la Virgen, el Papa quiere transcurrir unos momentos con vosotras, las numerosas religiosas aquí presentes, que representáis a las más de veinte mil dispersas por toda la geografía mexicana y fuera de la patria.

Sois una fuerza importantísima dentro de la

Iglesia y de la misma sociedad, esparcidas en innumerables sectores como el de las escuelas y colegios, las clínicas y hospitales, el campo caritativo y asistencial, las obras parroquiales, la catequesis, los grupos de apostolado y tantos otros. Formáis parte de diversas familias religiosas, pero con un mismo ideal dentro de diferentes carismas: seguir a Cristo, ser testimonio vivo de la perennidad de su mensaje.

Es la vuestra una vocación que merece la máxima estima por parte del Papa y de la Iglesia, ayer como hoy. Por eso os quiero expresar mi gozosa confianza en vosotras y alentaros a no desmayar en el camino emprendido, que vale la pena proseguir con renovado espíritu y entusiasmo. Sabed que el Papa os acompaña con su oración y se complace de vuestra fidelidad a la propia vocación, a Cristo, a la Iglesia.

Al mismo tiempo, sin embargo, me vais a permitir que añada algunas reflexiones que propongo a vuestra consideración y examen.

Visión profunda de fe, mantenida por la oración

Es cierto que en una gran parte de religiosas prevalece un encomiable espíritu de fidelidad al propio compromiso eclesial, y que se advierten aspectos de gran vitalidad en la vida religiosa con un retorno a una visión más evangélica, una creciente solidaridad entre las familias religiosas, una mayor cercanía a los pobres, objeto de una justa atención prioritaria. Son éstos motivos de gozo y optimismo.

Mas tampoco faltan ejemplos de confusión acerca de la esencia misma de la vida consagrada y del propio carisma. A veces se abandona la oración, sustituyéndola con la acción; se interpretan los votos según la mentalidad secularizante que difumina las motivaciones religiosas del propio estado; se abandona con cierta ligereza la vida en común; se adoptan posturas socio-políticas como el verdadero objetivo a perseguir, incluso con bien definidas radicalizaciones ideológicas.

Y cuando se oscurecen, a veces, las certezas de la fe, se aducen motivos de búsqueda de nuevos horizontes y experiencias, quizá con el pretexto de estar más cerca de los hombres, acaso de grupos bien concretos, elegidos con criterios no siempre evangélicos.

Queridas religiosas: No olvidéis nunca que para mantener un concepto claro del valor de vuestra vida consagrada necesitaréis una profunda visión de fe, que se alimenta y mantiene con la oración (cf. *Perfectae caritatis* 6). La misma que os hará superar toda incertidumbre acerca de vuestra identidad propia, que os mantendrá fieles a esa dimensión vertical que os es esencial, para identificaros con Cristo desde las bienaventuranzas y ser testigos auténticos del reino de Dios para los hombres del mundo actual.

Sólo con esta solicitud por los intereses de Cristo (cf. 1 Cor 7,32), seréis capaces de dar al carisma del profetismo su conveniente dimensión de testificación del Señor. Sin opciones por los pobres y necesitados que no dimanen de criterios del Evangelio, en vez de inspirarse en motivaciones sociopolíticas que —como dije recientemente a los superiores generales religiosos en Roma— a la larga se manifiestan inoportunas, contraproducentes.

Apertura a la dimensión de eternidad

Habéis elegido como método de vida el seguimiento de unos valores que no son los meramente humanos, aunque también éstos debéis estimar en su justa medida. Habéis optado por el servicio a los demás por amor de Dios. No olvidéis nunca que el ser humano no se agota en la sola dimensión terrestre. Vosotras, como profesionales de la fe y expertas en el sublime conocimiento de Cristo (cf. Flp 3,8), abridles a la llamada y dimensión de eternidad en la que vosotras mismas debéis vivir.

Muchas otras cosas os diría. Tomad, como dicho a vosotras, cuanto indiqué a las superioras generales religiosas en mi discurso del 16 de noviembre último. ¡Cuánto podéis hacer hoy por la Iglesia y por la humanidad! Ellas esperan vuestra generosa entrega, la dedicación de vuestro corazón libre, que alargue insospechadamente sus potencialidades de amor en un mundo que está perdiendo la capacidad de altruismo, de amor sacrificado y desinteresado. Recordaos, en efecto, que sois místicas esposas de Cristo y de Cristo crucificado (cf. 2 Cor 4,5).

La Iglesia os repite hoy su confianza: sed testimonios vivientes de esa nueva civilización del amor, que acertadamente proclamó mi predecesor Pablo VI.

Para que en esa empresa magnífica y esperanzadora os corrobore la fuerza de lo alto, que os mantenga, en una renovada juventud espiritual, fieles a estos propósitos, os acompaño con una particular bendición, que extiendo a todas las religiosas de México.

PROMOCION Y DEFENSA
DE LA FAMILIA

*Homilía del Santo Padre en la
misa celebrada en Puebla de los
Angeles, 28 de enero.*

Amadísimos hijos e hijas:

Puebla de los Angeles: el nombre sonoro y
expresivo de vuestra ciudad se encuentra hoy
día en millones de labios a lo largo de América
Latina y en todo el mundo. Vuestra ciudad se
vuelve símbolo y señal para la Iglesia latinoamericana. Es aquí, de hecho, donde se congregan a
partir de hoy, convocados por el Sucesor de Pedro, los obispos de todo el continente para reflexionar sobre la misión de los pastores en esta
parte del mundo, en esta hora singular de la historia.

Puebla, nuevo cenáculo

El Papa ha querido subir hasta esta cumbre
desde donde parece abrirse toda América Latina. Y es con la impresión de contemplar el di-
seño de cada una de las naciones que, en este
altar levantado sobre las montañas, el Papa ha

querido celebrar este sacrificio eucarístico para invocar sobre esta Conferencia, sus participantes y sus trabajos, la luz, el calor, todos los dones del Espíritu de Dios, Espíritu de Jesucristo.

Nada más natural y necesario que invocarlo en esta circunstancia. La gran Asamblea que se abre es, en efecto, en su esencia más profunda una reunión eclesial: eclesial por aquellos que aquí se reúnen, pastores de la Iglesia de Dios que está en América Latina; eclesial por el tema que estudia, la misión de la Iglesia en el continente; eclesial por sus objetivos de hacer siempre más viva y eficaz la aportación original que la Iglesia tiene el deber de ofrecer al bienestar, a la armonía, a la justicia y a la paz de estos pueblos. Ahora bien, no hay asamblea eclesial si ahí no está en la plenitud de su misteriosa acción el Espíritu de Dios.

El Papa lo invoca con todo el fervor de su corazón. Que el lugar donde se reúnen los obispos sea un nuevo cenáculo, mucho más grande que el de Jerusalén, donde los apóstoles eran apenas once en aquella mañana, pero, como el de Jerusalén, abierto a las llamas del Paráclito y a la fuerza de un renovado Pentecostés. Que el Espíritu cumpla en vosotros, obispos aquí congregados, la multiforme misión que el Señor Jesús le confió: *intérprete de Dios,* para hacer comprender su designio y su palabra inaccesibles a la simple razón humana (cf. Jn 14,26), abra la inteligencia de estos pastores y los introduzca en la verdad (cf. Jn 16,13); *testigo de Jesucristo,* dé testimonio en la conciencia y en el corazón de

ellos y los transforme a su vez en testigos coherentes, creíbles, eficaces durante sus trabajos
(cf. Jn 15,26); *Abogado o Consolador,* infunda
ánimo contra el pecado del mundo (cf. Jn 16,8) y
les ponga en los labios lo que habrán de decir,
sobre todo en el momento en que el testimonio
costará sufrimiento y fatiga.

Dios es una familia

Os ruego, pues, amados hijos e hijas, que os
unáis a mí en esta Eucaristía, en esta invocación
al Espíritu. No es para sí mismos ni por intereses personales que los obispos, venidos de todos
los ambientes del continente se encuentran aquí;
es para vosotros, Pueblo de Dios en estas tierras, y para vuestro bien. Participad, pues, en
esta III Conferencia también de esta manera:
pidiendo cada día para todos y para cada uno de
ellos la abundancia del Espíritu Santo.

Se ha dicho, en forma bella y profunda, que
nuestro Dios en su misterio más íntimo no es
una soledad, sino una familia, puesto que lleva
en sí mismo paternidad, filiación y la esencia de
la familia, que es el amor. Este amor, en la Familia divina, es el Espíritu Santo. El tema de la
familia no es, pues, ajeno al tema del Espíritu
Santo. Permitid que sobre este tema de la familia —que ciertamente ocupará a los obispos durante estos días— os dirija el Papa algunas palabras.

Sabéis que con términos densos y apremiantes

la Conferencia de Medellín habló de la familia. Los obispos, en aquel año de 1968, vieron, en vuestro gran sentido de la familia, un rasgo primordial de vuestra cultura latinoamericana. Hicieron ver que, para el bien de vuestros países, las familias latinoamericanas deberían tener siempre tres dimensiones: ser educadoras en la fe, formadoras de personas, promotoras de desarrollo. Subrayaron también los graves obstáculos que las familias encuentran para cumplir con este triple cometido. Recomendaron «por eso» la atención pastoral a las familias, como una de las atenciones prioritarias de la Iglesia en el continente.

**Acoger a los invitados
al banquete de la vida**

Pasados diez años, la Iglesia en América Latina se siente feliz por todo lo que ha podido hacer en favor de la familia. Pero reconoce con humildad cuánto le falta por hacer, mientras percibe que la pastoral familiar, lejos de haber perdido su carácter prioritario, aparece hoy todavía más urgente, como elemento muy importante en la evangelización.

La Iglesia es consciente, en efecto, de que en estos tiempos la familia afronta en América Latina serios problemas. Ultimamente algunos países han introducido el divorcio en su legislación, lo cual conlleva una nueva amenaza a la integridad familiar. En la mayoría de vuestros países se lamenta que un número alarmante de niños, porvenir de esas naciones y esperanzas para el futuro, nazcan en hogares sin ninguna estabilidad o, como se les suele llamar, en «familias incompletas». Además, en ciertos lugares del «Continente de la esperanza», esta misma esperanza corre el riesgo de desvanecerse, pues ella crece en el seno de las familias, muchas de las cuales no pueden vivir normalmente, porque repercuten particularmente en ellas los resultados más negativos del desarrollo: índices verdaderamente deprimentes de insalubridad, pobreza y aun miseria, ignorancia y analfabetismo, condiciones inhumanas de vivienda, subalimentación crónica y tantas otras realidades no menos tristes.

En defensa de la familia, contra estos males, la Iglesia se compromete a dar su ayuda e invita a los Gobiernos para que pongan como punto clave de su acción: una política socio-familiar inteligente, audaz, perseverante, reconociendo que ahí se encuentra sin duda el porvenir —la esperanza— del continente. Habría que añadir que tal política familiar no debe entenderse como un esfuerzo indiscriminado para reducir a cualquier precio el índice de natalidad —lo que mi predecesor Pablo VI llamaba «disminuir el número de los invitados al banquete de la vida»—, cuando es notorio que aun para el desarrollo es indispensable un equilibrado índice de población. Se trata de combinar esfuerzos para crear condiciones favorables a la existencia de familias sanas y equilibradas: «aumentar la comida en la mesa», siempre en expresión de Pablo VI.

Además de la defensa de la familia, debemos hablar también de promoción de la familia. A tal promoción han de contribuir muchos organismos: Gobiernos y organismos gubernamentales, la escuela, los sindicatos, los medios de comunicación social, las agrupaciones de barrios, las diferentes asociaciones voluntarias o espontáneas que florecen hoy día en todas partes.

Verdadera Iglesia doméstica

La Iglesia debe ofrecer también su contribución en la línea de su misión espiritual de anuncio del Evangelio y conducción de los hombres a la salvación, que tiene también una enorme repercusión sobre el bienestar familiar. ¿Y qué puede hacer la Iglesia uniendo sus esfuerzos a los de los otros? Estoy seguro de que vuestros obispos se esforzarán por dar a esta cuestión respuestas adecuadas, justas, valederas. Os indico cuánto valor tiene para la familia lo que la Iglesia hace ya en América Latina, por ejemplo, para preparar los futuros esposos al matrimonio, para ayudar a las familias cuando atraviesan en su existencia crisis normales que, bien encaminadas, pueden ser hasta fecundas y enriquecedoras, para hacer de cada familia cristiana una verdadera *ecclesia domestica,* con todo el rico contenido de esta expresión, para preparar muchas familias a la misión evangelizadora de otras familias, para poner de relieve todos los valores de la vida familiar, para venir en ayuda de las familias incompletas, para estimular a los gobernantes a suscitar en sus países esa política socio-familiar de la que hablábamos hace un momento. La Conferencia de Puebla ciertamente apoyará estas iniciativas y quizá sugerirá otras. Alégranos pensar que la historia de Latinoamérica tendrá así motivos para agradecer a la Iglesia lo mucho que ha hecho, hace y hará por la familia en este vasto continente.

Abríos a los demás

Hijos e hijas muy amados: El Sucesor de Pedro se siente ahora, desde este altar, singularmente cercano a todas las familias de América Latina. Es como si cada hogar se abriera y el Papa pudiese penetrar en cada uno de ellos; casas donde no falta el pan ni el bienestar, pero falta quizá concordia y alegría; casas donde las familias viven más bien modestamente y en la inseguridad del mañana, ayudándose mutuamente a llevar una existencia difícil pero digna; pobres habitaciones en las periferias de vuestras ciudades, donde hay mucho sufrimiento escondido, aunque en medio de ellas existe la sencilla alegría de los pobres; humildes chozas de campesinos, de indígenas, de emigrantes, etc. Para cada familia en particular el Papa quisiera poder decir una palabra de aliento y de esperanza. Vosotras, familias que podéis disfrutar del bienestar, no os cerréis dentro de vuestra felicidad; abríos a los otros para repartir lo que os sobre y a otros les falta. Familias oprimidas por la pobreza, no os desaniméis y, sin tener el lujo por ideal ni la riqueza como principio de felicidad, buscad con la ayuda de todos superar los pasos difíciles en la espera de días mejores. Familias visitadas y angustiadas por el dolor físico o moral, probadas por la enfermedad o la miseria, no acrecentéis tales sufrimientos con la amargura o la desesperación, sino sabed amortiguar el dolor con la esperanza. Familias todas de América Latina, estad seguras de que el Papa os conoce y quiere conoceros aún más porque os ama con delicadezas de Padre.

Esta es, en el cuadro de la visita del Papa a México, la Jornada de la Familia. Acoged, pues, familias latinoamericanas, con vuestra presencia aquí, alrededor del altar, a través de la radio o la televisión, acoged la visita que el Papa quiere hacer a cada una. Y dadle al Papa la alegría de veros crecer en los valores cristianos que son los vuestros, para que América Latina encuentre en sus millones de familias razones para confiar, para esperar, para luchar, para construir.

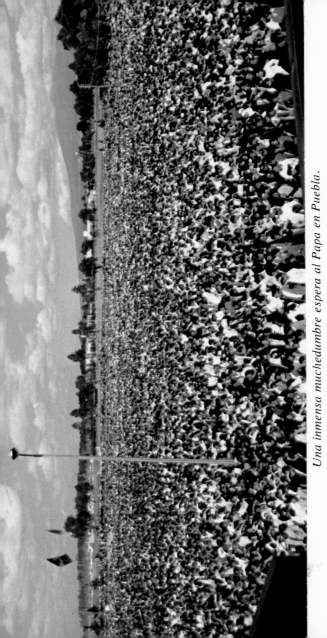

Una inmensa muchedumbre espera al Papa en Puebla.

Camino de Puebla, «Mexicum semper fidele».

El Papa, mensajero perpetuo de la paz.

El Papa bendice a la mult

...gregada ante la basílica guadalupana.

Homenaje de la juventud católica de Oaxaca.

Audiencia en Puebla a los observadores no católicos.

Tras la misa celebrada en el Seminario de Puebla.

AUDACIA DE PROFETAS
Y PRUDENCIA EVANGELICA
DE PASTORES

Discurso del Santo Padre al inaugurar los trabajos de la III Conferencia General del Episcopado Latinoamericano, 28 de enero.

Amados hermanos en el episcopado:

Esta hora que tengo la dicha de vivir con vosotros, es ciertamente histórica para la Iglesia en América Latina. De esto es consciente la opinión pública mundial, son conscientes los fieles de vuestras Iglesias locales, sois conscientes sobre todo vosotros que seréis protagonistas y responsables de esta hora.

Es también una hora de gracia, señalada por el paso del Señor, por una particularísima presencia y acción del Espíritu de Dios. Por eso hemos invocado con confianza a este Espíritu, al principio de los trabajos. Por esto también quiero ahora suplicaros como un hermano a hermanos muy queridos: todos los días de esta Conferencia y en cada uno de sus actos, dejaos conducir por el Espíritu, abríos a su inspiración y a su impulso; sea El y ningún otro espíritu el que os guíe y conforte.

Bajo este Espíritu, por tercera vez en los veinticinco últimos años, obispos de todos los países, representando al episcopado de todo el continente latinoamericano, os congregáis para profundizar juntos el sentido de vuestra misión ante las exigencias nuevas de vuestros pueblos.

La Conferencia que ahora se abre, convocada por el venerado Pablo VI, confirmada por mi inolvidable predecesor Juan Pablo I y reconfirmada por mí como uno de los primeros actos de mi pontificado, se conecta con aquella, ya lejana, de Río de Janeiro, que tuvo como su fruto más notable el nacimiento del CELAM. Pero se conecta aún más estrechamente con la II Conferencia de Medellín, cuyo décimo aniversario conmemora.

En estos diez años, cuánto camino ha hecho la humanidad, y con la humanidad y a su servicio, cuánto camino ha hecho la Iglesia. Esta III Conferencia no puede desconocer esta realidad. Deberá, pues, tomar como punto de partida las conclusiones de Medellín, con todo lo que tienen de positivo, pero sin ignorar las incorrectas interpretaciones a veces hechas y que exigen sereno discernimiento, oportuna crítica y claras tomas de posición.

Os servirá de guía en vuestros debates el Documento de Trabajo, preparado con tanto cuidado para que constituya siempre el punto de referencia.

Pero tendréis también entre las manos la exhortación apostólica *Evangelii nuntiandi* de Pablo VI. ¡Con qué complacidos sentimientos el gran Pontífice aprobó como tema de la Conferencia: «El presente y el futuro de la evangelización en América Latina»!

Lo pueden decir los que estuvieron cerca de él en los meses de preparación de la Asamblea. Ellos podrán dar testimonio también de la gratitud con la cual él supo que el telón de fondo de toda la Conferencia sería este texto, en el cual puso toda su alma de Pastor, en el ocaso de su vida. Ahora que él «cerró los ojos a la escena de este mundo» (cf. *Testamento de Pablo VI)*, este documento se convierte en un testamento espiritual que la Conferencia habrá de escudriñar con amor y diligencia para hacer de él otro punto de referencia obligatoria y ver cómo ponerlo en práctica. Toda la Iglesia os está agradecida por el ejemplo que dais, por lo que hacéis, y que quizá otras Iglesias locales harán a su vez.

El Papa quiere estar con vosotros en el comienzo de vuestros trabajos, agradecido al «Padre de las luces..., de quien desciende todo don perfecto» (Sant 1,17), por haber podido acompañaros en la solemne misa de ayer, bajo la mirada materna de la Virgen de Guadalupe, así como en la misa de esta mañana. Muy a gusto me quedaría con vosotros en oración, reflexión y trabajo: permaneceré, estad seguros, en espíritu, mientras me reclama en otra parte la *«sollicitudo omnium Ecclesiarum:* preocupación por todas las Iglesias»* (2 Cor 11,28). Quiero al menos, antes de regresar a Roma, dejaros como

prenda de mi presencia espiritual algunas palabras, pronunciadas con ansias de pastor y afecto
de padre, eco de las principales preocupaciones
mías respecto a la vida de la Iglesia en estos
queridos países.

I. Maestros de la verdad

Es un gran consuelo para el Pastor universal
constatar que os congregáis aquí, no como un
simposio de expertos, no como un parlamento
de políticos, no como un congreso de científicos
o técnicos, por importantes que puedan ser esas
reuniones, sino como un fraterno encuentro de
pastores de la Iglesia. Y como pastores tenéis la
viva conciencia de que vuestro deber principal
es el de ser maestros de la verdad. No de una
verdad humana y racional, sino de la verdad que
viene de Dios; que trae consigo el principio de la
auténtica liberación del hombre: «Conoceréis la
verdad y la verdad os hará libres» (Jn 8,32); esa
verdad que es la única en ofrecer una base sólida para una «praxis» adecuada.

I. 1. •Vigilar por la pureza de la doctrina, base
en la edificación de la comunidad cristiana, es,
pues, junto con el anuncio del Evangelio, el deber primero e insustituible del pastor, del maestro de la fe. Con cuánta frecuencia ponía esto de
relieve San Pablo, convencido de la gravedad en
el cumplimiento de este deber (cf. 1 Tim 1,3-7.
18-20; 11,16; 2 Tim 1,4-14). Además de la unidad

en la caridad, nos urge siempre la unidad en la verdad. El amadísimo papa Pablo VI, en la exhortación apostólica *Evangelii nuntiandi,* expresaba: «El Evangelio que nos ha sido encomendado es también palabra de verdad. Una verdad que hace libres y que es la única que procura la paz de corazón: esto es lo que la gente va buscando cuando le anunciamos la Buena Nueva. La verdad acerca de Dios, la verdad acerca del hombre y de su misterioso destino, la verdad acerca del mundo... El predicador del Evangelio será aquel que, aun a costa de renuncias y sacrificios, busca siempre la verdad que debe transmitir a los demás. No vende ni disimula jamás la verdad por el deseo de agradar a los hombres, de causar asombro, ni por originalidad o deseo de aparentar... Pastores del Pueblo de Dios: nuestro servicio pastoral nos pide que guardemos, defendamos y comuniquemos la verdad, sin reparar en sacrificios» (*Evangelii nuntiandi* 78).

Verdad sobre Jesucristo

I. 2. De vosotros, pastores, los fieles de vuestros países esperan y reclaman ante todo una cuidadosa y celosa transmisión de la verdad sobre Jesucristo. Esta se encuentra en el centro de la evangelización y constituye su contenido esencial: «No hay evangelización verdadera mientras no se anuncie el nombre, la doctrina, la vida, las promesas, el reino, el misterio de Jesús de Nazaret, Hijo de Dios» (ibíd., 22).

Del conocimiento vivo de esta verdad dependerá el vigor de la fe de millones de hombres. Dependerá también el valor de su adhesión a la Iglesia y de su presencia activa de cristianos en el mundo. De este conocimiento derivarán opciones, valores, actitudes y comportamientos capaces de orientar y definir nuestra vida cristiana, y de crear hombres nuevos y luego una humanidad nueva por la conversión de la conciencia individual y social (cf. ibíd., 18).

De una sólida cristología tiene que venir la luz sobre tantos temas y cuestiones doctrinales y pastorales que os proponéis examinar en estos días.

I. 3. Hemos, pues, de confesar a Cristo ante la historia y ante el mundo con convicción profunda, sentida, vivida, como lo confesó Pedro: «Tu eres el Mesías, el Hijo de Dios vivo» (Mt 16,16).

Esta es la Buena Noticia, en un cierto sentido única: la Iglesia vive por ella y para ella, así como saca de ella todo lo que tiene para ofrecer a los hombres, sin distinción alguna de nación, cultura, raza, tiempo, edad o condición. Por eso «desde esa confesión (de Pedro), la historia de la salvación sagrada y del Pueblo de Dios debía adquirir una nueva dimensión» (JUAN PABLO II, *Homilía del Santo Padre en la inauguración oficial de su pontificado,* 22 de octubre de 1978).

Este es el único Evangelio y, «aunque nosotros o un ángel del cielo os anunciase otro evangelio distinto... ¡sea anatema!», como escribía con palabras bien claras el Apóstol (Gál 1,8).

I. 4. Ahora bien, corren hoy por muchas partes —el fenómeno no es nuevo— «relecturas» del Evangelio, resultado de especulaciones teóricas más bien que de auténtica meditación de la palabra de Dios y de un verdadero compromiso evangélico. Ellas causan confusión al apartarse de los criterios centrales de la fe de la Iglesia y se cae en la temeridad de comunicarlas, a manera de catequesis, a las comunidades cristianas.

En algunos casos o se silencia la divinidad de Cristo, o se incurre de hecho en formas de interpretación reñidas con la fe de la Iglesia. Cristo sería solamente un «profeta», un anunciador del reino y del amor de Dios, pero no el verdadero Hijo de Dios, ni sería, por tanto, el centro y el objeto del mismo mensaje evangélico.

En otros casos se pretende mostrar a Jesús como comprometido políticamente, como un luchador contra la dominación romana y contra los poderes, e incluso implicado en la lucha de clases. Esta concepción de Cristo como político, revolucionario, como el subversivo de Nazaret, no se compagina con la catequesis de la Iglesia. Confundiendo el pretexto insidioso de los acusadores de Jesús con la actitud de Jesús mismo —bien diferente— se aduce como causa de su muerte el desenlace de un conflicto político y se calla la voluntad de entrega del Señor y aun la conciencia de su misión redentora. Los evangelios muestran claramente cómo para Jesús era una tentación lo que alterara su misión de Servidor de Yavé (cf. Mt 4,8; Lc 4,5). No acepta la posición de quienes mezclaban las cosas de Dios con actitudes meramente políticas (cf. Mt 22,21; Mc 12,17; Jn 18,36). Rechaza inequívocamente el recurso a la violencia. Abre su mensaje de conversión a todos, sin excluir a los mismos publicanos. La perspectiva de su misión es mucho más profunda. Consiste en la salvación integral por un amor transformante, pacificador, de perdón y reconciliación. No cabe duda, por otra parte, que todo esto es muy exigente para la actitud del cristiano que quiere servir de verdad a los hermanos más pequeños, a los pobres, a los necesitados, a los marginados; en una palabra, a todos los que reflejan en sus vidas el rostro doliente del Señor (cf. *Lumen gentium* 8).

I. 5. Contra tales «relecturas», pues, y contra sus hipótesis, brillantes quizá, pero frágiles e inconsistentes, que de ellas derivan, «la evangelización en el presente y en el futuro de América Latina» no puede cesar de afirmar la fe de la Iglesia: Jesucristo Verbo e Hijo de Dios, se hace hombre para acercarse al hombre y brindarle por la fuerza de su misterio, la salvación, gran don de Dios (cf. *Evangelii nuntiandi* 19 y 27).

Es ésta la fe que ha informado vuestra historia y ha plasmado lo mejor de los valores de vuestros pueblos y tendrá que seguir animando, con todas las energías, el dinamismo de su futuro. Es ésta la fe que revela la vocación de concordia y unidad que ha de desterrar los peligros de guerras en este continente de esperanza, en el que la Iglesia ha sido tan potente factor de integración. Esta fe, en fin, que con tanta vitalidad y de tan variados modos expresan los fieles de América Latina a través de la religiosidad o piedad popular.

Desde esta fe en Cristo, desde el seno de la Iglesia, somos capaces de servir al hombre, a nuestros pueblos, de penetrar con el Evangelio su cultura, transformar los corazones, humanizar sistemas y estructuras.

Cualquier silencio, olvido, mutilación o inadecuada acentuación de la integridad del misterio de Jesucristo que se aparte de la fe de la Iglesia, no puede ser contenido válido de la evangelización. «Hoy, bajo el pretexto de una piedad que es falsa, bajo la apariencia engañosa de una predicación evangélica, se intenta negar al Señor Jesús», escribía un gran obispo en medio de las duras crisis del siglo IV. Y agregaba: «Yo digo la verdad, para que sea conocida de todos la causa de la desorientación que sufrimos. No puedo callarme» (SAN HILARIO DE POITIERS, *Ad Ausentium* 1-4). Tampoco vosotros, obispos de hoy, cuando estas confusiones se dieren, podéis callar.

Es la recomendación que el papa Pablo VI hacía en el discurso de apertura de la Conferencia de Medellín: «Hablad, hablad, predicad, escribid, tomad posiciones, como se dice, en armonía de planes y de intenciones, acerca de las verdades de la fe defendiéndolas e ilustrándolas, de la actualidad del Evangelio, de las cuestiones que interesan la vida de los fieles y la tutela de las costumbres cristianas...» (PABLO VI, *Discurso a la Asamblea del Episcopado Latinoamericano,* 24 de agosto de 1968).

No me cansaré yo mismo de repetir, en cumplimiento de mi deber de evangelizador, a la humanidad entera: ¡No temáis! ¡Abrid, más todavía, abrid de par en par las puertas a Cristo! Abrid a su potestad salvadora, las puertas de los Estados, los sistemas económicos y políticos, los extensos campos de la cultura, de la civilización y del desarrollo (JUAN PABLO II, *Homilía del Santo Padre en la inauguración oficial de su pontificado,* 22 de octubre de 1978; *L'Osservatore Romano,* Edición en Lengua Española, 29 de octubre de 1978, p.4).

Verdad sobre la misión de la Iglesia

I. 6. Maestros de la verdad, se espera de vosotros que proclaméis sin cesar y con especial vigor en esta circunstancia, la verdad sobre la misión de la Iglesia, objeto del Credo que profesamos y campo imprescindible y fundamental de nuestra fidelidad. El Señor la instituyó «para ser comunión de vida, de caridad y de verdad (cf. *Lumen gentium* 9) y como cuerpo, *pléroma* y sacramento de Cristo, en quien habita toda la plenitud de la divinidad (cf. ibíd., 7).

La Iglesia nace de la respuesta de fe que nosotros damos a Cristo. En efecto, es por la acogida sincera a la Buena Nueva, que nos reunimos los creyentes en el nombre de Jesús para buscar juntos el reino, construirlo, vivirlo (cf. *Evangelii nuntiandi* 13). La Iglesia es «congregación de quienes, creyendo, ven en Jesús al autor de la salvación y el principio de la unidad y de la paz» (*Lumen gentium* 9).

Pero, por otra parte, nosotros nacemos de la Iglesia: ella nos comunica la riqueza de vida y de gracia de que es depositaria, nos engendra por el bautismo, nos alimenta con los sacramentos y la Palabra de Dios, nos prepara para la misión, nos conduce al designio de Dios, razón de nuestra existencia como cristianos. Somos sus hijos. La llamamos con legítimo orgullo nuestra Madre, repitiendo un título que viene de los primeros tiempos y atraviesa los siglos (cf. HENRI DE LUBAC, *Meditación sobre la Iglesia* p.211ss).

Hay, pues, que llamarla, respetarla, servirla, porque «no puede tener a Dios por Padre quien no tiene a la Iglesia por Madre» (SAN CIPRIANO, *De la unidad* 6,8); «¿cómo va a ser posible amar a Cristo sin amar a la Iglesia», a quien Cristo ama? *(Evangelii nuntiandi* 16), y «en la medida que uno ama a la Iglesia de Cristo, posee el Espíritu Santo» (SAN AGUSTÍN, *In Ioannem tract.* 32,8).

El amor a la Iglesia tiene que estar hecho de fidelidad y de confianza. En el primer discurso de mi pontificado, subrayando el propósito de fidelidad al concilio Vaticano II y la voluntad de volcar mis mejores cuidados en el sector de la

eclesiología, invité a tomar de nuevo en la mano
la constitución dogmática *Lumen gentium* para
meditar «con renovado afán sobre la naturaleza
y misión de la Iglesia. Sobre su modo de existir
y actuar... No sólo para lograr aquella comunión
de vida en Cristo de todos los que en El creen y
esperan, sino para contribuir a hacer más amplia
y estrecha la unidad de toda la familia humana»
(JUAN PABLO II, *Mensaje a la Iglesia y al
mundo*, 17 de octubre de 1978; *L'Osservatore
Romano*, Edición en Lengua Española, 22 de octubre de 1978, p.3).

Repito ahora la invitación, en este momento
trascendental de la evangelización en América
Latina: «La adhesión a este documento del
Concilio, tal como resulta iluminado por la Tradición y que contiene las fórmulas dogmáticas
dadas hace un siglo por el concilio Vaticano I,
será para nosotros, pastores y fieles, el camino
cierto y el estímulo constante —digámoslo de
nuevo— en orden a caminar por las sendas de la
vida y de la historia» (ibíd.).

I. 7.   No hay garantía de una acción evangelizadora seria y vigorosa sin una eclesiología
bien cimentada.

Primero, porque evangelizar es la misión
esencial, la vocación propia, la identidad más
profunda de la Iglesia, a su vez evangelizada (cf.
Evangelii nuntiandi 14-15; *Lumen gentium* 5).
Enviada por el Señor, ella envía a su vez a los
evangelizadores «a predicar, no a sí mismos, o sus
ideas personales, sino un Evangelio del que ni
ellos ni ella son dueños y propietarios absolutos

para disponer de él a su gusto» *(Evangelii nuntiandi* 15). Segundo, porque «evangelizar no es para nadie un acto individual y aislado, sino profundamente eclesial», una acción de la Iglesia (ibíd., 60), que está sujeta no al «... poder discrecional para cumplirla según los criterios y perspectivas individualistas, sino en comunión con la Iglesia y sus pastores» (ibíd., 60). Por eso una visión correcta de la Iglesia es fase indispensable para una justa visión de la evangelización.

¿Cómo podría haber una auténtica evangelización, si faltase un acatamiento pronto y sincero al sagrado Magisterio, con la clara conciencia de que, sometiéndose a él, el Pueblo de Dios no acepta una palabra de hombres, sino la verdadera Palabra de Dios? (cf. 1 Tes 2,13; *Lumen gentium* 12). «Hay que tener en cuenta la importancia "objetiva" de este Magisterio y también defenderlo de las insidias que en estos tiempos, aquí y allá, se tienen contra algunas verdades firmes de nuestra fe católica» (JUAN PABLO II, *Mensaje a la Iglesia y al mundo,* 17 de octubre de 1978).

Conozco bien vuestra adhesión y disponibilidad a la Cátedra de Pedro y el amor que siempre le habéis demostrado. Os agradezco de corazón, en el nombre del Señor, la profunda actitud eclesial que esto implica, y os deseo el consuelo de que también vosotros contéis con la adhesión leal de vuestros fieles.

I. 8.   En la amplia documentación, con la que habéis preparado esta Conferencia, particularmente en las aportaciones de numerosas Iglesias, se advierte a veces un cierto malestar respecto de la interpretación misma de la naturaleza y misión de la Iglesia. Se alude, por ejemplo, a la separación que algunos establecen entre Iglesia y reino de Dios. Este, vaciado de su contenido total, es entendido en sentido más bien secularista: al reino no se llegaría por la fe y la pertenencia a la Iglesia, sino por el mero cambio estructural y el compromiso sociopolítico. Donde hay un cierto tipo de compromiso y de praxis por la justicia, allí estaría ya presente el reino. Se olvida de este modo que: «La Iglesia... recibe la misión de anunciar el reino de Cristo y de Dios e instaurarlo en todos los pueblos, y constituye en la tierra el germen y el principio de ese reino» *(Lumen gentium* 5).

En una de sus hermosas catequesis, el papa Juan Pablo I, hablando de la virtud de la esperanza, advertía: «Es un error afirmar que la liberación política, económica y social coincide con la salvación en Jesucristo; que el *Regnum Dei* se identifica con el *Regnum hominis»*.

Se genera en algunos casos una actitud de desconfianza hacia la Iglesia «institucional» u «oficial» calificada como alienante, a la que se opondría otra Iglesia popular «que nace del pueblo» y se concreta en los pobres. Estas posiciones podrían tener grados diferentes, no siempre fáciles de precisar, de conocidos condicionamientos ideológicos. El Concilio ha hecho presente cuál es la naturaleza y misión de la Iglesia. Y cómo se contribuye a su unidad profunda y a su permanente construcción por parte de quienes tienen a su cargo los ministerios de la comunidad, y han de contar con la colaboración de todo el Pueblo de Dios. En efecto, «si el Evangelio que proclamamos aparece desgarrado por querellas doctrinales, por polarizaciones ideológicas o por condenas recíprocas entre cristianos, al antojo de sus diferentes teorías sobre Cristo y sobre la Iglesia, e incluso a causa de sus distintas concepciones de la sociedad y de las instituciones humanas, ¿cómo pretender que aquellos a los que se dirige nuestra predicación no se muestren perturbados, desorientados, si no escandalizados?» *(Evangelii nuntiandi* 77).

Verdad sobre el hombre

I. 9. La verdad que debemos al hombre es, ante todo, una verdad sobre él mismo. Como testigos de Jesucristo somos heraldos, portavoces, siervos de esta verdad que no podemos reducir a los principios de un sistema filosófico o a pura actividad política; que no podemos olvidar ni traicionar.

Quizá una de las más vistosas debilidades de la civilización actual esté en una inadecuada visión del hombre. La nuestra es, sin duda, la época en que más se ha escrito y hablado sobre el hombre, la época de los humanismos y del antropocentrismo. Sin embargo, paradójicamente, es también la época de las más hondas angustias del hombre respecto de su identidad y destino, del rebajamiento del hombre a niveles antes insospechados, época de valores humanos conculcados como jamás lo fueron antes.

¿Cómo se explica esa paradoja? Podemos decir que es la paradoja inexorable del humanismo ateo. Es el drama del hombre amputado de una dimensión esencial de su ser —el Absoluto— y puesto así frente a la peor reducción del mismo ser. La constitución pastoral *Gaudium et spes* toca el fondo del problema cuando dice: «El misterio del hombre sólo se esclarece en el misterio del Verbo Encarnado» (n.22).

La Iglesia posee, gracias al Evangelio, la verdad sobre el hombre. Esta se encuentra en una antropología que la Iglesia no cesa de profundizar y de comunicar. La afirmación primordial de esta antropología es la del hombre como imagen de Dios, irreductible a una simple parcela de la naturaleza, o a un «elemento anónimo de la ciudad humana» (cf. ibíd., 12,3 y 14,2). En este sentido, escribía San Ireneo: «La gloria del hombre es Dios, pero el receptáculo de toda acción de Dios, de su sabiduría, de su poder, es el hombre» *(Tratado contra las herejías* III 20,2-3).

A este fundamento insustituible de la concepción cristiana del hombre, me he referido en particular en mi Mensaje de Navidad: «Navidad es la fiesta del hombre... El hombre, objeto de cálculo, considerado bajo la categoría de la cantidad... y al mismo tiempo uno, único e irrepetible... alguien eternamente ideado y eternamente elegido: alguien llamado y denominado por su nombre» (JUAN PABLO II, *Mensaje de Navidad* 1, 25 de diciembre 1978).

Frente a otros tantos humanismos, frecuentemente cerrados en una visión del hombre estrictamente económica, biológica o psíquica, la Iglesia tiene el derecho y el deber de proclamar la verdad sobre el hombre, que ella recibió de su Maestro Jesucristo. Ojalá ninguna coacción externa le impida hacerlo. Pero, sobre todo, ojalá no deje ella de hacerlo por temores o dudas, por haberse dejado contaminar por otros humanismos, por falta de confianza en su mensaje original.

Cuando, pues, un pastor de la Iglesia anuncia con claridad y sin ambigüedades la verdad sobre el hombre, revelada por Aquel mismo que «conocía lo que en el hombre había» (Jn 2,25), debe animarlo la seguridad de estar prestando el mejor servicio al ser humano.

Esta verdad completa sobre el ser humano constituye el fundamento de la enseñanza social de la Iglesia, así como es la base de la verdadera liberación. A la luz de esta verdad, no es el hombre un ser sometido a los procesos económicos o políticos, sino que esos procesos están ordenados al hombre y sometidos a él.

De este encuentro de pastores saldrá, sin duda, fortificada esta verdad sobre el hombre que enseña la Iglesia.

II. Signos y constructores de la unidad

Vuestro servicio pastoral a la verdad se completa por un igual servicio a la unidad.

Unidad entre los obispos

II. 1. Esta será ante todo unidad entre vosotros mismos, los obispos. «Debemos guardar y mantener esta unidad —escribía el obispo San Cipriano en un momento de graves amenazas a la comunión entre los obispos de su país— sobre todo nosotros, los obispos, que presidimos en la Iglesia, a fin de testimoniar que el episcopado es uno e indivisible. Que nadie engañe a los fieles ni altere la verdad. El episcopado es uno...» (*De la unidad de la Iglesia* 6-8).

Esta unidad episcopal viene no de cálculos y maniobras humanas, sino de lo alto: del servicio a un único Señor, de la animación de un único Espíritu, del amor a una única y misma Iglesia. Es la unidad que resulta de la misión que Cristo nos ha confiado, que en el continente latinoamericano se desarrolla desde hace casi medio milenio, y que vosotros lleváis adelante con ánimo fuerte en tiempos de profundas transformaciones, mientras nos acercamos al final del segundo milenio de la redención y de la acción de la Iglesia. Es la unidad en torno al Evangelio, del cuerpo y de la sangre del Cordero, de Pedro vivo en sus sucesores, señales todas diversas entre sí, pero todas tan importantes, de la presencia de Jesús entre nosotros.

¡Cómo habéis de vivir, amados hermanos, esta unidad de pastores, en esta Conferencia que es por sí misma señal y fruto de una unidad que ya existe, pero también anticipo y principio de una unidad que debe ser aún más estrecha y sólida! Comenzáis estos trabajos en clima de unidad fraterna: sea ya esta unidad un elemento de evangelización.

Unidad con los sacerdotes, religiosos, pueblo fiel

II. 2. La unidad de los obispos entre sí se prolonga en la unidad con los presbíteros, religiosos y fieles. Los sacerdotes son los colaboradores inmediatos de los obispos en la misión pastoral, que quedaría comprometida si no reinase entre ellos y los obispos esa estrecha unidad.

Sujetos especialmente importantes de esa unidad serán asimismo los religiosos y religiosas. Sé bien cómo ha sido y sigue siendo importante la contribución de los mismos a la evangelización en América Latina. Aquí llegaron en los albores del descubrimiento y de los primeros pasos de casi todos los países. Aquí trabajaron continuamente al lado del clero diocesano. En diversos países más de la mitad, en otros la gran mayoría del presbiterio, está formado por religiosos. Bastaría esto para comprender cuánto importa, aquí más que en otras partes del mundo, que los religiosos no sólo acepten, sino que busquen lealmente una indisoluble unidad de miras y de acción con los obispos. A éstos confió el Señor la misión de apacentar el rebaño. A ellos corresponde trazar los caminos para la evangelización. No les puede, no les debe faltar la colaboración, a la vez responsable y activa, pero también dócil y confiada de los religiosos, cuyo carisma hace de ellos agentes tanto más disponibles al servicio del Evangelio. En esa línea grava sobre todos, en la comunidad eclesial, el deber de evitar magisterios paralelos, eclesialmente inaceptables y pastoralmente estériles.

Sujetos asimismo de esa unidad son los seglares, comprometidos individualmente o asociados en organismos de apostolado para la difusión del reino de Dios. Son ellos quienes han de consagrar el mundo a Cristo en medio de las tareas cotidianas y en las diversas funciones familiares y profesionales, en íntima unión y obediencia a los legítimos pastores.

Ese don precioso de la unidad eclesial debe ser salvaguardado entre todos los que forman parte del Pueblo peregrino de Dios, en la línea de la *Lumen gentium*.

III. Defensores y promotores
de la dignidad

**La dignidad humana,
valor evangélico**

III. 1. Quienes están familiarizados con la
historia de la Iglesia, saben que en todos los
tiempos ha habido admirables figuras de obispos
profundamente empeñados en la promoción y en
la valiente defensa de la dignidad humana de
aquellos que el Señor les había confiado. Lo han
hecho siempre bajo el imperativo de su misión
episcopal, porque para ellos la dignidad humana
es un valor evangélico que no puede ser despre-
ciado sin grande ofensa al Creador.

Esta dignidad es conculcada, a nivel individual, cuando no son debidamente tenidos en
cuenta valores como la libertad, el derecho a
profesar la religión, la integridad física y psíquica, el derecho a los bienes esenciales, a la vida... Es conculcada, a nivel social y político,
cuando el hombre no puede ejercer su derecho
de participación o está sujeto a injustas e ilegí-
timas coerciones, o sometido a torturas físicas o
psíquicas, etc.

No ignoro cuántos problemas se plantean hoy
en esta materia en América Latina. Como obispos, no podéis desinteresaros de ellos. Sé que os
proponéis llevar a cabo una seria reflexión sobre
las relaciones e implicaciones existentes entre

evangelización y promoción humana o liberación, considerando, en campo tan amplio e importante, lo específico de la presencia de la Iglesia.

Aquí es donde encontramos, llevados a la práctica concretamente, los temas que hemos abordado al hablar de la verdad sobre Cristo, sobre la Iglesia y sobre el hombre.

La promoción eclesial de la dignidad humana

III. 2.   Si la Iglesia se hace presente en la defensa o en la promoción de la dignidad del hombre, lo hace en la línea de su misión, que aun siendo de carácter religioso y no social o político, no puede menos de considerar al hombre en la integridad de su ser. El Señor delineó en la parábola del buen samaritano el modelo de atención a todas las necesidades humanas (cf. Lc 10,30), y declaró que en último término se identificará con los desheredados —enfermos, encarcelados, hambrientos, solitarios—, a quienes se haya tendido la mano (cf. Mt 25,31ss). La Iglesia ha aprendido en estas y otras páginas del Evangelio (cf. Mc 6,35-44) que su misión evangelizadora tiene como parte indispensable la acción por la justicia y las tareas de promoción del hombre (cf. *Documento final del Sínodo de los Obispos,* octubre de 1971; *L'Osservatore Romano,* Edición en Lengua Española, 12 de diciembre de 1971, p.6-9), y que entre evangelización y promoción humana hay lazos muy fuertes de orden antropológico, teológico y de caridad (cf. *Evangelii nuntiandi* 31); de manera que «la evangelización no sería completa si no tuviera en cuenta la interpelación recíproca que en el curso de los tiempos se establece entre el Evangelio y la vida concreta personal y social del hombre» (ibíd., 29).

Tengamos presente, por otra parte, que la acción de la Iglesia en terrenos como los de la promoción humana, del desarrollo, de la justicia, de los derechos de la persona, quiere estar siempre al servicio del hombre; y al hombre tal como ella lo ve en la visión cristiana de la antropología que adopta. Ella no necesita, pues, recurrir a sistemas e ideologías para amar, defender y colaborar en la liberación del hombre: en el centro del mensaje del cual es depositaria y pregonera, ella encuentra inspiración para actuar en favor de la fraternidad, de la justicia, de la paz, contra todas las dominaciones, esclavitudes, discriminaciones, violencias, atentados a la libertad religiosa, agresiones contra el hombre y cuanto atenta a la vida (cf. *Gaudium et spes* 26.27 y 29).

III. 3. No es, pues, por oportunismo ni por afán de novedad que la Iglesia, «experta en humanidad» (PABLO VI, *Discurso a la ONU*, 5 de octubre de 1965), es defensora de los derechos humanos. Es por un auténtico *compromiso evangélico*, el cual, como sucedió con Cristo, es, sobre todo, compromiso con los más necesitados.

Fiel a este compromiso, la Iglesia quiere mantenerse libre frente a los opuestos sistemas, para optar sólo por el hombre. Cualesquiera sean las miserias o sufrimientos que aflijan al hombre, Cristo está al lado de los pobres; no a través de la violencia, de los juegos de poder, de los sistemas políticos, sino por medio de la verdad sobre el hombre, camino hacia un futuro mejor.

La enseñanza de la Iglesia sobre la propiedad

III. 4. Nace de ahí la constante preocupación de la Iglesia por la delicada cuestión de la propiedad. Una prueba de ello son los escritos de los Padres de la Iglesia a través del primer milenio del cristianismo (SAN AMBROSIO, *De Nabuthae* c.12 n.53: PL 14,848). Lo demuestra claramente la doctrina vigorosa de Santo Tomás de Aquino, repetida tantas veces. En nuestros tiempos, la Iglesia ha hecho apelación a los mismos principios en documentos de tan largo alcance como son las encíclicas sociales de los últimos Papas. Con una fuerza y profundidad particular, habló de este tema el papa Pablo VI en su encíclica *Populorum progressio* (23-24; cf. también JUAN XXIII, *Mater et magistra* 104-115).

Esta voz de la Iglesia, eco de la voz de la conciencia humana, que no cesó de resonar a través de los siglos en medio de los más variados sistemas y condiciones socioculturales, merece y necesita ser escuchada también en nuestra época, cuando la riqueza creciente de unos pocos sigue paralela a la creciente miseria de las masas.

Es entonces cuando adquiere carácter urgente la enseñanza de la Iglesia, según la cual sobre toda propiedad privada grava una *hipoteca social.* Con respecto a esta enseñanza, la Iglesia tiene una misión que cumplir: debe predicar, educar a las personas y a las colectividades, formar la opinión pública, orientar a los responsables de los pueblos. De este modo estará trabajando en favor de la sociedad, dentro de la cual este principio cristiano y evangélico terminará dando frutos de una distribución más justa y equitativa de los bienes, no sólo en el interior de cada nación, sino también en el mundo internacional en general, evitando que los países más fuertes usen su poder en detrimento de los más débiles.

Aquellos sobre los cuales recae la responsabilidad de la vida pública de los Estados y naciones deberán comprender que la paz interna y la paz internacional sólo estará asegurada si tiene vigencia un sistema social y económico basado sobre la justicia.

Cristo no permaneció indiferente frente a este vasto y exigente imperativo de la moral social. Tampoco podría hacerlo la Iglesia. En el espíritu de la Iglesia, que es el espíritu de Cristo, y apoyados en su doctrina amplia y sólida, volvamos al trabajo en este campo.

La primacía de lo espiritual

Hay que subrayar aquí nuevamente que la solicitud de la Iglesia mira al hombre en su integridad.

Por esta razón, es condición indispensable para que un sistema económico sea justo, que propicie el desarrollo y la difusión de la instrucción pública y de la cultura. Cuanto más justa sea la economía, tanto más profunda será la conciencia de la cultura. Esto está muy en línea con lo que afirmaba el Concilio: que para alcanzar una vida digna del hombre, no es posible limitarse a *tener más,* hay que aspirar *a ser más* (*Gaudium et spes* 35).

Bebed, pues, hermanos, en estas fuentes auténticas. Hablad con el lenguaje del Concilio de Juan XXIII, de Pablo VI: es el lenguaje de la experiencia, del dolor, de la esperanza de la humanidad contemporánea.

Cuando Pablo VI declaraba que el desarrollo es el nuevo nombre de la paz (*Populorum progressio* 76), tenía presentes todos los lazos de interdependencia que existen no sólo dentro de las naciones, sino también fuera de ellas, a nivel mundial. El tomaba en consideración los mecanismos que, por encontrarse impregnados no de auténtico humanismo, sino de materialismo, producen a nivel internacional ricos cada vez más ricos a costa de pobres cada vez más pobres.

No hay regla económica capaz de cambiar por sí misma estos mecanismos. Hay que apelar también en la vida internacional a los princi-

pios de la ética, a las exigencias de la justicia,
al mandamiento primero, que es el del amor.
Hay que dar la primacía a lo moral, a lo espiritual, a lo que nace de la verdad plena sobre
el hombre.

He querido manifestaros estas reflexiones,
que creo muy importantes, aunque no deben dis-
traernos del tema central de la conferencia: al
hombre, a la justicia, llegaremos mediante la
evangelización.

Las violaciones de los derechos humanos

III. 5.   Ante lo dicho hasta aquí, la Iglesia ve
con profundo dolor «el aumento masivo, a veces, de violaciones de derechos humanos en
muchas partes del mundo... ¿Quién puede negar
que hoy día hay personas individuales y poderes
civiles que violan impunemente derechos fundamentales de la persona humana, tales como el
derecho a nacer, el derecho a la vida, el derecho
a la procreación responsable, al trabajo, a la
paz, a la libertad y a la justicia social; el derecho
a participar en las decisiones que conciernen al
pueblo y a las naciones? ¿Y qué decir cuando
nos encontramos ante formas variadas de violencia colectiva, como la discriminación racial
de individuos y grupos, la tortura física y psico-
lógica de prisioneros y disidentes políticos?
Crece el elenco cuando miramos los ejemplos de
secuestros de personas, los raptos motivados
por afán de lucro material que embisten con
tanto dramatismo contra la vida familiar y trama

social» (JUAN PABLO II, *Mensaje a la ONU*, 12 de diciembre de 1978; *L'Osservatore Romano*, Edición en Lengua Española, 24 de diciembre de 1978, p.13). Clamamos nuevamente: ¡Respetad al hombre! ¡El es imagen de Dios! ¡Evangelizad para que esto sea una realidad! Para que el Señor transforme los corazones y humanice los sistemas políticos y económicos, partiendo del empeño responsable del hombre.

Recta concepción cristiana de la liberación

III. 6. Hay que alentar los compromisos pastorales en este campo con una recta concepción cristiana de la liberación. La Iglesia tiene el deber de anunciar la liberación de millones de seres humanos..., el deber de ayudar a que nazca esta liberación (cf. *Evangelii nuntiandi* 30); pero siente también el deber correspondiente de proclamar la liberación en su sentido integral, profundo, como lo anunció y realizó Jesús (cf. ibíd., 31). «Liberación de todo lo que oprime al hombre, pero que es, sobre todo, liberación del pecado y del maligno, dentro de la alegría de conocer a Dios y de ser conocido por El» (ibíd., 9). Liberación hecha de reconciliación y perdón. Liberación que arranca de la realidad de ser hijos de Dios, a quien somos capaces de llamar *Abba!,* ¡Padre! (cf. Rom 8,15), y por la cual reconocemos en todo hombre a nuestro hermano, capaz de ser transformado en su corazón por la misericordia de Dios. Liberación que nos empuja, con la energía de la caridad, a la comunión, cuya cumbre y plenitud encontramos en el Señor. Liberación como superación de las diversas servidumbres e ídolos que el hombre se forja y como crecimiento del hombre nuevo.

Liberación que dentro de la misión propia de la Iglesia «no puede reducirse a la simple y estrecha dimensión económica, política, social o cultural..., que no puede nunca sacrificarse a las exigencias de una estrategia cualquiera, de una praxis o de un éxito a corto plazo» (cf. *Evangelii nuntiandi* 33).

Para salvaguardar la originalidad de la liberación cristiana y las energías que es capaz de desplegar, es necesario a toda costa, como lo pedía el papa Pablo VI, evitar reduccionismos y ambigüedades; de otro modo, «la Iglesia perdería su significación más profunda. Su mensaje de liberación no tendría ninguna originalidad y se prestaría a ser acaparado y manipulado por los sistemas ideológicos y los partidos políticos» (ibíd., 32). Hay muchos signos que ayudan a discernir cuándo se trata de una liberación cristiana y cuándo, en cambio, se nutre más bien de ideologías que le sustraen la coherencia con una visión evangélica del hombre, de las cosas, de los acontecimientos (cf. ibíd., 35). Son signos que derivan ya de los contenidos que anuncian o de las actitudes concretas que asumen los evangelizadores. Es preciso observar, a nivel de contenidos, cuál es la fidelidad a la palabra de Dios, a la tradición viva de la Iglesia, a su magisterio. En cuanto a las actitudes, hay que ponderar cuál es su sentido de comunión con los obispos, en primer lugar, y con los demás sectores del Pueblo de Dios; cuál es el aporte que se da a la construcción efectiva de la comunidad, y cuál la forma de volcar con amor su solicitud hacia los pobres, los enfermos, los desposeídos, los desamparados, los agobiados, y cómo, descubriendo en ellos la imagen de Jesús «pobre y paciente, se esfuerza en remediar sus necesidades y procura servir en ellos a Cristo» (*Lumen gentium* 8). No nos engañemos: los fieles humildes y sencillos captan espontáneamente cuándo se sirve en la Iglesia al Evangelio y cuándo se lo vacía y asfixia con otros intereses.

Como veis, conserva toda su validez el conjunto de observaciones que sobre el tema de la liberación ha hecho la *Evangelii nuntiandi*.

La doctrina social de la Iglesia

III. 7.   Cuanto hemos recordado antes constituye un rico y complejo patrimonio, que la *Evangelii nuntiandi* denomina doctrina social o enseñanza social de la Iglesia (cf. ibíd., 38). Esta nace a la luz de la Palabra de Dios y del Magisterio auténtico, de la presencia de los cristianos en el seno de las situaciones cambiantes del mundo, en contacto con los desafíos que de ésas provienen. Tal doctrina social comporta, por tanto, principios de reflexión, pero también normas de juicio y directrices de acción (cf. PABLO VI, *Octogesima adveniens* 4).

Confiar responsablemente en esta doctrina

social, aunque algunos traten de sembrar dudas y desconfianzas sobre ella, estudiarla con seriedad, procurar aplicarla, enseñarla, ser fiel a ella es, en un hijo de la Iglesia, garantía de la autenticidad de su compromiso en las delicadas y exigentes tareas sociales, y de sus esfuerzos en favor de la liberación o de la promoción de sus hermanos.

Permitid, pues, que recomiende a vuestra especial atención pastoral la urgencia de sensibilizar a vuestros fieles acerca de esta doctrina social de la Iglesia.

Hay que poner particular cuidado en la formación de una conciencia social a todos los niveles y en todos los sectores. Cuando arrecian las injusticias y crece dolorosamente la distancia entre pobres y ricos, la doctrina social, en forma creativa y abierta a los amplios campos de la presencia de la Iglesia, debe ser precioso instrumento de formación y de acción. Esto vale particularmente en relación con los laicos: «Competen a los laicos propiamente, aunque no exclusivamente, las tareas y el dinamismo seculares» *(Gaudium et spes* 43). Es necesario evitar suplantaciones y estudiar seriamente cuándo ciertas formas de suplencia mantienen su razón de ser. ¿No son los laicos los llamados, en virtud de su vocación en la Iglesia, a dar su aporte en las dimensiones políticas, económicas, y a estar eficazmente presentes en la tutela y promoción de los derechos humanos?

IV. Algunas tareas prioritarias

Muchos temas pastorales, de gran significación, vais a considerar. El tiempo me impide aludir a ellos. A algunos me he referido o me referiré en los encuentros con los sacerdotes, los religiosos, los seminaristas, los laicos.

IV. 1. Los temas que aquí os señalo tienen, por diferentes motivos, una gran importancia. No dejaréis de considerarlos, entre tantos otros que vuestra clarividencia pastoral os indicará.

a) *La familia:* Haced todos los esfuerzos para que haya una pastoral familiar. Atended a campo tan prioritario con la certeza de que la evangelización en el futuro depende en gran parte de la «Iglesia doméstica». Es la escuela del amor, del conocimiento de Dios, del respeto a la vida, a la dignidad del hombre. Es esta pastoral tanto más importante cuanto la familia es objeto de tantas amenazas. Pensad en las campañas favorables al divorcio, al uso de prácticas anticoncepcionales, al aborto, que destruyen la sociedad.

b) *Las vocaciones sacerdotales y religiosas.* En la mayoría de vuestros países, no obstante un esperanzador despertar de vocaciones, es un problema grave y crónico la falta de las mismas. La desproporción es inmensa entre el número creciente de habitantes y el de agentes de la evangelización. Importa esto sobremanera a la comunidad cristiana. Toda comunidad ha de procurar sus vocaciones, como señal incluso de su vitalidad y madurez. Hay que reactivar una intensa acción pastoral que, partiendo de la vocación cristiana en general, de una pastoral juvenil entusiasta, dé a la Iglesia los servidores que necesita. Las vocaciones laicales, tan indispensables, no pueden ser una compensación suficiente. Más aún, una de las pruebas del compromiso del laico es la fecundidad en las vocaciones a la vida consagrada.

c) *La juventud:* ¡Cuánta esperanza pone en ella la Iglesia! ¡Cuántas energías circulan en la juventud, en América Latina, que necesita la Iglesia! Cómo hemos de estar cerca de ella los pastores, para que Cristo y la Iglesia, para que el amor del hermano calen profundamente en su corazón.

Conclusión

IV. 2. Al término de este mensaje no puedo dejar de invocar una vez más la protección de la Madre de Dios sobre vuestras personas y vuestro trabajo en estos días. El hecho de que este nuestro encuentro tenga lugar en la presencia espiritual de Nuestra Señora de Guadalupe, venerada en México y en todos los otros países como Madre de la Iglesia en América Latina, es para mí un motivo de alegría y una fuente de esperanza. «Estrella de la evangelización», sea Ella vuestra guía en las reflexiones que haréis y en las decisiones que tomaréis. Que Ella alcance de su divino Hijo para vosotros: audacia de profetas y prudencia evangélica de pastores; clarividencia de maestros y seguridad de guías y orientadores; fuerza de ánimo de testigos, y serenidad, paciencia y mansedumbre de padres.

IV. 3. **El Señor bendiga vuestros trabajos.** Estáis acompañados por representantes selectos: presbíteros, diáconos, religiosos, religiosas, laicos, expertos, observadores, cuya colaboración os será muy útil. Toda la Iglesia tiene puestos los ojos en vosotros, con confianza y esperanza. Queréis responder a tales expectativas con plena fidelidad a Cristo, a la Iglesia, al hombre. El futuro está en las manos de Dios, pero, en cierta manera, ese futuro de un nuevo impulso evangelizador, Dios lo pone también en las vuestras. «Id, pues, enseñad a todas las gentes» (Mt 28,19).

FIDELIDAD EN LA UNIDAD

*Alocución del Papa a los partici-
pantes en un encuentro ecumé-
nico en Puebla, 28 de enero.*

Amados hermanos en Cristo:

Permitidme que ante todo os exprese mi sincero agradecimiento por este encuentro.

Deseo aseguraros que también yo me siento
muy complacido de estar con vosotros y compartir esta vivencia espiritual, sintiendo que
Cristo, el Maestro nuestro, el Señor, el Redentor, Cristo nuestra esperanza, está en medio de
nosotros. El sigue exhortándonos con su apremiante mandato: que sean uno, Padre, como tú
y yo lo somos.

Por parte mía, ya dije desde el principio de mi
pontificado que la preocupación ecuménica será
uno de mis objetivos.

Pidamos, hermanos, al Señor Jesús que El nos
dé la fidelidad a El, la fidelidad en la unidad que
El ha querido para nosotros, para que el mundo crea.

A fin de que así sea, os invito a recitar todos
juntos el padrenuestro.

EL PAPA REZA POR LOS NIÑOS ENFERMOS

Saludo del Santo Padre en su visita al hospital infantil de Ciudad de México, 29 de enero.

Queridos hijos:

Al venir a pasar estos momentos entre vosotros, quiero saludar a los dirigentes del centro, a todos los niños y niñas enfermos de este hospital infantil y a todos los niños que sufren en sus hogares, en cualquier parte de México.

La enfermedad no os permite jugar con vuestros amigos; por eso ha querido venir a veros otro amigo, el Papa, que tantas veces piensa en vosotros y reza por vosotros.

Saludo también a vuestros padres, hermanos, hermanas, familiares y a cuantos se preocupan de vuestra salud y os atienden con tanto esmero y afecto.

Os invito ahora a rezar un avemaría a la Virgen de Guadalupe por vosotros, que tan pronto encontráis el dolor y la enfermedad en vuestra vida.

Queridos niños: El Papa os seguirá recordando y se lleva vuestro sonriente saludo de brazos abiertos, dejándoos su abrazo y su bendición.

RESPETO A VUESTRAS RAICES

Respuesta del Santo Padre al discurso de bienvenida en Oaxaca, 29 de enero.

Señor arzobispo, hermanos e hijos queridísimos:

Muchas gracias a todos por este recibimiento tan cordial que me habéis dispensado, llegando a estas tierras de Oaxaca. Muchas gracias también al señor arzobispo por sus palabras de bienvenida.

No salgo de mi admiración, emocionada y agradecida, al ver con cuánta afabilidad, con cuánto entusiasmo me acogéis entre vosotros: signo sin duda alguna de que os habéis sentido desde siempre muy cercanos en el afecto al Vicario de Cristo, Pastor de la Iglesia universal y, por tanto, también vuestro.

En este primer encuentro con vosotros, deseo solamente manifestaros mi profundo respeto y aprecio por esta tierra de Oaxaca, rica de historia, tradiciones y religiosidad; cuna además de diversos pueblos nativos de esta zona, que han dejado huella imborrable en la historia mexicana. Pueblos y hombres que os han dejado en herencia algo que vosotros cultiváis como genuino patrimonio: una profunda estima por los valores morales y espirituales.

Saludo también muy cordialmente a cuantos no han podido venir por estar impedidos, en particular a los enfermos y ancianos. A todos, a ellos y a vosotros, mi mejor bendición.

EL PAPA QUIERE SER VUESTRA VOZ

Discurso del Santo Padre en Cuilapán a los indígenas y campesinos, 29 de enero.

Amadísimos hermanos indígenas y campesinos:

1. Os saludo con alegría y agradezco vuestra presencia entusiasta y las palabras de bienvenida que me habéis dirigido. No encuentro mejor saludo, para expresaros los sentimientos que ahora embargan mi corazón, que la frase de San Pedro, el primer Papa de la Iglesia: «Paz a vosotros los que estáis en Cristo». Paz a vosotros, que formáis un grupo tan numeroso.

Llamamiento universal a la santidad

También vosotros, habitantes de Oaxaca, de Chiapas, de Cuilapán y los venidos de tantas otras partes, herederos de la sangre y de la cultura de vuestros nobles antepasados —sobre todo los mixtecas y los zapotecas—, fuisteis «llamados a ser santos, con todos aquellos que invocan el nombre de nuestro Señor Jesucristo» (1 Cor 1,2).

2. El Hijo de Dios «habitó entre nosotros» para hacer hijos de Dios a aquellos que creen en su nombre (cf. Jn 1,11ss) y confió a la Iglesia la continuación de esta misión salvadora allí donde haya hombres. Nada tiene, pues, de extraño que un día, en el ya lejano siglo XVI, llegaran aquí por fidelidad a la Iglesia, misioneros intrépidos, deseosos de asimilar vuestro estilo de vida y costumbres para revelar mejor y dar expresión viva a la imagen de Cristo. Vaya nuestro recuerdo agradecido al primer obispo de Oaxaca, Juan José López de Zárate, y tantos misioneros franciscanos, dominicos, agustinos y jesuitas, hombres admirables por su fe y por su generosidad humana.

Ellos sabían muy bien cuán importante es la cultura como vehículo para transmitir la fe, para que los hombres progresen en el conocimiento de Dios. En esto no puede haber distinción de razas ni de culturas, «no hay griego ni judío..., ni esclavo ni libre, sino que Cristo es todo en todos» (cf. Col 3,9-11). Esto constituye un desafío y un estímulo para la Iglesia, ya que, siendo fiel al mensaje genuino y total del Señor, ha de abrirse e interpretar toda realidad humana para impregnarla de la fuerza del Evangelio (cf. *Evangelii nuntiandi* 20 y 40).

Solidaridad del Papa con los hombres del campo

3. Amadísimos hermanos: Mi presencia entre vosotros quiere ser un signo vivo y fehacien-

te de esta preocupación universal de la Iglesia. El Papa y la Iglesia están con vosotros y os aman: aman vuestras personas, vuestra cultura, vuestras tradiciones. Admiran vuestro maravilloso pasado, os alientan en el presente y esperan tanto para en adelante.

4.   Pero no sólo de eso os quiero hablar. A través de vosotros, campesinos e indígenas, aparece ante mis ojos esa muchedumbre inmensa del mundo agrícola, parte todavía prevalente en el continente latinoamericano y un sector muy grande, aún hoy día, en nuestro planeta.

Ante ese espectáculo imponente que se refleja en mis pupilas, no puedo menos de pensar en el idéntico cuadro que hace diez años contemplara mi predecesor Pablo VI, en su memorable visita a Colombia y más concretamente en su encuentro con los campesinos.

Con él quiero repetir —si fuera posible, con acento aún más fuerte en mi voz— que el Papa actual quiere ser «solidario con vuestra causa, que es la causa del pueblo humilde, la de la gente pobre» (PABLO VI, *Discurso a los campesinos*, 23 de agosto de 1968). El Papa está con esas masas de población «casi siempre abandonadas en un innoble nivel de vida y a veces tratadas y explotadas duramente» (ibíd.).

5.   Haciendo mía la línea de mis predecesores Juan XXIII y Pablo VI, así como la del Concilio (cf. *Mater et Magistra, Populorum progressio, Gaudium et spes* 9 y 71, etc.), y en vista de una situación que continúa siendo alarmante, no muchas veces mejor y a veces aún peor, el Papa

quiere ser vuestra voz, la voz de quien no puede hablar o de quien es silenciado, para ser conciencia de las conciencias, invitación a la acción, para recuperar el tiempo perdido, que es frecuentemente tiempo de sufrimientos prolongados y de esperanzas no satisfechas.

Urgen reformas audaces

El mundo deprimido del campo, el trabajador que con su sudor riega también su desconsuelo, no puede esperar más a que se reconozca plena y eficazmente su dignidad no inferior a la de cualquier otro sector social. Tiene derecho a que se le respete, a que no se le prive —con maniobras que a veces equivalen a verdaderos despojos— de lo poco que tiene; a que no se impida su aspiración a ser parte en su propia elevación. Tiene derecho a que se le quiten las barreras de explotación, hechas frecuentemente de egoísmos intolerables y contra los que se estrellan sus mejores esfuerzos de promoción. Tiene derecho a la ayuda eficaz —que no es limosna ni migajas de justicia— para que tenga acceso al desarrollo que su dignidad de hombre y de hijo de Dios merece.

6. Para ello hay que actuar pronto y en profundidad. Hay que poner en práctica transformaciones audaces, profundamente innovadoras. Hay que emprender, sin esperar más, reformas urgentes (cf. *Populorum progressio* 32).

No puede olvidarse que las medidas a tomar

han de ser adecuadas. La Iglesia defiende, sí, el legítimo derecho a la propiedad privada, pero enseña con no menor claridad que sobre toda propiedad privada grava siempre una *hipoteca social,* para que los bienes sirvan a la destinación general que Dios les ha dado. Y si el bien común lo exige, no hay que dudar ante la misma expropiación, hecha en la debida forma (cf. ibíd., 24).

Importancia del mundo agrícola

7. El mundo agrícola tiene una gran importancia y una gran dignidad: él es el que ofrece a la sociedad los productos necesarios para su nutrición. Es una tarea que merece el aprecio y estima agradecida de todos, lo cual es un reconocimiento a la dignidad de quien de ello se ocupa.

Una dignidad que puede y debe acrecentarse con la contemplación de Dios que favorece el contacto con la naturaleza, reflejo de la acción divina, que cuida de la hierba del campo, la hace crecer, la nutre y fecunda la tierra, enviándole la lluvia y el viento, para que alimente también a los animales que ayudan al hombre, como leemos al principio del Génesis.

El trabajo del campo comporta dificultades no pequeñas por el esfuerzo que exige, por el desprecio con el que a veces es mirado o por las trabas que encuentra, y que sólo una acción de largo alcance puede resolver. Sin ello, continuará la fuga del campo hacia las ciudades, creando frecuentemente problemas de proletarización extensa y angustiosa, hacinamientos en viviendas indignas de seres humanos, etc.

8. Un mal bastante extendido es la tendencia al individualismo entre los trabajadores del campo, mientras que una acción mejor coordinada y solidaria podría servir de no poca ayuda. Pensad en esto, queridos hijos.

A pesar de todo ello, el mundo campesino posee riquezas humanas y religiosas envidiables: un arraigado amor a la familia, sentido de la amistad, ayuda al más necesitado, profundo humanismo, amor a la paz y convivencia cívica, vivencia de lo religioso, confianza y apertura a Dios, cultivo del amor a la Virgen María y tantos otros. Es un merecido tributo de reconocimiento que el Papa quiere expresaros y al que sois acreedores por parte de la sociedad. Gracias, campesinos, por vuestra valiosa aportación al bien social. La humanidad os debe mucho. Podéis sentiros orgullosos de vuestra contribución al bien común.

Resolver situaciones injustas

9. Por parte vuestra, responsables de los pueblos, clases poderosas que tenéis a veces improductivas las tierras que esconden el pan que a tantas familias falta, la conciencia humana, la conciencia de los pueblos, el grito del desvalido, y sobre todo la voz de Dios, la voz de la Iglesia

os repiten conmigo: no es justo, no es humano, no es cristiano continuar con ciertas situaciones claramente injustas. Hay que poner en práctica medidas reales, eficaces, a nivel local, nacional e internacional, en la amplia línea marcada por la encíclica *Mater et Magistra* (parte tercera). Y es claro que quien más debe colaborar en ello, es quien más puede.

10. Amadísimos hermanos e hijos: Trabajad en vuestra elevación humana, pero no os detengáis ahí. Haceos cada vez más dignos en lo moral y religioso. No abriguéis sentimientos de odio o de violencia, sino mirad hacia el Dueño y Señor de todos, que a cada uno da la recompensa que sus actos merecen. La Iglesia está con vosotros y os anima a vivir vuestra condición de hijos de Dios, unidos a Cristo, bajo la mirada de María, nuestra Madre santísima.

El Papa os pide vuestra oración y os ofrece la suya. Y al bendeciros a vosotros y a vuestras familias, se despide de vosotros con las palabras del apóstol San Pablo: «Llevad un saludo a todos los hermanos con el ósculo santo». Sea esto una llamada a la esperanza. Así sea.

SED LEVADURA QUE TRANSFORME EL MUNDO

Homilía pronunciada en la catedral de Oaxaca con motivo de la ordenación de seis lectores y cuatro acólitos, 29 de enero.

Queridísimos hermanos y hermanas:

Esta ceremonia, en la que con inmenso gozo voy a conferir algunos ministerios sagrados a descendientes de las antiguas estirpes de esta tierra de América, confirma la verdad de lo dicho por una alta personalidad de vuestro país a mi venerado predecesor Pablo VI: Desde el comienzo de la historia de las naciones americanas, fue sobre todo la Iglesia quien protegió a los más humildes, su dignidad y valor como personas humanas.

La verdad de tal afirmación recibe hoy una nueva confirmación, ya que el Obispo de Roma y Pastor de la Iglesia universal llamará a algunos de entre ellos a colaborar con los propios pastores en el servicio de la comunidad eclesial, para su mayor crecimiento y vitalidad (cf. *Evangelii nuntiandi* 73).

Colaboradores de Dios

1. Es sabido que estos ministerios no transforman a los laicos en clérigos: quienes los reciben siguen siendo laicos, o sea, no dejan el estado en que vivían cuando fueron llamados (cf. 1 Cor 7,20). También cuando cooperan, como suplentes o ayudantes, con los ministros sagrados, estos laicos son, sobre todo, colaboradores de Dios (cf. 1 Cor 3,9), que se vale también de ellos para dar cumplimiento a su voluntad de salvar a todos los hombres (cf. 1 Tim 2,4).

Más aún, precisamente porque estos laicos se comprometen de manera deliberada con tal designio salvífico, a tal punto que ese compromiso es para ellos la razón última de su presencia en el mundo (cf. SAN JUAN CRISÓSTOMO, *In Act. Ap.* 20,4), deben ser considerados como arquetipos de la participación de todos los fieles en la misión salvífica de la Iglesia.

Difundir y defender la fe

2. En realidad, todos los fieles, en virtud del propio bautismo y del sacramento de la confirmación, tienen que profesar públicamente la fe recibida de Dios por medio de la Iglesia, difundirla y defenderla como verdaderos testigos de Cristo (cf. *Lumen gentium* 11). O sea, están llamados a la evangelización, que es un deber fundamental de todos los miembros del Pueblo de Dios (cf. *Ad gentes* 35), tengan o no tengan par-

ticulares funciones vinculadas más íntimamente con los deberes de los pastores (cf. *Apostolicam actuositatem* 24).

A este propósito dejad que el Sucesor de Pedro haga un ferviente llamado, a todos y cada uno, a asimilar y practicar las enseñanzas y orientaciones del concilio Vaticano II, que ha dedicado a los laicos el capítulo IV de la constitución dogmática *Lumen gentium* y el decreto *Apostolicam actuositatem*.

Renovar los hombres y las cosas

3. Deseo además, como recuerdo de mi paso entre vosotros, aunque también con la mirada puesta en los fieles del mundo entero, aludir brevemente a cuanto es peculiar de la cooperación de los laicos en el único apostolado de la Iglesia (cf. *Apostolicam actuositatem* 33) y que otorga a todas sus expresiones, ya individuales, ya asociadas, su característica determinante. Para ello voy a inspirarme en la invocación a Cristo, que leemos en la plegaria de *Laudes* de este lunes de la cuarta semana del tiempo litúrgico ordinario: «Tú que actúas con el Padre en la historia de la humanidad, renueva los hombres y las cosas con la fuerza de tu Espíritu».

En efecto, los laicos, que por vocación divina comparten toda la realidad mundana, inyectando en ella su fe, hecha realidad en la propia vida pública y privada (cf. Sant 2,17), son los protagonistas más inmediatos de la renovación de los hombres y de las cosas. Con su presencia activa de creyentes, trabajan en la progresiva consagración del mundo a Dios (cf. *Lumen gentium* 34). Esta presencia se compagina con toda la economía de la religión cristiana, la cual es una doctrina, pero es sobre todo un acontecimiento: el acontecimiento de la Encarnación, Jesús Hombre-Dios que ha recapitulado en sí el universo (cf. Ef 1,10); corresponde al ejemplo de Cristo, quien ha hecho también del contacto físico un vehículo de comunicación de su poder restaurador (cf. Mc 1,41 y 7,33; Mt 9,29ss y 20,34; Lc 7,14 y 8,54); es inherente a la índole sacramental de la Iglesia, la cual, hecha signo e instrumento de la unión de los hombres con Dios y de la unidad de todo el género humano (cf. *Lumen gentium* 1), ha sido llamada por Dios a estar en permanente comunión con el mundo para ser en él la levadura que lo transforma desde dentro (cf. Mt 13,33).

El apostolado de los laicos, así entendido y puesto en práctica, confiere pleno sentido a todas las manifestaciones de la historia humana, respetando su autonomía y favoreciendo el progreso exigido por la naturaleza propia de cada una de ellas. Al mismo tiempo nos da la clave para interpretar en plenitud el sentido de la historia, ya que todas las realidades temporales, como los acontecimientos que las manifiestan, adquieren su significado más profundo en la dimensión espiritual que establece la relación entre el presente y el futuro (cf. Heb 13,14). El desconocimiento o la mutilación de esta dimensión, se convertiría, de hecho, en un atentado contra la esencia misma del hombre.

Haced Iglesia

4. Al dejar esta tierra, me llevo de vosotros un grato recuerdo, el de haberme encontrado con almas generosas que desde ahora ofrecerán su vida por la difusión del reino de Dios. Y al mismo tiempo estoy seguro de que, como árboles plantados junto a ríos de agua, darán frutos abundantes a su tiempo (cf. Sal 1,3) para la consolidación del Evangelio.

¡Animo! ¡Sed levadura dentro de la masa (cf. Mt 13,33), haced Iglesia! Que vuestro testimonio vaya despertando por doquier otros anunciadores de la salvación: «Cuán hermosos son los pies de los que evangelizan el bien» (Rom 12,15). Demos gracias a Dios que «ha comenzado esta obra buena y la llevará a cumplimiento hasta el día de Jesucristo» (Flp 1,6).

FIDELIDAD A LA IGLESIA

Discurso del Santo Padre a los representantes de las Organizaciones católicas nacionales de México, Ciudad de México, 29 de enero.

Amadísimos hijos de las Organizaciones católicas nacionales de México:

Bendito sea el Señor que me permite también —en mi permanencia en esta querida tierra de Nuestra Señora de Guadalupe— tener el gozo de un encuentro con vosotros.

Agradezco vuestras vivas demostraciones de afecto filial y puedo confesaros cuánto me gustaría detenerme con cada cual de vosotros para conoceros personalmente, para saber más de vuestro servicio eclesial, para abundar sobre tantos aspectos fundamentales de vuestra proyección apostólica. Deseo, de todos modos, que estas palabras sean testimonio elocuente de compañía, aprecio, estímulo y orientación de vuestros mejores esfuerzos como laicos —y como laicado católico organizado— por parte de quien ha sido llamado al servicio, como Sucesor de Pedro, de todos los servidores del Señor.

Promoción del laicado

Vosotros sabéis bien cómo el concilio Vaticano II recogió esa gran corriente histórica contemporánea de «promoción del laicado», profundizándola en sus fundamentos teológicos, integrándola e iluminándola cabalmente en la eclesiología de la *Lumen gentium,* convocando e impulsando la activa participación de los laicos en la vida y misión de la Iglesia. En el Cuerpo de Cristo constituido en «pluralidad de ministerios pero unidad de misión» *(Apostolicam actuositatem* 2; cf. *Lumen gentium* 10 y 32), los laicos, en cuanto fieles cristianos «incorporados a Cristo por el bautismo, constituidos en Pueblo de Dios y hechos partícipes a su manera de la función sacerdotal, profética y real de Jesucristo», están llamados a ejercer su apostolado, en particular, «en todas y cada una de las actividades y profesiones» que desempeñan, «así como en las condiciones ordinarias de la vida familiar y social...» *(Lumen gentium* 31) para «impregnar y perfeccionar todo el orden temporal con el espíritu evangélico» *(Apostolicam actuositatem* 5).

En el cuadro global de las enseñanzas conciliares y especialmente a la luz de la «constitución sobre la Iglesia», se han abierto vastas exigencias y renovadas perspectivas de acción de los laicos en muy variados campos de la vida eclesial y secular. Sin mengua del apostolado individual, reconocido como su presupuesto ineludible, el decreto *Apostolicam actuositatem* señalaba también el aprecio de la Iglesia por las formas asociativas del apostolado seglar, congeniales al ser comunitario de la Iglesia y a las exigencias de evangelización del mundo moderno.

Vosotros sois, pues, signos y protagonistas de esa «promoción del laicado» que tantos frutos ha dado a la vida eclesial en estos años de aplicación del Concilio. A vosotros —y a través de vosotros, a todos los laicos y asociaciones laicales de la Iglesia de América Latina— invito a renovar una doble dimensión de vuestro compromiso laical y eclesial. Por una parte, a testimoniar valientemente a Cristo, a confesar con alegría y docilidad vuestra plena fidelidad al Magisterio eclesial, a asegurar vuestra filial obediencia y colaboración a vuestros pastores, a buscar la más adecuada inserción orgánica y dinámica de vuestro apostolado en la misión de la Iglesia y, en particular, de la pastoral de vuestras Iglesias locales. Muchos y muy probados ejemplos de ello ha dado y da el laicado mexicano. Y es con alegría y agradecimiento que quiero recordar en particular la conmemoración, en este año 1979, del *cincuentenario de la Acción Católica Mexicana,* columna vertebral del laicado organizado en el país. Me complazco de ello.

**Proyección apostólica:
campos principales**

La III Conferencia General del Episcopado Latinoamericano es un momento fuerte de gracia que exige conversión personal y comunitaria, para renovar vuestra comunión eclesial, vuestra confianza en los pastores, vuestro vigor y relanzamiento apostólico.

Por otra parte, desde esa perspectiva eclesial, quiero invitaros a reavivar vuestra sensibilidad humana y cristiana en la otra vertiente de vuestro compromiso: la participación en las necesidades, aspiraciones, desafíos cruciales con que la realidad de vuestros prójimos interpela vuestra acción evangelizadora de laicos cristianos.

De entre la vastedad de los campos que exigen la presencia del laicado en el mundo, y que señala la exhortación apostólica *Evangelii nuntiandi* —esa carta magna de la evangelización—, quiero señalar algunos espacios fundamentales y urgentes en el acelerado y desigual proceso de industrialización, urbanización y transformación cultural en la vida de vuestros pueblos.

La salvaguardia, promoción, santificación y proyección apostólica de la vida familiar deben contar a los laicos católicos entre sus agentes más decididos y coherentes. Célula básica del tejido social, considerada por el concilio Vaticano II como «Iglesia doméstica», exige un esfuerzo evangelizador, para potenciar sus factores de crecimiento humano y cristiano y superar los obstáculos que atentan contra su integridad y finalidades.

Los «mundos» emergentes y complejos de los intelectuales y universitarios, del proletariado, técnicos y dirigentes de empresa, de los vastos sectores campesinos y poblaciones suburbanas sometidas al impacto acelerado de cambios económico-sociales y culturales reclaman una particular atención apostólica, a veces casi misionera, por parte del laicado católico en la proyección pastoral del conjunto de la Iglesia.

¡Cómo no señalar también la presencia, en medio de esa muchedumbre interpelante, de la juventud, en sus inquietas esperanzas, rebeldías y frustraciones, en sus ilimitados anhelos a veces utópicos, en sus sensibilidades y búsquedas religiosas, así como en sus tentaciones por ídolos consumísticos o ideológicos! Los jóvenes esperan testimonios claros, coherentes y gozosos de la fe eclesial que los ayuden a reestructurar y encauzar sus abiertas y generosas energías en sólidas opciones de vida personal y colectiva.

La caridad, savia primordial de vida eclesial, se despliega por medio de los laicos cristianos también en la solidaridad fraterna ante situaciones de indigencia, opresión, desamparo o soledad de los más pobres, predilectos del Señor liberador y redentor.

¿Y cómo olvidar el mundo todo de la enseñanza, donde se forjan los hombres del mañana; el mismo terreno de la política, para que siempre responda a criterios de bien común; el campo de los Organismos internacionales, para que sean palestras de justicia, de esperanza y entendimiento entre los pueblos; el mundo de la medicina y del servicio sanitario, donde son posibles tantas intervenciones que tocan muy de cerca el orden moral; el campo de la cultura y del arte, terrenos fértiles para contribuir a dignificar al hombre en lo humano y en lo espiritual?

Las comunidades de base

En esa doble vertiente de renovado compromiso cristiano, vuestra fidelidad eclesial —recogiendo y vigorizando la tradición del laicado mexicano— os relanzará con nuevas energías para operar como fermento hacia más amplias perspectivas de convivencia social.

La tarea es inmensa. Vosotros sois llamados a participar en ella, asumiendo y prosiguiendo lo mejor de la experiencia de participación eclesial y secular de los laicos en los últimos años; dejando progresivamente a un lado las crisis de identidad, contestaciones estériles e ideologizaciones extrañas al Evangelio.

Uno de los fenómenos de los últimos años en el que se ha manifestado con creciente vigor el dinamismo de los laicos en América Latina y en otras partes, es el de las llamadas comunidades de base, que han ido surgiendo en coincidencia con la crisis del asociacionismo católico.

Las comunidades de base pueden ser un instrumento válido de formación y vivencia de la vida religiosa dentro de un nuevo ambiente de impulso cristiano, y pueden servir, entre otras cosas, para una penetración capilar del Evangelio en la sociedad.

Pero para que eso sea posible, es necesario que se mantengan bien presentes los criterios tan claros que se enuncian en la *Evangelii nuntiandi* (n.58), a fin de que se alimenten de la Palabra de Dios en la oración y permanezcan unidas, no separadas, y menos contrapuestas, a la Iglesia, a los pastores y a los otros grupos o asociaciones eclesiales.

Vocación a la santidad

Que vuestras asociaciones sean como hasta hoy —y mejor aún— formativas de cristianos con vocación de santidad, sólidos en su fe, seguros en la doctrina propuesta por el Magisterio auténtico, firmes y activos en la Iglesia, cimentados en una densa vida espiritual, alimentada con el acercamiento frecuente a los sacramentos de la penitencia y de la eucaristía, perseverantes en el testimonio y acción evangélica, coherentes y valientes en sus compromisos temporales, constantes promotores de paz y justicia contra toda violencia u opresión, agudos en el discernimiento crítico de las situaciones e ideologías a la luz de las enseñanzas sociales de la Iglesia, confiados en la esperanza del Señor.

Vaya mi bendición apostólica a vosotros, a todos los laicos de vuestras asociaciones, a vuestros asistentes eclesiásticos y al conjunto del laicado mexicano. Y también a los millones de laicos latinoamericanos que elevan su oración y ponen su esperanza en Puebla. A todos os encomiendo a la protección maternal de la Virgen María, en su advocación de Guadalupe.

PROCLAMAD CON HECHOS Y PALABRAS VUESTRA FE

Discurso del Santo Padre a los estudiantes católicos en el Colegio «Miguel Angel», Ciudad de México, 30 de enero.

Queridos jóvenes:

Estoy contento de poder encontrarme hoy con vosotros en esta escuela católica «Instituto Miguel Angel». Formáis un grupo numeroso de todas las edades, tanto los que estudiáis en este centro cuanto los venidos de muchas otras escuelas privadas y católicas. En vuestra juventud veo y siento presentes a todos los estudiantes del país. A todos os saludo con un afecto particular, porque veo en vosotros la esperanza prometedora de la Iglesia y de la nación mexicana del mañana.

También quiero saludar afectuosamente a vuestros profesores, a los representantes de las instituciones formadoras y de los padres de familia. Todos merecéis mi respeto porque entre todos estáis formando a las nuevas generaciones.

Formación integral

1.   Las dificultades que las escuelas católicas en México han sabido superar en el cumplimiento de su misión, es un motivo más de mi reconocimiento al Señor y al mismo tiempo un estímulo para vuestra responsabilidad, a fin de que la escuela católica lleve a cabo la formación integral de los futuros ciudadanos sobre una base auténticamente humana y cristiana.

«La Iglesia, en cuanto a su misión específica, debe promover e impartir la educación cristiana a la que todos los bautizados tienen derecho, para que alcancen la madurez en su fe. Como servidora de todos los hombres, la Iglesia busca colaborar mediante sus miembros, especialmente laicos, en las tareas de promoción cultural humana, en todas las formas que interesan a la sociedad» (Medellín, *Educación* 9).

Muy antigua es la tradición cristiana en esta ciudad de México; y ha sido también pionera en introducir la doctrina social de la Iglesia en los planes de estudio escolares. Esto ha sido germen de un mayor respeto a los derechos de todos los hombres, especialmente de los que sufren en la miseria o en la marginación social.

La juventud, fuerza renovadora

2.   La Iglesia contempla con optimismo y profunda esperanza a la juventud. Vosotros, los jóvenes, representáis a la mayor parte de la po-

blación mexicana, de la cual el 50 por 100 no llega a los veinte años. En los momentos más difíciles del cristianismo en la historia mexicana, los jóvenes han dado un testimonio heroico y generoso.

La Iglesia ve en la juventud una enorme fuerza renovadora, que nuestro predecesor el papa Juan XXIII consideraba como un símbolo de la misma Iglesia, llamada a una constante renovación de sí misma, o sea, a un incesante rejuvenecimiento.

Preparaos a la vida con serenidad y diligencia. En este momento de la juventud, tan importante para la maduración plena de vuestra personalidad, sabed dar siempre el puesto adecuado al elemento religioso de vuestra formación, el que lleva al hombre a alcanzar su dignidad plena, que es la de ser hijo de Dios. Recordad siempre que sólo si os apoyáis, como dice San Pablo, sobre el único fundamento que es Jesucristo (cf. 1 Cor 3,11), podréis construir algo verdaderamente grande y duradero.

Caminad al encuentro de Cristo

3. Como recuerdo de este encuentro tan cordial y gozoso, quiero dejaros una consideración concreta.

Con la vivacidad que es propia de vuestros años, con el entusiasmo generoso de vuestro corazón joven, caminad al encuentro de Cristo: sólo El es la solución de todos vuestros problemas; sólo El es el camino, la verdad y la vida; sólo El es la verdadera salvación del mundo; sólo El es la esperanza de la humanidad.

Buscad a Jesús esforzándoos en conseguir una fe personal profunda que informe y oriente toda vuestra vida; pero sobre todo que sea vuestro compromiso y vuestro programa amar a Jesús con un amor sincero, auténtico y personal. El debe ser vuestro amigo y vuestro apoyo en el camino de la vida. Sólo El tiene palabras de vida eterna (cf. Jn 6,68).

Vuestra sed de lo absoluto no puede ser saciada por los sucedáneos de ideologías que conducen al odio, a la violencia y a la desesperación. Sólo Cristo, buscado y amado con amor sincero, es fuente de alegría, de serenidad y de paz.

Pero después de haber encontrado a Cristo, después de haber descubierto quién es El, no se puede no sentir la necesidad de anunciarlo. Sabed ser testigos auténticos de Cristo; sabed vivir y proclamar, con hechos y palabras, vuestra fe.

Vosotros, queridísimos jóvenes, debéis tener el ansia y el deseo de ser portadores de Cristo a esta sociedad actual más que nunca necesitada de El, más que nunca a la búsqueda de El, a pesar de que las apariencias puedan tal vez hacer creer lo contrario.

«Es necesario —ha escrito mi predecesor Pablo VI en la exhortación *Evangelii nuntiandi*— que los jóvenes, bien formados en la fe y arraigados en la oración, se conviertan cada vez más en los apóstoles de la juventud» (n.72). A cada

uno de vosotros espera la tarea entusiasmante
de ser un anunciador de Cristo entre vuestros
compañeros de escuela y de diversión. Cada uno
de vosotros debe tener en el corazón el deseo de
ser un apóstol entre los que están a vuestro alrededor.

Comprometeos en cosas grandes

4.   Quiero ahora confiaros un problema que
llevo muy dentro de mí. La Iglesia es consciente
del subdesarrollo cultural existente en muchas
zonas del continente latinoamericano y de vuestro país. Mi predecesor Pablo VI, en su encíclica *Populorum progressio,* afirmaba: «...la
educación básica es el primer objetivo de un
plan de desarrollo» (n.36).

En la dinámica acelerada de cambio, característica de la sociedad actual, es necesario y, a la
vez, urgente que sepamos crear un ambiente de
solidaridad humana y cristiana en torno al acuciante problema de la escolarización. Ya lo re-
cordaba el Concilio en su documento sobre la
Educación: «Todos los hombres, de cualquier
raza, condición y edad, por poseer la dignidad
de persona, tienen derecho inalienable a una
educación...» (n.1).

No es posible permanecer indiferente ante el
grave problema del analfabetismo o semi-
analfabetismo.

En uno de los momentos decisivos para el futuro de América Latina, hago un fuerte llamado

en nombre de Cristo a todos los hombres y, de modo particular, a vosotros los jóvenes, para que prestéis hoy y mañana vuestra ayuda, servicio y colaboración en esta tarea de escolarización. Mi voz, mi súplica de Padre se dirige también a los educadores cristianos para que, con su aportación, favorezcan la alfabetización y «culturización», con una visión integral del hombre. No olvidemos que «un analfabeto es un espíritu subalimentado» (*Populorum progressio* 35).

Confío en la colaboración de todos para ayudar a resolver este problema, que toca un derecho tan esencial del ser humano.

¡Jóvenes, comprometeos humana y cristianamente en cosas que merecen esfuerzo, desprendimiento y generosidad! ¡La Iglesia lo espera de vosotros y confía en vosotros!

El Papa cuenta con los jóvenes

5. Pongamos esta intención a los pies de María, a la que los mexicanos invocáis como Nuestra Señora de Guadalupe. Ella estuvo asociada íntimamente al misterio de Cristo y es un ejemplo de amor generoso y de entrega al servicio de los demás. Su vida de fe profunda es el camino para robustecer nuestra fe y nos enseña a encontrarnos con Dios en la intimidad de nuestro ser.

Al volver a vuestras casas, asociaciones juveniles y grupos de amigos, decid a todos que el Papa cuenta con los jóvenes. Decid que los jó-

venes son el consuelo y la fuerza del Papa, que
desea estar con ellos para hacerles llegar su voz
de aliento en medio de todas las dificultades que
comporta el situarse en la sociedad.

Os ayude y estimule a cumplir vuestros propósitos la bendición apostólica que os imparto
de corazón a vosotros, a vuestros seres queridos
y a cuantos se dedican a vuestra formación.

Latinoamérica, continente de la esperanza.

En Cuilapán, con el sombrero de la «Danza de las plumas»

l cardenal Baggio saluda al Papa, al inaugurarse la III Con-
ferencia del CELAM.

VII

El Papa inicia los trabajos de la **III** Conferencia del CEL

...n su discurso sobre la evangelización en Latinoamérica.

Ofrenda floral de un campesino en San Miguel Xoxtla.

El Papa premia la tradición católica de la América Latina.

Conversando en Oaxaca con un grupo de sacerdotes.

ME PARECE ESTAR
EN MI CASA

Respuesta del Santo Padre al saludo del señor cardenal José Salazar López a su llegada a Guadalajara, 30 de enero.

Señor cardenal, hermanos, hijos amadísimos:

Agradezco de todo corazón al señor arzobispo de Guadalajara el saludo que ha tenido a bien dirigirme en el instante de mi llegada a esta querida arquidiócesis. El Papa se siente emocionado de la acogida tan humana, tan cristiana y tan familiar. Me parece estar entre los míos, en mi casa.

En la historia de este gran país, los habitantes de este Estado y de esta ciudad os habéis siempre distinguido por vuestra religiosidad y vuestra laboriosidad. Habéis sabido aunar lo espiritual y lo material en una síntesis que supone la auténtica vivencia del mensaje del Hijo de Dios.

Amadísimos todos: Mi saludo se dirige a los aquí presentes y de modo particular a los sacerdotes, religiosos y a todos aquellos que trabajan en la construcción del reino de Dios en esta arquidiócesis, rica en testimonio de fe cristiana,

que se manifiesta en tantas maneras y especialmente en vocaciones a la vida religiosa.

Gracias por la oportunidad que brindáis a
vuestro Padre de estar con vosotros, hijos míos,
en esta visita.

¡Qué el Señor os bendiga!

EL PAPA OS AMA PORQUE SOIS LOS PREDILECTOS DE DIOS

Saludo del Santo Padre en su visita al barrio pobre de Santa Cecilia, Guadalajara, 30 de enero.

Queridos hermanos y hermanas:

He deseado vivamente este encuentro, habitantes del barrio de Santa Cecilia, porque me siento solidario con vosotros y porque, siendo pobres, tenéis derecho a mis particulares desvelos.

Yo os digo en seguida el motivo: el Papa os ama porque sois los predilectos de Dios. El mismo, al fundar su familia, la Iglesia, tenía presente a la humanidad pobre y necesitada. Para redimirla envió precisamente a su Hijo, que nació pobre y vivió entre los pobres para hacernos ricos con su pobreza (cf. 2 Cor 8,9).

Como consecuencia de esa redención, llevada a cabo en quien se hizo uno de nosotros, ahora ya no somos pobres siervos, somos hijos, que podemos llamar a Dios: Padre (cf. Gál 4,4-6). Ya no estamos desamparados, ya que, si somos hijos de Dios, somos también herederos de los bienes, que El ofrece con largueza a aquellos

que lo aman (cf. Mt 11,28). ¿Podremos descon-
fiar de que un padre dé cosas buenas a sus hijos? (cf. ibíd., 7,7ss). El mismo Jesús, Salvador
nuestro, nos espera para aliviarnos en la fatiga
(cf. ibíd., 11,28). Al mismo tiempo cuenta con
nuestra colaboración personal para dignificarnos
cada vez más, siendo artífices de nuestra propia
elevación humana y moral.

A la vez, ante vuestra agobiante situación, invito con todas mis fuerzas a todo el que tiene
medios y se siente cristiano, a renovarse en la
mente y en el corazón para que, promoviendo
una mayor justicia y aun dando de lo propio, a
nadie falte el conveniente alimento, vestido, ha-
bitación, cultura, trabajo; todo lo que da dignidad a la persona humana. La imagen de Cristo
en la cruz, precio del rescate de la humanidad,
es una llamada acuciante a gastar la vida po-
niéndonos al servicio de los necesitados, a ritmo
con la caridad, que es desprendida y que no
simpatiza con la injusticia, sino con la verdad
(cf. 1 Cor 13,2ss).

Os bendigo a todos, pidiendo al Señor ilumine
siempre vuestros corazones y vuestras acciones.

ARTIFICES DE JUSTICIA
Y DE VERDADERA LIBERTAD

Discurso del Papa pronunciado ante una concentración de obreros en el estadio de Jalisco, Guadalajara, 30 de enero.

Queridos hermanos, hermanas, obreros y obreras:

Llego hasta aquí a este cuadro maravilloso de Guadalajara, donde nos encontramos en el nombre de Aquel que quiso ser conocido como el Hijo del Artesano.

Vengo hasta vosotros trayendo en mis ojos y en mi alma la imagen de Nuestra Señora de Guadalupe, vuestra Patrona, hacia la que profesáis un amor filial que he podido constatar no sólo en su santuario, sino incluso pasando por las calles y ciudades de México. Donde hay un mexicano, allí está la Madre de Guadalupe. Me decía un señor que el 96 por 100 de los mexicanos son católicos, mas el 100 por 100 son guadalupanos.

La familia, agente de bien y de amor

He querido venir a visitaros, familias obreras de Guadalajara y de otros lugares, en esta arquidiócesis que se distingue por su adhesión a la fe, por su unidad familiar y por sus esfuerzos para responder a las grandes exigencias humanas y cristianas de la justicia, de la paz, del progreso, según Dios.

Me presento ante vosotros como un hermano, con alegría y con amor, después de haber tenido la oportunidad de recorrer los caminos de México y de ser testigo del amor que aquí se profesa a Cristo, a la Virgen Santísima y al Papa, peregrino y mensajero de la fe, de la luz, de la verdad, de la esperanza y de la unión entre los hombres.

Deseo manifestaros desde el primer momento cuánto agrada al Papa que este encuentro sea de obreros, de familias obreras, de familias cristianas, que desde sus puestos de trabajo saben ser agentes de bien social y de respeto, de amor a Dios en el taller, en la fábrica, en cualquier casa o lugar.

Estad orgullosos de vuestros padres

Pienso en vosotros, niños y niñas, jóvenes de familias obreras; me viene a la mente la figura de Aquel que nació en el seno de una familia artesana, que creció en edad, sabiduría y gracia, que de su Madre aprendió los caminos humanos del bien, que en aquel varón justo que Dios le dio por padre tuvo el maestro en la vida y en el trabajo cotidiano. La Iglesia venera a esa Madre y a ese hombre, a ese santo, obrero también él y modelo de hombre y de obrero.

Nuestro Señor Jesucristo recibió las caricias de sus recias manos de obrero, manos endurecidas por el trabajo, manos abiertas a la bondad y al hermano necesitado. Permitidme entrar en vuestras casas —¿queréis tener al Papa como huésped y amigo vuestro?— y dadme el consuelo de ver en vuestros hogares la unión, el amor familiar que descansa tras la jornada de fatiga, el respeto mutuo y afectuoso que reinaba en la Sagrada Familia. Dejadme ver, queridos niños y jóvenes, que os estáis preparando de manera seria para el mañana; os lo repito, sois la esperanza del Papa.

No me neguéis el gozo de veros caminar por senderos que os conducen a ser auténticos seguidores del bien y amigos de Cristo. No me neguéis la alegría de ver vuestro sentido de responsabilidad en los estudios, en las actividades, en las diversiones. Estáis llamados a ser portadores de generosidad y honestidad, a ser luchadores contra la inmoralidad, a preparar ese México más justo y sano, más feliz para los hijos de Dios e hijos de nuestra Madre María.

Vosotros sabéis muy bien que el trabajo de vuestros padres está presente en el esfuerzo común de crecimiento en esta nación y en todo lo que contribuya para que los beneficios de la civilización contemporánea lleguen a todos los mexicanos. Estad orgullosos de vuestros padres y colaborad con ellos en vuestra formación de jóvenes honrados y cristianos. Os acompañan mi afecto y aliento.

Firmeza en las horas duras

El afecto del Papa se dirige también a las trabajadoras, madres y esposas presentes, y a todas aquellas que escuchan mi palabra a través de los medios de comunicación social. Recordad a aquella Virgen Madre que supo ser causa de alegría para el esposo y guía solícita para el Hijo. En los momentos de dificultad y de prueba, cuando hay preocupaciones y limitaciones, recordad que Dios escogió a una Madre pobre, y que Ella supo permanecer firme en el bien, aun en las horas más duras.

Muchas de vosotras trabajáis también en alguna de las múltiples actividades que hoy se abren a la capacidad femenina; muchas de vosotras sois también sustento para no pocos hogares y ayuda continua para que la vida familiar sea cada vez más digna. Estad presentes con vuestra creatividad en la transformación de esta sociedad; la manera de vida contemporánea ofrece oportunidades y empleos cada vez más importantes para la mujer; llevad vuestra aportación iluminada por vuestro sentido religioso a todos los puestos y aun a las más altas magistraturas.

Amigos, hermanos trabajadores, existe un concepto cristiano del trabajo, de la vida familiar y social que encierra grandes valores y que reclama criterios y normas morales que orientan a quien cree en Dios y en Jesucristo, para que el trabajo se realice como una verdadera vocación de transformación del mundo, en un espíritu de servicio y de amor a los hermanos, para que la persona humana se realice a sí misma y contribuya a la creciente humanización del mundo y de sus estructuras.

Testigos y agentes de la justicia

El trabajo no es una maldición, es una bendición de Dios que llama al hombre a dominar la tierra y a transformarla, para que con la inteligencia y el esfuerzo humanos continúe la obra creadora y divina. Quiero deciros con toda mi alma y fuerzas: me duelen las insuficiencias de trabajo, me duelen profundamente las injusticias, me duelen los conflictos, me duelen las ideologías de odio y violencia que no son evangélicas y que tantas heridas causan en la humanidad contemporánea.

Para el cristiano no basta la denuncia de las injusticias; a él se le pide ser en verdad testigo y agente de justicia. El que trabaja tiene derechos que ha de defender legalmente, pero tiene también deberes que ha de cumplir generosamente. Como cristianos estáis llamados a ser artífices de justicia y de verdadera libertad. La técnica contemporánea crea toda una problemática nueva y a veces produce desempleo, pero abre también grandes posibilidades que reclaman en el trabajador una preparación cada vez mayor y una aportación de su capacidad humana e imaginación creadora. Por ello, el trabajo no ha de ser una mera necesidad; ha de ser visto como una verdadera vocación, un llamamiento de Dios a construir un mundo nuevo en el que habite la justicia y fraternidad, anticipo del reino de Dios, en el que no habrá ya ni carencias ni limitaciones.

Construir un mundo mejor

El trabajo ha de ser el medio para que toda la creación esté sometida a la dignidad del ser humano e hijo de Dios.

Ese trabajo ofrece la oportunidad de comprometerse con toda la comunidad sin resentimientos, sin amarguras, sin odios, sino con el amor universal de Cristo, que a nadie excluye y que a todos abraza.

Cristo nos ha anunciado el Evangelio, por el que sabemos que Dios es amor, que es Padre de todos y que nosotros somos hermanos.

El misterio central de nuestra vida cristiana, que es el de la Pascua, nos hace mirar al cielo nuevo y a la tierra nueva. En el trabajo debe existir esa mística pascual, por la que los sacrificios y fatigas se aceptan con impulso cristiano para hacer que resplandezca más claramente el nuevo orden querido por el Señor, y para hacer un mundo que responda a la bondad de Dios en la armonía, el amor y la paz.

Amadísimos hijos: pido al Señor por vosotros todos y por vuestras familias. Pido al Señor por la unidad y estabilidad de los matrimonios, y por que la vida del hogar sea siempre plena y gozosa. La fe cristiana ha de ser más fuerte que todos los factores de crisis contemporánea. La Iglesia, como el Concilio nos ha enseñado tan luminosamente, ha de ser la gran familia en la que se vive la dinámica de unidad, de vida, de gozo y de amor que es la Trinidad Santísima. El mismo Concilio ha llamado a la familia «pequeña Iglesia»; en la familia cristiana tiene su principio la acción evangelizadora de la Iglesia. Las familias son las primeras escuelas de educación en la fe; solamente si esa unidad cristiana de la familia se conserva, será posible que la Iglesia cumpla su gran misión en la sociedad y en la misma Iglesia.

Amigos y hermanos: gracias por haberme ofrecido la posibilidad de participar en este gran encuentro con el mundo obrero, con el que me siento siempre tan a gusto. Sois para el Papa amigos y compañeros. Gracias.

Esta ciudad de Guadalajara se ha distinguido en todo México por el impulso dado a las actividades deportivas que porporcionan a la familia el crecimiento físico y espiritual y la alegría de una mente sana en un cuerpo sano. La corona de futbolistas que nos acompaña pone un nuevo color a nuestra gran reunión. El Papa os da su bendición a todos y cada uno. Ella os aliente en vuestro compromiso apostólico con generosa entrega fraternal y con la seguridad de que Dios trabaja con vosotros para que construyáis un mundo más hermoso, más amable, más justo, más humano, más cristiano. Así sea.

ACTUALIDAD DE LA VIDA CONTEMPLATIVA

Encuentro del Santo Padre con las religiosas de clausura en la catedral de Guadalajara, 30 de enero.

Queridas religiosas de clausura:

En esta catedral de Guadalajara quiero saludaros con esas bellas y expresivas palabras que repetimos con frecuencia en la asamblea litúrgica: «El Señor esté con vosotras» (Misal Romano). Sí, que el Señor, al que habéis consagrado toda vuestra vida, esté siempre con vosotras.

Aprecio por la vida contemplativa

¿Cómo podría faltar durante la visita a México un encuentro del Papa con las religiosas contemplativas? Si a tantas personas yo quería ver, vosotras ocupáis un puesto especial por vuestra particular consagración al Señor y a la Iglesia. Por ese motivo, el Papa también quiere estar cerca de vosotras.

Este encuentro quiere ser la continuación del

que tuve con las demás religiosas mexicanas; muchas cosas les decía también para vosotras, pero ahora deseo referirme a lo que es más específicamente vuestro.

¡Cuántas veces el Magisterio de la Iglesia ha demostrado su gran estima y aprecio por vuestra vida dedicada a la oración, al silencio, y a un modo singular de entrega a Dios! En estos momentos de tantas transformaciones en todo, ¿sigue teniendo significado este tipo de vida o es algo ya superado?

El Papa os dice: Sí, vuestra vida tiene más importancia que nunca, vuestra consagración total es de plena actualidad. En un mundo que va perdiendo el sentido de lo divino, ante la supervaloración de lo material, vosotras, queridas religiosas, comprometidas desde vuestros claustros en ser testigos de unos valores por los que vivís, sed testigos del Señor para el mundo de hoy; infundid con vuestra oración un nuevo soplo de vida en la Iglesia y en el hombre actual.

Testimonio silencioso del reino

Especialmente en la vida contemplativa se trata de realizar una unidad difícil: manifestar ante el mundo el misterio de la Iglesia en el mundo presente y gustar ya aquí, enseñándoselo a los hombres, como dice San Pablo, «las cosas de allá arriba» (Col 1,3).

El ser contemplativa no supone cortar radicalmente con el mundo, con el apostolado. La contemplativa tiene que encontrar su modo específico de extender el reino de Dios, de colaborar en la edificación de la ciudad terrena, no sólo con sus plegarias y sus sacrificios, sino con su testimonio silencioso, es verdad, pero que pueda ser entendido por los hombres de buena voluntad con los que esté en contacto.

Para ello tenéis que encontrar vuestro estilo propio que, dentro de una visión contemplativa, os haga compartir con vuestros hermanos el don gratuito de Dios.

Vuestra vida consagrada arranca de la consagración bautismal y la expresa con mayor plenitud. Con una respuesta libre a la llamada del Espíritu Santo, habéis decidido seguir a Cristo consagrándoos totalmente a El. «Esta consagración será tanto más perfecta, dice el Concilio, cuanto, por vínculos más firmes y más estables, represente mejor a Cristo, unido con vínculo indisoluble a su Iglesia» *(Lumen gentium* 44).

Las religiosas contemplativas sentís una atracción que os arrastra hacia el Señor. Apoyadas en Dios, os abandonáis a su acción paternal, que os levanta hacia El y os transforma en El, mientras os prepara para la contemplación eterna, que constituye nuestra meta última para todos. ¿Cómo podríais avanzar a lo largo de este camino y ser fieles a la gracia que os anima, si no respondierais con todo vuestro ser, por medio de un dinamismo cuyo impulso es el amor, a esta llamada que os orienta de manera permanente hacia Dios? Considerad, pues, cualquier otra actividad como un testimonio, ofrecido al

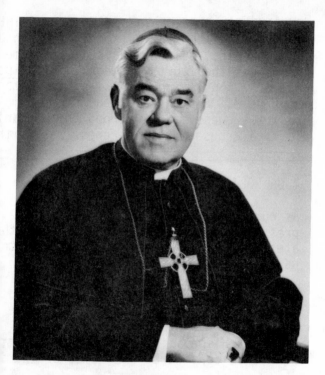

BISHOP NEVIN W. HAYES

FUNDAMENTAL PLEA OF THE STATEMENT TO THE
nections between the National Conference
encia General del Episcopado Latinoamer
ourselves the fourth largest Spanish Spe
tal U.S. population and 25% of the Catho
ment read. "And that was the first time
real awareness of how strong the Hispani
To have aroused that awareness was worth

YOUR HOLINESS JOHN PAUL:

As our shepherd who has felt the pain a
pression; as one who is committed to th
ates a vision of a more just and equita
us the following requests:

1. That in all dioceses of the United
percent or more a Hispanic Ordinary be

2. That Hispanic priests truly committ
people be considered and named ordinari

3. That any diocese with twenty percer

Señor, de vuestra íntima comunión con El, para
que os conceda aquella pureza de intención, tan
necesaria para encontrarlo en la misma oración.
De este modo contribuiréis a la extensión del
reino de Dios, con el testimonio de vuestra vida
y con «una misteriosa fecundidad apostólica»
(*Perfectae caritatis* 7).

Conservar la sencillez

Reunidas en nombre de Cristo, vuestras comunidades tienen como centro la Eucaristía,
«sacramento de amor, signo de unidad, vínculo
de caridad» (*Sacrosanctum Concilium* 47).

Por la Eucaristía también el mundo está presente en el centro de vuestra vida de oración
y de ofrenda, como el Concilio ha explicado: «y
nadie piense que los religiosos, por su consagración, se hacen extraños a los hombres o in-
útiles para la sociedad terrena. Porque, si bien en
algunos casos no sirven directamente a sus con-
temporáneos, los tienen, sin embargo, presentes
de manera más íntima en las entrañas de Cristo
y cooperan espiritualmente con ellos, para que
la edificación de la ciudad terrena se funde
siempre en el Señor y se ordene a El, no sea que
trabajen en vano quienes la edifican» (*Lumen
gentium* 46).

Contemplándoos con la ternura del Señor
cuando llamaba a sus discípulos «pequeña grey»
(cf. Lc 12,32), y les anunciaba que su Padre se
había complacido en darles el reino, yo os su-

plico: conservad la sencillez de los «más pequeños» del Evangelio. Sabed encontrarla en el trato íntimo y profundo con Cristo y en contacto con vuestros hermanos. Conoceréis entonces «el rebosar de gozo por la acción del Espíritu Santo» que es de aquellos que son introducidos en los secretos del reino (cf. Exhortación apostólica sobre la renovación de la vida religiosa, 54).

Que la Madre amadísima del Señor, que en México invocáis con el dulce nombre de Nuestra Señora de Guadalupe, y bajo cuyo ejemplo habéis consagrado a Dios vuestra vida, os alcance, en vuestro caminar diario, aquella alegría inalterable que sólo Jesús puede dar.

Como un gran saludo de paz que no se agota en vosotras aquí presentes, sino que se extiende invisiblemente a todas vuestras hermanas contemplativas de México, recibid de corazón mi bendición apostólica.

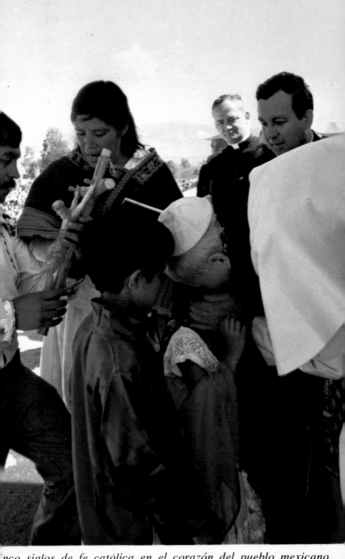

...nco siglos de fe católica en el corazón del pueblo mexicano.

Guadalajara recibe al Papa con el colorido de sus bailes típicos.

Monterrey aclama a Juan Pablo II.

La religiosidad del pueblo como capí

damental de la evangelización.

En Monterrey, tocado con el casco de un obrero metalúrgico.

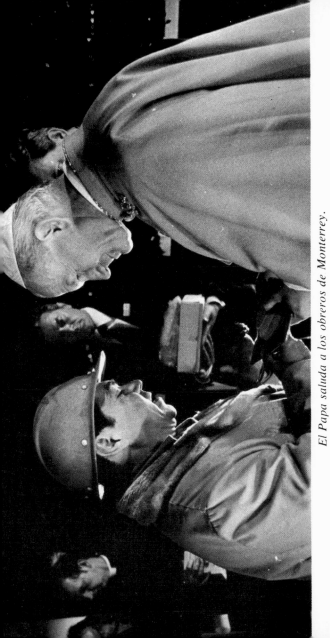

El Papa saluda a los obreros de Monterrey.

Magna concentración de los católicos mexicanos en Monterrey.

SOMOS RESPONSABLES
LOS UNOS DE LOS OTROS

Homilía del Santo Padre en el santuario de Nuestra Señora de Zapopán, Guadalajara, 30 de enero.

Queridos hermanos y hermanas:

1. Henos aquí reunidos hoy en este hermoso santuario de Nuestra Señora de la Inmaculada Concepción de Zapopán, en la gran arquidiócesis de Guadalajara. No quería ni podía omitir este encuentro en torno al altar de Jesús y a los pies de María Santísima, con el Pueblo de Dios que peregrina en este lugar. Este santuario de Zapopán es, en efecto, una prueba más, palpable y consoladora, de la intensa devoción que, desde hace siglos, el pueblo mexicano, y con él, todo el pueblo latinoamericano, profesa a la Virgen Inmaculada.

María en la piedad del pueblo

Como el de Guadalupe, también este santuario viene de la época de la colonia; como aquél,

sus orígenes se remontan al valioso esfuerzo de
evangelización de los misioneros (en este caso,
los hijos de San Francisco) entre los indios, tan
bien dispuestos a recibir el mensaje de la salvación en Cristo y a venerar a su Santísima Madre,
concebida sin mancha de pecado. Así. estos
pueblos perciben el lugar único y excepcional de
María en la realización del plan de Dios (cf. *Lumen gentium* 53ss), su santidad eminente y su
relación maternal con nosotros (ibíd., 61 y 66).
De aquí en adelante, Ella, la Inmaculada, repre-
sentada en esta pequeña y sencilla imagen,
queda incorporada a la piedad popular del pueblo de la arquidiócesis de Guadalajara, de la nación mexicana y de toda América Latina. Como
María misma dice proféticamente en su cántico
del *Magnificat:* «Me llamarán feliz todas las generaciones» (Lc 1,48).

Expresión de la fe

2.   Si esto es verdad de todo el mundo católico, cuánto más lo es de México y de América
Latina. Se puede decir que la fe y la devoción a
María y sus misterios pertenecen a la indenti-
dad propia de estos pueblos y caracterizan su
piedad popular, de la cual hablaba mi predecesor Pablo VI en la exhortación apostólica *Evangelii nuntiandi* (n.48). Esta piedad popular no es
necesariamente un sentimiento vago, carente de
sólida base doctrinal, como una forma inferior
de manifestación religiosa. Cuántas veces es, al

contrario, como la expresión verdadera del alma de un pueblo, en cuanto tocada por la gracia y forjada por el encuentro feliz entre la obra de evangelización y la cultura local, de lo cual habla también la exhortación recién citada (n.20). Así, guiada y sostenida, y, si es el caso, purificada, por la acción constante de los pastores, y ejercida diariamente en la vida del pueblo, la piedad popular es de veras la piedad de los «pobres y sencillos» (ibíd., 48). Es la manera cómo estos predilectos del Señor viven y traducen en sus actitudes humanas, y en todas las dimensiones de la vida, el misterio de la fe que han recibido.

Esta piedad popular, en México y en toda América Latina, es indisolublemente mariana. En ella, María Santísima ocupa el mismo lugar preeminente que ocupa en la totalidad de la fe cristiana. Ella es la madre, la reina, la protectora y el modelo. A Ella se viene para honrarla, para pedir su intercesión, para aprender a imitarla, es decir, para aprender a ser un verdadero discípulo de Jesús. Porque como el mismo Señor dice: «Quien hiciere la voluntad de Dios, éste es mi hermano, mi hermana y mi madre» (Mc 3,35).

Lejos de empañar la mediación insustituible y única de Cristo, esta función de María, acogida por la piedad popular, la pone de relieve y «sirve para demostrar su poder», como enseña el concilio Vaticano II (*Lumen gentium* 60), porque todo lo que Ella es y tiene le viene de la «superabundancia de los méritos de Cristo, se

apoya en su mediación» y a El conduce (ibíd.).
Los fieles que acceden a este santuario bien lo
saben y lo ponen en práctica, al decir siempre
con Ella, mirando a Dios Padre, en el don de su
Hijo amado, hecho presente entre nosotros por
el Espíritu: «Glorifica mi alma al Señor» (Lc
1,46).

Apertura al don de Dios

3.   Precisamente, cuando los fieles vienen a
este santuario, como he querido venir yo tam-
biën hoy, peregrino en esta tierra mexicana,
¿qué otra cosa hacen sino alabar y honrar a Dios
Padre, Hijo y Espíritu Santo, en la figura de María, unida por vínculos indisolubles con las tres
Personas de la Santísima Trinidad, como también enseña el concilio Vaticano II? (cf. *Lumen
gentium* 53). Nuestra visita al santuario de Zapopán, la mía hoy, la vuestra tantas veces, significa por el hecho mismo la voluntad y el esfuerzo de acercarse a Dios y de dejarse inundar
por El, mediante la intercesión, el auxilio y el
modelo de María.

En estos lugares de gracia, tan característicos
de la geografía religiosa mexicana y latinoamericana, el Pueblo de Dios, convocado en la Iglesia
con sus pastores, y en esta feliz ocasión con
quien humildemente preside a la Iglesia en la caridad (cf. SAN IGNACIO DE ANTIOQUÍA, *Ad
Rom.* prol.), se reúne en torno al altar y bajo la
mirada materna de María, para dar testimonio

de que lo que cuenta en este mundo y en la vida humana es la apertura al don de Dios, que se comunica en Jesús, nuestro Salvador, y nos viene por María. Esto es lo que da a nuestra existencia terrena su verdadera dimensión trascendente, como Dios la quiso desde el principio, como Jesucristo la ha restaurado con su muerte y su resurrección, y como resplandece en la Virgen Santísima.

Ella es el Refugio de los pecadores (*Refugium peccatorum*). El Pueblo de Dios es consciente de la propia condición de pecado. Por eso, sabiendo que necesita una purificación constante, «busca sin cesar la penitencia y la reconciliación» (*Lumen gentium* 8). Cada uno de nosotros es consciente de ello. Jesús buscaba a los pecadores: «No tienen necesidad de médico los sanos, sino los enfermos, y no he venido yo a llamar a los justos, sino a los pecadores» (Lc 5,31-32). Al paralítico, antes de curarlo le dijo: «Hombre, tus pecados te son perdonados» (Lc 5,20); y a una pecadora: «Vete y no peques más» (Jn 8,11).

Si la conciencia del pecado nos oprime, buscamos instintivamente a Aquel que tiene el poder de perdonar los pecados (cf. Lc 5,24) y lo buscamos por medio de María, cuyos santuarios son lugares de conversión, de penitencia, de reconciliación con Dios.

Ella despierta en nosotros la esperanza de la enmienda y de la perseverancia en el bien, aunque a veces pueda parecer humanamente imposible.

Ella nos permite superar las múltiples «estructuras de pecado» en las que está envuelta nuestra vida personal, familiar y social. Nos permite obtener la gracia de la verdadera liberación, con esa libertad con la que Cristo ha liberado a todo hombre.

Testigos del amor de Cristo

4. De aquí parte también, como de su verdadera fuente, el compromiso auténtico por los demás hombres, nuestros hermanos, especialmente con los más pobres y necesitados, y por la necesaria transformación de la sociedad. Porque esto es lo que Dios quiere de nosotros y a esto nos envía, con la voz y la fuerza de su Evangelio, al hacernos responsables los unos de los otros. María, como enseña mi predecesor Pablo VI en la exhortación apostólica *Marialis cultus* (n.37) es también modelo, fiel cumplidora de la voluntad de Dios, para quienes no aceptan pasivamente las circunstancias adversas de la vida personal y social, ni son víctima de la «alienación», como hoy se dice, sino que proclaman con Ella que Dios es «vindicador de los humildes» y, si es el caso, «depone del trono a los soberbios», para citar de nuevo el *Magnificat* (cf. Lc 1,51-53). Porque Ella es así «tipo del perfecto discípulo de la ciudad terrena y temporal, pero tiende al mismo tiempo a la celestial y eterna, que promueve la justicia, libera a los necesitados, pero sobre todo es testigo de aquel

amor activo que construye a Cristo en las almas» *(Marialis cultus* 37).

Esto es María Inmaculada para nosotros en este santuario de Zapopán. Esto es lo que hemos venido a aprender hoy de Ella, a fin de que Ella sea siempre para estos fieles de Guadalajara, para la nación mexicana y para toda América Latina, con su ser cristiano y católico, la verdadera «Estrella de la evangelización».

Pastoral adecuada

5. Pero no querría acabar este coloquio sin añadir algunas palabras que considero importantes en el contexto de cuanto antes he indicado.

Este santuario de Zapopán, y tantos otros diseminados por toda la geografía de México y América Latina, adonde acuden anualmente millones de peregrinos con un profundo sentido de religiosidad, pueden y deben ser lugares privilegiados para el encuentro de una fe cada vez más purificada, que les conduzca a Cristo.

Para ello será necesario cuidar con gran atención y celo la pastoral en los santuarios marianos, mediante una liturgia apropiada y viva, mediante la predicación asidua y de sólida catequesis, mediante la preocupación por el ministerio del sacramento de la penitencia y la depuración prudente de eventuales formas de religiosidad que presenten elementos menos adecuados.

Hay que aprovechar pastoralmente estas ocasiones, acaso esporádicas, del encuentro con almas que no siempre son fieles a todo el programa de una vida cristiana, pero que acuden guiadas por una visión a veces incompleta de la fe, para tratar de conducirlas al centro de toda piedad sólida, Cristo Jesús, Hijo de Dios Salvador.

De este modo la religiosidad popular se irá perfeccionando, cuando sea necesario, y la devoción mariana adquirirá su pleno significado en una orientación trinitaria, cristocéntrica y eclesial, como tan acertadamente enseña la exhortación apostólica *Marialis cultus* (n.25-27).

A los sacerdotes encargados de los santuarios, a los que hasta ellos conducen peregrinaciones, les invito a reflexionar maduramente acerca del gran bien que pueden hacer a los fieles, si saben poner por obra un sistema de evangelización apropiado.

No desaprovechéis ninguna ocasión de predicar a Cristo, de esclarecer la fe del pueblo, de robustecerla, ayudándolo en su camino hacia la Trinidad Santa. Sea María el camino. A ello os ayude la Virgen Inmaculada de Zapopán. Así sea.

CONSAGRARSE AL HOMBRE POR CRISTO

Discurso del Santo Padre a los seminaristas mayores, diocesanos y religiosos, en el seminario de Guadalajara, 30 de enero.

Queridos seminaristas, diocesanos y religiosos, de México:

¡La paz del Señor sea siempre con vosotros!

El entusiasmo desbordante y afectuoso con que me recibís esta tarde me hace sentir profundamente conmovido. Es un gozo inmenso el que pruebo al compartir con vosotros estos momentos, que por vuestra parte corroboran sin lugar a duda el aprecio que sentís por el Papa delante de Dios, y esto me infunde consuelo y nuevo aliento (cf. 2 Cor 7,13).

A través de vosotros, mi alegría interior se extiende a los queridos hermanos en el episcopado, a los sacerdotes, religiosos y a todos los fieles. Vaya a todos mi más entrañable agradecimiento por tantas atenciones y tanta cordialidad filiales, y más aún por su recuerdo en las plegarias al Señor. Puedo aseguraros que vuestra correspondencia unánime a esta mi «visita pastoral» a México, ha ido dando consistencia

en mí, durante estos días, a un grato presenti-
miento. Os lo diré con palabras del Apóstol:
«Me alegra poder contar con vosotros en todo»
(2 Cor 7,16).

La alegría de decir sí a Dios

1. Es para mí un motivo de satisfacción saber que los seminarios tienen una larga y gloriosa
tradición, que se remonta a los tiempos del concilio de Trento, con la creación del colegio «San
Pedro» en esta ciudad de Guadalajara, el año
1570. A él se han ido sumando en el tiempo
otros muchos centros de formación sacerdotal,
diseminados por todo el territorio nacional,
como demostración persistente de una fresca,
pujante vitalidad eclesial. No quiero pasar por
alto el ya centenario Colegio Mexicano en
Roma, que tiene una misión tan importante:
mantener viva la vinculación entre México y la
Cátedra del Papa. Considero un deber ineludible
de todos ayudarlo y sostenerlo para que cumpla
tan primordial cometido con plena fidelidad a las
normas del Magisterio y a las orientaciones dadas por la Sede de Pedro.

Esta solicitud histórica por crear nuevos seminarios, suscita en mí sentimientos de compla-
cencia y aplauso; pero lo que de modo especial
me llena de esperanza, es el continuo floreci-
miento de vocaciones sacerdotales y religiosas.
Me siento feliz de veros aquí a vosotros, jóvenes
rebosantes de alegría por haber dicho sí a la in-

vitación del Señor, a servirlo con cuerpo y alma en su Iglesia, por el sacerdocio ministerial. Al igual que San Pablo, quiero abriros de par en par mi ánimo para deciros: «Siento el corazón ensanchado...; pagadme con la misma moneda» (2 Cor 6,11-13).

Invitad a todos al banquete

2. Hace poco más de dos meses, cuando apenas había comenzado mi pontificado, tuve una «audiencia eucarística» con los seminaristas romanos. Como a ellos, también hoy a vosotros os invito a escuchar atentamente al Señor que os habla al corazón, principalmente en la oración y en la liturgia, para iros descubriendo y enraizando, en lo hondo de vuestro ser, el sentido y el valor de la vocación.

Dios, que es verdad y es amor, se nos ha manifestado en la historia de la creación y en la historia de la salvación: una historia incompleta aún, la de la humanidad, que «aguarda impaciente a que se revele lo que es ser hijos de Dios» (cf. Rom 8,18). El mismo Dios nos ha escogido, nos ha llamado para infundir nueva fuerza en esa historia, ahora ya sabiendo que la salvación «es don de Dios, no viene de las obras, y que somos hechura suya, creados en Cristo Jesús» (Ef 1,8-10). Una historia que es en los designios de Dios también la nuestra, porque nos quiere obreros en su viña (cf. Mt 20,1-16), nos quiere embajadores suyos para salir al encuentro de todos e invitarlos a entrar en su banquete (cf. ibíd., 22,1-14), nos quiere samaritanos, que usan misericordia con el prójimo desvalido (cf. Lc 10,30ss).

Incorporados al quehacer divino

3. Ya esto bastaría para vislumbrar de cerca cuán grande es la vocación. Experimentarla es un acontecimiento único, indecible, que únicamente se percibe como un soplo suave a través del toque desvelante de la gracia: un soplo del Espíritu que, al mismo tiempo que da perfil auténtico a nuestra frágil realidad humana —vaso de arcilla en manos del alfarero (cf. Rom 9,20-21)—, enciende en nuestros corazones una luz nueva, infunde una fuerza extraordinaria que, cimentándonos en el amor, incorpora nuestra existencia al quehacer divino, a su plan de re-creación del hombre en Cristo, es decir, la formación de su nueva familia redimida. Estáis, pues, llamados a construir la Iglesia —comunión con Dios—, algo muy por encima de lo que uno puede pedir o imaginar (cf. Ef 3,14-21).

Para los demás

4. Queridos seminaristas, que un día seréis ministros de Dios para plantar y regar el campo del Señor: aprovechad estos años en el seminario para llenaros de los sentimientos del mismo

Cristo en el estudio, en la oración, en la obediencia, en la formación del propio carácter. Veréis cómo a medida que va madurando vuestra vocación en esta escuela, vuestra vida irá asumiendo gozosamente una marca específica, una indicación bien precisa: la orientación a los demás, como Cristo que «pasó haciendo el bien y sanando a todos» (Act 10,38). De este modo, lo que humanamente podría parecer un fracaso, se convierte en un radiante proyecto de vida ya examinado y aprobado por Jesús: no existir para ser servido, sino para servir (cf. Mt 20,28).

Como bien comprenderéis, nada más lejano de la vocación que el aliciente de ventajas terrenas o la búsqueda de beneficios u honores: muy lejos también de ser la evasión de un ambiente de ilusiones frustradas o que se ofrece hostil o alienante. La Buena Nueva, para el llamado al servicio del Pueblo de Dios, además de ser un llamamiento a cambiar y mejorar la propia existencia, es llamamiento a una vida ya transformada en Cristo que hay que anunciar y propagar.

Os baste con esto, queridos seminaristas. El resto lo sabréis poner vosotros con vuestro corazón abierto y generoso. Una cosa quiero añadir: amad a vuestros directores, educadores y superiores. A ellos incumbe la grata pero también difícil tarea de llevaros de la mano por el camino que conduce al sacerdocio. Ellos os ayudarán a adquirir el gusto de la vida interior, el hábito exigente de la renuncia por Cristo, del desprendimiento y, sobre todo, os contagiarán del «suave olor del conocimiento de Cristo» (cf. 2 Cor 2,14). No tengáis miedo. El Señor está con vosotros y en todo momento es nuestra mejor garantía: «Sé de quién me he fiado» (2 Tim 1,12).

Abrid el corazón

Con esta confianza en el Señor, abrid vuestro corazón a la acción del Espíritu Santo; abridlo en un propósito de entrega que no sabe de reservas; abridlo al mundo que os espera y necesita; abridlo a la llamada que ya os dirigen tantas almas a las que un día podréis dar a Cristo en la eucaristía, en la penitencia, en la predicación de la palabra revelada, en el consejo amigable y desinteresado, en el testimonio alegre de vuestra vida de hombres en el mundo sin ser del mundo.

Vale la pena dedicarse a la causa de Cristo, que quiere corazones valientes y decididos; vale la pena consagrarse al hombre por Cristo, para llevarle a El, para elevarlo, para ayudarle en el camino hacia la eternidad; vale la pena hacer una opción por un ideal que os procurará grandes alegrías, aunque os exija también no pocos sacrificios. El Señor no abandona a los suyos.

Vale la pena vivir por el reino ese precioso valor del cristianismo: el celibato sacerdotal, patrimonio plurisecular de la Iglesia; vivirlo responsablemente aunque os exija no pocos sacrificios. ¡Cultivad la devoción a María, la Madre Virgen del Hijo de Dios, para que os ayude y aliente a realizarlo plenamente!

Formad santos apóstoles

Mas quiero reservar también una palabra especial a vosotros, educadores y superiores de casas de formación seminarística. Tenéis entre manos un tesoro eclesial. Cuidadlo con el mayor esmero y diligencia para que pueda producir los frutos esperados. Formad a estos jóvenes en la sana alegría, en el cultivo de una rica personalidad adaptada a nuestro tiempo. Pero formadla bien sólida en la fe, en los criterios del Evangelio, en la conciencia del valor de las almas, en un espíritu de oración capaz de afrontar los embates del futuro.

No recortéis la visión vertical de la vida ni rebajéis las exigencias que la opción por Cristo impone. Si proponemos ideales desvirtuados, son los jóvenes los primeros en no quererlos, porque desean algo que valga la pena, que sea ideal digno de una existencia. Aunque cueste.

¡Responsables de las vocaciones, sacerdotes, religiosos, padres y madres de familia! Dirijo a vosotros esas palabras. Comprometeos con generosidad en la tarea de procurar nuevas vocaciones, tan importantes para el futuro de la Iglesia. La escasez de vocaciones requiere un esfuerzo consciente por remediarlo. Y esto no se logrará si no sabemos orar, si no sabemos dar a la vocación al sacerdocio, diocesano o religioso, el aprecio y estima que merece.

Os doy a todos mi bendición. ¡Jóvenes seminaristas, Cristo os espera! No podéis defraudarle.

SINTESIS ENTRE FE Y CULTURA

Encuentro del Santo Padre con los universitarios católicos de México, Ciudad de México, 31 de enero.

Queridos hermanos y hermanas del mundo universitario:

1. Con inmensa alegría y esperanza acudo a esta cita con vosotros, estudiantes, profesores y auxiliares de las Universidades de México, en los que veo también al mundo universitario de América Latina entera.

Recibid mi saludo más cordial. Es el saludo de quien se encuentra tan a gusto entre la juventud, en la que cifra tantísimas esperanzas, sobre todo cuando se trata de sectores tan calificados como los que van pasando por las aulas universitarias, preparándose para un futuro que será determinante en la sociedad.

Permitidme que en primer lugar ponga un recuerdo para los miembros de la Universidad Católica La Salle, en cuyo recinto debía celebrarse este encuentro. Pero no es menos cordial mi recuerdo para las otras Universidades mexicanas: Universidad Ibero Americana, Universidad

Anáhuac, Universidad de Monterrey, Instituto Superior de Ciencias de la Educación de Ciudad de México, Facultad de Contaduría Pública de Veracruz, Instituto Tecnológico y de Estudios Superiores de Occidente en Guadalajara, Universidad Motolinia, Universidad Femenina de Puebla, Facultad canónica de Filosofía con sede en esta ciudad, y Facultad —todavía en ciernes— de Teología, igualmente en esta metrópoli.

Comprometidos por el reino de Dios

Se trata de universidades jóvenes. Tenéis, sin embargo, una antepasada venerable en la Real y Pontificia Universidad de México, fundada el 21 de septiembre de 1551, con la finalidad explícita de que en ella «los naturales y los hijos de los españoles fuesen instruidos en las cosas de la santa fe católica y en las demás facultades».

Hay también entre vosotros —y ciertamente son numerosísimos en todo el territorio mexicano— profesores y estudiantes católicos que enseñan o estudian en las universidades de diversa denominación. A ellos igualmente dirijo mi afectuoso saludo y manifiesto mi profundo gozo al saber que todos estáis comprometidos de la misma forma en la instauración del reino de Cristo.

Alarguemos ahora la vista por el vasto horizonte latinoamericano. Así mi saludo y pensamiento se detendrá complacido en tantos otros

Centros Católicos Universitarios, que en cada nación son motivo de legítimo orgullo, donde convergen tantas miradas ilusionadas, de donde se irradian la cultura y civismo cristianos, donde se forman las personas en un clima de concepción integral del ser humano, con rigor científico y con una visión cristiana del hombre, de la vida, de la sociedad, de los valores morales y religiosos.

Desarrollo completo de la persona

2. Y ahora, ¿qué más os puedo decir en estos momentos que necesariamente habrán de ser breves? ¿Qué puede esperar el mundo universitario católico mexicano y latinoamericano de la palabra del Papa?

Creo poder resumirlo, bastante sintéticamente, en tres observaciones, siguiendo la línea de mi venerado predecesor el papa Pablo VI.

a) La primera es que la Universidad Católica debe ofrecer una aportación específica a la Iglesia y a la sociedad, situándose en un nivel de investigación científica elevado, de estudio profundo de los problemas, de un sentido histórico adecuado. Pero esto no basta para una Universidad Católica. Esta debe encontrar su significado último y profundo en Cristo, en su mensaje salvífico, que abarca al hombre en su totalidad, y en las enseñanzas de la Iglesia.

Todo esto supone la promoción de una cultura integral, es decir, la que mira al desarrollo com-

pleto de la persona humana, en la que resalten
los valores de la inteligencia, voluntad, conciencia, fraternidad, basados todos en Dios Creador
y que han sido elevados maravillosamente en
Cristo (cf. *Gaudium et spes* 61): una cultura que
se dirija de modo desinteresado y genuino al
bien de la comunidad y de toda la sociedad.

b) La segunda observación es que la Universidad Católica debe ser formadora de hombres
realmente insignes por su saber, dispuestos a
ejercer funciones comprometidas en la sociedad
y a testimoniar su fe ante el mundo (cf. *Gravis-
simum educationis* 10). Finalidad que hoy es in-
dudablemente decisiva. A la formación científica
de los estudiantes conviene, pues, añadir una
profunda formación moral y cristiana, no considerada como algo que se añade desde fuera, sino
como un aspecto con el que la institución aca-
démica resulte, por así decirlo, especificada y
vivida. Se trata de promover y realizar en los
profesores y en los estudiantes una síntesis cada
vez más armónica entre fe y razón, entre fe y
cultura, entre fe y vida. Dicha síntesis debe pro-
curarse no sólo a nivel de investigación y enseñanza, sino también a nivel educativo-
pedagógico.

c) La tercera observación es que la Universidad Católica debe ser un ámbito en el que el
cristianismo sea vivo y operante. Es una vocación irrenunciable de la Universidad Católica
dar testimonio de ser una comunidad seria y sin-
ceramente comprometida en la búsqueda científica, pero también caracterizada visiblemente

por una vida cristiana auténtica. Eso supone, entre otras cosas, una revisión de la figura del profesor, el cual no puede ser considerado únicamente como un simple transmisor de ciencia, sino también y sobre todo como un testigo y educador de vida cristiana auténtica. En este privilegiado ambiente de formación, vosotros, queridos estudiantes, estáis llamados a una colaboración consciente y responsable, libre y generosa, para realizar vuestra misma formación.

Dad la mano a quien busca el bien común

3.   La implantación de una pastoral universitaria, ya sea como pastoral de las inteligencias, ya sea como fuente de vida litúrgica, y que debe atender a todo el sector universitario de la nación, no dejará de encontrar frutos preciosos de elevación humana y cristiana.

Queridos hijos que os dedicáis completa o parcialmente al sector universitario católico de vuestros respectivos países, y todos vosotros que, en cualquier ambiente universitario, estáis comprometidos en implantar el reino de Dios:

— cread una verdadera familia universitaria, empeñada en la búsqueda, no siempre fácil, de la verdad y del bien, aspiraciones supremas del ser racional y bases de sólida y responsable estructura moral;

— perseguid una seria actividad investigadora, orientadora de las nuevas generaciones hacia la verdad, hacia la madurez humana y religiosa;

— trabajad infatigablemente para el progreso auténtico y completo de vuestras patrias. Sin prejuicios de ningún tipo, dad la mano a quien se propone, como vosotros, la construcción del auténtico bien común;

— unid vuestras fuerzas de obispos, sacerdotes, religiosos y religiosas, de laicos, en la programación y realización de vuestros centros académicos y de sus actividades;

— caminad alegres e infatigables bajo la guía de la Santa Madre Iglesia, cuyo Magisterio, prolongamiento del de Cristo, es garantía única para no perder el justo camino, y guía segura hacia la herencia imperecedera que Cristo reserva a quien le es fiel.

Os encomiendo a todos a la eterna Sabiduría: «esplendente e inmarcesible es la sabiduría; fácilmente se deja ver de los que la aman y es hallada por los que la buscan» (Sab 6,12).

¡Que la Sede de la Sabiduría, a la que México y toda América Latina venera en el santuario de Guadalupe, os proteja a todos bajo su manto maternal! Así sea. Y muchas gracias por vuestra presencia.

SERVIR A LA VERDAD

Encuentro del Santo Padre con los representantes de los medios informativos, Ciudad de México, 31 de enero.

Queridos amigos del mundo de la información:

En muchas ocasiones, durante estas jornadas que el entusiasmo de los mexicanos ha hecho febriles y emocionadas, momentos llenos de belleza y significación religiosa transcurridos en lugares y ambientes inolvidables, he tenido la oportunidad de observaros mientras acudíais de un lugar a otro llenos de la determinación y empeño que distingue vuestra tarea informativa.

Me encuentro ahora a punto de regresar a Roma, después de haber asistido al inicio de este importante acontecimiento eclesial, maravilloso por su significado profundo de unidad y creatividad de futuro de la Iglesia, que es la Conferencia de Puebla, y haber peregrinado por las inolvidables tierras de la Virgen de Guadalupe. Y agradezco a la Providencia que en este momento me dé la esperada ocasión de encontrar a los profesionales de la información, que han querido acompañarme en este viaje.

Gratitud a los medios de comunicación

Muchos continuaréis aquí, para seguir llevando a la opinión pública el acontecer de Puebla, otros me acompañarán en mi regreso, mientras otros se verán reclamados por otras misiones. En todo caso vale la pena arrancar unos minutos a nuestro apretado horario para poder estar juntos, reflexionar y charlar un poco, esta vez de persona a persona. Por una vez sin tener como intermediario ningún medio de transmisión o estar en función de hacer presentes espiritualmente auditorios lejanos. Disfrutemos sin más de la alegría de estar juntos.

Desde luego, no se me olvida que detrás de las cámaras se encuentra una persona, que una persona es la que habla a través del micrófono, que es una persona la que perfila y corrige cada línea del artículo que publicará el periódico de mañana. Quisiera, en este breve encuentro, ofrecer a todos mi gratitud y respeto, y dirigirme a cada uno con su nombre. Siento el deseo y la necesidad de agradecer a cada cual el trabajo de estos días y el que va a continuar en Puebla, que reflejará una Iglesia que acoge todas las culturas, talantes e iniciativas, con tal que vayan dirigidas a la construcción del reino de Dios.

Comprendo las tensiones y dificultades en las que se desarrolla vuestro trabajo. Sé bien el esfuerzo que requiere la comunicación de la noticia. Imagino la fatiga que supone trasladar, montar y desmontar, de una parte a otra, todo este complicado utillaje vuestro. Me doy cuenta también de que el vuestro es un trabajo que exige largos desplazamientos y os separa de la familia y amigos. No es una vida fácil, pero, en compensación, como toda actividad creativa, en especial la que significa un servicio a los demás, os ofrece un especial enriquecimiento. Seguro que todos tenéis experiencia de ello.

Podéis prestar gran servicio a la humanidad

Recuerdo ahora una ocasión análoga, hace pocas semanas, en que tuve ocasión de charlar con los profesionales que acudieron a informar sobre mi elección e inauguración del pontificado. Hice referencia a esta profesión como una *vocación*. Uno de los documentos más importantes de la Iglesia, sobre las comunicaciones sociales, declara que «es necesario que el hombre de nuestro tiempo conozca las cosas plena y fielmente, adecuada y exactamente» *(Communio et progressio* 34), y proclama que cuando una información así viene facilitada por los medios de comunicación social, «todos los hombres se hacen partícipes... de los asuntos de toda la humanidad» (ibíd., 19).

Con vuestro talento y experiencia, vuestra competencia profesional, la necesaria inclinación y los medios que están a vuestra disposición, podéis facilitar este gran servicio a la humanidad. Y sobre todo, como lo mejor de vosotros mismos, queréis ser buscadores de la verdad, para ofrecerla a todo aquel que quiera oírla. Servid ante todo a la verdad, a lo que construye, a lo que mejora y dignifica al hombre.

En la medida en que persigáis este ideal, os aseguro que la Iglesia permanecerá a vuestro lado, porque éste es su ideal también. Ella ama la verdad y la libertad: libertad de conocer la verdad, de predicarla, de comunicarla a los demás.

Ha llegado el momento de saludarnos y de renovaros mi gratitud por el servicio prestado a la difusión de la verdad que se manifiesta en Cristo, y que se está expresando estos días en actos de la mayor importancia para la vida de la fe en estos países americanos, tan próximos a la Iglesia. Nos despedimos con respeto y amistad, dispuestos a ser consecuentes con nuestros mejores ideales. El Papa se complace en saludaros y bendeciros, recordando los medios que representáis: diarios, cadenas televisivas, emisoras radiofónicas, y también a vuestras familias. Por vosotros y por ellas ofrezco frecuentemente mi oración. Que el Señor os acompañe.

LA DIGNIDAD DE LA PERSONA HUMANA

Discurso de Juan Pablo II a los trabajadores de Monterrey, 31 de enero.

Queridos hermanos, campesinos, empleados y, sobre todo, obreros de Monterrey:

¡Gracias! A todos y a cada uno ¡muchas gracias!

1. Os agradezco de corazón esta acogida tan calurosa y cordial en vuestra ciudad industrial de Monterrey. En torno a ella discurre vuestra existencia y se desarrolla vuestro trabajo diario para ganaros el pan y el pan de vuestros hijos. Ella es también testigo de vuestras penas y de vuestras aspiraciones. Ella es obra vuestra, obra de vuestras manos y de vuestra inteligencia, y en este sentido, símbolo de vuestro orgullo de trabajadores y un signo de esperanza para un nuevo progreso y para una vida cada vez más humana.

2. Me siento feliz de encontrarme entre vosotros como hermano y amigo vuestro, como compañero de trabajo en esta ciudad de Monterrey, que es para México algo parecido a lo que significa Nowa Huta en mi lejana y que-

rida Cracovia. No olvido los años difíciles de la guerra mundial, en los que yo mismo tuve la experiencia directa de un trabajo como el vuestro, de su fatiga cotidiana y su dependencia, de su pesadez y su monotonía.

He compartido las necesidades de los trabajadores, sus justas exigencias y sus legítimas aspiraciones. Conozco muy bien la necesidad de que el trabajo no enajene ni frustre, sino que corresponda a la dignidad superior del hombre. Puedo dar testimonio de una cosa: en los momentos de mayor prueba, mi pueblo de Polonia ha encontrado en su fe en Dios, en su confianza en la Virgen María, Madre de Dios, en la comunidad eclesial unida en torno a sus pastores, una luz superior a las tinieblas, y una esperanza inquebrantable.

Preocupación prioritaria por los necesitados

3. Sé que estoy hablando a trabajadores que son conscientes de su condición de cristianos y que quieren vivir esa condición con todas sus energías y consecuencias. Por eso el Papa quiere haceros algunas reflexiones que tocan vuestra dignidad como hombres y como hijos de Dios. De esa doble fuente brotará la luz para conformar vuestra existencia personal y social. En efecto, si el espíritu de Jesucristo habita en nosotros, debemos sentir la preocupación prioritaria por aquellos que no tienen el conveniente alimento, vestido, vivienda, ni tienen acceso a

los bienes de la cultura. Dado que el trabajo es fuente del propio sustento, es colaboración con Dios en el perfeccionamiento de la naturaleza, es un servicio a los hermanos que ennoblece al hombre. Los cristianos no pueden despreocuparse del problema del desempleo de tantos hombres y mujeres, sobre todo jóvenes y cabezas de familia, a quienes la desocupación conduce al desánimo y a la desesperación. Los que tienen la suerte de poder trabajar aspiran a hacerlo en condiciones más humanas, más seguras, a participar más justamente en el fruto del esfuerzo común en lo referente a salarios, seguridad social, posibilidades de desarrollo cultural y espiritual. Quieren ser tratados como hombres libres y responsables, llamados a participar en las decisiones que conciernen a su vida y a su futuro. Es derecho fundamental suyo crear libremente organizaciones para defender y promover sus intereses y para contribuir responsablemente al bien común.

4. La tarea es inmensa y compleja. Se ve complicada hoy por la crisis económica mundial, por el desorden de círculos comerciales y financieros injustos, por el agotamiento rápido de algunos recursos, y por los riesgos de contaminación irreversible del ambiente biofísico.

Para participar realmente en el esfuerzo solidario de la humanidad, los pueblos de América Latina exigen con razón que se les devuelva su justa responsabilidad sobre los bienes que la naturaleza les ha confiado, y las condiciones generales que les permitan conducir un desarrollo en conformidad con su espíritu propio, con la participación de todos los grupos humanos que lo componen. Se hacen necesarias innovaciones atrevidas y renovadoras para superar las graves injusticias heredadas del pasado y para vencer el desafío de las transformaciones prodigiosas de la humanidad.

Revisar el progreso que atrofia los valores del espíritu

En todos los niveles, nacional e internacional, y por parte de todos los grupos sociales, en todos los sistemas, las realidades nuevas exigen aptitudes nuevas. La denuncia unilateral del otro, y el fácil pretexto de las ideologías ajenas, fueren cuales fueren, son coartadas cada vez más irrisorias. Si la humanidad quiere controlar una evolución que se le escapa de la mano, si quiere sustraerse a la tentación materialista que gana terreno en una huida hacia adelante desesperada, si quiere asegurar el desarrollo auténtico a los hombres y a los pueblos, debe revisar radicalmente los conceptos de progreso que, bajo sus diversos nombres, han dejado atrofiar los valores espirituales.

5. La Iglesia ofrece su ayuda. Ella no teme denunciar con fuerza los ataques a la dignidad humana. Pero reserva lo esencial de sus energías para ayudar a los hombres y grupos humanos, a los empresarios y trabajadores, para que tomen conciencia de las inmensas reservas de bondad

que llevan dentro, que ellos han hecho ya fructificar en su historia y que hoy deben dar frutos nuevos.

La Iglesia ha dejado huella en el campo social

El movimiento obrero, al que la Iglesia y los cristianos han aportado una contribución original y diversa, particularmente en este continente, reivindica su justa parte de responsabilidad en la construcción de un nuevo orden mundial. El ha recogido las aspiraciones comunes de libertad y de dignidad. Ha desarrollado los valores de solidaridad, fraternidad y amistad, en la experiencia compartida; ha suscitado formas de organización originales, mejorando sustancialmente la suerte de numerosos trabajadores, y contribuyendo —por más que no siempre se quiera decirlo— a dejar una huella en el mundo industrial. Apoyándose en este pasado, deberá comprometer su experiencia en la búsqueda de nuevas vías, renovarse a sí mismo y contribuir de manera aún más decisiva a construir la América Latina del mañana.

6. Hace diez años que mi predecesor, el papa Pablo VI, estuvo en Colombia. Quería traer a los pueblos de América Latina el consuelo del Padre común. Quería abrir a la Iglesia universal las riquezas de las Iglesias de este continente. Algunos años después, celebrando el octogésimo aniversario de la primera encíclica social,

la *Rerum novarum*, escribía: «La enseñanza social de la Iglesia acompaña con todo su dinamismo a los hombres en su búsqueda. Si bien no interviene para dar autenticidad a una estructura determinada o para proponer un modelo prefabricado, ella no se limita simplemente a recordar unos principios generales. Se desarrolla por medio de una reflexión madurada al contacto con situaciones cambiantes de este mundo, bajo el impulso del Evangelio como fuente de renovación desde el momento que su mensaje es aceptado en su totalidad y en sus exigencias. Se desarrolla con la sensibilidad propia de la Iglesia, marcada por una voluntad desinteresada de servicio, y una atención a los más pobres. Finalmente se alimenta en una experiencia rica de muchos siglos, lo que permite asumir en la continuidad de sus preocupaciones permanentes la innovación atrevida y creadora que requiere la situación presente del mundo». Son palabras de Pablo VI.

Atención a los emigrantes

7.   Queridos amigos: En fidelidad a esos principios, la Iglesia quiere hoy llamar la atención sobre un fenómeno grave y de gran actualidad: el problema de los emigrantes. No podemos cerrar los ojos a la situación de millones de hombres que, en búsqueda de trabajo y del propio pan, han de abandonar su patria y muchas veces la familia, afrontando las dificultades de un am-

biente nuevo no siempre agradable y acogedor, una lengua desconocida y condiciones generales que les sumen en la soledad y a veces en la marginación a ellos, a sus mujeres y a sus hijos, cuando no se llega a aprovechar esas circunstancias para ofrecer salarios más bajos, recortar los beneficios de la seguridad social y asistencial, a dar condiciones de vivienda indignas de seres humanos. Hay ocasiones en que el criterio puesto en práctica es el de procurar el máximo rendimiento del trabajador emigrante sin mirar a la persona. Ante este fenómeno, la Iglesia sigue proclamando que el criterio a seguir, en este como en otros campos, no es el de hacer prevalecer lo económico, lo social, lo político, etc., por encima del hombre, sino que la dignidad de la persona humana está por encima de todo lo demás y a ello hay que condicionar el resto.

Crearíamos un mundo muy poco habitable si sólo se mirase a tener más y no se pensara ante todo en la persona del trabajador, en su condición de ser humano y de hijo de Dios, llamado a una vocación eterna; si no se pensara en ayudarle a *ser* más. Ciertamente, por otra parte, el trabajador tiene unas obligaciones que ha de cumplir con lealtad, ya que sin ello no puede haber un recto orden social.

A los poderes públicos, a los empresarios y a los trabajadores invito con todas mis fuerzas a reflexionar sobre estos principios y a deducir las consecuentes líneas de acción. No faltan ejemplos, hay que reconocerlo también, en los que se ponen en práctica con ejemplaridad estos principios de la doctrina social de la Iglesia. Me complazco de ello. Alabo a los responsables, y aliento a imitar este buen ejemplo. Ganará con ello la causa de la convivencia y hermandad entre grupos sociales y naciones. Podrá ganar aun la misma economía. Y sobre todo ganará ciertamente la causa del ser humano.

Abríos a Dios

8.   Pero no nos quedemos en el solo hombre. El Papa os trae también otro mensaje. Un mensaje que es para vosotros, trabajadores de México y de América Latina: abríos a Dios. Dios os ama. Jesucristo os ama. La Madre de Dios, la Virgen María, os ama. La Iglesia y el Papa os aman y os invitan a seguir la fuerza arrolladora del amor, que todo puede superar y construir. Hace casi dos mil años, cuando Dios nos envió a su Hijo, no esperó a que los esfuerzos humanos hubieran eliminado previamente toda clase de injusticias. Jesucristo vino a compartir nuestra condición humana con su sufrimiento, sus dificultades, su muerte. Antes de transformar la existencia cotidiana, El supo hablar al corazón de los pobres, liberarlos del pecado, abrir sus ojos a un horizonte de luz y colmarlos de alegría y esperanza. Lo mismo hace hoy Jesucristo. Está presente en vuestras Iglesias, en vuestras familias, en vuestros corazones, en toda vuestra vida. Abridle todas las puertas. Celebremos todos juntos en estos momentos con alegría el

amor de Jesús y de su Madre. Nadie se sienta excluido, en particular los más desdichados, pues esta alegría que proviene de Jesucristo no es insultante para ninguna pena. Tiene el sabor y el calor de la amistad que nos ofrece Aquel que sufrió más que nosotros, que murió en la cruz por nosotros, que nos prepara una morada eterna a su lado y que ya en esta vida proclama y afirma nuestra dignidad de hombres, de hijos de Dios.

9.   Estoy con amigos trabajadores y me quedaría con vosotros mucho más tiempo. Pero he de concluir. A vosotros aquí presentes, a vuestros compañeros de México, y a cuantos compatriotas vuestros trabajan fuera del suelo patrio, a todos los obreros de América Latina, os dejo mi saludo de amigo, mi bendición y mi recuerdo. A todos, a vuestros hijos y familiares, mi abrazo de hermano.

QUEDA CON VOSOTROS
MI PALABRA

Mensaje del Papa a los Episcopados de América Central y de las Antillas antes de dejar México.

Queridos hermanos:

Antes de dejar el suelo de México siento la necesidad de enviar a vosotros y, por vuestro conducto, a todos los fieles confiados a vuestros cuidados pastorales un paterno saludo.

Saludo marcado con el signo de la pena por no haber podido visitar a esos queridos hijos, aun estando tan cerca de vuestros países.

Pena que se traduce en una expresión más profunda de amor.

Decidles que el Papa, en los días que ha vivido en el Nuevo Continente, ha pensado mucho en ellos y ha rezado mucho por ellos.

La vecindad material debida a mi visita a México, me ha hecho sentir más vivamente mi afecto y mi interés por toda la América Latina, y en particular he recordado con especial amor a todo el archipiélago de las Antillas durante mi breve estancia en Santo Domingo.

Ahora que mi pensamiento y mi afecto está

más cercano a vosotros, viene a mi memoria de manera especial el recuerdo de las calamidades materiales que aún hace poco tiempo flagelaron a algunos países, muy singularmente a Guatemala y Nicaragua. Damos gracias a Dios que el proceso de reconstrucción continúa realizándose satisfactoriamente.

¡Si pudieseis comprender cuánto desea el Papa que las gentes de estos países fuesen comprendidas en toda su dimensión de seres humanos, y que los que tienen en sus manos las posibilidades y el poder lo ejercitaran con una justicia cabal, que es condición de la paz y el desarrollo de los pueblos!

El Papa regresa a Roma, pero queda con vosotros su palabra: que sea un estímulo constante a que sigáis trabajando con renovado esfuerzo cada día para que el gran amor a vuestras patrias se manifieste a través de vuestro empeño en favor del bien y de la convivencia fraterna de esa gran familia que componen todos y cada uno de los países del continente americano.

Al impartir a los obispos, y por su medio a todos los pueblos de estas tierras, la bendición, el Papa desea consolidar, acrecentar y hacer más profundos estos lazos que se han establecido gracias a su misión pastoral.

Sea alabado Dios omnipotente que nos ha permitido, con motivo de la Conferencia del Episcopado Latinoamericano, hacer por unos días el centro de la Iglesia en tierras de América, días todos importantes para el presente y el futuro de la evangelización en ese amado y gran continente.

LAS BAHAMAS

ESPERANZA EN EL FUTURO

Discurso del Papa en Nassau, Islas Bahamas, 31 de enero.

Os estoy agradecido por esta acogida. Es para mí una gran alegría poder detenerme en Nassau a mi vuelta a Roma, la alegría grande de encontrarme con el querido pueblo de Bahamas.

Mi primer agradecimiento va a las autoridades de esta nación joven, independiente desde hace poco. Amablemente habéis dado facilidades para mi visita, y deseo expresaros mi agradecimiento cordial por ello. Además, podéis estar seguros de mis oraciones por el cumplimiento fiel de las importantes tareas que estáis llamados a cumplir al servicio de los hombres y mujeres de esta nación.

Al encontrarme esta tarde aquí entre vosotros, se me presenta la oportunidad de manifestaros mis mejores deseos para toda la población de Bahamas. Abrigo la esperanza de que cada uno avance constantemente a lo largo del camino del progreso humano auténtico e íntegro. Ojalá todo el pueblo de estas islas, convencido profundamente de la dignidad eminente de la persona humana, contribuya con su aportación individual y específica al bien común que tiene

en cuenta los derechos personales y los deberes
de todos los ciudadanos.

La solidaridad con
todos los católicos

Estar con vosotros es también compartir la
esperanza de que, como nación soberana dentro
de la familia de las naciones, aportaréis vuestra
parte propia y especial a la sociedad, es decir,
ayudaréis a construir el edificio de la paz mundial sobre las sólidas columnas de la verdad y la
justicia, la caridad y la libertad. Dios bendiga
vuestros esfuerzos y os ayude a cumplir esta
importante tarea para bien de esta generación y
de las que están por venir.

En esta ocasión maravillosa quiero dirigir una
palabra de particular saludo a todos los hijos e
hijas de la Iglesia católica. Os digo todo mi amor
en nuestro Señor Jesucristo, y confío en que mi
presencia es prueba auténtica de los lazos de fe
y caridad que os vinculan a los católicos de todas las partes del mundo. Rezo para que esta
solidaridad y amistad os dé fuerza y alegría, y
para que seáis testimonio constante de vuestras
creencias a través de la autenticidad de vuestra
vida cristiana. Las palabras de Jesús son un reto
continuo para todos nosotros: «Así ha de lucir
vuestra luz ante los hombres, para que viendo
vuestras buenas obras, glorifiquen a vuestro Padre que está en los cielos» (Mt 5,16).

Unidos en el respeto de la dignidad humana

Con profundo respeto y amor fraterno deseo saludar también a todos los otros hermanos cristianos, a todos los que confiesan con nosotros que «Jesús es el Hijo de Dios» (1 Jn 4,15). Estad seguros de nuestro deseo de colaborar leal y perseverantemente para obtener de Dios la gracia de la unidad querida por Cristo el Señor. Mi expresión de amistad va asimismo a todos los hombres y mujeres de buena voluntad que residen en esta región del océano Atlántico. Cual hijos de un único Padre celestial, estamos unidos en la solidaridad del amor y en el afán por impulsar hasta la plenitud la incomparable dignidad de la persona humana.

Por tanto, en estos momentos de breve parada siento la misma esperanza que tenéis vosotros, pueblo de Bahamas, la esperanza de un futuro grande como el océano que os rodea. Tengo el privilegio de compartir esta esperanza con vosotros y de manifestárosla ahora con la confianza de que ello os dará aliento en vuestros meritorios esfuerzos como pueblo unido. Pido a Dios que os guíe hasta el logro pleno de vuestro destino. Que El otorgue bendiciones copiosas y continuas al pueblo de Bahamas. Que socorra a los pobres, conforte a los enfermos, guíe a la juventud y conceda paz a todos los corazones. Dios bendiga a Bahamas hoy y por siempre.

POR UN MUNDO MAS PACIFICO Y MAS HUMANO

Palabras del Papa, en el aeropuerto de Fiumicino, a su regreso de México, 1 de febrero.

He recibido con viva satisfacción, Señor Presidente del Consejo de Ministros, las amables palabras de saludo y parabién que ha querido dirigirme, también en nombre del Gobierno italiano.

Al final de este primer viaje apostólico que me ha llevado más allá del Océano a la tierra noble y querida de México, prevalece un sentimiento sobre tantos como se agolpan en mi ánimo estremecido y emocionado: el sentimiento de gratitud.

Ante todo, doy gracias al Señor y a la Santísima Virgen de Guadalupe por la ayuda constante con que me han favorecido en estos días, permitiéndome coronar felizmente una iniciativa delicada e importante emprendida en cumplimiento del mandato universal que el mismo Cristo me ha confiado llamándome a la responsabilidad de Vicario suyo en la Sede de Pedro.

Pienso también con muy vivo reconocimiento en tantas demostraciones de atención, devoción y afecto de que me han hecho objeto los pueblos con quienes me he encontrado en el curso de mi peregrinación, y especialmente mis venerados hermanos en el episcopado reunidos en Puebla en representación de toda la jerarquía católica de América Latina. Mi corazón ha podido latir al unísono con el suyo: he gozado, sufrido, esperado con ellos, implorando al Padre común la venida de un mundo más pacífico, más justo, más humano por la adhesión sincera al mensaje de amor de su Hijo encarnado.

Y ahora, a mi regreso a esta sede romana, en la que el orbe católico reconoce el centro y la fuente de su unidad, vuestra acogida tan espontánea y cordial suscita en mí una nueva y grata emoción: por tanto, saludo con deferencia y gratitud al Señor cardenal Secretario de Estado y demás personalidades eclesiásticas, a las autoridades políticas, civiles y militares italianas, a los miembros del Cuerpo Diplomático y a todos vosotros que no habéis parado mientes en incomodidades con tal de poderme dar personalmente vuestra bienvenida.

Quiera Dios recompensaros tanta cortesía y con vosotros colme también de sus favores a cuantos se han entregado generosamente para el feliz resultado del viaje, comenzando por los directivos, pilotos y personal de las Compañías Aéreas, a quienes debo que la travesía haya sido encantadora y confortable. En confirmación de estos deseos me complazco en impartir a los aquí presentes, a la querida ciudad de Roma y a cuantos me han acompañado con el pensamiento y la oración, una especial y confortadora bendición apostólica.

REALIDAD HUMANA Y CRISTIANA DE MEXICO

Discurso del Papa a los cardenales a su llegada a Roma, 1 de febrero.

Señores cardenales:

1. En el momento en que concluye mi primer viaje misionero, elevo a Dios la más sentida acción de gracias por la gran experiencia que me ha concedido vivir en la plenitud de un trabajo apostólico que ha ocupado con intensidad particular cada hora de los días pasados.

2. Creí deber mío emprender este viaje (vinculado al desarrollo de la III Asamblea General del Episcopado Latinoamericano en Puebla, anunciada hace tiempo), siguiendo en esto el ejemplo de mi predecesor Pablo VI, de venerada memoria, que quiso inaugurar esta forma de cumplir el ministerio papal en la Iglesia.

3. Es difícil hablar cumplidamente de esta inolvidable experiencia cuando aún resuenan en mi ánimo las mil voces escuchadas y todavía están recientes los recuerdos de cuanto he podido ver, de las personas con quienes he podido encontrarme, de los temas que he tenido ocasión de afrontar.

4. Será preciso volver sobre todo esto durante mucho tiempo con la oración, la reflexión y el corazón; pero ya desde ahora puedo afirmar que este viaje, tras la breve pero significativa etapa en Santo Domingo, ha sido un encuentro excepcional con México en su realidad humana y cristiana; un encuentro con el Pueblo de Dios de este país, que ha respondido con un gran acto de fe a la presencia del Papa y que, comenzado en el corazón de la Iglesia mexicana que es Guadalupe, se prolongó hasta alcanzar las etapas de Puebla, Oaxaca, Guadalajara y Monterrey.

5. Este encuentro ofrece en cierto sentido, con la riqueza de sus contenidos y la multiplicidad de sus manifestaciones, un contexto vivo a las tareas que juntamente con los obispos de América Latina hemos afrontado en el ámbito de la III Asamblea general de aquel Episcopado, que, como sabéis, comenzaron el 27 del pasado enero, con la solemne concelebración en el santuario de la Virgen de Guadalupe, y continúan en Puebla con el tema «La evangelización en el presente y en el futuro de América Latina», para concluir el próximo día 13 de febrero.

Para introducir sus trabajos dirigí el 28 de enero, con gran esperanza y confianza, un mensaje a la Iglesia sudamericana, que ha hecho universal concretamente la presencia de los medios de comunicación social y los profesionales de la información (que han querido seguir con amplitud de tiempo cada etapa de mi breve pero intenso viaje).

Ciertamente, será preciso hablar más de una

vez del significado de los trabajos de Puebla y de cada uno de los problemas afrontados allí, volviendo sobre sus diversos temas.

6. Ahora, al regresar a la Sede Apostólica, después de siete días, siento la necesidad de agradecer de todo corazón a cuantos han contribuido, a todo nivel, a preparar y organizar este viaje, que ha resultado tan bien, a pesar de haberse desarrollado en tan escaso tiempo.

También querría dar las gracias a cuantos han soportado conmigo el peso de este viaje: a los monseñores Caprio, Casaroli, Martin, Marcinkus, Noe y a las demás personas del séquito, de la prensa, radio y televisión, a todos los laicos que me han acompañado a lo largo de todo el viaje.

7. Permitidme, en fin, que os dirija un ¡gracias! particular, por la acogida que me habéis dispensado, a todo el Colegio de Cardenales, a quienes he sentido muy cercanos con la oración y el corazón en el curso de estas inolvidables jornadas, y de modo muy especial al cardenal Decano, que ha sabido interpretar tan bien los sentimientos de todos vosotros, y al cardenal Secretario de Estado por el valioso trabajo desarrollado con disponibilidad generosa en los días de mi ausencia.

La Virgen de Guadalupe, a la que he rezado tanto en estos días, dé fuerza con su intercesión a nuestro empeño para que no se defrauden las esperanzas suscitadas por el viaje que hoy ha terminado.